# GANGS

## An International Approach

### Sean Grennan

*Long Island University–C.W. Post Campus*

### Marjie T. Britz

*The Citadel*

### Jeffrey Rush

*Murray State University*

### Thomas Barker

*Jacksonville State University*

Prentice Hall
Upper Saddle River, New Jersey 07458

**Library of Congress Cataloging-in-Publication Data**

Gangs : an international approach / Sean Grennan . . . [et. al.].
  p. cm.
  Includes bibliographical references and index.
  ISBN 0-13-324856-9 (paper)
  1. Gangs—United States.  I. Grennan, Sean.
  HV6439.U5  G3593  2000
  364.1'06'6'0973—dc21

99–26803
CIP
Rev.

Acquisitions editor: *Neil Marquardt*
Production editor: *Trish Finley*
Production liaison: *Barbara Marttine Cappuccio*
Director of manufacturing and production: *Bruce Johnson*
Managing editor: *Mary Carnis*
Manufacturing buyer: *Ed O'Dougherty*
Creative director: *Marianne Frasco*
Cover design: *Bruce Kenselaar*
Formatting/page make-up: *The Clarinda Company*
Printer/binder: *R.R. Donnelley & Sons Company*

Printed in the United States of America

10 9 8 7 6 5 4 3 2 1

ISBN 0-13-324856-9

Prentice-Hall International (UK) Limited, *London*
Prentice-Hall of Australia Pty. Limited, *Sydney*
Prentice-Hall Canada Inc., *Toronto*
Prentice-Hall Hispanoamericana, S.A., *Mexico*
Prentice-Hall of India Private Limited, *New Delhi*
Prentice-Hall of Japan, Inc., *Tokyo*
Pearson Education (Singapore) Pte. Ltd.
Editora Prentice-Hall do Brasil, Ltda., *Rio de Janeiro*

*Sean Grennan dedicates the work he did in this book to some very important people who will always be in his life: Mollie, Megan, Carmine C., Lauren, and Linda F.*

*Marjie Britz dedicates her work in loving memory to her father, the greatest man she has ever known, Theodore Albert Britz.*

# Contents

CHAPTER **5**

# Outlaw Motorcycle Gangs / 54

CHAPTER

# 6

## Supremacists and Militias / 81

CHAPTER

## 7

## Street Gangs / 121

CHAPTER

## 8

## Jamaican and Nigerian Gangs / 128

CHAPTER

## Chinese Gangs / 181

CHAPTER

# 10

## Japanese, Vietnamese, and Korean Gangs / 219

# Hispanic Gangs / 276

# Russian and Israeli Gangs / 336

# Other Worldwide Organized Crime Groups / 366

CHAPTER

# 14

## Conclusions / 413

# Preface

Gangs have been a subject of a great deal of research over the past fifty years. Whether the gangs are traditional or nontraditional, as some theorists have labeled these different types of groups, the vast majority of these gangs are adept at committing crimes that ultimately help them make money. Although some theorists are tediously searching for what causes people to join gangs, the authors of this book decided to research and write about the formation of gangs, the history of the gangs' criminal activities, and the future of the these gangs in our society. Gangs that are hardly mentioned in other organized crime books are thoroughly investigated and discussed in this book.

A number of college textbooks discuss the issue of gangs in the United States, and in many cases the past, present, and future of many of these diversified gangs are only discussed lightly. However, the authors of this text researched gangs throughout the world. Every gang discussed in this book is viewed historically, territorially, and economically in an effort to provide a complete package of all the global gangs. This informational package includes historical background on the formation of each gang, including how and why members formed the gang. The ethnic, racial, or religious makeup of the gang is discussed along with each group's initiation rites (if any exist), length of membership (day by day or lifetime), and the availability of upward mobility. The illegal activities that gang members participate in or refer to as "work"—from filing false insurance claims to kidnapping, terrorism, and murder—are thoroughly examined and discussed in this book. Possible worldwide government participation in gang activity is also explored.

This book gives students an in-depth perspective on gangs that no other book on the market offers. With this text students not only gain knowledge concerning local gangs but they also grasp information concerning gangs worldwide and a basic history of what caused the formation of each gang in its country of origin. Students read this book and enthusiastically discuss how much they enjoyed the subject matter. Written with the college student in mind, this book contains meaningful information that grants the student a greater knowledge and understanding of organized criminal gangs. Such information assists students during their course work and gives them a better understanding of the operations of global crime groups.

## ACKNOWLEDGMENTS

The authors are grateful for the assistance of the Southern Poverty Law Center; Major Steve Smith, South Carolina State Law Enforcement Division; Todd Cranor, the Southern Poverty Law Center; and the Charleston, South Carolina, Police Department. They also extend their appreciation to the individuals who reviewed the book: Ronald Graham, Fresno City College; James McKenna, Villanova University; Anthony Smith, California State University–Long Beach; and Micheal S. Turner, Pellissippi State University.

As he is one of the greatest procrastinators on earth, Sean Grennan would especially like to thank Cheryl Adam for her patience. Also, he never would have completed this project without Linda F. Morrissey's guidance, editing, direction, and devotion. He will always be indebted to her for her gracious and devoted assistance (458).

# 1

# Gangs in History

He saw them silhouetted against the morning sun. Three, no four, maybe even five riders. From that direction he guessed they were probably strangers. Coming into town. For what? "I'd better let the sheriff know," he thought.

This scene or one like it is played out in almost every Western ever made. Of course, being a Western, it is a scene that "reflects" life in the 1850s or earlier. Those movies depict people such as Jesse and Frank James, Butch and Sundance, the Youngers, the Daltons, and many others. And these depictions show the workings of their gangs: the Hole in the Wall gang, the James gang, and the Dalton gang, to name but a few. Gangs in the Wild West and gangs in the 1990s—their similarities far outnumber their differences. Surprising? It shouldn't be.

Let us return for a moment to the earlier 1800s and the War of 1812 against England. Andrew Jackson needed assistance to protect New Orleans from the British. And so he called on Jean Lafayette and his gang, or rather his band of buccaneers. Whether you call them buccaneers or gangsters, a rose by any other name is still a rose. Hiring gangsters or buccaneers to help the law-abiding fight crime is absurd, right? Or was it a political necessity of the time? A historical anomaly? Look at the city of Fort Worth, Texas. They recently began a program to hire former gangsters to assist the police in their dealing with gangs and gangsters. It is a case of back to the future, in real life.

Historically, many gangs roamed the West. From the Cowboys of Arizona to the Jameses in Missouri, gangs, each sharing a deadly purposefulness, existed throughout those years when the law was spread thin. As the lawman Bat Masterson said of the gangsters he knew, when it came to dispute resolution, any one of them "would not have hesitated a moment to put up his life as the stake to be played for" (Trachtman, 1974: 8). Scott (1994) makes a similar point about being a 1990s gangster.

While the West saw many different gangs composed of many different gangsters, their living by the gun gave them a shared identity. Says Trachtman, "They were recognized, and recognized themselves as a distinct fraternity in Western society; when any one of them made his appearance on a scene, his very presence could inspire awe and dread" (1974: 35). Similar observations have been made of today's gangs. As with today's gangsters, an affront to a gangster of the West brought the wrath of his fraternity brothers. When Luke Short was "run out" of Dodge City, Kansas, within months—because travel took a while—Bat Masterson, Wyatt Earp, Doc Holliday, Shotgun Collins, and a whole host of lesser-known gangsters that were all buddies of Short, descended on Dodge City to "renew old acquaintances." It is truly amazing that Mr. Short was able to return to business in Dodge City under new negotiated settlements with his old rivals. This scenario sounds strangely reminisicent of today, an individual gangster is "run out of town" and yet soon returns, after his friends (homies, brothers, etc.) have a "conversation" with those who ran him out of town.

The gunfighters and gangsters of old, like the gangsters of today, "belonged to a species that courted its own destruction, readily—even eagerly—putting their lives on the line for any issue they deemed important" (Trachtman, 1974: 39). And like their counterparts of today, monikers and reputation mean everything, whether deserved or not. The reputation is the element that gave them an edge with an often nervous opponent. As Scott (1994) relates, his moniker of "Monster" helped to get him out of as many situations as it placed him in. This nickname (i.e., a reputation) gave his rivals, and occasionally the police, something to think about; and while they were thinking, he was acting. As it was in the West, reputation is what gangsters strive for, for it is one aspect—including length of tenure in the gang, number of incidents you are involved with, and how the other members think of you—that will make you an original gangster (OG). So, gangsters must have the following goals:

1.  Strive to build the reputation of their name as an individual

2.  Build their name in association with their particular set, so that when their name is spoken, their set is also spoken of in the same breath, for they are synonymous

3. Establish themselves as a promoter of their gang (adapted from Scott, 1994: 15)

So, what was the driving force behind the proliferation of gangs? For many, and certainly at the top of the list for all, it was the monetary rewards, the lure of quick money. But other reasons were a big part of the picture as well. Henry Starr, a gang leader in the Indian Territory (what is now Oklahoma and Arkansas) said, "Life in the open, the rides at night, the spice of danger, the mastery over men, the pride of being able to hold a mob at bay —it tingles in my veins. I love it. It is wild adventure" (Trachtman, 1974: 53). Ask a gangster today what attracts him or her, and you will receive a similar answer.

Though we think that today's gangs evolved from today's society, reality is based in a long tradition of gang banging. Gurr (1989) reports that no less than 500 vigilante groups existed between 1760 and 1900. During the economic depression of the early nineteenth century people were especially fearful of the harassing and assaultive behavior of juvenile gangs. The editors of a Philadelphia newspaper expressed fear and concern over the "new" juvenile street gangs,

> A few nights ago, a number of boys assembled in Fifth-street, between Market and Chestnut streets, to divert themselves with firing squibs. A gentleman on horseback and a servant driving a carriage, with a pair of horses, happened to pass by at the same instant; and also several persons on foot, who might have had their limbs shattered, if the horses had broken loose. The boys [saw this as] a fine opportunity for sport and mischief, and eagerly seized the moment, to light a squib, and fling it towards the horses. Luckily, indeed, the beasts were in good hands, and, though frightened, were prevented from [running off]. Had not this been the case, the newspapers might [be reporting] a list of five or six persons killed or wounded" (Sanders, 1970: 326).

By the early 1800s teenage gangs were a fixture, albeit unwanted, of most large cities. It was not just juveniles, however, that were the problem. The Forty Thieves is identified as the first modern adult criminal gang (Illinois State Police, 1989). This Irish-American immigrant gang was formed in 1820 in the Five Points district of New York City. As did so many adult gangs then and now, the Forty Thieves produced several auxiliary or subgangs composed of juveniles, with appropriate names (e.g., the Forty Little Thieves). While many of these gangs engaged in relatively low threat behavior, clearly many juvenile gangs "chose a variety of targets: lonely pedestrians, police officers, younger adolescents . . . and isolated members of competing ethnic or racial populations" (Johnson, 1979: 83). Along with the Forty Thieves, there were the Kerryonians, the Dusters, the Plug Uglies and the Dead Rabbits, to name just a few (Asbury, 1927/1971). It was generally believed that these gangs,

> were formed by young men rebelling against their low social status. They came from areas of overcrowded, substandard housing, poor or nonexistent health care facilities, broken homes, and few economic opportunities. . . . Their original intent may have been simple camaraderie born of shared frustration at perceived social or economic injustices. Whatever the reason, their original purpose eventually degenerated to social resentment and ultimately they manifested that resentment in criminal activity (Illinois State Police, 1989: 2).

This description sounds strangely similar to today's gangs.

Again, the early gangs appeared to reflect the definitions of the day: play groups, secret clubs, social clubs, athletic teams, and adolescent groups. Despite what they were initially called, as they evolved over time and were influenced by their adult counterparts, gangs "took on increasingly darker tones" (Goldstein, 1991: 8). How did these changes happen? Thrasher, in his seminal work, provides some insight into this process:

> It does not become a gang . . . until it begins to excite disapproval and opposition. It discovers a rival or an enemy in the gang in the next block; its baseball or football team is pitted against some other team; parents or neighbors look upon it with suspicion or hostility . . . the storekeeper or the cops begin to give it shags [chase it]; or some representative of the community steps in and tries to break it up. This is the real beginning of the gang, for now it starts to draw itself more closely together. It becomes a conflict group (1927/1963: 26).

The Bloods of Los Angeles are instructive here.

Although gangs existed in Los Angeles at least as far back as the 1920s, the rivalry that exists between the Crips and the Bloods have captured much attention. After winning a fight with the Avenue Gang, the Crips developed in the early 1970s out of the Los Angeles high schools and formed to terrorize and extort money from other students. Following Thrasher's model, the Bloods developed as a response to the Crips. How does one protect himself from the Crips? One joins up, runs, exists as a continuous victim, or looks for help. Because neither law enforcement nor school officials could provide 24-hour protection, these "victims" formed their own gang—the Bloods—for protection. (See Chapter 7 for a more extensive discussion of street gangs including Crips and Bloods.) A similar chronology can be found in every city where gangs exist.

Gangs have existed throughout history, most often consisting of racial or ethnic groups (e.g., Jews, Italians, Irish, black) who perceived themselves as being at the bottom of the social economic class. The gang was seen as useful in achieving either group or individual status, providing an outlet for physical activity, or gaining economic resources (i.e., money). Indeed, money may be the sole reason for existing, because with money comes power and status. Their existence has been chronicled by many, and, except for Thrasher, the explanations of their beginnings appear to have followed the current mode of thinking. Puffer, for example, chose Darwinism as the explanation, noting that

> the boy's gang [is] the result of a group of instincts inherited from a distant past. . . . We must suppose that these gang instincts arose in the first because they were useful once, and that they have been preserved to the present day because they are, on the whole, useful still (1912: 83).

The gang was useful for _____. (Fill in the blank: Jesse James, Luke Short, etc.) It will, therefore, be useful for me.

Thrasher, anticipating many current explanations for and explorations of gangs, attempted to look for a combination of factors involving the youth *and* the community in which he resided. Thrasher saw the gangster as "a rather healthy, well-adjusted, red-blooded American boy seeking an outlet for normal adolescent drives for adventure and expression" (Hardman, 1967: 7). The youth, however, was also influenced by his environment, where inadequacies in the family, housing, jobs or the ability to find one, schools, etc., all combined to motivate the youth to look elsewhere for life satisfaction and rewards (Goldstein, 1991). That elsewhere was the gang.

Since Thrasher, social causation has persisted as a major determinant for gang formation. As we entered the 1980s era of gangs, more inclusive perspectives on gang formation appeared. Miller, for example, observes that

> youth gangs persist because they are a product of conditions basic to our social order. Among these are a division of labor between the family and the peer group in the socialization of adolescents, and emphasis on masculinity and collective action in the male subculture; a stress on excitement, congregation, and mating in the adolescent subculture; the importance of toughness and smartness in the subcultures of lower-status populations; and the density conditions and territoriality patterns affecting the subcultures of urban and urbanized locales (1982: 320).

Similarly, Edgerton proposed a causative explanation focusing on the idea of multiple marginality,

Contributing to the formation of gangs is residential segregation in low-income areas, poverty, poor school performance, little parental supervision, discrimination, and distrust of law enforcement. In these conditions, young people spent much of their lives together on the streets where a gang served them . . . as surrogate family, school, and police. We also hear from gang members . . . about the appeal that gang membership has for them—friendship, pride, prestige, belongingness, identity, self-esteem, and a desire to emulate their uncles and older brothers who were gang members before them (1988: x).

More recently, Hagedorn (1991) has suggested that, at least in Milwaukee, Thrasher was right. He goes further, suggesting that gang formation follows a pattern parallel to the economic and social trends in American society, most importantly, the changes in American economy. This idea is supported by Jackson (1991) who found that as American society moves from a manufacturing economy to a service one, gang formation appears to be a natural consequence, although unintended. Gangs flourish in such an environment because the more moderating influences of successful adults and stable families decline. Beyond economics, "The social order in gang communities is further disturbed by population movement and the disorganization created when there are rapid ethnic or racial changes in an area" (Spergel, cited in Conly, 1993: 8).

Gangs, then, have existed throughout history, responding to the social and economic structure of the time. Populated primarily by social, racial, or ethnic minorities, the gangs existed as a buffer against or as a mechanism to deal with and fight back against the real or perceived inequities of society, most probably projected upon them. Often, gangsters saw themselves as gladiators, fighting the good fight. In other cases, gangsters saw themselves as simply getting "their piece of the pie." In still other cases, gangsters saw themselves as simply responding to the threat posed by other gangs, which included the police. Nevertheless, the idea that "our" gangs are "new" is simply not true. Nor is it true that "our" gangs are more violent. All that is new, all that has changed, are the "tools of the trade," and the economic incentives (drugs). Clearly both have provided avenues for increased violence but not necessarily more violence—a semantic difference, perhaps, but an important one.

From Dickens's Artful Dodger to the Posses, gang formation, structure, and membership have remained remarkably consistent. As the community and family break down and without parental and social controls, juveniles left on their own with little to do but "hang out" become ripe to be influenced by the adult criminals, gangsters, and gangs that exist in their neighborhood. Indeed, even with strong adult role models, the pushes and pulls are enormous. The movie *A Bronx Tale* is instructive here. As Santayana noted, if we do not learn from history, we are doomed to repeat it. Though information on the history of gangs is relatively sparse, and almost every specific gang has its own history, what we know of the general history of gangs tells us much. Can we learn from it? Or are we doomed to repeat the mistakes of those who have come before?

CHAPTER 2

# What Is a Gang?

The previous chapter introduced the basic idea that what a gang is and does has not changed significantly over the years. How they carry out their activities, the tools they use, and the criminal activity they engage in may change, but the gang itself does not. Nevertheless, it is important to be able to have at least a working definition of what a gang is, because a definition affects program responses. However, when working with and studying gangs, a common definition is not always available.

Goldstein (1991), for example, offers 14 different definitions of a gang. These range from 1912 to 1990 and include definitions offered by academics and professionals. Conly et al. (1993) offer six definitions, again using those provided by academics and professionals. Neither the 14 definitions in one study nor the six in the other are the same. So what? The community's response and the resources it provides for combating the "gang problem" will rely heavily (if not completely) on how gangs and the "gang problem" are defined. Thus, being able to define the problem leads one to the response and the available resources. If we cannot define the problem, we cannot address it. The absence of a common definition is surprising given that interest in gangs goes as far back as the 1890s, if not earlier. In fact, it could also be argued that the Capulets and Montagues of Shakespeare's *Romeo and Juliet* could be considered gangs.

The professional community, in looking for advice and direction in this area, would probably find yet another reason to see academia as not being useful, because we cannot agree among ourselves about what a gang is. Miller (1980) sees this problem as significant, and calls on the "social scientists to define what a gang is to counteract the manipulation of the term by people outside the social science research community" (in Horowitz, 1990: 43). Miller goes on to argue that law enforcement and the media (you could add corrections, juvenile justice, etc.) broaden or narrow their definition as it suits their own particular cause. One of the problems that arises is the inability to compare information about gangs across cities or times. Decker and Kempf (1991) note that even within the same jurisdiction, different parts of "the system" define the problem differently. This lack of a clear definition forces public officials to respond to an ill-defined problem, and could make them look as if they do not know what is going on in their own community. It often results in a denial that a gang problem exists, and/or in the over-identification of gangs, gang members, and the gang problem (Huff, 1990). The search for a definition may also overshadow our purpose in looking at gangs and in solving the gang problem. Ryan (1995) makes the point that we may be spending too much time defining gangs rather than addressing strategies to deal with, prevent, and intervene with them.

It may, however, be beneficial that a firm definition does not exist. Every group involved in working with gangs have their own interests and assumptions and would probably never agree on a specific definition in the first place. Second, a firm definition might restrict research on gangs and the topics studied. With a firm definition in place, new questions or foci could be discouraged. As it is, every study of gangs and the gang problem offers its own definition of what a gang is. Typically these definitions rely on the definitions imposed on gangs by those from whom the information is sought (e.g., law enforcement, gangsters themselves, etc.). While these variations make cross-jurisdictional comparisons difficult, knowing the definitions assigned by those involved assists in understanding the interplay between the justice system personnel, the community, and the gang. It also affects the publicity, or lack of it, afforded the problem, the distribution of resources, and how the gangster is treated by the system. Zatz (1985) has noted that issues of definition do affect the way a suspected gangster is identified and treated by the justice system.

Clearly, as gangs have evolved, so too have the definitions. Can we identify some commonalities, some characteristics that are common to the Hole in the Wall Gang and the Rolling 60s? Miller (1974) surveyed more than 100 criminal justice and youth services agencies about their respective definitions of what makes up a gang. In terms of consensus, he identified six major elements:

1. Being organized

2. Having identifiable leadership

3. Identifying with a territory

4. Continual association

5. Having a specific purpose

6. Engaging in illegal activities

Within many of the definitions one encounters, these six general elements will appear. They also make evident how the character of gangs has changed. While we believe that each of Miller's six elements is characteristic of all gangs, whether juvenile or adult, clearly other elements must also be considered. One element is the increase in violent behavior. Noted gang researcher Irving Spergel in testimony before the Senate's juvenile justice subcommittee commented that the gang problem is "amorphous and complex, . . . that we seem to know what to do rather than what not to do, but that violence is a major consideration" (December 19, 1994). While Spergel made this comment in December 1994, Miller in 1975 noted, "Contemporary youth gangs pose a greater threat to public order and a greater danger to the safety of the citizenry than at any other time during the past" (in Goldstein, 1990: 7). Given that we have made little current progress in addressing the gang problem, one can only speculate about what the next century will bring. It is important to note also, that in his same testimony, Spergel commented that he did not believe the savagery itself had radically changed, but the instruments of violence certainly had. Newer and more deadly instruments of violence result in a more certain end for those involved in the violence.

Besides more serious firepower, these new instruments are often used impersonally. The escalation of violence also appears to have an intergenerational dynamic to it. In those gangs that contain an intergenerational connection, primarily Hispanic and some Chicago gangs, younger gangsters seem to want to match or outdo their predecessors. Still others want to live up to their moniker. Spergel identifies some other nonbehavioral reasons: gangs today have more weapons; they are more sophisticated; they have a greater ability to "hit and run" (e.g., drive-bys); and membership may have grown (1990). Also, gangs appear more willing to use weapons and see them as signs of power (Hynes, 1991; Conly et al., 1993). It must also be remembered that violence has in many ways become an acceptable response to life's obstacles.

The other new element is drugs. Many gangs are involved in the drug trade, and some, such as the Jamaican Posses, appear to exist exclusively for that purpose. Some are involved in selling drugs, others in doing drugs; drugs are a defining element in many if not all of the current gang activities. Any current gang definition needs, in some form, to consider the increase in violence and drug activity. It should be noted, however, that if drugs were to be removed from society, or legalized, that gangs would still exist. They would simply find another illegal outlet for making money.

Returning to the idea of violence, it must be understood that violence is not the *primary* activity of most gangs. "Hanging out" and partying (certainly not criminal activities) are still staple gang activities, as is participation in many truly conventional activities, most notably athletics. In fact, most gang activity is not violent. However, violence permeates gang life and gang activity. A gang cannot be territorial without the willingness to use violence to exert and maintain control of their territory. Violent events do much to provide cohesion for the gang, and as Klein has commented, violence has a mythic quality (Decker, 1995). Gang members talk about it, retell the story, and use it as a focal point for the next violent episode. Even though very little gang time is taken up with violence, as Sanders notes, "It is the *willingness to do violence* that makes a gang a gang" (1994: 12, emphasis in the original). For those who interact with the gang, the knowledge that the group will use violence is what sets it apart from other groups—gang or nongang, juvenile or adult, criminal or noncriminal. Using violence is proof positive of the ongoing willingness to do violence. Violence, even if used sparingly, then plays a key role in defining a gang and gang behavior.

What, then, makes a gang a gang, at least as most people think of them? It is violence. Even Miller (1975), who did not want to overemphasize violence, used it to differentiate street groups from gangs. So, if it is violence that defines a gang, what kind of violence, and how does it work with respect to the gang? Sanders (1994) provides us with some answers. First, a gang must use deadly force. They must use or be prepared to use enough force to kill another. This killing can occur in a defensive or offensive posture, but death is the key.

Second, the violence must be used in the name of the gang. The members, when engaging in a violent crime, recognize that it is done for or with the gang. This intent is most evident with drive-by shootings. As Davis noted in his study of drive-bys, those involved in the shootings "dressed in ways that marked them as gang members" (1995: 17). The gang members in his study saw any sign of disrespect as an affront that warranted attack, and the members "accepted the implied responsibility of being willing to commit a violent crime for the organization" (1995: 18). For Garfinkel (1967) the violence and the gang are mutually enforcing. Violence defines the event as gang related, and the gang is seen as causing the violence.

Third involves gang solidarity. Violence serves as a solidifying force for the gang. Group solidarity increases in the face of external threats to the group. Because gangs have few sources of internal cohesion, the external threats posed by the police and rival gangs serve to maintain group cohesion (Klein and Crawford, 1967). Whether viewed as appropriate or not, the violence serves as a solidifying force. This cohesion, however, is a unique balancing act for gangs. Too much external pressure, usually in the form of a law enforcement response or several deaths, can have the opposite effect. If the belief is "we're getting shot at or arrested everywhere we go, the gang can become viewed as a source of problems and disunity" (Sanders, 1994: 18). Thus, it must be "the right amount of violence" at the "right time" against the "right people" to maintain group cohesiveness. Violence therefore is generally not the gang's all-consuming passion. It must be balanced with other activities, legitimate and otherwise.

Fourth involves territoriality. Many gang definitions talk about territory or turf. Although this aspect is changing somewhat, gangs are identified by their turf. Implied in this notation is, again, the use of violence. A gang cannot keep territory without being willing to use violence in keeping it. Thus violence is necessary to maintain territorial integrity (Sanders, 1994).

While violence is a defining behavior for gangs, it is not and does not need to be constant or engaged in by all members. As a group, a gang is composed of a variety of individuals, many of whom will prove their loyalty to the gang in ways other than violence (e.g., stealing, pimping, etc.). The frequency and intensity of the gang's violence may also vary. Many gangs may go years without a violent act. It is their *reputation* for violence that keeps them a gang. Indeed, when a gang feels their reputation is in jeopardy, they are likely to resort to violence to renew their gang status, to let everyone around know they are still here, and more important, still violent.

As important as violence is in defining a gang, it is not the sole determinant. Also important is the transpersonal nature of membership. A gang is defined not by its specific members at any given point in time, but as a phenomenon transcending its membership. The gang exists no matter who its members are. The gang as a unit, as a force to be reckoned with, remains. This idea is important for identifying a gang, for it differentiates a gang from what Yablonsky (1962) called a "near group," ad hoc, impermanent and transitory.

What then is a gang? Not wanting to reinvent the wheel, and recognizing the merit present in each state's criminal justice agencies' own definitions, we generally like Sanders's (with some exceptions):

A youth gang is any transpersonal group of youths that shows a willingness to use deadly violence to claim and defend territory, and attack rival gangs, extort or rob money, or engage in other criminal behavior as an activity associated with its group, and is recognized by itself and its immediate community as a distinct dangerous entity. The basic structure of gangs is one of age and gender differentiation, and leadership is informal and multiple (1994: 20).

We would take exception with two points. One, we believe that a youth gang (by definition) is no different from an adult gang. Adult gangs are also defined by transpersonality, a willingness to use violence, and engaging in criminal behavior with and for the gang. Because of benefits associated with gang membership, many gangsters are remaining in the gang longer or for life, which is especially true of Hispanic gangs. Thus, we believe the tag "youth" should be removed. A gang is a gang is a gang, no matter the age of its members.

Our other exception has to do with Sanders's point about leadership. It is our contention that not one gang, but rather a multiplicity of gangs and gang types exist, each with the "basics": a willingness to use deadly violence to claim and defend territory, and attack rival gangs, extort or rob money, or engage in other criminal behavior as an activity associated with its group, recognized by itself and its immediate community as a distinct dangerous entity but each having unique qualities as well. For many, this uniqueness is its leadership. The importance of leadership is certainly true of organized crime, many Asian gangs, some Hispanic gangs, and the Disciples and Vice Lords. Many of these have a well-defined leadership structure with policies in place for replacement, succession, etc. Clearly this structure is formal and singular rather than informal and multiple. The same can be said of many Wild West gangs. We would argue that most gangs whose leadership is informal and multiple are probably not transpersonal and cease to exist when their leadership is arrested or dead. Thus, using much from Sanders, we would offer the following definition of a *gang:*

> A gang is any transpersonal group of individuals that shows a willingness to use deadly violence to claim and defend territory, and attack rival gangs, extort or rob money, or engage in other criminal behavior as an activity associated with its group, and is recognized by itself and its immediate community as a distinct dangerous entity. The basic structure of gangs is one of gender and leadership differentiation unique to its particular location and history.

For many, knowing what a gang is, is important for deciding what a gang-related crime is. Unfortunately, not all agencies define a gang-related incident in the same way, and just because the police call an incident gang-related (or nongang-related) does not necessarily make that definition correct. Often, this definition occurs because the individual involved has been identified as a gangster; however, as Katz (1989) argues, even though a criminal has been identified as a gangster it does not mean that the crime was caused by gang involvement. Spergel and Chance suggest that "a gang crime incident is an incident in which there was gang motivation, not mere participation by a gang member" (1991: 23). They believe that a gangster's nongang crime should, however, be recorded although differentiated from his gang crime. For example, Sanders notes the shooting of a rival lover by a gangster. Even though the rival was not a gangster and the violent act was not one in the name of the gang but rather in the name of love, because the shooter was a gangster the police identified the crime as gang related.

Being in a gang will result in criminality. Often it will be direct, at other times indirect, but it will be criminal nevertheless. In fact, it is the criminality that directs our attention to the gang. A gang itself is not illegal; being in a gang is not illegal. What is illegal is gang members' criminal behavior. Is it necessary—other than as an academic exercise—to really know the difference, to categorize the difference? Does knowing the difference assist us in dealing with gangs? We think not. In many gangs, a gangster cannot commit a crime on his/her own. The gang will get its "cut" somehow. Thus the gangster who goes into the local "stop and rob," empties the cash register, and uses the money for his personal good and is subsequently disciplined by the gang for either bringing too much pressure on them or for not giving them their cut, did he not do a gang-related crime? In other instances, the individual gangster may engage in criminal behavior he could not "pull off" were it not for his gangster status. Is this not also gang related? We believe the gang- and nongang-related crime distinction is an artificial one that does nothing but cloud the issues here. If an identified hard-core gangster commits a crime, it is gang related, and should be recorded as such.

A gang, then, is a group of individuals willing to use violence in pursuit of their goals, who engage in criminal behavior individually or collectively, and have a specific structure defining themselves. A street group is not, then, a gang because it is not willing to use violence in pursuit of their objectives. Hate groups, although willing to use violence in pursuit of their goals, are not gangs because, generally, they do not keep and maintain territory (i.e., a defining structure). Yablonsky's near groups are not gangs because they are transitory. With some exceptions, a group that is not willing to use violence, or is transitory, or does not claim territory is, therefore, not a gang. That they are not gangs does not make them any less worthy of study, or dangerous; it does, however, make them different from a gang, and will generally require a different response.

# 3

# Gang Structure and Organization

As with any organization, gang members go a long way in defining a gang's structure and organization. Given that criminality, especially violent criminality, is key in defining gangs and their activity, why would an individual want to join a gang? Keep in mind that, while gang members are of all ages, it is rare that one joins or begins gang life as an adult. Clearly some individuals learn about gangs while in prison, and upon their release join the local gang, but for the most part, gang membership begins during youth and adolescence. Unfortunately, little research has been done on why one would join a gang, and even less research on how one leaves a gang. This point is important from a preventive view, because if we knew more about how and why an individual joins a gang, programs could be established to reduce these risk factors. Additionally, some evidence suggests that gang formation and one's entry into a gang vary with the location or context of the gang.

## WHY PEOPLE JOIN

For example, in Los Angeles, city and suburban gangs developed differently, with violence being the flashpoint for gang formation in the city, followed by drug dealing. In the suburbs of Los Angeles, drug dealing came first, followed by gang formation and recruitment, then violence. In Milwaukee, Wisconsin, gangs developed out of dance groups, when fights broke out after the dance competitions. In addition, traditional corner groups also coalesced around the fighting. As was noted in the previous chapter, when groups are threatened, they respond with and are solidified by violence. Thus, gangs form and individuals join them for a variety of reasons associated with the individuals and with the community where they reside. And while gangs are not exclusively ethnic or racial, the contexts associated with being an ethnic or racial minority provide an impetus for gang formation. Throughout history, when any ethnic group (e.g., Jews, Irish, Italian) was at the bottom, gangs were formed.

Certainly one explanation that is frequently offered is that the gang fills a void in the individual's life. Typically, for this type of individual, the traditional family does not exist, leaving the individual to believe she or he is alone and must cope with her or his problems alone. The gang, then, becomes a surrogate family providing the individual with personal attention and sense of identity.

Johnston identified several factors that increased the chance that one might choose gangsterism: community characteristics, social and insititutional attachments, and a definition of self (1983: 283). Many of the gangsters in Johnston's study tended to be from communities where the perception of racial tension was high. Most of the gangsters did, in fact, come from single-parent families with little parental control. These gangsters also tended to have problems in school as well as low self-esteem and relatively low self-confidence in any setting. The gang, then, could provide these youth with the status, a sense of self-worth, and a place of acceptance that they at least perceived they did not have in their family life. Again, however, this scenario is not unusual for disenfranchised ethnic groups.

Individuals join gangs for a variety of reasons, including individual needs for identity, recognition, protection, love and understanding, status, money, and opportunity. Wade (1991) identifies the following reasons for joining a gang: acceptance, recognition, a sense of belonging, status, power, discipline (or consistency), structure, unconditional love, shelter, food, clothing, nurturing, activities, economic support, and respect. She goes on to comment that many gang members tell her that their families only provide three or four of these.

Despite the criminality and violence associated with being in a gang, joining up may be viewed as normal and respectable. The criminality and violence may be seen as secondary to the excitement, fun and frolic, and associating with peers of similar class, interest, need, and persuasion (Sarnecki, 1986). Deukmajian (1981) and Reosenbaum and Grant (1983) suggest that the consequences of being a gangster may not be recognized by adolescents and young adults. We would disagree. While youths generally do not have the same maturity as adults, they do know right from wrong and know

—or should know—that criminality and violence are wrong. That they do not know the consequences provides them a way out or an excuse for their behavior. We believe they do know the consequences of their behavior, and either do not care, or their need for status, recognition, etc., overwhelms their rationality, or the police and juvenile courts do not do a sufficient job of attaching punishment and accountability to their behavior when they are caught, particularly the first time.

Not only may joining a gang be viewed as normal by the individual, but it may also be seen as desireable and expected in certain communities. Particularly in lower-class white ethnic and Hispanic communities, honor, loyalty, and fellowship are viewed as compelling reasons for joining gangs. The gang is seen as the vehicle for preserving the neighborhood and protecting its honor (Torres, 1980; Horowitz, 1983). In these communities and for these residents, the gang is an extension rather than a substitute of the family and development of the clan. For many individuals, especially Hispanics, multi-generational gang membership is the norm rather than the exception.

Gang membership may also be seen as a way of providing protection from real or perceived threats, perhaps even from the gang itself. This reason may be especially true for the new kid in school or town. Members of the family may be harassed, intimidated, or attacked, thus he or she joins the gang to be protected. While the gang member may feel safer within the gang, Savitz, Rosen, and Lalli (1980) point out that being a gangster increases the likelihood of attack, at least by another gangster. So, while the individual may believe his or her safety is tenuous, joining a gang, ironically, actually increases his or her chances of becoming a victim.

In addition to the social and psychological reasons espoused for joining a gang, many individuals join a gang for financial reasons. The gang becomes a vehicle for the individual to develop contacts and the "know-how" for further criminality. In addition, the gangster attracts the attention of older gangsters, including those involved in traditional organized crime; many become proteges and go on to an adult criminal life. This pattern is well depicted in *The Godfather* movie series. Most recently, the gang has become a place for contact with drug dealers and to prepare for a career as a dealer, hit man, or enforcer (Miller, 1975).

We believe that an individual chooses to become a gangster for a variety of reasons; the process of joining up, however, is hardly one-sided. Like the military, gangs have a vested interest in recruitment of the "right" people, especially in communities where intergenerational gang membership cannot be relied on. The gang has utilitarian reasons for recruiting and enrolling members who have the interests and skills the gang needs. Jankowski (1991) observes that gangs allow their members a certain latitude in developing and pursuing individual interests as long as those interests do not conflict with gang goals.

## HOW PEOPLE JOIN

Little information is available on how one goes about the process of actually joining a gang. It may be as simple as hanging around with and being accepted by other gangsters. As Spergel notes, "Forced recruitment is not common and intimidation is more indirect than direct . . . although on occasion a youth who refuses to join can be severely beaten" (1993: 57). Some gangs have a formal process of initiation (jumping in) where the member must run the gauntlet in order to join. For others, the process is more informal, relying on family members, friends, and drug-dealing activities to join. Fagan (1993) suggests that

> recruitment is a courtship. The degree of formality varies across gangs, depending on how well organized the gang is. Factors that play a part include the degree of ethnic solidarity in a community, which can serve as a facilitator, and the degree of opposition from the larger society (cited in Conly, 1993: 19).

Moore (in Conly, 1993) suggests that most people who join Chicano gangs in East Los Angeles want to join. When recruitent occurs, it is generally those individuals who

1. are a part of a single-parent family.

2. have a need for social acceptance.

3. lack a positive role model at home or school.

4. are having difficulty in school.

5. have dropped out of school.

6. are generally part of a lower socioeconomic status (SES) group.

7. are not able to become gainfully employed.

8. lack access to community recreational facilities.

9. have little exposure to religion (adapted from Williams, Terrell and Leonard, 1991: 7).

# 4

# Italian Organized Crime

> Slum-area youngsters joined gangs and turned to delinquent behavior at an early age. Unlike most of their contemporaries, who also belonged to corner gangs and were involved in occasional mischief-making, the criminal-in-the-making had little or nothing to do with legitimate labor, which they believed was only for "suckers," men who worked long hours for low pay and lived in overcrowded tenements with their families. It appears that all the prohibition-era racketeers, whether born in the United States or brought here as infants or children, started their careers in one or another gang. The corner gang became their school (Nelli, 1976: 107).

Perhaps the most feared criminal organization within U.S. boundaries—the Sicilian mafia—is also the least understood. Historical accounts of Italian organized crime are peppered with gross inconsistencies and inaccuracies to such an extent that their repetition has obliterated all but the sensational. In fact, romanticized depictions of leading mob figures are so prevalent that their viciousness is often obscured. Thus, an "accurate" or "academic" account is an almost insurmountable task. However, compilation of the various accounts may be helpful in developing a basic understanding of the underpinnings of the organizational structure, ideology, and individual similarities.

Few accounts have paralleled the similarities between the Italian syndicate of organized crime and other ethnic factions. Like contemporary street gangs who prey on their own communities, early mafia activities may be characterized as predatory. Relying primarily on income gained through strong-armed robberies and extortion, young Italians concentrated on the most vulnerable and available targets—members of their own communities. In fact, without the proceeds from these predatory activities, it is highly unlikely that the transition from street thuggery to sophisticated criminal activity would have been possible.

It was not until the passage of the Volstead Act in 1919 (Figure 4-1) that a hierarchical, sophisticated organization emerged. Prohibition not only enabled the Sicilian branch of the American underworld to capitalize on the public's lust for liquor, it also provided them with working capital to enter legitimate enterprises. Contemporary groups have carefully masqueraded as

---

The Eighteenth Amendment was ratified on January 16, 1919. Its contents clearly forbade the manufacture, sale, import, or export of intoxicating beverage. However, the amendment proved to be useless prior to passage of the Volstead Act. The Volstead Act of 1919, which was passed by Congress on October 27, 1919, but went into effect on the one-year anniversary of the Eighteenth Amendment, was actually more significant because it defined the language of the amendment. "Intoxicant," for example, was defined as any beverage containing more than one-half of one-percent alcohol by volume. It also authorized federal agents to enforce any and all provisions of the amendment. Further it specified rather harsh penalties for individuals convicted of booze trafficking. Ironically, it did not provide for criminal acts deriving from the actual imbibement of such intoxicants. Rather, like today's drug laws, it was not a crime to drink or to feel its intoxicating effects. As a result, mainstream America had little to lose by enjoying the product, while at the same time they actually were directly responsible for all of the violence surrounding its existence.

The period between the ratification of the Eighteenth Amendment and the enactment of the Volstead Act enabled enterprising young criminals to stockpile homemade liquor. In addition, warehouses that housed unconsumed legitimate alcohol were raided and burglarized by these criminals. And, finally, the "legitimate" alcohol produced for medicinal or industrial purposes was manipulated by gangsters for consumption purposes. Speakeasies replaced bars and saloons, and because they were illegal in and of themselves, they were well stocked with a virtual smorgasbord of other vice-related activities (i.e., gambling and prostitution), which allowed mainstream America to enjoy their favorite pastimes, while actually supporting the criminal underworld.

Repealment of the Eighteenth Amendment, which had been designed to reduce criminal behavior, was actually a moot point. Some individuals who had once been socially undesirable (for example, Joe Kennedy, father of John and Bobby Kennedy) channeled their illicit profits into legitimate enterprises, buying their way into society's favor. Others who foresaw the end of Prohibition had already channeled their resources elsewhere. And so the era of Prohibition and the laws governing it abjectly failed in their efforts to reduce criminal behavior. In fact, Americans had never stopped drinking, and an economic foundation had been laid for a criminal syndicate that continues to flourish to this day.

**FIGURE 4-1**  Volstead Act of 1919 and the Eighteenth Amendment

legitimate corporations, and have monopolized a variety of regulated industries. This facade has successfully masked the violence inherent in such organizations, and has unfairly affected the playing fields on which law-abiding citizens and businesses compete. Though law enforcement efforts have become increasingly successful in criminal prosecutions, the ranks of the Italian mafia have remained resilient due to their ability to recruit young males.

## HOMELAND FOUNDATIONS AND AMERICAN MOBSTERS

Although some incidents in the history of the American mafia remain disputed, the success and longevity of the American mafia is not. Their propensity for violence coupled with their ability to corrupt governmental structures has enabled them to remain at the forefront of the criminal underworld. These characteristics, somewhat alien to earlier criminal gangs, are deeply rooted in their unique cultural and ethnic history, and are throwbacks to their Sicilian heritage where lines between criminal organizations and governmental institutions are not clearly drawn.

Perhaps the most powerful of all organized crime syndicates in the annals of history is the original Sicilian mafia, which emerged in Italy in the 1800s as a result of an immobile class system. Originally utilized as arbitrators by feudal landowners, early mafiosi were tasked with mediating disputes between peasant classes and absent landlords. Thus empowered, these street-level bandits soon represented a pseudojudiciary, arbitrarily extorting tithes and demanding fines from peasant and landlord alike. Inevitably, this system encouraged violence and mistreatment of the poor, and resulted in greater levels of economic disparity. While landowners were originally satisfied with this system, they proved to be very shortsighted. In fact, the introduction of a "middle" class shook the foundations of a traditionally dichotomous economic superstructure. Dissatisfied with their current standing, mafiosi exploited their role, and eventually became powerful in their own right, with a power that far exceeded legitimate government institutions (Jamieson, 1989).

Jamieson (1989) identifies four main components of this overarching power structure: (1) manpower, (2) the power of violence, (3) political power, and (4) financial power. Likening it to a country, Jamieson explains that these powers enabled the mafia structure to be antistate and assert its authority over a democratic nation. Accordingly, the Sicilian mafia may be characterized as a state within a state—one that contains its own government, army, financial resources, and territorial competence, all of which corrupt legitimate structures with little or no repercussions (Jamieson,

1989). In fact, the mafia has become so entrenched in the welfare of the country that Sicilian authorities are powerless to combat it. Recent prosecution efforts and the assassination of high-ranking governmental officials indicate that Italy is in a state of civil war, one destined to be perpetual in nature.

Unlike their homeland counterparts, American factions of Italian organized crime do not routinely assassinate federal judges, prosecutors, or politicians, and are not as intrinsically interwoven in national politics. This apparent distance is not to suggest, however, that their more subtle approach has not affected governmental policy, prosecution efforts, and local politics. Indeed, past experience indicates that much of the success and continuing longevity enjoyed by the American mafia lies in their ability to manipulate governmental institutions, policies, and interests. Thus, the difference in the two is not the outcome, but the approach. American mobsters, perhaps recognizing the futility of armed conflict in a militarily strong environment, rely on the power of economic persuasion through corruption of poorly paid, street-level officers and local politicians. While both approaches have advantages, the American approach traditionally allowed mobsters to limit occupational fatalities from outsiders. By limiting violence to insiders only, they also successfully achieved a facade of respectability within their communities and beyond, allowing them to enjoy tolerance and even outright acceptance among the American public (see Figure 4-2). On the surface, then, it may appear that the American criminals are far removed from their Sicilian counterparts. On the contrary, Sicilian ideals of loyalty and tradition permeate the mafia subculture and provide a blueprint for organizational consistency as well as lay the foundations for organizational structure.

## STRUCTURE

Unlike some contemporary gangs, who seem to lack formalized structures and hierarchy, the American mafia is a highly organized, formally structured, and well-oiled criminal machine. Strictly patriarchal, the American mafia has never been an equal opportunity employer. Traditionally, only card-carrying Sicilian males were eligible for membership. Homeland prejudices and ethnic stereotypes, brought over by immigrants, separated some Italian communities and subsequent organized crime families. Cultural differences in dress, style, and language, undetectable to non-Italians were, in some cases, as divisive as race or religion. Although the increasing lack of ethnic purity has moderated these hostilities and blurred ethnic lines, cultural manifestations often hint at individual lineage. For example, Sicilian gangsters such as

## Community Groups and Facades of Legitimacy

The most powerful of the decision makers . . . are not even known to the public. These names . . . are rarely if ever seen in print, for leadership in the brotherhood requires a shunning of the limelight and headlines. The true mafiosa maintains a reticence and humility, an unassailable facade of respectability.

He is the owner of a small business on a sidestreet in a great American city. A kindly man who gives small sums to the needy, who contributes to the church and local charities, a wise and graying don, accepted and beloved in the neighborhood.

Tonight he meets with a few old friends in the back of a restaurant. One man is a corporation head. Two others are known figures in the rackets. Two are neighborhood dons. One is a man who has served time for murder. They drink red wine and talk in Sicilian dialect. The terms are archaic, the phrases obscure. The meanings and ideas are a mixture of superstition, ritual, fraternal loyalty, and cynical ruthlessness.

This is a court of underworld law. A brother has failed to pay a debt as ordered by the council. The defendant is their long-time friend and associate. He has often sat with them as a judge and passed the sentenced of death on others. However, he has been unfortunate; he tried to raise the money and failed. They know it is not a willing default; but what you owe, you pay.

The defendant is on the spot. In the society of silence, the word somehow spreads. No one will help him, no one will hide him, no one will take up his cause. The laws forbid.

He is stripped of the protection of the invisible worldwide government. Even his kin turn from him. There is no place to run, no place to hide. Sooner or later hired mafia executioners find him and shoot him down as he walks a street, or paints his front porch, or relaxes in a barber chair.

In his neighborhood world, the white-haired don continues to play his quiet role, an obscure symbol of wisdom and love and charity. The racketeers slip back into their own well-protected circles. Whatever they make, a share goes to the brotherhood leader. The corporation head returns to his board of directors, his civic committees, his political efforts to improve local government and get rid of the rackets.

This is the picture, this goes on, these are the men who control and corrupt whole communities—not a century ago, but in the 1960s, in the United States of America.

**FIGURE 4-2**  Community Patronage and Murder in the 1960s
*Source:* Anslinger and Ousler, 1961, pp. 77–78.

Carlo Gambino and Paul Castellano are subdued and somber by nature, disdaining the flamboyance exhibited by Neapolitan John Gotti (Jamieson, 1989).

Ethnicity, in and of itself, does not guarantee entrance into this criminal subculture. Prospective members are often recruited in childhood or adolescence, acting as runners or valets for neighborhood "wiseguys," i.e., "made" members, or those formally recognized as family members. In fact, many youths actively pursued the mafia, drawn to the mystique and apparent wealth of neighborhood mobsters. As William Fopiano remembers:

> Tony [the "Canadian" Sandrelli] always looked like a million dollars. Me and the other kids used to watch him stepping out of his shiny new Cadillac in cashmere coats and two-hundred-dollar mohair suits with lapels sharper than our dads' razors. The man who had me go get Tony's suit was his friend, Henry Salvitella . . . . You could always find Henry and Tony at a table in the Florentine with a frail, quiet man with a thick Sicilian accent. His name was Frank Cucchiara [boss of Boston family], and he was known as the "Cheeseman" for a cheese importing business he owned a few blocks away on Endicott Street.
>
> We all knew that these men were mobsters. We knew it from street talk and what we read in the papers, even if we were too young to have any idea exactly what they did or where their power came from. That was something we couldn't see. There were no machine guns or tough-guy bodyguards or bulletproof limousines around. All we knew was that they were better off than everybody else and people treated them as if they were important. They seemed to move in some exciting, secret world that was invisible to anyone who wasn't one of them.
>
> Everybody worked, and worked hard. They just never got paid much. Sure, they were better off than our grandparents who got stuffed into disease-infested rat holes as soon as they stepped off the boat and were expected to be grateful for any dirty job . . . our fathers would take anything they could get. They were construction workers, factory workers, bricklayers, storekeepers, truck drivers, waiters, janitors, stevedores. A few of the really lucky ones had civil service jobs. No one had any real money, except, of course, the wiseguys (Fopiano and Harvey, 1993: 7–9).

> Everybody wanted to be a hoodlum. There were degrees—some guys got into it just a little, some more than a little. Me, I was in all the way. Before I was fifteen I was a veteran of holdups and heists. The gang I put together robbed payrolls and broke into stores, restaurants and businesses all over Boston. In those days no place had an alarm, so it was almost hard to get caught. In school, we did what we had to do to get by, and for the most of us school was about to become a memory. But when it came to the ins and outs of stealing, no students were more enthusiastic or attentive. We learned how to break open safes that boasted six inches of manganese steel with just a sledgehammer, a two-pound, and an awl. And when burglar alarms eventually did become a problem, we were soon well-versed on the latest technology and the best methods of getting around it (Fopiano and Harvey, 1993: 1).

As young adults, these individuals are expected to exhibit criminal entrepreneurship, contribute to family coffers, and pay homage to local wiseguys. Often these youngsters develop their own gangs or "crews" with one youth acting as leader. Moneymaking enterprises traditionally include credit card scams, merchandise hijacking, and residential burglary. Entire groups and individual leaders passing muster are quickly recognized and recruited by local mafiosi, which is the first major step toward organizational entry.[1]

Prospective recruits must be sponsored by at least one family member. Those individuals successfully being "called up" or "straightened out" are then formally inducted into their respective family with as much solemnity as High Mass. Recollections of induction ceremonies by government witnesses are remarkably similar to that described by Salvatore "Sammy the Bull" Gravano while testifying at the trial of Gambino crime boss and long-time friend, John Gotti:

> [Paul Castellano] asked me if I liked everybody there. I told him yes. He asked me a few questions. One of the last questions he asked me was would I kill if he asked me to. I told him yes.
>
> He told me what was my trigger finger. I pointed to my trigger finger. He pinched it, blood came out. He put it on the saint, and started to burn the saint in my hand. He said, honor the oath. He said to me, that if I divulge any of the secrets of this organization that my soul should burn like the saint.
>
> I kissed him on both cheeks. I kissed everybody. I went around the table and kissed everybody. I sat down. They got up. They locked hands. They unlocked hands. They made me get in the middle of it.
>
> They locked hands again and told me, at that point, I was part of the brotherhood. I was a made member and I belonged (Maas, 1997).

This formal recognition represents an important milestone in the recipient's criminal career. As one wiseguy related to undercover special agent Joseph Pistone, "Getting made is the greatest thing that could ever happen to me . . . I've been looking forward to this day ever since I was a kid" (Pistone and Woodley, 1987). Organizational jargon recognizes family affiliation and graduation from associate status, as new members are introduced as "friends of ours." These newly recognized "soldiers" are assigned to a *capo* or *caporegime*. Usually, this individual is one with whom they have previous criminal association. Entering on the bottom rung of the organizational hierarchy, new soldiers must again prove their worth through moneymaking

---

[1]The importance of these neighborhood gangs cannot be overstated, as the majority of adolescent groupings become adult organizations.

criminal enterprise and "tithing" a predetermined percentage of their profit to their captain. Capos in turn direct group profits to the higher-ups, paying homage directly to the family boss. Underbosses and consiglieres (i.e., family advisors) receive their portion from the head of the family (Fopiano, 1986; Cressey, 1969; Bonavolonta and Duffy, 1996; Pistone and Woodley, 1987).

Independent as they may appear, individual families are supervised by an executive board—the Commission. This governing body is composed of the bosses from the five New York families (i.e., Gambino, Lucchese, Bonanno, Colombo, Genovese). This governing body controls relationships and mediates disputes that erupt periodically between and within the 24 American families. "Hits" or murders between warring factions must receive the blessing of the Commission. Individual members or families who violate Commission rulings face the most severe of sanctions—death.

In addition to regulations formally mandated by the Commission, La Cosa Nostra (LCN) groups have traditionally shared a complex system of rules deeply rooted in ethnic heritage and religious ideology. Projecting maxims found among those incarcerated, Cressey (1969: 175–178) identified five universal rules of conduct among criminal organizations:

1. *Be loyal to members of the organization. Do not interfere with each other's interests. Do not be an informer.* . . . [This rule] is a call for unity, for peace, for maintenance of the status quo, and for silence.

2. *Be rational. Be a member of a team. Don't engage in battle if you can't win.* [This rule demands] the corporate rationality necessary to conducting illicit businesses in a quiet, safe, profitable manner . . . violence involving other Cosa Nostra [sic] members and stealing from members is to be avoided.

3. *Be a man of honor. Always do right. Respect womanhood and your elders. Don't rock the boat* . . . emphasis on honor actually functions to enable despots to exploit their underlings. It is the right and duty of every member to question every other member's conduct, even that of a boss or underboss, if he suspects that the other man is not "doing right."

4. *Be a stand-up guy. Keep your eyes and ears open and your mouth shut. Don't sell out* . . . must be able to withstand frustrating and threatening situations without complaining or resorting to subservience . . . shows [sic] courage and heart . . . does not whine or complain in the face of adversity, including punishment, because "If you can't pay, don't play."

5.  *Have class. Be independent. Know your way around the world.* . . .
    To be straight is to be a victim: . . . a man who is committed to regular
    work and submission to duly constituted authority is a sucker . . . [be]
    concerned with [your] own honesty and manliness as compared with the
    hypocrisy of corrupt policemen and corrupt political figures.

Unfortunately, Cressey's depiction loses something in the translation.
Admonitions of "respect your elders and womanhood" fly in the face of contemporary mafia groups. Elders are respected based on the position that
they hold and the power that they wield. Castellano's ignominious demise on
the curb outside Sparks Steak House illustrates the amount of respect extended to organizational elders. And while reserving Friday night as official
"wives night out" may spare them the discomfort of an introduction to their
girlfriend, it would probably not result in high marks on most morality tests.
Indeed, it would appear that the rules proposed represent an earlier breed
of criminal, one rarely exposed to external cultural or religious ideologies.
These apparent contradictions do not suggest, however, that identifiable
similarities of conduct did not exist historically. In fact, a compilation of informant accounts and government sources indicate it was the following similarities that granted early Italians the leverage to achieve the highest echelons of the criminal underworld. In fact, many authors suggest that the
breakdown of these traditional norms has resulted in an increase in successful criminal prosecutions.

Other rules that have apparently been forsaken by the newer generation
are as follows:

1.  Economically support your community.

2.  Keep street-level drugs out of your community.

3.  Maintain church ties.

These patterns of behavior are directly related to the early economic success
of the Italian mafia. Poverty-stricken communities, desperate for any means
of economic support, unwittingly supported an institution that was most
harmful to them. However, the superficiality expressed by early mafiosi with
the activities in the preceding list enabled them to gain legitimacy and support from the communities that spawned them. Later generations, forsaking
this tradition, have found that Italian communities that once embraced them
and their kind would forcibly expel them if given the opportunity. Indeed, it
appears that while contemporary street groups are attempting to emulate
the model of the Italians, Italian youths are abandoning structural and cultural mainstays.

The most glaring and self-serving of all is, of course, *omerta*—code of silence. While every successful criminal organization has a code of secrecy, none has been more successful than LCN groups in ensuring its compliance. Traditionally, this code of *omerta* insulated mafia families from criminal prosecutions. Indeed, mafia informants were virtually an unheard of phenomenon prior to Valachi's 1963 appearance at the McClellan Committee (aka Subcommittee on Investigations of the U.S. Senate Committees on Operations). Recent years have seen an increase in governmental informants and organizational turncoats. In fact, John Gotti, head of the Gambino crime family, and Philadelphia boss Nicky Scarfo are but two of many high-ranking mafia officials who have organizational informants to thank for their lengthy prison sentences. Though various authors have attributed the decrease in organizational loyalty to increasing prosecution efforts, the answer may lie in an overall disregard for culturally mandated conduct by fourth generation Italians. Indeed, Cressey's (1969) identification of five universal rules of conduct are based on outdated generational constructs.

## A BRIEF HISTORY IN THE UNITED STATES

### The Black Hand

Some authors suggest that Italian organized crime existed long before Prohibition. These individuals suggest that much of the early criminality displayed by the Italians was far removed from highly industrialized areas such as New York and Chicago. Indeed, much weight is given to an incident occurring in the late 1800s in the southern city of New Orleans. Many accounts argue that the murder of Chief David Hennessey was in retaliation for this officer's involvement in earlier "mafia" cases in which numerous individuals were convicted. However, one of the few academic studies of the phenomenon negates this supposition. In fact, Nelli (1976: IX) states that:

> so many writers have accepted and repeated myths and distortions of fact so many times that inaccuracies have become accepted as truths. Furthermore, most of the studies have concentrated on the experience in one city, New York, and have generalized from that situation about the entire country. Certainly New York has been of great importance in the emergence and growth of syndicate crime in the United States; at the same time, significant differences among cities did exist, and still exist.

In fact, it is unclear whether an "organized" criminal syndicate existed as has often been argued. Nelli (1976) points out that revisitations of the incident alternatively blame the *mafia* or the *cammora*.[2] This inconsistency reveals a pattern of sensationalism and inaccuracy. It appears that contemporary authors have actually perpetuated the myth of a nationwide Italian syndicate by relying on editorial comments made during the time of the trial. These editorial comments, and much of the remaining text, was inherently laden with anti-Italian/anti-immigrant sentiment based on WASP distrust of Catholicism. Caricatures showing crazed Italians warned of the danger of this new "breed" of homo sapiens. In fact, a review of court transcripts and official proceedings indicate a veritable buffet of circumstantial evidence based on little more than ethnic stereotypes. In any event, the acquittal of all defendants charged in the murder of Chief Hennessy reaffirmed city residents' perceptions of a wide-scale criminal society, one that could corrupt even their most Christian neighbors. The subsequent lynching of those acquitted, which was accomplished with the assistance of prison personnel, extended the myth of the "black hand," a secret criminal society (Nelli, 1976). And so began the American mafia.[3]

By the turn of the century, ethnic criminal gangs sprouted across the country. Metropolitan areas experiencing an influx of immigrants reported criminal activity perpetrated by bands of Southern Italian immigrants. For the most part, these groups were highly unstructured, and preyed primarily on their own communities. Extortionists and common thugs abounded quickly becoming known as the *Black Hand*. Although the origin of such a title is debated (some authors attribute it to secret Sicilian societies, while others proclaim it to be a term used for resistance groups during the Spanish Inquisition), it seems apparent that the name was selected due to its ominous nature (Nelli, 1976). Extortion letters demanding specific sums and threatening dire consequences if ignored were sent to a variety of successful businessmen. These letters, signed *La Mano Nera,* proved to be a lucrative enterprise for their authors. It was a rare exception, indeed, when these letters failed to elicit the desired response. Shortsighted individuals who re-

---

[2]Historical accounts of the development of organized crime in Italy have traditionally dichotomized criminal groupings according to their geographic origin. The *mafia,* by far the most recognized grouping in this country, is comprised primarily of individuals from Palermo, Sicily; whereas members of the *cammora* trace their roots to Naples. Both groups are remarkable in that organizational expectations are consistent with their cultural heritage. Neopolitans, for example, are known for their flamboyance; whereas their Sicilian counterparts disdain the limelight and are more sedate in appearance and behavior.

[3]It is unclear which came first—the mafia or its myth. Ethnic succession theorists who suggest that the mafia developed due to a lack of legitimate avenues may argue that it was this event, signalling an all-out distrust and contempt for Italian-Americans, that actually encouraged the development of such a phenomenon.

fused to bow to these extortion attempts quickly lost their homes and businesses to explosions set by the Black Handers. Other individuals were either assaulted or murdered. It appeared to local residents that these extortion bands were invulnerable. Schools, churches, and government institutions all bowed to the Black Hand. However, these individuals were largely unorganized and lacked the organizational longevity soon displayed by the Italian mafia. For the most part, individuals engaging in Black Hand activities were not members of the more structured mafia. In fact, some of the most powerful figures in organized crime were victimized by the Black Hand. For example, Ignazio "Lupo the Wolf" Saietta, one of the most successful counterfeiters in New York, reportedly paid $10,000 to the Black Hand when members of his family were threatened. The apparent confusion or bifurcation of the groups seems to have originated because

> Italian gangs of this era used the Black Hand reputation and known techniques as covers, eliminating rivals in such a manner as to suggest Black Hand operations to the police and to the public (Nelli, 1976: 79).

Prosecution efforts and law enforcement resources were not completely helpless against Black Hand extortionists, however. One officer in particular, Lieutenant Petrosino, was particularly effective in identifying Italian criminals. Rising quickly through the ranks, he was appointed head of the "secret service branch" of the New York City Police Department (NYPD), and was tasked with eliminating Black Hand and anarchist activity. He was gunned down in the streets of Palermo while cooperating with Italian authorities. While no one was arrested for his murder, Sicily's most powerful crime boss, Don Vito Cascio Ferro, bragged that he had personally carried out the hit (Nelli, 1976).

Several factors eventually culminated in the death of La Mano Nera. The continuation of Petrosino's secret squad, community groups such as the White Hand, and the cessation of Italian immigration all combined to reduce the feasibility of Black Hand extortion. The introduction of federal postal regulations coupled with the severity of sanctions for violations further decreased the cost-benefit ratio associated with such activity. In addition, the well-publicized retaliation from intended victim Big Jim Colosimo, in which all three extortionists were murdered by Johnny Torrio and company, illustrated the vulnerability of individual gangs. Most importantly, the passage of the Volstead Act, which prohibited the sale and manufacture of alcoholic beverages, dramatically expanded vice-related opportunities. Some Black Handers, such as Frank Uale (Yale) and the extremely volatile and violent Genna brothers, moved into the increasingly lucrative business of booze.

## Chicago, Capone, and Prohibition

It must be pointed out that implanted Old World traditions were but one of many characteristics that resulted in organizational longevity for the American mafia. Emphasis on organizational loyalty, hierarchical structure, rule codification, and the like enabled Italian-Americans to rise the top of the underworld food chain, surpassing early Jewish and Irish rivals. However, the primary impetus for their ascension was not of their own making. Rather, it was the result of two seemingly unrelated and government initiated events —the passage of the Volstead Act in 1919 and Mussolini's purge.

The passage of the Volstead Act in 1919 opened a market ripe for criminal organizations. With the same farsightedness displayed by their homeland predecessors, criminally minded Italian-Americans saw Prohibition as a way to circumvent traditional social and economic roadblocks faced by recent immigrants. As one FBI agent put it:

> When Prohibition went into effect in 1920, well, they might have well have put up billboards all over Sicily with big arrows pointing toward America: attention thieves, smugglers, and confidence men. This way to the land of crooked deals and fat profits. Of course, criminal groups from other countries came to the United States, too, but the Italian mafia was tougher and better organized. And their consciences were less troubled, I think, by the idea of preying on their own kind (Bonavolonta and Duffy, 1996: 56–57).

Although a variety of sources, such as academic textbooks, popular media, etc., credit Alphonse "Scarface" Capone with bringing organized crime to Chicago, this distinction is sorely misplaced. Not only other Italians but other ethnicities preceded Capone as well. Like New York, the foundations for organized crime in Chicago must be attributed to the Irish, a group that brought a semblance of order to a chaotic underworld. Originally involved in prostitution rackets and gambling, the Irish established a foothold in both economic and political circles. In fact, it was the Irish who created a sophisticated "wire" service, which effectively cornered the market for off-track betting, preventing the "past-posting" that had been so costly to gambling operators.[4] Indeed, it appears that the Irish criminals had a finger on the pulse of society's deviant side. However, increasing numbers of Italian immigrants coupled with the advent of Prohibition signaled the end of Irish dom-

---

[4]"Past-posting" refers to the practice of placing a wager *after* a race is over and a winner established. A common practice prior to organized wire services, it is estimated that these "bets" cost gambling institutions considerably.

inance in Chicago. Their shortsightedness and the underestimation of the Italian threat resulted in their displacement as rulers of the underworld.

Prior to the passage of the Volstead Act of 1919, Italian criminals, like their Irish predecessors, engaged in a variety of illegal activities. Bookmaking, loansharking, and prostitution became mainstays in American culture due primarily to the efforts of organized crime groups. The demand for such services was exaggerated in industrialized areas, and the supply was provided by a long list of criminal entrepreneurs. Arguably, Irish criminals originally satisfied these demands. Individuals from the Irish community controlled New York's Tammany Hall and Chicago's First Ward. However, an influx of Italian immigrants into the Midwest reduced the power of Irish politicians and set the stage for one of the bloodiest conflicts in American history. Indeed, prior to World War II, Chicago's infamous organized crime figures proved to be more successful and far more recognized than their New York counterparts, who tended to keep a more low-key profile (Nelli, 1976).

One of the first individuals to capitalize politically on the growth of Italian communities was also one of the first to gain a foothold in vice activities on Chicago's South Side. Born in Calabria, Italy, James "Big Jim" or "Diamond Jim" Colosimo came to the South Side of Chicago as a young boy. Indiscriminate in his career choices, "Big Jim" alternated between legitimate employment and illegal enterprise. An accomplished thief and pimp, Colosimo nevertheless was essential in garnering support in the Italian community for Michael "Hinky Dink" Kenna. Rewarded with a precinct captaincy, Colosimo capitalized on his political power to ensure that his illegitimate enterprises would be unmolested by authorities. In 1902, Colosimo married a former whore and current madam, and took over the management of her flourishing prostitution business. A partnership with Maurice Van Bever in 1903 established a white slave trade that lured young girls with promises of grandeur and kept them through violence. The Mann Act of 1910[5] proved to be ineffective at best, and did not threaten Colosimo's position as king of prostitution on Chicago's South Side. Due to his expanding fortune, Colosimo became a target for Black Hand extortionists. Enter Johnny Torrio.

Like Colosimo, Johnny Torrio was brought to the United States at an early age. Settling in New York City's Lower East Side, Torrio quickly rose to

[5]The Mann Act of 1910 was enacted to halt an increase in white slavery and prostitution. In essence, this law made it a federal offense to transport women across state lines for "immoral" purposes. Unfortunately, this act had little success, and few victims were willing to testify against syndicate leaders. One notable exception was Colosimo's own partner, Maurice Van Bever, and his wife. Both were convicted of pandering and received a one-year sentence and a $1,000 fine. Colosimo and his nephew Johnny Torrio were implicated but never convicted (Nelli, 1976).

prominence as leader of the James Street Boys—a band of juvenile delinquents who would ascend to the highest echelons of Italian organized crime. Boyhood friends such as Paul (Vaccarelli) Kelly, Frankie (Uale) Yale, and Alphonse "Scarface" Capone proved to be instrumental in the expansion of Italian organized crime. Brought to Chicago in 1910 by his uncle, "Big Jim" Colosimo, Torrio quickly rose to prominence within his uncle's business by arranging the execution of a band of Black Hand extortionists. After the pandering indictment in 1910 proved unsuccessful and public pressure called for the abolishment of brothels, Torrio expanded Colosimo's operations to neighboring Cook County suburbs. The most famous of these, the Four Deuces (due to its location at 2222 Wabash Avenue), also housed Torrio's office, full-service gambling, and a well-stocked bar. With the arrival of New York's Alphonse "Scarface" Capone and the onset of Prohibition, Torrio's rise to the pinnacle of Chicago's underworld was all but secure. The one obstacle, his Uncle Jim, was fortuitously murdered on May 11, 1920, in the entrance hall of his nationally renowned restaurant, Colosimo's Cafe. Though it is unclear as to who was responsible for his murder (conflicting accounts point to any number of possible suspects, such as Frankie Yale, Al Capone, Colosimo's estranged wife, or Torrio himself), the benefits to Torrio and the young Capone were enormous. Torrio inherited Colosimo's empire, and Capone became his second in command.

Freed from his uncle's supervision, Torrio, a brilliant organizer and criminal mastermind, put together a criminal organization while maintaining a veneer of civility. Known throughout Chicago's First Ward as a devoted husband and devout Catholic, Torrio effectively separated his personal and professional life. Dealing in white slavery, gambling, bootlegging, and of course, violence, Torrio encouraged other criminal leaders to abandon traditional activities such as robbery and burglary, and assigned territories for alcohol distribution. Leaders across Chicago took note, and a new era of vice was born. High levels of violence and treachery characterized this era. Rival gangs, jockeying for position in Chicago's lucrative bootlegging business (some reports estimate the profits obtained by the Torrio-Capone organization alone was as much as $240 million), were often dissatisfied with their designated area and proceeded to rub out any and all competitors (Nelli, 1976). Torrio's better-staffed organization was originally resilient to this type of violence, but conflicts between other gangs resulted in a high number of casualties on all sides.

One of the most notorious battles waged between a group headed by Irish gangster and florist Dion O'Banion and the terrible Gennas, six Italian brothers known for their volatile tempers. While it remains unclear as to who started the conflict, the end result is not debated. On November 10, 1924, while preparing flowers for the funeral of Mike Merlo (reputed leader of Unione Siciliana), O'Banion was shot six times at close range. In retaliation, Hymie Weiss (aka Earl Wajciechowski) went after Capone and Torrio as reputed supporters of the Gennas. Capone escaped unscathed, but Torrio was not as lucky. Torrio was shot several times while walking with his wife. Though he survived the ordeal, Torrio did not return to Chicago after a nine-month prison stint arising from his involvement of a raid on one of O'Bannion's breweries. Some authors report that Torrio was actually shot not by Hymie Weiss and company, but was ordered murdered by none other than Al Capone himself (Giancana and Giancana, 1992).

Capone's ascension to the underworld throne was characterized by even greater levels of violence. Irish gangs, wary of Capone's increasing dominance, banded together to defeat the Neapolitan. Originally Capone enjoyed a high level of community support, being branded a hero after paying for the physician who treated a young mother who was injured by machine gun fire directed at Capone. However, Capone fell from grace after his gunmen murdered an assistant state's attorney. Several cease-fires were called due to waning business and public condemnation. Yet, peace was never long-lasting. Capone's violent rage erupted when it was reported that Frankie Yale (his one-time friend and benefactor) was hijacking shipments of Capone's liquor. Capone retaliated by killing the New York boss. In addition, Capone arranged the murder of "Bugs" Moran, a Chicago gangster who had inherited Weiss's bootlegging operation. In what became known as the St. Valentine's Day Massacre, seven Moran associates (six gangsters and a hanger-on) were cold-bloodedly murdered execution-style. Unfortunately for him, one of the victims closely resembled Moran, and some reports suggest that the gunmen believed Moran to be one of the victims. Witnesses reported seeing "policemen" enter the warehouse where the execution took place. In actuality, Capone's supporters lured their victims into the warehouse by masquerading as police inspectors.

Capone's rage was not restricted to his gangland rivals. In fact, three of Capone's leading soldiers—among them John Scalise and Albert Anselmi—were beaten to death at a banquet ostensibly held in their honor. Apparently, guests were given baseball bats and invited to join in the beating of the guests of honor. So zealous were the participants that coroners were hard pressed (no pun intended) to find a bone intact. After serving a prison sentence designed to protect Capone and allow tempers to cool, Capone returned to Chicago and developed a system of racketeering only to be reincarcerated in 1932 for income tax evasion. His 11-year sentence was shortened significantly when it was found that Capone was suffering from advanced syphilis. The most notorious and most feared man in Chicago's history died quietly at his Miami villa, struck down not by an assassin's bullet but by his own sexual behavior.

Organized crime (OC) in Chicago continued unaffected by Capone's incarceration and subsequent death. Frank Nitti, Sam Giancana, and others developed new marketplaces while maintaining a stranglehold on traditional OC activities of prostitution, gambling, etc. While revenue suffered immediately following the repeal of the Eighteenth Amendment, Chicago gangsters found an even more lucrative enterprise—narcotics. However, Chicago mafia dominance over Italian organized crime in the United States was soon supplanted by OC activity on the East Coast. Chicago mafiosi would never again enjoy the prominence enjoyed during the Dry Years. Indeed, a war, which had started in New York while Capone was still in power, would continue after his downfall, and would quickly overshadow Chicago's glory days.

## Unione Siciliana and the Castellammarese War

With the advent of massive Italian immigration, increasing persecution of Roman Catholics, and the passage of the Eighteenth Amendment, the stage was set for an explosion of criminal activity within poverty-stricken areas hit hard by discrimination. Enter Unione Siciliana. In essence, the Sicilian nation (i.e., the mafia) was transported to the United States where social discrimination necessitated the formation of Italian fraternal organizations. These organizations, originally tasked as insurance providers and neighborhood caretakers, quickly descended into illegitimate enterprise, transforming American norms of alcohol abstinence. As Inciardi (1975) put it:

> . . . the respectability and benevolence of the Unione declined as Prohibition approached. First in New York and later in distant city branches, cadres of gangsters began to infiltrate and pervert the association. L'Unione siciliana acquired a dual character: it was open and involved in good works among needy Sicilians, yet it was hidden and malevolent, dealing in theft, murder and vice (Inciardi, 1975: 115).

Inevitably, the increasing competition among Italian groups resulted in a subsequent increase in violence. For the most part, this violence was confined to mafia families and their members, though there were some exceptions. In 1931, this competition resulted in unprecedented levels of violence between two factions. In one corner, there was Salvatore Maranzano, a native Sicilian with roots in Castellammare del Golfo. Maranzano's group was comprised primarily of Sicilian immigrants, individuals such as Lucchese, Bonanno, Profaci. These mafiosi had been quite active in criminal activities in their homeland, and were heavily indebted to Maranzano, who had helped them flee from Mussolini's persecution. In the other corner, Giuseppe "Joe the Boss" Masseria gathered a multicultural army of Italians and Jews. Unfortunately for Masseria, the lack of ethnic consistency weakened the loyalty of his followers. Leading Americanized gangsters such as Charles "Lucky" Luciano, Vito Genovese, Frank Costello, Meyer Lansky, and Bugsy Siegel secretly abandoned Masseria when it became apparent that his defeat was imminent. In fact, it was this same group of Masseria followers who executed him in return for their own safety. With Masseria dead, Maranzano declared the war officially over and appointed himself "Boss of the Bosses" (Cressey, 1969). He also established the notion that

> there would be bosses beneath him, each with an underboss and a "caporegima," or "lieutenant," who, in turn, would have "soldiers" working for him. Maranzano did not invent this form of organization. He, or someone, lifted it bodily from the Sicilian mafia. According to Mr. Valachi, Maranzano then "went out and explained the rules," namely, that henceforth there would be a rational, hierarchical chain of command, with no individualistic, indiscriminate violence. He established his non-Castellammarese ally, Gagliano, as a boss. However, Maranzano ruled that anyone who had fought on his side in the war could remain with him. Valachi turned from Gagliano to Maranzano and "the boys from the Castellammarese," as did two more of Gagliano's mercenaries. Luciano's betrayal of Masseria was rewarded with position as a boss, and Genovese's reward took the form of underboss to Luciano (Cressey, 1969: 42).

This organizational structuring laid the foundation for all families operating at the time. The structure proposed by Maranzano, however, lasted far longer than his reign as mafia kingpin (see Figure 4-3). Fearing the increasingly powerful relationship between Luciano, Genovese, and Jewish organized crime figures, Maranzano placed a "contract" (order to murder) on Luciano. Unfortunately for Maranzano, Luciano commissioned a similar "hit," and his assassins struck first. On September 11, 1931, Maranzano was executed in his Park Avenue suite. This date came to be known as the "Night of the Sicilian Vespers" or "the Purge of the Moustache Petes" (Cressey, 1969). While these designations conjure up images of masked assassins roaming the country in search of Maranzano supporters while civilians cowered behind locked doors, no evidence supports media assertions that more than 40 mafiosi were killed. In fact, little if any evidence exists detailing even one mob-related murder.

In the wake of Maranzano's murder, other ranking members of the Italian mafia tacitly agreed to maintain peaceful relationships. Luciano convened a sit-down in Chicago, which was hosted by Capone, and members

Salvatore Lucania was born to a poor family in the hillside village of Lercara Friddi. Immigrating to the United States in 1906, Lucania gained employment as a general laborer. Disdaining the poverty surrounding him, Salvatore Lucania began preying on smaller children, demanding their lunch money in return for "protection." One of Lucania's intended victims, a small boy five years younger, refused to participate. For some unknown reason, his refusal actually endeared him to Lucania who liked his spunk. This friendship, between Lucania and Meyer Lansky, would become one of the first multicultural relationships in organized crime. Lansky was Jewish.

Although the two would soon go their separate ways—Lucania to reform school and Lansky to public school—they hooked up several years later. In the meantime, Lucania, leader of his own gang of ruffians, entered into an alliance with the head of the 104th Street Gang headed by Francesco "Frank Costello" Castiglia. This alliance, intended to be temporary, would last throughout Lucania's life, and would ultimately lead to one of the biggest shake-ups in organized crime history. After both served short prison sentences—Lucania for drug running and Castiglia for possession of a firearm—they created their own street gang where Lansky joined them, bringing his friend Benjamin "Bugsy" Siegel. By now the two were known as Charlie Luciano (a name picked up in prison, which was more preferable to the feminized nicknames of Sal or Sally) and Frank Costello (as a joke, Luciano had changed his friend's surname to an Irish one). These names would soon reverberate within the underworld and come to symbolize both power and intelligence.

Luciano and company soon rose to prominence within the Italian underworld. Lucrative business deals during Prohibition and carefully chosen alliances ensured Luciano's position. However, the older dons were apprehensive about this upstart. Masseria and Maranzano, competing for the ultimate power position, saw the profitability of an alliance with Luciano's crew. Luciano, along with his advisors, were not amenable to an alliance with either, recognizing the war between the two as self-defeating. They decided that both bosses had to be disposed of. But first, Luciano and his associates entertained noncompeting mobsters like Al Capone of Chicago, Nig Rosen of Philadelphia, and Moe Dalitz of Cleveland.

Once his plan was established, Luciano "joined" forces with Masseria, while carefully placing his pawns for his assassination. Captured and badly beaten by Maranzano, Luciano was released alive, if not severely scarred. (His release, after being "taken for a ride," earned him the nickname of Lucky.) Luciano arranged to have lunch with Masseria, and conveniently went to relieve himself when Albert Anastasia, Genovese, and Siegel filled Masseria with lead. Shortly thereafter Maranzano was executed on orders from Luciano, and a Commission was developed to prevent future bloodshed.

Luciano, Costello, and Lansky remained steadfast friends and loyal compatriots throughout their lives. Benjamin "Bugsy" Siegel was not so lucky. In 1947, Bugsy Siegel was shot to death in the home of his mistress, Virginia Hill. The hit was ordered by his boyhood friends, Costello and Lansky, after it was reported that he was skimming money that had been loaned to him to start a casino in Las Vegas. Almost ten years later, Frank Costello would be shot on orders from Vito Genovese. The bungled assassination attempt was carried out by Vincente "The Chin" Gigante, current boss of the Genovese crime family. Ah, to have such friends.

**FIGURE 4-3** Boyhood Friends, Powerful Leaders

formulated an organizational board of directors, dissolving the position of "boss of bosses," and establishing territorial boundaries. This newly formed Commission was originally comprised of the four remaining New York leaders: Lucky Luciano, Vincent Mangano, Joe Profaci, and Joe Bonanno; and two non-New Yorkers: Chicago's Al Capone and Cleveland's Frank Milano. (The current Commission also includes leaders from cities across the country, such as Detroit, Philadelphia, Kansas City, and others.) In addition, the Commission agreed to "freeze" membership, so rival groups could not out-recruit one another (i.e., build a supreme army). Beneath the Commission (and its six permanent members), 24 other families were recognized. This new approach was designed to decrease interfamily violence and provide a modicum of security for the bosses. Unfortunately for low-ranking organizational members, it did not provide any protection from their own family. Nor did it protect other ethnic leaders.

## FIVE FAMILIES FROM NEW YORK

The formulation of the Commission all but put an end to interfamily fighting in New York, although periodic outbreaks still occurred. Luciano, or perhaps Torrio, saw the negative repercussions experienced in Chicago. Thus, territorial boundaries, firmly established and uncontestable, divided New York into five recognizable factions.

### Luciano/Genovese Family

Born in 1897, the boy christened Salvatore Lucania began his life in the United States in a rat-infested tenement in New York's Little Italy at age nine. Perceiving the lack of legitimate opportunities to those of Italian descent, Charles "Lucky" Luciano (as he would come to be known) was a chronic truant and schoolyard bully. Extorting money from children during elementary school signaled his criminal entrepreneurial nature. Along with other delinquents—most notably Meyer Lansky, Benjamin "Bugsy" Siegel, and Francesco "Frank Costello" Castiglia—he formed the Five Points Gang (see Figure 4-4). It was an enterprising youth gang that relied on Luciano's uncanny criminal mind, Lansky's skill of deduction, and Siegel and Costello's brute force. While their scams tended to be successful, no one could have anticipated the heights that the foursome would reach among New York's criminal elite.

Luciano's role in the Castellammarese War cannot be overstated. Some authors suggest that the entire conflict was actually masterminded by Luciano. They argue that Luciano cleverly played both sides against the middle,

The Five Points Gang was one of the most vicious, violent, and most recognized multicultural youth gangs in New York City at the turn of the century. Ruling the area between the Bowery and Broadway, 14th Street and City Hall Park, the Five Points Gang specialized primarily in robbery, prostitution, and common thuggery.

**Paolo Antonio Vaccarelli (aka Paul Kelly):** leader of the Five Points Gang, at one point reputed to command the allegiance of 1,500 youths (Nelli, 1976). Unlike other Italian leaders, Vaccarelli actively pursued alliances with individuals from various ethnic backgrounds.

**Frankie Uale (Yale):** responsible for Al Capone's arrival in Chicago. Eventually the two would part ways, and Capone would order the execution of his one-time mentor.

**Charles "Lucky" Luciano:** perhaps one of the biggest leaders in Italian organized crime. Luciano has been described as a youth criminal, dropping out of school in the fifth grade at the age of 14.

**Johnny Torrio:** leader of his own youth gang—the James Street Boys—Torrio moved to Chicago on request from his uncle "Big Jim" Colosimo. Torrio has been credited with revolutionizing (and suburbanizing) the prostitution business in Chicago. He returned to New York after a failed assassination attempt and is often credited with the solidification of mafia leaders across the United States (i.e., the Commission) through his protege Lucky Luciano.

**Alphonse "Scarface" Capone:** undisputed leader of the Chicago Outfit from 1920 to 1931, Capone left school in the sixth grade shortly after his fourteenth birthday. A former bouncer for Frankie Uale (Yale), he received his nickname after an altercation left him with a four-inch scar across his left cheek. He was sent to Torrio under suspicion of two murders. Capone eventually placed a contract on Torrio's head, forcing him to flee to New York. On January 25, 1947, Al Capone died of pneumonia symptomatic of syphilis at his Palm Beach retreat.

**FIGURE 4-4** The Five Points Gang

ultimately emerging as the victor (Nelli, 1976). Whether this argument is supported, Luciano's prominence following the conflict is indisputable. Viewed as a first among equals, Luciano's "family" was granted the largest slice of organized crime in New York City. Luciano, credited with establishing peace between warring factions, successfully prevented his own assassination, but could not protect himself from criminal prosecution and subsequent deportation.

In 1936, Luciano was charged with more than 60 counts of prostitution and sentenced to 30–50 years in prison. His incarceration, however, proved to be little more than a hindrance. He continued to issue directives through underlings from his cell. His power was so absolute, in fact, that the U.S. government enlisted his aid during the early days of World War II. U.S. counterintelligence agents found it difficult to infiltrate the longshoreman's union, and could not monitor "suspicious" antigovernment activity on the docks.

Using "Socks" Lanza as a mouthpiece, Luciano paved the way for undercover government surveillance of anti-American activities. Furthermore, Luciano's cooperation ensured the absence of costly strikes or union problems. It was also rumored that Luciano was also instrumental in the invasion of Mussolini's Fascist Italy. While these rumors are largely unsubstantiated, it would appear that Luciano and a variety of other Italian-American criminals had a compelling reason to assist the U.S. government: Mussolini's purge of Italian mafiosi had left hundreds dead, incarcerated, or homeless. It was further rumored that in exchange for his cooperation (i.e., creating maps, deployment of personnel, and designation of "safe" areas), Luciano would receive a full pardon.

If indeed these rumors were true, Luciano was foolish to trust the U.S. government and Luciano's former nemesis-turned-governor, Thomas Dewey. Dewey did release Luciano, but ordered his deportation. The role played by Luciano following his deportation is hotly debated. Some authors suggest that Luciano actually continued to receive homage from U.S. gangsters during his exile (Demaris, 1975). While others suggest that Luciano and all members of the American mafia were held in contempt by their Sicilian counterparts (Barzini, 1972). In reality, it is not important if the two stories cannot be reconciled. Luciano's contribution to OC in New York City and La Cosa Nostra far exceeds whatever humble fate he may have endured: Luciano—above all other gangsters before or since—solidified mafia factions across the country.

During Luciano's imprisonment and subsequent deportation, his boyhood friend and fellow Five Pointer assumed control of Luciano's family. Francesco Castiglia (aka Frank Costello) was a juvenile delinquent turned powerbroker. Marriage and a prison stint transformed a neighborhood tough guy into a criminally astute and politically connected entrepreneur. One of the first OC leaders to actively pursue legitimate businesses (i.e., the Horowitz Novelty Company), Frank Costello channeled much of the revenue garnered by his criminal activity into his company. Of course, his novelty company complemented his criminal endeavors by producing and servicing punchboards and other gambling devices (Nelli, 1976). It was this appearance of legitimacy that angered law enforcement officials who finally achieved a conviction of contempt based on his lack of cooperation during the Kefauver Committee hearings, and a further conviction of income tax evasion, which was later reversed. Costello's reign ended "voluntarily" after a failed assassination attempt encouraged his "retirement."

Costello's successor was Vito Genovese, the individual for whom the family is now named. Genovese was a Neapolitan who had a long history of criminal activity. Prior to his ascension, Genovese had been an active proponent of narcotics trafficking, seeing it as an extension of Prohibition bootlegging. Genovese began his criminal life under the tutelage of Luciano. In fact, it has been reported that Genovese's narcotics operations were actually supported by and a product of Lucky Luciano. Unfortunately for Genovese, his dominance was short-lived. Vito Genovese was one of the first major players in Italian organized crime to be convicted of narcotics violations. Genovese died in prison while serving out a sentence.

Costello's would-be assassin, Vincent "The Chin" Gigante, assumed control of the Genovese family. The Genovese family's most important industry, however, is not narcotics. In fact, price-fixing, a newly recognized white collar or corporate criminal activity, was actually initiated by the Italian mafia. In 1923, Joseph "Socks" Lanza, developed the United Seafood Workers Union in New York City. As such, his control over the Fulton Fish Market affected seafood prices throughout New York and the rest of the country. Fishermen who refused to pay homage (i.e., percentages per pound) watched as their catch rotted on the New York docks. His control was so absolute, in fact, that even individuals desperate for work refused to unload or deliver cargo of those not in compliance. Though he served a two-year sentence for violation of the Sherman Antitrust Act, Lanza continued to rule the waterfront until his death in 1968 (Nelli, 1976). His successors in the Genovese family have continued to reap the profits from this most lucrative racketeering market. In addition, their current enterprises also include entertainment unions, a relatively new phenomenon. Much like their control over the Seafood Workers Union, the Genovese family (in alliance with their Chicago counterparts) has established a stranglehold on workers' unions within the entertainment field. With the exception of the Screen Actors Guild, virtually all organizations represented on movie locations are controlled through New York. It is this activity which most affects the U.S. population, and was the impetus for the passage of the RICO Act (see "Government Efforts" in this chapter). However, the Genovese family is not the only organization that has pursued this type of illicit activity. It is estimated that the Genovese family is second only to the Gambinos in strength and numbers. However, these estimates may be outdated because they do not account for recent prosecution efforts.

### Anastasia/Gambino Family

Though what is now considered the Gambino family was actually initiated by Al Manfredi (Mineo), his short reign does not grant him a place of prominence in the annals of organized crime. A close ally of Joseph Masseria at the onset of the Castellammarese War, Mineo never lived to see its completion.

Instead, Frank "Don Cheech" Scalise, a Masseria defector, was given the chieftain position after Masseria's death. He was replaced, however, upon Maranzano's execution and returned several years later as Albert "Executioner" Anastasia's underboss. Anastasia, a volatile individual, reportedly committed his first murder prior to his twentieth birthday and was the reputed leader of Murder, Inc. (see Figure 4-5). When he was not snuffing the life out of some unfortunate soul, Anastasia could be found ruling the Brooklyn waterfront via his leadership of the International Longshoremen's Union, Local 1814. Like Lanza, Anastasia virtually controlled the prices of any merchandise unloaded by his employees. In addition, Anastasia's group was responsible for millions of dollars of "hijacked" merchandise, and other nefarious schemes including loan-sharking. In fact, some suggest that the operation was cyclical in which individuals looking for employment were "encouraged" to "borrow" money from their employers. In 1955, the "Executioner" was executed while enjoying a visit to his favorite barbershop. His killers appear to have been supported by factions within his own organization, but supplied by either Joseph Profaci or Vito Genovese.

---

Murder, Inc. was the name given to one of the most notorious mercenary groups in American history. It began when the "Boys from Brooklyn"—Abe "Kid Twist" Reles, Philip "Pittsburgh Phil" Strauss, and Martin "Buggy" Goldstein—attempted to take over the pinball machine business in the East New York–Brownsville section of Brooklyn. Disregarding the proprietary interest expressed by the Shapiro brothers, the "Boys" hired a tough crew of Italian criminals to forward their interests. The war that commenced was quite bloody. However, the "Boys from Brooklyn" were the undisputed victors, quickly overtaking virtually all organized crime rackets in the area.

On the request of the newly formed Commission and under the direction of Albert "Executioner" Anastasia, the group soon saw the profitability of murder-for-hire. Acting as the enforcement arm of the formal syndicate, the group was responsible for at least one hundred murders across the country. Perhaps the most famous of these was the execution of Dutch Schultz. The group's prominence and notoriety grew in pace with their professionalism. Dress rehearsals, previously prepared graves, getaway cars, and the like heightened their efficiency.

The end of Murder, Inc. resulted when "Kid Twist" Reles was arrested on a variety of charges, including the murder of Alec "Red" Alpert. Unwilling to die in the electric chair, Reles became the proverbial singing canary. His testimony led to the conviction and electrocution of seven of his former partners, including Lepke Buchalter and Louis Capone. Before he could implicate Albert Anastasia, then crime boss of the current Gambino family, he became the canary that could sing but couldn't fly. While under police protection, he mysteriously plummeted to his death from a window on the sixth floor of a Coney Island hotel.

**FIGURE 4-5** Murder, Inc., Albert Anastasia and Company

Carlo Gambino was born in Palermo in 1902 and immigrated to the United States in 1921. He was one of the few mobsters in his day who did not immigrate with his family. Gambino came alone. His sole friend in the United States was Gaetano Lucchese, a quickly rising mobster associated with Albert Anastasia. As a soldier, Gambino started a lucrative bootlegging business that flourished well after Prohibition. Gambino, along with several other gangsters, made a fortune during World War II by appropriating and distributing ration stamps with the assistance of corrupt officials of the Office of Price Administration. He further expanded his fortune by engaging in a legitimate trucking industry. He ruled the family for almost two decades, but he is most notable for the repercussions of his untimely demise in 1976.

Mob tradition was such that Gambino's death should have resulted in the ascension of his underboss to the head of the family. However, Gambino's cousin and brother-in-law, Paul "Big Paul" Castellano, received the nod. Aniello "Neil" Dellacroce, Gambino's long-suffering underboss, took the insult better than anyone. A firm believer in tradition, Dellacroce opposed any plans to start a war or murder Castellano. Maintaining his position as underboss, Dellacroce urged his soldiers to obey directives from Castellano. Castellano demanded homage from his underlings, while restricting their activities to racketeering-type activities. Members dealing drugs, he said, would be executed. Dellacroce soldiers, however, were already immersed in the drug subculture, seeing an easy score and a quick profit. When Angelo Ruggiero, a Dellacroce nephew, was indicted for drug trafficking his life was spared only to appease Dellacroce and his supporters. However, entire Gambino family crews were starving without the proceeds from their drug enterprises. Tensions soared even higher when it was revealed that Castellano allowed Genovese soldiers to traffic in narcotics within his demographic fiefdom *if* they paid him a handsome profit. Dellacroce died of natural causes in 1985. Within two weeks of Dellacroce's funeral, Castellano and his newly appointed underboss, Tommy Bilotti, lay dead in the street outside of New York's Sparks Steakhouse. The hit was engineered by one of Dellacroce's most loyal supporters—John Gotti.

John "Johnny Boy" Gotti's entrance into the criminal underworld was all but predestined. One of thirteen children born to poor immigrants in the South Bronx and surrounded by poverty, the young Gotti's only view of wealth was those involved in mafia activities. After moving to the Brownsville-East section of New York at age 12, Gotti followed his older brother Peter into the Fulton-Rockaway Boys. The group frequented areas populated by Italian mobsters. Hanging around social clubs, the group gained the notice of some low-level mobsters due to their ability to fence stolen property. Johnny Boy, in particular, came to the attention of Carmine

Fatico, a capo for Albert Anastasia. Gotti began stealing cars and any other merchandise not tied down. Because Gotti was in and out of jails throughout the '60s, his wife was often forced to go on welfare to support her growing family. When not incarcerated, Gotti began to hang out at the Bergin Hunt & Fish Social Club in Queens. The Bergin was owned by Fatico and was conveniently located close to JFK International Airport. (Gotti's crew and the rest of the Gambino crime family were notorious hijackers.)

A big-time gambler and most often loser, Gotti controlled Fatico's gambling industry until Fatico was indicted on a variety of charges. Dellacroce replaced Fatico with 31-year-old Gotti—a move that shocked gangsters and law enforcement alike. Gotti, after all, was not even a made member. Gotti's star was on the rise. He received greater prominence after murdering James McBratney, a small-time Irish hood who reportedly kidnapped and murdered Carlo Gambino's son. Returning from his most recent prison stint, Gotti was rewarded with a brand new car, compliments of Carlo Gambino. It seemed that Gotti was unstoppable. He was not, however, immune to personal tragedy. In March 1980, Gotti's 12-year-old son, Frank, was struck and killed on a motorbike outside his Queens home. By all accounts, the driver of the vehicle, John Favara, a neighbor and father of Gotti playmates, was not at fault; Frank Gotti had darted out directly into the path of the moving car. The Gottis were devastated, but none more so than Frank's mother, Victoria. Two months after the accident, she attacked Favara with a baseball bat, but no charges were pressed. Shortly thereafter, Gotti and Victoria went to Florida on "vacation." Upon their return, they were notified of the mysterious disappearance of their neighbor, John Favara.

Gotti's murder of Castellano and Thomas Bilotti in 1985 may have been power motivated, but it was definitely a matter of self-preservation as well. Gotti and his crew had become heavily involved in heroin trafficking. Fearing his own murder, Gotti acted first. At age 45, he became boss of one of the most powerful organized crime syndicates in U.S. history. For a time it appeared that Gotti would actually continue his criminal enterprise for some time. His Armani suits and flashy lifestyle endeared him to a community looking for heroes. His ability to outwit law enforcement authorities and evade criminal prosecution earned him the name the "Teflon Don." But Gotti had an Achilles heel, and the government found it in 1991. Gotti was arrogant—carelessly so. Believing himself invulnerable after beating two RICO charges, Gotti ignored the lesson of recent RICO convictions within the Lucchese and Genovese families. Electronic surveillance equipment (i.e., bugs) were placed in all of Gotti's hangouts—the Ravenite Social Club, his home, and an apartment upstairs from the club. Federal investigators turned on their machines and heard the sweetest sound of all—John Gotti bragging about his criminal accomplishments and plans for the future. Armed with this overwhelming evidence, the feds approached Salvatore "Sammy the Bull" Gravano, who was Gotti's friend and underboss. Exposing a plot hatched by Gotti to murder Gravano, federal agents encouraged Gravano's testimony. In 1992, Gotti received five life terms—four of which offered no parole—and an additional 65 years. Current reports indicate that John Gotti, Jr., has assumed his father's role. However, the longevity of any such organization is questionable. Through the expensive attire and slick appearance, Gotti never displayed a level of intelligence comparable to his predecessors. Instead, Gotti's expensive image and sophisticated veneer was misleading. Though Gotti achieved a position far higher than the average street thug, his organization did not.

Currently, the Gambino family's main enterprises appear to be construction. Reportedly, no building contracts or permits in New York are free from mob supervision and manipulation. Their control ranges from cement workers unions to City Hall. They are extremely active in the garment industry, controlling prices and garment production. They are also involved in the trafficking of narcotics, like the majority of their organized crime counterparts.

## Lucchese Family

Gaetano "Tommy" Reina, a one-time supporter of Masseria, originally controlled the Lucchese family. Murdered in 1930, Reina did not live to see the end of the Castellammarese War. His successor, Gaetano Gagliano, served for more than two decades with Thomas "Three Finger Brown" Lucchese as his underboss. Lucchese arrived from Sicily in 1911. He was 11 years old. First arrested at the age of 21, Lucchese's career would span nearly half a century. Smaller in numbers than the other families, the Lucchese family originally concentrated on the organized crime mainstay of gambling. For the most part, Lucchese is most notable for his ability to stay out of trouble. His children were both college graduates and maintained a suburban existence, excluding the fact that his daughter married the son of Carlo Gambino. The same cannot be said of the current family. Changes in leadership and random violence are characteristic of the group's recent struggles. Currently, the group's largest moneymaking scheme appears to be air cargo heists from Kennedy airport. Recent indictments indicate that employees of Kennedy airport, members of local police departments, and associates of the family are all on the payroll.

## Profaci/Colombo Family

Already an ex-convict by age 25, Joseph Profaci saw the United States as the land of opportunity and immigrated there. Profaci was one of the few active gangsters who was able to remain neutral during the Castellammarese War. By all accounts a traditional mobster, Profaci was nevertheless one of the most successful in establishing legitimate businesses. Known as the "Olive Oil King," he was at one time the largest single importer of olive oil. Although his family remained stable and relatively free of violence during his reign, intrafamily rivalry and subordinate disloyalty marked the year prior to his death. Some members, most notably the Gallo brothers, were uncomfortable with the percentage demanded by Profaci as family boss. They were further dissatisfied with his practice of allowing blood relatives to attain positions of leadership above more deserving soldiers. Profaci, in his Old World ways, appeared to view his family as a kingdom to be inherited only through birth order. The Gallo brothers executed a number of Profaci's greatest allies. Profaci's response was to forgive them, superficially at least. He then lured the transgressors into vulnerable situations. Joseph "Joe Jelly" Gallo was murdered, but his brother was "rescued" from a similar fate. In fact, he was in the process of being murdered when a patrol officer happened upon the scene and the killers fled.

Profaci's death in 1962 was followed shortly by the death of his appointed successor, his brother-in-law Joseph Magliocco, in 1963. Both died from natural causes. The Commission appointed Joseph Colombo heir, after it was revealed that he had warned Carlo Gambino and Thomas Lucchese of murder contracts. In any event, the war that had been initiated by the Gallo brothers in 1961 set the tone of the new family. Since that time, war within the family has depleted much of their power and moneymaking abilities. One of their main operations continues to be racketeering. The Colombo family maintains control over cement unions in the New York area. Any new construction—skyscrapers, houses, sidewalks, and even streets—is affected by the Colombo's stranglehold of cement workers' unions. The family has proven to be especially vulnerable to law enforcement efforts in recent years due to the lack of loyalty and consistency of leadership within the organization. New associates are increasingly focusing on narcotics, which brings further violence to a family with more than its share.

## Bonanno Family

Joseph "Don Peppino" Bonanno arrived in the United States in 1924. According to his own autobiography, Bonanno was forced out of Italy due to his anti-Fascist activities. An early supporter of Maranzano, Bonanno was disappointed by the new generation of mafia that emerged under Luciano. However, he was pleased that he was appointed head of his own family (Bonanno and Lalli, 1983). Contrary to Bonanno's assertions, federal law enforcement sources indicate that one of their earliest enterprises was narcotics. Bonanno presents himself as a reformed mobster, whose legitimate endeavors into cheese manufacturing and garment-related enterprises have enabled him to survive.

In 1963, Bonanno reportedly put a contract on the heads of competing crime bosses Gambino and Lucchese—a charge he vehemently denies. Fleeing to Canada to escape retaliation, Bonanno allegedly left his son in charge. Unfortunately for his son, family members and the Commission alike opposed his promotion. Bonanno states that he was summoned to appear before the Commission. An offer he says he declined. He further suggests that he was abducted by armed gunmen on order of his cousins, Buffalo's Magaddino family. He then fled to Tucson in fear for his life (Bonanno and Lalli, 1983). This charge is highly questionable. While it is likely that Bonanno had reason to fear for his safety, it is absurd to think that he was kidnapped and released for no apparent reason—the mob is not characterized by high levels of forgiveness.

The struggle for dominance over the family was dubbed the "Banana War." The federal government finally convicted Bonanno on a minor charge in 1980, resulting in a one-year prison sentence imposed for his lack of cooperation in government proceedings based largely on his autobiography. By his own account, Bonanno retired after his prison stint, and ceased all criminal activity. Since his retirement, his family has been notorious for random violence and intrafamily conflicts. Their current criminal enterprises are largely unsophisticated and involve heroin trafficking.

## CRIMINAL PROSECUTION

### Narcotics and the Mob

Contrary to Hollywood versions of the American mafia, trafficking in illegal substances has long been an entrepreneurial mainstay among Italian groups. According to Anslinger and Ousler,

> [the mafia] have held for many years the dominant position in narcotics distribution throughout the United States. The narcotics syndicate in America came into being about the time Prohibition ended, in the early 1930s, when the gangsters were looking around for new opportunities. Dope had always been part of their operation; now it took on a bigger role. The syndicate put the operation on a businesslike basis. They hired a legal staff, set up a

supervisory board, a general manager, a traveling representative and a sales force (1961: 88).

In fact, some of the older bosses such as Paul Castellano and Angelo Bruno openly disdained narcotics endeavors by family members. However, these same bosses accepted drug proceeds from other families. (In fact, it was this hypocrisy that eventually resulted in the demise of both.) Other bosses such as Luciano and his successors saw vast potential in the narcotics trade following Prohibition. Much like their approach to bootlegging, Luciano's organization carefully cultivated local politicians and police officials. This low-level corruption proved to be the most successful.

One of the most famous cases in mafia history was dubbed "the Pizza Connection" due to the suspects' choice of cover—a pizzeria. The case, which concluded in 1987, involved Salvatore "Toto" Catalano, a Bonanno caporegime, and recent immigrant Gaetano Badalamenti. Badalamenti, once a prominent figure in the Sicilian mafia, was said to have transported over $1 billion in street-level heroin. This heroin was distributed through the auspices of the defendants' pizzerias. The individuals involved in this case routinely used coded language to discuss their drug transactions, thinking that it would protect them from criminal prosecution. This assumption proved to be extremely naive and shortsighted. This case was followed quickly by an additional one that involved members of the Gambino crime family. Thus, it appears that the Italian mob has not retreated from traditional criminal activity. Although many of them are involved in legitimate businesses, many others pursue traditional criminal activity. In fact, recent RICO arrests in Charlotte, North Carolina, and Oakland, California, suggest that many of the Italian families have actually created relationships between themselves and other criminal organizations such as outlaw motorcycle gangs, Colombian cartels, etc.

## Government Efforts

Traditionally, prosecution efforts directed at the mob were largely unsuccessful. Territorial jealousies and a general lack of cooperation within and between law enforcement agencies hampered large-scale prosecution efforts. Instead, only marginal successes occurred directed primarily at individuals. One of the first tactics used by federal prosecutors was an effort initiated not by the Federal Bureau of Investigation, but by Treasury agents. Individuals employed by the Internal Revenue Service waded through volumes of paperwork and news accounts of mob activity, and successfully prosecuted high-ranking mobsters like Al Capone. The individual who had refused to pay homage to any man forgot to pay homage to the IRS. In the end, the IRS got what was coming to them and so did Capone. Al "Scarface" Capone was removed permanently from the Chicago organized crime scene by slight individuals with pocket protectors. Waxey Gordon and Dutch Schultz were two other notables convicted on income tax invasion.

As stated, the Internal Revenue Service with their army of statisticians and bookkeepers did what the Federal Bureau of Investigation could not. Marked by competition and jurisdictional disputes, the agents of the FBI, who trained so zealously for physical combat with armed assailants, were all but useless. Bonavolonta, a former FBI agent assigned to the Organized Crime Division, elaborated on the lack of professionalism and the inadequacy of the FBI:

> At the time I got back there [New York], we had the one assistant director in charge. That was Welch [Neil]. But under Welch there were three separate FBI field offices, each one headed by one of the Hooverite bishops . . . we had the office in Manhattan . . . we had another one in Westchester County, up toward Connecticut. And then we had still another out in the borough of Queens in Rego Park.
>
> Having three different offices would have been fine, I suppose, except that each one was what you might call fussy about its geographic per-quisites. You might call it that, anyway; what I called it was . . . paranoid.
>
> Personalities aside, the arrangement was as screwed up as it could pos-sibly be, and the reason for that was—if you put it as a question—do you think Paul Castellano and his scuzzball, drug-dealing pizza parlors really stopped at the Westchester county line?
>
> What I'm saying is that the FBI, in its incomparable brilliance, had es-tablished a stupid-assed, monkey-minded bureaucracy that could not have been more conducive to exploitation by the wiseguys than if they had set it up themselves (Bonavolonta and Duffy, 1996: 63–64).

In addition, the RICO law, which had been on the books since 1970, was lost in this top-heavy bureaucracy because it was uncommunicated to the agents in the trenches for almost ten years.

> . . . that tells you something about the way Washington works . . . I'm sure some bright lawyer somewhere in the Department of Justice knew all about [RICO]. But without a clear signal from someone higher up in the organiza-tional food chain, that bright lawyer is going to keep his mouth shut, and RICO is going to sit on the books for a decade, as useless as if the law had never been passed.

Many believe that the acronym RICO (Racketeer Influenced and Corrupt Organizations statute, 18 U.S.C. Sections 1961–1968) was a clever play on a name from the 1930 mob movie *Little Caesar* in which Edward G. Robinson played small-town hood Enrico "Rico" Bandello (Bonavolonta and Duffy, 1996). This law, overwhelmingly simple in hindsight, concentrated on the fact that La Cosa Nostra was an organization developed to pursue criminal enterprise. Created by Bob Blakey, an attorney on the U.S. Senate Subcommittee on Criminal Laws and Procedures, RICO stated that

> It shall be unlawful for any person employed by or associated with any enterprise engaged in, or the activities which affect, interstate or foreign commerce, to conduct or participate, directly or indirectly, in the conduct of such enterprise's affairs through a pattern of racketeering activity or collection of unlawful debt.

| Name | Family/Position | Crime(s) | Sentence |
|------|-----------------|----------|----------|
| Joseph DeFede | Lucchese/acting boss | Extortion, racketeering (1999) | 5 years |
| John Gotti, Jr. | Gambino/boss | Racketeering, gambling, income tax evasion, loan-sharking (1999) | $5\frac{1}{2}$ to $7\frac{1}{4}$ years + $1 million |
| Andrew Russo | Colombo/boss | Jury tampering (1999) | Pending |
| Vincente "The Chin" Gigante | Genovese/boss | Racketeering, conspiracy to commit murder, i.e., John Gotti (1997) | Maximum of 20 years |
| Vittorio "Vic" Amuso | Lucchese/boss | Racketeering, murder (1992) | Life |
| John Gotti | Gambino/boss | Racketeering, murder, bribery, gambling (1990) | Life |
| Carmine "Junior" Persico | Bonanno/boss | Racketeering (1985) | 39 years (1985) + 100 years (1986) |

**FIGURE 4-6** RICO's Most Recent "Victims" among the Five New York Families

In essence, RICO enabled law enforcement to use specific criminal acts such as homicide, gambling, and loan-sharking as *pieces* of evidence, lessening the burden of proof. In other words, state offenses, such as homicide and burglary, could now be prosecuted under federal authority without actually *proving* criminal culpability beyond a reasonable doubt, a feat that had traditionally been almost impossible due to the lack of witnesses. In addition, RICO broadened the spectrum of probable cause, which dramatically increased the number of successful Title III applications.[6] It is perhaps this latter option that was more important to law enforcement in RICO cases where the majority of evidence is actually gathered through these technological mediums.

The importance of the RICO Act cannot be overstated. Nearing its second decade of implementation, RICO has successfully been utilized against numerous members of organized crime. More importantly, it is directly responsible for the successful prosecution of entire La Cosa Nostra families. RICO prosecutions of John Gotti and the Gambino family; Anthony "Fat Tony" Salerno and the Genovese family; and Carmine "The Snake" Persico and the Colombo family are but few of the many cases that have resulted in lengthy prison sentences for the highest ranking members of the Italian mafia (see Figure 4-6). While it must be noted that these organizations still exist and continue to engage in illicit criminal enterprise, their ranks appear to be dwindling as the risk-benefit ratio increases.

## CONCLUSIONS

Though many events in La Cosa Nostra history are often sensationalized to the point of absurdity, the evolution and transference of power has been well documented through government informants, electronic transmissions, and the like. Beginning with reports of the Black Hand, the concept of a formalized structure of Italian criminality has long frightened and fascinated faint-hearted Americans. As early as the nineteenth century, reports of criminal secret societies have permeated American folklore. Perhaps the earliest reports characterized criminal behavior among groups of Italian immigrants as a subversive, ethnic society composed of young Italians and referred to as

---

[6]In 1968 the Omnibus Crime Control and Safe Streets Act became the centerpiece for Richard Nixon's "war on crime." One of the most important changes from a law enforcement viewpoint was the inclusion of Title III, which allowed for electronic surveillance (e.g., wiretaps and recording or eavesdropping equipment). Interestingly, Title III was the brainchild of Bob Blakely, author of the RICO statute.

the Black Hand by apprehensive residents of New York City (Train, 1922). Indeed, incidents of strong-armed extortion were reported across the country. The murder of Police Commissioner David Hennessey in New Orleans in the late 1800s raised public hysteria to epidemic portions, and anti-Italian sentiment abounded. As stated, it is unclear whether this incident was in any way the result of an *organized conspiracy*. In fact, some authors argue that Italian criminality was anything but organized. Rather, they suggest that pockets of illegitimate entrepreneurs were actually an exception to the hordes of Italian immigrants who successfully pursued legitimate opportunities (Train, 1922). However, this distinction is often overlooked as the turn of the century brought a dramatic increase in organized crime within Italian-American communities. However, they are not the only ethnic group who has chosen this avenue.

During this century, the majority of incoming minority ethnic groups have solidified their masses in order to combat the reality of a hostile new world. Several individuals, dissatisfied with limited opportunities, banded together for the sole purpose of gaining economic independence through illicit means. Eventually, the activities of these groups became more sophisticated and expanded to international proportions. This process was marked by vicious power struggles in which many innocents and not-so-innocents were killed. After a time, the violence subsided as the Italians soon gained unequivocal domination over the criminal subculture. However, this struggle for underworld dominance has become much more pronounced as various ethnic groups clash over territorial boundaries, both materially and geographically.

The explosion of the narcotics industry in the Unites States, traditionally owned and operated by the Sicilian families, has resulted in the induction of various conflicting ethnicities. Although appearing more than disparate, certain similarities emerge regardless of ancestry. Contrary to popular media depictions that proclaim unprecedented levels of random street violence by young ethnic gangs, the early foundations of the American mafia were predicated on the same type of street-level activity. In fact, today's ethnic gangs closely resemble the humble beginnings of most recognized criminal syndicates in the country. Like their predecessors, contemporary urban gangs are primarily comprised of young males from marginalized segments of society. Denied access to legitimate avenues of success, these ethnic gangs, like the Italians, rely on proceeds from illegal activities. Finding the most vulnerable targets within their own communities, these groups prey on their own kind, developing criminal networks to increase their powers of intimidation.

The Sicilian mafia embodies the hierarchy and autonomy prevalent in police organizations, the armed forces, and other paramilitary organizations. A hierarchical structure has lent credence to the stability of La Cosa Nostra and enabled it to flourish for nearly a century. This bureaucratic structure is perpetuated by the use of territorial guidelines, the provision for regulation of violence, and mediation of disputes. A hierarchical approach has enabled it to flourish for over a century. However, a recent influx of contemporary youth has resulted in an increase in criminal prosecutions. Whether through careless behavior or misplaced bravado, many of today's criminals have seemed to bask in the media spotlight. Unfortunately for them, this media scrutiny is increasingly harmful to their criminal longevity. Recent organization-wide RICO cases have decimated many of the original Italian families. Even though these families continue to survive, the future may bring a significant decline in mafia-related activity.

CHAPTER

5

# Outlaw Motorcycle Gangs

Traditionally, organized crime groups have been predicated on similar ethnic, racial, or religious backgrounds. Created to circumvent institutional obstacles, these groups have found strength in their homogeneity and have successfully parlayed this solidarity into an increasingly global criminal syndicate. This globalization, however, has not been accomplished without sacrifice. Indeed, expansion of organized crime has resulted in concentrated efforts and increasing scrutiny from the law enforcement community. Even though this increased vigilance has negatively impacted traditional organized crime organizations, it has also obscured the threat of nontraditional criminal groups. In fact, formal definitions of organized crime groups that are based on stereotypical models have all but ignored criminal structures lacking ethnic, racial, or religious consistency. Many deviant subcultures have taken advantage of this oversight to establish themselves in the underworld superstructure and gain a foothold in the expanding vice market. Only recently recognized by some authorities as a significant threat, groups such as outlaw motorcycle gangs (OMGs) have proven particularly resilient to RICO prosecutions due largely to traditional characterizations of "organized crime."

With more than 300 clubs, 5,000 members, and at least 10,000 associates, OMGs have quickly become one of the nation's largest criminal organizations (Serwer, 1992). Although annual revenues of $1 billion pale in comparison to mob highs of $50 billion, OMGs have displayed a remarkable ability to adapt. This ability has enabled them to become major players in international drug markets, prostitution rackets, and arms trafficking.

However, the danger of these groups has often been overlooked because traditional stereotypes and media depictions promote images of poorly shaven, beer-swilling misfits. In fact, a sharp increase in sales of Harley-Davidsons and Hells Angels memorabilia to mainstream American males has indicated a growing cultural affinity for social outcasts and tolerance of lawlessness.

## HISTORY

Calling themselves POBOB (Pissed Off Bastards of Bloomington), the Hells Angels motorcycle club was originally comprised of disillusioned World War II veterans (SLED, 1997). Many of these returning veterans experienced feelings of disassociation and felt alienated from a society that largely expected them to resume their former lives as if their absence had been nothing more than an extended vacation. In fact, the group's original charter was little more than a fraternal organization of post-wartime camaraderie for nostalgic veterans. In this atmosphere, members were free from the strictures of polite society. Buoyed by the support of their brethren, members reveled in their newly found freedom from the traditional trappings of social conformity. Members allowed their hair and beards to grow to socially inappropriate levels to symbolize their disdain for the established order. Motorcycles, their transportation of choice, epitomized their rejection of societal expectations.

For the most part, these outward manifestations of rebellion did not indicate widescale criminal activity. Rather, organizational ideology, if articulated, encouraged members to squeeze the largest amount of fun out of every waking moment. This carefree atmosphere, however, would prove to be short-lived; circumstances soon forced members to choose between group association and legitimate lifestyles. Ironically, the event that propelled these former veterans into the criminal underworld occurred on Independence Day, a holiday associated with national patriotism and those of the armed services.

Although reports differ, most authors agree that a confrontation in 1947 between motorcycle enthusiasts and local law enforcement signalled the beginning of outlaw motorcycle gangs. This confrontation, sensationalized in the film *The Wild One,* was instigated by the general lawlessness displayed by POBOB members. Apparently, the authorities of Hollings, California, did not appreciate the manner in which many individuals entered establishments at full throttle, and responded by arresting bikers for even the smallest indiscretions. Their response and the appearance of reinforcements successfully quelled further disturbances but set in motion an antiestablishment movement far more sinister in its implications. In fact, law enforcement's actions exacerbated feelings of alienation and served as a rallying cry for future criminal behavior (Wolf, 1991; Lavigne, 1996; Thompson, 1966).

## THE BIG FOUR

Law enforcement sources list four main outlaw motorcycle gangs, each referred to as a "1%."[1] They contain formalized bureaucracies and pose a significant threat to domestic security. Without exception, these groups are highly structured and increasingly volatile. Perhaps the most dangerous and certainly the most recognizable of all outlaw motorcycle gangs is the Hells Angels. This organization, originally founded immediately following World War II, is indisputably the leader of the outlaw biker subculture. However, they are not alone in their criminal pursuits. In fact, other criminal organizations pepper the North American landscape, each unique in location and criminal pursuits. The Outlaws, based primarily in Chicago, Illinois, continue to control methamphetamine manufacturing in the Midwest. The Pagans, founded in 1959 in Prince George's County, Maryland, continue to dominate northeastern methamphetamine markets and are reported to have ties with other more traditional organized crime groups. Finally, the Bandidos, headquartered in Houston, Texas, are concentrated in the southern and western regions of the United States, and are reportedly used as enforcers for Colombian cocaine distributors. Accordingly, each of the Big Four motorcycle gangs poses a significant threat to U.S. society in general and the law enforcement community (SLED, 1997; Lavigne, 1996).

Thus, while the Angels were the first to exhibit a formal, highly bureaucratized structure, various other organizations have displayed an amazing aptitude for criminal adaptation as well. Unfortunately, inaccurate media depictions of biker subcultures have concentrated on the Hells Angels organization. Although organized criminal behavior by bikers is almost always attributed to the Hells Angels organization, territorial boundaries observed by rival groups contradict this representation. The Angels remain the most prominent and most dangerous of all OMGs, but they are not the sole proprietors of the outlaw biker ethos. Unfortunately, competing organizations, such as the Bandidos, Pagans, and Outlaws, have only recently been recog-

---

[1]The term "1%" was adopted by outlaw motorcycle gangs in response to a speech given by the president of the American Motorcyclist Association in which he stated that only 1% of all motorcycle enthusiasts were criminals. Outlaw motorcycle gangs flaunt their criminal lifestyles by wearing "1%" patches on their colors.

nized by law enforcement authorities as highly structured criminal organizations. This oversight has allowed a collection of bikers or outlaw motorcycle gangs to prosper throughout the continental United States.

## The Hells Angels and Sonny Barger

The designation *Hells Angels* was first adopted by the San Bernardino chapter in 1948. Originally comprised of POBOB members, this group adopted the winged deathhead insignia favored by WWII aviators. The "Berdoo" chapter (denoting the group's San Bernardino location) was originally the headquarters to the Hells Angels organization. In 1957, Ralph "Sonny" Barger, a 19-year-old veteran discharged for lying on his application, joined the ranks of the Oakland chapter. Even though his beginnings were anything but auspicious, this high school dropout would become somewhat of a second coming for the Hells Angels (Lavigne, 1996, 1987).

Barger's impact on contemporary OMGs cannot be overstated. His vision transformed a group traditionally characterized by chaos, violence, and self-destruction into a well-oiled, highly structured criminal organization. Like a general marshalling his troops, Barger successfully recruited the most intelligent Angels to serve as his administrative staff while arming them with the most vicious soldiers. Other jurisdictions, angered at his high-handedness, were quickly silenced through violence and intimidation. Subsequently, Barger created an iconoclastic empire and established the Oakland chapter as organizational headquarters and himself as the group's undisputed leader. Coupled with his paracorporate approach, this position enabled Barger to concentrate on expanding his domain.

Originally focusing on the West Coast, Barger targeted rival groups for absorption or dissolution. To accomplish Angel dominance, Barger forced competing gangs to choose between compliance or extinction—an early indication of Barger's corporate approach. According to Lavigne (1996), the majority of these takeovers were, for all pratical purposes, mutually beneficial business transactions. Targeted clubs, forced to abandon corporate colors and ideology for those of the new parent company, received professional counsel, economic resources, and additional personnnel when necessary. On the rare occasions when targeted groups failed to adequately appreciate the benefits of such a merger, violence ensued. The unprecedented and largely unanticipated success of this corporate approach encouraged Barger to monopolize international markets as well. To the dismay of law enforcement, Barger's Napoleonic tendencies resulted in an international criminal conglomeration.

By 1983, an estimated 56 chapters of Hells Angels existed worldwide as a result of these systematically initiated corporate takeovers. Alternately implementing public relation platforms and headbreaking strategies, the Angels successfully cornered the outlaw motorcycle gang market in locations across the globe. Increasingly sophisticated in his approach, Barger cultivated a cosmopolitan image by relying on bilingual "ambassadors" familiar with foreign customs to spread his message of group domination. This presentation, coupled with a reputation for violence, proved to be wildly successful. In fact, many organizations actively campaigned for Angel assimilation (Lavigne, 1996).

Their success in international markets formally elevated the Hells Angels to the top of the OMG criminal hierarchy. Other groups have followed their lead, hoping to mimic the success enjoyed by the Angels organization. However, it was not sheer criminal supremacy that propelled the Angels into the forefront. Group leaders, especially Barger, aggressively sought out legitimate safeguards. Formally incorporating their organization in the 1970s, the Angels were also successful in securing tax-exempt status. Establishment of a formal nonprofit charitable organization, The Church of the Angel, negated organizational responsibilities of taxation (Lavigne, 1996). The Angels even copyrighted their club logo! In fact, revenue garnered from copyright infringement cases has been used to fuel legal defense funds for members awaiting trial. As a result, the Angel assets swelled. Other groups have only been moderately successful.

### Becoming a Member

Contrary to popular belief, outlaw motorcycle gangs are quite selective in their membership. The desire to ride Harley-Davidsons and engage in criminal activity does not guarantee entrance into this biker subculture; these organizations are more selective of personnel than most law enforcement agencies. Extensive background checks on all prospective members all but negate the possibility of law enforcement infiltration. Members are most often recruited by patch-wearing members, and individuals displaying too much interest in the group are often discouraged from further inquiries.

According to Wolfe (1991), entrance into the outlaw subculture is closely guarded. The four-step initiation process assures compatibility and brotherhood. The majority of new members are scouted by incumbents for their general knowledge and appreciation of outlaw motorcycling values and behavior. These individuals are considered outsiders and interactions are guarded. Upon acceptance of and sponsorship by an individual member, new recruits are then introduced as "friends of the club." Unanimous approval is a prerequisite to "striking" or "prospecting," which is the next step in the initiation process. The graduation to this level is ritualized by the granting of preliminary colors—the bottom rocker designating the striker's club charter. The duration of this period may range from six months to three years. Prospects are expected to perform the most distasteful of duties without complaint. It is not uncommon for strikers to be responsible for providing entertainment, cleaning clubhouse bathrooms, and washing members' "iron" (i.e., motorcycles). Prospects are also required to serve security detail, and prove their worth by protecting established members. Most organizations even require prospects to engage in criminal assaults. This requirement is one of the most effective obstacles to governmental infiltration.

Prospects or strikers who successfully complete their probationary period are then inducted into the organization as full members with all the rights and privileges that the position implies. This rite of passage is symbolized by the granting of full "colors." Colors refer to the rockers and emblems worn on a member's jacket and are the most prized possession of outlaws. (In fact, colors are so important to outlaws that many individuals have them tattooed directly on their back. This "back pack" includes both the club emblem and the top and bottom rockers.) The "official uniform" of outlaw motorcycle gangs is a sleeveless denim or leather jacket. Featured on the back of the jacket are the club name, location, and logo. On the front are the member's moniker, office held, and various patches, pins, and medals. Colors are the property of the club and are to be worn only by club members, as they are regarded as sacred by outlaw motorcycle gang members. Once individuals are accepted as color-wearing members, they are entitled to vote in weekly "church" meetings and be appointed to executive offices. This thorough initiation process, coupled with a complex organizational structure, has allowed many OMGs to prosper in the criminal underworld (Wolfe, 1991; Lavigne, 1996; SLED, 1997).

## Organizational Structure

Hells Angels chapters have been reported in 17 countries across the globe. This unparalleled criminal expansion of the organization may be attributed to the group's hierarchical structure and corporate ideology. Each chapter has an executive staff similar to noncriminal organizations: president, vice president, secretary, treasurer, and sergeant at arms (see Figures 5-1 and 5-2). Generally speaking, the responsibilities attached to these positions mirror those in traditional clubs, with one exception. The sergeant at arms, responsible for club discipline, uses violence to ensure rule compliance.

Unlike the Pagans, Bandidos, and Outlaws, the Hells Angels do not have formal national or international presidents. Rather, the majority of the power

An example of OMG colors. Note the abbreviation M.C. (motorcycle club) on the front and the rockers on the back, designating location and affiliation. (Courtesy of South Carolina State Law Enforcement Division)

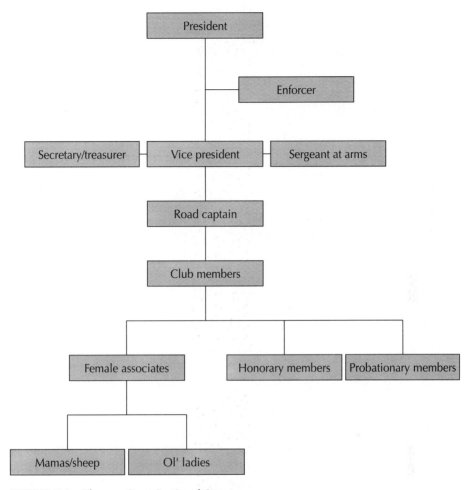

**FIGURE 5-1** Chapter Organizational Structure

remains with the Oakland chapter. Regional officers selected by individual charters represent their club at regional meetings. The U.S. component of the Hells Angels is divided into East Coast and West Coast factions in reference to their location to Omaha, Nebraska. Monthly meetings are held between the two factions, and each charter is expected to have representatives present. These meetings, however, are not intended to serve as governing entities. Rather, chapters remain somewhat autonomous, and meetings are likened to democratic elections in which a two-thirds majority is required to pass a major resolution. Criminal activities are not discussed at these meetings. This aspect, coupled with their superficial appearance of autonomy,

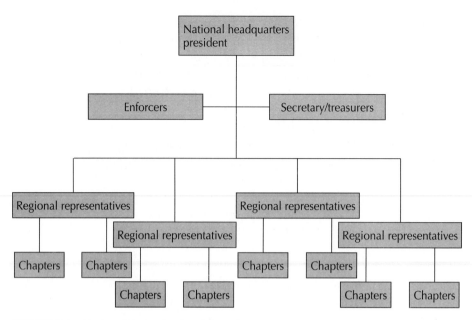

**FIGURE 5-2**  National Organizational Structure

insulates the club from RICO prosecutions, as chapters maintain an appearance of individuality. Ultimately, however, absolute power remains with Barger's Oakland chapter (SLED, 1997).

The annual "USA" motorcycle run is mandatory for all members and strikers not otherwise incapacitated (i.e., incarcerated, hospitalized, or dead). These national runs include mandatory meetings for all national presidents. An agenda prepared prior to the event (usually the last week of July) includes motions submitted by individual clubs. These motions are voted on by all members. Similar to presidential elections, smaller groups are at a distinct disadvantage. Again, a motion can only be passed by a two-thirds majority. The Oakland chapter remains the biggest, and its influence is immeasurable. Even World Runs are dominated by Barger's group, though he disavows any formalized position of power (SLED, 1997; Lavigne, 1996).

Contrary to the Angels who have not formalized a national presidency, the Outlaws, Bandidos, and Pagans maintain a national/international headquarters called "the mother club." The Outlaws and the Bandidos are remarkably similar in their organizational structures. Both groups have a governing board comprised of the national president and four regional vice presidents. In both organizations, the national president maintains total control over club policies, bylaws, and activities. The Pagans, on the other hand, maintain a governing body of former club presidents. Founded in 1959 in Prince George's County, Maryland, the Pagan Nation does not claim a particular location for its headquarters. Rather, promotion to the mother club is based on criminal performance. Each member presides over select Pagan chapters. Collectively, this governing board retains absolute power over Pagan members (SLED, 1997; Lavigne, 1987).

Each of the Big Four also maintains specialized positions to insulate themselves from law enforcement prosecution and protect themselves from rival gangs. During "runs" or other club sponsored events, road captains are appointed to coordinate security and run logistics (see Figure 5-3). These individuals are responsible for mapping out destination routes, emergency strong points, and refueling/refreshment centers. Road captains must also ensure that necessary equipment (e.g., spare motorcycle parts, guns, etc.) is included in "crash" cars. He is also responsible for run security and identifying safe locations in the event of threatening rival gangs (SLED, 1997). In addition, each organization maintains a staff of intelligence officers. These officers are responsible for gathering intelligence on law enforcement personnel, including addresses, phone numbers, financial information, children's names, etc. This facet, which will be discussed further, insulates OMG members from criminal prosecutions (Lavigne, 1996, 1987; SLED, 1997).

## Rules and Regulations

Like other criminal subcultures, outlaw motorcycle gangs have formalized rules and regulations that are violently enforced. Established to prevent law enforcement infiltration, these bylaws emphasize organizational loyalty and group solidarity. In most cases, OMGs require individuals to "befriend" incarcerated members—providing economic and emotional support upon demand. At all times, members must place group affiliation first, regardless of family or social responsibilities. Subsequently, members are expected to behave lawlessly and irresponsibly. Individual members who resist this all-encompassing lifestyle are ostracized or otherwise punished for their shortsightedness (Lavigne, 1997). In addition, compliance with other club regulations is mandated, and merging clubs are required to adopt organizational policy. International clubs are expected to adopt English as their official language and remain cognizant of the U.S. power structure. Regular attendance at chapter "church" meetings is also required, and traveling members are expected to attend "church" while on the road. These requirements ensure member accountability and organizational primacy (Lavigne, 1986, 1996; SLED, 1997).

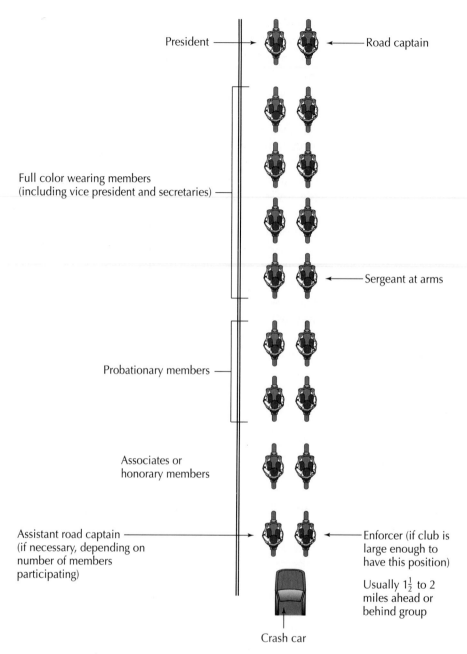

President →← Road captain

Full color wearing members
(including vice president and secretaries)

Sergeant at arms

Probationary members

Associates or
honorary members

Assistant road captain
(if necessary, depending on
number of members
participating)

Enforcer (if club is
large enough to
have this position)

Usually $1\frac{1}{2}$ to 2
miles ahead or
behind group

Crash car

**FIGURE 5-3**  Formation and Lineup During a Run

The majority of OMGs have strict requirements regarding racial identity. Equating nonwhites with other club enemies, traditional policies of "no cops, no niggers, no snitches" pervade most outlaw bylaws (Lavigne, 1996). Prospecting clubs are often forced to expel nonwhite members.[2] This supremacist ideology permeates the outlaw subculture and extends beyond the boundaries of club membership. In fact, attacks on innocent African Americans are encouraged by organizational ideology (Lavigne, 1996). However, exceptions to this rule do occur when exchange relationships are necessary in pursuit of criminal enterprise. One example of such complicity is the long-standing relationship between California Angels and Oakland's East Bay Dragons, a black motorcycle gang who received a 25-year Angel commemorative patch (Lavigne, 1996).

Much of the continuing success of OMGs is attributed to their strictly enforced code of silence. OMGs aggressively protect organizational secrets. However, OMGs do not restrict their violence to individual traitors. In fact, reports from law enforcement authorities indicate that OMGs extract their revenge from the most vulnerable targets—innocent women and small children. This unprecedented level of violence is of utmost concern to law enforcement agencies, because no formal limitations on violence and targeting of innocents may be identified. Unfortunately, governmental extensions of protection are disdained by those they seek to protect. Assurances of safety to significant others (primarily spouses or their informal counterparts) are met with tentative distrust and outright skepticism.

## Women and the Outlaw Subculture

Like other criminal organizations, outlaw motorcycle gangs are not equal opportunity employers. A strictly patriarchal phenomenon, females are not allowed to apply for or secure membership rights and privileges. Rather, females are relegated to marginal positions that are highly sexualized. Indeed, members vie for a variety of conquest patches—some socially deviant, some overtly criminal (see Figure 5-4). This contempt for traditional notions of commitment and monogamy, and the sexualization of the female gender have resulted in a highly structured stratification system within organizational boundaries. While promiscuity among males is encouraged, independent promiscuity among female companions is not tolerated. Females deviating from proscribed subservient roles are punished for their indiscretions.

---

[2]Although a strict "white only" policy is found in many organizational charters, there have been isolated exceptions. These exceptions, rare indeed, are only extended to avoid violent resistance among prospective clubs.

All outlaw motorcycle gangs have their own particular system of patches. Patches are awarded for participation in runs, official organizational designation, and most commonly for deviant sexual acts. The following is a sample listing of patches awarded to various members of OMGs. Keep in mind that awarding of such patches often requires eyewitness testimony to substantiate claims made.

| | |
|---|---|
| "1%" | Derives from a disclaimer by the American Motorcycle Association which stated that 99% of the country's motorcyclists belong to the AMA. The 1% patch designates the wearer as an outlaw. |
| "13" | Worn by an OMG member to symbolize the usage or distribution of marijuana. |
| "22" | Symbolizes that the wearer has previously been incarcerated. |
| "666" | Symbolizes the mark of Satan. |
| Eight ball | Patch worn on colors, earned by committing homosexual sodomy with witnesses present. |
| "POBOB" | Pissed Off Bastards of Bloomington—the original gang that later developed into the Hells Angels. |
| White-power fist | Patch worn on colors, which displays the gang's racial ideals and philosophies of white supremacy. |
| "MC" | Motorcycle club |
| "AFFA" | Angels Forever, Forever Angels |
| "OFFO" | Outlaws Forever, Forever Outlaws |
| "Nomad" | When worn as a bottom rocker on a member's colors means that the wearer does not belong to any individual chapter. In some clubs they are the enforcers. |
| Green wings | Patch earned when the wearer performs oral sex on a woman afflicted with some sort of venereal disease. |
| Purple wings | Patch earned when the wearer performs oral sex with a woman's corpse. |
| Golden wings | Patch earned when the wearer engages in sexual activity with a woman during a gang splash of more than 15 persons. |

**FIGURE 5-4** Patch Designations

This rigidity is not to suggest, however, that females are not an important part of the organizational subculture. In fact, many motorcycle gangs aggressively pursue associations with certain females. Their practice of recruiting and/or seducing individuals in sensitive positions is a large part of their intelligence gathering strategy. Reports of female associates in governmental or law enforcement occupations are increasing. Governmental intelligence reveals that some female employees of government agencies have provided counterintelligence information to OMGs. However, positions of power among female associates are nonexistent, because OMGs are strictly patriarchal in nature, and females are only used to service the entrepreneurial or sexual needs of the club.

According to Wolfe (1995), three distinct classes of females permeate the outlaw subculture. "Broads," the lowest class occupied by females, refers to individuals who have brief sexual associations with one or more members, or women in transitional stages of association who may eventually graduate to the higher levels of association—"mamas" or "ol' ladies." Many of these women articulate motivations similar to male associates. For some, the outlaw subculture embodies a spirit of social rebellion. For these women, the "heavy macho image . . . the intrigue of association . . . and the partying and excitement of the hedonistic lifestyle" act as powerful, though temporary, magnets (Wolfe, 1991: 145). On the average, the majority of these associations constitute little more than a fleeting flirtation. However, Wolfe's assertion that these encounters are entirely voluntary is somewhat misleading. Lavigne (1996: 32) suggests that the outlaw culture's "idea of female emancipation is to take the handcuffs off a woman after they've had her." Unfortunately, many females are unaware of the total lack of benevolence on the part of many OMGs. These individuals often find that this flirtation has serious implications for their personal safety. Indeed, some individuals have reported that their participation in sexual situations was anything but voluntary, and was the result of drug-induced states or threats of violence. In fact, communiqués between European and U.S. authorities report that "white slavery" and prostitution rings composed of unwilling females are increasingly becoming business favorites among outlaw motorcycle gangs (SLED, 1997; Lavigne, 1996).

For the most part, however, the majority of these females participate in the outlaw subculture quite willingly, albeit temporarily. Indeed, the bulk of these experiences represents a brief vacation to the "wild side" for these individuals. Most do not develop long-standing ties to specific outlaw members or the outlaw subculture in general. In fact, the same members who sample the wares of these females openly display contempt for their promiscuity. Ironically, the practice of group sex (i.e., "pulling trains") discourages members from establishing further relationships with these individuals, and all but negates the possibility of graduation to ol' lady status. However, a small minority of these females do establish a somewhat permanent association with the club.

Of the three groups delineated by Wolfe (1991), the least numerically represented are "motorcycle mamas." Hierarchically, these individuals occupy a position only slightly higher than that of broads. As such, they are accorded the same level of protection accorded to organizational mascots and club animals. Jacket rockers reading "Property of _____ (organizational name)" indicate their continuing favor among club members and their willingness to perform sexual acts with any (or all) club member. Their primary responsibilities are twofold: (1) sexually servicing club members and their visitors, and (2) providing continuous income for club coffers. Some clubs even employ mamas in their various sex-related enterprises, such as massage parlors, prostitution, etc. Their position within the organization, however, remains somewhat precarious, reliant upon acceptance by members and their ol' ladies (Wolfe, 1991; Lavigne, 1996; SLED, 1997).

The highest level of female association within outlaw motorcycle clubs is only achieved through a long-standing or monogamous relationship with one member. Females attaining such elevated status are affectionately known as "ol' ladies," and are accorded a measure of respect much higher than that of other female associates. This respect, however, is often hard-won, because female associates are exposed to heightened levels of scrutiny. Thus, organizational association and corresponding privileges are not extended without significant personal sacrifice.

Recognizing the compelling nature of intimate relationships, most OMGs have established informal mechanisms for ousting undesirable or nontrustworthy partners. Accordingly, indoctrination processes experienced by ol' ladies are more intense and demanding than those experienced by their male counterparts, and serve as evaluative measures for organizational acceptance. Females seeking elevation to this grandiose status are required to display high levels of humility, submission, and obedience to respective mates. Subservient at all times, ol' ladies must be passive complements to displays of gendered supremacy. Indeed, female adherence to traditional gender roles is considered to be a reflection of her partner's masculinity, and directly affects his organizational standing. As such, male members are highly encouraged—even expected—to disdain monogamy and act upon their "manly urges." This expectation of sexual promiscuity is one that is not reciprocated. Indeed, extramarital (or extra-relationship, whichever the case may be) affairs by ol' ladies often result in immediate expulsion from the group. This practice, necessary to preserve the sanctity of the brotherhood, also ensures the privacy of club activities. In some cases, groups have actually executed former ol' ladies whom they felt were privy to incriminating evidence (Lavigne, 1996).

Ol' ladies pose the greatest threat to group solidarity, and as such, are scrutinized more closely than organizational brethren. The significance of their role cannot be overstated; the acceptance of prospective members is often predicated on the behavior of their significant other. Members and/or strikers who are unable to adequately control the activities of their ol' ladies are harshly criticized, and are often forced to choose between their respective mates and their "brothers." Overwhelmingly, the group's primacy is maintained, as few members choose their female companions over the group. However, ol' ladies receiving organizational endorsement are often used to protect club assets from governmental forfeiture. For example, Barger's motorcycle repair shop, his home, and the Oakland headquarters for the Hells Angels are "owned" by his wife, Sharon.

In return for their loyalty, females who successfully pass muster are entitled to display their affiliation with modified colors. The primary modification, of course, is one that clearly indicates their subservient or secondary status. "Property of" rockers accompany the club emblems. Unlike colors sported by organizational hangers-on, bottom rockers displayed by ol' ladies boldly proclaim individual ownership. These outward manifestations of enslavement are not without significant rewards. Additional benefits of club affiliation include club protection, extended vacations from reality, etc. In reality, biker ol' ladies occupy a position far below a biker's iron or colors. With few exceptions, females in these positions are physically and emotionally abused. In many cases, the absence of formal marital contracts leaves little or no legal recourse for discarded ol' ladies. In the rare case that legal judgments of spousal or dependent support are secured, few are satisfied because process servers are reluctant to enter OMG strongholds.[3]

Summarily, marginalization of females appears to be a mainstay of the outlaw subculture. Sexualization of female associates serves to reinforce subcultural values and ideology, while encouraging male domination and female subservience. Contrary to popular belief, working- or lower-class females are not overrepresented within these organizations. On the contrary, broads, mamas, and ol' ladies appear to be attracted to the carefree lifestyle

---

[3]Some notable exceptions to this rule include, for example, Barger's motorcycle shop, the Oakland clubhouse, and various other Angel holdings that are "owned" by Barger's wife, Sharon. Their relationship has survived for more than two decades, and most describe them as "close." However, Barger's track record, coupled with the group's propensity for violence, suggests that this "closeness" would not protect Sharon in the event of a divorce. Nor would her "first lady" status remain in the event of a split.

espoused by OMGs *despite* economic background. Almost without exception, however, these females are only slightly postpubescent. Regardless of socioeconomic status, profession, or background, the younger generation is disproportionately represented among female associates, who are used until their physical beauty has faded and then they are traded in for newer models. Finding few takers outside the outlaw subculture, many of these women are forced to remain in abusive environments.

## CRIMINAL ACTIVITIES

Without exception, the informal goals of OMGs revolve around lawless lifestyles. Social institutions, including law enforcement agencies, are condemned as overly restrictive and hypocritical entities. As such, the laws they espouse are ignored. Instead, rules and regulations more consistent with the outlaw ideology are adopted. This alternative system actually encourages violent behavior and victimization of others. Subsequently, outlaw motorcycle gangs have been involved in criminal activities such as murder, aggravated assault, rape, arson, robbery, prostitution, and burglary. They have also established complex criminal networks involving drugs and weapons trafficking, prostitution, and protection rackets.

### Drugs

The primary source of revenue for outlaw motorcycle gangs is a compilation of illegal narcotics trafficking. Beginning in the late 1960s, the Hells Angels organization became one of the primary distributors of LSD in the San Francisco Bay area. Since that time, outlaw motorcycle gangs have been found to be active in the manufacturing, marketing, and distribution of heroin, cocaine, marijuana, seconal, STP, MDA, PCP, and amphetamines. Currently, OMGs, especially the Hells Angels, are considered to be the largest supplier of methamphetamines in the country (SLED, 1997; Lavigne, 1996). Subsequent by-products of their narcotics trade have included murder, extortion, and witness intimidation. In addition, various groups have become increasingly active in arms trafficking. Law enforcement authorities have seized from OMGs an array of sophisticated weaponry including but not limited to fully automatic weapons, silencers, explosive agents, and military antipersonnel devices (SLED, 1997; Lavigne, 1996).

Federal authorities have achieved limited success for their enforcement efforts, which have primarily concentrated on the Hells Angels organization. In the 1980s, Federal Bureau of Investigation Operations ROUGHRIDER and CACUS resulted in a number of narcotics-related convictions of Hells Angels in the northeastern and western portions of the United States. Additional enforcement efforts have resulted in a variety of arrests and seizures across the country. While the majority of these drug-related charges involve the manufacturing and distribution of methamphetamines, some governmental sources have documented links between northeastern Hells Angels chapters and the Medellin cartel of Colombia and other traditional organized groups. Links between other outlaw motorcycle gangs, such as the Bandidos, have also been established and are an increasing concern among law enforcement personnel (SLED, 1997).

As stated, the vast majority of drug-related enterprises among OMGs involve methamphetamines. Seizure of clandestine methamphetamine labs in California, Oregon, and Missouri indicate the growing demand for "ice" or "crank" within domestic markets, and illustrate an OMG monopoly. Increasingly, outlaw groups are contracting with nonmember clandestine lab operators to manufacture for them. Typically, OMGs maintain ownership over required chemical products, and simply pay for the "cooking" or actual manufacturing of the "ice." This practice has further insulated OMGs from criminal prosecution and law enforcement scrutiny. In addition, such activities have become so lucrative that many members have invested proceeds in legitimate businesses (SLED, 1997; Lavigne, 1996).

Outlaw motorcycle gangs are extremely protective of their drug distribution territories. Crossing territorial boundaries poses dire consequences not only for rival gangs but also for members dealing outside the confines of their individual chapters. To limit regional disputes, many OMGs have formed tenuous alliances with rival gangs. This agreement has greatly enhanced financial rewards through monopolistic jurisdictions that maintain economic regularity. In addition, strict organizational rules prohibiting "narcotics burns" (taking the goods without paying) amplify product marketability.

## Organized Crime Mainstays: Prostitution and Protection

Like organized crime groups of old, OMGs have also focused on vice activities to further enlarge club coffers. Surveillance reports have uncovered a complex system of prostitution rings and brothels. Members engaging in this sort of criminal activity act as pimps or procurers, earning a percentage of their prostitutes' wages. Unlike their predecessors, however, the females working in such establishments are not there of their own accord. Rather, drug addiction, threats, and other intimidation tactics are employed to maintain "company personnel." These tactics have been successful in discouraging government informants or cooperative witnesses. One exception, a former prostitute in an Angels' brothel in Vallejo, California, was murdered along with her six-year-old daughters (twins) and a male companion for her testimony. Unfortunately for her, government assurances of protection were inadequate in the face of the group's sophisticated counterintelligence unit; her location was divulged by a postal employee on the Angel payroll (Lavigne, 1996).

Steady income is also provided by a complex web of protection rackets. Unlike traditional organized crime groups who focused on a variety of legitimate businesses, outlaw motorcycle gangs tend to target drinking establishments and social clubs. Simply stated, members promise to appear en masse in full colors unless a small monthly fee is provided. Business owners, faced with the prospect of losing legitimate business, quickly agree to such charges. To protect these arrangements, scrupulous record keeping and weekly church meetings provide "off limits" establishments. For the most part, however, these admonitions are unnecessary because members tend to congregate in predominantly biker establishments (Lavigne, 1996).

## Other Criminal Activities

Traditional vice-related enterprises are not the only criminal activities engaged in by outlaw motorcycle gangs. Members are also involved in nonviolent criminal activities. Over the years, outlaw motorcycle gangs have exhibited an amazing aptitude for fraudulent activities. The most well known of these, insurance fraud, involves the false reporting of injury, destruction, or disappearance of real or personal property. "Legitimate" club businesses, such as motorcycle repair shops, present an aura of respectability while providing the opportunity to traffic "stolen" motorcycles, parts, and equipment. It is not uncommon for club property to burn down in the middle of the night and club "iron" to be stolen right out of club parking lots. As few individuals would venture onto OMG property and even fewer would dare to linger, such reports must be approached with a degree of skepticism.

Other activities engaged in by OMGs are standard, run-of-the-mill, violent felonies. The majority of these assaults, rapes, and murders are economically motivated and a by-product of a moneymaking enterprise such as narcotics distribution or prostitution. However, some of these violent attacks are not fiscally motivated but are, in fact, committed in retaliation of a rival gang, as punishment of a former member, or to intimidate a government witness/informant. Still other attacks are perpetrated against innocents, further negating media depictions of fun-loving, beer-swilling misfits. Documented accounts of such viciousness include the stabbing death of a five-year-old child. This incident, in which her parents and 17-year-old brother were also murdered, clearly illustrates the savage nature of OMGs. Indeed, it is this characteristic of outlaw motorcycle gangs that is most disturbing to law enforcement (Lavigne, 1996).

## Gang Wars

Although outlaw motorcycle gangs share a common ideology, territorial disputes have arisen between organizations. Perhaps the most violent and certainly the longest lasting feud originated in 1974 when Sandy Alexander, president of the New York Hells Angels, assaulted a member of the Outlaw organization for allegedly raping his ol' lady. In order to save face among his peers, the Outlaw claimed that he was blindsided by a band of Angels. Outlaw members tortured and executed three Angels in Florida in retaliation. Charlotte became the main battleground in the conflict when four Outlaws, one female associate, and the club's guard dogs were shot and killed in their clubhouse. (Some Outlaws wear the tattoo "7-4-79" to

Outlaws colors. (Courtesy of South Carolina State Law Enforcement Division)

commemorate the date.) The following year the Angel clubhouse in Charlotte was blown up by rival Outlaws (Lavigne, 1996). Although the feud is still brewing, periodic cease-fires have been observed. Some law enforcement sources predict that ensuing peace talks may result in an end to the conflict. However, increased occurrences of gang disputes overseas may negate this projection (SLED, 1997).

## LAW ENFORCEMENT

### Counterintelligence

Though outlaw motorcycle gangs are now recognized as a powerful organized crime group, law enforcement efforts have seen only limited success. Individual members have been successfully targeted for prosecution, but widescale organizational prosecution has not been effective. On the surface, it may appear that their emphasis on corporate-like strategies would increase their vulnerability to RICO prosecutions. However, OMGs have purposely separated the corporation and business side of the organization from the criminal activity perpetrated by its members. This functional separation does not suggest, however, that motorcycle gangs do not fit standard definitions of organized crime; rather, OMGs—beginning with Barger and the Hells Angels—have intentionally distanced themselves from officially sanctioned criminal activity. As such, OMGs as organizations have proven resilient to RICO convictions even though individuals have been convicted on a variety of charges. In fact, two of the first well-publicized cases were dismal failures for law enforcement and led to a great reluctance to seek RICO convictions. It has been suggested that the lack of prosecutorial success may be attributed to the seemingly unlimited source of funding among outlaw motorcycle gangs. For example, one author reported that the Hells Angels paid $100,000 for police reports during RICO trials in 1979–1981. These documents, labeled "confidential" and "for law enforcement eyes only," were then distributed to chapters worldwide (Lavigne, 1996).

Much of the success of outlaw motorcycle gangs may be attributed to their proactive approach in avoiding criminal prosecution. Unlike traditional organized crime (OC) groups, who develop subversive tactics to avoid technically advanced surveillance equipment, OMGs exploit technology and adopt government techniques and equipment until it is almost worthless to law enforcement efforts. OMGs employ state-of-the-art detection devices that uncover monitoring equipment such as electronic bugs and wires. They hold intelligence-training sessions where members are introduced to the latest technological advancements. Voice-stress analyzers on strikers and suspect members are used to determine the truthfulness of their responses and their loyalty to the club (Lavigne, 1996; SLED, 1997).

Further strengthening their position, OMGs rely on a loose network of informants to assist them in their counterintelligence endeavors. OMGs actively recruit associates from service occupations and have developed sources in the postal service, the electric company, the phone company, even the department of motor vehicles (DMV). These associates act as intelligence-gathering agents, compiling information on government agents, judges, and potential jurors. These information sources are estimated to be far superior to ones established by governmental agencies. Not restricted by legislative mandates, these individuals obtain private addresses, cellular phone numbers, even passenger information profiles from airline manifests (Lavigne, 1996). Associates have even infiltrated law enforcement agencies, a feat the government has not been able to reciprocate. In essence, then, law enforcement agencies are outstaffed and outfunded.

### Defense Funds and Bailbondsmen

In addition to their counterintelligence strategies, outlaw motorcycle gangs have further strengthened their organizations with in-house counsel. Keeping attorneys on retainer allows OMGs to secure the release of jailed members almost immediately. This expediency negates the possibility of jailhouse confessions and limits the power of law enforcement investigators. In addition, most OMGs have established defense funds to assist in legal expenditures. These funds are derived from mandatory donations, membership dues, and illegal revenues. Furthermore, some OMGs maintain agreements with bond companies to file individual surety. Members simply flash their club tattoo, and the bond is supplied. This "get-out-of-jail-free tattoo" is also used as a form of identification by some law enforcement agencies.

### Law Enforcement Successes

As stated, the government has only enjoyed minimal success through implementation of RICO statutes. Even the most concentrated efforts by law enforcement have fallen short of wholescale group prosecution. However, recent years have seen an increase in individual convictions. The most notable victory for law enforcement was a result of a lengthy multijurisdictional task force, which relied primarily on the efforts of a top-ranking Angels informant (see Figure 5-5). For the first time in history, federal agents were granted access via electronic surveillance to church meetings, annual motorcycle runs and rallies, and informal criminal discussions. Although this type of access is

Originally, Operation CACUS was the result of a disillusioned Angel. Anthony Tait, long a cop-wannabe, actually initiated the investigation and solicited law enforcement interest. Paid heavily by the Federal Bureau of Investigation, Tait allowed law enforcement to accompany him on his unprecedented rise to the highest echelon of the Hells Angels organization. His cooperation and unparalleled enthusiasm were especially significant, as his credibility was unchallenged.

Unlike many criminal informants whose cooperation is secured through promises of reduced sentences, Tait *voluntarily* came forward without provocation. Accordingly, criminal prosecutions against the highest ranking officers were successful. Although it did not result in RICO prosecutions, numerous individual convictions were obtained. For example:

*Ralph "Sonny" Barger: undisputed leader of the Hells Angels; convicted of conspiracy to violate federal law and conversion of government property; $3\frac{1}{2}$ years

*Kenneth Jay "K.O." Owen: touted as the world's best methamphetamine cook; convicted of distribution and possession of methamphetamine; 41 years, $2.1 million fine, forfeiture of over $2 million in real and personal property

*Charles Daniel "Chico" Manganiello: convicted of distribution of methamphetamine; $300,000 fine, special parole for life, forfeiture of real and personal property

*Edwin Floyd "Eddie" Hubert: president of Anchorage chapter; convicted of distribution of cocaine; 2 years in custody, 6 years supervised release

*Montgomery David "Monty" Elliott: Anchorage; convicted of distribution of cocaine; $4\frac{1}{2}$ years in custody, 3 years special parole, $10,000 fine

*Michael Vincent "Irish" O'Farrell: president of Oakland chapter; convicted of conspiracy to violate federal law and conversion of government property; $3\frac{1}{2}$ years

*Dennis E. "Bigfoot" Pailing: president of Fairbanks chapter; convicted of possession of cocaine, distribution of cocaine, possession of an unregistered machine gun; $1\frac{3}{4}$ years custody, 3 years probation

*Gerald Michael "Pee Wee" Protzman: treasurer/vice president of Anchorage chapter; convicted of conversion of government property; probation

*Richard Allen "Sleazy Ric" Rickleman: Anchorage chapter; convicted of possession of a firearm by a felon; 1 year in custody, $3,000 fine

*John Makoto "Fuki" Fukushima: San Francisco vice president and computer expert extraordinaire; convicted of possession of an unregistered firearm; $1\frac{1}{2}$ years custody, special parole with a nonassociation clause, $25,000 fine, forfeiture of $32,000

**FIGURE 5-5**  Operation CACUS

virtually unheard of, recent reports by law enforcement sources do indicate an increase in testimonial evidence.

Factors such as individual prosperity and heightened levels of intragroup violence have apparently weakened organizational bonds of loyalty and brotherhood. As such, an increasing number of turncoats have been successfully employed in prosecutorial capacities by law enforcement agencies. Though their testimonial evidence is highly self-serving, it is unclear whether their primary motivation is fear of incarceration or organizational retaliation. However, it is apparent that many individuals are frightened by intragroup violence and have turned to law enforcement for shelter. Interestingly, OMGs, which so closely resemble traditional OC groups and, in fact, mimic much of OC organizational structure, have overlooked the most important lesson: homicidal dictatorship invariably leads to organizational combustion. Thus, in many cases, the specter of group assassins may supercede the nightmare of incarceration. Motivation notwithstanding, it appears that law enforcement authorities are increasingly cognizant of subcultural structure and ideology. While much of this understanding may be attributed to the elevated numbers of organizational informants, private and public information clearinghouses are increasingly important.

Intelligence agencies that focus almost exclusively on outlaw motorcycle gangs are sprouting across the country. Some intelligence networks are funded through state and/or federal sources, but many of these information repositories are entirely capitalistic in nature; the privatization of intelligence gathering is quite lucrative. Although the majority of public intelligence networks are regional in scope, their purpose is to gather information on narcotics, drug-related offenses, and organizations profiting from illicit substances. These nonprofit organizations compile information from a variety of jurisdictions, both local and federal, and often coordinate multijurisdictional investigations and prosecutions (Lavigne, 1996). Like VICAP (Violent Criminal Apprehension Program), information may be obtained through modus operandi (MO), aliases, or location. Unfortunately, regional repositories are grossly underutilized. As is the case in many areas of law enforcement, jurisdictional boundaries and jealousies remain sacrosanct, and many potential opportunities for prosecution are lost.

## CONCLUSIONS

Unlike many gangs, outlaw motorcycle gangs do not share an ethnic identity. On the average, members are white males from working-class backgrounds. Like many criminal subcultures, outlaw motorcycle gangs are primarily an American phenomenon, though many groups are extending their focus to international alliances. Originally created as fraternal organizations, biker gangs have metamorphosed from a group of vandalizing, beer-swilling hell-raisers to a highly sophisticated, increasingly mainstream organization whose sophisticated criminal structure and entrepreneurial activities rival that of corporate giants like IBM.

Long underestimated by law enforcement authorities, OMGs remain a major player in the narcotics trade. Exhibiting a remarkable aptitude for adaptation, external trappings of organizational affiliation are increasingly

Changing times: Two Hells Angels at Bike Week. Note the short hair and clean-cut appearance of the member on the right. Various OMG members are becoming more mainstream in their appearance, making it more difficult for law enforcement investigations. (Courtesy of South Carolina State Law Enforcement Division)

passe. On the decline are the leather jackets, long hair, and unkempt appearance. In their place, a more sophisticated and harder to identify outlaw biker is emerging. Biker "iron," necessary for membership, is seldom used except in connection with limited club events. In fact, Nissan Pathfinders and Ford Explorers are quickly becoming the transportation of choice for club officers. This suburbanite appearance enables OMGs to exist in some communities virtually unnoticed. In fact, this superficial appearance of legitimacy cloaks increasingly sophisticated criminal activities.

Like their Italian counterparts, OMGs are entering legitimate markets at unprecedented levels. Motorcycle repair shops, silk screening businesses, and drinking establishments are but a few examples. These businesses protect both club and personal assets from govenmental forfeiture, and are titled to club associates or ol' ladies. Many of these "fronts" are actually quite successful, due primarily to unlimited capital, low shrinkages, and intimidation tactics. In fact, law-abiding citizens find it impossible to compete in legitimate markets where illegitimate practices are employed. When given the choice, nonoutlaw businesses are forced to choose between unholy alliances or outright extinction. Thus, the existence of OMGs has dire consequences for every segment of society, not just those practicing outside the law.

Although the majority of OMGs have not yet forged international alliances, many of the Big Four have successfully entered illegal markets around the globe. Official chapters of the Hells Angels, indisputably the largest and most dangerous of all OMGs, have been reported in at least 17 countries (Lavigne, 1996; SLED, 1997). OMG activity has been reported in England, Germany, Japan, Sweden, and Russia to name a few. Many of these chapters, perhaps influenced by pop culture, originally mirrored traditional stereotypes and primarily concentrated on street-level criminal behavior. However, recent reports indicate that these groups have quickly followed the lead of U.S. Angels. Developing elaborate criminal networks and abandoning superficial trappings of association, they are increasingly sophisticated in both their activities and their appearances. International members are also entering leadership positions within the organizational hierarchy. Ultimately, however, the power structure is contained within U.S. boundaries.

The unprecedented increase in international chapters may be attributed to Barger's monopolistic approach and the group's propensity for violence. However, this international explosion has not been accomplished without significant growing pains. Increasingly, reports of interchapter fighting dominate church meetings, and group leadership is struggling to maintain "brotherhood" among a culturally and socioeconomically diverse membership. Unfortunately for the Angels, cultural and socioeconomic differences are not easily reconciled, and formal rules and regulations are not applicable in all societies. In their ethnocentrism, the U.S. Angels may have sounded their own death knell in societies intolerant of intolerance. Many Eastern European countries are so burdened by historical baggage that criminal laws remain secondary to national policy. Indeed, Hamburg and like-minded cities act as an example for U.S. law enforcement. Utilization of antisupremacist statutes grants law enforcement greater latitude in group prosecution and organizational disbandment.

Recent reports by law enforcement authorities indicate a shift in power within the Hells Angels organization. OMGs appear to be in significant jeopardy from urban street gangs. Designed to protect them from law enforcement scrutiny, their "suburbanization" has increased their vulnerability to rival gangs. In fact, law enforcement authorities report that the Hells Angels are actually being forced out of areas such as Oakland. Though this hostility appears to be good news for urban authorities, gang mobilization in nonurban areas is anticipated. Many predict that formal power within the organization will move to the southeast region of the United States where competition from other criminal organizations is minimal. In addition, concentrated recruitment efforts have been initiated. Younger members, necessary to revitalize an aging organization, are increasingly targeted in prison, schoolyards, and drinking establishments.

Presently, outlaw motorcycle gangs are recognized as a strictly organized, highly sophisticated criminal syndicate. Increasingly low key in appearance and activity, OMGs are infiltrating legitimate marketplaces and monopolizing entire industries. Law enforcement efforts have had limited success. Personal convictions of patch-wearing members are increasingly common; however, RICO prosecutions have proven unsuccessful. Though group insularity has weakened in recent years, ties of brotherhood still abound.

# Supremacists and Militias

A brief survey of U.S. history reveals unrivaled levels of violence and intolerance. Nepotism, a British trademark and an early foundation of American society, ensured that the prosperity enjoyed by the desirables—white, male, Anglo-Saxon, Protestant landowners—continued. Social regulations, legislative mandates, even religious doctrines granted a foothold for the chosen few. Genocide, as distasteful as it sounds, was used repeatedly to ensure WASP succession. Beginning with the annihilation of Native Americans and continuing long after the abolishment of slavery, American culture reveals a pattern of intolerance inconsistent with democratic ideals. The seemingly limitless selection of white supremacist organizations is a manifestation of such bigotry. Inarguably, these organizations are the most visible and the most long-standing example of racial and religious intolerance upon U.S. soil; however, they are not unique in their radical rhetoric and violent practices.

Contrary to media depictions, white supremacists are not the sole proprietors of racist dogma. Although their continued longevity and subversive ideology is a great concern to contemporary law enforcement, the real danger lies in overlooking their nonwhite counterparts and the increasing popularity of antiestablishment sentiment, white and black, as evidenced in the examples provided in Figures 6-1 and 6-2. Long characterized as a white phenomenon, supremacist ideology among nonwhite groups has often been underestimated or entirely overlooked. However, membership increases in organizations such as the Black Muslims, a glorification of racist antiestablishment groups such as the Black Panthers, and a revisitation of the 1960's

### Gordon Kahl

In 1983, Gordon Kahl was killed in a shootout by Arkansas sheriff Gene Matthews. Kahl, an ardent member of the Posse Comitatus, had previously been involved in the shooting deaths of two U.S. marshalls and the wounding of several others. Declaring that government above the county level was not only repressive but inherently unconstitutional, Kahl refused to acknowledge the legitimacy of the Internal Revenue Service. His failure to comply with taxation laws resulted in the initial confrontation with law enforcement authorities. Supremacist and militia groups have promoted the incident as an example of the abuse of the federal government.

### Randy Weaver

In 1991, Randy Weaver was charged with selling two shotguns that were one-quarter inch shorter than the legal limit. After an extensive surveillance of 18 months by the Bureau of Alcohol, Tobacco, and Firearms (BATF), U.S. Marshall William Degan, 14-year-old Samuel Weaver, and his dog were killed during a shootout. Kevin Harris, a family friend, alerted the Weavers, who collected Samuel's body. After a lengthy standoff, FBI snipers wounded Randy Weaver and Kevin Harris. During the gunfire, Randy's wife, Vicky, was shot and killed while cradling her 10-month-old infant. Weaver and Harris were eventually charged and acquitted of the murder of Degan. Weaver's family was awarded more than $3 million in a subsequent civil suit.

### David Koresh

On April 19, 1993, at least 80 individuals, including 22 children, were killed at a rural retreat in Waco, Texas. The group's leader, David Koresh (formerly known as Vernon Howell), was a self-proclaimed messiah who claimed to have the answers to salvation. The incidents leading to the massacre remain questionable. Government reports indicate that four federal agents were killed while attempting to serve a warrant for weapons violations. After a 51-day standoff, the government, armed with CS gas and tanks, entered the compound. In the melee, Koresh and the majority of his followers were killed. Eleven Branch Davidians were subsequently tried for the murder of the four agents. During the trial, the defense relied heavily on a 911 tape in which the Branch Davidians were heard pleading with the dispatcher to halt the firing because children were at risk. The anguished cries of victims and the wailing of children intermingle with the sound of gunfire. All defendants were acquitted of the most serious charges. Militias and supremacists perceive the incidents of Waco to be indicative of an increasingly secretive and violent government —one that preys on its citizens. In fact, many individuals believe that the date of the Oklahoma City bombing was carefully planned to coincide with the anniversary of the Waco massacre.

**FIGURE 6-1**   Martyrs of the White Supremacist/Militia Movement

signal a revival of racist violence among nonwhite organizations. While the Nation of Islam may appear to have little in common with the Ku Klux Klan, their apparent differences are far outweighed by their similarities.

Both traditional and contemporary supremacist organizations have espoused anti-Semitic ideology. Bolstered by religious frameworks, these groups

### Elmer "Geronimo" Pratt

In 1972, former Black Panther Geronimo Pratt was convicted of the murder of Carolyn Olsen, a 27-year-old school teacher in Santa Monica. Pratt's attorney, Johnny Cochran of O. J. Simpson fame, argued that prosecutors withheld key evidence in the original trial in a successful attempt by the FBI to frame Pratt. The defense contended that the government's key witness, Julius Butler, was jealous of Pratt's position within the party and joined forces with the government in order to convict an innocent man. Bolstered by the FBI's counterintelligence program (COINTELPRO), aimed at undermining radicals, Pratt's conviction was primarily based on eyewitness testimony from the slain woman's husband. This testimony, coupled with the absence of alibi witnesses (not a single Black Panther testified on Pratt's behalf), resulted in a life sentence. In 1997, Pratt was awarded a new trial due to the efforts of Cochran and Jay McCloskey, whose Centurion Ministries, based in Princeton, New Jersey, specialize in exonerating those wrongly convicted.

### Mumia Abu Jamal

In 1981, Mumia Abu Jamal (aka Wesley Cook) was sentenced to death in the shooting death of Philadelphia police officer Daniel Faulkner. Jamal, a former minister of information for the Black Panther Party, has long alleged that the Philadelphia Police Department had intentionally framed him for the murder of Officer Faulkner due to his vocal condemnations regarding the city's MOVE fiasco. A radical print and radio journalist, Jamal has attracted an array of celebrities to his cause. His supporters argue that the city used intimidation tactics to coerce witnesses. They further argue that Jamal's political ideology sealed his fate. Jamal's case has mobilized individuals across the world, and protests have been staged as far away as Paris. In addition, many celebrities have vowed their support for Jamal. On October 29, 1998, the Supreme Court of Pennsylvania denied Jamal's petition for postconviction relief. As the U.S. Supreme Court has previously denied certiorari, it is anticipated that a new date will be set for Jamal's execution.

### MOVE

On May 13, 1985, six adults and five children were killed and more than 50 homes were destroyed in Philadelphia after law enforcement officials used incendiary devices while affecting an arrest. These devices (reportedly containing large amounts of C-4) were dropped on the roof of the MOVE headquarters. Neighborhood houses and non-MOVE residents were devastated by the resulting fire, which was allowed to burn undeterred for several hours. Ramona Africa, widow of the group's leader, argues that their group was targeted for annihilation due to their militant posturing. She argues that the group was actually a nonviolent resistance group, driven to violence by white authorities. (Nine members of the group were charged in a 1978 incident in which a Philadelphia police officer was shot and killed.) Under Ramona Africa's leadership, the group has been actively involved in the Black Militant movement. They have been quite vocal in their support of individuals "wrongfully convicted" such as Mumia Abu Jamal.

**FIGURE 6-2**    Martyrs of the Black Militant Movement

share a common enemy—those of Jewish ancestry. Branding Jews as slayers of Christ or infidels, respectively, these groups are extremely successful in inciting anti-Semitic violence. In addition, contemporary supremacist organizations, race notwithstanding, effectively target governmental institutions and figures by depicting them as a product of Jewish establishments and conspiracies. Indeed, many traditional white supremacist groups have refocused their attention on ZOG (Zionist Occupied Government). These groups

Although the Panthers argued that theirs was a self-defense movement, many of the group's publications proved to be most proactive. The following are reproductions of images that appeared in the infamous *Black Panther Coloring Book,* which was allegedly created by the Black Panther Party to indoctrinate children with their ideology. However, the Panthers have long disavowed any knowledge of its creation, claiming that the book was published by the federal government to discredit the Panthers' movement. Interestingly, the FBI also claims no knowledge of the book's creation.

Black brothers are tired of the white man in black communities.

Brothers and sisters deal with the white store owner that robs black people.

The junior Panther defends his mother.

**FIGURE 6-3** *Black Panther Coloring Book*

are increasingly dangerous, as they actively recruit young members for violent activity.

Preying on economically disadvantaged youths, both white and nonwhite supremacist organizations have traditionally targeted American youth due to their malleable nature (for example, see Figure 6-3). In fact, manipulation and exploitation of disillusioned generations have granted adult members the luxury of legitimization, while bastardizing their young members. Free from "fund-raising" responsibilities (i.e., criminal activities), many adult members have successfully attained political positions and developed legitimate platforms that are palatable to mainstream America but lacking in intent and substance. This superficial legitimacy is perhaps the greatest danger to U.S. society. Like their predecessors, contemporary racists minimize radical dogma while maximizing mainstream appeal.

It must be noted that while the techniques employed by contemporary supremacists are deeply rooted in traditional organizations, their modes of communication and propaganda have advanced significantly. Relying on technological advancements, such as computer bulletin boards and Internet Web sites, both white and black supremacists have successfully propelled their organizations toward the twenty-first century, radically enhancing outdated recruitment instruments. Coupled with bleak economic and occupational projections, this strategy has resulted in an increase in youth involvement. In addition, a climate of political inconsistency, which simultaneously praises and criticizes issues such as affirmative action, has created an atmosphere conducive to supremacist ideologies on both sides. This antagonism, though not unique to contemporary society, has reached proportions similar to those of the late 1960s and early 1970s. Thus, before reviewing contemporary supremacist gangs, a discussion of the roots of such racist ideology and the precursors to current racist organizations is required.

## MALCOLM X AND THE NATION OF ISLAM

I've never seen a sincere white man.

White people are born devils by nature.

Black, brown, red, yellow, all are brothers, all are one family. The white one is a stranger. He's the odd fellow.

Thoughtful white people know they are inferior to black people.

The time is near when the white man will be finished. The signs are all around us.

Like Martin Luther King, Jr., Malcolm Little (aka Malik Shabazz, aka El-Hajj Malik El Shabazz, aka Malcolm X) perceived himself as a religious leader. They were both born black in a time when racial harmony did not, and could not, exist. Both were sons of Baptist ministers. Both characterized American society as inherently racist and discriminatory. Both were extremely charismatic. Both touched thousands of lives, and both were struck down in the prime of life by assassins' bullets. These similarities, however, were superficial at best, overwhelmed by ideological differences and incompatible lifestyles. At 26, King completed his doctorate in systematic theology, became minister of his own congregation, and began a lifelong involvement in the civil rights movement. Malcolm, on the other hand, was completing a sentence of 8–10 years for burglary at Norfolk Prison Colony. A self-avowed atheist prior to his incarceration, Malcolm, like so many inmates, found God (in his case, Allah). This most personal discovery proved to be monumental in its consequences.

Following the teachings of Elijah Muhammad (aka Elijah Poole, aka Elijah Karriem), the self-proclaimed divine prophet, Malcolm denounced whites as "devils," a race genetically engineered by the mad scientist, Yacub, to punish Allah and his followers. Red (Native American) and yellow (Asian) people were by-products of the engineering process. These assertions, inconsistent with traditional Islamic teachings, not only promulgated an attitude of superiority but served as a justification for any violence directed at infidels (i.e., White or Jewish Americans). Seeking to increase both individual visibility and organizational credibility, Malcolm immersed himself in the works of the world's most prominent philosophers, such as Nietzsche, Pliny, and Thoreau. His usage of their words and theories within casual and formal discourse earned him the recognition of the media, the government, and Muhammad. But most importantly, his articulate style and militant posturing gained him a most ardent following among black youth. These youth delighted when Malcolm said Kennedy's assassination was "a case of the chickens coming home to roost," and characterized the death of 120 white passengers on a flight from the United States to Paris as "good news" (X and Haley, 1964: 305). This ideology was exactly what young males in urban poverty were seeking. Unfortunately for Malcolm, these statements, so cavalier yet consistent, signaled his exile from the Nation of Islam.[1]

---

[1] Although many sources imply that Malcolm chose to leave the Nation of Islam upon discovering its leaders' penchant for adultery, a practice specifically forbidden by the Muslim faith, Malcolm stated that it was primarily due to his increasing popularity. He argued that his very public dismissal, attributed by Muhammad as a punishment for disobedience, was a calculated move by Muhammad to destroy his credibility and isolate him from his followers. Malcolm further credited his dismissal as an attempt to conceal Muhammad's indiscretions, which he related to Malcolm prior to the split (X and Haley, 1964).

Malcolm's banishment from the Nation, coupled with a pilgrimage to Mecca, appeared to soften both Malcolm's actions and his rhetoric.[2] This new Malcolm or El-Hajj Malik El Shabazz, as he now called himself, stressed religious rather than racial brotherhood. His new organization, Organization of Afro-American Unity (OAAU), lacked consistency and was denounced by militants as too moderate, and by moderates as too militant. In many circles, he was branded a hypocrite. Indeed, while arguing that his was a nonviolent, strictly self-defensive group, he stated that his followers had to "be ready to go to jail, to the hospital, and to the cemetery." He further asserted that he would send "armed guerrillas into Mississippi," after classifying anything south of Canada as Mississippi (X and Haley, 1964: 418). On February 21, 1965, Malcolm X was shot to death in front of his family at the Audubon Ballroom by his former "brothers" of the Nation of Islam.[3] Malcolm's physical death did not result in the demise of his spiritual message. In fact, his death served as a rallying point for many young black males and initiated splinter black supremacist/antiestablishment gangs.

## The Current State of the Nation of Islam

As stated, the Nation of Islam was and still is particularly attractive for young black males in low-income areas (predominantly urban). Outlining certain unrealistic expectations, their platform is consistent with many international terrorist organizations. Like street gangs, members find safety in numbers and display a propensity for violence. Furthermore, this ideology eliminates individual responsibility and rationalizes economic and social failures in African-American communities. By promoting conspiracy theories and declaring white society the work of Satan, members are freed from personal responsibility. In and of itself, these tenets are especially appealing to urban youth that feel rejected by society. Like traditional street

---

[2]Space does not permit a thorough discussion of Malcolm X's (now El-Hajj Malik El Shabazz) transformation. However, in 1964, in an interview with Alex Haley, Malcolm recanted his earlier characterization of the white race as the devil race. He proposed that he had been blinded by Muhammad and that the Nation of Islam was more dissimilar than similar to the Islamic religion. He declared that all races could unite under one God, and he advocated a peaceful, nonviolent existence. This transformation, however, has been challenged as Malcolm continued to depict the United States as a racial battleground. While the legitimacy of Malcolm's transformation remains questionable, the outcome does not. Regardless of his sincerity, Malcolm X was assassinated before the hatred and rage he created among young black males could be extinguished.

[3]Betty Shabazz, Malcolm's widow, died on June 23, 1997, from burns sustained in a fire at her home. The blaze, determined to be arson, was set by her 12-year-old grandson.

gangs, who perceive legitimate avenues of economic success closed, Black Muslims denounce established institutions of authority. Both groups share perceptions of governmental persecution and harassment. Both groups use violence without hesitation, and both groups are extremely dangerous. Thus, both groups are a primary concern of local law enforcement. However, with its heightened focus, charismatic leaders, and definitive targets, the Nation of Islam promises to have organizational longevity, a characteristic not necessarily shared by street gangs. This variable, coupled with the ability of the Nation to disguise extremist rhetoric as political or intellectual discourse, has the greatest national implications as it creates a facade of legitimacy.

Unlike his predecessor who openly advocated guerilla-type tactics, Louis Farrakhan's message of racial supremacy is neatly packaged into a social policy platform. To a casual observer, it may even appear that Farrakhan is embracing concepts of personal accountability. (After all, his Million Man March called for black males to take responsibility for their offspring.) But a more careful analysis of his teaching reveals traditional notions of government conspiracies and blue-eyed, blond devils. In essence, then, it is not the platform or even the militancy that has changed within these organizations, only their methods.

Following is a compilation of the ten most frequently cited conciliatory requirements for Black Muslims (the Nation of Islam's holiday wish list).

1. We want freedom. We want a full and complete freedom.

2. We want justice. Equal justice under the law. We want justice under the law. We want justice applied equally to all, regardless of creed or class or color.

3. We want equality of opportunity. We want equal membership in society with the best in civilized society.

4. We want our people . . . whose parents or grandparents were descendants from slaves, to be allowed to establish a separate state . . . either on this continent or elsewhere. We believe that our former slave masters are obligated to provide such land and that the area must be fertile and minerally rich . . . [and] maintain and supply our needs in this territory for 20–25 years.

5. We want freedom for all Believers of Islam now held in federal prisons . . . for all black men and women under death sentence.

6. We want an end to the police brutality and mob attacks.

7. As long as we are not allowed to establish a state or territory of our own, we demand not only equal justice under the laws of the United States, but equal employment opportunities NOW.

8. We want the government of the United States to exempt our people from ALL taxation.

9. We want equal education—separate schools up to 16 for boys and 18 for girls on the condition that the girls be sent to women's colleges and universities. We want all black children educated, taught, and trained by their own teachers.

10. We believe that intermarriage or race mixing should be prohibited.

These demands begin rather benignly and are, in fact, somewhat reasonable. Certainly few Americans wish to deny equal justice or equal employment opportunities. Nor do the majority of Americans accept practices of police brutality or mob lynching. Indeed, these principles are noncontroversial on their face. However, further tenets are predicated on perceptions of societal persecution and smack of racism.

Black Muslims advocate the release of ALL black criminals. They argue that any criminal act perpetrated by an African American is justifiable. They further believe that the federal government owes them land, property, and wealth and the choice of an independent nation and government. They further believe that African Americans should be exempt from taxation because the existing government is neither representative or legitimate. Ironically, they also call for legislation imposed by this illegitimate government that would outlaw interracial marriages. This antiestablishment dogma, based on religious doctrines, is essentially identical to other African-American hate groups, white supremacists, and a number of militia groups across the country. Unfortunately, black supremacist groups such as the Nation of Islam and the Black Panther Party are not considered to be as noteworthy of surveillance as they once were. This oversight and reallocation of government resources accords black militants the freedom to spew their hatred unchecked, inciting antiestablishment rage and seducing many African-American youths.

It may be argued that many of these young black males are not aware of or even concerned with the fundamental religious and political principles of the Nation of Islam. Economic depression, the increasing threat of street violence, a shrinking job market, and the lack of educational opportunities promote feelings of despair among urban minorities. This sense of futility creates a need for identification and belonging and increases their vulnerability to subversive organizations and proviolence dogma. Traditionally, criminal street gangs have filled the void in these communities. Increasingly, however, a revisitation of 1960s culture has been promoted by the popular media (e.g., movies such as *Panther* and *Malcolm X*), the legal community (e.g., the freeing of Geronimo Pratt and appellate proceedings of Mumia Abu Jamal), and individual families (today's parents are yesterday's survivors). A resurgence of black nationalism and/or militance appears to be a foregone conclusion, one that the majority of Americans appear to have missed.

## BLACK PANTHERS

> I want 30 police stations blown up, one southern governor, two mayors, and 500 cops dead (James Foreman, prominent Panther leader).

> The Panthers held a national attraction for the young . . . who had been tempered in the crucible of ghetto life (Burns, 1971: xv).

Like their Black Muslim counterparts, the Black Panther Party gained national attention in the civil rights era. Founded in Oakland in 1966 by Bobby Seales and Huey Newton, the Black Panther Party for Self-Defense expanded premises set forth by Robert Williams, leader of the North Carolina–based Deacons for Self-Defense and author of *Negroes with Guns.* Their militant approach, which focused recruitment efforts toward young black males, and original platform were markedly similar to that of the Nation of Islam with one critical distinction: the Black Panther Party held no particular religious affiliation. This divergence greatly enhanced the marketability of the Panthers among the younger generation "who were looking for someplace to channel their anger and frustration about life" (Pearson, 1994: 45). The absence of religion was especially attractive to pre-adults chafing under parental restraint and reluctant to denounce pleasurable activities that were finally within their reach. The Panthers also freely enjoyed the increasing tide of anger and resentment within black communities, the culmination of the Nation's tireless efforts and costly sacrifices.

Unlike their sharply dressed and increasingly articulate counterparts, the Panthers adopted uniforms consistent with their "revolutionary" movement. Garbed in black leather jackets, black berets, and dark glasses, with ammunition draped over their shoulders, they patrolled the urban streets wreaking havoc on the sensibilities of white community residents. In many respects, their tactics were similar to ones employed by an older supremacist organization, the Ku Klux Klan. Like the Klan, they randomly selected their victims based on race. Like the Klan, who recently identified the federal government as their enemy, the Panthers had a history of antigovernment dogma, openly sympathizing with North Vietnam during the conflict in East

Asia. Furthermore, both groups have the same interpretation of the Second Amendment. In fact, a heavily armed Panther contingent entered the California legislature in 1967 to protest the Mulford Act, an early gun-control bill, long before militia groups became popular among white supremacists.

Two further incidents in 1967 propelled the Panthers into the national spotlight and earned them the prominence in the youth community they desired. The first was inadvertently initiated by black organizations in the Bay area and black elected officials across California. Although they had not yet gained credibility in the eyes of other black groups, they were called upon to serve security detail for Malcolm X's widow, Betty Shabazz. This act, misconstrued by many, did not signal their arrival in the legitimate black community. On the contrary, these leaders, unwilling to take responsibility for Shabazz's safety, called on the most expendable and least desirable organization, the Black Panthers. In fact, these leaders, frightened by the group's militant stance and menacing appearance, were probably hoping for a most public failure. Instead, this incident propelled the Panthers into the forefront of the racial conflict and gained them a most important supporter, Eldridge Cleaver, the author of one of the nation's first radical journals (Pearson, 1994).

The second incident that had a tremendous impact on the younger generation was the arrest of Panther cofounder Huey Newton (see Figure 6-4). Newton, arrested for the murder of a white police officer, soon became a symbol for American youth in general.[4] Panther chapters were developed in 48 states and many international areas. In fact, antigovernment youth gangs seemed to sprout in every community, regardless of race, economics, or religion. "Free Huey" was their motto, the Black Panther Party their model. Although the majority of these youth gangs proved to be short-lived, this unprecedented unification of American youth across racial, gender, religious, and economic lines was most significant (Pearson, 1994). The specter of omnipotence no longer immobilized the younger generation. For the first time in history, America's youth developed a collective, generational consciousness. A group realization that erupted into violence laid the foundation for contemporary antiestablishment ideology.

Many of these groups perceived the development of the Black Panthers as a long overdue movement to demand restitution and ensure racial equality. Riding the crest of their newfound popularity, the Party developed social programs in poor, urban communities. These initiatives, benignly

---

[4]Although originally convicted, Huey Newton continued to act as a rallying cry for many black organizations. He was released on bail in 1970, and all the charges concerning his involvement in the murder of Officer John Frey were dropped after two hung juries.

In 1966, Huey Newton and Bobby Seale founded the Black Panther Party for Self-Defense. Initially, Newton and Seale argued that the group's primary purpose was to increase the standard of living in black, urban areas. To their credit, they did organize a number of community programs designed to provide basic necessities for community residents. However, many contemporary authors overlook the vicious criminal enterprises that funded the programs and the theft of legitimate contributions by its founders. Recent Hollywood interpretations, for example, glorify Newton as a defender of the disadvantaged, using violence as a last resort. Nothing could be further from the truth.

Charged with his first murder in 1967, Newton became a national hero. The murder of Oakland police officer John Frey was considered justified by many and was consistent with the antiestablishment ideology sweeping the country. Incited by images of racist police action in the South, Newton came to symbolize governmental oppression; and his release on a technicality in 1970 was touted as a victory in the war to revolutionize American institutions. This hero-worship, it appears, was sorely misplaced.

After his release from prison, Newton's escalating drug problem was only outpaced by his murderous temper. He routinely assaulted individuals, including Party members, forcing many of them to quit. He even assaulted his lifelong friend and cofounder, Bobby Seale. In fact, "Newton dramatically beat Seale with a bullwhip and sodomized him so violently that his anus had to be surgically repaired by a physician" (Pearson, 1994). Within two weeks, Newton attacked and killed Kathleen Smith, a 17-year-old prostitute who made the mistake of calling him "Baby." Unfortunately, his arrest was not soon enough to prevent three other attacks.

**FIGURE 6-4** Huey Newton: The Man, the Myth, the Monster

*In his absence, Elaine Brown assumed the helm. Unfortunately, Brown displayed a level of violence and militance only slightly lower than Newton's. In her short reign, several bodies surfaced, including that of her former bookkeeper, Betty Van Patter.

referred to as "Survival Programs," appeared to be a straightforward attempt to increase the standard of living among minority communities. In reality, however, the militant stance of the Panthers and their proclivity for violence remained; these "survival pending revolution" programs were nothing if not self-serving. Educational initiatives, touted as enrichment programs, were actually more akin to platform indoctrination. The Free Breakfast for Children Program was actually initiated by a Catholic church in San Francisco and existed long before and long after the Panthers' wave of popularity. Other programs claimed by the Panthers appeared to be funded by magical fairies, because no governmental resources were allocated and few recognizable benefactors were identified. In retrospect, these programs were probably funded by the deluge of money gained through the Panthers' various criminal enterprises. Activities they vehemently denied (Pearson, 1994).

As stated, Newton's violence was directed at both members and nonmembers. A staff member at the Lamp Post was the recipient of a beating so severe that it knocked her glass eye right out of her head. Shortly thereafter, Newton attacked a female customer of the same establishment for "getting smart" with his bodyguard. Later the same day, Newton pistol-whipped his tailor for making the same mistake as Smith. The tailor received four skull fractures and underwent neurosurgery for his poor choice.

Newton, charged with a variety of crimes, including the murder of Smith, fled to Cuba in 1974 and remained there until 1977.* Newton's reemergence was well planned. He quickly intimidated his former tailor and plotted to kill the sole witness to his murder of Kathleen Smith. Unfortunately for Newton, his selection of assassins was poor and eventually led to the Party's demise.

A bungled assassination attempt left one Panther dead and one wounded. Nelson Malloy, the paramedic who treated the wound, was taken to Las Vegas, where he was summarily shot and left for dead. Discovered under a pile of rocks by two tourists, Malloy, permanently paralyzed, told investigators and the media that the failed attempt signaled Newton's effort to destroy any links between the botched assassination and Newton. For the first time, the Panthers were unable to blame law enforcement sources. Even Newton's elite squad of enforcers abandoned ship.

Although Newton escaped conviction in the Kathleen Smith murder, he experienced legal problems until his death. Oddly enough, the majority of these charges were not connected with his vicious behavior; rather, they included charges of fiduciary wrongdoing, more consistent with contemporary definitions of white-collar crimes. Newton was killed in 1989 during an argument over drugs. In fact, some have argued that Newton's death was long overdue.

Like many ethnic gangs before and since, the Panthers usually victimized businesses and residents in their own communities. Extortion and armed robbery, group favorites, appeared to have been their primary sources of income. Originally, the Panthers publicly endorsed these activities, claiming that they were the only opportunity available due to white oppression. Eventually seeking legitimacy, however, they quickly distanced themselves from members formally charged with these offenses and publicly disavowed any involvement in criminal activity. In reality, this public condemnation was superficial at best. Contrary to their public posturing, the Panthers continued their intimidation of neighborhood businesses, demanding "support" for their survivor programs. Any support other than cash advances, which were often used to support Newton's drug habit, were refused. Businesses not cooperating with Newton were quickly targeted for foreclosure. This intimidation, coupled with Newton's homicidal tendencies, resulted in the exodus of many adult members from the group. This flow was only temporarily stemmed when Newton fled to Cuba to escape prosecution for murder.

During Newton's self-imposed Cuban exile, Elaine Brown took over the Panthers' helm. Although Brown successfully obtained mainstream political favor and governmental recognition for her efforts, her public benevolence was merely a facade. Indeed, Brown was akin to a pampered rottweiler with her propensity for viciousness hidden behind perfectly coiffed hair and painted fingernails. Like Newton, Brown's violence was not restricted to outsiders. In fact, Brown was only slightly less violent than her predecessor. Brown's advocation of violence and lack of genteel sensibilities, however, proved futile in her quest to control the Party. Characterized by heightened levels of traditional gender stratification, many of the Party's younger members—especially Newton's elite squad of enforcers—rejected their female figurehead. This misogyny led to Newton's return and the Party's demise (Pearson, 1994; Foner, 1995).

Upon Newton's return, many of the Party's most prominent leaders, such as Bobby Seale, Stokely Carmichael, and David Hilliard, abandoned the movement and developed groups of their own. Newton's elite squad, comprised primarily of young black males, proved to be a bit more resilient. However, Newton's erratic behavior eventually distanced even the most ardent of his supporters. Following Newton's assassination attempt of two Panther enforcers, the remaining most fanatical youths abandoned ship. The majority of these disillusioned youths joined other militant organizations, such as the Black Muslims or the Black Guerilla Family, or continued their criminal behavior unsponsored.

Many reports date the Black Panther Party's waterloo sometime in the late 1970s. This characterization obscures the continuing interest in black militancy and the Black Panther Party in the United States. In 1989, for example, more than 10,000 mourners attended the funeral of Huey Newton. Many even paid their respects to the site of the drug-related murder. This resurgence also led to the republication of the Panthers' official party newspaper in 1991. Furthermore, many contemporary pop stars glorify Newton as a martyr, emulating his militance and posturing.[5] As is often the case in historical revisitations, negative characteristics are glossed over or ignored. Unfortunately, the impact of the popular media and the revisionist accounts they promote are often underestimated.

---

[5]In fact, some of these pop icons inadvertently brought violence upon themselves, such as the case of actor/recording artist Tupac Shakur. The son of one of the New York 21, Shakur's lifestyle mirrored the gangsta rap that made him famous. Unfortunately for Skakur, this mimicry resulted in his murder.

## BLACK GUERILLA FAMILY AND OTHER PRISON GANGS

Although prison gangs have existed in U.S. correctional institutions since their inception, most are founded as defensive mechanisms with promises of protection and insulation for their members. This basic definition does not suggest that the violent behavior they express is entirely reactionary. In fact, many of the more powerful gangs actively initiate violence towards other inmates. Much of this violence is executed as a demonstration of force. In addition, the majority of this activity appears to be racially motivated, usually targeted against outsiders. However, the majority of prison gangs (the Mexican Mafia, Nuestra Family, etc.) lack ideological consistency beyond the boundaries of racial awareness. One notable exception to this rule is the Black Guerilla Family.

Founded by former Panther George Jackson, the Black Guerilla Family (BGF) originated at San Quentin in 1966. Originally, the BGF was developed as an ancillary arm of the Black Panther Party. Its ideological framework, consistent with a Maoist philosophy, encouraged "political activism" on the part of its members. This activism included the assault, murder, and rape of nonblack inmates and prison officials. Like other prison gangs, the BGF has established partnerships with other nonideological gangs such as the Black Liberation Army. Both of these groups have aggressively recruited street gang members and have been successful in creating complex criminal networks. The recruitment of individuals from established street gangs, such as the Crips and the Bloods, has enabled the BGF to gain outside support. While this group's primary power remains ensconced within prison boundaries, the effect of supremacist indoctrination remains to be seen.

## SIMILARITIES AMONG BLACK SUPREMACIST GANGS

Although popular media accounts negate the existence of racist ideology by nonwhites, the gangs already mentioned are but a few examples of nonwhite supremacist organizations in the United States. While supremacist movements appear to be sporadic and short-lived, experience suggests that the ideological frameworks guiding their actions are not. Too often, racial violence, especially violence initiated by minorities, is miscategorized as random street crime, and the seriousness of its implications overlooked. Like its white counterpart, black supremacy has traditionally been characterized by intergroup conflict and competing recruitment strategies. Nevertheless, underlying similarities between these organizations have resulted in ideological longevity and sporadic increases in popular support.

Inarguably, black militance is most prevalent during periods of economic depression and political persecution. Like their predecessors, contemporary militant/nationalist gangs are fortified by religious ideologies and political dogma. Subsequently, these groups remain overwhelmingly patriarchal. Without exception, these groups share platforms of equality for all men, women not included. In keeping with religious teachings, these groups advocate a return to "traditional" family values. The most recent example, Farrakhan's Million Man March, called for black males to take responsibility for their offspring. This seemingly benign platform masked traditional inflammatory rhetoric espoused by Farrakhan and other supremacists.

These organizations, both traditional and contemporary, are extremely hierarchical in nature. Their bureaucratic approach is responsible for both the popularity and the legitimacy these groups enjoy. Garnering political support, these groups effectively camouflage their militant posturing in ideological rhetoric. This capability is directly responsible for societal indulgence and organizational forbearance. Effectively bridging generational differences, these groups maintain economic patronage from adult groups while enhancing their appeal to disadvantaged youth.

By concentrating their recruitment efforts on those most vulnerable, both traditional and contemporary organizations have successfully amassed a group of violent individuals, seemingly expendable in nature. Proclaiming self-empowerment and equality for all, black youths are manipulated and sacrificed like pawns in a conflict for mature audiences only. Often recruited while incarcerated, criminal-minded and/or violent youths are targeted. In addition, black militant groups mimic the efforts of their white supremacist counterparts, utilizing communication and technological advancements to recruit young members. Antiwhite, anti-Semitic, and antiestablishment dogma permeates cyberspace and pervades the most innocuous of documents. Queries into black leaders, scholars, investors, or historians, for example, often result in propagandist Internet addresses or links. Unfortunately, much of this literature is passed off and interpreted as legitimate. The result is more than an avenue of revolutionary rhetoric; it is an ideological and increasingly violent battleground, one with no definitive boundaries or targets.

## WHITE POWER

Unlike their black counterparts, which have traditionally concentrated on antiestablishment ideologies and are a relatively new phenomenon in American society, white supremacist organizations have had a history of intolerance only slightly shorter than the country itself. An evaluation of U.S. culture reveals a pattern of intolerance inconsistent with the much espoused notion of the melting pot society. The eradication of entire tribes of Native Americans and the persecution and execution of religious dissidents are just two of many examples of such intolerance. In a society in which government expresses racially intolerant policies it is not surprising that racist subcultures often emerge. What is remarkable, however, is that this intolerance, often manifested in targeted violence, is often predicated on religious ideologies.

Like many nonracists, hatemongers often use principles of Christianity and the Bible selectively. Citing only those passages that superficially support notions of homophobia, racism, and anti-Semitism, these hate groups recite selections religiously, using God's "word" as a justification for attacks on nonbelievers. Like their antigovernment counterparts, these gangs seem to focus exclusively on the Old Testament while proclaiming themselves to be chosen by the Savior found only in the text of the New Testament. Unfortunately, these much espoused ideologies mask the sociological factors that contribute to this type of violent fanaticism and fail to elucidate current patterns of youth involvement.

As stated, racial and religious intolerance appears to be an American mainstay, however, contemporary organizations are now more likely to have large numbers of juvenile members. Sociologists argue that this trend may be attributed to the increasing uncertainty of future job opportunities, an increase in civil disorder in general, and the desensitization to violence. Throughout history, periods of economic depression have invariably resulted in elevated levels of subversive dogma. Traditionally, however, these periods of fiscal deflation impacted mature members of society while leaving teens, who often filled unskilled labor positions and menial jobs, unscathed. For the first time in U.S. history, predictions are that future generations will not achieve or even maintain the economic levels enjoyed by their parents. This bleak projection coupled with increasingly graphic violence, racial conflict in schools, and the availability of hate-oriented material on the Internet has promulgated a sense of despair among many adolescents and increased their susceptibility to iconoclastic doctrines (Southern Poverty Law Center, 1997). This vulnerability has resulted in two significant developments in the white supremacist movement: (1) replenishment of dwindling resources in traditional organizations hard hit by criminal prosecution and civil liability (i.e., KKK, Aryan Nations, etc.), and (2) emergence of loosely formed, increasingly violent youth gangs.

## KKK

> . . . the success of anti-Semitism stemmed from the patness of the explanation it offered for the Klansman's anxieties: his fear of racial mixing, his financial and social insecurity, and his xenophobia . . . (Chalmers, 1965: 352).

> . . . Klaverns worked better when they could get down to local business . . . members might differ in their alarm about the Jews, the international bankers . . . but the pressures of Negro integration gave them a point of common concern . . . (Chalmers, 1965: 353).

The most recognized and most flamboyant of all supremacist organizations, the Ku Klux Klan, has historically been the poster child for hate groups across the country. Inarguably, the Klan has been the most powerful of all supremacist organizations. Their tactics, both overt and covert, have ranged from business blockades to church fires to murder. Their influence on U.S. history can not be overstated. Their history, intrinsically woven into the

White supremacist groups proclaim that their ideology is derived from biblical teachings. (Courtesy of Charleston, South Carolina, Police Department)

American fabric, has seen periods characterized by unquestionable political power interspersed with intervals of torpid infirmity. Perhaps most noted for their habit of burning crosses and wearing satin robes, the KKK has most recently been characterized by shock television as uneducated, misinformed buffoons whose greatest danger to the American public is a possible increase in dry cleaning prices. This characterization, lacking any historical overview, masks the danger of an organized group of violent individuals with only a single agenda of wholescale extermination of all races, ethnicities, and religions save their own.

## History of the Ku Klux Klan

Contrary to the group's contemporary ideology, the Ku Klux Klan, more commonly known as the KKK, was originally developed by six disenfranchised former Confederate soldiers as a thrill-seeking fraternal organization. Perhaps the behavior exhibited by this gang of young men, forced too young into the role of adulthood, was reminiscent of shared childhood experiences. Masquerading as ghosts, they draped white sheets over themselves and their horses, and played harmless pranks on friends and family under the cover of darkness (Chalmers, 1965; Zellner, 1995). However, this carefree behavior, lacking in malice, had an unfortunate by-product, one that would create a mean-spirited organization with far-reaching and deadly consequences.

## The Invisible Empire: Protecting the Old South (1865–1871)

With the emergence of sheet-clad apparitions, tales of otherworldly avengers bent on persecuting unruly blacks were rife among newly freed slaves. Acting on these superstitions, many white males, powerless under the stricture of Reconstruction, established an illegitimate power structure. By intimidating black voters and terrorizing black communities, white males were successful in manipulating, and ultimately disrupting, the legitimate political process. Consequently, newly freed blacks, emancipated from formal institutions of slavery and visible bondage, remained captives of their own fear, allowing racist franchises to flourish throughout the South.

As one might expect, the most notable figure to emerge during this preliminary period of Klan activity was a former slave owner and officer in the Confederate army, Nathan Bedford Forrest. Under the auspices of office, Forrest attempted to control an organization much akin to the Hydra of Greek mythology. Random violence and unspeakable acts of terror, not sanctioned by the newly developed bureaucracy, erupted across jurisdictional boundaries and outraged blacks and whites alike. Consequently, Forrest formally disbanded the Klan in 1869. However, the effectiveness of this proclamation was somewhat limited in scope. Indeed, it was not until martial law was imposed in 1871 that the last vestiges of the original Klan were eliminated (Chalmers, 1965).

## Family Values and Civil Rights (1920s–1960s)

Like other illegitimate organizations that experience periodic success, the KKK once again gained prominence during the 1920s. Once again preying on the fears of the American public, the Klan successfully recruited uneducated individuals fearful of mass waves of statue-worshipping heathens, namely Italians, Irish, and other recent immigrants. Newly arrived and fleeing from political and religious persecution, immigrants were often met with open hostility. Indeed, it would appear that intolerance and subsequent violence awaited the unwitting immigrant who stepped onto U.S. soil lost in dreams of equality and the "American dream." It may be argued that these immigrants, abruptly awakened to the reality of economic competition in a capitalist society, were the lucky ones. The true victims of the KKK during this era were those who passed the threshold unscathed and not forewarned of nor forearmed for institutional discrimination.

According to Chalmers (1965), the Klan's political influence during the 1920s was immeasurable. Representatives, senators, governors, even a Supreme Court justice (Hugo Black), all supported by, and in some cases card-carrying members of the Klan, created a governmental structure of white, Protestant supremacists. During this period, the Klan extended its appeal to groups heretofore reluctant to tie their wagon to extremist organizations. This far reaching influence enabled the Klan to invade large cross sections of the nation, establishing chapters in all regions. However, like their early predecessors, the new Klan's appeal was short-lived due to their inability to control autonomous local branches that perpetuated atrocities against children and innocents, which proved too extreme for mainstream America to ignore. Once again, the Klan lost favor, and membership fell to an all-time low during the 1930s.

Although seriously wounded by anti-Klan sentiment, the extremist ideology espoused did not die and resurfaced shortly after the desegregation action decided by the Supreme Court in 1954. This decision, monumental in its impact, allowed previously planted seeds of discontent to bear fruit (Zellner, 1995). Almost imperceptibly, separatist ideology pervaded societal institutions, and a broader scope of intolerance took root.

Seeking to widen their appeal, the Klan provided equal opportunity to all hatemongers during the 1960s, promising political revision and social change.

Ironically, Horace King, a well-known leader of the Klan, must receive permission from and follow the dictates of Charleston police chief Reuben Greenberg, an African-American Jew. (Courtesy of Charleston, South Carolina, Police Department)

Their platform was widely heard, and long smoldering embers erupted, most notably in the southern region of the United States. Violence primarily directed at blacks and Jews abounded in the South. Incidents of violence were reported in Florida, Georgia, Alabama, Mississippi, Virginia, Louisiana, and the Carolinas, while government silence gave tacit approval, if not downright legitimacy, to acts committed against nonwhite Protestants (Chalmers, 1965).

Not traditionally known for its trailblazing nature, the state of Alabama during the 1960s earned a permanent place in U.S. history as the undisputed leader of the anti-civil rights war. Indelible images of police brutality and political corruption, captured by photographers and newsreels, were indicative of the long simmering anger bubbling under the surface of many traditionally depressed areas in the state. Individuals faced with limited employment opportunities and economic deprivation were particularly vulnerable to inflammatory political rhetoric embraced by government officials. Examples set by Governor George Wallace, who blocked the threshold at the University of

Alabama in open defiance of federal integration mandates, and Chief Bull Connor (Birmingham), who encouraged white citizens to stamp out "insolent" black communities, promoted an atmosphere conducive to and supportive of violence.

The years following were marked by unsurpassed levels of civil unrest and disorder. While personal residences, community centers, even religious institutions were devastated through vandalism and arson, their attackers went unpunished, acting under the tacit approval of the establishment. Some cases were even characterized by active involvement of local law enforcement.[6] Perhaps the most important act was one that brought national attention and the media spotlight to the growing turmoil in the South. In 1963, a firebomb exploded at the 16th Street Baptist Church in Birmingham, Alabama, killing three young girls. Public reaction was swift and severe. This action, and its subsequent repercussions, signaled an end to public apathy. This apathy coupled with an increase in enforcement activity ultimately resulted in the dismantling of Klan groups across the country (George and Wilcox, 1992).

In 1964, tactics of harassment and intimidation of known Klansmen were launched by the FBI's counterintelligence program (COINTELPRO). Threats of public exposure and sanctions for employers hiring Klansmen induced many individuals to voluntarily hang up their robes. Use of informants resulted in the prosecution of some of the more steadfast members. Federal legislation was passed and congressional investigations (i.e., House Committee on Un-American Activities) featured hearings that exposed high-ranking Klan officials who had remained loyal to the cause and who had successfully evaded prosecution.[7] The end result was significant. In the years directly fol-

---

[6]Cecil Ray Price, chief deputy sheriff of Neshoba County, was convicted with six others for the 1964 slaying of three civil rights worker (George and Wilcox, 1992).

[7]It must be noted that many of the tactics employed by the FBI during this period have been harshly criticized. Some argue that COINTELPRO's main concern was not prosecution of felonious acts; rather, their activities were directed at disrupting legally protected avenues of communication and assemblage. Many also argue that these actions violated numerous constitutional rights. Subversive practices of intimidation and illegal wiretaps are just two of the examples given. Many of these critics question whether the ends justifies the means, citing the case of Gary Rowe. While acting as a paid federal informant, Rowe participated in the murder of Viola Liuzzo, a civil rights worker. Encouraging Rowe to continue his participation in criminal activity, agents protected Rowe from prosecution for a collection of felonious charges, including murder. It may be argued that this knowledge, coupled with their encouragement, indicated a gross disregard for the public they were allegedly protecting. Indeed these actions, consistent with many Hoover-era strategies, have been described as "cheap psychological warfare and dirty tricks" (George and Wilcox, 1992: 400).

lowing this federal scrutiny, Klan membership decreased by 75 percent (George and Wilcox, 1992).

## Education, Legitimacy, and Christianity (1970s to the present)

During the 1970s it was no longer acceptable for government to tolerate racial hatred and separatism. Due to federal antisegregation legislation, state and local governments were mandated to accept a multicultural society. The Klan, which had been devastated by enforcement efforts in the 1960s, was forced to regroup and redevelop recruitment strategies. Faced with a shortage of new members, divisive ideologies of future directions soon developed in regional chapters (George and Wilcox, 1992)

Long characterized by internal competition, regional Klans were now openly at war with one another. The most notable of the groups, Louisiana's Knights of the Ku Klux Klan, was headed by a charismatic young man named David Duke. Duke's approach, less violent and more discreet, would prove to be the most resilient, and the most dangerous.

By creating an image of a well-educated, highly intellectual organization, David Duke successfully elevated his Klan and subsequent racist organizations to a more sophisticated level. This practice had enormous impact and insulated his members from law enforcement scrutiny. By suggesting that the Klan was a fraternal organization comprised of hard-working middle-class individuals and by publicly condemning violence and criminal activity, Duke successfully recruited on college campuses, seducing a large number of educated youth. Duke extended invitations to females and Catholics, two groups that had previously been denied access. Duke's allure was so strong that he successfully pursued a bid for the Louisiana State House of Representatives. Perhaps Duke's quintessential contribution to the white supremacist movement was the establishment of the National Association for the Advancement of White People (NAAWP), an organization currently gaining popularity.

While Duke was successfully increasing membership in his organization, rival klaverns were decimated by criminal prosecution and civil litigation (see Figure 6-5). Overt violence and a flagrant disregard for legitimate authority proved once again to be their downfall. In fact, due primarily to the efforts of Morris Dees and the Southern Poverty Law Center (SPLC), many chapters were forced to disband and declare bankruptcy. Profits from the auction of the assets were awarded to the various victims.

It has been argued that these judgments have collectively signaled the imminent demise of the KKK (George and Wilcox, 1992). Indeed, recent

In 1981, a federal court ruled against the Texas Klansmen who were "patrolling" Galveston Bay, burning boats and threatening Vietnamese fishermen, after a lawsuit was filed on behalf of the Vietnamese fishermen by Klanwatch, a branch of the Southern Poverty Law Center. The court ordered immediate termination of such activity and forced Louis Beam to disband his 2,500-member paramilitary army. (A similar ruling in 1986 forced the North Carolina–based White Patriot Party, led by Glenn Miller, to disband and resulted in a military order that prohibited servicemen from participation in such organizations.)

In 1987, Klanwatch was successful in obtaining a $7 million judgment against United Klans of America (UKA) for the mother of Michael Donald, a 19-year-old man who was found hanging from a tree. Klanwatch investigators were also responsible for much of the evidence presented at the criminal trial that resulted in the conviction of three men, including two UKA officials. One of these individuals, Henry Hays, son of the group's Grand Titan, was executed on June 6, 1997. He was the first white man executed for the murder of an African American in Alabama since 1913.

In 1988, an Ethiopian man, Mulugeta Seraw, was beaten to death by a group of neo-Nazi skinheads. A lawsuit, filed by Klanwatch, successfully argued that the teenagers were encouraged to violence by Tom Metzger, the founder of White Aryan Resistance (WAR), and his son, John. A $12.5 million judgment effectively bankrupted Metzger, whose assets were seized and auctioned to satisfy the judgment (Dees, 1996).

In 1993, a Klanwatch lawsuit resulted in a judgment against the Invisible Empire, once the largest and most violent of the Klans. The judgment called for immediate disassembly and liquidation of all assets—including its name—and payment to civil rights marchers injured in a confrontation in Forsythe County, Georgia.

In 1995, a default judgment of $1 million was awarded to the family of Harold Mansfield. The victim, an African-American sailor who had served in the Gulf War, was murdered by a member of the Church of the Creator. In an attempt to avoid payment, the Church transferred ownership to William Pierce, a well-known racist and author of *The Turner Diaries*. A subsequent judgment of $85,000 was awarded due to the fraudulent nature of the transaction.

In 1998, the Southern Poverty Law Center successfully secured the largest judgment ever awarded against the Christian Knights of the Ku Klux Klan, Grand Dragon Horace King, and four others. The judgment, $37.8 million, was secured for Macedonia Baptist Church, which was burned on June 21, 1995.

**FIGURE 6-5**  Judgments against the Klan

*Sources:* Southern Poverty Law Center, *Intelligence Reports,* 1996, 1997, 1998.

Youth involvement in white supremacist movements is growing. (Courtesy of Southern Poverty Law Center/Klanwatch)

statistics have indicated that membership in Klan-like groups has significantly decreased (Southern Poverty Law Center, 1997). However, many of the movement's most prominent—and most deadly—leaders have emerged as powerful figures in the growing antigovernment/antiestablishment movement and have increasingly used the newly developed information superhighway to attract younger members. Individuals such as Louis Beam and Tom Metzger, minimizing overt racist rhetoric and promoting themselves as constitutional defenders, have been successful in luring disenchanted youths to their cause. This usage of uncensored Internet resources has resulted in a new wave of white supremacist/antiestablishment hatemongers. So, while many have sounded the death knell for the Klan, this tolling may be both premature and dangerously misleading. In fact, the Klan's most important contribution to the legacy of intolerance is the foundation it laid for future organizations, such as the Order,[8] White Aryan Resistance, Aryan Nations, and various other neo-Nazi–type groups.

## WHITE ARYAN RESISTANCE

> The skinheads are white mean machines who deliver honest casualty reports (Tom Metzger [Hamm, 1993: 63]).

In the early 1980s a new plague of racial intolerance reached epidemic proportions. Many of these groups maintained traditional Klan-like ideology, but concentrated primarily on disassociated youth. Targeting young individuals apprehensive of shrinking job markets, these groups, primarily founded and presided over by adults, were successful in establishing a network of hate-filled teenagers with a penchant for violence. Perhaps the most influential leader to emerge during this period was former Klansman Tom Metzger. Metzger, a former Duke supporter and friend, was denounced by the Klan for his extremist ideology and passion for violence. One of the first to promote far right paramilitary structure and training, Metzger routinely distributed works such as *The Anarchist's Cookbook, The White Man's Bible,* and the supremacist favorite, *The Turner Diaries.* Metzger periodically found popular support for his extremist ideology as evidenced by his winning a California congressional primary and placing fourth in a later Senate primary (Hamm, 1993). After his expulsion from the Klan, Metzger formed several organizations, each of which proved to be short-lived. His dream of a perfect hate-fueled machine of destruction went unfulfilled until he discovered the ultimate youth medium—music.

Metzger, recognizing the influence of pop culture on malleable audiences and the increasing interest of rebellious youth, abandoned traditional notions of ritualism and organization and embraced icons of the British skin-

---

[8]Although short-lived, the importance of Robert Matthews' group, the Order, cannot be overlooked in an evaluation of youth racism in the United States. Perhaps the most militant of all previous organizations, the Order was responsible for several execution-style murders, including that of a government informant and Alan Berg, an outspoken Jewish radio personality. The Order was also responsible for a variety of criminal acts designed to illicit funds for future violent activities, including but not limited to several armored car heists, bank robberies, racketeering enterprises, and arms trafficking. The Order's ignominious reign of terror was concluded with the death of its founder, Robert Matthews, in a standoff with government agents. Unfortunately, the allure of the Order was only heightened by the execution of Matthews. Touted as a martyr, his death served to collectify various factions of the militant right. Often declared the first "casualty of war" by many militant groups, Matthews accomplished something in his death that he could not have achieved had he lived—immortality.

head community. Ian Stuart and his band, Skrewdriver, echoed strains of rebellion, nonconformity, and frustration resounding within the youth psyche. Their music, purely antiestablishment, stressed individuality and encouraged teens to take control. Universal in its message, it was wildly successful in inciting passion and rage among its young listeners. This gateway to the youth subculture granted Metzger superficial legitimacy with American teens and allowed him to channel these elevated emotions into his newly formed White Aryan Resistance (W.A.R.).

Promoting a specter of an evil establishment, Metzger preached to his targeted audience of the absence of any real future for young white males in a society controlled by Jews, minorities, and homosexuals. He justified violent acts as a means necessary to an end. He published a newspaper devoted to young people and their concerns, peppering articles with sophisticated cartoons and musical lyrics from antiestablishment rock groups. He created a television program called *Race and Reason* that cultivated his image as a highly polished, respectable businessman. He appeared as a guest on shock talk shows, portraying himself as an intellectual under attack by an antiwhite society. He developed complex computer networks and chat groups, uniting skinheads and hate groups across the country. For those not connected or lacking access to his W.A.R. board, he developed a W.A.R. hotline.

Apparently, this community is intolerant of skinhead activity. (Courtesy of Southern Poverty Law Center/Klanwatch)

Metzger directed his message to an existing subculture of young people, the skinheads. Members of this subculture, initially attracted by their mutual musical preferences, distinguished themselves from other groups by their apparel of Doc Martens, military bomber-style jackets, and shaved heads. Although lacking aesthetic value, this ensemble was more mod than sinister. Indeed, the most striking aspect of this existing subculture was the absence of malice. In fact, a variety of cultures were represented in the skinhead subculture prior to Metzger's seizure of the Aryan Youth Movement (A.Y.M.)[9] (Hamm, 1993).

The takeover of A.Y.M. had widespread consequences. Appointing his son, John, as the new leader, Metzger parlayed this relationship into a successful means of recruiting high school and college students. More importantly, it allowed Metzger to repaint the canvas of the skinhead prototype. Metzger called for a decrease in visibility. By placing his son, a photogenic, conservative-looking young man, in the position of leadership, Metzger was able to convince many followers to tone down their radical appearance. This outward appearance allowed members to carry out their missions covertly and hampered law enforcement efforts in adequately enumerating their strength. In fact, it has been suggested that this new approach was so successful that Metzger's soldiers infiltrated every government institution, including the military and the police (Hamm, 1993).

## ARYAN NATIONS

It was also during this period that exiled Klan leader Louis Beam assumed control of Richard Butler's Aryan Nations in Hayden Lake, Idaho. Beam, disgraced after a civil judgment in Texas, joined forces with "Reverend" Richard Butler, a vanguard of the militant right, and invited American teens to reclaim their lost heritage and take their rightful place in society (Dees, 1996). Beam's Aryan Nations quickly gained national recognition through violence and radical propaganda. Beam also recognized the value of the information superhighway and was responsible for establishing the first of many hate libraries on the Internet. He was also responsible for developing a widely publicized "point" system. This point system targeted federal officials, civil rights workers, and other undesirables for assassination. In 1987, Beam, indicted for numerous counts of sedition and conspiracy, fled to Mexico. Upon his capture, he was found not guilty on all counts. Beam, increasingly antigovernment,

---

[9]Shortly after denouncing his racist past, Greg Withrow, the founder of A.Y.M., was found near death. He had been beaten, stabbed repeatedly, and nailed to a wooden board (Hamm, 1993).

quickly became a leader in the newly emerging Patriot movement. As publisher of *The Seditionist,* Beam outlined a new approach to a revolutionary takeover. His "leaderless resistance" platform called for the purposeful disassembly of all existing Patriot organizations, which was intended to insulate members from full-scale prosecution. This ideology, coupled with a remarkable ability to move people, has made him one of the most powerful leaders in the antigovernment movement and has assured his ideological longevity.

## CONTEMPORARY GANGS: SKINHEADS AND BEYOND

Although the skinhead phenomenon gained national attention primarily due to the efforts of Tom Metzger and Louis Beam, American skinheads actually emerged on the California music scene in the 1970s. Initially multicultural, skinheads were primarily known for their preferences of shaved heads and on-the-fringe performers. It was not until the emergence of Skrewdriver and Tom Metzger in the early 1980s that skinheads began to develop "white power" ideologies consistent with the youth angst previously displayed by British teens.

The first notable gang of nonorganized "skinheads" appears to have been in the increasingly depressed Haight-Ashbury district. Economic depression and the musical influence of British groups such as Skrewdriver resulted in a wave of racially motivated assaults. Stereotyping minorities, Jews, and homosexuals as amoral provided an explanation for the country's decreasing economic prosperity and identified enemies to be targeted. Taking their cue from British skins, Metzger's "Resisters," and basic societal distaste, American youth gangs adopted uniforms of shaved heads, Doc Martens, and leather jackets. Unfortunately, most of these groups were incorrectly linked by law enforcement agencies, government sources, and media reports to Metzger's W.A.R. While Metzger's group was certainly a cause for concern, this inaccurate depiction masked unique characteristics that may have been useful in intelligence gathering strategies of local law enforcement and federal agencies. This miscategorization, however, did have some positive byproducts. In 1990, for example, Metzger, his son John, and W.A.R. were found to be civilly responsible in the racially motivated murder of Mulugeta Seraw, an Ethiopian immigrant.[10] This judgment ordered the Metzgers and

---

[10]In 1988, Mulugeta Seraw, an Ethiopian immigrant, was beaten to death by three members of a Portland skinhead gang, East Side White Pride. Although this group had no formal ties with Metzger or W.A.R., racist propaganda written by Metzger and published and distributed under the auspices of W.A.R. were found in the defendants' apartment. The subsequent civil lawsuit successfully argued that this publication was responsible for the hatred expressed by the defendants and the techniques used in the attack on Seraw.

their organization to pay $10 million to the Seraw family. The lawsuit, initi-
ated by Morris Dees and the Southern Poverty Law Center, effectively shut
down the operation of W.A.R. (Zellner, 1995).

While the Metzgers' formalized hate institution was mortally wounded,
the ideology it espoused was not. On the contrary, skinhead groups and
other racist gangs emerged across the country. The primary difference in
these groups and their traditional counterparts appears to be the lack of formalization, recognizable leaders, and identifiable targets For example, in
1996 a Boston gang of racist skinheads invaded a party armed with knives,
chains, ax handles, and broomsticks. The incident resulted in the beating
and stabbing death of Jayson Linsky, an individual who had previously asked
the group to leave after they drew swastikas on their hands. This episode
was particularly troubling to Massachusetts authorities, who had considered

---

### Boston, Massachusetts

John Tague was convicted of first degree murder on December 4, 1997, and sentenced to life without parole. Tague along with more than a dozen members of a
Boston skinhead group terrorized partygoers in the fall of 1996. Jason Linsky of
Boston, Massachusetts, was beaten and stabbed to death after asking Tague to leave
the party after he was seen drawing swastikas on his hands.

### Huntington Beach, California

A Native-American male was stabbed more than 25 times by skinhead youth, amid
shouts of "white power."

### Redlands, California

A homeless man died after four months in a coma that resulted from an assault by
a number of United Bulldog Skins.

### Brockton, Massachusetts

The 15-year-old son of an African-American police officer was attacked and severely beaten by skinheads as he walked home from a football game.

### Fayetteville, North Carolina

James Burmeister, a former Army paratrooper, was convicted of capital murder in
the shooting deaths of an African-American couple in December 1995. Burmeister
was an avowed skinhead who randomly targeted the couple for termination.

### Allentown, Pennsylvania

Two skinhead brothers were convicted of murder in the beating deaths of their parents who allegedly disagreed with their supremacist ideology.

---

**FIGURE 6-6** Recent Skinhead Activity
*Source:* The Southern Poverty Law Center.

their area immune to racial violence. Unfortunately, this incident was just one of many that occurred in 1996. Many argue that incidents of skinhead violence, absent in recent years, are becoming increasingly common. Figure 6-6 describes a few recent examples of skinhead violence. In fact, Klanwatch estimates indicate that youth involvement in racially motivated assaults more than doubled between 1995 and 1996 (Southern Poverty Law Center, 1997). This estimate, disturbing in its implications, is made more so due to the lack of adequate measurement tools and the inability of traditional law enforcement agencies to closely approximate hate crime activity.

While traditional skinhead ideologies of intolerance and racial supremacy are surfacing across the country, it is sociologically relevant to note that most of these groups are concentrated in areas rich in cultural diversity *and* economic deprivation. A Marxist approach might argue that the reemergence of skinhead dogma may be attributed to economic competition between sections of the lower class. Indeed, this perspective may have some merit. In a time of relative prosperity, it appears that the middle class in the United States, if there is one, is spontaneously combusting. Racial hostility among lower- and middle-class members appears to be growing. This self-destruction is not only signalled by the growth of formalized subversive organizations, but also by the escalation of intolerance sporadically displayed by informal and largely unstructured dissident youth gangs.

## OTHER NOTABLE GROUPS

The resilience and longevity displayed by traditional gangs are a major concern for law enforcement agencies. While concentrated efforts have successfully reduced membership and mainstream appeal, the underlying foundation of racial dominance enforced by violence has not been affected. In fact, this framework has been adopted by a variety of volatile youths. These youths often mimic the ideologies and activities of traditional groups, but eschew formalized institutions of hate and the superficial trappings they require (e.g., shaved heads, satin robes, etc.), thereby insulating themselves from governmental interest.

Like self-styled satanists or nondenominational churches, these gangs disavow formalization, perceiving organizations as inherently corrupt. These gangs are especially dangerous due to their ability to draft hate-filled scenarios free from law enforcement scrutiny. Inadvertently, this autonomy also allows crimes motivated by hatred to remain undetected. Unfortunately, this lack of detection reflects the gross inadequacy of current crime prevention measures and illustrates the need for a more careful perusal of incident reports. Furthermore, it is impossible to determine the depth of this new

Like street gangs, many young hatemongers mark their territory with graffiti. (Courtesy of Southern Poverty Law Center/Klanwatch)

infestation of intolerance, because these types of gangs are only identified *if* their criminal activity results in prosecution.

One such gang, the Lords of Chaos, only came to law enforcement attention after they had successfully committed a variety of hate-motivated crimes ranging from car theft to murder. A plot to kill African Americans at Disney World was uncovered after the arrest of several of the group's leaders. This Fort Meyers, Florida, gang was comprised of white teens, some of whom had intelligence quotients bordering on genius levels. Although not charged with more serious crimes, such as armed robbery and murder, members of the Crew, a New Jersey gang, are suspected of various counts of intimidation and harassment. Like the Lords of Chaos, members of this gang also display high IQs and are led by a Cornell University student (Southern Poverty Law Center, 1997). These groups are just two examples of a growing number of informal racist gangs.

## SIMILARITIES AND DIFFERENCES AMONG GROUPS

Like their black counterparts, white supremacist organizations may be characterized by ideological similarities and intergroup conflict. The majority of these organizations are predicated on far-right Christian principles. This perspective advocates a return to traditional family values and emphasizes familial responsibility and authority. Without exception, these groups are increasingly critical of governmental legislation, portraying law enforcement agencies as evil entities intent on destroying the most powerful of all institutions—the American family. Thus, white supremacist organizations are increasingly antiestablishment. The significance of this ideological transformation cannot be overstated when looking at their successful appeal to a cross section of American society.

In recent years, political conservatism has become increasingly popular. Economic uncertainty, diminishing occupational opportunities, tax increases, and the rising cost of health care have increased the attractiveness of right-wing politics. The once ridiculed "religious right" has become a political force in contemporary society. The increasing vulnerability of the middle class in the United States has been successfully targeted by traditional supremacist organizations. Downplaying their racist rhetoric and focusing on disillusioned youth, traditional groups have achieved new life, one anticipated to be long-lasting. Without exception, these groups successfully exploit young members, granting only superficial leadership and reserving the most unpopular and distasteful tasks for those most expendable.

## COMMONALITIES BETWEEN SUPREMACIST GANGS AND STREET GANGS

A comparison of supremacist gangs and traditional street gangs reveals a multitude of similarities often overlooked in the popular media. Like their counterparts in street gangs, members in supremacist groups are primarily concentrated in economically deprived areas. Contrary to popular belief, the vast majority of supremacist movements originate in highly urbanized and industrialized communities and do not fit the backyard "Bubba" stereotype promoted by the media. Membership is also characterized by low educational attainment and perceptions of institutional persecution or discrimination. In addition, members tend to share common dysfunctional family situations. Many of these members come from single-parent homes or physically abusive situations.

It must be noted that involvement in supremacist organizations is most common during periods of economic or social unrest. These increased levels may be attributed to an elevated level of disassociation. Overwhelmed by community disorder, uncertain futures, and familial circumstances, low-income youths join supremacist gangs for a sense of belongingness and brotherhood. In essence, these groups become pseudofamilies for these youth, providing structure, ideology, and most importantly, fraternity. This sense of fellowship, however, does not come without significant expectations and responsibilities. Members are expected to sever any and all ties with outsiders, including but not limited to family members and nonconforming significant others. Subsequently, the malleability and vulnerability of these disassociated youth are often manifested in criminal and violent activities.

Like their street gang counterparts, racist groups provide explanations for economic deprivation. Both street gangs and supremacist groups perceive themselves as victims of institutionalized discrimination. However, their response to this perceived persecution differs. While criminal gangs engage in illicit activity to circumvent these formalized structures of oppression, supremacist groups actively attack them. These varying modes of adaptation are predicated on ideological discrepancies and signify the most compelling difference between the two.

## DISTINGUISHING BETWEEN SUPREMACIST GANGS AND STREET GANGS

As stated, ideological foundations act as a dividing line between the two groups. Street gangs, best known for their overt criminal activity and seemingly random violent behavior, lack ideological consistency. Though brought together by marginalization, few members can articulate theoretical boundaries and constraints. Supremacist groups, on the other hand, gain strength through ideological dogma and religious rhetoric. Whether spouting "Christian identity" verbiage or pseudo-Islamic dialogue, both white and black supremacist organizations are bolstered by articulable ideals, principles, and targets. This commonality has allowed extremist ideologies to continue throughout periods of relative prosperity. This characteristic, however, has often been overlooked by law enforcement personnel. Assuming that civil litigation and criminal prosecution have neutralized supremacist groups, such as the Klan and the Panthers, some enforcement agencies have been caught unaware by the recent resurgence of antiestablishment ideology. Such an oversight, coupled with their subversive abilities, has enabled supremacist or antiestablishment organizations to stockpile a significant amount of hidden resources such as munitions, personnel, literature, etc. In actuality, victories for law enforcement have proven to be superficial at best.

Characterized by unprecedented levels of adaptability, supremacist groups have recently refocused their attention and their anger on a more vulnerable and socially acceptable target. Bowing to political correctness, both white and black supremacist groups have increasingly targeted those of Jewish ancestry. Recent accounts of anti-Semitic activity reveal an intolerance only exceeded by the Nazis of Germany. This redirection, more palatable to a society socialized to be wary of non-Christians, has resulted in successful membership drives in virtually all supremacist organizations. In addition, by characterizing formalized governmental structures as Jewish-owned or controlled, supremacists have effectively seduced American youth, race notwithstanding, into antiestablishment ideologies. The delusion has also reinforced traditional stereotypes and elicited a number of adult members. Unfortunately for American society, it has resulted in a cyclical pattern of antagonism and intolerance.

While both supremacists and street gang members are overwhelmingly gathered from dysfunctional familial situations, an increasing number of young supremacists are recruited from the realms of nuclear families. These nuclear families, however, are anything but traditional in nature. Unlike Rockwell's depictions, these youngsters are not reared in fireside or cozy environments sprinkled with love and forgiveness; rather, elders are responsible for passing on family values that encourage extremism and racism. The importance of socialization through kinship cannot be overstated. Just as street gang members emulate community elders, young supremacists find affirmation for supremacist ideology within their families, communities, and churches. Thus, it may be argued that predestination for supremacist youths is all but guaranteed by sociological factors. Like their street-affiliated counterparts, supremacist youths are surrounded not only by support but by encouragement of their extremist ideology. However, unlike their street peers, who graduate from group illegal activity to independent illicit entrepreneurship, the majority of young racists do not fully evolve. In fact, racist activity is rarely, if ever, perpetrated by individuals.

Three remaining characteristics distinguish street gangs from their supremacist counterparts. The first appears too obvious to mention. While criminal activity perpetuated by street gangs is inherently profit driven, supremacist organizations engage in these endeavors to create revenue for the successful overthrow of ZOG and further spreading ideological rhetoric. Increasingly, these organizations have utilized tools of mass media and technological advances in communication mediums to promote their subversive dogma. These strategies, unheard of in strictly criminal organizations, have enabled supremacist organizations to reach a cross section of American youth. The accessibility of and the lack of censorship on the Internet have radically enhanced traditional recruitment strategies. Figure 6-7 lists only a few of the many supremacist-supported Internet Web sites. Finally, organizational longevity of supremacist groups has been secured through successful platforms of political legitimacy and mainstream appeal. Unlike their street counterparts, leaders in racist groups have successfully camouflaged their proclivity for violence and subversive activities in political agendas. For the most part, criminal street gangs are often characterized as shortsighted due to their reluctance to cultivate political patronage

www.natvan.com
Home page of the National Alliance, this site features the "teachings" of "Dr."
William Pierce, author of *The Turner Diaries*. The rhetoric tends to lament the discrimination directed toward whites in political, social, and economic areas. Their
monthly newsletter has argued that the media is actually a Semitic tool designed to
extinguish any and all racial unity among whites.

www.nidlink.com/~aryanvic
One of many Aryan Nations home pages, this site is particularly good at identifying
acts they define as atrocities committed against whites by minorities. This site includes writing from hatemongers such as Richard Butler. Their literature supports
both separation and violence as a means to an end.

www.wpww.com
Home of White Pride World Wide, this site appeals to those individuals in need of
white-only holidays. Some of the most notable include Robert E. Lee's birthday (January 20), Stonewall Jackson Day, and Adolf Hitler's birthday (April 20). This site also
details "Jewish conspiracies" within the United States. This site has periodically advocated the boycott of certain products for their antiwhite policies. These include
McDonald's for their refusal to fly the Georgia flag because it contains the Confederate battle flag; AOL and Geocites due to their censorship of racist Web pages; and
Miller Brewing Company for their support of the Thurgood Marshall Fund.

www.whitepride.net
Promoted as an entertainment site, this page promotes various white supremacist
bands such as Skrewdriver and Berserkr, bands known for their intolerant and homicidal propaganda. This site also includes sections of ethnic jokes. Like many supremacist organizations, this site spouts religious rhetoric to support their views of
racial oppression, separation, and annihilation.

**FIGURE 6-7**  Web of Hate

or associations. Thus, it is anticipated that supremacist ideology will continue to outpace and endure far longer than groups solely motivated by
fiduciary gain.

## CONCLUSIONS

Contrary to popular media depictions that characterize hate-motivated violence as a white phenomenon, racial violence is an equal opportunity activity. Many incidents perpetuated by nonwhites are presented as reactionary
or defensive. Too often, the underlying motivations in these activities are un-
dermined or ignored. Take for instance the 1993 mass murder of six com-

www.naawp.com

The official Web page of the National Association for the Advancement of White People claims to debunk "myths" promoted by a variety of racial and religious minority groups. Viewers may, for example, view "real" crime statistics, which indicate that African Americans tend to prey on whites. This site also provides links for those individuals searching for similar organizations.

www.stormfront.com

One of the most popular racist sites on the Net, Stormfront's home page offers a variety of options for interested parties. Hatemongers, for example, can find like-minded partners on the new Aryan Dating Page and shop for racist artifacts in the gift shop. This site also provides a comprehensive list of links to other supremacist Web pages. The authors have developed a "legal defense fund" for their founders, readers, and publications. They warn that a Jewish conspiracy is preventing Gentiles from expressing their constitutional privileges and detail an agreement between America Online and the Anti-Defamation League of B'nai B'rith and the Simon Wiesenthal Center to censor the Internet. This group also provides links to political pages, such as that of David Duke.

www.duke.org

David Duke's home page mirrors his political campaigns of old. This page espouses an intolerance for nonwhites and argues that many black politicians are actually dyed-in-the-wool criminals or morally bankrupt. He argues that the media have fallen into the hands of antiwhite individuals who pose a significant threat to white America. Careful to distance himself from hatemongers, Duke claims to have no harsh feelings toward minority groups. To the contrary, Duke claims to be a race lover—infatuated with the notion of being white.

muters on a 12-car commuter train. Media accounts of this shooting suggest that Colin Ferguson, a Jamaican immigrant, simply chose to vent his rage over unrealized expectations, much like a disgruntled postal worker. These accounts frequently omit the racial singularity of those *not* targeted, African Americans. This misrepresentation, likening Ferguson to a delusional misfit, negates the seriousness of racial conflict in contemporary society. Other examples of racial violence (see Figure 6-8) indicate a growing division in American society. Many individuals foresee a resurgence in racial supremacy that will surpass the unrest of the civil rights era. It is anticipated that youth involvement in the impending racial war will be significant. In fact, the opening salvos may have already been exchanged.

Tampa, Florida, 1993
Randomly selecting a black tourist, two white men doused the man in gasoline before igniting him.

Guthrie, Kentucky, January 14, 1995
Nineteen-year-old Michael Westerman was shot and killed while driving down the road with his wife. The perpetrators, young African-American males, executed Westerman after they became angry at the Confederate battle flag flying from the rear of Westerman's truck.

South Carolina, 1996
An elderly white couple were found guilty of second-degree lynching for their involvement in an attempted lynching. Their children were also involved, allegedly beating, kicking, and attempting to strangle a young black male.

Ohio, 1996
Damico Watkins, a 17-year-old African-American prison inmate, was stabbed to death by members of the Aryan Brotherhood, a white supremacist gang.

California, 1996
An African-American male was called racial slurs, beaten, and set on fire by a reported skinhead.

Vermont, 1996
A white woman was attacked by Roy Towsley, a 19-year-old African American, who was charged with aggravated assault, simple assault, and committing a hate crime after he threw the victim to the ground while shouting racial epithets.

California, 1996
Four white males, including three teenagers, attacked a Latino man, stabbing him repeatedly while yelling racial epithets.

California, 1996
Two white high school students were attacked by a gang of Asian youths. Two teens involved in the incident were charged with a hate crime and assault with a deadly weapon.

California, 1996
Three black teenagers were charged with a hate crime and assault with a caustic chemical for urinating on two white males.

North Carolina, 1996
A white high school student was attacked by two black teenagers after an exchange of racial epithets.

New York, 1996
A Jewish family was beaten by a group of young black males who shouted anti-Semitic remarks.

**FIGURE 6-8** Racial Violence: An Equal Opportunity Activity

Mobilization of disassociated youth is increasingly universal in these more radical, ethnocentric groups. Of particular concern are the religious and political ideology these organizations espouse. This indoctrination, whether veiled or overt in its approach, creates a complex network of like-minded individuals and legitimizes violence. Drawing on generational consciousness, adult leaders actually manipulate those individuals seeking empowerment. Utilization of mass communication interfaces further propagates racial intolerance. An unanticipated by-product is the multiplication of less formalized splinter groups. These gangs, many founded by and presided over by teens, are often the most unpredictable and the most deadly. Unfortunately, law enforcement efforts are directed at the more formalized and more traditional groups, such as the Ku Klux Klan and the Black Panthers.

The dismantling of the Black Panther Party, the assassination of Malcolm X, and the successful criminal and civil prosecution of klaverns and their leaders by the Southern Poverty Law Center are perceived by many governmental agencies as social victories, monumental in their impact. On the surface, these events taken collectively do appear to have reduced the desirability of hate-motivated activity, and most would agree that any progress in enforcement efforts is deserving of applause. However, these events do not signal the demise of gang-related hatemongering nor do they indicate widespread multicultural tolerance. On the contrary, recent exposés of the annual "good old boys" roundup epitomize the *lack* of social understanding or awareness. Societal divisiveness and subsequent racial violence appear to be a foregone conclusion, one that some agencies seem to have missed.

Traditionally, periods of supremacist affiliation and organizational prominence have been short-lived. Each period of prosperity enjoyed by supremacist organizations was invariably ended due to their own propensity for self-destruction and *not* as the result of law enforcement efforts. In fact, their emphasis on local control and lack of self-regulation created associations particularly vulnerable to the antics of individual members. Had they been able to reconcile minor ideological and jurisdictional disputes (e.g., issues of affirmative action, gay and lesbian rights, school prayer, community programs, etc.), their impact might have significantly altered the face of current social policy. Thus, it is impossible to contemplate the implications for contemporary society had they been more foresighted in their endeavors. In spite of themselves, however, they were successful in planting seeds of racism. Much like weeds, the products of such seeding are unpredictable and unbelievably resilient to the most concentrated efforts.

Recent occurrences of racial violence and elevated levels of anti-Semitism have indicated a growing unrest in American society. The resurgence of racist ideology further indicates that criminal and civil proceedings against these organizations have not been successful in "curing" social intolerance. Metaphorically speaking, the venomous hatred espoused by supremacist organizations may be likened to a prevaccine epidemic. In the quest for quick-fix inoculations, root causes and the effects of short-term exposure to racist rhetoric have been overlooked, allowing pathological mutations to fester. The repercussions of such an oversight have not yet been evaluated.

# CHAPTER 7

# Street Gangs

By now you might be asking, "I thought all the gangs previously discussed were street gangs," and to a large extent you would be right. Clearly all gangs "work the street." What we mean by street gangs in this chapter are those gangs traditionally referred to as black gangs (Bloods, Crips, Disciples, and Vice Lords). To refer to them as black gangs would create a misnomer as well as problems for those who work and deal with gangs. While black gangs may have once been the appropriate term, we believe it is no longer either appropriate or accurate. First, many of the traditional black gangs now have white members. Indeed, in the city of Chicago whites are the fastest growing segment of the Gangster Disciples (Sebeck, 1998). If those involved in gang work believe only blacks are Disciples and Bloods, then they will not see many facets crucial to understanding gangs. Second, many ethnic gang types are black, again creating a problem because the wrong assumptions about the black gangster may be the result. And, when dealing with gangs and gangsters, assumptions can literally get one killed. Third, we believe that to refer to these individuals as black gangsters gives fuel to white supremacists, including skinheads, thus creating a more difficult situation and possibly grounds for increased membership recruiting.

The two general types or styles of street gangs, Los Angeles and Chicago, are often referred to as West Coast and East Coast gangs. Many people assume that street gangs got their start in Los Angeles, a notion arising from media coverage in the 1980s in Los Angeles. The Chicago-based gangs have been in existence much longer than the L.A. gangs and were probably the forerunners of the groups Thrasher (1963) wrote about.

## CHICAGO-BASED STREET GANGS

The current Chicago gangs had their origination in the 1960s under the leadership of two charismatic individuals, David Barksdale and Jeff Fort. "King David" Barksdale formed the Devil's Disciples, and Fort, the Black P. Stone Rangers. Each gang or set in Chicago acted independently of each other, however, most formed at least loose alliances with either Barksdale or Fort. Barksdale and his two protegés, Larry Hoover and Shorty Freeman, ruled the Disciples until Barksdale was killed in a drive-by shooting. After Barksdale's death, Hoover and Freeman engaged in a power struggle for control of the Disciples with Hoover coming out on top. Once firmly entrenched, Hoover restructured and renamed the gang Black Gangster Disciple Nation. Known for their narcotics distribution and their use of extreme violence, Disciple leadership, especially Hoover, then went about consolidating power by convincing many other Chicago gangs to join the Disciple organization and follow one philosophy.

Hoover was successful in this endeavor; however, in the mid 1970s he had been convicted and sentenced to prison for the murder of a rival gangster. Many thought his prison term would mean the end of Hoover's reign and perhaps the Disciple Nation itself, but nothing could have been further from the truth. While in Stateville prison, Hoover continued to lead and direct the Black Gangster Disciple Nation, which got stronger and more broad based and eventually evolved into the FOLK Nation. Originally developed in prison for protection "inside," the FOLK Nation consists of a number of different gangs, allied for the purposes of protection and distribution of narcotics. Larry Hoover, despite his current incarceration in the SuperMax Federal Prison in Colorado, continues as undisputed leader and the one to whom loyalty is shown. The alliance adopted mutually acceptable symbols and a philosophy that would identify members of FOLK, which means simply Follow Our Loving King.

Always at odds with the Disciples, Fort and the Black P. Stones could not stand by idly and watch the Disciples grow and become an overpowering force. Aligning themselves with the various gangs that had been opposed to Hoover and the Disciples, they formed the People Nation and also adopted mutually acceptable signs and symbols to identify themselves as "one," and as NOT FOLK.

Both FOLK and People have a variety of race and ethnic types within their nations, including blacks, Hispanics, whites, and in some cases Asians.

Their influence and expansion has created a network of affiliates throughout the United States. What distinguishes one from another is not their race or ethnic heritage but rather their style of dress, symbols, and language.

## LOS ANGELES GANGS

Probably because it is Los Angeles (L.A.), gangs there are better known or at least more familiar with more written about them than are gangs in Chicago, even though their patterns of "modern development" appear to be remarkably similar. Street gangs in Los Angeles can be traced to at least the 1940s, primarily in the ghettos and low-income areas, and as today, famous people and athletes were reported to be gang members. Boxing champion Don Jordan (Geronimo) was one such individual and was affiliated with the Purple Hearts of the Aliso Housing Project. During the years of the Korean conflict and for some time afterward, L.A. gang activity experienced a lull. A reemergence of gang activity occurred in 1958 and continued on until 1965 with such gangs as Huns, Del Vikings, Roman Pearls, the Gladiators, and the Slausons, "which displayed the first gang hand sign, displaying a 'V' for Slauson Village" (Bell, 1998: 7). In times of conflict, the weapons of choice were knives, jacks, chains, and zip guns, with fistfights as the major method of confrontations. During this period, drug and alcohol use by gangsters emerged.

As with the 1950s, a lull in gang activity occurred between 1965 and 1969, which coincided with the time of the Vietnam War. Certainly the draft put many of these gang members and potential gangsters in the armed forces in service of our country. Bell (1998: 7) notes, "[I]t's no wonder that since the change in drafting young men to serve our country that there has been nothing to change the flow of young men in our communities." The military removed young men from the community and changed many into responsible adults. On the other hand, the Vietnam War also provided many young men with the discipline and training necessary to be better gangsters, especially after the "disrespect" the received upon their return from the war.

The period immediately after Vietnam is known as the pre-Crips era. Again, many gangs formed, with names like Al Capone, the Smacks, and Charlie Browns. Some of the principals in this era and their monikers were Angelo White (Barefoot-Pookie), Raymond Washington (Truck), Michael Concepcion (Shaft), and Melvin Hardy (Skull). Notice the strong or tough sound of the monikers. After fighting with and beating the Avenue gang, the Smacks (led by Raymond Washington) began to skip school and hang out together, becoming the Crips. While many different versions of the origin of the name "Crip" continue the float around, the most commonly accepted version is that its source is the Vincent Price movie *Tales from the Crypt,* and is the phonetic spelling of crypt. Why crypt (crip)? The gangsters wanted to convey an image that just as dead people were placed in crypts, anyone who messed with them—the Crips—would end up in one also.

Another term, *cuzz,* which was used in reference to a fellow Crip, came from a gang member who was called Young Cousin, which was shortened to just Cuzz. Originally one big gang (set) as the result of suspensions, expulsions, and school transfers, the Crips separated into a variety of subsets. Their adoption of the color blue came about because the L.A. county jail issued bandanas to the inmates. Crips "picked" the color blue, and as members returned to the streets so did the bandanas and the color.

As the Crips grew in numbers and strength, many individuals did not want to join up, yet they realized that they probably could not survive without a "group" of their own. The Bloods formed as a response, essentially to protect its members from the Crips. Early Bloods leaders included Sylvester Scott (Puddin), Bobby Lavender, and Tam. Beginning on Piru Street, Bloods have always been fewer in number than the Crips but have been able to stick together much better than the Crips who, in addition to being bitter enemies of the Bloods, continue to engage in feuds and violence among themselves. Red bandanas are the signature mark of the Bloods. Besides being the color of blood it was also the color of choice for the Blood gangster who wanted to survive and hang with his homies while incarcerated in the L.A. county jail.

## THE GANGSTERS' "NEW" FACE

After the riots following the acquittal of the Los Angeles police officers in the Rodney King incident, the Crips were able to convince the federal government that they were a charitable organization and thus received some of the federal rebuilding funds. Their ingenuity in this situation should come as no surprise because the Gangster Disciples have done much the same thing. In the early 1990s, under the leadership of Larry Hoover (who was and still is in prison), an organization known as Blueprint for Growth and Development (aka BGD–Black Gangster Disciples) was formed.

Under the leadership of Wallace "Gator" Bradley, Hoover's most trusted lieutenant (and second in command), Blueprint for Growth and Development and its subsidiary, 21st Century Voices of Total Empowerment, or 21st Century V.O.T.E., have succeeded in convincing many that they have given up the gangster life to "save" all those who might have been led to gangs. They claim to have found solutions to many urban problems, including drugs, gang violence, unemployment, and homelessness. So convincing were Bradley and Hoover (through Bradley) that many prominent Chicagoans, including former mayor Eugene Sawyer, state representative Coy Pugh, the NAACP, and many other people and organizations attempted, unsuccessfully, to get Hoover paroled in 1993.

Bradley, a convicted felon and enforcer for the Gangster Disciples, has run for city alderman on at least two separate occasions, forcing a runoff in his most recent campaign. In addition, Bradley has been invited to the White House to meet with President Clinton, the Reverend Jesse Jackson, Angela Davis (a convicted cop killer), and two other individuals to discuss the problems of urban America. It would seem the federal government is also interested in the new image of the Gangster Disciples.

In another apparent contradiction, a gang summit sponsored by the federal government occurred in 1992 with the slogan STOP THE VIOLENCE, in an attempt to get us all to live together in peace and harmony, accompanied by the singing of the Coca Cola song, "I'd Like to Teach the World to Sing." Rather than peace and harmony, however, what resulted was the country divided among the gang factions, a national approach begun by Larry Hoover. The result: the FOLK Nation (Gangster Disciples, etc.), the Crips, and the Surenos (the Mexican Mafia) aligned themselves against the People Nation (Vice Lords, Latin Kings, etc.), the Bloods, and the Nortes. So the traditional rivalries continue to exist, only now each side has greater numbers.

## GANG IDENTIFIERS

With the gang alliance of 1992, symbols of gang identy have become interchangeable within the alliances but continue to differ between the alliances. In general, the FOLK Nation adopts the right side, the color blue, the six-point star (aka the Star of David), and the pitchfork. The People Nation adopts the left side, the color red, the five-point star, and the three-point crown. Interestingly enough, with the Chicago Bulls' three national championships, Chicago gangs gravitated toward the color red and the Bulls' symbols, which have become interchangeable between the gangs. This attraction to successful sports teams is not necessarily the case outside of the Chicago area, however.

Many gang researchers look for deep psychological reasons for the adoption of various colors, sports team apparel, monikers, and meanings. The reality probably is that the simplest explanation is probably the best. One must remember that many of these gangsters are uneducated, common kids who select images they like and that express what they want to portray. Still others sit around, drink beer, smoke dope, and come up with definitions for terms. The wearing of earrings is a good example. Gangsters, particularly L.A. gangsters, began wearing earrings because they liked the way the

Barbarians looked wearing earrings in the movie *The King and I.* Again, no deep-seated psychological explanation is appropriate—simply watching a movie, saying "that's neat," and doing it provide all the explanation necessary. The process is not unlike how many kids "become gangsters" today, or what some have called *video* or *MTV gangsters.*

## INFLUENCE OF RAP MUSIC

Whether rap music is the music of the streets or not, it is "certainly impacting and defining a generation" (Stallworth, 1998). Interestingly enough, it seems to have a greater impact on white kids than on black kids. Indeed white, middle-class youth have made rap music so popular. Contradictions abound in this aspect too. While many of the leading rappers are gang members, Stallworth notes that neither Tupac Shakur nor Suge Knight were gang members even though Shakur was killed for alleged gang affiliations, and the Bloods hold Knight in high esteem. Nevertheless, rap music has had a negative effect on the youth of today through its images (right or wrong) of life "on the street," which lead many to emulate what they hear in the music.

Just like the different styles of gangs (east and west, Chicago and L.A.), rap music has been similarly divided into East Coast and West Coast, generally referred to as Eastside and Westside. Rap music started in the South Bronx, but the West Coast soon dominated, which required a response from the East. While originally playfully done in the tradition of Otis Redding and Carla Thomas, the idea of disrespect was taken to a new level when Tim Dog recorded the song "F*** Compton." With this song, Dog seemed to be attacking an entire generation of South Central youth, and in so doing, made it personal. This animosity is easy to understand when one remembers that the gang lifestyle is all about respect and reputation. Disrespecting another leads to a fight, whether that disrespect occurs face up, to one's girlfriend or family member, or through song.

The Eastside/Westside war took on a life of its own with the shooting of Tupac Shakur in 1995. As a result, a continuing battle of words, actions, and lyrics rages as each side tries to disrespect the other. In the tradition of gangs, rap music (at least gangsta rap) is legal dope directed at the youth of this country. As Robert Bobb, city manager of Richmond, Virginia, notes, "Sure, the streets are tough, but we need to promote a different set of values" (*Insight,* 1989: 55). One must also understand that even though rap music does not cause a young person to join a gang, it is safe to say that the influences of gangsta rap are certainly not beneficial for young people, especially those fighting the temptations of the street.

## STRANGE FACTS

Strange facts about Bloods and Crips frequently surface. Whether they are true is certainly conjecture, but given the unusual nature of street gangs, their veracity would hardly be surprising. About the Bloods: They often eat and hang out at Kentucky Fried Chicken (KFC) because KFC stands for "Kill F*****g Crips." Hardcore Bloods will not eat at Burger King because BK stands for "Blood Killer." One should note as well that the Kentucky Fried Chicken chain is now primarily called KFC and most of the restaurants are red and white—Blood colors. Was this name change an attempt to simplify marketing or a welcome to the Bloods? (Food for thought, so to speak.) About the Crips: They hang out at Burger King because BK stands for "Blood Killer." And when Crips began throwing Molotov cocktails at Bloods, they called them BK broilers, like the sandwich. When Crips joined the FOLK Nation, they adopted the eight ball as a symbol because the two hand signs put together look like the number eight.

## CONCLUSIONS

Like other gangs mentioned in this text, street gangs have unique histories, beliefs, behaviors, and identifying features. And like other gangs, they are just as deadly, perhaps more so, because they are often simply overlooked as misguided youth. Perhaps white street gangsters are overlooked because they are not black. Nevertheless, at this point street gangs may pose the greatest threat to our society. Why? Because unlike most other gangs, street gangs prey on all of us and in some areas and jurisdictions they are overlooked by law enforcement and school personnel. Some of these professionals do not want to see gangs or gangsters and so deny, ignore, and delay their response, which can only lead to further trouble. Unfortunately, while perhaps not the smartest individuals in the world, street gangsters recognize their effect and influence and the response it illicits and use it for their gain. The results of such behavior on both parts could be disastrous to us all.

CHAPTER

# 8

# Jamaican and Nigerian Gangs

The Jamaican and Nigerian organizations are the two major black organized crime groups. Jamaican gangs have been active in organized crime activities since the mid 1960s, while Nigerian activity began in the early 1970s. Most Jamaican gangs have been mentioned as growers and distributors of marijuana worldwide. In reality, it goes beyond marijuana and drugs; this group has become involved in as many unlawful activities as any other group.

## JAMAICAN ORGANIZED GANGS

The island of Jamaica was at one time a British colony in the West Indies. A majority of the island inhabitants are descendants of Africans who were brought to the islands as slaves several hundred years ago. Jamaica has a heterogeneous society that includes Asian as well as European citizens. The literacy rate in Jamaica is 90 percent, which has created a proud citizenry that has a productive as well as diversified culture. Most citizens are either Protestant or Roman Catholic, but a considerable increase has occurred in the number of people participating in the Rastafarian religious movement.

The immigration of Jamaican citizens to the United States began in the early 1900s. During World War II, a noteworthy increase of Jamaican immigrants was the result of the decrease in the number of workers available in the United States due to the war. A majority of these immigrants settled in

New York City. The number of Jamaican newcomers to the United States decreased after 1952 and the passage of the McCarron-Walter Act. It limited the number of Jamaicans entering the United States to 100 per year. In 1965 the passage of the Hart-Cellar Act increased the quotas on Caribbean people entering the United States.

One of the first groups of Jamaican immigrants to arrive in the United States, after the passage of the Hart-Cellar Act, was the Rastafarians. At first they were considered by many to be members of some type of gang because of their outward appearances and religious beliefs. The Rastafarians are considered by many law enforcement officials to have been the precursor of today's Jamaican Posses. Their reputation came primarily from Rastafarian participation in the growth, sale, and use of marijuana in Jamaica and the United States. The Rastafarians however turned out to be more of a religious group than a gang, although some people are still of the opinion that the Jamaican gangs are made up of Rastafarians. Although the Rastafarian sect does not have an inflexible or a numbered set of principles that guide them, most sect members conform to a ten-point code. These membership standards include the following:

1. They object to the use of sharpened instruments to shave the hair off one's body or to put tattoos on the body.

2. They scorn the eating of pork, shellfish, scaleless fish, and snails; many sect members are vegetarians.

3. They pay homage to Ras Tafari or the living God (Ras Tafari was inaugurated as the King of Ethiopia on November 2, 1930, and he was immediately named the Imperial Majesty Haile Selassie, which means the might of the Trinity), who is comparable to Jesus in the Christian religion and Mohammed in the Moslem religion.

4. They love the brotherhood of man.

5. They detest hatred, jealousy, envy, deceit, and other similar vices.

6. They disagree with modern-day society and all its evils.

7. They seek a society that consists of one brotherhood.

8. They want to supply benevolence to any brother in anguish.

9. They must comply with the ancient Ethiopian principles.

10. They must shun assistance and accolades extended by a nonmember (Jamaican Information Service, 1998).

Several other features make it fairly easy to distinguish a member of the Rastafarian religious group from Jamaican gang members. The first is the unusual way that the Rastafarians style their hair. This type of hair styling has been called dreadlocks and is worn as a symbol of defiance. They also believe that a person's strength has something to do with the length of one's hair. Another feature of the Rastafarian cult is reggae music. The attachment to reggae comes from their use of this type of music to express their protest against the way they were treated by the police and the local government in Jamaica. The third characteristic of a person practicing the Rastafarian religion is the use of ganja or marijuana. The practice of smoking ganja goes back to the inception of this group and it is considered part of the Rastafarian religious ritual (Jamaican Information Service, 1998).

An understanding of the Rastafarian sect would cause anyone to doubt that a member of this religion would be a participant in gang activity. Rastafarians may have been involved in the sale of marijuana, but such activity was done, in many cases, on an individual basis to enable a particular person to support himself or herself. In fact, the only probable interaction that would take place between a Rastafarian and a Jamaican gang member would be when a Rastafarian purchases marijuana from a gang drug operative.

The Jamaican street gangs that are present in our society today have evolved over the past 25 years. During that time these gangs have gained an expertise in the way their criminal operations function. These same gangs developed in the Jamaican ghettos during the early 1970s. Like their counterparts in the United States, these enterprising tough and young Jamaican street kids discovered that they could recruit a number of other adolescents from their neighborhoods. In turn, they could then form their own criminal organization to control a specific territory. The gangs took up the name "Posses," taken from old American western movies. These posses were formed on the similitude of the neighborhood, political alliances, and/or notoriety. In most cases, the gang took a name that was associated with their local district. The Waterhouse Posse is from the Waterhouse area of Kingston, Jamaica. They usually maintain a further affiliation with either of the political groups, the Jamaican Labor Party (JLP) or the Peoples National Party (PNP). A connection to a political party and its elected officials affords the gang favoritism when that specific party is in power. The types of unfair preference that can be bestowed upon the gangs include public works projects that allow the gangs the right to provide jobs for gang and nongang members in the community. Preferential treatment may also be granted to gang members seeking asylum from other authorities or just to avoid some type of required governmental procedure. The gangs provide monetary support—that in most cases is accumulated from their participation in drug trafficking activities—to the political parties as well as any other type of secondary support (Interpol, 1998).

The influx of Jamaican street gangs into the United States started in the late 1970s. A majority of the first arrivals in the United States had prior criminal records in Jamaica and were escaping the Jamaican justice system. They arrived in the United States as illegal aliens. These fugitives from Jamaican justice formed their own posses or assisted others in the expansion of the Jamaican street gangs. The results of this work have placed most of these people in either a mid-level or high-ranking status within the posse. The more advanced posse members saw immigration to the United States as an opportunity to improve their ranking in Jamaican society by creating and operating some type of criminal enterprise. Recruiting new members into the posses can be fairly easy, because Jamaica is an extremely poor country. When a gang member returns to Jamaica with cash assets obtained in the United States, impressionable Jamaican youths see gang membership as a way to obtain a better lifestyle. Law enforcement sources in the United States indicate that most of the street-level drug and gun dealers are recruited from within the local Jamaican community (ATF, 1993).

During the 1980s law enforcement agencies throughout the United States were able to recognize, take advantage of, and start major criminal prosecutions that capitalized on the deficiencies within these Jamaican criminal organizations. Some of the major defects resulted from the composition of the Jamaican criminal group. Most of these gangs had a large and identifiable membership who made little or no effort to hide their gang affiliation. This behavior ultimately led to the imprisonment, deportation, or murder of many gang members by the same or rival gangs (ATF, 1989).

The Jamaican groups were industrious enough to realize their weaknesses and adjusted their structure and operations in order to become a more impressive opponent for the U.S. law enforcement system. These gangs quickly decreased their size and became more secretive organizations. The leaders of the Jamaican Posses, through the use of a tier structure in their organization, have managed to isolate themselves from the street-level drug dealings. Such a pyramid type of organization places the leaders or bosses at the top without any direct connection to the street narcotics' dealings but with a majority of the unlawful profits being delivered to them. A leader then handpicks underbosses or lieutenants to supervise the day-to-day operations of gang activities. The average street gang worker is an illegal alien brought to the United States to fill jobs within the gang (U.S. Customs, 1993).

## Drug Trafficking

A short time after their arrival in the United States the Jamaican Posses managed to take over a large portion of the street marijuana operations and then set up their own system for trafficking the marijuana. During the 1980s, the Jamaican Posses took over a large number of various types of drug markets, previously controlled by blacks and other ethnic groups (see Figure 8-1). In just about all the cases, it was done through the use of violence. As the Jamaican Posses participation in drug trafficking activities increased in the United States so did the gang's membership and wealth.

The centralized location of Jamaica has made it an important transshipment site for the large amounts of Colombian-grown cocaine and marijuana that are routed for the United States (see Figures 8-2 and 8-3). Estimates established by federal law enforcement sources indicate that approximately 25 percent of the marijuana shipped from Jamaica to the United States is also grown in Jamaica (U.S. Customs, 1993). Over the past ten years, law enforcement intelligence information indicates that the Jamaican Posses are the major street marijuana dealers in the United States. However the gang's recent involvement in the crack cocaine market indicates the group's desire to increase their wealth and power in the United States drug market. Since

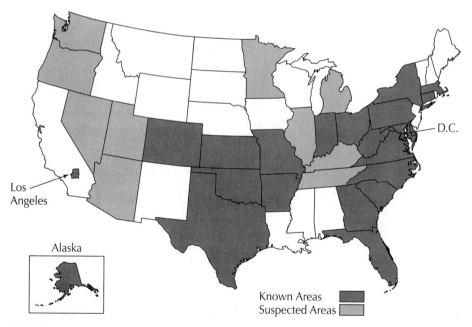

**FIGURE 8-1** Jamaican Narcotics Trafficking Within the United States
*Source:* U.S. Department of Justice, 1994.

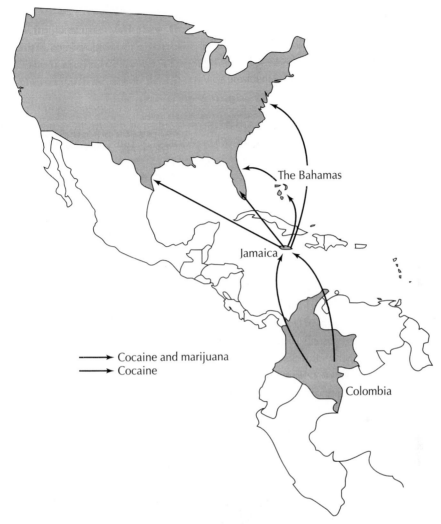

**FIGURE 8-2** Cocaine and Marijuana Routes
*Source:* U.S. Drug Enforcement Agency, 1995.

the early 1990s the Jamaican Posses have become heavily involved in the crack-cocaine trafficking business. The gang's in-depth participation in this drug enterprise has expanded to include the operation of street-level or crack houses, setting up and managing drug distribution centers or stash houses and safehouse locations throughout the United States. The street-level or crack facilities set up by the Jamaican gangs are usually rented by females and managed by armed members of the Jamaican Posses. These street-level facilities are often referred to as gatehouses by gang members. A

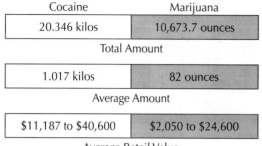

| Cocaine | Marijuana |
|---|---|
| 20.346 kilos | 10,673.7 ounces |

Total Amount

| 1.017 kilos | 82 ounces |
|---|---|

Average Amount

| $11,187 to $40,600 | $2,050 to $24,600 |
|---|---|

Average Retail Value

**FIGURE 8-3** U.S. Customs Service Seizures of Cocaine and Marijuana Carried by Jamaicans 1991 to 1994

*Source:* Financial Crimes Enforcement Network.

*Note:* These statistics represent typical Jamaican courier activity. Bulk seizures are excluded.

majority of the Jamaican drug business takes place within these well-fortified facilities. Included within the definition of a gatehouse facility are houses, apartments, convenience stores, record shops, restaurants, and commercial buildings. Once a location is selected by the gang, construction workers are employed to buttress this stronghold by barricading doors and windows, and installing escape doors and hatches and other devices that could kill or seriously injure anyone who breaches the security of the gatehouse. The types of traps put down in the gatehouses include holes in floors that are covered by rugs with beds of nails on the floor below; live electrical wires placed in windows and doorways; gates and bars on entrances; exits and windows electrically wired; floor surface underneath windows cut away and razor wire laid across open area; bucket-type devices filled with nails or other metal objects and attached to trip wires; and hanging objects containing phosphorous, alcohol, and potassium chloride placed in aluminum foil that will explode on any type of contact. The exchange of money and drugs is done through plexiglass shields and, in most cases, the buyer must be known by the dealer. An abundant quantity of various types of narcotics and guns are stored in the distribution or stash houses by the gang members. On a daily basis, gang members remove small amounts of narcotics from these locations to be delivered to the crack house for distribution to local street dealers. In turn, all of the profit made by the gang from the prior drug sales is returned to the stash house. The gang's bookkeeper maintains records of all of the monetary and narcotics transactions made between the gatehouses and the stash house. These security devices are set up to prevent law enforcement agencies from preparing a successful action that could be used to shut down the Jamaican gangs' drug operations. Higher-ranking members of the Jamaican Posses may live in these stash houses. The safe house or control point is were the gangs store their weapons and keep a hidden reserve of narcotics that is used to restock the stash houses (FBI, 1992; FLETC, 1989).

The amount of drugs found on Jamaican gang members at any given time is usually small. This precaution stems from the gang's awareness of the penalties associated with federal and state drug laws. Gang members are of the opinion that if they are arrested with a smaller amount of drugs, they have a lesser chance of being fined or sentenced to a term in jail. It is also easier for the gangs to continually distribute the drugs in smaller amounts without attracting attention from local law enforcement agencies. The success of Jamaican Posses in the narcotics business has been due to its ability to operate not only as small-time importers but also as industrious drug retailers. The profit gained by Jamaican Posse drug merchants can be exemplified as follows: The Jamaican Posses' purchase a kilo of cocaine from a Colombian drug trafficker for $15,000. A Posse member then moves the cocaine up the East Coast to New York City or Washington, D.C., and transforms the cocaine into 15,000–20,000 rocks of cocaine. This rock cocaine's street value will then exceed $125,000, which brings the Jamaican gang a profit of at least $110,000. It also makes the Jamaican Posses' drug business far more profitable than the Colombian trafficker who originally purchased the cocaine for $5,000 and then sold it to the Jamaican gang members for $15,000 (U.S. Customs, 1993).

Street-level drug dealing for the Jamaican Posses is usually conducted by African Americans who are recruited by gang members. The African Americans are enlisted into the Posse but are never truly accepted or depended upon by the Jamaican members of the gang. Street sales persons are only entrusted with a small quantity of the drugs that they are assigned to sell. They are required to respond back to the gatehouse or stash house as soon as possible to turn in their profits to a Jamaican gang lieutenant and replenish their drug supply. In some cases, Jamaican gang members become involved in street drug sales but in the greater majority of situations the Jamaican street dealer is far more cautious and secretive than a street drug dealer from any other ethnic group.

Since the late 1980s the Jamaican gangs have expanded their activities throughout the United States. These Posses have moved their operations into cities such as Houston, St. Louis, Dallas, Kansas City, Philadelphia, Boston, Richmond, Washington, D.C., and rural West Virginia (see Figures 8-4 and 8-5). In some of these cities, the Jamaican Posses have joined forces with other gangs (such as the Bloods and Crips in Kansas City, the Nigerians in Washington, D.C., and the Dominicans in Philadelphia and Boston), to enhance their drug trafficking capabilities. The Jamaican gangs further strengthen their control over their drug empire through the use of violence.

One instance of the gang's ability to recruit new members and then increase their affinity with violence is shown in the case of John C. Smith. Smith

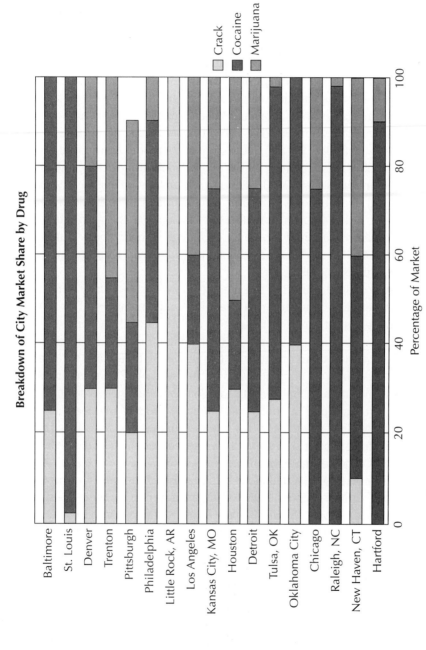

**FIGURE 8-4** Cities Where Jamaicans Are Responsible for UNDER 25 Percent of the Total Narcotics Market

*Source:* U.S. Department of Justice, 1994.

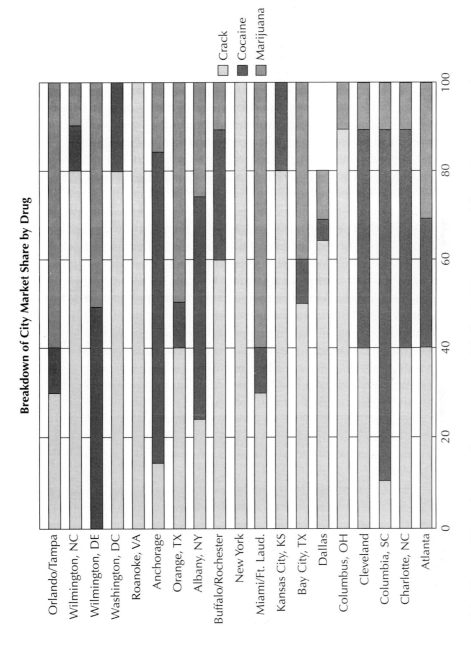

**FIGURE 8-5** Cities Where Jamaicans Are Responsible for OVER 25 Percent of the Total Narcotics Market

*Source:* U.S. Department of Justice, 1994.

137

first became involved in drug dealing when he was 13 years old. Three years later Smith was recruited by Jamaican Posse members to deal drugs in Dallas. He was given a plane ticket to Dallas and $100 spending money. A short time after his arrival he was selling crack out of a Dallas apartment making an estimated $5,000 a day for the gang. Smith always carried a 9-millimeter semi-automatic pistol with him. Two months after his arrival in Dallas, Smith was arrested and charged by the Dallas police with three murders. According to the Dallas police, Smith went on a 36-hour rampage while under the influence of drugs and killed three people. Smith shot one of the victims 11 times, including the soles of the feet. He is presently serving an 18-year sentence in a Texas correctional institution for the three murders that he admitted committing just eight weeks after his arrival in Dallas (Meier, 1989).

In an attempt to destroy the New York–Dallas drug and gun rings, a combined NYPD and FBI task force raided premises in Brooklyn, Albany, Uniondale, Long Island, and Dallas. The gang's headquarters at 1367 Sterling Place in the Crown Heights section of Brooklyn, New York, known as the "White House" or the "killing house," was seized by the police. This location was often used by drug leaders as a place to assassinate rival drug leaders and gang members who stole drugs or money from the gang. It was also a location from which the gang sold drugs in the hallways 24 hours a day, 365 days a year (McKinley, 1990).

This gang, known as the Gulleymen, who take their name from a neighborhood in Kingston, Jamaica, known as McGregor's Gulley, rented cars in New York to ferry drugs to Dallas. Upon arrival in Dallas the autos were filled with dozens of illegal firearms for their return to New York. Members of the Gulleymen who were arrested by the federal task force were also charged with 10 homicides. A total of 15 guns and $150,000 in U.S. currency was seized during the raids conducted by this federal task force. Evidence gathered by federal authorities indicates that this group invested their unlawfully obtained profits in real estate in Brooklyn and Long Island while some portion of the money was shipped back to Jamaica. Federal authorities have indicated that some of this gang's drug money has been used to support political candidates in Jamaica (McKinley, 1990).

### Firearms Trafficking

The Jamaican Posses have managed to excel in their ability to deal illegal guns. Jamaican gangs obtain the weapons for their firearms trafficking business in several ways.

1. *Purchase*—A gang member sets up a residence and all the necessary documentation in a state where a specific amount of time in residency

(usually 30–90 days) is the main requirement to purchase guns. Once all the residency requirements are met, the gang members can, in a short period of time, buy all the pistols/guns they desire. These guns are then transported to New York City or some other large urban center where the guns are sold, usually on the street, for two to three times their original price.

2. *Straw Purchase*—This type of purchase is similar to the previous type of purchase except a person with a gang affiliation, who already has residence and documentation, buys the firearms for the gang member. This person usually receives a percentage of the gun purchase price (10–15 percent is common). Guns are then transported to major urban centers and sold for high profit levels.

3. *Firearms Theft*—In these cases the gang member(s) either break into gun dealerships or commit gun dealership robberies. Weapons are taken instead of money, and the guns are once again transported to a major urban location where they are sold for profit.

4. *Home Invasion Robberies*—The gang forcibly enters private residences where they know a great deal of guns are located and forcibly take the weapons from the owner. These guns are also transported to a large city where they are sold for profit.

5. *Hijacking*—When possible the gang will steal a vehicle carrying weapons or, if necessary, use whatever force required to obtain the weapons that will be ultimately sold at street level.

6. *Theft from Military Bases*—Posses members break into a military installation and remove all of the weapons accessible to them.

7. *Mail Theft*—A gang member or gang associate who works for the U.S. Postal Service steals packages containing weapons and gives said firearms to the gang for use or profit.

Just about all the purchases of firearms by gang members take place in Texas, Virginia, Georgia, and Florida. Almost all the guns are transported back to New York City for distribution throughout the United States. Some of these firearms are transported back to Jamaica where the profit margin is far more remunerative than the U.S. market but far more dangerous because of the strict gun laws. The gang is required to use several methods to smuggle firearms into Jamaica:

1. Transporting the weapons in commercial containers that hold other items such as food or machinery

2. Enlisting female merchants as weapon carriers (these females are chosen because they are Jamaican and regularly travel between Miami and Jamaica)

3. Using small planes

4. Concealing guns somewhere in a vehicle that is shipped to Jamaica from the United States

The Jamaican gangs do their best to remove all identifiable marking on these weapons before selling them.

## Economic Crimes

### Money Laundering

The Jamaican gangs have become familiar with the laws in the United States related to the laundering of currency under the U.S. Bank Secrecy Act (BSA). A majority of the Jamaican and most of the other active criminal organizations in the United States avoid currency transactions through conventional financial establishments. Yet, the vast amount of profit from the gangs' drug operations needs to be moved out of the United States as quickly and safely as possible. The leaders of the Jamaican Posses have undoubtedly managed to successfully transport large amounts of currency to Jamaica without any major interference by U.S. law enforcement agencies. Upon the arrival of the money in Jamaica a majority of the currency is quickly invested in legitimate businesses such as resorts, apartment buildings, restaurants, and other investment holdings.

In most cases, individual members of the Jamaican gang will transport the currency somewhere on their bodies or within very close proximity of themselves. Another alternative used by the gangs involves the transfer of U.S. currency into some type of commodity, which is then transported to Jamaica. Usually merchandise such as electronic equipment, automobile components, and retail garments are the commodities shipped to Jamaica by the gangs. The Jamaican Posses have come up with some far-reaching and complicated currency laundering and money smuggling conspiracies, including the following:

*Street Higglers.* Street traders or dealers are perceived as higglers within Jamaican society. Street higglers regularly visit the United States to buy articles that they will ultimately sell in Jamaica. In some cases, the higgler is financed by a Jamaican Posse. In other instances, a Jamaican gang will pay the higgler's round-trip transportation costs and on the higgler's arrival in the United States he is given money to procure retail merchandise. Said merchandise is then transported to Jamaica where the items are sold and the money redeemed from the sales returned to the Posse. The money has been, therefore, laundered by the gang (see Figure 8-6).

*Use of 55-Gallon Drums for Transporting Money.* A Jamaican gang member will fill 55-gallon drums with currency and then transport the drums to Jamaica. A corrupt airline employee or a gang member who is employed by an airline at a local U.S. airport receives the drum, and the employee guarantees that the drum will be put on a plane to Jamaica. Upon its arrival in Jamaica the drum is moved off the plane and through Jamaican Customs without being detected.

*Use of Airline Employees.* An employee of any airline, who constantly flies into Jamaica is paid a fee to carry money from the United States to Jamaica without claiming the funds at either United States or Jamaican Customs. Once the employee arrives in Jamaica and passes through Jamaican Customs the money is returned to the gang.

**FIGURE 8-6** Higgler Money Laundering
*Source:* U.S. Dept. of Justice, 1994.

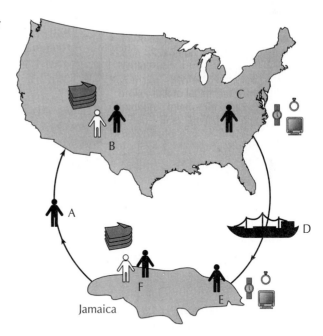

A. Higgler travels to the United States.
B. Gang in the United States provides money to higgler.
C. Higgler buys goods in United States.
D. Goods shipped to Jamaica.
E. Goods sold in Jamaica.
F. Money returned to gang in Jamaica.

*Use of Currency Couriers.*   The Jamaican gangs, as most other criminal organizations, are highly aware of possible problems they face when transporting currency. Jamaican Posse leaders, after a great deal of discussion, came up with the idea of using many couriers carrying lesser amounts of cash to make identification and apprehension a lot less possible. A great deal of the money that travels between New York, Miami, and Washington, D.C. is transported by an emissary in a rental car. Information gathered from police agencies conducting enforcement duties on routes of travel used by Jamaican gang members, to move moneys between New York, Washington, D.C., and Miami, indicate that seizures by local police authorities have taken place. Couriers who were apprehended fit into the following categories:

1.   The amount of money in their possession is usually between $10,000 and $15,000 dollars in U.S. currency, which is considered a small amount that would not hurt a million-dollar drug business.

2.   The sum is considered small by the gang leaders and, therefore, the courier has been told that he or she should not claim ownership of the money.

3.   The person(s) chosen as couriers have a low profile and the same basic characteristics as anyone else traveling the highways of the United States. In some cases, three or four people who have never met before are placed in a vehicle and travel as a "family." The only problem with this type of operation is that if the gang's "family" gets stopped by the police and the police question the alleged family members, none of the group can answer questions about other family members. This situation immediately makes the police highly suspicious of the group (DEA, 1993).

The gang's purpose, in most cases, is to move currency from its nationwide locations to one central site (see Figure 8-7). If U.S. law enforcement organizations manage to stop and seize money from one out of every 20 couriers the whole operation set up by the gang is still a success.

*Use of Automobiles.*   A member of the Posse will purchase a new vehicle at a car dealership. This automobile will be purchased with cash (up to $10,000 in U.S. currency), checks, and financial assistance. This type of buying is done so that the gang can avoid filling out an Internal Revenue Service Form 8300, which must be used when a purchase is paid for in U.S. currency and that payment exceeds $10,000. These cars are then shipped to Jamaica where they are sold on the open market, and the money originally paid out by the gang is refunded to them.

*Use of Barrels.*   In this case, the gang contacts an express shipping company that supplies the gang with one of a variety of types of barrels. The

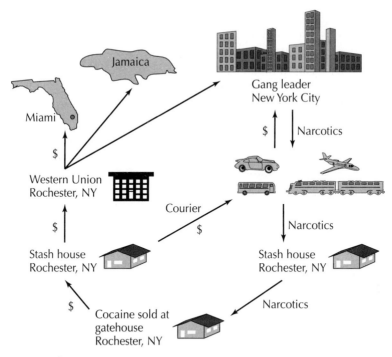

**FIGURE 8-7** Drugs into Currency
*Source:* U.S. Customs Service, 1994.

barrel is filled with money by the gang and returned to the shipper who transports the barrel to any location in Jamaica. These companies are present in most Jamaican neighborhoods throughout the United States and are frequently used by Jamaicans living in the United States to ship items back to their families in Jamaica.

*Use of Express Mail.* The illegally obtained drug money can be moved back to Jamaica by the gangs through the use of overnight Express Mail. The gangs have found this method to be safe as well as cheap.

*Use of Western Union.* Jamaican gangs have discovered that they can easily transfer their money to Jamaica through the use of wire transfer companies. The gangs move their money from one location to another in the United States before finally transferring it to a Jamaican Western Union office. In order to avoid the ever present U.S. government required Currency Transfer Report (CTR) the gangs will transfer amounts that are smaller than $10,000. One gang member may transfer a total of $20,000 in U.S. currency but will take at least three transactions to do so. In such cases, the Western Union office is not required to have the person transferring the money make out a CTR. The only problem is that Western Union records provide police agencies with a paper trail that may ultimately lead to the indictment of gang officials involved in laundering illegally obtained drug money.

*Use of Legitimate Companies.* The Jamaican gangs, after having observed the successes of other organized criminal groups, are investing their unlawfully obtained funds into legitimate companies. Some of these businesses may be used by the gangs to assist them in their illegal narcotics trafficking operations. Major portions of these enterprises are kept free of narcotics trafficking and are used to furnish a way for the gangs to turn illegally obtained funds into legitimate currency.

*Race Track Deceit.* Jamaican gang members have discovered a legitimate way to change a large amount of smaller numbered U.S. currency bills into larger denomination U.S. currency bills. The majority of U.S. race tracks have machines where chits can be purchased for wagering. U.S. bills in smaller denominations ($1, $5, $10, and $20) are placed in the machine and a chit for that amount is returned to the person who entered the money into the machine. A chit can be used to place a bet or can be cashed in with other chits for larger denomination bills at a wagering window at the race track. In many cases, the Posse member purchases chits of all different U.S. currency denominations until all of the drug money in his possession has been changed into chits. These chits are then cashed in for U.S. currency bills in larger amounts ($50 and $100) in order to reduce the quantity of the bills for shipment to Jamaica.

*Use of Banks to Launder Money.* Up until recently, most law enforcement agencies considered it doubtful that Jamaican Posses would ever use banks to launder their money because these gangs were so aware of the money tracing devices used by federal law enforcement. These assumptions have been found to be false. The Jamaican gangs, like all the other organized crime syndicates, are also using banks as a means to launder their money. They move the money through either a few or many bank accounts with the currency concluding its journey when it arrives at a Jamaican bank. Late in 1991, a Jamaican marijuana trafficker placed more than $70,000 into a U.S. bank. Currency transaction reports indicate that Jamaican Posses are depositing money into U.S. savings and loan associations as well as commercial banks. It seems apparent from the number of currency transaction reports, currency or monetary instrument reports, foreign bank and financial accounts reports, and Internal Revenue Form 8300 (Report of cash payments over $10,000) handled by federal investigative agencies, that the Jamaican gangs have become heavily involved in the use of banks to launder their unlawfully obtained funds (Financial Crimes Enforcement Network, 1992).

*Use of Money for Subsistence Expenses.* Information gathered by law enforcement agencies throughout the United States indicates that some Jamaican gang leaders keep large amounts of U.S. currency in their stash houses. It has also been confirmed that in some cases both the gang leaders and their lieutenants spend large sums of money to assure themselves the same lifestyle from day to day. The daily routine of some Jamaican gang members includes a stop at the local race track and the betting of large sums of money without any remunerative return. This behavior seems to indicate that a small number of Jamaican Posse leaders are wagering with what one could consider disposable earnings.

*Counterfeiting.* Like many other ethnic groups, Jamaican Posses have been involved in the production and use of counterfeit U.S. bills. The Jamaicans use forged currency along with legal currency to purchase drugs in what is usually a planned drug scam. These currency reproductions are sold at about 40–50 percent of their real market value. Just about all of the forged money is produced in Jamaica. Forged bills are then transported to the United States by either courier or some other safe and easy transfer method. Most of the participants in these counterfeiting conspiracies are also heavily involved in drug trafficking.

## Other Criminal Activities

### Immigration Fraud

The past decade has seen a sharp increase in the number of illegal Jamaican aliens entering the United States. Illegal Jamaican aliens account for approximately 25 percent of the membership of the Jamaican Posses. U.S. authorities have a difficult task ascertaining the identities of many of these illegal Jamaican immigrants because of their ability to skillfully use counterfeit identification.

Jamaican gangs have skillfully set up several different types of operations to service illegal Jamaican aliens entering or already residing in the United States including:

*Marriage Fraud.* A classic example of a Jamaican marital scam includes an illegal Jamaican immigrant and a U.S. citizen, usually a lawyer with an expertise in immigration law with a gang affiliation. They arrange for another U.S. citizen who will act as the marriage partner, set up the marriage contract, train the pair for their meeting with a U.S. Immigration official, and prepare all the necessary government forms. In most situations, the female partner is supplied by the facilitator/lawyer and paid a fee of $1,000 to

$10,000. The women who become short-term partners in these marriage schemes are either junkies or prostitutes. The facilitators/lawyers who assist the illegal Jamaican immigrants in completing these spurious plots can make a great deal of money in a short period of time. If the facilitator/lawyer is a gang member, proceeds of this scam return to the gang's liquid asset's coffer; if the facilitator/lawyer has an affiliation to the gang a specific fee is paid to this person.

*Document Counterfeiting.* Investigators from the U.S. Immigration and Naturalization Service (INS) have identified eight different Jamaican Posse groups as the generators of a number of counterfeit documents. The major benefit gangs reap from these schemes is that they are conducted in Jamaica, away from any threat of arrest and prosecution that U.S. government investigative agencies may pose. The gangs specialize by producing only one or two types of forged documents, U.S. Virgin Island or Canadian birth certificates. Another gang may generalize and produce many types of forged instruments. The Mavis Anglin Posse produces Jamaican, Canadian, and U.S. passports; Jamaican and U.S. Virgin Island birth certificates, U.S. voter registration cards, U.S. and Canadian military identification, U.S. birth certificates, and many other types of false documentation. This gang was able to gather community support for their unlawful activities by putting some of the profits from their illegal operations back into the community (FinCEN, 1992).

*Green Card Fraud.* Another scam conceived by the Jamaican Posses involves fraudulently acquiring green cards. (These cards are to be carried by immigrants who are legally in the United States awaiting an opportunity to become a legal resident of this country.) This scheme requires a gang member with a legally obtained green card or a gang member who is an illegal alien to pose as the owner of the green card and falsely report to federal authorities that their green card was lost or stolen. Once this report is made to the U.S. Immigration and Naturalization Services, the deceitful gang member obtains a fingerprint card from the legal green card owner and submits an application for a substitute green card. Once the green card is obtained a gang member will acquire all the other legal forms necessary to properly identify him or her as a being a legal immigrant in the United States (state driver's license, social security, etc.). It is also possible to revise the identity on the replacement green card once it is secured from the government (U.S. Customs Service, 1992).

*Other Illegal Ways of Entry into the United States.* Jamaican gangs have conceived other ways of smuggling illegal aliens into the United States. One way the gangs have been successful involves the use of a gang member or gang associate who is a U.S. citizen. This person takes a cruise ship to Jamaica and disembarks upon arrival in Jamaica. The boarding pass is then sold to a designated Jamaican citizen who then takes the ship back to Miami. Once the boarding pass is sold, the U.S. citizen flies back to the United States. An alternative to this scheme involves a gang member passenger, who upon boarding the ship, takes an extra boarding pass and fills it out with all of the required information. Upon arrival in Jamaica, the gang member immediately sells the extra boarding pass to an appointed Jamaican citizen. In many cases, the Jamaican boarding pass purchaser will travel back to the United States with the gang member and they will disembark separately upon the ship's arrival in Miami. U.S Immigration authorities cannot easily identify the duplicate boarding passes unless they are found and a comparison is made. In fact, the possibility of either one of these schemes being discovered during the trip back or immediately after docking is unlikely. It was only after an investigation by the U.S. Immigration Service that this scam was uncovered. The gangs will charge anywhere from $1,000 to $5,000 to any person willing to seek this type of illegal entry into the United States (U.S. Immigration Service, 1992).

## Legitimate Businesses

The Jamaican Posses, like their organized crime counterparts, put their illegally obtained funds into legitimate businesses. Through the use of legitimate businesses the Jamaican gangs make it more difficult for law enforcement agencies to confiscate illegally obtained resources. The Jamaican Posses use family members as well as close acquaintances to purchase both commercial and residential properties, in order to conceal the true property owners. Another method used by the Jamaican gangs to hide their involvement in the acquisition of legal ventures involves the use of both Jamaican and Black American females to purchase land and other types of possessions. Gang members who lease apartments, houses, or cars usually put the lease in the name of a female associate. Some of the Jamaican Posse leaders have made so much money in the drug market that they have built million-dollar houses in Jamaica.

In the United States the Jamaican gangs have managed to reinvest some of their money in restaurants, nightclubs, grocery stores, record stores, boutiques, garages, and car services that are located within a local Jamaican community. Originally, these businesses were supposed to remain legitimate after their purchase but in many cases they become part and parcel of the Jamaican gangs' drug empire after only a brief time. They are used to launder money as well as dispense drugs. The nightclubs are turned into after hours clubs; the restaurants sell food as well as marijuana; the grocery stores sell milk, soda, beer, and crack; and the car services transport drugs and guns that are to be sold or dropped off throughout the area.

## Activities Outside of the United States

The Jamaican gangs have managed to increase their drug activities through working relationships with Nigerian, Dominican, and Asian gangs. These alliances have helped the gangs strengthen their operations throughout North America and Europe.

### Europe

The international connections set up by the Jamaican gangs pose a major threat of increased drug activity throughout Great Britain. Already, in several incidents, the Jamaican gangs have used violent tactics during confrontations with the British police. A few of these events involved the shooting of English police officers. Since these incidents took place British authorities have begun to see an increase in the amount of violence used by Jamaican gangs. The increased Jamaican gang participation in narcotics trafficking stems from the gang's ability to move drugs between the United States and England. Jamaican gangs use the same basic drug smuggling methods in Great Britain as Asian, Nigerian, and Colombian groups use to import illegal drugs into the United States. The drug market in England provides the gang with a considerably greater amount of profit than the U.S. drug marketplace (FinCEN, 1992).

### Canada

The Jamaican Posses have managed to set up subsidiary groups throughout Canada to move money and drugs between the United States and Canada (see Figure 8-8). The gangs in Canada are also involved in the Jamaican gangs' illegal alien smuggling activities. U.S. Immigration Service has gathered information that indicates that many of the drug gatehouse workers are smuggled into the United States from Canada to work in these drug dens (1992). Forged documents are also readily available to illegal Jamaican aliens by the Jamaican Posses. Canadian law enforcement authorities indicate that one of the finest Jamaican document counterfeiters is part of a Jamaican gang in Canada that is producing most of the forged U.S. and Canadian passports (RCMP, 1992).

Subsidiary gangs that have been put in place in Canada are all answerable to the parent groups in the United States. Currency and drugs are con-

| | |
|---|---|
| Bantom Posse | Maryland, New York, and Pennsylvania |
| Barker Organization | Philadelphia, Pennsylvania |
| Brooks Organization | Philadelphia, Pennsylvania |
| Bulbeye Posse | Ontario |
| Bungy Posse | Quebec |
| Cocaine Cowboys | Philadelphia, Pennsylvania |
| Cuban Posse | Pennsylvania and Virginia |
| Delta Force Posse | New Jersey |
| Douglass Organization | Pennsylvania |
| Dunkirk Posse | Pennsylvania |
| Forbes Organization | Philadelphia, Pennsylvania |
| Glanro Posse | Quebec |
| Gulleymen Posse | New York City and Philadelphia, Pennsylvania |
| Hot Steppers Posse | Pennsylvania |
| Jungle Massive | Ontario |
| Jungle Posse | Maryland, New York, and Pennsylvania |
| Lawrence Organization | Philadelphia, Pennsylvania |
| (The) Mob | Philadelphia, Pennsylvania |
| Montego Bay Posse | Pennsylvania |
| Powerhouse Posse | Ontario |
| Red Shirt Massive | Philadelphia, Pennsylvania |
| Reema Posse | New Jersey and Pennsylvania |
| Shower Posse | Maryland, New Jersey, New York, Ohio, and Pennsylvania |
| Solid Gold Posse | New Jersey |
| Spangler Posse | Maryland, New Jersey, New York, Ohio, and Pennsylvania |
| Spanishtown Posse | Pennsylvania |
| Sterling Organization | Philadelphia, Pennsylvania |
| Strikers (Strikas) Posse | Ontario and Pennsylvania |
| (The) Syndicate | Philadelphia, Pennsylvania |
| Tel Aviv Posse | Pennsylvania |
| Tower Hill Posse | Pennsylvania |
| Trinidad Posse | Pennsylvania |
| Uptown Posse | Quebec |
| Waterhouse Posse | New Jersey, New York, Ohio, and Pennsylvania |
| Wet Shirt Massive | Philadelphia, Pennsylvania |

**FIGURE 8-8** Jamaican Organized Crime Groups Currently Operating on East Coast and Canada

veyed between the United States (New York) and Canada (Toronto), with drugs going north and money coming south. In some cases, Western Union is used to transfer money from the United States to Canada, and then the money is sent to its final destination in Jamaica.

Jamaican gangs in Canada sell drugs on two levels. The first involves dealing drugs out of a house where the buyer uses the drug at the location right after its purchase. These types of places are considered smoke houses rather than gatehouses. Presently, no U.S.-type of gatehouses are set up in Canada. A second type of drug dealing involving Jamaican gangs evolves around government housing projects in Canada. Just about all of the Jamaican Posses' participation in street drug sales in Canada is done in the housing project environment. As has been seen in the United States, the Jamaican gangs in Canada have started to move their unlawfully gained profits into legitimate businesses. Some of these ventures remain legitimate while others are used to enhance profits from their illegal activities.

Since the early 1990s, the number of violent incidents involving Jamaican Posses in Canada has increased sharply. As the involvement of the Jamaican gangs in drug dealing has increased so have the battles over the control of certain areas of government housing projects in Toronto. These Canadian housing projects are the main street drug sale locations for the Jamaican gangs, and the battles among the various gangs for this turf have been regular and increasingly violent. Toronto police have found that victims of this gang violence seldom appear in court to sign complaints against gang members. Most victims are bought off by the gang leaders for a few pieces of crack, currency, or a free trip to Jamaica (Mascoll and Pron, 1992).

The gang leaders do not live in the projects that they control. A number of the gang bosses live with what they call "baby mothers" in houses on the outskirts of the projects. The heads of these Posses have 6–12 of these wives who not only serve as mothers for their children but also conceal their drug supplies and money (Mascoll and Pron, 1992).

## NIGERIAN ORGANIZED CRIME

The early 1970s brought a new phenomenon upon the New York banking industry. Banks were suddenly receiving fraudulent loan and credit card applications (see Figure 8-9) with the names and addresses of legitimate university professors. It was later determined that these loans had been submitted by a group of Nigerian students attending universities throughout the New York metropolitan area. A police investigation ascertained that the Nigerian students were obtaining a majority of the information that they used in their criminal enterprises from university yearbooks (IACCI, 1984).

This particular scam was the beginning of what has turned out to be a major organized criminal operation, controlled by several Nigerian organized crime groups. Since the early 1980s Nigerian groups have expanded their illegitimate activities to include several other types of crime including the importation of drugs to the United States and Europe. Drug enforcement officials have also noticed a drastic increase in the amounts of heroin being

The following fraud traits should be considered as alerts and cause for further investigation. Any one trait or combination of traits is an indication of the *possibility* of fraud; however, they should not be considered as absolute without confirmation through additional investigative procedures.

A. *Name*
   1. Unusual name configuration such as two first names, i.e., John N. James, Dennis L. George, etc.
   2. Unusual foreign-sounding names that are difficult or nearly impossible to pronounce, i.e., Oprig/sn Ameolinadunl, etc.
   3. Foreign-sounding first or last name coupled with a common American name, i.e., Richard Ameadonilyme, Oyemeni Miller, etc.
   4. Names of known personalities, i.e., George Burns, Robert Young, George Allen, etc.

B. *Address*
   1. Addresses are usually "drop" numbers and are not kept for long. Consequently, the address is usually not a pertinent trait. At times, an unusually high number of fraudulent applications may be received from certain cities or locales; but, in general, the organized fraud is widespread throughout the country and no particular area should be considered as "safe."
   2. P.O. box at large city—always investigate.

C. *Employment/Salary*
   1. Job title misspelled.
   2. Job title unusual or does not appear to fit type of employment.
   3. Salary appears out of range for type of employment.
   4. Monthly salary includes cents or unusual symbols after base salary.
   5. Years employed don't correlate with age.

D. *Credit References*
   1. Often will look "too good." They know what you are looking for and, at times, "overdo" what usually would be normal for the references given.
   2. Bad account number configurations; approximately 40% of fraudulent applications have bad account numbers. Familiarize yourself with as many configurations as possible, i.e., American Express all begin with 37, Diners with 30 or 38, MasterCard with 5, Visa with 4, etc.

E. *Nearest Relative*
   1. The nearest relative is often shown as a doctor in an attempt for credibility.

F. *Signatures*
   1. Signatures are *usually* scrawled and undecipherable.
   2. Written over as if made a mistake on first try.
   3. Often underscored and angled off signature line.

G. *Miscellaneous*
   1. Use of periods. The Nigerian Group often use periods incorrectly or in unusual places, i.e., after zip code, last name, account numbers, signature, etc.
   2. Use of the letter "Y." The Nigerian Group usually make the "Y" as _____.
   3. Fraudulent applications in general are usually printed, a few handwritten, but, to date, very few have been typed.
   4. Most of the Nigerian Group we have talked with speak very broken English.
   5. Unusual abbreviations, i.e., Street = Str., Company = Com., Avenue = Aven., etc.

**FIGURE 8-9** Traits of Fraudulent Applications

*Source:* NYPD, 1991.

smuggled into the United States by Nigerian groups. The number of seizures from Nigerian drug smugglers has increased more than a hundred-fold since early 1980 when law enforcement made a total of two arrests.

## Historical Overview

Nigeria is located on the west coast of Africa and is approximately twice the size of the state of California. It consists of 19 states and 1 territory. This area encompasses about 554,262 square miles and is bordered by the countries of Benin, Chad, Niger, and Cameroon. Nigeria's coastline extends approximately 511 miles on the Gulf of Guinea. The natural resources of Nigeria include crude oil, tin, columbite, iron ore, coal, limestone, lead, zinc, and natural gas (U.S. Dept. of State, 1992).

The population of Nigeria was estimated at 115.5 million in 1990, making it the most populated country in Africa, with nearly one-quarter of the continent's population. The majority of these people are members of 250 tribes that are broken into four groups. The major northern tribes are the Housa (21%) and Fulani (9%), while the Yoruba (20%) tribe resides in the southwest and the Ibos (50%) reside in the southeast. Even though English is the official language of Nigeria, an extensive spectrum of tribal languages consists of 141 dialects throughout the country. The religious makeup is approximately 50 percent Muslim, 40 percent Catholic, and 10 percent unknown. The literacy rate in Nigeria is somewhere between 25 and 30 percent (U.S. Dept. of State, 1992).

Native witchcraft also has a strong influence on Nigerian superstitions and beliefs. The majority of the Nigerian population live in what can be considered an impoverished environment with an average annual income of $700 and a life expectancy of 50 years. In addition, the Nigerian population has experienced a high incidence rate of HIV.

As previously mentioned, the official language of Nigeria is English, which is the result of British influence in that country dating back to the mid 1780s. In 1914, Nigeria was formally united as a British colony and remained that way until October 1, 1960, when she was granted independence. The Nigerian constitution was adopted on October 1, 1979, and further amended on February 9, 1984. The present military government banned all political parties in December 1983. This military system of administration had originally promised that a national election for president would take place in the year 1992 (U.S. Dept. of State, 1992). An election finally took place in 1993 and Moshood K. O. Abiola was elected president of Nigeria. Mr. Abiola's tenure as president was short because he was imprisoned by the military rulers soon after the election. These same corrupt military leaders have run this country since freedom from British rule was gained by Nigeria in 1960 (U.S. Dept. of State, 1992).

The economy of Nigeria shifted in the early 1970s from one of agriculture to one that now relies on oil for 95 percent of export earnings and for 70 percent of the federal budget resources. This focus also resulted in a mass migration in the population from agriculture to industry workers.

The oil boom of the late 1970s and early 1980s increased the opportunity for people to obtain a higher financial position in Nigeria but helped to "erode traditional Nigerian moral values and ethics" (Penn, 1985: 1). According to Larry Diamond, a specialist in Nigerian culture, the oil boom "generated staggering corruption. Public servants became wealthy, basically through white collar crime," with these corrupt officials becoming "role models" for a countless number of Nigerian students (Penn, 1985: 1). The never-ending corruption in Nigeria is a contributing factor in the success of most criminal activities within and without the country. The desire for bribes (known as "dash" in Nigeria) is open and bribes are solicited by corrupt officials at all levels of government. Nigeria, a country with an abundant amount of oil resources, has gone from what most economic analysts regard as a middle income nation to one of Africa's poorest countries, because its oil-producing industry is still not efficiently productive.

## Organizational Structure

Nigerian organized crime groups are still somewhat loosely knit and, as of yet, not really comparable to the established La Cosa Nostra organized crime families in the United States (Magloclen, 1990). Most traditional Italian organized crime families in the United States control a considerable number of criminal activities in a specific geographical area. In contrast, any referral to the makeup of Nigerian organized crime groups is far more connected to the structure and its network and not actually connected with any definitive territorial area of control (see Figure 8-10).

The Nigerian criminal systems can be compared to an octopus with its head (body) located in the African home base, specifically Nigeria, and the tentacles reaching to other important areas in Asia and the Far East to Europe in the north and the United States (Figure 8-11) and Canada in the northwest. New tentacles have recently emerged to the west in South America, specifically Colombia, in a quest to increase Nigerian control over the cocaine network throughout Africa and Europe.

The leader of a Nigerian criminal group is known as the *baron* (see Figure 8-12). He is the person who is more than qualified to make an investment in a criminal operation. Transactions usually involve the pur-

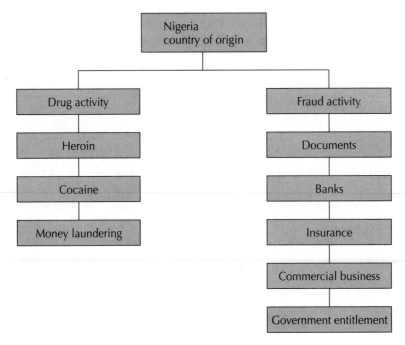

**FIGURE 8-10** Nigerian Organized Crime
*Source:* FBI, 1996.

**FIGURE 8-11** Cities with Large Nigerian Populations

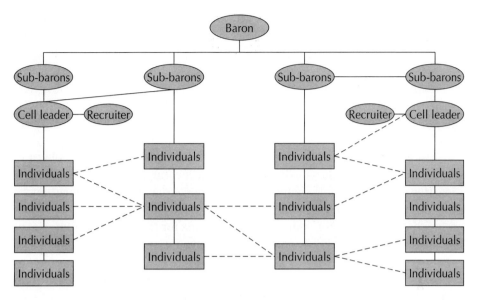

**FIGURE 8-12**  Typical Nigerian Criminal Organization
*Source:* FBI, 1996.

chase and transport of drugs out of the Far East in bulk into Nigeria for further cutting of the heroin. It is then repackaged for distribution to the African, European, and American markets. A baron provides the collateral for subbarons or captains to commence the purchase of heroin in either southeast or southwest Asia. Once the procured drug consignment arrives in Nigeria it is prepared for shipment or sold in bulk to a group of subbarons. They then receive profit once the drug is distributed to the gangs' major market places.

In this sense a strong disparity is obvious between Nigerian and American organized crime. Most of the barons encourage their mid-level employees to go out on their own, which helps establish a broader base for the leader's supply of drugs. Any type of individual effort by members of the La Cosa Nostra would probably result in that individual's death, especially if it occurred in what is considered the traditional U.S. organized crime structure. Because a La Cosa Nostra crime boss, or family capo (which are positions that can be considered comparable to the Nigerian gang leader or baron), would more than likely control access to the retail market within his territory, he would, without a doubt, never tolerate any individual enterprise by his subordinates. The Nigerian baron does not have that advantage because the activities of the gang members are worldwide and difficult to oversee. Consequently, the baron concedes that an underling who decides to go out on his own can broaden the baron's markets and increase profits by encouraging mid-level subordinates to branch out. Nigerian organized crime families, in some respects, closely resemble the corporations that distribute their products through sales and promotion in the United States. It is similar to companies that inspire mid-level employees to establish their own networks to supply. This kind of operation expands the base of distribution for the product with the demand and profit continuing all the way to the main source of the product, the corporation.

Just about every Nigerian organized crime group is divided into cells, and the members of the cells usually participate in several different criminal activities. It is entirely possible that a Nigerian criminal may be involved with more than one gang and in some instances may operate as a singular entity, especially an individual who creates counterfeit documents for the gangs. A great deal of interaction takes place between the different groups and their cells. The gangs exchange knowledge related to their banking and credit schemes, corrupt contacts in both the public and private sector, mail drops, and any other information that may be relevant to their operations (Magloclen, 1991).

Figure 8-13 is a list of indicators common among Nigerian organized crime groups. A majority of the members of this highly organized crime group have an above average education. One thing that is highly unusual about the Nigerian gangs has been their ability to avoid internal conflict. Thus far, little or no internal resentfulness, strife, or violent confrontations between members have characterized Nigerian criminal organizations. It is

---

Indicators of an organized criminal group:

- Nonideological
- Hierarchical
- Has limited or exclusive membership
- Perpetuitous
- Uses violence and bribery
- Demonstrates specialization and division of labor
- Governed by explicit rules and regulations
- Monopolistic

Criminologists define an organized criminal group as a secret, exclusive society with its own rules and regulations. These groups have been studied by sociologists and psychologists for decades.

---

**FIGURE 8-13** Nigerian Organized Crime
*Source:* FBI, 1996.

apparent that Nigerian groups go out of their way to work with each other. Law enforcement sources have identified several instances where Nigerian groups in the United States and Africa have sent stolen credit cards in overnight mail to gang associates in Europe so that the cards can be used for several more days. European police have recently uncovered a scam involving Nigerian gang members who pilfer credit cards from the Nigerian postal service. Then over a period of three days to a week gang members fly all over Africa and Europe purchasing items costing up to $1,500 from airline gift catalogs. (The limit for the amount of purchases that can be made on an airline without verification of the card is $1,500.) Once the member disembarks from the plane the card and the items puchased are handed off to other gang members who proceed to either reuse the card on another flight and/or transport property purchased to a safe house. The use of a credit card on airlines continues until at least $10,000 is run up on the card (Europol, 1996).

Since the early 1970s, the number of criminal activities involving members of the Nigerian community in the United States has sharply increased. Nigerian groups originally participated in several different types of banking and government frauds. The majority of their fraudulent activities involved the swindling of currency from financial institutions. Some of their most popular schemes involve making false insurance claims through the use of crime reports; purchasing autos and other valuable items with a legitimate down payment but using false credit sources; establishing phony credit accounts at large major department stores and purchasing expensive items; opening fraudulent checking and credit card accounts; creating life insurance policies for bogus relatives and then presenting false documents to verify their deaths; and using false identification to participate in schemes that bilk government agencies of large sums of money (Harris County Sheriffs Dept., 1986; Penn, 1985; and IACCI, 1984).

The ability of the Nigerian criminal element to obtain fraudulent documents has expanded its participation in illegal activities. Individuals involved in these schemes have no problems obtaining unlimited counterfeit Nigerian passports. Once they arrive in the United States they proceed to make the right contacts to obtain the necessary fraudulent U.S. or state government documents. Obtaining forged Social Security, nondriver identification, and insurance cards poses no major inconvenience to these groups. Investigators have uncovered, on several different occasions, that these suspects have at least a dozen different driver and nondriver identification cards that contain the same suspect's photo on the front (Duga and Balsamini, 1990).

## Involvement in Fraudulent Schemes

Early Nigerian Gang Scams

A raid by federal agents on a Brooklyn, New York, apartment in 1982 turned up four Nigerian students who had fraudulently obtained more than $100,000 in federal student loans (Agres and Seper, 1986). In 1985 evidence was presented in the *Wall Street Journal* that 35 percent of all student loan frauds since 1979 were perpetrated by Nigerian students (Penn, 1985). J.C. Penny discovered that in 1983 six Nigerians, all using the same address, submitted more than 400 credit card applications using fabricated credentials (Penn, 1985). The ability of the Nigerian gangs to manipulate the credit card companies becomes even more apparent when the gang uses credit cards to fraudulently obtain new high-priced, high-profile vehicles. In fact, a New York City police department investigation into a Nigerian gang operating out of Park Hill Avenue in the Staten Island section of New York City turned up 30 vehicles that had been fraudulently obtained by gang members (Duga and Balsamini, 1990). It was estimated in 1985 that Nigerian crime groups were becoming more and more responsible for the ever-increasing amount (1,200 percent increase in eight years) of credit cards rip-offs since 1977 (Duga and Balsamini, 1990; Agres and Seper, 1986; and Penn, 1985). A principal U.S. banking agency recently issued an investigative report that places the amount of money swindled from U.S. businessmen by the Nigerian gangs at $1 billion a year. This report also pronounced that 75,000 of the 100,000 Nigerians living on the U.S. East Coast are actively participating in the gangs' fraudulent activities (*South China Morning Post,* 1992).

Many of these criminal groups are comprised of illegal aliens from Nigeria, but U.S. Immigration investigators have confirmed intelligence reports that verify the fact that a small portion of the members of these groups are from Liberia and Ghana (U.S. Immigration and Naturalization, 1990; and Duga and Balsamini, 1990). Federal law enforcement agencies have also been able to substantiate the fact that the people involved in these frauds have attended and graduated from crime training schools in Nigeria or have been trained in the United States by Nigerians with expertise in fraudulent crimes (Duga and Balsamini, 1990; Agres and Seper, 1986; Penn, 1985; Cohon, 1985; Harris County Sheriff's Dept., 1986; and IACCI, 1984).

Welfare Fraud

A short time after a Nigerian gang member arrives in the United States, he or she is introduced to the U.S. welfare system. The ability of Nigerians to speak English fluently and their knowledge of the American culture make it fairly easy to participate illegally in the welfare system. A Nigerian gang member usually enters the United States legally with either a visitor or student visa. The gang member acquires fraudulent identification documents that identify him or her as being born in the U.S. Virgin Islands, which entitles the gang member the right to apply for welfare. Within a short period of time, the gang member is on the public assistance rolls. Once this status is obtained most gang members get jobs driving gypsy cabs that are owned by members of the gang using a different set of forged credentials. Private vehicles are used as gypsy cabs, and the Nigerian gang members usually rent a car (using a fraudulently obtained credit card), and then put gypsy cab plates from another vehicle on the car. The gang member runs his or her fraudulent activities while maintaining his or her job driving a taxi cab. Most Nigerians, because of their ability to speak English, are easily assimilated into most black communities in the United States. It is, therefore, easy for them to work in these communities as well as live in them.

## Student Loans

In the early 1980s Nigerian gangs arrived on U.S. shores under the guise of being foreign students. Once these alleged students prepared to settle in at a local university they realized that money could be made by applying for and being awarded guaranteed student loans or Pell Grants. It was not long before these students (gang members) were creating fraudulent identification documents and submitting them in order to gain entrance into that university. Upon gaining admission to said university the gang member would go to a loan institution with the letter of acceptance and the forged identification documents and apply for a student loan. In a short period of time the bank would approve the loan and forward the check to the gang member who never intended to attend the university nor repay the loan.

Federal investigations into student loan fraud have shown that in some cases Nigerian "students" have submitted several different fraudulent identifications and letters of acceptances at many different universities in order to obtain multiple student loans from the banks at the same time. One Nigerian "student" in Baltimore had managed to accrue 15 different loan accounts at three different universities. At the time of his arrest he had collected $28,000 of the $42,000 that he had submitted for on the student loans. In another case, a Nigerian student using an assortment of forged credentials collected a total of $36,000 in student loans while enrolled in three different colleges in Alabama and one in Maryland (Senate Permanent Subcommittee on Investigations, 1991).

## Insurance Fraud

Nigerian criminals have managed to become experts in the area of insurance fraud. The Nigerian groups have developed skills that assist them in submitting fraudulent personal injury, car theft, death, property damage, and loss claims. Once again, the gang's ability to produce numerous fraudulent documents makes it easy for one gang member to participate in numerous insurance scams at one time. Some insurance claims are submitted for property theft of merchandise recently purchased with a stolen or fraudulently obtained credit card. The property allegedly stolen is identified by a sales draft and once the claim is submitted the gang member ships the appliance to Nigeria where it can be sold for four to five times the purchase price on the black market. This scam is interesting considering that no one ever paid for the appliance. A fraudulent credit card was used, a false insurance claim was made and the item will be sold for four to five times its actual value in another country. Another scam involves the use of a fraudulent credit card to buy a vehicle. The auto is purchased within a short period time after the gang member receives the credit card. Within a month the auto is shipped to Nigeria where it will be sold for several times its value. Shortly after being transported the vehicle is reported stolen to the police and a U.S. insurance company. In May of 1991, U.S. Customs Service agents seized 40 recently purchased new vehicles at J.F.K Airport prior to being shipped to Nigeria.

The ever-increasing proficiency of the Nigerian gang members involved in insurance scams is evident from the prosperity they have procured from their activity in staged accident schemes. The gangs participate in several major scams that evolve around staged vehicular accidents. One type of scheme requires a Nigerian gang member to have multiple insurance policies on his car. A short time after all of the policies become effective a claim is filed by the insured stating that an unidentified vehicle caused damage to the Nigerian's auto by forcing it off of the road. Appointments for the insurer's appraisal are made, estimates on repair costs are then evaluated along with the damage to the vehicle and each insurance company, unaware of the other policies, makes what is considered an equitable payment to the insured party. Insurance companies are also unaware that in a majority of these cases the Nigerian gang member either buys a vehicle that is already damaged or intentionally damages the auto prior to making an insurance claim.

Another type of preplanned accident scam involves the use of two vehicles. Vehicles owned by the group, usually containing three or four gang members in each vehicle, collide at a prearranged location. Police respond to the scene, one of the drivers claims the accident was all his fault, and both the drivers and passengers claim personal injuries. A police report is prepared containing all the facts surrounding the accident. Each of the participants in this accident visits a doctor, obtains a diagnosis of an injury sustained in the accident, and then proceeds to hire an attorney. The doctor submits a bill and medical report to the insurance company confirming that the accident has debilitated the victim and that the victim is unable to work at this time. Once all of this information is evaluated the insurance company will make an out-of-court settlement that is equitable to all parties.

An additional deviation from the first two types of staged accidents involves the use of counterfeit documents. Usually two or more Nigerian gang members set up a paper trail that revolves around a bogus vehicular accident. This claim, when filed with an insurance company, contains all of the necessary information concerning vehicles, drivers, passengers, statements of witnesses, and extent of injuries to those in the involved vehicles. This type of conspiracy seldom has any type of police report or documentation of medical assistance being rendered at the scene. A necessary degree of integrity is added to this scam through the use of doctors who verify "injuries," and attorneys who set up civil suits. The possibility that the doctors and lawyers treating and defending the gang members are part and parcel of this criminal operation is likely. Once again, to avoid complications, the start of court proceedings can almost assure the claimant that the insurance company will come to a monetary settlement that is equitable to both parties.

A life insurance policy scheme requires that a gang member apply for a life insurance policy using phony identification with another gang member named as the beneficiary. In many cases, a number of policies are applied for in a short period of time using the same identification and usually include an accidental death or double indemnity clause. Several months after the life insurance policies become effective a death claim is filed by the heir. In this death claim, the beneficiary indicates that the insured died in an accident while on either a business trip or vacation in Nigeria. The insurance company is supplied with a death certificate, burial certificate, a newspaper obituary report, a police report of the accident, funeral bills, and in some cases, a newspaper report of the accident. Due to the fact that most insurance companies have neither the capabilities nor the facilities to properly investigate or refute the evidence produced by members of the Nigerian gangs, either a deal is made on the amount of payment or the claims are paid in full by the company. This scheme has been so successful that members of Nigerian crime groups have put together what they call a "death kit." A Nigerian death kit comes equipped with necessary instructions and copies of the fraudulent credentials that will be required in order to perpetrate the scam.

## Bank Fraud

The average Nigerian gang member is a resourceful con artist who has the ability and knowledge to pilfer currency from U.S. banks through the use of what can be considered unsophisticated check and loan scams (see Figures 8-14 and 8-15). The three major characteristics involved in these swindles include the following:

1.  The individual opens a bank checking account using counterfeit identification. In almost every case, a hundred dollars is deposited in the account.

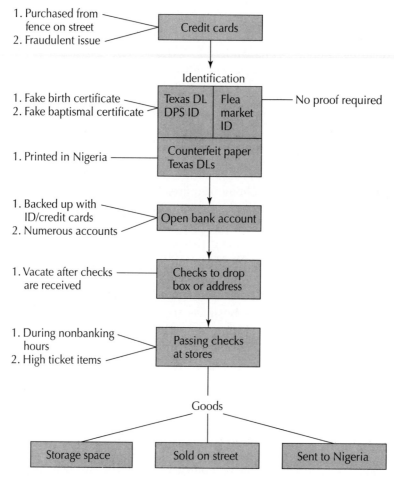

**FIGURE 8-14**   Nigerian Check Scheme
*Source:* FBI, 1996.

CHAPTER 8

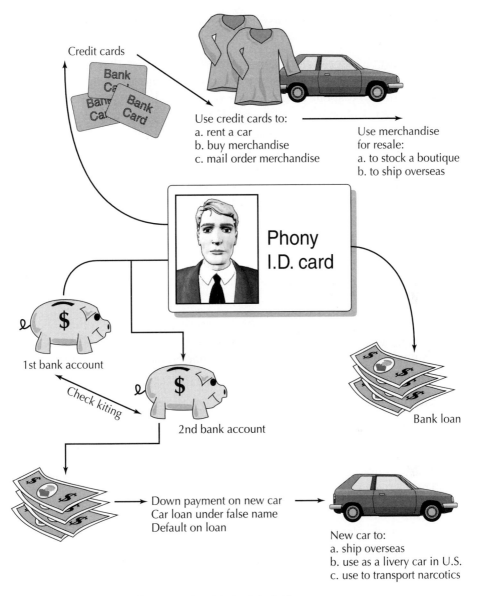

Credit cards

Use credit cards to:
a. rent a car
b. buy merchandise
c. mail order merchandise

Use merchandise
for resale:
a. to stock a boutique
b. to ship overseas

Phony
I.D. card

1st bank account

Check kiting

2nd bank account

Bank loan

Down payment on new car
Car loan under false name
Default on loan

New car to:
a. ship overseas
b. use as a livery car in U.S.
c. use to transport narcotics

**FIGURE 8-15** Using a Phony I.D. for Criminal Activities
*Source: Staten Island Advance,* 1990, p. 7.

2.  The initial deposit is followed up with the deposit of two checks from an out-of-town bank, which are made out to the person who opened the checking account. Within a short period of time, these checks will be identified as written on bogus checking accounts or drawn on closed ac-

counts or accounts that have insufficient funds to cover the amount of the check.

3.  The gang member reviews the account to make sure that the checks deposited have cleared through the bank. The money placed in this account must be spent as quickly as possible. The ultimate result is that the gang member will go out on a Friday and write as many checks as possible until Monday morning. They know that the stores cannot check the balance in a checking account over a weekend. The checks will then come back to the bank and the bank is responsible for these checks. It soon becomes apparent to the bank that all of the identification presented to the bank was counterfeit (Duga and Balsamini, 1990).

### Credit Card Fraud

The Nigerian gang members are also well versed on credit card scams. Nigerian credit card scams are skillfully planned and easily perpetrated by the gangs in several ways:

1.  The individual obtains legitimate employment as either a member of a security force or as a health care worker in order to gain personnel data on people who work for the company that employs the gang member.

2.  The gang member then sets up a credit line using the information that was obtained illegally.

3.  Fraudulent identification documents are prepared for a gang member who has a thorough understanding of U.S. culture and banking practices.

4.  A temporary change of address is filed through the U.S. Postal Service. The new address is usually a mail drop that is run by a private company.

5.  A gang member then starts ordering credit cards in the name of one of the company employees whose personnel records were illegally reviewed.

6.  The mail is inspected by a gang member until all of the credit cards arrive at the phony address and then the U.S. Postal Service is notified to deliver all of the mail to the original address.

7.  The gang member then proceeds to go on a buying spree using all of the illegally acquired credit cards.

In most cases, this type of scam is not discovered until the victim receives the bills in the mail or when a collection agency employee appears at the victim's door and informs the victim of the unpaid credit card bills. The gang member who perpetrated this crime is long gone as are the illegally obtained credit cards. In many cases, the property that was secured is on its way to Nigeria.

The majority of the Nigerian aliens involved in committing these fraudulent criminal acts credit most of their success to some or all of the underlying components:

1. The creation and availability of counterfeit identification translates into many financial benefits through the use of phony checking accounts, credit cards, and loan applications.

2. By avoiding avaricious practices, these groups advance their criminal activities through numerous smaller swindles rather than one big rip-off. The use of many minor scams takes advantage of the numerous loopholes within the U.S. economic system and avoids any lengthy punishment by the criminal justice system if apprehended.

3. Through family allegiance, Nigerian organizations are established on the abilities of their lower-level workers. Nigerian criminal groups are both well organized and structured family factions where everyone is someone else's cousin.

4. Training schools in Nigeria successfully tutor people to adapt to the American culture and how to run schemes that will defraud the American public. These schools inform their pupils on what is the most esteemed identification to obtain, how to acquire these credentials, and how to best utilize these documents in obtaining money and merchandise after the students arrive in the United States. Federal agents recently raided a church in Brooklyn, New York, and arrested 14 gang members for conspiracy to commit bank fraud and illegally obtain welfare or social security benefits. The church was being used as a school to train Nigerian gang members on how to participate in various fraudulent schemes and obtain forged documents (Duga and Balsamini, 1990).

5. The accessibility of gang members as contacts for colleagues newly arrived from Nigeria is highly effective in assisting the new gang member in obtaining all the documents necessary for this immigrant to become a participant in the illegal activities of the group of which he or she is a member (Duga and Balsamini, 1990; and U.S. Customs Service, 1989).

Recent Nigerian Gang Scams

As early as 1990, Nigerian gang members were instituting new con schemes to lure money away from greedy businesspeople. One such scam involves the alleged finding of large sums of money ($10–$50 million in U.S. currency) by a government employee, owed by the Nigerian government to several corporations throughout the world. The Nigerian government worker sends a letter or letters out to English and American businessmen, soliciting their help to obtain these funds by defrauding the Bank of Nigeria. In these letters the Nigerian employee suggests that he will have no problem modifying both bank and government documents so that the money will be conveyed to this businessperson. The victim is informed that the Nigerian worker needs the victim's foreign bank account to transfer the funds and that the victim will be rewarded with 30 to 40 percent of the total amount extricated from the Bank of Nigeria, which will be left in the victim's bank account as a payment for cooperation.

Once this businessperson joins in this venture, he is informed that blank invoices and business letterhead must be forwarded to the contact in Nigeria. The victim is assured that this step is necessary in order to make his corporation appear as the legitimate legatee of these funds. After a period of several months, during which a continual interchange of letters, phone calls, and faxes occurs between the Nigerian worker and the victim, the victim finally receives a phony fax message or telegram that is allegedly from the Bankers Trust Company. This message informs the victim that the time has come for the Bank of Nigeria to transfer the money to his business account. In many cases, this notification to the businessperson comes on a Friday and the victim waits patiently until Monday. When the money does not arrive a phone call is made to the Nigerian worker. At this point the worker informs the victim that it is necessary for him to pay a standard Nigerian foreign exchange tax of 2.5 percent before the money can be forwarded to him. The businessperson, figuring that he is going to receive millions of dollars, forwards by wire transfer the 2.5 percent, or whatever that amount may be, in currency to the worker. Needless to say, that is both the last time the victim ever hears from his contact in Nigeria or sees his money (Duga and Balsamini, 1990).

An off-shoot of this scheme involves contacting an American or European businessperson by sending him or her what appears to be an authentic business letter requesting his or her assistance in administering a multimillion dollar fund. The person who receives the letter is also informed that he or she will receive a percentage of the total sum of the account plus remuneration for taking care of the fund (see Figure 8-16).

One example of this scheme involved the chief executive officer of a Virginia-based corporation who was contacted by several members of a Nigerian group to participate in this scam. A short time after he received the letter from Nigeria concerning a $28.5 million fund this person was asked to forward a deceptive statement to the Nigerian government for $18.5 million and also to send a check for $715,000 to take care of expenses until the

DR. BLESSING JONAH
NO. 4 HASSAN IDOWU STREET
OFF SANYA ROAD
AGUDA SURULERE
LAGOS – NIGERIA

12th OCTOBER, 1991.

ATTN: THE PRESIDENT

FIRST CARD SERVICES
60 CHIARLES LINDBERGH BLVD
UVONDALE, NY 11553 U.S.A.

Dear Sir,

I am the special assistant to the Chief Accountant of Federal Ministry of Aviation and got your particulars through one of your numerous customers. Your customer gave good recommendation of you hence my writing you. I write to intimate you of an opportunity I would like to utilize.

A contract was awarded by ny Ministry for the supply of Aviation equipments to our New Federal Capital (Abuja) and Kaduna. This contract was over inflated to the tune of $30.M (Thirty Million US Dollars) to favour the Chairman of the contract Approval Board and other top government functioneries. Now that our government is changing from Military to Civilain rule, I myself and other top officers are interested in politics. With this our mind, we have vital documents that will enable us transfer US $30.M to any incorporation account Overseas. After the transfer for the money, we will resign from our job and go straight into partical politics– The money realised from the transaction will help us in our political campagns.

It is in this regard I am writing you to assist us so that the money will be paid into your account. The mode of sharing is 35% for you as the account owner, 55% for us while 10% is reserved for miscellaneous expenses.

If this proposal satisfies you, please forward to me without delay the following data and documents:–

(1) Company's bank account number an Address of the Bank.
(2) Three copies of BLANK SIGNED AND STAMPED company's Proforma invoice.
(3) Three copies of BLANK signed and stamped company's letter headed papers.
(4) Personal telex number, Fax and Telephone –numbers.

The blank signed and stamped invoices and letter heading will be used in describing the nature of work done and writingl letter of claims respectively. The documents will then be forwarded to the Ministry where our men who are aware of the transaction will approve the payments. The money, enters the account all the parttis involved will come to your country for our shares after which the documents used in the transaction will be destroyed. Also reply and inform us in time whereby you are not interested.

Please treat as ver y urgent ans confidential. Reply through DHL or call on me through any of the above telecommunication means. The business is 100% risk free.

Thanks for your anticipated co-operation.

Yours faithfully,


BLESSING JONAH (DR.)

**Figure 8-16**   Scam Letter 1
*Source:* Grennan, 1991.

government finally released the money in the fund. The victim quickly fulfilled both requests. Solicitations for money to pay advance fees for this fund from the Nigerian gang members continued as did the money being sent to them by this victim. In 1993, the victim, who paid out $4.4 million to these Nigerian gang members, and the company $1 million in arrears due to his involvement in this scam, informed the F.B.I. of what had happened to him. Ultimately, the U.S. Department of Justice handed down indictments on the three Nigerian gang members involved in this scam but, as of yet, no apprehensions have been made by federal authorities (*Newsweek*, 1994).

In almost every case, the victim of this type of crime will receive a letter, telex or fax from a person who claims to be a Nigerian prince, doctor, government dignitary, or notable businessperson who will pay the victim a large fee if he will help the Nigerian citizen secure a multimillion dollar fund from the Nigerian government. It is not only businesspeople who are contacted, however, but any person or organization the Nigerian gangs feel is susceptible to greed. It can also include religious as well as benevolent groups who are approached, in most cases, by a person who presents himself as emissary of an affluent patron.

A sinister spin-off of this scheme concentrates on prior victims of these Nigerian scams. These victims are contacted and informed that they will be compensated for their monetary losses by the Nigerian government's "Presidential Task Force of Debt Repayment." The victim is informed that this repayment can be accomplished by forwarding all financial data, including bank account numbers and signatures, to the Nigerian person who forwarded this information within 48 hours or the offer will be nullified. This information, when made available to a Nigerian gang member, is as good as a certified check made out to this criminal group. Once this information is in the hands of the swindler, he can easily forge the victim's signature and move money to gang accounts, and the target of this crime is victimized a second time.

Members of these criminal organizations are not only proficient in speaking and writing the English language but they also have available to them a plentiful number of counterfeit government documents. Gang members involved in these schemes even go as far as listing addresses and telephone numbers where the victim can contact them. In some cases, they even invite the target to Nigeria in order to build the victim's confidence, and hopefully entice him to participate in this scheme (*Newsweek*, 1994).

Placement of a conspirator inside a stock or trading company has helped the Nigerian gangs create another new scam. This scheme involves rerouting to a gang member a company check specified for one of the company's vendors. A mutual fund money market account is opened using the name of a gang member and within a short period of time the gang member has fund checks mailed to checking accounts with disparate identities in a number of banking facilities throughout the area. Once the checks have cleared they are cashed as quickly as possible but, in most cases, in a way that will arouse as little suspicion as possible. All the steps involved in creating and working this scheme evolve around the length of time it will take the stock or trading company to realize that the check has not been sent to the vendor. The conspirator, who was employed by the company, leaves his position a short time after the vendor checks were mailed to coconspirators. Like all the other gang members involved in running scams this person used forged documents to identify himself to this employer, and it is doubtful that his identity will ever be ascertained by investigators.

ATM machines that make it possible for people to get cash advances at an ATM location through the use of a credit card have made the theft of credit far more lucrative to the Nigerian gangs. Members of the Nigerian gangs have found it much easier to go to an ATM machine prior to midnight and withdraw the amount allocated for each card holder on a daily basis (usually $500) and then right after midnight make another withdrawal for the same amount. Illegally obtaining funds from ATM machines is a whole lot easier for the gangs than obtaining appliances and other goods and selling these items at a tangible discount or shipping the items to Nigeria and waiting a long period of time prior to finally being reimbursed for their illegal activities.

The participation of Nigerian gang members in what is known as visa scams has increased dramatically since early 1990. These unlawful operations involve a written solicitation to the president of either a British, American, or European company to come or to send a high-ranking official of the firm to Nigeria and participate in what a businessperson would perceive as a tantalizing business proposal. This business executive is informed that the Nigerian government wants to buy some of the corporation's merchandise. It is further indicated that an agreement with the Nigerian government could be reached immediately or as soon as the businessperson arrives in Nigeria. The invitation also informs the executive that a visa is not required because the contact can get him through immigration and customs without a visa. All the information the business executive receives is supported by documents containing the letterhead of the Nigerian Defense Ministry or the Nigerian Petroleum Corporation. These letters also suggest that a high-ranking official of the corporation visit Nigeria as soon as possible to show the Nigerian government that this company is interested in obtaining the contract. The corporation makes a commitment and informs the contact that a company executive will be leaving for Nigeria. Upon the arrival of this high-ranking company official in Nigeria, he is immediately rushed through immigration and customs and then taken to a remote residence outside of Lagos (Noble, 1992).

A short time after the business executive's arrival, this person is informed by his original contact(s) that he is no longer free to leave and that the only way out of this predicament is to pay an ample amount of ransom money or for him and/or his corporation to partake with his kidnappers in an unlawful act, possibly illegally laundering money for this gang. The gang members emphasize the fact that the executive can be arrested and prosecuted because he does not have a visa stamp on his passport and the only way out is to pay or participate in the scheme (Noble, 1992).

The outcome of some of these schemes indicates that Nigerian gangs may be prone to violence. In July 1991, David Rollings, a British businessman, traveled to Lagos in an attempt to recover $4 million that had been previously defrauded from a fellow British business official. A short time after Mr. Rollings arrival he was found shot to death in his hotel room (*Newsweek,* 1994). Within the same year, Gerald Scruggs, a U.S. businessman who was under the impression that he was a participant in a authorized business venture was murdered by some of the Nigerian gang members who initiated the scam. Scruggs was first "garroted" with an auto tire and then burned to death outside of the Sheraton Hotel in suburban Lagos after he refused to continue participating with Nigerian gang members (*Newsweek,* 1994).

One other type of fraud that has been established by the Nigerian gangs involves contacting corporate executives who have been doing business in Nigeria. The executive receives a proposition for the purchase, at a discount price, of a tanker full of oil worth a million dollars. He is informed that this oil exceeds the amount of oil that Nigeria, as an OPEC nation, is allowed to produce and once a surplus of oil is deemed in excess of an OPEC designated amount it can be sold at a cheaper price on the open market. Once an agreement is made all of the necessary papers are forwarded on bogus Nigerian National Petroleum Corporation (NNPC) letterhead or from communication terminals "on the tanker" confirming the particulars of this transaction (see Figure 8-17). The gang con artist then requests the sum of $250,000 to offset the costs of licenses, taxes, and port duties. A victim then forwards this money, in good faith, to his contact. A short time after the transaction is completed the victim contacts the oil company in an effort to obtain the oil shipment. He is then informed that the deal is phony and that the oil cargo belongs to either the Nigerian government or some major petroleum company. It is also conceivable that this oil has already been removed from the vessel. It has been established by the Nigerian government that in most of these schemes several different victims usually claim ownership of the petroleum (Vick, 1992).

```
FROM THE DESK OF:
DR. BASIL ONUOHA
NIGERIAN NATIONAL PETROLEUM CORPORATION
CHAIRMAN: CONTRACT REVIEW COMMITTEE
FALOMO OFFICE COMPLEX, LAGOS –NIGERIA.        TEL/FAX:234–1–820123
                                              FAX: 234–90–405621
                                              TEL/FAX: 234–1–5891200
                                              LAGOS – NIGERIA

                                              4th SEPTEMBER, 1996.
```

STRICTLY CONFIDENTIAL

Dear Sir,

Your esteem particulars was given to me by a valid associate of yours in neighborhood who assured me of your ability and reliability to champion the course of this business transaction requiring maximum confidence.

I am an accountant and a member of "Tender Committee Board" with Nigerian National Petroleum Corporation (NNPC).

We have thirty million U.S. dollars only (US$30,000,000.00) which we got from over inflated contracts from crude oil contract awarded to some foreign contractors in the Nigerian National Petroleum Corporation. We are seeking for your assistance and permission to remit this amount into your account because as civil servants (government workers) the Code of Conduct Bureau made it an offence for us to own or operate a foreign account.

Mode of sharing: It has been agreed upon by all the officials that if you or any company of your choice can take the liberty as the beneficiary, the person or the company will retain 30% of the total amount, 60% for the officials involved, while 10% will be set aside to off-set any bill (expenses) that may come up during the course of the transaction.

Please notify me of your acceptance to do this business urgently through my private phone and fax number. The men involved are men in government, therefore, there is no risk in either side. More details will be sent to you by fax as soon as we hear from you.

For the purpose of communication in this matter, may we have your private phone (home) and fax numbers.

Note: Your entire bank particulars should be included also. Please treat as most confidential. All replies strictly by the above fax and phone number.

The officials involved have agreed to establish viable business venture in your country which you will be a pioneer member on successful transfer of this fund.

Thanks for your co-operation.

Best regards,

DR. BASIL ONUOHA

**Figure 8-17**   Scam Letter 2
*Source:* Grennan, 1996.

Nigerian gang members also run oil tanker scams with nothing but an empty tanker. Members of the gang will board a tanker and compel the ship's captain to allow them to operate the fax or telex. A prospective buyer is contacted and convinced to participate in this deal. Arrangements are made between the gang members and the client for docking facilities for the tanker. A request is then made by the gang to the purchaser for payment of a fee, usually $250,000, to cover unexpected business expenses such as bribes or other fees. When the buyer attempts to procure the oil he will find that there is no oil and that he is out the money invested in the scheme (*South China Morning Post*, 1992).

Another fraudulent scheme that must be touched upon involves the shipment of merchandise to Nigeria. In this scam, European and U.S. corporations are informed that the Nigerian government wants to purchase a considerable amount of products from their companies. The Nigerian gang members further authenticate this scheme by forwarding all of the required documents on the letterhead of the Nigerian government purchasing office. A letter is also sent that guarantees that a check in full payment will be sent once the product arrives in Nigeria and is audited by government employees. Most companies will then ship the requested products to Nigeria only to find out within a short period of time that the check they receive is no good. In a large number of these cases, the bank on which the check is drawn does not exist or the account is closed (*African Business*, 1992).

One such scheme took place in 1990 when one Bisola Chalmers contacted the Belgium-based Quarante Import/Export Company and informed this company that his auto dealership was one of the larger car dealerships in Nigeria. Chalmers proceeded to order twenty 1990 Mercedes-Benz model 260 Es at a cost of 952,500 Belgian francs. A forged irreversible credit letter, that was purportedly validated by London-based Barclay's Bank, was forwarded to the Quarante Import/Export Company by this Ibadan-based corporation. A short time after the arrival of this letter the Quarante Company realized that the instrument forwarded to them was fraudulent and the signatures were counterfeit. As of 1994, the Quarante company has been unable to locate its cars or receive any type of payment for the vehicles (Imasa, 1991).

## Drug Trafficking

The deterioration of economic conditions in Nigeria has precipitated a significant increase in the involvement of Nigerian nationals in international drug trafficking. Nigeria is not what would be considered a supply depot for heroin or cocaine because neither opium nor cocoa leaves are grown in Nigeria. Therefore, the participation of Nigerian criminals in a drug trafficking enterprise revolves around their ability to transport heroin from the Golden Triangle (Thailand, Burma, and Laos) in southeast Asia and the Golden Crescent (Iran, Afghanistan, and Pakistan) in southwest Asia to other countries in Europe and the United States. They also import cocaine from South America for distribution to other African Nations and Europe (see Figure 8-18). Enterprising Nigerian traffickers use both bogus and bona fide passports to travel to heroin-producing Asian countries such as Pakistan, India, and Afghanistan to purchase heroin. In most cases, they fly into Karachi, Pakistan, allegedly on vacation, and then fly or drive to Islamabad or Peshawar, Pakistan, to purchase heroin at $6,000 to $8,000 per kilogram. Once the heroin is obtained and properly concealed the smugglers return to Nigeria. The heroin is then prepared for transportation to the United States or Europe. An estimated 5 percent of all Nigerian drug couriers are apprehended by the U.S. Customs Service agents. See Table 8-1. An indication of the type of Nigerian citizens involved in the drug trade was made apparent in 1987 when Captain Billy Eko, a celebrated Nigeria Airlines pilot, was arrested with 7.5 pounds of brown and white heroin by U.S. Customs officers at Kennedy International Airport (Ogar, 1989).

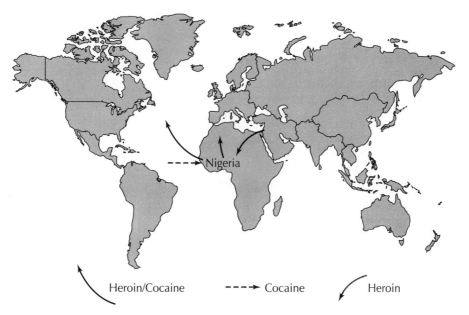

Heroin/Cocaine     - - - -> Cocaine     Heroin

**FIGURE 8-18** Narcotics Movement in and out of Nigeria
*Source:* U.S. Customs Service, 1992.

**TABLE 8-1**  Arrests of Nigerian Drug Smugglers by United States and Foreign Drug Enforcement Agencies from 1985 to June 30, 1994

| Year | United States | Foreign | Total |
|------|---------------|---------|-------|
| 1985 | 105 | 258 | 363 |
| 1986 | 129 | 357 | 486 |
| 1987 | 44 | 456 | 500 |
| 1988 | 36 | 724 | 760 |
| 1989 | 217 | 504 | 721 |
| 1990 | 290 | 632 | 922 |
| TOTAL | 821 | 2931 | 3752 |

*Source:* U.S. Customs Service, 1991.

An assessment by U.S. Customs officials of Nigerian drug smuggling rings indicates that it would not be unusual to have 30 to 40 smugglers on any given flight out of various airports in West Africa. These couriers are paid anywhere from $2,000 to $5,000 per trip and the smugglers, in most cases, are accompanied on their flight by a member of the gang who is known as a controller. Nigerian smugglers utilize several methods to export their product to the United States (see Figure 8-19). The techniques used are body cavity, body carry (packages taped to body), swallowing, heels of shoes and false bottom luggage (U.S. Dept. of Justice, 1989; and Treaster, 1992). In an effort to avoid customs authorities the Nigerian gangs have created many new international transportation routes for their couriers to travel and the gangs have recruited smugglers from all over Europe and Africa. A smuggler may make 2–5 stops at various transportation terminals throughout the world before arriving at a final destination. The Nigerian drug traffickers, like their Chinese counterparts, have been using Canada as a stop off location en route to the United States (*North Star,* 1993). The participation of the Nigerian gangs in drug trafficking has consistently been as a supplier and not a street dealer. Thus far, the Nigerian gangs have been identified as the entrepreneurs who supply various other gangs with heroin to be sold at street level. The two major purchasers of this illicit Nigerian product are Jamaican and Dominican gangs. The profits that are stimulated by the sale of heroin are immense when one considers that a kilogram of heroin sells for about $22,000 in Nigeria and more than $200,000 in the United States. This profit margin remains approximately the same when the sale of cocaine is examined because cocaine sells at a much higher price in Britain and Europe than it does in the United States. The Nigerian gangs, who are quite aware

Drug Activity
Methods of Shipment

Followed standard scenarios

- Luggage or carry-on items
- Carry on body
- Laundry powder in luggage
  - Clothes, shoes, hair, turbans
  - Baby bottles, liquid heroin

- Body cavities
  - Primarily females
  - Rectal or vaginal

- Extreme cases
  - Dead baby, surgically implanted

Smugglers Profile — Nigerians

- Primarily male; females have been apprehended
  - Age 24–35

- Youngest, 14, male, 662 grams, JFK, 1989
  - Oldest, 60, male

- Average quantity — 700 grams, 1.3 lbs. (60–80 condoms per)
  - Largest seizure — 1,450 grams swallowed

- Schooled before flight

Tools of Drug Traffickers

- Condoms supplied by the United States
- Black electrical tape
- Cream of okra soup
- Heroin for packaging
- Schools for couriers — in Africa
- Schools for fraud activities in U.S. and Africa
- Controllers on flights, not known to couriers
- Intel analysts
- Dry runs to see what works
- "Witch Doctor"

**FIGURE 8-19**   Nigerian Organized Crime

*Source:* Duga and Balsamini, 1990.

*Note:* As of 1991, other West Africans as well as other nationalities have been recruited as couriers, resulting in a drop in purity of heroin, due to the increase in shipment fee.

of the differences in monetary gain, deal their drugs only in the markets that provide the greatest dividends for them (Magloclen, 1991).

In April 1994, the U.S. State Department disclosed that somewhere between 35 and 40 percent of all the heroin entering the United States is supplied by Nigerian organized criminal gangs. See Tables 8-2 and 8-3. According to the

**TABLE 8-2** Amount of Heroin Seized from Nigerian Drug Smugglers, 1979–1989

| Year | United States | Total Grams | Total Pounds |
|---|---|---|---|
| 1983 | 19 | 7,193 | 15.9 |
| 1984 | 114 | 27,858 | 61.4 |
| 1985 | 66 | 20,568 | 45.3 |
| 1986 | 85 | 42,211 | 93.1 |
| 1987 | 44 | 26,049 | 61.8 |
| 1988 | 36 | 21,604 | 47.6 |
| 1989 | 217 | 225,975 | 497.7 |
| 1990 | 263 | 247,673 | 597 |
| TOTAL | 844 | 619,131 | 1419.8 |

*Source:* U.S. Customs Service, 1991.

State Department report the international drug activities of these gangs are supported by members of the Nigerian government. Robert Gelbard, the Assistant Secretary of State for International Narcotics Matters, went on to say:

> Nigeria has become a major source of trafficking around the world, as Nigerian trafficking organizations have become one of the most extraordinary, organized phenomena of carrying heroin and cocaine both in the United States and Europe. We calculate that some 35 to 40 percent of all heroin coming

**TABLE 8-3** Total Heroin Seizures and Arrests by Federal Agents at U.S. Ports of Entry*

| Year | Nigerian Sz. | Nigerian Amt. | Nigerian Arst. | African Sz. | African Amt. | African Arst. | Other Sz. | Other Amt. | Other Arst. | Total Sz. | Total Amt. | Total Arst. |
|---|---|---|---|---|---|---|---|---|---|---|---|---|
| 1986 | 85 | 93 | 103 | 19 | 24 | 31 | 277 | 575 | 395 | 381 | 692 | 529 |
| 1987 | 44 | 62 | 71 | 6 | 6 | 9 | 445 | 567 | 383 | 495 | 633 | 463 |
| 1988 | 36 | 48 | 41 | 3 | 3 | 5 | 279 | 1,300 | 681 | 318 | 1,351 | 727 |
| 1989 | 217 | 498 | 341 | 9 | 23 | 19 | 213 | 985 | 282 | 489 | 1,057 | 642 |
| 1990 | 281 | 471 | 421 | 19 | 55 | 32 | 231 | 979 | 507 | 531 | 1,505 | 960 |
| 1991 | 271 | 539 | 404 | 65 | 146 | 86 | 334 | 2,075 | 1,021 | 670 | 2,760 | 1,511 |
| 1992 | 283 | 602 | 362 | 162 | 402 | 220 | 423 | 1,206 | 596 | 868 | 2,210 | 1,176 |

*Source:* U.S. Customs Service, 1993.

*Numbers include non-African smugglers employed by Nigerian gangs.

Note: sz. = seizures, amt. = amount (in pounds), arst. = arrests.

into the United States comes from Nigerians who bring it into this country. The smugglers are not random mules, or individuals who are doing this on a free-lancing basis. These people are working for very organized groups, which we have felt is with the protection of Government officials" (Sciolino, 1994: A1, A11).

Enterprising Nigerian drug merchants have increased their deployment of non-Nigerian citizens as drug couriers. Within the past ten years drug seizures made in numerous countries throughout the world indicate that citizens of West African countries as well as Great Britain, Europe, and the United States are employed by Nigerian drug lords as drug runners. The Nigerian couriers are informed that if they are apprehended by law enforcement officials, their families will be provided for until they are released from prison. These drug runners agree to remain secretive and withhold any information they may have pertaining to the Nigerian gangs. Their silence is also motivated by fear of retaliation against their families by Nigerian gang members. Just about every Nigerian courier receives training from the drug lords. The training relates to how the drug runner is to avoid apprehension, how to respond if challenged by authorities, and how to answer questions if confronted by law enforcement personnel (Kraft, 1994). The following two cases indicate the use of foreign nationals by Nigerian drug groups:

1.  In October 1984, DEA agents in Seattle seized 334 grams of heroin that had arrived aboard a Japan Airlines flight. It was later learned that the heroin had been originally obtained in Bombay, India, by English females working for Nigerian drug lords. The heroin was transported from Bombay to Tokyo, Japan, where it was repackaged into smaller lots and then dispensed to these same couriers for travel to the United States and Great Britain (U.S. Dept. of Justice, 1985).

2.  In September 1988, Japanese police raided the residence of a Nigerian national in Tokyo, Japan, and seized 16 pounds of heroin. At that location the police arrested one Nigerian national and four U.S. citizens. It was later ascertained that the four U.S. citizens had been recruited by a Nigerian drug dealer to supply heroin to several locations in the United States (U.S. Customs Service, 1989).

Since 1985 one major Nigerian heroin exporter has been using Abidjin, Ivory Coast, as his base of operations. This move was due to an increase in enforcement efforts by the Nigerian government (U.S. Dept. of Justice, 1985).

One of the major problems facing the Nigerian government's drug enforcement efforts is corruption. A good deal of the progression and prosperity of the heroin transporters has been due to the dishonesty of government officials. In many instances, administrative authorities in middle and lower level positions have become involved in corrupt activities with drug dealers. Investigative efforts in Nigeria have indicated that corrupt officials assist drug dealers by providing protection and police intelligence data, aiding drug carriers, supplying fraudulent documents, and functioning as "couriers and controllers" (U.S. Dept. of Justice, 1985: 7).

In 1984 the following government officials in Lagos, Nigeria, were identified as skilled conspirators who were using their positions within the government to assist the Nigerian gangs' drug smuggling enterprises (U.S. Dept. of Justice, 1985: 8):

> Chief of Immigration, Alagbon Close Street
> Chief of Security, Murtala Mohammed Airport
> Chief of Criminal Investigation Division, Yaba

In an effort to correct this problem the government cracked down on corruption by either discharging/firing or forcing retirement on many of the police, customs, immigration, and National Security personnel. To some extent this endeavor was successful in that it led to the arrest of a number of drug runners at Lagos airport and a dishonest customs official who was involved in narcotic trafficking; it helped eliminate corrupt officials from the National Security Office; it forced the Nigerian drug gangs to seek new transportation routes for their drugs in an effort to avoid Lagos; and it forced the military government in Nigeria to create a law that makes drug smuggling a capital offense with a provision related to the forfeiture of suspects' assets (U.S. Dept. of Justice, 1985).

In an effort to control drug trafficking by Nigerian nationals the Nigerian government created the National Drug Law Enforcement Agency in December of 1989. This agency increased the government's participation in enforcement of state laws related to narcotics transactions by the Nigerian gangs. This endeavor has doubled the amount of arrests of Nigerian gang members for drug smuggling, as shown in Table 8-4.

## Money Laundering

Employees in private industry have also been exposed for their participation with the gangs in drug conspiracies. Included as active partakers are airline and bank personnel. It has been substantiated by U.S. federal investigators that several privately owned companies have established affiliations with the Nigerian drug cartels. These companies have become active participants in the drug import and export industry and in assisting the drug cartels in the laundering of illicitly obtained money. Some of the Nigerian businesses that

**TABLE 8-4** Nigerian National Drug Enforcement Agency
Activity, 1994

| Year | Arrests | Amount Seized (in kilograms) |
|------|---------|------------------------------|
| 1986 | 3 | 2.2 |
| 1987 | 6 | 4.7 |
| 1988 | 16 | 11.25 |
| 1989 | 25 | 34.5 |
| 1990 | 116 | 36.9 |
| 1991 | 131 | 145.32 |
| 1992 | 81 | 67.2 |
| 1993 | 149 | 194.8 |
| 1994 | 300 | 217 |

*Source:* Duga and Balsamini, 1990.

were exposed during this investigation include the following (U.S. Dept. of Justice, 1985):

Vago Associates, Export and Import
O.P.S. International, Ltd.
Ibrahim International
Cool Art Store
Mosun Fayemiwo Trading Company
Lourdes Disco

The majority of Nigerian gang members smuggle money from drug operations back to Nigeria because U.S. currency is much stronger than the Nigerian naira. This transfer is accomplished in several ways: through couriers who carry large amounts of U.S. currency, usually $50 or $100 bills, in their luggage; bank or wire transfers; purchasing goods that can be resold in Nigeria for profit; or negotiable instruments. Several Nigerian gang leaders have attempted to establish offshore banking operations similar to those on islands in the West Indies. Drug money, however, is not the only currency that the Nigerian gangs would be trying to launder (see Table 8-5). As a group they are just as deeply entrenched in unlawful schemes as they are in drug trafficking, although these gangs are aware that the turnover of money is quicker in drug dealing than in scams (U.S. Dept. of Justice, 1995).

Intelligence gathered by U.S. government investigative sources indicates that some Nigerian drug dealers have become identified as active participants in both political and terrorist operations by supplying these groups with monetary support. In one specific inquiry it was discovered that Niger-

**TABLE 8-5** Results of U.S. Secret Service Investigations into Criminal Activities of Nigerian Organized Crime Groups, 1988–1991

| Year | Cases | Arrests | Total Amount Seized |
|------|-------|---------|---------------------|
| 1988 | 97 | 97 | $ 2,558,863 |
| 1989 | 84 | 67 | 4,008,652 |
| 1990 | 128 | 185 | 3,840,467 |
| 1991 | 159 | 272 | 7,603,834 |
| TOTAL | 468 | 621 | 18,011,816 |

*Source:* U.S. Customs Service, 1992.

ian drug groups were using drug money to fund the activities of the Palestine Liberation Organization. In another U.S. government investigation into the activities of the Nigerian gangs, it was ascertained that a terrorist arms supplier was affiliated with these same Nigerian groups (U.S. Dept. of Justice, 1992). Therefore, not all the money obtained from participating in drug trafficking is being put in gang leaders' pockets.

## CONCLUSIONS

As this chapter indicates the Jamaican and Nigerian organized crime groups continue to be two of the most futuristic gangs operating worldwide. They have little or no participation of street gangs except when they occasionally use these gangs to sell their imported drugs on the street. Surely, the ability of the Nigerian groups to send unlawfully obtained property—from hand-held calculators to luxurious automobiles—back to the gangs' headquarters in Nigeria for profitable resale indicates their creativity and resourcefulness as criminal groups.

# *9* Chinese Gangs

## ASIAN ORGANIZED CRIME GROUPS

Prior to 1965, crime within Asian communities in the United States was considerably low in comparison to crime in other ethnic neighborhoods. The vast majority of immigrants from China, Japan, and other Asian countries were law-abiding citizens who worked hard and avoided trouble whenever possible (McGill, 1938; Tracy, 1980). Almost all Asian immigrants worked long hours (in a sweatshop-type environment), on a daily basis for minimal pay, which left little or no time to supervise their children. Yet, most Asian youths growing up under these conditions spent a major portion of their time concentrating on schoolwork and avoiding trouble.

The involvement of Asian youths in street gang crime prior to the 1970s was minimal, but we must also consider that the reason for this scarcity of criminal activity was due to the low numbers of Asian adolescents at that time. Asians as a group were treated as second-class citizens by many members of our society. Our legislators passed laws that suppressed the immigration of Asians (Chinese Exclusion Act of 1882 and the Natural Origins Acts of 1924) and incarcerated Japanese citizens and immigrants living in the United States during World War II. We must remember that prior to 1965 Japanese and Chinese ethnic groups were just about the only people of Asian descent in this country, and the crimes these groups were involved in, if any, had no impact on society (Chin, 1990; Kaplan and Dubro, 1986; FBI, 1985).

| | 1 | Organizational structure |
| | 2 | Continuing criminal conspiracy |
| Continuing and self-perpetuating criminal conspiracy fed by fear and corruption and motivated by greed. | 3 | Purpose— generation of profits |

**FIGURE 9-1** Organized Crime
*Source:* FBI, 1992.

The modification of the immigration quotas in the mid 1960s and the Vietnam War increased the number of Asians immigrating to the United States. These factors consequently led to a substantial increase in the population of Asian communities in the United States. The sudden addition of these immigrants caused a breakdown in the stability within the Asian communities. This breakdown occurred because the majority of the immigrants were Chinese, and the large influx of these new arrivals led to the fragmentation of any substantial social support groups available to these new immigrants (Chin, 1990). Figure 9-1 illustrates the purpose of organized crime within a society.

## CHINESE GROUPS

When we discuss Chinese organized crime groups we must note some of the major factors that have helped increase Chinese gang activity in the United States and many other locations throughout the world.

1. The increasing migration of Chinese immigrants (legal and illegal) to the United States since the mid-1960s. See Table 9-1. It is entirely possible that the figures could increase anywhere from 25 to 100 percent if the number of illegal immigrants entering this country were considered.

| Year | Legal Immigrants |
|------|------------------|
| 1960 | 237,292 |
| 1970 | 435,063 |
| 1980 | 812,718 |
| 1990 | 1,371,435 |

*Source:* U.S. Dept of Justice, 1994.

2. The increase in Chinese gangs and their memberships since the 1970s has also led to the expansion of crimes and criminal activities (murder, kidnapping, robbery, extortion, drug dealing) from within a small Chinatown-type of community to any locale where affluent Chinese people may live or congregate.

3. During the 1970s and most of the 1980s Chinese gangs only exploited other ethnic Chinese individuals. But many Chinese gangs, like their Vietnamese counterparts, have expanded their criminal horizons to include any other Asian groups who supply a service or prevent a Chinese gang from controlling a specific enterprise.

4. Law enforcement officials believe that Chinese organized crime syndicates will take over the Mafia crime businesses. This shift, in reality, is quite doubtful because the Mafia has been entrenched in the illegitimate as well as the legitimate workplace for several decades and will not be easy to supplant.[1] The Chinese have gained a foothold in some criminal activities but so have Colombian, Nigerian, Japanese, Vietnamese, and Russian groups. Too much competition is present in the organized crime marketplace for any one group to displace the Mafia.

5. The gang connection in Hong Kong, now part of China, has been expanding its workbase from Hong Kong to the United States, Canada, Southeast Asia, and Australia. The Hong Kong consortium controls a majority of the heroin imported from Southeast Asia, which has been force-fed into the world heroin market. (Chin, 1990; U.S. Dept. of Justice, 1988; Dombrink and Song, 1996). Figure 9-2 shows Chinese organized crime groups and their criminal activities.

## HISTORY

During an internal revolt against the Ming dynasty military leaders from the Ming government requested assistance from the Manchus, a barbarian tribe from Mongolia. The Manchus realized that most of the resistance emanated from the Shaolin Buddhist monastery in Foochow and sent a large military

---

[1]The theory related to the Chinese crime gangs taking over the La Cosa Nostra empire is nothing more than a fantasy created by the FBI to implement their funding. We must not forget that La Cosa Nostra is deeply entrenched in illegitimate businesses and has been for several decades. At this point in time, they will not be easily overthrown. Also, presently, too many other criminal syndicates operate in the United States, not one of which has the power or ability to eliminate the La Cosa Nostra. The reality is that these other groups are only operating because La Cosa Nostra allows them to operate and most likely collects homage from them.

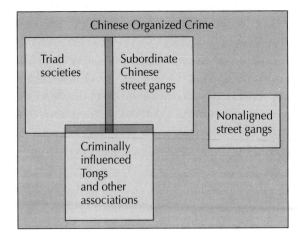

Criminal Activities
- Alien smuggling
- Armed robbery
- Arson
- Blackmail
- Bombings
- Bribery
- Burglary
- Contract murder
- Copyright violations
- Drug trafficking
- Extortion
- Illegal gambling
- Infiltration of legitimate businesses
- Investment fraud
- Loansharking
- Money laundering
- Murder
- Prostitution
- Public corruption
- Tax evasion
- Weapons smuggling

**FIGURE 9-2** Interrelation of Chinese Crime Groups in the United States
*Source:* McKenna, 1996.

force to kill the rebellious monks. One hundred and twenty-three monks were killed by the invaders, and the five that escaped formed the first Triad group (Booth, 1991).

Chinese organized gang activities did not just suddenly appear on the American scene. As students and observers of gang operations we must review what brought about these criminal/gang activities from within a fairly stable Chinese society. China's culture stresses a Confucian code, which projects that if all persons fulfilled their duties toward themselves, their families, states, and the world, a "Great Harmony" would prevail (Booth, 1991).

When we discuss the evolution of the Chinese gangs, we must also view the impact that Triads have had on these groups. Triad (triangle of heaven, earth, and humans) groups first appeared in China in the late seventeenth century. These groups were formed in an attempt to overthrow the Quig (Ch'ing) government that had been created by Manchu invaders. It wasn't until 1912 that the Quig regime finally collapsed. Some Triad leaders and members attempted to place themselves in the newly created Republic of China government. A large portion of those not assimilated into the new government reestablished themselves within their Triad associations in order to maintain some type of authority within their own associations. The secretive Triad organizations, which were originally civic minded and devoted religious fellowships, were slowly but surely deteriorating into what is known as organized crime factions. This degradation took place once the leadership of the Triads was consumed by self-serving individuals who were able to impose their own standards of conduct on the organization for self-stature and self-gain (Chin, 1990; Booth, 1991).

Triad societies' involvement in criminal activities increased during the first half of the twentieth century when many Chinese citizens became more uneasy with the various officials struggling to control the government. Several influential organizations recruited Triad members and sanctioned strong-arm methods and violent tactics to ensure that the average person in society followed the organization's rules. The Triads were then authorized by these associations to set up and control prostitution, gambling, and opium houses (Seagrave, 1985). As the Triads' enforcer status for the powerful political associations increased, their patriotic interests decreased and the ability of their leaders to control illegal activities of the membership declined (Chin, 1990).

Then in 1949, the Red Army defeated Chang Kai-Shek's Kuomintang Party, which led to a mass migration of Kuomintang party supporters to Taiwan and Hong Kong. It wasn't long after the defeat of Chang Kai-Shek's army that the Chinese Communist party started harassing and executing Triad members (Posner, 1988). Triad groups were quickly reformed in Hong Kong, and soon the ranks of the Hong Kong police department contained Triad members. This infiltration helped control most criminal activities in Hong Kong and continued the deterioration of a once proud and patriotic group to a sleazy criminal enterprise (Posner, 1988). In fact, an investigation into the officers assigned to the Hong Kong police department's Triad Society Division disclosed that most of its members also held active Triad membership. This investigation further exposed unbridled corruption within the Triad Society Division. Five police sergeants (Five Dragons)[2] were the leaders of this corrupt organization, and the investigation ultimately led to the indictments and exodus of more than 40 police officers and the theft of millions of dollars by people who had sworn to uphold the law (U.S. Dept. of Justice, 1987). Figures 9-3 and 9-4 show the symbolism and formation of Triad groups.

---

[2]The Five Dragons were identified as Choi Bing Lung, Chen Cheng You, Nam Kong, Hon Kwing Shum, and Laui Lok, all active members of the 14K Triad.

Heaven

Earth        Man

In 1844 China was conquered by foreign Manchus, who established the Ch'ing Dynasty. The third Ch'ing emperor issued an edict against secret societies, i.e., the Society of Heaven and Earth, whose aims were the moral reform of the people, the maintenance of religious belief and practice, and the encouragement of Chinese nationalism and patriotism. Its famous motto, which remains relevant today in Triads, was "Overthrow the Ch'ing and restore the Ming."

**FIGURE 9-3**    Triad Symbolism
*Source:* NYPD, 1993.

## Hong Kong Connection

Triad societies have been active in Hong Kong since the seventeenth century but the Hong Kong groups' participation in criminal activities started a lot sooner. Hong Kong was transferred to British control in 1842, and three years later the Triads created a number of social disorders with their unlawful operations. These disruptions forced the British government in Hong Kong to enact an Ordinance for the Suppression of Triads (the Societies Ordinances). The statutes banned Hong Kong citizens from becoming members of Triad groups or partaking in any Triad activities (U.S. Dept. of Justice, 1987; Chin, 1990; Booth, 1991). These laws helped to control the actions of

| | |
|---|---|
| Belief | Hung—Heaven, Earth, and Man |
| Seventeenth century | 36 oaths—goodness: patriotism, brotherhood, security, secrecy, "one for all and all for one"<br>36 strategies—badness |
| Eighteenth century | Formation of Triads overseas |
| Nineteenth century | Tongs formed in North America: King Sor, Kung Kuam, Hui; protection for Chinese workers and new immigrants to America; Tong values almost carbon copy of Triads |
| Twentieth century | Street gangs formed and used as enforcers by Triads and Tongs; no values, strictly part of criminal enterprise |

**FIGURE 9-4**    Formation of Chinese Secret Societies
*Source:* Royal Hong Kong Police, 1994.

Triad groups by moving most of their operations out of public view until the early twentieth century when Triad groups started resurfacing in Hong Kong. The Triads were reestablished as organizations to provide protection for territories chosen by peddlers. Triads, once again, started to flourish in Hong Kong but not without conflict. A major portion of the problems revolved around the confrontations over the territorial rights of the vendor-Triad members. Triad associations found that members of different Triads had been working the same locations. In an effort to settle these conflicts the Triad organizations held a joint meeting to start a unification process and to form one association to supervise the activities and settle the disputes. During this conference all of the attendees voted to use the word "Wo" (peace) prior to the symbolic name of each Triad (Wo Sun Ye On). Ultimately, these "Wo" groups evolved into some of the most powerful and disreputable chapters of the Hong Kong Triads (Postner, 1988; Chin, 1990; Booth, 1991).

Some early factors that effected the increased growth and success of the Hong Kong Triad groups were:

1. The ability of members to infiltrate, recruit within, and then take control of labor unions.

2. The Triad cooperation with the Japanese military government during World War II. The Triads embellished their control over illegal activities by supporting the Japanese officials, who in turn, destroyed cooperating Triad members with prior criminal histories and permitted the Triad informers and enforcers to control gambling, prostitution, and opium operations in Hong Kong.

3. Once the war ended, the Hong Kong Triads continued their rapid growth, but with this increased growth came the loss of control over Triad membership, camaraderie, righteousness, and secrecy. A segment of the Hong Kong Triads' membership had already sacrificed their nationalism when they joined forces with the Japanese during World War II. After the war other members also relinquished all the other values of these secret societies by becoming involved in criminal activities. All these factors plus the doing away with membership registration led to the further criminalization of what now could be considered fractious criminal organizations (Chin, 1990; Booth, 1991; U.S. Dept. of Justice, 1987).

All these factors plus the sudden reemergence of Chinese Triad groups created severe problems for the citizens of Hong Kong. In 1956 and 1967 disturbances between anti-Communist workers and pro-Communist workers created havoc in Hong Kong. Altercations between these same groups erupted due to the "cultural revolution" that was occurring in China. The results of all the changes in Triad customs and the anti/pro communist issue has led to a dramatic takeover of almost all the Triads of Hong Kong by mainland Chinese groups—Sun Ye On, 14K, Ching Societies, Wo On Lok, and Big Circle (Postner, 1988). These drastic changes began in the 1970s, and since that time most Triads of Hong Kong have become nothing more than groups of street criminals pretending to be nationalistic.

The structures of Triad societies may differ slightly, but most organizations are arranged in the same basic manner (see Figures 9-5 and 9-6). Numbers play an important role and are used as signs of identification related to

| FBI | Chin | San Francisco PD | Job Description |
|---|---|---|---|
| Leader<br>Elder Brother<br>489 | Shan Chu<br><br>489 | Shan Chu<br>Leader<br>489 | Group Leader<br>Boss of Group<br>Older Brother<br>Slang Tai Lo |
| Deputy<br>Incense Burner<br>Vanguard Leader<br><br>438 | Yee Lu Yuan<br>Fu Shan Chu<br><br>438 | Fu Shan Chu<br>Deputy Leader<br>Heung Chu<br>Incense Master<br>438 | Second Brother<br>Slang Yee Lo |
| Red Pole<br>Enforcer<br>426 | Hung Kwan | Sin Fung<br>Vanguard<br>Sheung Fa<br>Double Flower<br><br>Hung Kwan<br>Fighter Official | High Priest<br><br>Status Rank<br>General Affairs<br>Recuiter<br>Enforcer<br>Responsible for gang<br>protection and<br>implementing punishment |
| White Paper<br>Fan Advisor<br>415 | Park Tse Sin<br><br>415 | Park Tse Sin<br>White Paper Fan<br>415 | Planner and advisor |
| Grass Sandal<br>Messenger<br>432 | Cho Hai<br>Liaison<br>432 | Cho Hai<br>Grass Sandal<br>432 | Messenger<br>Liaison<br>Spy<br>Infiltrate police and<br>other groups |
| Members<br><br>49 | Sey Kow Jai<br>Worker<br>49 | Ordinary Member<br><br>49 | |
| Recuits<br>36 | | | |

**FIGURE 9-5** Designations of Leaders and Members of Triads

CHAPTER 9

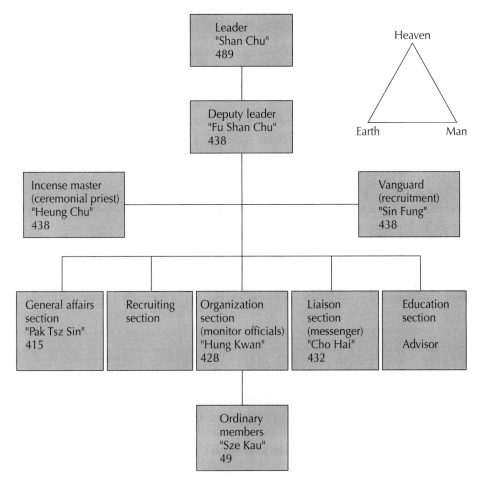

**FIGURE 9-6** Triad Headquarters Structure
*Source:* FBI, 1993.

Triad history. When the number four (4) is used as the first number in a specific numerical figure it signifies the ancient Chinese belief that earth is surrounded by four great seas.

As with most other secret societies, newly recruited members must participate in a simple initiation ceremony known as "hanging the blue lantern." The participants in the ceremony are accepted into the Triad as members once they proclaim the 36 oaths of loyalty, secrecy, and brotherhood (U.S. Dept. of Justice, 1987; Booth, 1991). Chinese groups are defined in Figure 9-7, and the modern Triad structure is shown in Figure 9-8.

With the 1997 ceding of Hong Kong by the British to the People's Republic of China, the tentacles of the major Hong Kong Triads established

| Subordinate | Triad |
|---|---|
| **Gangs** | **Societies** |
| Chinese and Vietnamese street gangs that are affiliated with criminally influenced Tongs. Subordinate gangs are used as enforcers for illegal gambling operations. | Ancient secret criminal societies that trace their roots to 17th century China. Today, there are approximately 50 Triads based in Hong Kong and Taiwan. The Royal Hong Kong Police estimate worldwide membership of Triads to be in the tens of thousands. |
| **Nonaligned** | **Chinese** |
| **Gangs** | **Tongs** |
| Chinese gangs that are not affiliated with any Chinatown–based association or Triad society | Chinese fraternal and business organizations with chapters in major U.S. cities. The membership of Tongs is composed largely of noncriminals. However, criminal investigations have determined that some have ties to organized crime. |

**FIGURE 9-7**   Chinese Organized Crime Definitions
*Source:* FBI, 1993.

new bases of operation in the United States, Canada, and Australia. The most powerful and largest Triad group in Hong Kong, Sun Yee On, has vastly increased its membership over the past decade (Dombrink and Song, 1996). This group is heavily involved in extortion, money laundering, loansharking, drug trafficking, arms sales, prostitution, gambling, credit card fraud, and illegal alien smuggling. The most important gains by Sun Yee On have been within the film industry. This activity has allowed Sun Yee On the opportunity to form a potent alliance with members of the Chinese Public Security Bureau. Movies shot on location in China help to provide employment for local citizenry and illegal money to local politicians and party leaders. Sun Yee On's control over the film industry in China has afforded them the power base they were seeking with the Chinese government. Historically, Sun Yee On was formed in 1796 and first appeared in Hong Kong in 1841. The majority of the membership were postal workers using the name Sun On Tong Triad. Within a year members from Chiu Chow created the Man On Triad. In 1919 the Yee On Triad was forged with Henry Chin inducted as Dragon Head. The original income of Yee On came from the import/export business. In 1922 Henry Chin changed the name of the organization to Sun Yee On. These societies continued to grow over the years and in 1987 Hong Kong police estimated the membership of this Triad at 35,000 members

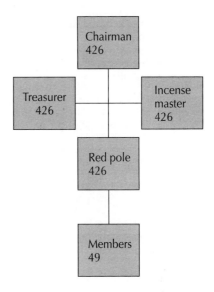

**FIGURE 9-8** Modern Triad Structure
*Source:* Royal Hong Kong Police, 1991.

(Dobson, 1993). A recent estimation places membership at approximately 65,000 members (*South China Morning Post,* January 29, 1994).

Until recently, the majority of Triads had been anti-Communist and pro-nationalist but Hong Kong's change of hands has prompted a meaningful shift in loyalty. A major portion of the leaders of Sun Yee On are direct descendants of the people who migrated from Chiu Chow to Hong Kong and have become highly supportive of the government in Beijing. According to police intelligence reports the Sun Yee On has been working with members of the Beijing government since a meeting between the two groups in Kowloon in 1988. This meeting helped form advantageous alliances that have grown powerful over time. In reality, this association has given Sun Yee On the opportunity to make investments in the People's Republic of China and allowed some members of the Chinese government's Public Security Bureau to enhance their monetary accounts (Dobson, 1993; Torode, 1993). Figure 9-9 shows the criminal activities and affiliations of the Sun Yee On society.

The Wo Triad group is a combination of societies that, prior to World War II, controlled a major portion of the labor market in Hong Kong. During the Japanese occupation of Hong Kong most Wo groups aggregated their power base under the aegis of the Japanese military. After the defeat of the Japanese, the British returned to Hong Kong while the three major Wo organizations, Wo Shing Tong, Wo Yung Yee and Wo Hop To, not only expanded their business ventures but continued to keep a tight control over their labor holdings. An investigation conducted by the Hong Kong police after the war in-

**International Affiliations**
- **Hong Kong**
- **Canada**
- **Dominican Republic**
- **Australia**

Portland
Boston
New York City
Philadelphia
San Francisco
Los Angeles
Miami

**Interaction with U.S.–based groups**
- **Born to Kill gang** New York
- **Ghost Shadows gang** New York
- **Tung On Tong** New York
- **Tung On gang** New York
- **Flying Dragons gang** New York
- **Wah Ching gang** San Francisco
- **Tsun Tsing association** New York
- **Chinese Freemasons** New York
- **On Leong Tong** New York

**Criminal Activities**
- **Alien smuggling**
- **Extortion**
- **Loansharking**
- **Illegal gambling**
- **Blackmail**
- **Prostitution**

**FIGURE 9-9** Sun Yee On Society Criminal Activities and Affiliations in the United States
*Source:* Royal Hong Kong Police, 1993.

dicated that the same Wo group members managed to accumulate up to 15 million Hong Kong dollars a year by charging local street vendors both legal and illegal initiation fees to operate in districts controlled by the Wo groups (Posner, 1988; Booth, 1991).

During the 1950s the Wo groups continued their growth by assimilating many other Wo societies into their Triad grouping. The variations in the sizes of these associations are from 6,000 to 20,000 members (Posner, 1988; Booth, 1991). The Wo Triad groups have continued to increase over the past 30 years with an estimated membership of 29,000 in 1995. The Wo group has extended its illegal activities by increasing its participation in drug dealing as well as extortion, prostitution, gambling, and the labor market.

The 14K Triad was originally the Hung Tat Shan part of the Chung Yee Wui society, which was a mixture of different segments of Triad groups brought together to strengthen Triad support of the anti-Communist Nationalist government in the mid 1940s. A massive recruitment drive attracted close to a million new members. A group this size eventually dissipated into smaller and more cohesive groups. The late 1940s brought about the defeat of the Nationalist movement and the integration of members of this Triad from mainland China into Hong Kong because the communist government did not want organized crime groups operating in China. Originally, the movement of the 14K Triad into Hong Kong was met with animosity by other local Triad groups and caused many conflicts throughout the 1950s (Posner, 1988; Booth, 1991). During the 1950s, the 14K became the second largest Triad as its total membership increased to over 80,000. Presently, the 14K has branches in Japan, Taiwan, Macao, Europe, Southeast Asia, Canada, and the United States (U.S. Dept. of Justice, 1987).

Another Hong Kong group that must be mentioned is the Dai Huew Jai or the Big Circle Triad, which was originally composed of members from mainland China. This group's roots originated from the cultural revolution and reeducation camps in mainland China during the 1960s. Most members of this organization remained in mainland China until the Tienanmen Square massacres. This society has attracted a large number of mainland Chinese refugees and ex-Chinese Red Guard Army personnel who are heavily involved in violent activities. The U.S. Drug Enforcement Agency lists this group as a major heroin importer to the United States (Grennan, 1992). One of its members, Johnny Kon, was arrested and convicted of importing more than 100 pounds of heroin into the United States between 1984 and 1987 (*South China Sunday Morning Post,* 1992).

## Hong Kong Triad Operations Outside the United States

Hong Kong Triads have managed to enhance their worldwide criminal operations by setting up a base in Canada. The Kung Luk Triad has active illegal programs in place in Toronto, Montreal, Ottawa, Vancouver, Hamilton, and many other urban areas in Canada. This North American Triad is different from the Triad/Tong fusion groups operating in the United States. The Canadian Kung Luk Triad is a prototypical Triad that operates in the same fashion as the Hong Kong-based Kung Luk Triad. Members of the Kung Luk Triad are constantly traveling between Canada, the United States, and Santo Domingo, most likely because Lau Wing Kui, a reputed leader of the Kung Luk who was deported from Canada, owns an interest in several gambling clubs in Santo Domingo. The President's Commission on Organized Crime indicated that Kung Luk Triad members used the casino in Santo Domingo to launder money prior to depositing the currency in U.S. accounts. We must also remember that a large amount of the heroin brought into the United States by Chinese groups is distributed to Dominican organized crime groups who then handle street sales (U.S. DEA, 1993). The Kung Luk Triad, through its connection in the Dominican Republic, has managed to set up a drug distribution ring that has been very profitable to all of the participating groups (President's Commission on Organized Crime, 1986).

Several members of the Dai Huen Jai or Big Circle Triad were recently arrested in Hong Kong for smuggling heroin into Canada. A joint investigation involving Canadian and Hong Kong police led to the arrests of a Mr. Kong and a Mr. Chu for importing 6.9 kilos of 97 percent pure heroin into Canada. Police believe that the purity of this heroin led to more than 70 drug overdoses in 1993 (Hughes, 1993)

Australia is another country chosen by Hong Kong Triads as a base for their criminal operations. Since the mid 1980s several Hong Kong Triads have set up operations in Australia. These groups include Sun Yee On, 14K, Wo Yee Tong, and Wo Shing Wo Triads. Evidence gathered by the Australian police has thus far led to several large seizures of Southeast Asian heroin and the arrests of Chinese drug importers. In 1988 Australia police, in conjunction with Hong Kong police, seized 43 kilograms of heroin that was departing Hong Kong for Australia. A 50 kilograms seizure was made at Port Vila, Vanuatu, in 1989. This heroin shipment had departed Hong Kong en route to Sydney, Australia. Two major seizures were made in Australia, the first was 21.5 kilograms of heroin imported from Taiwan, and the second was a 12.7 kilograms seizure from three Singapore nationals at Perth airport (Pierce, 1992).

**Triads in Taiwan**

The operations of Triad associations in Taiwan are basically the same as the Hong Kong Triads. The major difference is that the Taiwan Triads, known as "right handed" groups, support the anti-communist government in Taiwan, while the Hong Kong Triads, known as "left-handed" groups, have recently started swinging their allegiance towards the government of the People's Republic of China. Hundreds of gangs in Taiwan are associated with the six to eight dominant local Triad criminal organizations. Bamboo United is the most powerful Triad in Taiwan with a membership of approximately 30,000–40,000. The Four Seas Triad, formerly the number two gang in Taiwan, maintained control over a major portion of the prostitution, gambling, and protection rackets in Taiwan (U.S. Dept. of Justice, 1989).

In an attempt to take control over the Triads the Taiwanese government put an amnesty program in place in early 1997. This program allowed Triad members to turn themselves into the police and renounce their lives of crime in an effort to avoid prosecution under the new and very strict Organized

Crime Prevention Act. Police authorities claim that approximately one third of Taiwan's 1,200 gangs were disbanded during the amnesty period known as Operation Self-Renewal. Officials indicated that the second largest gang in Taiwan, the Four Seas Triad, was dissolved by its leader, Chao Ching-hua (Hajari, 1997).

## Tongs

Chinese immigrants started arriving in the United States shortly after the discovery of gold in California in the late 1840s. Most of the early Chinese settlers were from the southern coastal areas of China. These new arrivals on U.S. soil learned the meaning of discrimination quickly and found themselves being considered as outcasts because of their ethnic backgrounds. Soon small Chinatowns sprang up at almost every gold rush location. Family and local associations were set up according to the province in China where the majority of the residents were born. Ultimately, these fraternal organizations were combined and designated as Tongs.

The history of Chinese Tongs goes back to the mid-nineteenth century. Tongs, a term used to describe meeting halls, were originally formed to protect Chinese businesses and new immigrants against the alien and hostile American communities. As time passed some Tongs were formed to serve new members of Chinese communities to locate relatives or friends and to assist immigrants in locating a place to stay/live. Research indicates that Low Yet, a Triad member and a leader of the Taiping rebellion, was the founder of Tongs in San Francisco. Yet formed the Chee Kong Tong, which had more than 1,000 members in 1887. This Tong was modeled after the Triad Yet had been a member of in Hong Kong (FBI, 1996).

The majority of Tongs are national organizations whose members are legitimate people involved in assisting community businesses, ethnic societies, and politics. A small percentage of Tong members use these organizations to benefit themselves and other members of organized crime groups (President's Commission on Organized Crime, 1986; Chin, 1990). Although Tongs were conceived on the North American continent, Chinese Triads undoubtedly had a hand in creating these associations. The Federal Bureau of Investigation (FBI) has stated that a major portion of all of the crimes in Chinatowns throughout the United States can be traced back to high-ranking Tong officials. In fact, both the FBI San Francisco and New York offices have linked murder, extortion, gambling, drug trafficking, and prostitution to the local Chinatown Tongs (U.S. Dept. of Justice, 1987; U.S. Dept. of Treasury, 1995).

The administrative structure of Tongs is similar to that of La Cosa Nostra.

| Mafia | Tongs |
|---|---|
| Boss | Chairman |
| Underboss | Vice Chairman |
| Consigliere | English-Speaking Secretary |
| Caporegime | Tong Treasurer |
| Capo | Tong Social Secretary |

Source: (U.S. Dept. of Justice, 1987).

The godfather-type of rank in the mafia would also be a highly influential position in the Tongs but one that is shared by a group of members who are perceived as "the elders." The lower ranks of the Tong structure contain the largest proportion of members known as soldier/workers. Figure 9-10 shows the Tong hierarchy, and Figure 9-11 illustrates the Tong structure.

Tongs have no restrictions as to the number or background of newly recruited members. This openness has led to the rapid growth of membership in the Tongs within a short period of time. Tongs have embraced the same basic type of socialization process as the Triads. Initiation rites are mandatory for all new members, as is the reciting of oaths of loyalty, nationalism, and brotherhood. Like the Triads, the Tongs maintain a highly covert operation that restricts the identification of the leadership. This secrecy leaves a majority of the membership without any knowledge of the daily activities within the Tong. One problem facing the Tongs is that the politics within the Tong are usually fragmented because of the number of various factions in each association. An elected Tong leader in many cases can be considered nothing more than a puppet who is controlled by many factions instead of a strong leader elected by the majority (Chin, 1990; U.S. Dept. of Justice, 1987). The Tong associations (presently 100 in New York City) are also part of the Chinese Consolidated Benevolent Association, which is highly influential within the political circles of Chinatowns throughout the United States (U.S. Dept. of Justice, 1987).

The United States is home to several major Tong associations. According to the Federal Bureau of Investigation the top three Tongs are: On Leong, Hip Sing, and Hop Sing (U.S. Dept. of Justice, 1987).

The first On Leong Chapter was established in Boston in 1894. After the turn of the century On Leong moved its headquarters to New York City's Chinatown (Chin, 1990). This group gained prominence in the mid 1980s when control of this association was taken over by Chan Tse Chin or Eddie Chan.

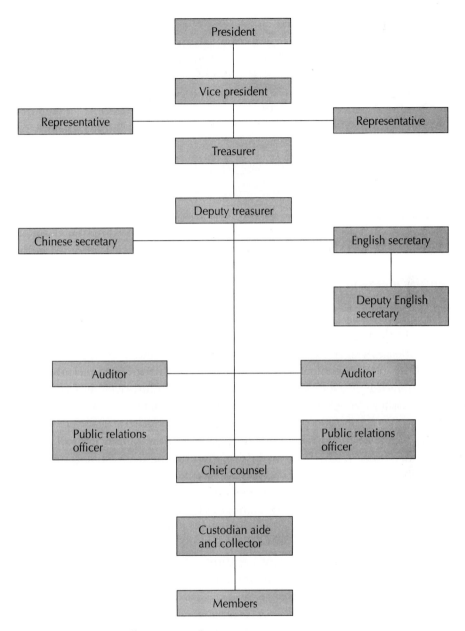

**FIGURE 9-10**   Tong Officers Hierarchy

*Source:* NYPD, 1993.

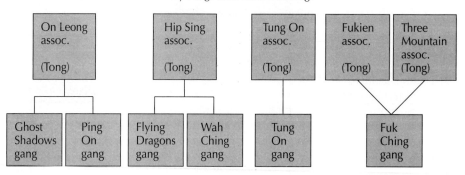

Primary Tongs and Affiliated Gangs

**FIGURE 9-11**   Structure of Chinese Organized Crime
*Source:* FBI, 1993.

Chan was an ex-Hong Kong police sergeant who immigrated to Mexico during the Five Dragons police scandal in Hong Kong (see footnote 2) in the 1970s. Within a short period of time Chan arrived in New York City's Chinatown and set up several successful businesses. This success led to his election as president of the On Leong Tong. Chan proceeded to tighten the connection between On Leong Tong and the Ghost Shadows street gang using them whenever possible to protect his criminal enterprises and to strong-arm any other groups or persons attempting to move in on his criminal empire.

It was not long before a power struggle broke out between Chan and Nicky Louie, head of the Ghost Shadows street gang, over the distribution of money. Louie moved his operation to Chicago where he was the victim in an attempted murder. It was later alleged that Chan had ordered the shooting of Louie and other discontented members of the Ghost Shadows in Chicago. Chan had purported that Louie had extorted money from him. Chan had also formed the Continental King Lung Group, a financial investment company, as a front to conduct his fraudulent ventures. Chan was later identified by a Hong Kong Triad member as the Dragon Head (crime boss) of New York's Chinatown (President's Commission on Organized Crime, 1984b). Chan helped the On Leong build and control many illegal enterprises prior to fleeing the United States after being subpoenaed to testify in front of the President's Commission on Organized Crime.

The present leader of the On Leong, Chan Wing Yeung, owns fifty percent of Frankwell Management Services, which was recently seized by federal authorities for participating in illegal trading activities. Frankwell Management is a subsidiary of Frankwell Holdings Limited in Hong Kong. Chan

Wing Yeung was previously named as a coconspirator with On Leong Tong in 1990 for participating in gambling and racketeering activities in Chicago. The trial ended with a hung jury (Chan, 1994).

The On Leong Tong's illegal activities have continued to flourish. Presently On Leong Tong has chapters in 26 U.S. cities. Thus far, in nine of these cities the Ghost Shadows street gang is affiliated with On Leong Tong.

The Hip Sing Tong, like the On Leong, is based in New York City's Chinatown. Its leader until recently was Lei Lo Chat whose street name is Benny Ong, Uncle Seven, or Uncle Benny. Ong was convicted of murder in 1936 and served 18 years in prison. Besides his criminal record little else is known about Ong except that he has been influential in New York City politics. The Hip Sing has chapters in 16 major cities, and it has affiliations with the Flying Dragons street gang in nine of these locations (U.S. Dept. of Justice, 1987; Chin, 1990).

The Hop Sing Tong operates out of the western section of the United States with chapters in more than 12 cities. This Tong is associated with the Hop Sing Boys street gang in nine of these cities. The Hop Sing has been involved in an ongoing turf war with the Bing Hung Tong. Since 1983 these two groups have been involved in more than a dozen different violent confrontations over the control of illegal activities in both Seattle and San Francisco (U.S. Dept. of Justice, 1987).

The Fukienese American Association/Tong did not really come to light until June of 1993 when a ship named the *Golden Venture*, full of illegal immigrants, ran ashore off Rockaway Beach, New York. In the 1980s this organization started to grow and its street gang, the Fuk Chow/Ching, started getting involved in criminal activities in the Chinatown area of New York City. A 1990 investigation into the smuggling of illegal Chinese immigrants into Canada provided Toronto police with a conversation, through a phone tap, between the alien smugglers and the Fukienese Association's chairperson. The address of this association had also been given as a drop off point for money to release a kidnap victim. Federal authorities have indicated that members of this Fukienese Tong are undoubtedly involved in the criminal activities of the Fuk Ching gang but have, thus far, avoided any type of prosecution (Kleinknecht et al., 1993).

Tung On Association/Tong is considered one of the largest in New York City. Clifford Wong, the long-time president of Tung On Tong was charged with operating a criminal enterprise involved in the murder of ten people and numerous other crimes. The investigation of this case disclosed how Tong leaders use members of their affiliated street gangs to safeguard and expand their business empires (Faison, 1994). Federal prosecutors portrayed Mr. Wong as a successful businessman who managed to acquire a thoroughbred horse racing stable and a chain of restaurants from New York to Florida. Wong had been the leader of the Tung On since 1984 while his brother Steven controlled the Tung On street gang until his 1988 narcotics conviction. Mr. Wong built a profitable criminal federation within the Tung On Tong during his tenure as president (Faison, 1994).

The Tongs discussed are the five most powerful Tongs operating in the United States today. All these Tongs have many members who are legitimate individuals, but other Tong members constantly participate in illicit activities. Tong members who are involved in criminal actions usually sanction Chinese street gangs who, in turn, are affiliated with the Tongs and carry out most of their criminal operations.

Most of these gangs can be considered violent. A great proportion of the gang membership is composed of newly immigrated adolescents who are easily recruited into the gangs. The gang members tend to be in their late teens and early twenties while gang leaders are usually older, some over thirty. A majority of the youths who are recruited into the Chinese street gangs are school dropouts whose ability to communicate in the English language is poor. They have few opportunities to obtain decent paying jobs. A major portion of these adolescents join the gangs willingly, but some members are compelled to join the gangs. A number of these Chinese gangs have some type of induction ritual that is patterned after the customary Triad subcultural ceremony. Although the organizational configuration of most Chinese gangs appears diversified, just about every gang has some type of power structure. The upper echelon of the gangs contains leaders who are known as "Dai-los," or big brothers. The Dai-los direct the operations of the gangs and do not normally participate in any of the criminal activities involving gang members. The leaders are also the emissaries who will have contact with other gangs, Tongs, or Triads. Another segment contains members known as "Sai Lo," or underboss; they are considered lieutenants and control street gang members. The third level of the gang contains ordinary members known as "Ma-Jai," which means little horses, or street soldiers who follow the orders of the bosses. The Chinese gangs support themselves in two basic ways:

1. They do what might be considered freelancing, which consists of the gang's participation in criminal behavior that they initiate such as extortion, robbery, drug trafficking or kidnapping.

2. The gangs are contracted by either Tongs or Triads as protectors or enforcers of a legal or illegal enterprise.

## CHINESE STREET GANGS

### West Coast Gangs

Chinese street gangs started developing in San Francisco during the 1950s. The Chinese gangs were formed and structured in the same manner as other ethnic youth gangs. A street gang known as the Beigs was one of the first street gangs formed by American-born Chinese. This gang's area of criminal expertise was burglary and they could be easily identified by the "Beatle" type of outfits they wore (Chin, 1990).

The Wah Ching (Youth of China) was the first immigrant gang. This gang was formed to prevent assaults on foreign-born Chinese immigrants by American-born Chinese. Modifications in the U.S. immigration laws led to an increase in the number of immigrants arriving from mainland China. The Wah Ching took advantage of these changes to become a more powerful gang by recruiting many of the younger immigrants as new members of their organization. The power of this gang was soon recognized by members of the Chinese community who hired gang members to run errands and provide strong-arm protection for gambling operations (Posner, 1988; Chin, 1990). Figure 9-12 shows the criminal activities and affiliations of the Wah Ching gang.

The Hop Sing Tong, seeing the advantages of being associated with a street gang, brought the Wah Ching under the Hop Sing control by creating a youth branch within the Tong. A short time later, the Suey Sing Tong created a youth gang known as the Young Suey Sing or the Tom Tom Street gang. Conflict between the Wah Ching and the Young Suey Sing led to many street confrontations (Office of Attorney General of California, 1991). One group, the Yau Lai (Yo Le) or Joe Fong Boys, was formed in 1969 by discontent members of the Wah Ching gang who left the gang because of restrictive controls placed on the gang members by the Hop Sing Tong (Chin, 1990).

During the early 1970s both the Wah Ching and the Joe Fong Boys expanded their criminal activities by targeting people in the Asian community as victims of their crimes. The growing membership of the Wah Ching and Joe Fong Boys multiplied the number of violent conflicts between the two groups over territorial rights, especially during 1973–1977, when 27 people were killed in gang-related incidents. On one occasion five people were killed and eleven seriously injured (not one a gang member) during a vicious attack by members of the Joe Fong Boys (Chin, 1990).

The San Francisco area probably has the largest amount of Chinese gang activity on the West Coast. The Hop Sing Boys, the Kit Jars, the Asian Inva-

**International Affiliations**
- Hong Kong
- Canada
- Taiwan

**Triad Interaction**
- **14K group** Hong Kong
- **Sun Yee On** Hong Kong
- **Luen Lok** Hong Kong
- **United Bamboo gang** Taiwan
- **Wo group (confrontational)** Hong Kong

**Criminal Activities**
- Murder
- Weapons violations
- Loansharking
- Illegal gambling
- Drug trafficking
- Extortion
- Arson
- Bombings
- Prostitution
- Police corruption
- Copyright violations
- Tax evasion
- Infiltration of legitimate businesses

**FIGURE 9-12** Wah Ching Gang Criminal Activities and Triad Affiliations
*Source:* FBI, 1993.

sion, and the Local Motion are some of the Chinese gangs that operate criminal enterprises in the Bay area. Wah Ching is considered the largest street gang in California with about 600–700 active members of which 200 can be considered highly cohesive. The Wah Ching gang formed an alliance with the Sun Yee On Triad in 1987 (*San Francisco Examiner,* May 10, 1987: B1; U.S. Dept. of Justice, 1987).

The Los Angeles branch of the Wah Ching was formed in 1965 by Wah Ching members from San Francisco. Wah Ching was formed in Los Angeles to stop the constant harassment of newly immigrated Chinese youths by Mexican gang members. Despite the formation of the Chinese gangs conflicts did not cease and have continued until the present.

One specific area outside of Los Angeles, Monterey Park, saw its Chinese population double between the late 1970s and the early 1980s. The population increase in Monterey Park resulted from a crackdown by Taiwan police covert individuals in the late 1970s and early 1980s, forcing a multitude of criminals to seek asylum in the United States. Many of these individuals then settled in Monterey Park because the majority of Chinese residents in Monterey Park were from Taiwan.

The transgressors who arrived from Taiwan brought with them enough gang experience to set up two new gangs. The Four Seas gang originally appeared in Taiwan in 1955 only to dissipate within several years. A short time later the Four Seas gang was resurrected under new leadership that fortified the gang's economic status by opening and controlling houses of prostitution and gambling casinos. Membership in the Four Seas increased as legal and illegal Taiwanese gang members reached the U.S. shores. The Four Seas gang was soon expanding its criminal enterprise to include legal as well as illegal ventures (Booth, 1991; Posner, 1988).

Another Taiwanese gang that set up operations in Monterey Park is United Bamboo. This gang was dispersed by the Taiwanese police in 1958 only to reemerge in the 1960s as a dominant street gang. During the 1980s, United Bamboo expanded its operations into the entertainment business. It increased its membership and listed 17 new branches for a total of 25 chapters. Although total membership in the United States is unknown, it is estimated that the United Bamboo in Taiwan has more than 10,000 members (Posner, 1988).

The United Bamboo gang gained nationwide attention in 1984 when some of its leaders were involved in the murder of Henry Lui, a formidable Chinese writer. Lui wrote a biography that made derogatory statements about the then Taiwanese president and was preparing a manuscript related to the unethical practices of Taiwanese politicians. Media reports indicate that two United Bamboo leaders, Chen Chi-li and Swei Yi Fund, and the chief of Taiwan's Military Intelligence Bureau, Vice Admiral Wong Shi-Lin, met in 1984 and discussed punishing Lui for what they considered "traitorous acts." Originally, the Los Angeles United Bamboo was to take some action against Lui but was unable to carry out this mission. Vice Admiral Wong then had Chen and Swei trained to fulfill the contract on Lui. Upon Chen's arrival in the United States he was joined by United Bamboo's West Coast enforcer Wu Tun. Another member from Taipei, Tung Kwei-Sen, soon joined Chen and Wu to partake in this conspiracy. A short time after Tung's arrival Wu and Tung entered Lui's house and murdered him (*New York Times*, November 30, 1986; Chin, 1990). Besides being involved in the most notorious murder of a Chinese-American writer, the United Bamboo are also heavily involved in heroin importing, extortion, and gun running (Grennan, 1992) (see Figure 9-13).

**International Affiliations**
- Taiwan
- Hong Kong
- Philippines
- Thailand
- Japan
- Saudi Arabia

Chicago
New York City
Atlantic City
Boulder
San Francisco
Denver
Los Angeles
Phoenix
Honolulu
Houston
Miami

**Interaction with U.S.–based groups**
- **Wah Ching** San Francisco
- **Fuk Ching** New York
- **Flying Dragons gang** New York
- **Ghost Shadows gang** New York

**Criminal Activities**
- Contract murder
- Illegal gambling
- Money laundering
- Loansharking
- Weapons violations
- Public corruption
- Drug trafficking
- Investment fraud
- Extortion
- Armed robbery
- Prostitution

**FIGURE 9-13** United Bamboo Gang Criminal Activities and Affiliations in the United States
*Source:* FBI, 1993.

## East Coast Gangs

Prior to the immigration law changes in 1965, the only Chinese street gangs in New York City were the Continentals. This gang was formed in 1961 to protect Chinese students from attacks on them by other ethnic groups. The Continentals were made up of American-born Chinese youths who did not get involved in street crimes nor were they associated with any of the Chinatown Tongs (Chin, 1990).

Then in 1964, the On Leong Tong formed the On Leong Youth Club, which became known as the White Eagles gang. This gang was made up of foreign-born Chinese youths who were deployed throughout Chinatown to prevent any type of discriminatory activities by outsiders against Chinese businesses and residents (Chin, 1990). Another gang known as Chung Yee appeared on the streets of Chinatown. Like its antecedent, On Leong, the membership of the Chung Yee was made up of new arrivals from mainland China. This gang operated in the same fashion as the On Leong, protecting the rights of Chinatown citizens and businesspeople. Chinese street gangs continued to increase and gangs like the Quen Ying, Liang Shan, Flying Dragons, and Black Eagles appeared on the streets of Chinatown. The early history of these gangs indicates that they were all martial arts clubs used to prevent visitors from harassing local businesses and residents (Chin, 1990).

The early 1970s saw an increase in the amount of violence used by Chinese gangs. The two elements that caused an elevation of the amount of disorder by Chinese gangs were the increase in the availability of weapons and the conflict between the growing number of street gangs coupled with the "restlessness" of the new immigrant youths whose violent behavior threatened all of the residents of Chinatown (Posner, 1988).

During this period, the youth gangs extorted money and food from local business establishments through the use of fear and strong-arm tactics and then extended their criminal activities by forcefully robbing local gambling dens. The Tongs, seeing their businesses being extorted and robbed, hired the gang members to perform private security as the Tongs' enforcers and protectors. This affiliation led to some of the gangs becoming part of the Tong family (White Eagles with the On Leong Tong, and Flying Dragons with the Hip Sing Tong) (Posner, 1988).

The problem with the Chinese street gangs was that by 1974 some of the gangs were completely out of control. The White Eagles' gang members, hired by the On Leong Tong to protect On Leong members and businesses, were openly robbing, extorting, and humiliating the Tong members on Chinatown streets. The On Leong Tong started to disassociate itself from the White Eagles by stopping all monetary payments and weapons to the gang and recruiting the Ghost Shadows street gang to replace the White Eagles as the On Leong Tong's street gang (Chin, 1990).

After a short struggle the Ghost Shadows took charge of the most profitable locations in Chinatown while the White Eagles removed themselves from the On Leong's portion of Chinatown. A realignment of all the territories within Chinatown was completed a short time after the removal of the White Eagles, and all the gangs, seemingly content about territorial adjustments, went back to their criminal ventures. The hostilities between the gangs continued as did an increase in street violence (Posner, 1988).

The year 1976 turned out to be Chinatown's most violent year as internal and external gang hostilities increased sharply. Most of the gangs' criminal activities expanded to include the use of coercion, which was so intimidating that the majority of Chinatown's businessmen feared for their lives

(Posner, 1988). During this time, several gunfights between the Flying Dragons and the Ghost Shadows resulted in the killing of one Ghost Shadow and one innocent restaurant customer, and the wounding of one Flying Dragon and five innocent bystanders (Posner, 1988).

During the gang warfare between the territorial Chinatown gangs the presence of Wah Ching gang members in the Chinatown vicinity increased drastically. Local gang leaders concerned about the Wah Ching's propinquity set up a meeting of gang leaders to announce the termination of the gang warfare and that gang members would be seeking employment. After this announcement, it appeared that the gangs were working together to prevent a turf invasion by outside groups, but purported gang unity and promises of peace were not to last long. Within a month a dispute over turf rights broke out between the Ghost Shadows and the Black Eagles gangs. It resulted in the wounding of Black Eagle Leader, Paul Ma, and four other Black Eagle associates. A short time later a Ghost Shadow member was shot and killed, followed in a week by the killing of a Black Eagle gang member (Posner, 1988).

Prior to 1976 the majority of confrontations were between opposing gangs over the rights to certain areas in Chinatown. During 1976 problems within different gangs surfaced and struggles ensued over control and money causing increased internal conflict within several of the major New York City gangs. The intragang hostilities continued as did the gangs' ability to increase their turf holdings. The escalating violence became apparent when the owners of a midtown-Manhattan Chinese restaurant were murdered for refusing to pay extortion money to the Black Eagles gang (Posner, 1988). Another indication of how far out of control gang violence had become was the attempted murder of Man Bun Lee. Lee, the former president of the Chinatown Community Business Association, gained media attention by requesting that additional police enforcement units be assigned to remove the gangs from Chinatown. This action resulted in Lee being stabbed five times. Lee survived the assault, and his assailant was arrested and convicted of this crime. But both of these incidents sent a positive message to the Chinese community not to cross the gangs because they controlled the streets. Another factor related to Chinatown street gangs was the fact that it did not matter which or how many gang members were arrested and/or convicted by law enforcement authorities. Even since the mid 1970s when the police started taking action against the Chinese gangs, the gangs have continued to participate in their chosen crime ventures without any serious interruptions from either federal or local law enforcement.

Since the early 1980s several new street gangs have appeared in the Chinatown area. Fuk Ching, White Tigers (which were a result of intragang warfare), Tung On, Green Dragons, and Born to Kill are names of some of the new gangs. The criminal activities of these gangs have expanded gang operations to all five boroughs of New York City. In most cases these new gangs have attempted to avoid conflict with the original older ones by not impinging on the older groups' territories. Instead, the new gangs have taken control of turf outside of Chinatown and, in some cases, outside of Manhattan. One aspect that is apparent is that these new gangs are more violent than their predecessors.

## THE GANGS

### Flying Dragons

The Flying Dragons have continued to grow. Presently, this gang has five factions, three of which control gang operations in Chinatown and Manhattan. The fourth group maintains gang business in Queens, and the fifth part is a flying squad used as needed throughout the metropolitan area to provide strong-arm assistance to other gang members. This gang is, fundamentally, the best run street gang in Chinatown. The Hip Sing Tong keeps tight reins on this gang and, in doing so, has kept them out of law enforcement's limelight. Benny Ong, the recently deceased head of Hip Sing, set up the original guidelines for the operation of this street gang and never let the organization get out of control. A majority of the members are ethnic Chinese. The Flying Dragons, like other Chinese groups, do use Vietnamese or Korean gang members to handle the extortion, kidnapping, or robbery of Vietnamese or Korean businesses or citizens. The Flying Dragons gang is involved in narcotics trafficking, extortion, gambling, and robbery (see Figure 9-14). It has chapters in San Francisco, Los Angeles, Houston, and Boston.

### Ghost Shadows

Like the Flying Dragons, the Ghost Shadows are an established Chinatown gang with a long-standing association with the On Leong Tong. The Ghost Shadows have two factions in Chinatown and one associate gang. One of the two factions is located on Bayard Street while the other operates on Mott Street. The associate gang, the White Tigers, operates in Queens under the tutelage of the Ghost Shadows. The Ghost Shadows are a notorious gang known for its use of violence. In 1990, the Ghost Shadows got involved in a turf war with the Vietnamese gang Born to Kill (BTK). BTK was infringing on Ghost Shadows territory by robbing Tong-controlled gambling establishments. A warning was given to BTK to cease and desist its crimi-

**International Affiliations**
• Hong Kong
• Canada

Boston
New York City
Philadelphia
Newark
San Francisco
Los Angeles
Fairfax County,
VA (VFD)
Dallas
Houston

**Triad Interaction**
• **14K group** Hong Kong
• **Sun Yee On** Hong Kong
• **United Bamboo gang** Taiwan

**Criminal Activities**
• **Murder**
• **Weapons violations**
• **Loansharking**
• **Illegal gambling**
• **Drug trafficking**
• **Extortion**
• **Armed robbery**

**FIGURE 9-14**   Flying Dragons Gang Criminal Activities and Triad Affiliations
*Source:* FBI, 1993.

nal activities in Ghost Shadows' territories but BTK refused to stop. A short time later Vinh Vu, the second highest ranking BTK member, was shot to death.

Members of BTK then proceeded to hold an elaborate funeral procession through the streets of Chinatown. During the burial rites in Linden, New Jersey, three of the mourners who were actually Ghost Shadows gang members opened fire with automatic weapons injuring numerous grieving attendees. The members of this gang are used as mid-level heroin couriers by the On Leong Tong. The members are also actively involved in loansharking, extortion, robbery, and alien smuggling (see Figure 9-15). The Ghost Shadows gang has vigorously recruited Vietnamese gang members because of their reputation for being violence-prone, leading to 25 percent Vietnamese membership in the Ghost Shadows. The Ghost Shadows' affinity for violence has had something to do with the recruitment of Vietnamese members.

## Tong On Boys

The Tong On Boys have jurisdiction over portions of East Broadway, Market, Division, and Catherine Streets in Chinatown. The Tong On Boys are made up of two separate groups. The first is the Tong On Boys, and the second

**International Affiliations**
- Hong Kong
- Canada
- Philippines

**Triad Interaction**
- **14K group** Hong Kong
- **Sun Yee On** Hong Kong
- **United Bamboo gang** Taiwan

**Criminal Activities**
- **Murder**
- **Weapons violations**
- **Loansharking**
- **Kidnapping**
- **Bribery**
- **Drug trafficking**
- **Extortion**
- **Burglary**
- **Alien smuggling**
- **Gambling**
- **Robbery**

**FIGURE 9-15**   Ghost Shadows Gang Criminal Activities and Triad Affiliations
*Source:* FBI, 1993.

gang is known as the Sun Yee On. Most of the leaders of the Tung On are also members of the Sun Yee On, which is listed by law enforcement agencies as a Triad.

The Tong On Boys are associated with the Tung On Tong/Association that is run by Clifford Wong and the Tsung Tsen Tong run by Kwok Too Lai. The main operations of this group are in the New York and Philadelphia areas with a smaller branch in Portland, Maine. Like the other gangs, the Tung On Boys are involved in drug trafficking, prostitution, extortion, alien smuggling, and gambling.

### Fuk Ching

Many of the Fuk Ching gang members are from the Fukien province of China. They are associated with the Fukien American Association/Tong. This gang controls parts of East Broadway, Christie, Allen, and Eldridge Streets in New York City's Chinatown. The Fuk Ching gang is perceived as one of the most vicious and dauntless Asian gangs. In the recent past the Fuk Ching has gained a great deal of media attention because of its participation in three major events. The first involved the kidnapping and unlawful imprisonment of 61 illegal Chinese immigrants; gang members locked their victims in a Jersey City, New Jersey, warehouse. These Chinese immigrants were being held until they could reimburse the smugglers who brought them to the United States. The second incident involved a triple murder in Teaneck, New Jersey. Two of the victims of this murder were the brothers of Fuk Ching gang leader Ling Kee Kwk (aka Ah Kay). Within a short period of time law enforcement arrested five Fuk Ching gang members for this crime. The most publicized event was the grounding of the *Golden Venture,* a ship used to transport illegal aliens into the United States. The ship belonged to gang leader Ah Kay who has made millions of dollars smuggling illegal immigrants into North America.

## Green Dragons

This Queens-based gang evolved from within the Fuk Ching gang. The Green Dragons can be located in the Jackson Heights, Flushing, Elmhurst, Woodhaven, and Long Island City sections of Queens. Most of the gang members are from the Fukien province of China. The White Tigers gang is the main adversary of the Green Dragons, and the two have maintained a restless respite over the control of specific areas of Queens. The Green Dragons are a gang the Federal Bureau of Investigation claimed it "had by the tail" (Rosario, 1991: 13). This claim might have been somewhat true when a high-ranking gang member, Stu Man "Sonny" Wong, testified about the participation of other gang members in crimes of murder, kidnapping, robbery, and extortion. Law enforcement officials dubbed Wong the Chinese, Sammy "the Bull" Gravano, because of the specificity of his information on the gang's involvement in crimes. All gang members in this case were found guilty and given terms of life imprisonment for their participation in these crimes (Dao, 1992: A1).

The pressure from law enforcement failed to dismantle the Green Dragons gang, however. They have once again been resurrected and the gang is operating in the same Queens neighborhoods from where law enforcement officials "allegedly" removed them. This gang has continued to thrive by recruiting newly arrived Chinese adolescents and promising them friendship, protection, flashy cars, and plenty of money. The gang's increased activity in extortion, drug dealing, and robbery attests to the fact that it was hardly wounded by the federal government's indictments and convictions.

## Born to Kill (BTK)

Also known as the Canal Street Boys, the membership of this gang is ethnically Vietnamese. It was founded by former members of the Flying Dragons gang. They are not associated with any Tong or Triad but they do infringe on the territories of other gangs. BTK is still being used by Chinese Tongs and gangs as enforcers and drug couriers. This gang can be found in Queens, Brookyn, and Jersey City, New Jersey. A more in-depth analysis of this gang is provided in the Vietnamese section of this book.

## White Tigers

This gang is an affiliate of the Ghost Shadows and has branches in Chinatown and Flushing, Queens. They are sanctioned by the Ghost Shadows to operate in Chinatown. This gang also has an ongoing feud with the Green Dragons over territorial rights in Queens. Gang leader Gary Soo Kee Tam was recently indicted by federal authorities for paying other gang members $7,000 each to murder his sister, brother-in-law, and their infant son (*New York Times,* August 20, 1994: B7).

## Gum Sing

This gang materialized after a major portion of the higher echelon of the Vietnamese BTK gang was arrested. Gum Sing, although not associated with any Tong or Triad, is based out of what is considered Brooklyn's Chinatown (8th Avenue from 40th to 60th Streets). Membership is basically Vietnamese with a marginal number of members from other Asian ethnic groups. As a gang, they are quite mobile and move around the five boroughs of New York City committing various crimes such as drug trafficking, home robberies, and extortion.

The original purpose of Chinese gangs was to protect Chinatown businesses and citizens from the harassment of other ethnic groups without any cost to Chinese citizens. It was not long before the profiteers of illegal activities began hiring gang members to protect their illegitimate businesses. In turn, members of the Chinese street gangs realized that they could make money by shaking down businesses for protection money. The gangs then set up a systematic collection arrangement and started moving into other types of criminal enterprises.

## CRIMINAL ACTIVITIES

### Extortion

A short time after their inception, Asian street gangs realized that by extorting money from legitimate as well as illegitimate businesses the gangs could support themselves. Extortion quickly became the principal moneymaking scheme for the gangs. The gangs also discovered various methods to use to extort money or goods:

1. Money was solicited from business owners as an investment or contribution to an illegal goal.

2. Gang members received a sizable deduction on products made or sold by a business.

3. Companies were forced to buy materials connected with specific Chinese holidays.

4. Business owners were ordered to pay a specific amount of protection money on a monthly basis.

5. Business owners paid "lucky money" for specific events or the opening of a new business.

6. Business owners were required to put video gambling machines inside their stores.

7. Business owners were compelled to purchase either equipment or other merchandise from the gang.

The sum of money demanded by the gang usually is based on a classification of the enterprise and the intake of that business. A business owner who either declines to make or misses a payment will find gang retaliation in the form of violence against either him or the business. Any type of operation that does not pay is usually connected to the gang or Tong. Small profit businesses are usually charged less (e.g., $108–208 per month), while high profit businesses such as restaurants pay $300 or more per month. They are also forced to buy specialty items from the gangs such as mooncakes, which cost about $7 each in a bakery, but for which they pay $50–200 each. The money is usually extorted monthly with additional monies extracted on Chinese holidays, grand openings, and the sale of special objects. In most cases, the gangs only extort money from businesses within gang-controlled territories (U.S. Senate, 1991).

Recently gangs in New York City's Chinatown began forcing business owners to put illegal video gambling machines that contain black jack and joker poker games into their business establishments. The owner of the location is then obligated to split the profits from the machines with gang members.

## Alien Smuggling

The smuggling industry has become extremely profitable for the Chinese gangs. The shipping in of illegal immigrants was brought to the attention of the U.S. government when a ship called the *Golden Venture* ran aground off Rockaway Beach in New York. The ship contained approximately 300 illegal Chinese aliens who were paying anywhere from $30,000 to $50,000 each to be taken to the United States. Information gathered by law enforcement sources indicate that the illegal immigrants must pay at least half of the amount prior to departure (Treaster, June 9, 1993: 1, B2).

Two kingpins of the illegal alien trade are Cheng Chui Ping known as "Foudu (Stealing Passage) Queen," and Guo Liang Chi also known as "Ah Kay," the leader of the Fuk Ching gang. Cheng Chui Ping has been in the smuggling business for the past ten years and operates out of a variety store called Yung Sim on East Broadway in Chinatown. She purchased the variety store for $3 million and paid in cash. Cheng Chui Ping also runs a money transfer business that charges a fee of $25 for the first $1,000 and $20 more for every $1,000 after that sent to China. She guarantees a prompt three-day delivery period. The other major smuggler is Ah Kay, the notorious leader of the Fuk Ching gang. Ah Kay was indicted for two counts of murder after he allegedly ordered the murders of three members of an opposing faction within Fuk Ching. The hit resulted in the killing of two of Mr. Kay's adversaries. Kay was seized in a gambling den in Hong Kong. Federal agents seized two crates that contained the business records of the Fuk Ching gang (Faison, August 30,1993: B1).

Alien smuggling has become an increasingly lucrative business for the Fuk Ching gang. An estimate by the U.S. Immigration and Naturalization Service indicates that the Fuk Ching gang has smuggled well over 100,000 illegal immigrants from the Fukien province in China over the past two years. For a rate of approximately $30,000 per person the smugglers would bring in about $3 billion before expenses, which would be minimal. Its profitability is why alien smuggling has become such a popular short-term investment for Triad, Tong, and gang leaders (*U.S. News and World Report,* June 21, 1993).

The smugglers, known as "Snakeheads," also provide forged documentation to their customers. Once the person seeking to go to the United States obtains an exit visa from the People's Republic of China he or she travels to Bangkok where a gang member supplies him or her with counterfeit identity documents. The individual is placed on an airline and taken to another country from where he/she will travel to the United States by automobile, airplane, or boat. A number of routes are used by the gangs to transport the aliens to the United States. Almost all these routes run through South and Central America. Countries such as Panama, Bolivia, and Belize are willing to provide the smugglers with necessary visas for the right price (U.S. Senate, 1991). The smugglers have few problems finding corrupt officials in most South and Central American countries who can provide routes for bringing illegal immigrants to the United States. These same corrupt officials have been helpful to the alien smugglers who are also involved in drug smuggling.

### Home Invasion Robberies

Subjects of home invasions are targeted after gang members gather information related to large sums of money or jewelry being kept in a specific house or location. Gang members will follow the subject to the residence to verify the site. A short time after the verification of the address gang members use either subterfuge or force to enter the premises. After entry into the location, the occupants are tied up and the house is thoroughly searched for valuables. If the anticipated amount of money, jewelry, or other valuables is not found the victims may be menaced, tortured, beaten or raped, or a family member may be kidnapped until the family provides a ransom to the gang for that person's release. Gang members who participate in this crime must be extremely mobile.

### Business Invasion Robberies

Chinese street gangs have also been involved in the robberies of garment factories in Chinatown. The gangs forcibly enter these factories and then rob all the employees. On two occasions female employees were raped by gang members. In one instance three gun-carrying males entered a factory at 150 Lafayette Street and robbed 50 women employees. These robberies take place in the daytime, and thus far 16 businesses have been robbed at gunpoint by gang members (DeStefano, 1991: 18).

### Credit Card Fraud

Triads and gangs have gotten involved in credit card fraud. The Big Circle Boys gang uses counterfeit credit cards that are produced through the use of silk screening and are encoded with the information of a credit card customer. Cards that have been lost or stolen are modified and imprinted with different numbers and names. Authorities say that these groups can produce a credit card that defies detection. These cards have fairly high limits on them, which are often reached in 30–60 days.

In March 1992, Hong Kong police raided a factory that was used to produce fraudulent credit cards. Nineteen employees were arrested and the police confiscated 50 counterfeit Visa and MasterCard cards and more than 200 different credit card numbers, counterfeit currency, numerous pawn slips, and guns. Then on April 16, 1992, Montreal police expropriated 60 forged credit cards from gang members during a raid on a Chinese gambling den (CleuLine, November 1992).

## Commodity Scams

A commodity scam set up by Chan Wing Yeung of the On Leong Tong in New York's Chinatown managed to swindle millions of dollars from more than 300 people. The Evergreen International Development Corporation purported to be trading in gold bullion and foreign currency, while the corporation was really channeling money to Hong Kong. According to Kathy Palmer, a U.S. government prosecutor, "There were no legitimate transactions." At least half of the Evergreen Company was owned by Frankwell Management Service, Inc., controlled from China by Eddie Chan, a fugitive from U.S. authorities' charges of murder and racketeering (Smith and Chan, August 31, 1994: 10). An investigative report by the *New York Daily News* discovered that Chan Wing Yeung and Eddie Chan were closely connected to the Sun Yee On Triad in Hong Kong. Federal authorities say the scam had well over 1,000 investors, most of whom worked for the company. Victims indicated that they were guaranteed training, good jobs, and big profits. Ironically, not one of these pacts will ever be fulfilled (Smith and Chan, August 31,1994: 10).

## Prostitution

Chinese criminal groups have been involved in controlling houses of prostitution or massage parlors for many years. The participation of these criminal enterprises in prostitution has increased over the past 20 years with the large increase of Asian male immigration into the United States. Originally, these houses of prostitution were filled with Korean females and run by Korean entrepreneurs. In most cases the Chinese groups have, by whatever strategy necessary, taken over control of these houses of prostitution and filled them with Korean, Taiwanese, and/or Vietnamese prostitutes. Most of these women are little more than indentured hostages who must work for the group controlling the house of prostitution until all the costs of their immigration to the United States are paid.

## Narcotics Trafficking

According to the U.S. Drug Enforcement Agency (DEA), import of South-eastern Asian heroin into the United States has increased dramatically. Southeast Asian heroin is grown in the poppy fields of the Golden Triangle, Myanmar (formerly Burma), Laos, and Thailand. The heroin, once it is processed, is then sent through Hong Kong on its way to some destination in the United States. Seventy percent of all heroin seized by federal authorities in New York was identified as being from the Golden Triangle.

Recently confiscated heroin from the Golden Triangle has been found to be 41 percent pure. The purity of this heroin is considerably higher than heroin expropriated by law enforcement authorities several years ago. In fact, the purity of Southeast Asian heroin has consistently increased over the past ten years. The cost of a kilogram of heroin in the United States will vary from one ethnic group to another. An example would be if one Chinese group sold a kilo of heroin to another Chinese group, the cost would be $60,000–80,000 while the cost of the kilo of heroin increases $100,000–140,000 if a Chinese group sells to a non-Chinese group.

Evidence gathered by U.S. enforcement agencies indicates that not all of the members of Triads, Tongs, and street gangs are involved in narcotic trafficking but information shows that Triad-linked groups control more than $200 billion worth of the international heroin transactions (U.S. Senate, 1991). The documented information gathered by the U.S. investigative agencies shows that specific members of the Chinese Triads, Tongs, and street gangs have been regularly involved in the importation of heroin from Southeast Asia. Evidence indicates that the majority of these Triad, Tong, and street gang members act on their own or with the help of one or two other members, but without the assistance of the whole organization. Until recently, most Chinese groups have avoided selling heroin on the street. In most cases, the heroin was wholesaled to other ethnic groups who then sold the heroin at street level. This arrangement has recently changed as New York Chinese street gangs are becoming heavily involved in the street sale of heroin on the outskirts of Chinatown (U.S. Senate, 1991). The monetary gain that heroin trafficking produces encourages greater involvement of Triads, Tongs, and street gangs in street distribution of heroin.

## Money Laundering

The Chinese groups, like all other organized crime groups, have become involved in money laundering because of their participation in criminal activities. It has been difficult thus far for U.S. law enforcement agencies to make any headway in dissolving these criminal networks. The only dent made by law enforcement was in Boston where Goon Chun Yee (aka Harry Mook, the past president of the Hung Mun Chinese Freemasons Association), pleaded guilty to administering and participating in a multimillion-dollar worldwide money laundering scheme that was headquartered in Boston's Chinatown. This case also resulted in the arrest of several Boston police officers who were paid off by Mook to overlook his gambling operations (U.S. Senate, 1991).

## SPECIFIC GEOGRAPHIC AREAS

The Chinese groups, in some cases Triads, Tongs, and street gangs, have set up operations throughout the world. In the United States the Tongs and the street gangs have made a definite impact on all major urban centers. The areas discussed in the following paragraphs have seen a large influx of Asian immigrants over the past several years.

As Atlanta's Chinese population increased so did crimes involving Asians. Thus far the Hip Sing and On Leong Tong have set up chapters in Atlanta as have the Ghost Shadows street gang. Chicago, like New York, San Francisco, and Los Angeles, has a long-established Chinatown area, dominated by the On Leong Tong and the Ghost Shadows street gang. Chicago is one of the locations where Chinese organized crime groups and Italian organized crime groups work together. Both of these groups are involved in gambling operations and attempting to locate corrupt public officials to help run their other illegal activities. Law enforcement authorities in Houston have found that Chinese street gangs are present and have formed a bond with Vietnamese and Jamaican groups in running drug houses. The Alcohol, Tobacco, and Firearms enforcement agency (ATF) has unearthed evidence that clearly indicates that Chinese groups are investing in properties in Mexico, Belize, and Venezuela. In most cases, the Chinese groups buy legitimate businesses in these countries to launder their illegally obtained money (ATF, 1993).

Philadelphia has about 17 gangs, half of which are Chinese. Representatives from the Flying Dragons, Ghost Shadows, Ping On, Golden Eagles, and Black Eagles are present in Philadelphia, but a major portion of the membership are transients fleeing New York or returning to New York after committing a crime elsewhere. Atlantic City has become a center for some of the Chinese groups. Triads such as Sun Yee On, Wo Hop To, 14K, and Kung Luk, along with On Leong, Hip Sing, and Tong On Tongs, have operations in Atlantic City. Gambling is popular with the Chinese, as is money laundering. During the FBI operation "White Mane," one of the Chinese groups was found to be running money through the casinos. The Sun Yee On Triad pulled a $3 million baccarat scam at one casino while Herbert Liu, Freemason Tong member, put on shows at the Sands Hotel. Along with the Chinese groups has come an increase in the extortion of Asian businesses, drug trafficking, weapons smuggling, and home invasion robberies in all the major metropolitan areas where the groups have made their bases.

## CONCLUSIONS

The information presented in this chapter is meant to increase reader awareness of Chinese groups' impact on violence and crime in our society. Most likely, gang activity will get worse before it gets better, therefore, there is an explicit need for organization in our society to stop gang activities. Until such organization becomes effective, a decrease in gang activity by the Chinese groups is doubtful.

## ADDITIONAL READING

Appendix A lists the oaths and strategies of Chinese gangs.

# 10

# Japanese, Vietnamese, and Korean Gangs

The remaining three Asian organized crime groups include the Japanese (Yakuza), the Korean, and the Vietnamese. Japanese organized crime has been effectively operating throughout Japan for more than 300 years. Over the past several decades they have broadened their bases of operation, as well as their criminal activities, to almost everywhere in Asia, Australia, and the United States. Korean organized crime has extended only to locations outside of Korea during the past two decades with a great deal of their operations being controlled by street gangs in the United States. A majority of the Vietnamese criminal groups were formed in the United States during and after the Vietnam War. An association was formed with Chinese street gangs and from this alliance came what is now known as Vietnamese organized crime groups.

## JAPANESE ORGANIZED CRIME

The threat of Japanese organized crime to the United States and the world was expressed by U.S. Attorney General William French Smith in December 1982 when he noted that Japanese organized crime members were expanding from Hawaii to the whole North American continent. During U.S. congressional hearings on organized crime, evidence showed that members of Yakuza, the Japanese organized crime group, had held meetings with members of the La Cosa Nostra in both Hawaii and Las Vegas (*Cleu*, 1993). In fact, law enforcement agencies in Hawaii recorded Michael Zaffarino, a Bonanno family leader, displaying how profitable the pornography business could be for Japanese organized crime families (FBI, 1992). According to FBI intelligence reports, contacts between bosses of the La Cosa Nostra and leaders of the Yakuza have increased drastically over the past decade (FBI, 1992).

This threat was enhanced by the fact that the Yakuza is one of the richest organized crime families in the world and that for years they have been investing in properties both offshore and in the mainland of North America. Again in December 1987 another warning was set forth about the threat of Japanese organized crime to the United States. This time the warning was given by the FBI through a report published on Asian organized crime in the United States. The FBI stated that the Boryokudan group would create a consequential crime dilemma for most police agencies in the western part of the United States. Apparently these predictions were sufficiently established but totally understated considering the fact that the Boryokudan has become established in both Guam and the Northern Marianas Islands. The influence of this Yakuza group continues to grow in Hawaii and on both the east and west coasts of the United States. Local U.S. law enforcement agencies that should anticipate the growth of Japanese organized crime groups in their cities include: Honolulu, San Francisco, Los Angeles, Las Vegas, Newark, New York City, Boston, Atlanta, Seattle, Portland, and Washington, D.C. Four Japanese gangs that have been continually moving parts of their operations into the United States are the Yamaguchi-Gumi, Sumiyoshi-Kai, Inagawa-Kai, and Toa Yuai Jigyo Kumiai (FBI, 1992).

The Boryokudan may become a more dangerous threat to the United States than any other organized crime group because of their ability to launder illegally obtained currency and to penetrate and bankrupt legitimate companies. They use colleagues to combine legally obtained money with unlawfully acquired money to purchase a legitimate company, then all of the money effectively becomes legal currency. The victims of the Japanese gangs are usually members of the Japanese community.

Approximately 850,000 people of Japanese ancestry currently live in the United States. Just about 88 percent of this population is American-born, and a major portion of this group lives in either Hawaii or California. For this reason, Japanese gang activity is far more common on the West Coast. Areas of Hawaii, California, Oregon, Washington, and Vancouver, B.C., are major vacation spots for Japanese visitors. These locations provide members of Japanese organized crime an opportunity to set up fraudulent vacation activities that exploit these foreign travelers. Although these types of activities can be considered trivial they can also be viewed as a training ground for new members who will ultimately become involved in far more elaborate illegal schemes (FBI, 1992).

Organized crime groups first appeared in Japan more than 300 years ago. What can be considered the start of organized crime groups occurred when the feudal Japanese monarchs did away with Samurai warriors. The new government leaders saw no need for these inordinate soldiers who had served Japan's feudal barons during the sixteenth and seventeenth centuries. The once-proud Samurai warriors found themselves cast adrift by the leaders for whom they would have sacrificed their lives. They soon became an undisciplined group of mercenaries who were unable to contend with peaceful times. Many of these warriors found themselves roaming the countryside committing crimes against local merchants and farmers to support themselves (Kata, 1964). Eventually, the Samurai members were to become a major part of what is known today as the Yakuza (a gambling term for numbers that are considered worthless or useless). Other Japanese organized crime definitions are given in Figure 10-1.

Groups known as the Tekiya or Yashi (street traders), or Bakuto (street gamblers) were formed along with a larger group, the Boryokudan (violent ones), which has been in existence for more than 300 years and at one time was committed to old customs and the cultural traditions of Japan. Many of the early members of Boryokudan regarded themselves as direct descendants of the Samurai warriors. The Boryokudan recruited a vast majority of its members from the buraku (ghetto), from a group that constantly complained that they were abused and discriminated against by the rest of Japanese society. Another ghetto group that became a part the Boryokudan

---

**Oyabun**
Literally, "father role," the overall boss of the Rengo, Gumi, Kai.

**Kobun**
Literally, "child role," the member of a gang, obligated to his Oyabun as a child is to its father.

**Yakuza** (yahk-za)
Literally, "8-9-3," a term derived from the worst possible score in a card game "Hanafuda." Totalling "20" the player automatically "loses." Thus, he is a loser, "good for nothing." This term is preferred by Japanese gangsters.

**Boryokudan**
"Violent ones," the term preferred by the Japanese National Police Agency (NPA) when referring to the Yakuza. The NPA has defined "Boryokudan" as an organization which collectively or habitually engages in, or has the possibility of engaging in, violent and unlawful acts.

---

**FIGURE 10-1** Japanese Organized Crime Definitions
*Source:* U.S. Dept. of Justice, FBI, 1993.

was the Eta, meaning "much contamination." They worked jobs that Japanese society considered the most repugnant (slaughtering animals, washing and dressing dead bodies, etc.). This group was stigmatized with the name "sangoku-jin" or third country people. The ghetto associates were comprised of different ethnic members including Chinese and Korean who were seeking ways to rid themselves of poverty. These ghetto-bred individuals quickly became the most violent members of the Boryokudan.

Prior to World War II members of the Yakuza adopted the American gangster dress style and strut. Most gang participants have ornate tattoos all over their bodies. Many tattoos relate to the Samurai warriors who most members identify as the original founders of the group. One must also remember that tattooing was initially used in feudal Japan to classify the criminal elements in its society. The gang embraced the tattooing as an additional trademark of its mobster image. These modern-day criminals are known as "koika boryokudan" or the chic violent ones.

When the leader of the Yakuza group decides that one of the members has violated group policy, the member must atone for his mistake by cutting off the joint of his last finger (a ceremonial ritual known as *yubitsume*) and presenting it to his boss. It is then up to the boss to decide whether all is forgiven. This type of action may be required with other fingers anytime a mistake is made by a "koban" soldier and the reparation is accepted by the leader. If cutting off a finger is not acceptable as atonement by the boss, then the member might have to commit "seppuku" or suicide the dignified way by self-disembowelment. Many of the gangs portray themselves as "mutual aid societies," but most people are aware of this deceptive label. At the conclusion of World War II, a large number of social and economic problems permitted the Yakuza to gain control quickly over the newly created black market. They then extended their activities to include gambling, extortion, prostitution, labor racketeering, and drug trafficking. A number of new gangs consisting mostly of delinquents known as "chimpira" began to appear in Japan. Some of these newly organized gangs were known as "gurentai" or "seishonen-furyo dan." A significant amount of turbulent contention arose among the new and old gangs. Ultimately these new groups were assimilated into either the "bakuto" or "tekiya" (U.S. Customs Service, 1993).

The Yakuza permanence lies in the gangs' ability to control power and money, and the major purpose of this group is to increase the organization through force. Presently, approximately 2,300 Yakuza gangs contain about 87,000 members. A gang member's rank is decided by that person's productivity as an procurer of assets for his bosses. The higher the person's status in the organization, the larger the amount of funds that are allocated to him while still responsible to the higher-ranking officials in the group.

The Yakuza maintains a competitive association designed to pressure each member to maintain a high level of productivity. Yakuza members are always seeking ways to create new ventures to gratify their bosses. In fact, the two most important functions of Japanese gang members are remaining loyal and productive to their superiors and being responsible to their specific group.

The ability of the Japanese people to adapt is evident from the way Japan's industries rebounded after World War II. This resurgence was accomplished through the use of Western society's management and business techniques and without losing sight of their own traditions. Japanese gangs, like the society surrounding them, are just as capable of modifying their work styles in order to adjust to the organizational systems of criminal gangs in the United States. We must remember that the Yakuza has already formed a relationship with La Cosa Nostra (LCN), and with its assistance the Yakuza would easily adapt to U.S. activities.

The Yakuza, like many other gangs, has a membership initiation ritual that permeates the growth of kinship and cohesiveness between the leaders and the workers. This rite is similar to the ceremonial installation conducted by LCN but the Japanese investiture involves a greater commitment to the organization and its objectives. Another component of Yakuza membership requires the newly installed person to become a "sworn brother" to all other members. The ritual is called *Engumi* (Figure 10-2) and is the first of a three-part initiation rite of passage referred to as the "Sakazuki-goto," the union of a blood kinship. A second type of rite, a "Shumei," involves the selection of a new leader after either the death or retirement of the present boss. The last ritual, "Teuchi," relates to two groups that have been involved in a number of violent encounters, meeting to agree to a peaceful truce. These rites are ties that remain between the present-day Yakuza and its predecessor, the Samurai (FBI, 1992). Figures 10-3 and 10-4 show the group and subgroup structures of the Yakuza.

## THE GANGS

### Yamaguchi-Gumi

The largest Yakuza group is known as the Yamaguchi-Gumi. This gang contains 750 branches that have approximately 20,000 members and control about 80 percent of Japan's prefectures (see Figures 10-5 and 10-6). This group has been beleaguered by hostilities within the ranks and with opposing gangs. A major portion of the Yamaguchi-Gumi's problems started after the death of their Oyabun, Kazuo "The Bear" Taoka, in 1981. Then in 1982,

In order for the binding to be fully consummated, the presence of the following people is required:

Toji-Sha—the persons who are to form the relationship by the exchange of cups.
Torimochi-Nin—a mediator, or go-between.
Mitidoke-Nin—a witness to the ceremony.

The foregoing represent the minimum of individuals who must be involved. However, in most cases where there are considerably large families involved or when a family requires strict adherence to formality, other attendants are required as follows:

Koken-Nin—a guardian, or elder. Usually the boss or mentor of the person involved.
Tokubetsu-Koken-Nin—a special guardian, assistant to the mentor.
Maishaku-Nin—a matchmaker who performs the ceremony instead of the Torimochi-Nin.
Kenbun-Nin—an examiner, a special high-ranking witness.
Suisen-Nin—a character witness who recommends the suitability of the person concerned.
Honso-Nin—an assistant in the mediation process.
Sashizoe-Nin—an assistant concerned with the formation of the brother relationships.
Tachiai-Nin—lower-ranking attendants.

Originally, the Torimochi-Nin used to perform the Sakazuki-Goto (Engumi) ceremony, but now the Baishaku-Nin performs the ceremony almost exclusively. Conducted in a specially designated ceremonial room, containing a Saidan, or altar, preparations for the ceremony begin with the placing of the likenesses of the Japanese gods upon the top tier, the most honorable place. The gods that are invoked during this ceremony are the following:

Hackiman-Dai-Bosatsu—a god of bravery
Amaterasu-Oomi-Kami—original god
Kasuga-Dai Myojin—a god of bravery
Katori-Dai Myojin—the god of military/martial arts

On the second tier of the Saidan, offerings to the gods, in the form of food placed on square plates, are arranged. On either side of the Saidan are arranged large name plates reading:

Toji-Sha
Koken-Nin
Torimochi-Nin
Honso-Nin
Suisen-Nin
Baishaku-Nin

**FIGURE 10-2**   Engumi Initiation Ceremony
*Source:* U.S. Dept. of Justice, FBI, 1993.

On both sides of the ceremonial room, name plates for the Mitadoke-Nin and the Tachiai-Nin are placed in order of their ranking, beginning from the upper seat in the room. A long, bleached cotton sheet is spread in the center of the room from the center of the Saidan and extending to the lowest seat in the room, similar to the red carpet used for dignitaries. Sacred sake, called Omiki, is set upon the Sango, or cloth, decorated with origami, folded paper in the form of male and female butterflies. Sacred salt, in the form of a hardened pyramid is also placed on the Sanpo, along with fresh fish (usually red snapper), and a set of long chopsticks. After everything has been arranged, all attendants enter the room and take their reserved seats. In the case of a two-party Engumi, the two participants take their places face-to-face in front of the Saidan. If there are three or more, the participants take their seats facing the attendants. The Baishaku-Nin takes his seat facing the Saidan at the very end of the room. The Torimochi-Nin and the Honso-Nin sit on the right side of the Baishaku-Nin who begins the ceremony with an opening speech after which he places the Sanpo with the sacred sake upon the altar and briefly prays. Then, placing three Sanpos in front of the participants, the Baishaku-Nin places the salt, fish, and sake upon each Sanpo from left to right. Taking a Sanpo in front of himself he then places an unglazed sake cup upon it, bows his head and again prays to the gods. Then, removing the male and female butterflies and the sacred sake bottles, he fills the unglazed cup, drinks it, and declares that the sake is not poisoned. The Baishaku-Nin then fills the remaining two cups on the Sanpo with the sacred sake and again silently prays. After pouring the sake, he touches the sacred salt and the fish with the chopsticks and, moving the chopsticks over the cups, he mingles the salt and the blood of the fish with the sake. Placing the Sanpo with the sake cups on it between the persons concerned, he instructs them to drink half of it. He then mixes the rest of the sake, adding some to the already mingled sake and presents them to the Torimochi-Nin, confirming that they are well blended, thus concluding the first drinking ceremony.

The second drinking ceremony begins with the Baishaku-Nin approaching the participants again and instructing them to finish the sake in one gulp. The Baishaku-Nin then declares the completion of the Engumi. After finishing the sake, the participants place the sake cups upside down on the Sanpo, wrap them with paper whereupon each participant places the cup into the breast folds of his kimono. In another version, the Baishaku-Nin takes the handle of a dagger and smashes the sake cups to pieces upon the Sanpo, thus symbolizing that as the cups can never resurrect, never can the newly formed relationship be canceled. The Baishaku-Nin then steps to the Torimochi-Nin and reports the final consummation of the Engumi. Occupying the upper seat, the Torimochi-Nin faces the two participants and instructs them to join hands with each other, at the same time joining his hands with theirs. He then advises them to make their best efforts to help each other, while the participants pledge themselves to each other forever. The Mitadoke-Nin and the Tachiai-Nin clap their hands to celebrate the finality of the Engumi and to confirm it. The Baishaku-Nin declares the conclusion of the Engumi to all of the attendees, whereupon the participants express their gratitude to all in attendance. Finally, a sumptuous banquet is held in celebration.

**FIGURE 10-2 *continued*** Engumi Initiation Ceremony

*Source:* U.S. Dept. of Justice, FBI, 1993.

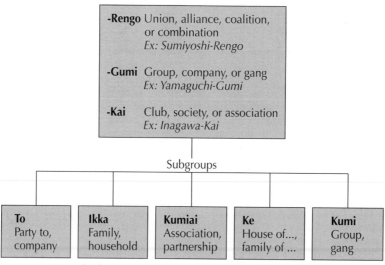

| **To** Party to, company | **Ikka** Family, household | **Kumiai** Association, partnership | **Ke** House of..., family of ... | **Kumi** Group, gang |

-**Rengo** Union, alliance, coalition, or combination
 *Ex: Sumiyoshi-Rengo*

-**Gumi** Group, company, or gang
 *Ex: Yamaguchi-Gumi*

-**Kai** Club, society, or association
 *Ex: Inagawa-Kai*

Subgroups

A Boryokudan group may include in excess of 100 subgroups

**FIGURE 10-3** Yakuza Group Structure
*Source:* U.S. Dept. of Justice, FBI, 1993.

the obvious successor to Taoka, Ken Yamamoto, died in prison. These deaths left two other Yamaguchi-Gumi leaders, Hiroshi Yamamoto and Masahisa Takenaka, vying for the top position. Ultimately, Takenaka was chosen as the new boss of the Yamaguchi-Gumi. In June 1984, an angry Yamamoto proceeded to withdraw from the Yamaguchi-Gumi along with 18 top lieutenants and 13,000 members to form a new group known as the Ichiwa-Kai. Takenaka remained calm and offered the dissidents an expanded benefits package that included amnesty and a retirement income plan. This offer by Takenaka was accepted by 10,000 of the defectors who were welcomed back by the Yamaguchi-Gumi gang. A short time after many gang members had reaffiliated themselves with Yamaguchi-Gumi, Takenaka and two of his top aides were assassinated by four members of the Ichiwa-Kai. These murders resulted in an emergency meeting of the Yamaguchi-Gumi leaders who named Kazuo Nakanishi the new boss and pledged an all-out war against the Ichiwa-Kai.

Over the next six months, Japanese riot police found themselves on constant alert seizing weapons and arresting gang members. During this time period about 200 shootings took place, 26 of which resulted in the death of a Yakuza member.

As the number of confrontations increased the Yamaguchi-Gumi's need for weapons became more apparent to gang leaders. One such member,

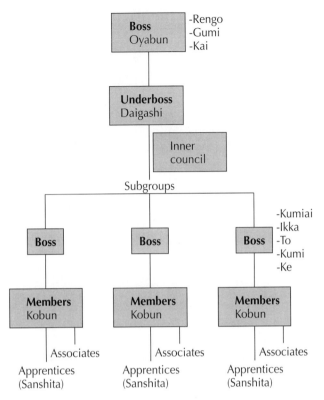

**FIGURE 10-4** Yakuza Subgroup Structure

*Source:* U.S. Dept. of Justice, FBI, 1993.

Masashi Takenaka, set out to obtain new weapons for the gang but in doing so he made a major mistake. Takenaka approached two undercover U.S. federal agents and offered to trade 8½ kilos of heroin and another 8½ kilos of methamphetamine for 3 rocket launchers, 5 machine guns, 100 handguns, and a executioner (hit man) to murder the entire upper echelon of the Ichiwa-Kai by firing a rocket into the headquarters of the Ichiwa-Kai. This conspiracy resulted in the arrest of ten members of the Yamaguchi-Gumi and the subsequent conviction of only one, Koyoshi Kajita, with the acquittal of the other nine members. Even without what would be considered a sufficient amount of guns, the unwavering attacks on the Ichiwa-Kai by the Yamaguchi-Gumi resulted in the disintegration of the Ichiwa-Kai. The Yamaguchi-Gumi assimilated a major portion of the membership of the dismantled Ichiwa-Kai gang.

The Yamaguchi-Gumi gang has a total of 92 leaders. The head of the group is known as the fifth boss, and each of the other 91 leaders has his

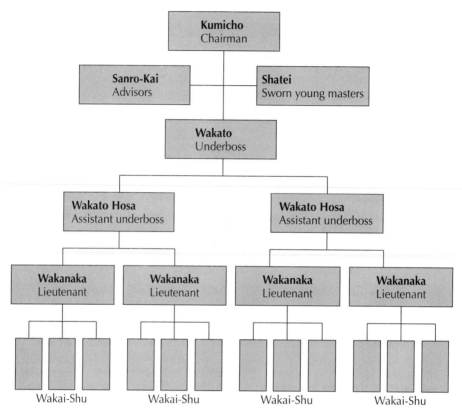

**FIGURE 10-5** Yamaguchi-Gumi Organization Structure
*Source:* U.S. Dept. of Justice, FBI, 1993.

own subdivision of the gang. If a member of one of these subbranches manages a prosperous business, he can, in turn, establish his own subgroup of the gang. The power of the Yamaguchi-Gumi as a group comes from the gang's ability to recruit new members and maintain the largest membership of all the Japanese groups. According to estimates the Yamaguchi-Gumi has approximately 25,000 members. Some of the gang's subgroups have been using corporate classifications to disguise their true identities and unlawful activities from law enforcement agencies (FBI, 1992).

Prior to the Yamaguchi-Gumi's selection of a new leader the organization embraced a cooperative leadership style of management. Under this type of supervision the gang avoided controversy by staying out of the media limelight. This anonymity did not last long because the appointment of the new leadership brought with it a desire to aggrandize the treasury and territories of the Yamaguchi-Gumi by moving into regions under the control of other

**Prefectures and Cities**

| | | | | | |
|---|---|---|---|---|---|
| 2. **Akita** | Akita | 18. **Kagoshima** | Kagoshima | | |
| 3. **Aomori** | Aomori | 19. **Kanagawa** | Yokohama | 35. **Saitama** | Urawa |
| 4. **Chiba** | Chiba | 21. **Kumamoto** | Kumamoto | | |
| | | | | 39. **Tochigi** | Utsunomiya |
| 10. **Gumma** | Maebashi | | | 41. **Tokyo** | |
| 11. **Hiroshima** | Hiroshima | | | | |
| 14. **Ibaraki** | Mito | 29. **Niigata** | Niigata | 45. **Yamagata** | Yamagata |
| | | | | 46. **Yamaguchi** | Yamaguchi |
| 16. **Iwate** | Morioka | | | 47. **Yamanashi** | Kofu |

**FIGURE 10-6** Yamaguchi-Gumi Sphere of Influence

*Source:* U.S. Dept. of Justice, FBI, 1993.

gangs. Encroaching on other gangs' areas precipitated skirmishes between the Yamaguchi-Gumi and these other Yakuza groups. In fact, on December 4, 1990, a meeting in Isogo-ku, Yokohama, was attended by members of the Yamaguchi-Gumi gang to formulate tactics to move in on the Tokyo territories of the Sumiyoshi-Kai. The decision made by Yamaguchi-Gumi was to set up business offices as "operational bases" in Tokyo, which would be used to recruit new members. The Sumiyoshi-Kai, in turn, responded by forewarning the Yamaguchi-Gumi that the Sumiyoshi-Kai would never allow the Yamaguchi-Gumi to interfere in the criminal enterprises controlled by the Sumiyoshi-Kai in Tokyo.

The Yamaguchi-Gumi, in an effort to increase membership, defied an age-old Yakuza rule that forbids enlisting membership from rogue groups; the Yamaguchi-Gumi has continued to seek out and enroll these outlaw groups into their gang. Strife within the ranks of the Yamaguchi-Gumi has plagued the gang. This discord has been caused by what some members of the gang consider disparity in the reparations for distinguished deeds performed during the skirmishes with the Ichiwa-Kai and the treatment of members recently infused from other gangs.

One member of the Yamaguchi-Gumi who has been highly visible in the media in the past two years is Masaru Takumi, the Wakagashira or underboss of the Yamaguchi-Gumi gang. Takumi was refused admittance to Paris in 1992, was linked to tour companies in Vancouver, and purchased houses in Vancouver and in Australia (Hogben, August 6, 1992, and March 20, 1993). Takumi was also arrested in July 1992 for violations of the Foreign Exchange Control Law after he purchased the home in Vancouver, Canada. Takumi was one of the first members of the Yakuza to be arrested under a new foreign exchange law that is part of a set of laws used by police to arrest and prosecute members of Japanese organized crime.

Under this new antigang legislation, known as the Boryokudan Countermeasures Laws, which took effect on March 1, 1992, crime groups in Japan can be certified by the police as being boryokudan or violent organized criminal gangs. This new law makes the certification of these gangs relatively easy because the police need only to prove that approximately four percent of the gang members have criminal histories. With regard to the number of members of the Yakuza gangs with criminal records, a study conducted by the Hyogo Prefecture Police indicates that 50 percent of the Yamaguchi-Gumi's senior members have criminal records, while 34 percent of the Inagawa-Kai membership and 27 percent of the Sumiyoshi-Kai have previous criminal histories (FBI, 1992). Once a gang is recognized as a violent group the police can raid its business offices, confiscate its weapons, and arrest members without a warrant. Another part of the legislation deals specifically with prosecuting individuals who are involved in money laundering.

## Sumiyoshi-Kai

This group is considered a "bakuto" or gambling-oriented organization. A major part of this gang's revenue has been obtained from illegal gambling operations in Japan. The Sumiyoshi-Kai is based in Tokyo and its top leader is Masao Hori who prefers that this group stay out of the limelight. This Sumiyoshi-Rengo-Kai gang consists of 177 different subsections and it is considered the most powerful Yakuza group in Eastern Japan. Masao Hori combined all the Sumiyoshi-Kai groups along with other gambling associations under the Sumiyoshi-Rengo organization in 1969. Since that time Hori has completely changed the hierarchy of the gang and the areas that the gang controls in Eastern Japan. Then in 1988, Hori took control of the gang by making himself the "Sosai" or president of the group (FBI, 1992). Within his newly structured group, Hori created new positions to enable change in the organization that would help his alliance sustain its power and not be overtaken by the Yamaguchi-Gumi or the Inagawa-Kai. The Sumiyoshi-Kai uses what can be considered a management team to make decisions. Representatives of this group are chosen from the leadership of the Sumiyoshi-Kai subgroups and they are responsible for providing the organization with deliberate and concise group decisions. The one major advantage to this process is that once a decision is made by the board, their determination can be easily administered without any major opposition within the group. The Sumiyoshi-Kai's use of this type of management resolution may ultimately assist this group in becoming quite successful in their criminal ventures in North America (FBI, 1992). See Figures 10-7 and 10-8.

Gambling is becoming more and more acceptable throughout the United States and Canada. Legalized gambling has been operating for years in Las Vegas and Atlantic City. Recently several states have passed laws to legalize gambling. In other states it is legal for casino gambling to be operated on Indian reservations. In Japan, betting on pachinko (a pinball-type game), bicycle racing, horse racing, and speedboat racing is legal and run by local organizations. Presently, Japan has more than 10,000 pachinko parlors, and the Sumiyoshi-Kai direct a major portion of these operations. The Sumiyoshi-Kai also controls illegal casinos, off-track bookmaking, a portion of the entertainment industry, pornography, prostitution, stimulant trafficking, and gun running. A majority of these illegal practices would prosper in either an Atlantic City or Las Vegas environment.

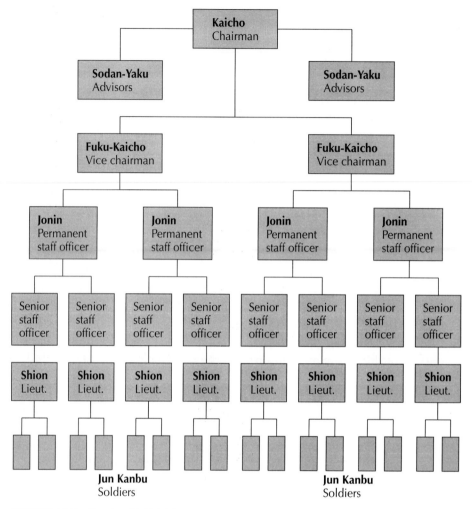

**FIGURE 10-7** Sumiyoshi-Kai Management
*Source:* U.S. Dept. of Justice, FBI, 1993.

## Inagawa-Kai

The Inagawa-Kai is considered the number three Yakuza group in Japan. This gang is made up of 313 subgroups with a membership of more than 6,700 in 20 prefectures throughout Japan (see Figure 10-9). The leader of this group is Kakuji Inagawa. The hierarchy of this gang consists of 18 fixed administrative positions with Kakuji Inagawa at the top. The Inagawa-Kai is run quite differently from the Sumiyoshi-Kai in that all policy judgments are made by Kakuji Inagawa and not by a board of managers like the Sumiyoshi-

| Prefectures and Cities | | | | | | | |
|---|---|---|---|---|---|---|---|
| 1. **Aichi** | Nagoya | | | | | | |
| | | 18. **Kagoshima** | Kagoshima | | 34. **Saga** | Saga | |
| | | | | | 35. **Saitama** | Urawa | |
| 4. **Chiba** | Chiba | 20. **Kochi** | Kochi | | 36. **Shiga** | Otsu | |
| 5. **Ehime** | Matsuyama | 21. **Kumamoto** | Kumamoto | | 37. **Shimane** | Matsue | |
| 6. **Fukui** | Fukui | 22. **Kyoto** | Kyoto | | 38. **Shizouka** | Shizouka | |
| 7. **Fukuoka** | Fukuoka | 23. **Mie** | Tsu | | | | |
| | | 24. **Miyagi** | Sendai | | 40. **Tokushima** | Tokushima | |
| | | 25. **Miyazaki** | Miyazaki | | | | |
| 11. **Hiroshima** | Hiroshima | 27. **Nagasaki** | Nagasaki | | 42. **Tottori** | Tottori | |
| | | 28. **Nara** | Nara | | 43. **Toyama** | Toyama | |
| 13. **Hyogo** | Kobe | 29. **Niigata** | Niigata | | 44. **Wakayama** | Wakayama | |
| 14. **Ibaraki** | Mito | 30. **Oita** | Oita | | | | |
| 15. **Ishikawa** | Kanazawa | 31. **Okayama** | Okayama | | 46. **Yamaguchi** | Yamaguchi | |
| 16. **Iwate** | Morioka | 32. **Okinawa** | Naha | | 47. **Yamanashi** | Kofu | |

**FIGURE 10-8**   Sumiyoshi-Kai Sphere of Influence

*Source:* U.S. Dept. of Justice, FBI, 1993.

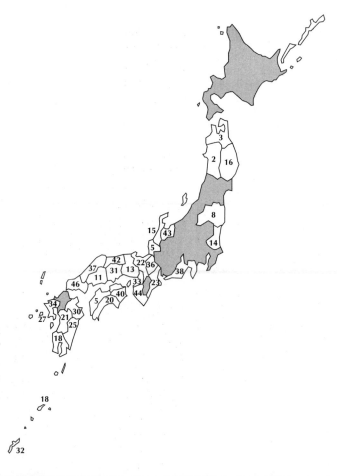

## Prefectures and Cities

| 1. **Aichi** | Nagoya | 17. **Kagawa** | Takamatsu | 33. **Osaka** | Osaka |
|---|---|---|---|---|---|
| 2. **Akita** | Akita | 18. **Kagoshima** | Kagoshima | 34. **Saga** | Saga |
| 3. **Aomori** | Aomori | | | 35. **Saitama** | Urawa |
| | | 20. **Kochi** | Kochi | 36. **Shiga** | Otsu |
| 5. **Ehime** | Matsuyama | 21. **Kumamoto** | Kumamoto | 37. **Shimane** | Matsue |
| 6. **Fukui** | Fukui | 22. **Kyoto** | Kyoto | 38. **Shizouka** | Shizouka |
| | | 23. **Mie** | Tsu | | |
| 8. **Fukushima** | Fukushima | | | 40. **Tokushima** | Tokushima |
| | | 25. **Miyazaki** | Miyazaki | | |
| | | | | 42. **Tottori** | Tottori |
| 11. **Hiroshima** | Hiroshima | 27. **Nagasaki** | Nagasaki | 43. **Toyama** | Toyama |
| | | | | 44. **Wakayama** | Wakayama |
| 13. **Hyogo** | Kobe | 30. **Oita** | Oita | | |
| 14. **Ibaraki** | Mito | 31. **Okayama** | Okayama | 46. **Yamaguchi** | Yamaguchi |
| 15. **Ishikawa** | Kanazawa | 32. **Okinawa** | Naha | | |
| 16. **Iwate** | Morioka | | | | |

**FIGURE 10-9** Inagawa-Kai Sphere of Influence

*Source:* U.S. Dept. of Justice, FBI, 1993.

Kai. The Inagawa-Kai's organizational composition is similar to that of La Cosa Nostra, and like La Cosa Nostra this gang also assigns communications and coordination activities to chosen supervisors. The Inagawa-Kai equivalents in the Yamaguchi-Gumi and Sumiyoshi-Kai partake in a tariff procedure. Although the leader of the Inagawa-Kai, Kakuji Inagawa, demands that his membership pay a much higher levy than most other groups (FBI, 1992).

Inagawa-Kai has sustained an ongoing friendly relationship with Yamaguchi-Gumi and has managed to improve their long-term alliances with the Aizu-Kotetsu-Kai based in Kyoto and the Doya-Kai of Nagoya. As this group moves its activities into other districts of Japan, the gang also continues to assimilate other smaller gangs into the Inagawa-Kai. In an effort to avoid both police and media attention, this gang went as far as to remove its symbol from the front of its headquarters. In recent years, the Inagawa-Kai, like the Sumiyoshi-Kai, has set its goals on higher stakes by advancing into more complex scams within the financial affairs area.

In the past several years, dissension has increased among members of this gang over escalating amounts of tariffs they are forced to pay. Another factor causing conflict is Kakuji Inagawa's practice of maintaining an unreasonable number of older members in higher-ranking positions within the Inagawa-Kai, which in turn denies upper mobility to younger members of this gang. Kakuji Inagawa has also stirred up dissatisfaction by attempting to place his son Chihiro Inagawa, who is 50 years old, in the number two position without any consideration for some far more productive and deserving high-ranking gang officials. In fact, some of the recent moves by Kakuji Inagawa have been more harmful than helpful to the gang.

An investigation by the U.S. Department of Justice has recently concluded that the Inagawa-Kai is investing a great deal of its capital in Hawaii, California, and Nevada. Early in its investigation the FBI discovered direct links between the Yamaguchi-Gumi, the Inagawa-Kai, and the Toa Yuai Jigyo Kumiai. The information gathered by the FBI indicates that these groups have formed partnerships in order to make investments in various business enterprises in the United States and Canada (FBI, 1992).

### Toa Yuai Jigyo Kumiai

The Toa Yuai Jigyo Kumiai (TYJK), which is also known as the East Asia Friendship and Enterprise Union, and previously (prior to 1979) known as the Tosei-Kai, consists of six subgroups with a total of 850 members. Although the membership of this group seems small, they actively participate in criminal conduct in the United States, Japan, and Canada. TYJK controls more than 20 prefectures throughout Japan. The scope of their power is remarkable when compared to the Inagawa-Kai, which has 313 subgroups and more than 6,700 members and controls about the same total number of prefectures. TYJK is one of the few Yakuza groups that has a number of other ethnic Asians within the membership. Approximately 15 percent of the TYJK is ethnic Koreans, and a major portion of the TYJK's power structure has Korean lineage (FBI, 1992).

Information gathered by the FBI shows that one of the top leaders of the TYJK is a formidable Japanese billionaire entrepreneur. According to Japanese police and FBI intelligence information this businessman controls a Tokyo-based corporation that has a large number of companies and land resources all over the United States and Canada (FBI, 1992).

TYJK has been identified by both the FBI and the U.S. DEA as being heavily involved in drug trafficking in Hawaii. This type of activity presents a major problem to the U.S. government because of the ability of Japanese gangs to set up sophisticated networks of drug importation and the Yakuza's ever increasing competency in the money laundering business. Figure 10-10 is a list of terms used by Yakuza members to describe occupations, crimes, and group organization and relationships.

## CRIMINAL ACTIVITIES OF YAKUZA

### Money Laundering/Business Activities

The Yakuza has a profound ability to launder the proceeds of their criminal activities without attracting attention from law enforcement agencies throughout the world. The United States and Canada have become primary locations for Yakuza groups to launder their money (see Figure 10-11). Federal authorities have pinpointed Yakuza money laundering operations in Hawaii, Los Angeles, San Francisco, Las Vegas, Colorado, Washington State, and New Jersey. In most areas, the Yakuza has penetrated into lawful Japanese and American (usually Japanese-American) companies to launder their money that in most cases was illegally obtained in Japan.

One thing about the Yakuza that must always be remembered is their ability as a group to make legal profit through the use of illegal funds. Yakuza gang members are using what can be considered fees assessed on their membership along with money expropriated from gang-owned businesses to finance their ventures into Kabutocho, Tokyo's stock market. They then retrieve their earnings and distribute the accumulated funds to participating gangs. The Inagawa-Kai, for example, has managed to accumulate well over a hundred million yen in profits through their dealings in the Tokyo stock ex-

**Typical Crimes**
Likely to be found on Japanese "rap sheets"

Baishun Boshiho Ihan – Violation of
  antiprostitution law
Boko – Simple assault
Chakufuku – Embezzlement
Fuhu Kyoki Shoyo – Illegal possession
  of deadly weapon
Gizo – Forgery
Kakuseizai – Stimulant drugs
  (slang - Shabu or Piropon)
Kenka – Fighting
Kinshi Yakuhin – Prohibited drugs
Kyogino Chinjutsusho – False written
  statement
Kyogino Moshitate – False oral statement
Kyohaku – Extortion
Mayaku – Narcotics
Sagi – Fraud
Satsujin – Homicide
Shogai – Assault and battery
Shogai Chishi – Assault and battery
  resulting in death
Tabaku – Gambling
Wairo – Bribery
Yukai – Kidnapping
Zenka – Criminal record

**Typical Occupations**
Likely to be found on visa applications

Doboku – Civil engineering (usually work
  obtained by graft)
Fundosan – Real estate
Kanekashi – Money lending (loan shark)
Kensetsu – Construction
Kinyugaisha – Loan company
Kogyo Nushi – Promoter
  (entertainment, theater)
Unso of Unyo – Transportation

**Organization and Relationship**

Anikibun – Superior (in rank or position)
Bakuto – Gambler
Boryokudan – Violence groups
  (also Soshiki Hanzai)
Gumi – Association, company, gang
Gruentai – Hoodlum
Jiageya – Thugs who remove tenants by
  threats and force
Kai – Association, society
Kobun – Common Boryokudan,
  "child role"
Kuromaku – Behind-the-scenes power
  broker link to legitimate world
Ototobun – Inferior (in rank or position)
Oyabun – Boss, godfather, "parent role"
Rengo – Federation
Riji – Important advisor and link to
  legitimate world
Sarakin – Loan sharks, salary man
  financiers
Sokaiya – Corporate extortionists,
  financial racketeers
Tekiya – Street stall operator, con-man
  (slang - Yashi)
Tokushu Kabunushi – Corporate
  extortionists
Yubitsume – Slicing part of the finger off
  in apology

**FIGURE 10-10** Yakuza-Related Terminology
*Source:* U.S. Dept. of Justice, FBI, 1993.

change. In fact, the Inagawa-Kai created its own stock transaction company, Hokusho Sangyo, located in Chiyoda-Ku, Tokyo. The president of this stock exchange firm is Susumu Ishii who was the number two man in the Inagawa-Kai gang until his death in September 1991 (FBI, 1992).

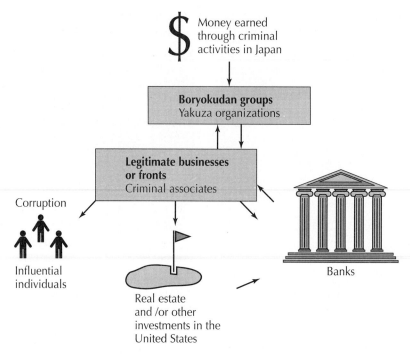

**FIGURE 10-11** Yakuza Investments Money Laundering in the United States
*Source:* U.S. Dept. of Justice, FBI, 1993.

Under the leadership of Susumu Ishii, the Hokusho Sangyo company expanded its investments to include real estate. The success of this company can be measured by the 12.2 million yen that it earned in 1987. Hokusho Sangyo's company then proceeded to build its home office in Kojimachi where the average 3.3 square yard plot cost approximately 50 million yen in 1988. Three specific circumstances helped the Inagawa-Kai become highly successful in its stock and real estate market ventures (FBI, 1992):

1. The group's innate ability to legally dispose of illegal funds

2. The procurement of funds from the Showa Lease, a finance company associated with the Kyowa Bank of Japan

3. The affirmed support of a major conveyance company

A subgroup of the Yamaguchi-Gumi, the Kyushu, has managed to scrupulously advance a substantial amount of currency to a local monetary affairs corporation by diverting the money via a financial consultation firm directed by a Sokaiya or corporate mobster. This company has been so successful that in 1989 it disbursed millions of yen in profits from its stock ventures to the upper echelon of this Kyushu organization (FBI, 1992).

Historically, stock market investments made by the Yakuza remained hidden from the public view. Most of the money made by these gangs involved tentative stock or bond ventures. In the past ten years, Yakuza groups have freely and assertively participated in stock market trading.

The Yakuza is constantly demonstrating its ability to adapt to the world around it in its money-making endeavors. The capability to adjust makes the Yakuza a conglomerate of criminal groups controlling an assorted collection of legal and illegal money-making operations. As a group they have their own stock market and real estate ventures. Recently they have entered into the oil painting market by offering to lengthen elevated percentage loans with the prestigious works of art as insurance against default on the loan. When the Gekkoso, a distinguished art gallery in the highly trendy Ginza district of Tokyo, foreclosed recently almost all of the gallery's 100 world-renowned paintings were acquired by a gallery associated with the Sumiyoshi Rengo-Kai gang. The Yakuza capabilities are enhanced by groups and/or agencies seeking to attract them to locations outside of Japan.

Gambling casinos in Las Vegas hire Japanese personnel in an effort to entice affluent Japanese businessmen, whether legitimate or illegitimate, to Las Vegas to disburse some of their money. This invitation, of course, entices Yakuza membership who are looking to get rid of or transfer over some of their unlawfully obtained funds. These trips to Las Vegas led to the formation of friendly relationships between Yakuza and La Cosa Nostra members in the early 1970s.

## Sokaiya (Corporate Extortion)

The ability of the Yakuza to diversify its legal and illegal operations has caused great concern among members of Japanese society. Japanese citizens have requested an expansion of police participation to impede the growth of these gangs. Recently, the police have attempted to control the activities of the gangs participating in Sokaiya.

The Sokaiya was originally a separate entity from the Yakuza. Recently they joined forces, with the Yakuza as the muscle part of the operation and the Sokaiya as the central processing unit. Sokaiya was initially a word used to refer to a competent individual who managed to procure an adequate amount of stock in a company so that this person could attend the stockholders meetings and attempt to disrupt the proceedings. The maneuvers used by the Sokaiya might be as slight as injecting a suitable phrase or as impertinent as disrupting the meetings. Doing so may make stockholders aware of the unethical or immoral activities of either the corporation or members of the company's executive board. In most cases, the Sokaiya receives a dividend from his stock holdings, which is usually some type of fee from the person who hired him to take this action. Some of these Sokaiya have claimed to be "grass-roots shareholders campaigners" but in reality are nothing more that con artists who use these methods to extort money from corporate executives (Jones, 1993).

These types of acts have been replaced by a modern-day Sokaiya who will act in whatever manner necessary to extort money from the corporation, including threats of publishing outrageous facts about corporate officials in unethical newspapers. These actions would not only damage the image of the company executives, it would also tarnish the reputation of the organization.

Shortly after the end of World War II the number of cases involving the Sokaiya increased at about the same rate as the Japanese economy. The 1980s brought along the Yakuza members as more active participants in these types of crimes. Until 1993 about 90 percent of all Sokaiya throughout Japan were controlled by members of the Yakuza. Early in 1980 approximately 1,800 active corporations in Japan reported that they had been extorted by the Sokaiya. If one considers the total number of corporations in Japan, the total of 1,800 companies reporting these incidents is small. In 1992 three senior executives of the Ito-Yokado Company, a Seven-Eleven convenience store chain, met with Sokaiya members on three occasions and delivered more than 27 million yen to these gangsters. A short time later both the company executives and the Sokaiya members were arrested for their participation in this criminal activity. These payoffs were given to the Sokaiya because they guaranteed the Ito-Yokado Company that Sokaiya members would refrain from making any humiliating revelations at the corporation's annual meetings in June (*New York Times*, 1992).

One recent incident in Japan involved the murder of Juntaro Suzuki, a senior executive of Fuji Film Company, who was hacked to death with a samurai sword near his residence in Tokyo on Monday, February 28, 1994. This horrible murder was preceded by numerous attempts by Sokaiya to extort money from the Fuji Film Company. During a Fuji Corporation meeting in January 1994 about 20 Sokaiya members created a disturbance by badgering Minoru Ohnishi, president of Fuji Film, over company policy related to dividends and other transactions. While the proceedings were continuing, one of the Sokaiya directly connected to the Yamaguchi-Gumi was arrested for tossing three different liquor bottles at Ohnishi (*Toronto Star*, 1994).

During 1981, three Sokaiya who were members of the Yamaguchi-Gumi, Koulchi Masada, Chiyousei T. Wada, and Yoshiki Asada, were in attendance at the stockholder meetings of International Telephone and Telegraph, the Bank of America Corporation, and the Pacific Gas and Electric Corporation, all in San Francisco. Afterwards, they then attended the meeting of the Chase Manhattan Bank in New York City. Information gathered on the three Yakuza members who attended these meetings by federal investigative sources indicated that the Yakuza gangs were "testing the waters" in an effort to ascertain whether to start using Sokaiya methods to extort U.S. corporations (Japan National Police Agency, 1993; FBI, 1992).

Information gathered by the National Police Agency of Japan indicates that Yakuza members with college educations are being recruited to attend U.S. universities in an effort to obtain advanced degrees in business. This strategy is an attempt to eventually infiltrate and ultimately extort U.S. industries. Subsequent data denotes that a Los Angeles Sokaiya group has been formed by both Japanese and Caucasian individuals who have been using the misleading identity "Japanese Defense Society" (1993).

The Yakuza can apply Sokaiya methods to U.S. corporations in an effort to build a foundation for movement into legitimate businesses. Once the Sokaiya establishes a base within U.S. business the Yakuza can then either extort money from these enterprises or use them to launder money. The Yakuza's average yearly profits are $10 billion. A major portion of these earnings have to be laundered through a number of phony companies and financial enterprises and ultimately put back in with other assets of the Yakuza.

## Investments

The Yakuza, like the scrupulous members of Japanese society, have recently become involved in real estate ventures, including investment in U.S. properties. In Hawaii alone, prior to 1990, Japanese real estate speculators invested more than $6 billion with an expected $1.3 billion in other land deals waiting to be consummated. Since 1988, a company owned and operated by a former member and present associate of the Yamaguchi-Gumi has acquired several parcels of land in Oahu valued at over $164 million, including the Turtle Bay Hilton Resort (U.S. Senate, 1993).

One recent real estate deal that went bad involved one Ken Mizuno, owner of Ken International Company of Tokyo and an associate of the Toa Yuai Jigyo Kumiai criminal organization (U.S. Senate, 1993). Mizuno used his corporation to transfer more than $265 million in what both the United States and Japanese governments consider "illegally obtained proceeds" from Japan to the United States. It is estimated that $100 million of the laundered money was used to purchase the Indian Wells Country Club and Hotel near Palm Springs, California, and the Royal Kenfield Country Club in Henderson, Nevada. Mizuno also bought a DC-9 jet, a $2.8 million home and a $2.3 million condominium in Beverly Hills. He also acquired three houses and a vacant lot in Hawaii. Between 1989 and 1991 Mizuno managed to lose more than $60 million playing the baccarat tables in Las Vegas. Mizuno reputedly has strong ties to the Yakuza (Schoenberger, 1993).

In another real estate deal a Tokyo developer, Minora Isutani, bought the Pebble Beach Country Club on the Monterey Peninsula in 1990. Testifying before a U.S. Senate Committee on Governmental Affairs a Yakuza associate using the name "Bully" described how Isutani and Japanese gangsters collaborated with the Itoman Corporation of Osaka, Japan, to purchase Pebble Beach and then offer for sale $1 billion worth of $100,000 memberships in a special club at the golf course (*San Francisco Examiner,* 1993).

The Riviera Country Club, on the bluffs overlooking the Pacific Palisades, was purchased by a Japanese investment firm in 1989. The group that acquired the Riviera, the Watanabe family, is presently under investigation by the U.S. government for possibly being involved in a money laundering scheme. Hiroyasu Watanabe, along with two others, was indicted by the Japanese government for providing $15.7 billion to corporations affiliated with Yakuza organized crime syndicates. Japan's second largest organized crime group, the Inagawa-Kai, received a total of 95.2 billion yen (*South China Morning Post,* 1992). Investigators are analyzing connections between the Watanabes and Shin Kanemaru, the most notorious Japanese political power broker in whose house the Japanese police recently found more than $50 million in cash and securities. He has also been implicated in a tax evasion case and being financially connected to members of the Yakuza. Although no definitive evidence at this time points to money laundering, U.S. government officials claim the Watanabes concealed the identity of their investors even after an agreement had been reached and a total of $53 million for the purchase was paid in cash (Schoenberger, 1993). Watanabe has been accused by the National Police Agency of Japan of hiring Susumu Ishii, the head of the Inagawa-Kai Yakuza group, to remove a group that was denouncing Prime Minister Noboru Takeshita, who was at that time involved in a campaign to be elected Prime Minister of Japan. The group known as Nippon Kominto was ultimately removed from the area. Watanabe was also charged with unlawfully utilizing family business funds to make loans and credit warranties of approximately $765 million to corporations that were used as fronts by the Inagawa-Kai and other Yakuza groups. This money allegedly produced kickbacks to Japanese politicians (*New York Times,* 1992).

Atlantic City and Las Vegas gambling casinos are other locations where the Yakuza have attempted to gain a foothold. During 1978, Takashi

Sasakawa, whose father Ryoichi Sasakawa is closely associated with the Yakuza, attempted to purchase the Shelburne Hotel in Atlantic City with Benihana restaurant chain owner Hiroaki "Rocky" Aoki in order to convert the old hotel into a casino. This effort ultimately failed because of the lack of financial assistance and increasing inquiries by both state and federal law enforcement agencies.

Then in 1982, Ken Mizuno first appeared on the Las Vegas scene and proceeded to open a restaurant in the Tropicana Hotel. The Aladdin Hotel and Casino in Las Vegas was purchased in 1986 by Ginji Yasuda, whose funding came from a finance company operated by Yasumichi Morishita who had direct links to the Yakuza. Morishita apparently used members of the Sumiyushi-Kai Yakuza group as enforcers to collect money owed to him (U.S. Senate, 1991). Yasuda soon became the first Japanese citizen to be issued a Las Vegas casino license. Minori Isutani, another Yakuza associate, purchased the Barcelona Hotel in Las Vegas in 1988 and attempted to obtain a casino license but retracted his application before the Nevada Gaming Board's intensive investigation was finished.

## Drugs

Approximately 33 percent of the Yakuza's earnings are obtained from drug trafficking. The principal drug dealt by Yakuza groups is crystal methamphetamine, known as "shabu," the primary drug of Japan's drug culture. In the United States this drug goes by the name "ice."

About 100 percent of the methamphetamine market in Japan is controlled by the Yakuza. In an effort to cultivate a U.S. market for this drug product the Yakuza started smuggling crystal methamphetamine into Hawaii in the early 1980s. The first indication of trafficking of crystal methamphetamine into the United States was in 1984 when undercover U.S. federal agents were approached by members of the Yamaguchi-Gumi in Hawaii who then attempted to sell the agents 40 kilograms of ice and 8 kilograms of heroin (U.S. DEA, 1984). The crystal methamphetamine dilemma has increased consistently since the mid 1980s. A total of 32 deaths was attributed to an overdose of crystal methamphetamine between 1985 and 1988 in Honolulu, while during the first half of 1989 an additional 12 people died from an overdose of crystal methamphetamine. This problem has reached serious levels on the mainland of the United States. "Ice" is now being produced in the United States as evidenced by the seizure of major "ice" laboratories in Portland, Oregon, and Sacramento, California. Korea, Taiwan, and the Philippines are the principal suppliers of "ice." An affluent ethnic Korean member of the Yakuza group TYJK, who is a major property owner in Hawaii, has been identified by federal sources as a significant "ice" vendor who distributes more than 30 kilos of crystal methamphetamine a month (FBI, 1992).

Another drug that has attracted some attention from members of the Yakuza is cocaine. The number of arrests and total amounts of cocaine seized have increased more than 50 times over the past five years. Japanese police intelligence reports also indicate that large amounts of cocaine are presently stored in Tokyo. One reason this cocaine supply has not hit the street is the ongoing conflict between Yamaguchi-Gumi and Nibiki-Kai over control of certain areas of Tokyo. One must consider that most Japanese citizens are inclined to follow trends previously started by citizens in other nations and, with that in mind, cocaine becomes appropriate for members of the Japanese society. Another possibility is that the cocaine is to be exchanged for guns, which are of great value in Japan because of the strict laws regarding the sale or possession of firearms.

## Other Business

The Yakuza has expanded its boundaries throughout the nations and territories of the Pacific Basin. The Yakuza has found that Guam, the Philippines, and the Commonwealth of the Northern Marianas Islands (CNMI) are well suited for both their legal and illegal business ventures. A major portion of all of the "Hajika" or "heaters" (guns) as Yakuza members call them are made in the Philippines, Guam, or CNMI. A primary source of the weapons purchased by Yakuza groups is Los Angeles, California.

Both CNMI and Guam have been thoroughly swamped by members of the Yamaguchi-Gumi, Sumiyoshi-Kai, and the Inagawa-Kai. To make matters worse, a heavy infiltration of a number of the smaller Yakuza groups has also occurred in these countries. These Yakuza groups have managed to take control of the tourist trade throughout these islands and are currently exploiting the real estate business by creating and operating building contracting firms and phony investment corporations.

The expansion of Yakuza operations on the islands continued during the 1980s. Along with this growth, the amount of miscellaneous types of drugs being transported through and being used on these islands has also increased. Law enforcement investigations indicate that the Yakuza also has a reapportioning point somewhere in Japan. The Yakuza's participation in heroin smuggling is purely for profit because a pound of heroin costs about $100,000 on Palau and can be retailed for approximately $1 million in Los Angeles (U.S. DEA, 1993).

The amount of Japanese organized crime activity in Canada has multiplied tenfold over the past ten years. Canadian police found that the Japanese pavilion at Expo 86 in Vancouver was funded by Ryoichi Sasakawa, one of Japan's leading organized crime figures. Sasakawa, a billionaire, recently contributed $1 million to York University in Ontario (Stovern, 1993).

A 1989 heroin conspiracy investigation and arrest in Vancouver turned up Atsuki Nagamine of the Matsuba-Kai Yakuza gang as one of the participants. In 1991 Masaru Takumi of the Yamaguchi-Gumi gang purchased a home in Vancouver through a company of which he is one of the directors, the TM Canada Investment Corporation. Investigative information gathered by the RCMP in 1993 indicates that an Osaka-based Yakuza group is actively involved in transporting drugs from South America to Vancouver and to Japan for dispersal. Police sources also verified a significant number of meetings have taken place in British Columbia involving leaders of several Yakuza groups (Stovern, 1993).

Besides the United States and Canada, the Yakuza has also secured a foothold in Australia. A cooperative investigation involving the Japanese and Australian police led to the arrest of two Japanese gang members. The first arrest was made in Melbourne by the Australian police of one Kazuto Furuichi who was caught smuggling heroin into Australia. A continued investigation by Australian police, who passed information on to the Japanese police, led to the arrest of coconspirator Hideo Nistumoto in Japan. An ongoing investigation by the Australian Federal Police has looked into the Yakuza's participation in buying a Queensland casino. During Australian Senate hearings it was determined that Japanese organized crime was involved in more than 25 percent of all the real estate deals in Queensland (Roberts, 1992). In an effort to dissuade Yakuza groups from conducting business in Australia, the Australian government refused to sell a piece of property in Kobe to members of the Yamaguchi-Gumi (Shigemasa, 1994; *Japan Times Weekly*, 1992).

Recently, the Yakuza crime syndicate has been moving some operations into the lower part of the Yangtze River basin in southern China. Yakuza syndicates working together with Triad members from Taiwan are using lawful establishments such as karaoke bars and hotels in an effort to open up and operate their unlawful businesses. A study conducted by a Shanghai professor discovered that Yakuza gangs are located in both the lower Yangtze and the Guangzhoa areas of China as well as more than 400 Japanese companies operating in the lower Yangtze sector. The presence of the Yakuza signals strong possibilities that the gangs are checking out the profitable companies so that the crime syndicates can extort money from them in Japan (*Japan Times Weekly,* 1994).

The Japanese gangs, like the Chinese gangs, have recently become involved in illegal alien smuggling. In 1993, three members of the Yamaguchi-Gumi were arrested by Japanese police for attempting to smuggle 145 Chinese aliens into Japan. In fact, the total number of illegal Chinese aliens arrested in Japan jumped from 18 in 1990 to 335 in 1993 (*Japan Times Weekly,* 1994).

As the criminal activities of the Yakuza continue to be augmented in both legal and illegal ways, Vietnamese organized crime groups are also broadening their unlawful operations to new bases in Asia and the United States.


## VIETNAMESE ORGANIZED CRIME

The Vietnamese people have dealt with more than 2,000 years of conflict that go back to the Chinese invasion of Vietnam around the time of Christ. Approximately 800 years later the Chinese were finally removed from power in Vietnam, but the Vietnamese culture was certainly affected by years of Chinese rule. Vietnam as a country remained fairly stable until the arrival of the French in the mid 1800s. The French invaded Vietnam and within a short period of time took over control of this Southeast Asian country. The French played an important role in influencing the present-day culture of Vietnam.

The French controlled Vietnam from the mid 1800s until their defeat by the Vietnamese army at Dien Bien Phu in 1954. During their rule in Vietnam, the French changed the way the government controlled the Vietnamese people and the whole lifestyle of society in Vietnam. The French changed the educational system in Vietnam to model the French system without giving any consideration to the long-established Vietnamese educational system. The French administation in Vietnam even went as far as to remove village leaders and replace them with people who had an allegiance to the French administration in either Saigon or Hanoi. The French went a step further by changing the various written dialects of the Vietnamese language and consolidating them with the French language.

The changes made by the French represented their perspective of the people in this Third World nation. The notion that all people who were racially or somewhat ethnically different from the French were subject to exploitation by people from European nations was not only a French perception, but was a belief that extended throughout Europe and Great Britain. The European opinion that the destruction of a nation's culture would also bring a society to its knees was not to hold true in Vietnam's case. In 1954 the Vietnamese fought and defeated the French at Dien Bien Phu and chased them out of Southeast Asia.

Not long after the demise of the French, U.S. military advisors started appearing in Vietnam to support the democratic government in Saigon against the communist regime in Hanoi. History tells us the ultimate result of this U.S. intervention, but along the way the American interference uprooted more than 25 percent of the villagers in Vietnam. Village and family are central factors to the Vietnamese people, because family loyalty is the most important aspect of this society and a major portion of this family allegiance is inherited from the village philosophy. The Vietnamese family notions have been conveyed to the Vietnamese street gangs whose members work closely together like a family.

The demise of the democratic government in Saigon signalled the retreat of the U.S. military out of Vietnam in 1975. Once the U.S. troops withdrew from Vietnam, a large influx of Southeast Asian immigrants poured into the United States. Many of these immigrants were perceived to be Vietnamese although some were actually Laotian, Cambodian, and ethnic Chinese from Vietnam. The first wave of Vietnamese emigrants were important citizens who left the country because of their relationship with the U.S. military and, due to this association, feared retaliation by the Vietcong regime. Many had good educational backgrounds and would easily adapt to the lifestyle in the United States because of their relationships with U.S. military personnel in Vietnam. These new arrivals considered themselves well qualified and of no actual threat to U.S. citizens. They felt because of their credentials they should be easily incorporated into the American community and become fruitful members our society. The members of this group who were participants in criminal activities fit right into the Vietnamese communities. They became active within their local communities and quickly got mixed up in fraudulent types of scams including money transfer schemes and welfare swindle. An example of the type of criminal operation that the Vietnamese person would participate in took place in 1984 when 60 Vietnamese pharmacists and physicians deceitfully billed the California Bureau of Medi-Cal for $25 million (FBI, 1993). In most cases these purported professional people used Vietnamese gang members as their couriers.

The first groups that arrived from Vietnam managed to quickly create a number of communities throughout the United States. A major portion of these neighborhoods were located on the West Coast. These communities would soon become home bases for a second group of arrivals from Vietnam that contained more of a criminal element than the first group (FBI, 1993).

The second wave of Vietnamese were what had to be considered true refugees and not immigrants. These expatriates were, in most cases, both socially and educationally different from the people who arrived in the first group. Most of them were from rural regions or coastal communities and had fled Vietnam in boats packed with other fleeing emigrants who suffered the abuses of pirates from Thailand who constantly tormented the fleeing "Boat People." Within this group of new arrivals were people who arrived with their families and friends, and those who disembarked alone. A large number of unescorted children and older sons arrived alone with a strategy that included finding a job and working as hard as possible in order to gather sufficient funding to bring the remaining members of the family to the United States.

These newly arrived Vietnamese can be classified as refugees for several reasons. First, the refugee is compelled to leave his or her homeland. Second, the circumstances surrounding this person's escape are life threatening; and third, the refugee is without any specific direction or destination. This whole episode totally traumatized most of the refugees. Another problem facing the new refugees can be described as culture shock. The culture shock encountered by Vietnamese refugees created a stress that affected the entire Vietnamese family. Such stress is further complicated by the anxiety of learning a new language within a different culture. Stress seems to especially affect the adolescent members of this society, therefore it is not unusual for a youthful member of a family to set up family members as victims of home robberies. The situation for some adolescents becomes even worse if no family unit is available for the youth who in many cases has already become a gang member. Once a gang member, this teenager adopts the gang as his/her family and responds to stressful situations by using violence (FBI, 1993).

Over the past several years many of the Vietnamese street groups have progressed from undisciplined and out-of-control groups to the designation as street gangs. Most of these gangs have joined together to form tightly knit organizations that are coupled to Vietnamese groups throughout the United States. This type of union meets some basic needs of other members of the Vietnamese gangs who are basically linked together for self-preservation and for participation in the profits from gang ventures. The protection of members is of utmost importance to all of the membership because of the tight family relationships within Vietnamese society. Gang members in different areas of the United States must be capable of providing refuge to members of traveling gangs who may be en route to commit a crime or who may be retreating from having just committed a crime.

## VIETNAMESE GANGS

The description of a Vietnamese traveling gang must be preceded by the definitions of what can actually be considered a street gang. As a group they:

1. collaborate to perpetrate or commit a transgression against a specific person or group for profit.

2. identify themselves through the use of a name, sign, or symbol or through a distinguishable leader.

3. participate in criminal activities, which is unusual in comparison to other identifiable groups.

4. proclaim that the group will be operating in a specific area.

5. distinguish themselves through their garments, tattoos, and the way they act, appear, or communicate with other members (FBI, 1993).

6. adopt the gang as family because they are, in the case of Vietnamese gangs, usually adolescents who came to the United States without any other family member traveling with them or already living in the United States.

7. come from a paternal type of society where everything evolves around a tightly knit family that is totally controlled by the father whose authority is never challenged. This adolescent now enters a foreign society whose members have throughout time questioned authority. It is not long before conflict between the father and son develops, which will ultimately, in some cases, cause the son to become ostracized from the rest of the family and seek out the family affinity supplied by the gang members.

Almost every street gang referred to in this book fits into the first five aforementioned categories. It has taken a longer time for the Vietnamese gangs to adapt to gang ideology because of categories six and seven. In most of the other gangs, members did not come out of a war-ravaged and chaotic homeland. Many Vietnamese youths entered the United States bewildered and unstable. They came from a basically agrarian society that in most cases lacked any gang-like organizations or groups to emulate upon their arrival in the United States.

Vietnamese gangs in the United States have carefully done their apprenticeship under the guidance of Chinese street gangs. This experience has helped Vietnamese gangs grow into what now can be considered an organized and well-trained criminal element. The gangs that have come to the forefront from the training they received from the Chinese gangs are Born to Kill, who learned under the guidance of the Flying Dragons gang, and Hung Pho, who were taught by the Wo Hop To gang. Most of the members of the gangs that have associated with the Chinese gangs are ethnically Viet-Ching gangs that could be easily assimilated into either group because of their ability to speak both languages and understand both cultures.

The Vietnamese traveling "hasty" or "phantom" gangs can be considered gangs originally created to perform special tasks. Like members of all other Vietnamese gangs, traveling gang members also receive their fair share of the profits, and they are more apt to seek some type of shelter or asylum after leaving the scene of a crime. The criminal activities that these gangs are involved in are anything but recklessly committed. Almost every criminal act they participate in is thoroughly planned and carried out by skilled gang members. In fact, gang members who are actively involved with the traveling gangs routinely recruit members who are experienced in perpetrating the same types of crimes that these gangs members will be committing.

Almost all these gangs surface prior to the crime and then vanish within a short period of time after the successful completion of the crime. Activities involving these gangs are preplanned, and the target of the crime selected long before traveling gang members are chosen to participate in the criminal act. The members of these gangs are usually selected from locations throughout the United States. This strategy makes identification of the perpetrators more difficult for the victims and the police. It also makes it easy to understand why these gangs are considered "phantom" gangs when few of the participants have the same home base. It is possible that the only common identifying factor in these cases is that the participants are members of the same gang but from different locations in the United States. The traveling gang members are usually between the ages of 12 and 25.

The Asian population in California, the largest within the United States, gave rise to the first Vietnamese gang in Los Angeles in 1978. In 1980, the Vietnamese population in Southern California was approximately 110,000, and about 45,000 in Northern California. Within a short period of time, Vietnamese gangs showed up in Santa Ana, Anaheim, Westminister, and Garden Grove. In 1982 five organized Vietnamese gangs were operating in Southern California. The Vietnamese gangs concentrated all of their criminal activities within the Vietnamese community. The gangs relied on the crime of extortion of Vietnamese businessmen, vehicle theft, business takeovers, and protection rackets in order to make their gangs profitable. The early Vietnamese gangs received a great deal of attention from the media. Many early gang members were thought to be elite military personnel who had received many hours of high-tech military training including in-depth instruction in the use of explosives and underwater demolition. A large percentage of this media grandiosity has been found to be untrue. The persons chosen to lead the gangs were usually experts in the use of violence and cold-blooded murder.

One of the first Vietnamese gangs to appear in Southern California was the Frogmen (Nguoi Nhu) whose name came from an elite Vietnamese military underwater demolition team. The major criminal activities of this gang, based out of Garden Grove, California, are gambling, murder, prostitution, drugs, extortion, and robbery. During the early 1980s an internal struggle took place within the Frogmen gang, resulting in the gang splitting into three different factions, Tai's Gang, Cac's Gang, and Phong's Gang.

The second gang is known as the Thunder Tigers (Loi Ho), based out of Houston, Texas, with a second base established in 1981 in Orange County, California. The membership of this gang is also made up of ex-military personnel. The third group was the Catalina Boys, located in both Los Angeles and Orange County, California. This gang was involved in several criminal incidents with the Thunder Tigers. The fourth gang, the Pink Knights, is named for a bar in Saigon and operates in the Anaheim area. Their major criminal activity is extortion. The last gang is the Luns or Little People. Most members of this gang are between 13 and 20 years old and attend Costa Mesa High School. They are involved in the crimes of extortion and robbery and were associated with the Frogmen gang.

These early Vietnamese gangs had their problems. In fact, in 1981 two separate violent incidents involved Vietnamese gang members. The first incident took place on February 5, 1981, when a gun battle occurred between members of the Frogmen and a combined force of Catalina Boys and Thunder Tigers. Then on February 12, 1981, Nguyen Dang, a Los Angeles restaurant owner, was shot and killed in front of his market by gang members because of his refusal to pay extortion demands by Vietnamese gangs. Another incident took place on October 11, 1981, when two masked gunmen entered the restaurant hangout of the Tai Gang brandishing shotguns. The exchange of gunfire resulted in the death of one woman and the wounding of eight others (LAPD, 1982).

The original street gangs were the forerunners of the present-day Vietnamese street gangs; some of these still coexist with the newer and more violent Vietnamese street gangs of today. The number of Vietnamese refugees coming into the United States has tripled since the 1980s, causing a widespread increase in the number of gangs, which is especially evident in the number of Vietnamese gangs on the West Coast. The home base for almost every Vietnamese gang in the United States is in California. A majority of these new street gangs are easily identifiable by their names: Viet Ching, King Cobra Boyz, Natoma Boyz, or Oriental Boyz. The makeup of most of these gangs, however, is ethnically diverse. A number of female street gangs of Vietnamese origin have become visible in Southern California as well. Among them are the South Side Scissors, Asian Girlz Hood, Oriental Raider Girls, and the IBK (Innocent Bitch Killers). The female gangs will at times work hand-in-hand with the male gangs, but on several occasions female gangs have been in direct conflict with their male counterparts. Most of these Vietnamese gangs wear specific gang colors and are very aware of the territory they control. Like most other California gangs, Vietnamese gangs have also adopted hand symbols to gesture loyalty to the gang and/or to notify other members and avoid verbal communications. Some use graffiti to mark boundary lines of their territories, to deliver a challenge to a rival group, or to declare the gang's opinion of other members of society, especially the local police establishment. Gang affiliation can sometimes be ascertained by tattoos and other imprints gang members have on their bodies.

When discussing California Asian gangs one must consider the Viet-Ching element of the Vietnamese gangs. Prior to the fall of Saigon, a major portion of this group was considered professional people who owned and operated businesses in Saigon, and another portion was involved in medical occupations. The Viet-Ching had acquired the reputation of being an elitist group in Saigon. A great deal of the financing, money lending, and banking throughout Asia was always controlled by the Chinese, so it was not unusual that the Viet-Ching or Cholon Chinese dominated the financial environment of South Vietnam. Most of the ethnic Chinese were from the Cholon district of Saigon and took time to form their own limited triad groups. These triads may well be present in the "Little Saigons" that have appeared throughout Vietnamese communities in California. Law enforcement sources in the United States believe that these Viet-Ching triads control the activities of the Viet-Ching gangs operating in and around local Vietnamese districts (FBI, 1993).

The Viet-Ching businesspeople have set up their own criminal networks throughout the United States. This system allows Viet-Ching entrepreneurs to become leaders as well as operatives who advise the street gangs. This advice usually relates to potential victims of home invasion robberies. The other advantage these networking Viet-Ching groups have is that the secluded Vietnamese community rarely communicates its secrets to any members of outside communities, including the police whom the Vietnamese hold in low esteem. The Viet-Ching gangs have to be considered the most well-structured Vietnamese criminal organization operating in the United States today (FBI, 1993). Most of the Viet-Ching gangs are based in Orange and Los Angeles Counties in Southern California, but they also have large groups operating in San Jose and San Francisco in Northern California and in Houston, Texas.

Many of the Vietnamese street gangs are under the tutelage of a "Dai Ka" or big brother who was at one time a South Vietnamese military officer. These big brothers use the advisor position with the street gangs to revitalize their prior military prowess. The gangs are modeled after the military unit that their advisor served in during the Vietnam War, although in some cases the alleged ex-military personnel from South Vietnam who are now working with the gangs as advisors were not old enough to participate in the Vietnam War.

The Vietnamese gangs consist of three different types of membership (see Figure 10-12). The first type of member has to be considered hard core because he requires membership in the gang to survive. A majority of these members are the gang leaders and control the criminal activities that involve gang members. They can also be considered the most violent members of the gang and have the power to select the gang members who are to participate in criminal activities. Almost all of these hard-core leaders are well liked by the members. The second type of gang member is the associate who participates with the gang to gain some type of status and/or notoriety from peer group members outside of the gang. These members need to belong and other gang members fulfill their aspirations. The third and final type of member is a peripheral member. This type of member participates in gang activities as long as the criminal operations interest him. In many cases, it would be easy for this type of member to become either an associate or hard-core member.

One of the major weapons used by Vietnamese street gangs to control crime victims before, during, and after the crime is intimidation. The gang members use both verbal and nonverbal methods of intimidation. Verbal communication is done through the use of various threats that will make the victim fearful of gang members from the start to the finish of the crime. Some of the verbal warnings may contain threats of killing, raping, or kidnapping another family member or friend. The nonverbal method is used along with verbal techniques and usually includes the use of force or violence. It might encompass sticking guns down victims' throats, burning people with cigarettes or scalding water, and physically striking victims. Another type of nonverbal intimidation used by Vietnamese gangs involves leaving a knife or one bullet in plain view so it will be found by the victim. It sends the message that he or she is not safe and that gang members may return at any time to inflict harm or injury on the victim or his or her family (LASD, 1992). This type of intimidation was evident on April 5, 1991, when four members of the Vietnamese street gang the Oriental Boys entered a store in Sacra-

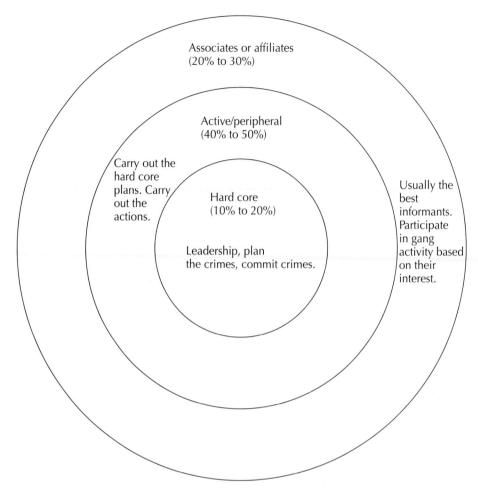

**FIGURE 10-12**  Gang Makeup
*Source:* California Department of Justice, 1993.

mento, California, and held 41 people hostage for 8½ hours. In an effort to intimidate the police the gang members shot a hostage in the leg and sent him out of the store. During the ensuing siege with the police, one of the gang members ran down along a line of hostages shooting the hostages one by one. When the siege was finally over, three gang members and three hostages were dead and 15 other people were wounded (Gross, 1991).

Many more Vietnamese gangs operate on the West Coast than on the East Coast. In fact, information gathered by law enforcement agencies in the United States indicates that the Vietnamese gang population in California is at least ten times greater than in any other location in the United States (FBI,

1993). Yet, the gang members commit crimes throughout the United States and have gang or other Vietnamese connections in most areas of the United States. This widespread criminal activity is evident in the ability of the traveling gangs to hastily move around this country. For example, on October 15, 1990, police in Westbrooke, Maine, broke up a residential robbery and found Vietnamese gang members Tai Ho and Tho Quang Ton in what they considered a gateway vehicle. A week later both Tai Ho and Tho Quang Ton were arrested in San Francisco for robbing a local Vietnamese mechanic inside his garage (S. Chin, 1991). According to San Francisco police Sergeant Dan Foley, the Vietnamese travel all over the United States committing robberies. Foley states, "They might drive from Texas to Los Angeles, for example, and stop off in Phoenix and do a couple of robberies on the way. Then they will go to Los Angeles, visit some people, do a robbery, and then come up to San Francisco and meet a big brother, who might have a couple more robberies for them to perpetrate" (S. Chin, 1991).

One phenomenon of West Coast Asian gangs is girl gangs. At least 25 Asian girl gangs presently operate in Southern California. A majority of these girl gangs are ethnically Vietnamese, but Filipino, Korean, Cambodian, and Laotian female gangs exist as well. They have been arrested for their involvement in home invasion robberies with male gang members and by themselves. Each one of these female adolescent gangs is affiliated with one or more male gangs. The girl gangs usually average anywhere from 10–20 members who are somewhere between 14 and 28 years old. Most of the members are fearless and tough. They will challenge female as well as male members from opposing gangs to fight and then pull a knife and use it, if necessary, during the brawl. At first, it was believed that girl gang members only carried weapons for male gangs, but that presumption was found to be untrue because the female gang members are involved in crime almost as often as their male counterparts (Efron, 1989; LACSD, 1992).

An East Coast connection to the West Coast gangs is the Born to Kill (BTK) Vietnamese street gang. This gang operates throughout the United States but has established a large operation in the New York City metropolitan area. The BTK, originally known as the Canal Street Boys, is known for its cruel and vicious behavior. Most members of this gang were originally associated with the Flying Dragons Chinese street gang until 1986 when they broke away and formed their own gang under the leadership of David Thai. BTK is one of the few street gangs that does not have any connections to either a Chinese Tong or Triad. Their territory includes parts of Canal Street, but the gang infringes on the territories of all of the Chinese gangs to extort money from Chinese businesses. The BTK gang is presently operating in Chinatown, Coney Island in Brooklyn, Jackson Heights, and Flushing,

Queens. Members sport tattoos of a coffin with three candles on it, which means that members are not afraid to die.

The number one criminal activity of the BTK gang is home invasion robberies. They also are involved in extortion, gambling, prostitution, and the production and sale of counterfeit watches. The counterfeit watch business was discovered when law enforcement personnel went to the apartment of the head of the BTK gang, David Thai, to question him in a murder investigation. Thai was ultimately arrested and convicted of conspiring and committing the murder of Sen Von Ta, a Chinatown jewelry store owner, of attempted murder, and of a number of robberies and extortions. Federal prosecutors and law enforcement agencies were hopeful that the convictions of Thai and six other BTK members would seriously weaken the BTK. However, it seems to have only temporarily weakened this gang's New York City operations. The BTK gang is a formidable force similar to other Asian gangs and just as capable of quickly replacing imprisoned leaders with little loss of authority, territory, or monetary operations.

Another New York City Vietnamese street gang is the Gum Sing. This gang is an offshoot of the BTK gang. Its headquarters are in Brooklyn's Chinatown between 40th Street and 60th Street on Eighth Avenue. Like the BTK, the Gum Sing gang has no connection to either a Triad or Tong. The Gum Sing is a highly mobile gang made up of Vietnamese adolescents and a few other ethnic Asian youths. Gum Sing moves freely throughout the New York City metropolitan area to perpetrate their criminal activities. The Gum Sing is involved in drug dealing, home invasions, extortion, and kidnapping (NYPD, 1994).

Local BTK Vietnamese gangs have terrorized Chinatown businesspeople and residents by staging daytime shootouts on the bustling streets of Chinatown. These activities are an attempt to wrestle away control of the booming Chinatown extortion business. In another instance, members of the BTK entered a garment factory, locked all the doors, and then proceeded to rob the owners and all the employees (*Law Enforcement News,* 1991).


## CRIMINAL ACTIVITIES OF VIETNAMESE GANGS

### Home Invasion Robberies

One of the most vicious crimes adopted as a common gang activity by all types of Vietnamese street gangs is home invasion robberies. The Vietnamese gangs have perfected their approach by:

1. gathering all known facts on each and every target prior to making a decision on whether a specific location is worth robbing by being sure that

a specific amount of valuables will be at the location when they commit the crime. In most cases the ideal target for the gangs is either a wealthy business owner or a large group of new refugees living in the same location who have little faith in the U.S. banking system or are trying to avoid the IRS.

2. properly arming all gang members for participation in this crime and supplying them with stolen autos.

3. keeping the number of active gang participants in this crime limited to 5–8 members whenever possible.

4. requiring that gang members involved in these crimes practice the tasks they are required to perform during the crime

5. binding and gagging all victims in one specific location in the structure.

6. initiating an act of violence, assault, or rape against one of the victims for no apparent reason. This violence may be used to obtain more valuables, ascertain whether victims will notify police, or to further terrify victims.

7. demanding all valuables in the house or that the family owns. Gangs sometimes threaten to kidnap and/or rape a family member to obtain more valuables; sometimes gang members rape and sexually abuse victims just for fun (*Law Enforcement News,* 1991).

8. leaving at the crime scene various types of transportation to take members to Vietnamese safe houses located throughout the United States after the crime has been committed (Office of Attorney General of California, 1991).

## Computer Chip Theft

The theft of computer chips has become a profitable business for Vietnamese gangs. These crimes are prevalent on the West Coast, especially California, but recent thefts have taken place in Florida and Texas. In fact in 1991, approximately $1 million worth of computer chips was stolen from a St. Petersburg, Florida, company. During this robbery the ten employees of the company were tied up, gagged, and blindfolded by the five Vietnamese robbers. Stolen chips can be used in almost any computer and the average cost is $300–700 each.

Vietnamese gangs were the first group to realize that theft of computer chips is an attractive activity, because the computer chips resell at about 80 percent of their value. Computer chips are also difficult to trace because they do not have any type of serial numbers. Computer chips are illegally obtained by Vietnamese crime groups in a number of ways:

1.  Street gangs commit the robberies of computer chip companies using methods similar to those used during the commission of a home invasion robbery.

2.  Asian individuals who become indebted to Vietnamese gangs through gambling are forced to steal chips for the gangs.

Presently, law enforcement authorities have identified five major computer chip fencing rings in Southern California alone. The chips are taken by these groups, repackaged, and then auctioned off to the highest bidder. Many of the pilfered chips are sold at computer swap shows or transported to Taiwan, Thailand, or Hong Kong for resale.

Another type of scam involving Vietnamese gangs involves the stealing of what are known as "valueless chips." The price of these valueless chips may be next to nothing in the ever-evolving high-tech market, but in Third World countries where nations are a lot less scientifically advanced, these chips have value. This chip may have some value because it was made with some type of precious metal. Vietnamese criminals are known to have been participants in the theft of valuable metals and gems for years, and the jewelry markets of Asia ask few questions about the legitimacy of the metals or gems.

### Extortion

Three types of extortion are practiced by Vietnamese groups identified by law enforcement officials. In the first instance a person who is affiliated with a newspaper or periodical with a limited distribution contacts businesspeople within the Vietnamese community and informs them that if they do not financially support the periodical they will be named as members of the communist party or subject to some other type of harrassment. The second type of Vietnamese extortion involves a member of an alleged Vietnamese resistance organization who approaches a businessperson and informs that person that only a contribution to the resistance organization will provide "protection" against some type of violence. With the third type of extortion, the Vietnamese gangs directly sell protection to community business owners. These behaviors are typical of street gang extortion rings (FBI, 1987).

### Prostitution

Most of the prostitution activity within the Vietnamese community involves massage parlors and escort services. Many of the female participants in these prostitution rings were forced into this activity by Vietnamese street gangs that run both the massage parlors and the escort services. Gang members who run the prostitution rings have kept them well organized and under tight control. These illegal operations help the Vietnamese street gangs operate other unlawful activities including currency transfer, narcotics sale, gambling, and violence.

## Gambling

Gambling operations are sometimes set up in residences and the street gangs are used to protect and act as lookouts for these illegal businesses. The street gangs also check out the big winners and may ultimately be involved in a home invasion robbery of a patron. The Vietnamese favor gambling games involving the use of cards. The card games they enjoy betting on are Xap Zam or thirteen card, and Tu Sac, a game involving a deck containing 112 small, multicolored cards that have Chinese imprints on them.

## Drug Trafficking

The Vietnamese have observed the profit made by other gangs in drug dealing, and they are becoming involved in the drug trade. Vietnamese gangs are active participants in the crack cocaine business. In both New Orleans and New York City the Vietnamese gangs have been mixed up in the drug business. At first in New York City the Vietnamese gangs moved heroin for the Chinese gangs, but once they realized the profitability in drugs the Vietnamese gangs quickly became active in the drug market (ATF, 1993).

## Auto Theft

Since the mid 1980s Vietnamese gangs have been involved in vehicle theft. The gangs made up their own modified keys to gain entrance into the auto. In many cases the cars stolen were either Toyotas or Datsuns. The modified keys can be used on any Datsun or Toyota manufactured since 1967 to gain entrance within a short period of time (5 seconds). Other people can purchase these keys from Vietnamese gangs members for $20 each. It is estimated that every member of Vietnamese traveling gangs has access to one of these modified keys (New Jersey State Police, 1990).

The Vietnamese gangs are active in almost every major metropolitan area in the United States. Recently, these Vietnamese gangs have been appearing in countries outside of the United States. Toronto, for instance, has had an increase in the number of home invasion robberies and shootings by

Vietnamese street gangs. The Canadian police have identified BTK gang members from New York City as the main culprits in most of these home invasion robberies and shootings. According to Canadian law enforcement the BTK gang has a number of criminal associates in Toronto, Montreal, Calgary, and Vancouver (Project North Star, 1993).

Australia has also had a recent increase in criminal activity involving Vietnamese gangs. The Australian police have found that the Vietnamese gangs make a science out of extortion. They have investigated four main types of extortion practiced by Vietnamese gangs:

1. Five or more gang members enter a specific restaurant, and each gang member sits at a separate table and stays for two or more hours. This method decreases the number of patrons who can eat at the location. The gang leader then refuses to pay any of the dinner bills. Gang members will return to a restaurant until the owners pay a specific amount of extortion monies to the gang.

2. Gang members block business entrance ways forcing anyone who wants to enter the location to squeeze past or push the gang member out of the way. The person who is attempting to enter the store is then subject to ridicule from the gang members. Gang members will continue this practice until the business owner pays them the required protection money.

3. A gang leader offers to supply protection to the nightclub owners for a specific fee. If the club owners refuse to pay extortion to the gang, the gang members will enter the club and cause problems by starting fights and damaging property. These activities by the gang will continue until the owners succumb to the extortion demands of the gang.

4. Gang members will enter a general store and demand that the store owner loan them some money. Most of the store owners ultimately submit to these extortion requests (Victoria Police, 1992).

Like their American counterparts, the Asian members of the Australian community seldom report these types of incidents to the police.

Australian police have found the Vietnamese gangs to be similar to the Vietnamese gangs in California. The leader is usually older than the other gang members, and all gang members have tattoos that identify them as members of a specific gang. The Vietnamese gangs in Australia are involved in the armed robberies of gas stations and convenience stores, theft of motor vehicles, home invasion robberies, burglary, and drug trafficking. The police have found that most gang members have guns readily available to them (Victoria Police, 1992).

All these Asian organized crime groups have prospered from their unlawful ventures whether they be corporate extortion, theft of computer chips, or smuggling prostitutes into other countries. Each group has created its own specialties. If it is a good scam, other groups will use it. Yet, like other organized crime groups, not one of their home countries has taken any major steps to obliterate these groups, which gives rise to concerns about the widespread influence of these groups and the extent of corruption that allows them to continue to operate.

## KOREAN ORGANIZED CRIME

Federal law enforcement officials have documented a sharp increase in Asian organized crime activities in the United States over the past decade. In fact, within the New York City metropolitan area is the second largest Asian population in the United States. During 1992 approximately one-third of all legal immigrants arriving in New York were from Asian countries. The large influx of these settlers from abroad has created in New York City some of the largest Asian ethnic communities in the United States.

One of the largest Asian ethnic groups to settle in the New York City area is of Korean descent. Most Korean immigrants have not been well assimilated into the ways of this society. They have maintained the same moral standards and hard work ethics that were instilled in them during their upbringing in Korea. Instead of becoming a splintered group within a new environment, the Koreans have formed their own communities in the United States. Korean immigrants have started their own businesses and created housing within that same community. A perfect example of this type of Korean neighborhood exists in both Flushing, New York, and Koreatown, Los Angeles. The only problem with this kind of community in New York City is that sooner or later it will attract the attention of the Asian criminal element from either that neighborhood or an adjoining area. At first, it was Chinese gangs who were attracted to Flushing from Chinatown in Manhattan because of the Chinese businesses in the area but a short time later Korean gangs who were originally affiliated with the Chinese gangs started to appear on the streets of Queens. Presently, approximately six Korean street gangs operate in this area of the city.

Korean involvement in organized crime dates back to the early 1800s when an organized group of Korean businessmen was formed to smuggle jewels and drugs out of China to be used by the Korean nobility. Soon after the formation of this group, other criminal associations started to appear in Korea. The Japanese occupation of Korea during World War II promoted the development of many of these criminal associations in Korea by allowing corruptive types of activity to control the environment. These conditions ultimately led to the evolution of one of the most powerful Korean organized crime groups in the mid 1940s (U.S. Customs, 1993).

This group, the Samurai Pa gang, became the most powerful force in Seoul by taking over control of the central business district and the entertainment area known as Chong No. A major portion of the membership of this gang was made up of ethnic Japanese with the minority group comprised of Koreans who were low in rank within the gang. The Samurai Pa gang was protected by the Japanese army because they cooperated with the military and provided the army with certain services such as call girls. The gang also gathered information related to the activities of the Korean freedom fighters, for dissemination by the Japanese military rulers. Another Korean gang, Chong No Pa, was quickly formed when Tu Hwan Kim, a radical Korean Independent freedom fighter, reappeared with his associates in Korea.

Immediate conflict arose between the Samurai Pa and the Chong No Pa gangs. Most of these hostilities evolved over control of the Chong No district in Seoul. The strife continued until the Chong No Pa defeated the Samurai Pa and took over control of the Chong No district.

At the end of World War II, Korea was hit with an unusual amount of societal chaos. The outcome of all this turmoil was a large number of unemployed workers, creating a segment of vagrants, beggars, and criminals within Korean society.

During these cataclysmic times the criminal element within this society, especially Chong No Pa, continued to prosper. This prosperity encouraged new gangs, which began to appear throughout Seoul. Members were recruited from among the unemployed workers, with most gangs concentrating on recruiting membership from a specific region, town, or village, or the same clan in an effort to firmly stake out the area they would control. Gang activity and recruitment was extremely intense in the Cholla do section of the Korean peninsula. These new gangs had problems with previously entrenched rival gangs such as the Chong No Pa. Most gangs operated on a hit-or-miss basis on local businesses and stores. This type of activity lasted until the gangs were finally able to take over some of the territories previously controlled by the Chong No Pa (FBI, 1993).

Some of the gangs that survived these unstable times were Myong Dong, Tong Dae Moon Pa, Sodae Moon and Mookyo Done Pa. These gangs regulated different areas of Seoul including sections from which they took their original names. Each gang is a separate entity that functions within a broad and adaptable organized crime system working either together or apart.

CHAPTER 10

During the 1950s, Korean organized crime syndicates were classified into categories.

## THE GANGS

### Political Gangs

The most dominant gangs in Korea are the political gangs because of their attachment to corrupt politicians. They were employed by corrupt politicians to use whatever method necessary to make opposing bureaucrats withdraw from an election race, relinquish their elected position, or throw their support to the criminal syndicates.

Most political gangs, besides being dominant, were well-established organizations that were substantially well-connected with government officials. This association put the political gangs in a favorable position against the Korean National Police (KNP) who were essentially rendered ineffective against the gangs. In fact, the KNP seldom interceded in any activities involving the gangs.

Once police interference was eliminated the Chong No Pa, the Mookyo Dong Pa and the Tong Dae Moon Pa could do whatever they pleased without any interruptions. These criminal syndicates were able to operate their illegal activities (loan sharking, prostitution, gambling, smuggling). During this time investigations by the KNP and the Korean Central Intelligence Agency indicated that the Korean gangs, specifically the Chong No Pa, renewed their relationships with the Japanese gangs. Although contact with the Yakuza was established, the effects of 35 years of occupation and poor treatment at the hands of the Japanese during their reign in Korea strained the relationship significantly. A working relationship between the Japanese and the Koreans was finally reestablished in the 1960s and firmed up in the 1970s (U.S. Customs, 1993).

### Street Gangs

The second form of Korean gang is the street gang. Gangs of paltry lawbreakers roamed the streets of Korea victimizing local businesses and amusement areas. The street gangs' main method of financing their operations was extorting funds from businesses within the area of their operation and having the rights to blackmarket goods. The street gang members were characterized as street urchins by both the citizens and the police of Korea. In most cases, the Korean street gangs did not create the same major type of violent threat to society as do present-day street gangs.

## Gangs on the Run

Early in 1961, a military coup established General Park Chong Hee as the new leader over South Korea. Park immediately commanded his underlings to arrest all known gang members and place them in military camps to be reeducated on how to get out of the criminal lifestyle. The military rounded up hundreds of gang members and petty criminals and sent them to a desolate island off the coast of Inchon. A large portion of the gang leaders and their membership were either put to death by members of the military or opposing gang leaders, or died because of poor prison conditions. The reeducation programs created by General Park Chong Hee were basically unsuccessful; the only thing that these camps accomplished was the killing of numerous gang leaders and members. Ultimately, those who did not die in these camps were released by the government in early 1964 (U.S. Customs, 1993).

## New Gangs

The Korean government's attempts to quell gang activities was short term, because once the government started releasing gang members from the prison camps the gangs, once again, started to sprout up all over Korea. San-chong Sin, a camp releasee and a prior member of Chong No Pa, quickly established a new gang, the Cholla Do Pa, with a new membership that included hundreds of onetime Chong No Pa members. Within a short time this gang had taken control of almost all parts of the Cholla do business and entertainment area in Seoul.

Another gang, the Bon Gae Pa, was formed by Chong-sok Pak, a former captain in the Chong No Pa. The Bon Gae Pa (the lighting faction) gang was soon to become the major rival of the Cholla Do Pa. These two groups continually battled over control of the main business and entertainment areas in Yongdongp'o, Cholla do, and other similar areas in the major cities of South Korea. After several years of hostilities the Bon Gae Pa attacked the headquarters of the Cholla Do Pa and killed Cholla leader San-chong Sin and many of his underbosses. This action helped the Bon Gae Pa become the strongest and most feared gang in Seoul. During the mid 1970s the Bon Gae Pa membership increased so much that the gang was divided into three different groups—the Sobang Pa, the Yang Un Pa, and the Ob Pa—with Chong sok Pak in charge (KNP, 1994).

Pak delegated the power to run these new gangs to several of his underbosses. Tae chon Kim and Chong chol Oh were appointed as leaders of the Sobang Pa. The Yang Un Pa was named after and controlled by Yang un Cho, who had participated with Pak in a political gang prior to being imprisoned by the military. The leader of the Ob Pa gang was Tong chae Yi who also ran the Ho Rang Yi Pa (the Tiger faction) gang. Yi took over the leadership of the Ob Pa gang by murdering Pak while Pak was visiting one of his criminal operations in Kwangju, Cholla do. A short time later, Tong chae Yi moved his headquarters, along with most of his Ob Pa gang, to Seoul. Yi made sure he would remain in control over his unlawful activities in Kwangju by leaving a sufficient number of Ob Pa gang members in Kwangju to supervise operations there (KNP, 1994).

## Contemporary Gang Activity in Korea

During the 1970s the Korean gangs expanded their criminal operations by taking control of covert economic activities throughout Korea. The profit gained by the gangs from these illegal operations was then reinvested into sanctioned businesses. Most major media organizations in Korea have professed for years that members of the Korean organized crime gangs financed some of Korea's major corporations during the early stages of their development (U.S. Customs Service, 1994).

One Korean organized crime syndicate, the KTA (Korean Tourist Association) or KK (Korean Killers), instituted a scam in the late 1970s that provided it with an increasingly profitable scheme. This conspiracy involved the use of Korean females to work as prostitutes in both Korea and the United States. The KK devised a perfect way for females to gain entry into the United States as U.S. citizens (see Figure 10-13).

The KK use Korean prostitutes who are in many cases purchased from their families while they are in their early adolescence. These young females are sent to what are called farms, locations owned and controlled by the KK, where they serve as prostitutes for members of the Korean military. They then work in local bars, massage parlors, and hotels owned by members of the KK that provide sexual services to members of the U.S. military. Gang members who own massage parlors or houses of prostitution in the United States contact KK members in Korea and make arrangements for a sham marriage to be arranged between a U.S. serviceman and a Korean prostitute. A KK member expedites all the required documents and marital paperwork, travel arrangements, and details concerning the location where the female will work upon her arrival in the United States (KNP, 1994). Upon their arrival in the United States, these women are obligated to the Korean gangs and must work a number of years to pay back their liability to the gang. In most cases, the women barely survive during the years they are working for a gang, which pays them less than a minimal wage to work long and arduous hours (FBI, 1993).

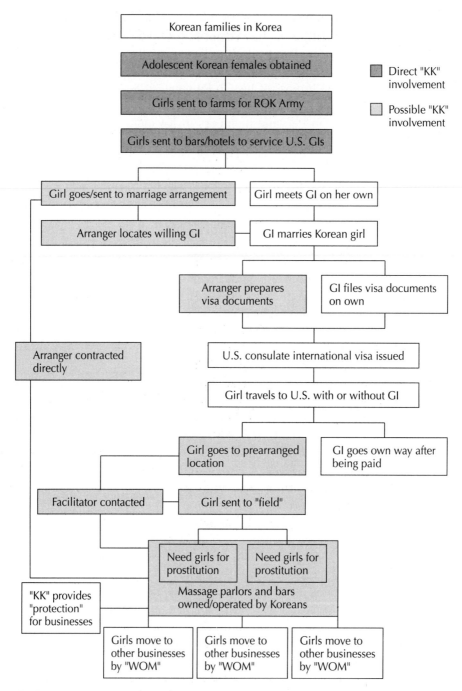

**FIGURE 10-13**  KK or KTA Involvement in Korean Marriage Fraud/Prostitution Schemes
*Source:* U.S. Immigration and Naturalization Service, 1994.

As the KK was building its empire, other Korean gangs were also increasing their membership and business opportunities. The Cholla Do gang continued to grow by continuously recruiting new gang members and absorbing smaller gangs under the control of Cholla Do membership. The constant expansion of the gangs into legitimate businesses led to greater complexity within the associations and to the growth of other organized criminal syndicates in Korea.

Some of the largest criminal syndicates are the Hoguk Ch' Ongyon Yonhap Hae or the Korean National Defense Youth Federation, which was formed and controlled by Sung wan Yi. A short time later, Tae chon Kim organized the Sin U Hae (the Trusted Friendship Association), after his liberation from prison where he had served time for gang-connected crimes. During his tenure in prison Kim became affiliated with the Full Gospel Christian Church. After his release from prison he induced members of the Full Gospel Church to join his group under the pretense that his association was involved in benevolent work. The Korean government views the Full Gospel as a religious organization whose membership is made up of Korean dissidents. The Full Gospel Church has expanded to the United States where it presently has numerous members and houses of worship. One other group that should be included is the Songhap Hae or the Pine Tree Association, which is controlled by Hang Hak Kim (U.S. Treasury Dept., 1994).

Besides the larger criminal organizations, a number of smaller syndicates are influential and should be part of our discussion. Included in this group are the Yang Un, Suwon Pa, Ho Rang Yi Pa, Mokpo Pa, Taejon Pa, Tong Song Pa, Hyan Chon Pa, Chil Song Pa, E Sheep Sa Gae Pa, Tae Ho Pa, Tong A Pa, Kukchae Pa, Pusan Yongdo Pa, Piba Ram Pa, and Yong O Pa Uichong Hae Pa, to name a few. Korean gangs, large and small, are heavily involved in drug trafficking, control of the allotment of liquor and food within the entertainment areas, owning and operating gambling casinos, loan sharking, money laundering, political corruption, and credit card and tax fraud in Korea. Most of these organized crime syndicates have created and maintained exhaustive lists of local and worldwide contacts in both legitimate and illegitimate businesses.

## Activities Outside of Korea

Prior to the mid 1980s, most Korean organized crime groups were considered nothing more than a small subdivision of either the Japanese or the Chinese organized crime groups in the United States. Only in the past several years have federal law enforcement sources come to the conclusion that Korean crime syndicates are a considerable threat to American society. Korean criminal groups are involved in a diverse amount of illegal operations in the United States including drug trafficking, money laundering, and the production and dispersal of bogus brand-name goods. A prime example, the Korean gangs' active participation in the trafficking of crystal methamphetamine, or ice, is one indicator of the ability of the Korean syndicates to grow and change within our society.

Investigative data gathered by several federal law enforcement agencies in the early 1990s indicate that approximately 152 different Korean criminal syndicates exist in the United States with about 35 percent of them actively participating in criminal activities. Estimates place membership in active Korean gangs in the United States at 2,000–3,000 (U.S. Dept. of Justice, 1994).

Three major issues arise when considering Korean gangs in the United States. The first one is the increasing influence of Korean Power gangs within Korean communities in the United States. The second issue is the long-standing relationship between the Japanese gangs, who are becoming increasingly active in the United States, and the Korean criminal gangs. Presently, almost all transactions between the Koreans and Japanese involve the distribution of methamphetamine (ice); both of these groups have recognized the potential they have in working together. The third concern is the extent of unlawful operations involving the already-entrenched Korean groups who are linked to gangs in both Korea and the rest of Southeast Asia. This attachment was quite evident during the recent seizure of more than 400 pounds of Southeast Asian heroin from Korean gang members (U.S. Customs Service, 1994).

## Korean Power and Other New York Street Gangs

In the early 1980s Korean Power gangs began to surface in several major cities throughout the United States. Newly immigrated Koreans were quick to form new Korean Power gangs in New York, Denver, Chicago, Los Angeles, and Washington, D.C. The Washington, D.C., group quickly expanded into both Maryland and Virginia. At first, the Korean Power groups were just interested in extorting money from local Korean businesses, but before long these groups extended their operations into other criminal activities.

Membership in the Korean Power gang in the New York metropolitan area has continued to grow over the past ten years. This has brought about a great amount of distress within the Korean community. These gangs intimidate local business owners in order to extort money from them, but they are equally likely to invade a person's home to commit a robbery. Five members of the Korean Power gang were arrested in May 1993 for terrorizing and extorting money from Korean-owned businesses in Midtown Manhattan between 28th and 48th Streets from Madison to 7th Avenues. Merchants were forced to pay anywhere from $50–200 per week plus feed gang members for free whenever coerced to do so (O'Shaughnessy, 1993). According to the NYPD, the Korean Power gang is in cahoots with the Korean Merchant Association of 124 West 24th Street, New York City. In fact, the Korean Merchant Association controls the activities of the Korean Power gang (1993). See Figure 10-14.

A direct spin-off of the Korean Power gang is the Junior Korean Power (JKP) gang, which has spread its tentacles throughout New York City. This gang is comprised of youths between the ages of 14 and 30 with an estimated membership of 75–100. The JKP gang's criminal activities include extortion, home invasion robbery, protection of bars and houses of prostitution, kidnapping, and weapons possession. Federal law enforcement investigative reports indicate that the JKP gang is heavily involved in the production and distribution of methamphetamine (ice) in New York. This gang is well organized, and in many cases the members are heavily armed. Members of this gang have been arrested for rape, robbery, and murder in recent years.

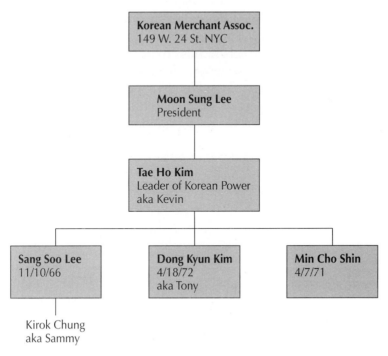

**FIGURE 10-14**   Korean Power, New York City
*Source:* NYPD, 1993.

White Tigers
Korean Power
Green Dragons
Korean Fuk Chings
Flying Dragons
Ghost Shadows
Taiwan Boys (Mandarin speaking)

**FIGURE 10-15**   Active Queens Gangs
*Source:* NYPD, 1994.

The Korean Fuk Ching gang is comprised of both an older and a younger faction. The elder members are involved in traditional organized criminal activities and direct the activities of the younger members (usually 14 to 30 years old), who participate in extortion, kidnapping, robbery, and drug dealing. Adolescent members are recruited from local high schools. This Korean gang is presently operating throughout Brooklyn and Queens (see Figure 10-15).

The Korean Flying Dragons are affiliated with the Chinatown Hip Sing Tong and their associates, the Chinese Flying Dragons. This gang operates throughout Queens and is involved in robbery, kidnapping, and extortion (see Figure 10-16). The members of this street gang are between 14 and 30 years old. In December 1992, seven members of the Korean Flying Dragons were arrested for the robbery of the World Taberah World Mission in Flushing, Queens. The suspects entered the church armed with a machine gun and several pistols. They beat the pastor and forced the parishioners to lie

Extortion
Massage parlors
Gambling
Narcotics trafficking
Firearms
Auto theft
Assault
Kidnapping
Burglary
Robbery
Credit card fraud
Protection

**FIGURE 10-16**   Gang Activities
*Source:* NYPD, 1994.

down on the floor while the robbers mocked and humiliated them. The robbers then compelled the congregation members to surrender their money, jewelry, and house keys (Sullivan, 1992).

## California Korean Street Gangs

The first Korean street gang to appear in California was the AB, or American Burger. This gang was formed to protect Korean high school students from being assaulted by other high school ethnic gang members. This gang led to the formation of other Korean street gangs.

One of the most vicious gangs to come out of this era was the Korean Killers street gang, known as KK or K75K, which stands for Korean (year the gang was established) Killers. The use of the year by this gang was a way of identifying different sections of the gang. Another Korean gang that appeared within the same time period was the BK, or Burger King gang. The Burger King gang was active in the Koreatown area of Los Angeles. The leader of this gang was BK Sam, or Mustang Sam, who went on to become one of the most notorious Korean gang members in Los Angeles (Martin, 1993).

Three other gangs are based out of Garden Grove, California. These gangs are known as the Garden Grove Boys or the Garden Grove Koreans. The total membership of this gang is somewhere around 50. Almost all of the activities of this gang take place in Los Angeles, and the gang has an ongoing conflict with the South Bay Killers and the Wah Ching. Two newer gangs that have appeared in Garden Grove are the Korean Town Mob and the Asian Town Koreans. These gangs have created problems for the Garden Grove Boys. Many predict direct conflict will occur between these gangs sometime in the near future (Martin, 1993).

The Los Angeles Korean gangs are similar to the local Vietnamese gangs in that most members in both gangs are between 16 and 25 years old. Both gangs have token white members, and the Koreans, like their Vietnamese counterparts, are mobile and concentrate their criminal efforts against other members of the Korean community. The Korean gangs and their criminal activities are known in all the Korean communities throughout the United States.

At one time respect was an important factor to all members of Korean gangs. More mature gang members came be be known as "older brothers" while youthful or newer members were referred to as "younger brothers." Respect helped the gangs maintain not only good relationships within their own gangs but also prevented gang members from becoming overzealous. This type of relationship has created a number of problems within the Korean gangs since the late 1980s. The dilemma created by this past affinity may ultimately produce gang warfare because the younger gang members of today are far more aggressively violent than their predecessors, who were guided by the need of all members to treat each other in a civilized manner.

The West Coast Korean gangs benefit greatly from both street and invasion robberies, either home or commercial, and in all cases the crimes are well planned by gang members. Victims of these crimes are commonly known to the gang members, and the victim is usually put under surveillance by the gang in order to gather information for a period of time prior to execution of the criminal act. Once information is gathered a plan is put in place that includes strategy for escape and a contingency plan in case something goes wrong with the first plan.

The Korean gangs are also involved in the crimes of burglary, extortion, kidnapping, and auto theft. California law enforcement authorities indicate that the Korean gangs are involved in street sales of rock cocaine and other illegal narcotics including marijuana and heroin, although the gangs' major area of narcotics trafficking is the distribution of methamphetamine (ice). In one instance, a Honolulu Organized Crime Drug Enforcement Task Force (OCDETF) investigation led them to Paciano Sonny Guerrero, a major dispenser of methamphetamine, who was the key figure in the introduction of methamphetamine throughout Hawaii. The inquiry also led the investigators to two Korean nationals, Dae Sung Lee, who established methamphetamine trafficking in Hawaii in the mid 1980s and controlled the supply of methamphetamine into the 1990s, and Ki Woon Kim, who forced Lee to flee to Korea and took over command of the methamphetamine importation business. The final results of this investigation showed that half of the drug supply of methamphetamine was produced in mainland communities such as Seattle, Tacoma, and Los Angeles, while the other half came from suppliers in Japan, South Korea, and Taiwan (ATF, 1993).

## CRIMINAL ACTIVITIES OF KOREAN GANGS

Connections between the Korean gangs and the Yakuza have already been explored in this chapter, but some aspects of the relationship between these two groups must be further discussed at this juncture. Intelligence gathered by Japanese, Korean, and U.S. law enforcement agencies shows that the Yamaguchi-Gumi and three large Japanese gangs, the Pusan Yongdo Pa, the Chil Song Pa (Seven Stars), and the E Sheep Sae Gae Pa (Twentieth Century), have been involved in smuggling methamphetamine, guns, and other restricted materials between Japan and Korea.

Another major Japanese group, the Toa Yuai Jigyo Kumiai (TYJK), has taken control over a large portion of the methamphetamine distribution in Hawaii and the West Coast of the United States. As previously mentioned in the section on Japanese organized crime, approximately 15 percent of the TYJK and most of the hierarchy of this gang are of Korean descent (FBI, 1992). The drug trafficking activities of the TYJK gang are connected to five Korean gangs, the Ho Sei Kai, the New Obi Group, Yung Gun Pae, Korean White Tigers, and the So Bon Pae. Further evidence turned up by federal law enforcement agencies shows that members of Yakuza gangs met for several days with the Pusan Yongdo Pa gang in Pusan, South Korea. Another factor that points to the formation of an affiliation between the Japanese and Korean groups was recently brought to light by the Korean police. The Korean police information shows that almost all of the Korean gangs have started adopting Yakuza guidelines related to the loyalty, responsibility, and morality of group members. The transferring of mandatory group membership provisions from Japanese to Korean gangs could definitely strengthen the development of the Korean gangs and their affiliation with the Yakuza (U.S. Customs, 1994).

U.S. and foreign law enforcement agencies are distraught over the ever-increasing criminal activity involving members of Korean organized crime. The emergence of Korean crime syndicates in the United States poses three major problems for law enforcement organizations throughout the world. One of the first critical issues facing authorities is the ability of the Korean gangs to easily establish bases for their illegal activities in major urban centers in the United States. Besides setting up bases for their gang operations, the Korean groups have also been able to set up and run their illegal criminal operations—specifically drug smuggling, money laundering, prostitution, and copying and marketing fraudulent brand-name goods—with little or no interference from any law enforcement agency.

The second major concern of law enforcement relates to the management and operation of the Korean organized crime syndicates. Most Korean groups seem to be loosely knit organizations that are strewn throughout the United States. These Korean gangs have been heavily involved in a number of serious criminal incidents including the smuggling of 440 pounds of heroin into the United States during the summer of 1993. Thus far, the only information connecting Korean gangs to larger organizations was detected by the NYPD, whose investigators were able to find a connection between the Korean Merchant Association in New York City and the Korean Power gangs. Information gathered by the NYPD indicates that this relationship is far more involved than was first anticipated by this law enforcement agency. In fact, the connection discovered between these two groups is similar to the relationship between the Hip Sing Tong and the Flying Dragons street gang. The gang protects the merchants' business enterprises, collects overdue payments from people who fail to repay a debt, loan, or bill, and forces competitors out of business (NYPD, 1994).

The third problem facing law enforcement relates to the sudden influx of Korean criminals into the United States. Korean media—through the use of Korean TV stations in Los Angeles and New York—informed U.S. law enforcement agencies that a large number of Korean criminals were immigrating to the United States. The information was verified through Korean law enforcement sources, which indicated that they had data showing well over 100 Korean criminals are presently developing and operating criminal enterprises in the United States (Interpol, 1993). Further intelligence has indicated that many of these Korean criminals have set up their operations in areas of Georgia, Florida, and the Carolinas, away from the previously established Korean communities in Los Angeles and New York. Law enforcement authorities believe these criminals will ultimately form Korean organized crime syndicates throughout the United States. The success of other Asian criminal syndicates in the United States has also played an important role in the recent immigration of Korean criminals into the United States.


## CONCLUSIONS

Korean criminal groups are now operating at an international level, thanks in part to the formidable relationship the Koreans forged with the Japanese gangs. Some criminal activities that the Korean gangs in the United States are already involved in are gambling, extortion, prostitution, alien smuggling, loan sharking, drug trafficking, and marketing counterfeit trademark products. Among the gangs that have surfaced in the United States are the Korean Power gangs, Korean Killers, Korean Flying Dragons, White Tigers, Green Dragons Korean Town Mob, Korean Honam Power, Jul Ra Do, and the Korean Fuk Ching. The majority of these gangs model themselves after the Chinese street gangs. In some cases, the Korean gangs are outgrowths of the Chinese gangs, having originally formed under Chinese tutelage. Presently, Korean gangs are operating in Los Angeles, Atlanta, Detroit, New Orleans, Philadelphia, New York, Chicago, Seattle, Baltimore, Boston, Honolulu, San Francisco, and Washington, D.C. The Korean groups' ability to set up their gangs and criminal operations in major U.S. cities points to a bright future for Korean organized crime syndicates throughout this country.

The growth of the newer Korean and Vietnamese organized crime groups has also been a result of the increase in the number of legal and illegal young immigrants entering the United States from both countries. This was especially true during the early 1970s when a large number of young Vietnamese immigrants came to the United States. With little or no parental guidance available to them some of these young men succumbed to the peer pressure placed on them by gang members and became active in Vietnamese street gang activity.

## ADDITIONAL READING

Appendix B is a brief of the most active Asian gangs.

# CHAPTER 11

# Hispanic Gangs

When Hispanic organized crime is discussed, the first group to come to mind would be either Colombian or Mexican groups because of their media notoriety. Historically, however, the original Hispanic organized crime group was Cuban. This group was at one time closely associated with La Cosa Nostra through their gambling activities. The Colombian crime families appeared only after they realized the profits that Cuban gangs were accumulating through the sale of cocaine. As the Colombian groups increased their fortunes through the distribution and sale of drugs, Mexican groups started making their mark by forming jail gangs. These gangs grew and expanded operations throughout the United States at the same time that other Mexican groups were expanding their drug operations in Mexico. Dominican organized crime groups, on the other hand, have only appeared on the scene in the last decade. Yet this group has risen to prominence because of the violence of its actions in controlling the street drug market, and through its use of violence, it has received the respect of all major drug importers.

## CUBAN ORGANIZED CRIME

The role of some Cuban crime groups is somewhat similar to that of the Italian mafia from which the Cuban organizational crime structure emanated several decades ago. Research indicates three basic types of Cuban groups: structured gangs, violent refugees, and members of Castro's regime. The original structured gang runs a majority of numbers, policy, and bolita locations from New York to Florida with the blessings of La Cosa Nostra. The second type of criminal group evolved out of the Mariel boatlifts of the early 1980s and is noted for its violence. The third group consists of members of Fidel Castro's Communist regime in Cuba.

Historically, the first Cuban organized criminal groups were strongly influenced by members of La Cosa Nostra. The relationship between Cuban organized crime and La Cosa Nostra was formed in Cuba during the Batista government regime when gambling and corruption were in vogue in Havana. Just about all of the gaming casinos in Havana were controlled by La Cosa Nostra under the guidance of Meyer Lansky. The first two Cuban organized crime groups were the Corporation and La Compania. These groups were formed by some of the early arrivals from Cuba and are considered to be:

1. more comprehensive and highly organized than later groups.

2. capable of forming lasting relationships with other crime groups.

3. less violent than future Cuban gangs.

4. heavily involved in gambling and narcotics trafficking with very little participation in other types of gang crimes.

5. qualified to create a structured criminal empire.

A short time after its formation, the Corporation became active in illegal gambling activities. Some of its original bolita and policy operations were set up and run in Dade County, Florida, during the early 1960s. Cuban gambling cartels established their illegal betting businesses so that each part of this enterprise would be capable of booking bets with another faction within the scheme rather than laying the bets off with the Italian gangs. Jose Miguel Battle, who is also known as El Gordo or Don Miguel, has been, since its inception, the "Godfather" or the boss of the Corporation. Battle was originally a soldier in the Cuban army and later became a police officer during the Batista government's control over Cuba. A short time after he fled Cuba, Battle joined Brigade 2506 and participated in the failed Bay of Pigs invasion. Upon his return to Miami, Battle set out plans to operate and control a Cuban gambling operation in Florida with the help of other veterans of the Bay of Pigs invasion. Once this first business was solvent, Battle set up a meeting with La Cosa Nostra bosses Joe Zicarelli and Santo Trafficante to get an okay to move his gambling operations north. The Italian gangs were slow in showing their support of Battle and he started using force whenever necessary to take over some of the northern policy operations. Another meeting was quickly arranged between Battle, Zicarelli, and James Napoli, and a settlement was negotiated that permitted Battle to run his policy and bolita operations, provided he would pay a specific percentage of the earnings to

La Cosa Nostra. Since the outset of this Italian-Cuban criminal conspiracy, the average gross weekly income is approximately $2.5–3 million, and the annual net profit is somewhere between $120 and $135 million (FBI, 1993).

Under the leadership of Jose Battle the Corporation has garnered hundreds of millions of dollars in profits from its gambling ventures. A great deal of this money has been reinvested in both domestic and foreign monetary establishments as well as in the purchase of other types of financial instruments. These investment ventures were coupled with the purchase of a vast amount of property throughout the state of Florida. Following are some of the legitimate companies associated with the Corporation (President's Commission on Organized Crime, 1986b).

Union Management and Mortgage Company
Union Finance Company
Union Financial Research Company
Union Travel and Tours
El Zapotal Realty

Jose Battle has had his problems with law enforcement representatives over the years. He was convicted under RICO (Racketeer Influenced Corrupt Organization Act) for which he served 13 months and was charged with weapon possession and the murder of a former member of the Corporation, Ernest Torres. This second conviction ultimately led to an 18-month sentence for Battle. Considering the time and effort spent by federal, state, and local law enforcement agencies in arresting and convicting Battle for these charges, Jose Battle easily won that round by doing only a total of 31 months in jail.

In 1982, Battle moved his base of operations from New York to Florida and quickly purchased more than $1 million in real estate for $800,000 cash. The purchase of real estate by these criminal organizations is probably the easiest way to launder money even though in most cases it can turn out to be a long-term investment.

The Corporation is consistently seeking ways to launder money so that the money can be utilized in legal ventures. Thus far, the Corporation has managed to build an elaborate network of influence within both the banking and real estate markets. The Corporation has invested large amounts of its gambling profits in the Capital National Bank of New York. It turns out that this bank redeems the largest total of food stamps within the United States. The large number of food stamp coupons retrieved by this bank comes from local bars and restaurants located in established Cuban neighborhoods in Northern New Jersey. According to federal officials, members of the Corporation purchase the coupons from food stamp recipients at rates that are anywhere from 10 to 25 percent higher than the actual value of the stamps.

They then allow customers, who receive the food stamps, to wager with the coupons in place of U.S. currency. In turn, the stamps are used as a device to launder illegally obtained gambling moneys (President's Commission on Organized Crime, 1986b).

The Corporation's involvement in money laundering scams does not cease with the purchase of food stamps. A joint federal investigation in 1985 discovered that members of the Corporation had become mixed up in a deceitful scheme that involved the purchase of winning tickets in the legitimate Puerto Rican lottery. Members of the Corporation had taken control over all U.S. distributors and/or salespersons of Puerto Rican lottery tickets. Lottery ticket agents, who worked for the Corporation, were notified to contact the Corporation with the names and addresses of any persons holding winning tickets with large-sum payouts. Corporation members would then contact the winning person and offer to purchase the ticket from him or her at a superior price. The usual amount paid for the ticket was anywhere from 20 to 25 percent higher than the actual amount won, so if the ticket paid $125,000 the Corporation would give the owner of the ticket anywhere from $150,000 to $160,000 for the ticket. A Corporation member would then cash the ticket in Puerto Rico and the proceeds, after taxes, would be approximately $80,000 in U.S. currency. This arrangement would enable the Corporation to launder money it had illegally obtained from gambling or narcotics operations. The currency would then be legally deposited in a financial institution or invested in stocks, bonds, or realty without any possible indication of the money's true origin. Federal law enforcement officials have confiscated more than $43 million in currency from the Corporation since the early 1960s. These same officials also assert that Corporation leaders have accumulated so much money in profits from gambling operations that they are more than willing to pay two dollars for one dollar in order to launder their money (President's Commission on Organized Crime, 1986b). In 1983, both Battle's son, Jose Jr., and a close associate, Humberto Davila Torres, were seized at two different locations with large amounts of U.S. currency.

The Corporation maintains a low profile in communities where it operates gambling enterprises. In fact, in the neighborhoods where the Cubans run gambling operations, most residents have no idea that the men running them are of Cuban descent. Strict enforcement of the gambling activities of organized criminal groups is considered a low priority by most law enforcement agencies. The Corporation membership is aware of this fact and they operate in the open marketplace using store fronts and bodegas as their bases of operation in most neighborhoods. In some cases, the Corporation has gone as far as to put slot machines into some of its gambling locations. During the fall of 1994, the New York City Police Department put a dent in the Corporation's illegal gambling operations when officers raided the gang's New York headquarters at 750 Kappock Avenue in the Bronx and also a number of other gambling locations throughout New York City. The raid resulted in the seizure of $280,000 in currency and approximately $270,000 in jewelry. Yet no significant information was obtained against Mr. Battle or any of his main operatives (Perez-Pena, 1994). Police have found that members of this organization refuse to cooperate with the police and inform on other gang members or activities. This loyalty is probably one of the major reasons, along with the gang's reluctance to get heavily involved in drug trafficking, why strict enforcement against this group has not been a police priority.

The other long-standing Cuban organized crime group, La Compania, was also formed in the 1960s, but its main activities involved the importation of cocaine, heroin, and marijuana. Prior to the takeover of the cocaine business by Colombian groups, the Cubans were the major suppliers of cocaine on the East Coast. Members of La Compania are still involved in the importation of both cocaine and heroin. Total membership of this gang is estimated at about 200 with its base of operations in Miami and other chapters of the gang in New York, Los Angeles, New Jersey, Las Vegas, Texas and Mexico. Information related to La Compania is somewhat limited because this close-knit group runs a covert drug-smuggling operation. Members are scattered throughout the United States with all their narcotics transactions being wholesaled to a select group of buyers and transpiring at concealed locations. This group has been fairly successful in avoiding the attention of both media and law enforcement.

## Marielitos Banditos

Just prior to Easter in 1980, 25 Cubans gained asylum at the Peruvian embassy in Havana. Castro had originally placed Cuban police around the embassy but decided that these people were now in the hands of the Peruvian government, and so let the Peruvian diplomats worry about them. This decision turned out to be a major blunder on Castro's part because on Easter Sunday morning the crowd outside the embassy had swelled to more than 10,000 people. Castro apparently had no idea how many disillusioned Cubans would seek asylum at the Peruvian embassy once the security forces left the embassy. Just about every member of the group at the embassy came from what can be considered the working class of Cuba. Several nations, including the United States, volunteered to accept some of these refugees, resulting in a quick departure of Cuban citizens from Mariel Harbor, about 30 miles outside of Havana, for the United States. Castro finally acceded to the departing refugees and charged each citizen $750 to leave Cuba. In an effort to cause embarrassment to the U.S. government, Castro ordered his military, police, and correctional personnel to locate all deviant persons not already incarcerated, whether they be ex-convicts, drug addicts, vagrants, delinquents, or persons suffering from mental disorders. Once these people were rounded up they were then confined to a high-security makeshift prison camp near the El Mosquito plantation outside of Mariel.

Through the use of this Mariel boatlift Castro was able to unload 25,000 people with criminal records onto the U.S. shores, or about 10 percent of the total number of refugees. A large portion of the Marielitos, as this criminal element/gang came to be known, were criminals who had spent a number of years confined to a torturous Cuban prison environment where cruelty and viciousness were common practice. It was this atmosphere that transformed many of these criminals, who were weak, poor, uneducated Afro-Cubans, into psychopaths.

A short time after this group's arrival on U.S. shores a gang network was set up. Some of the Marielitos were interviewed, issued residency cards, and released into society. Others were incarcerated while an in-depth check could be made on their criminal and psychological histories. Once the Marielitos with criminal backgrounds were released into local communities, they quickly established houses to be used for meeting gang members and organizing criminal activities. Through the use of these "safe houses," the leaders of this criminal organization were able to recruit and consolidate membership at several different locations. It gave the members of the Marielitos gang the opportunity to meet and socialize with other participants in gang operations, old friends, and newly recruited members in a friendly setting. These houses also presented the gang leaders with a chance to locate and sponsor the release of gang associates confined in detention centers since their arrival in the United States. This sponsorship was originally created to get gang members with special criminal skills out of the detention camps, but with the gang's greater involvement in criminal and drug activities, anyone with a criminal background was a possible new recruit for gang membership.

Gang members were recruited by the Corporation and La Compania as collectors for overdue gambling or narcotics debts. They were instructed to injure or maim anyone who refused to pay up past liabilities, or to kill anyone who declined to pay off large debts or, for that matter, anyone who was considered competition for these groups. The Colombian gangs found work for some of the Marielitos as drug couriers and hit men. Gang members also became involved in local vehicle theft. Most gang members set up their own criminal operations using money gained from their crimes to purchase high-powered handguns, shotguns, and rifles.

Along with the formation of the Marielitos gangs came a drastic increase in the amount of crime within as well as outside the Cuban community. Subtle increases in criminality are not always noticed in most U.S. communities, but the violence associated with the unlawful activities of the Marielitos brought an uproar in almost every community where the gang's criminal acts took place. This gang brought a new meaning to violent crime. Members of the Marielitos gang tended to finish almost every criminal incident with some type of brutal and vicious act. In some cases, body parts were cut off, words were carved on the body of the victim, or a victim was set on fire, while others were viciously raped, sodomized, and/or murdered in a ritualistic manner.

The Marielitos gang has a cultlike image surrounding its membership. Many gang members have little education in their backgrounds, but most have served in the Cuban military. Under Cuban law it is mandatory that everyone over a certain age serve time in the military and a portion of their military service typically took place in either the Congo or Central America. Most of the members have scars on their bodies that were either self-inflicted or the result of some type of religious ritual. Approximately 90 percent of the gang members have tattoos on their bodies. Marielitos' tattooing indicates that they realize they are considered pariahs by all other members of Cuban society. Tattooing is looked upon as a sign of disgrace by legitimate Cuban citizens who have labeled these criminals "guzanos" (worms) or "escoria" (scum). Gang members have a number of different types of tattoos on their bodies:

1. Saints or other Christian religious symbols

2. Writings or drawings associated with a special saint (e.g., St. Barbara who is the goddess of vengeance)

3. Names, writings, or drawings in an African dialect ("firmas," which means signatures)

4. Secret society emblem with words attached (Abakwa Secret Society or a Strawman)

5. Tombstones with names of deceased relatives

6. Drawings of American Indians, which usually have some type of religious meaning to them (e.g., drawing of a female Indian protects a person from danger)

7. Animals, usually predators such as sharks, snakes, or leopards

8. Women, pictured with predator animals, usually naked, and armed with a weapon

9. Locations of meaning to them (e.g., name of a prison)

10. Name of wife or girlfriend

Most of these tattoos are coarsely drawn or written during the gang member's time in prison. Dots drawn on the hands typically indicate prison time, while a tattoo inside the lower lip is usually a prisoner identification number. In some cases, five dots on a person's hand may denote that the person is a pickpocket while an arrow-shaped tattoo in the web of the hand indicates membership in the Abaqua religious sect. The tattooing tells outsiders that the members of the Marielitos gang do not trust anyone.

Tattooing in many cases is associated with the superstition and religious beliefs of the Marielitos gangs. Almost all of the Marielitos are members of an Afro-Cuban religious group known as Santeria. Santeria combines African religion, Christianity, and superstition into one religious sect. Some of the rudimentary doctrines of Santeria follow:

1. Every human being has an Orisha, which can be considered a patron saint or guardian angel who should be honored throughout this person's life.

2. Practicing members of this religious cult attain an ability to interpret omens.

3. The concept of ache pertains to the achievement of power.

4. Priests of Santeria are known as Santeros, Santeras, Babalawos, or Espirititas.

5. Believers in the Santeria religion usually undergo a number of rituals as initiation.

6. A believer may suffer torment from several different causes: a disregard for the Orishas or other departed souls; curses placed by another person (Brujeria, Bilongo); stealing the head (Eleda); being given the evil eye (Mal de Ojo); and failure to keep a pledge or doing something outlawed by the religion (DEA, 1990).

This religion gives the criminal a sense of power and confidence. Some of the saints the gang members pay homage to include Chango, who is St. Barbara, warrior and protector of criminals; Eleggua, the Christ child, who helps avoid trouble; Oshun, the saint of charity, love, and marriage; Babalu-aye, or St. Lazarus, a leper who walks with two dogs; and Oggun, or St. Peter, who watches over weapons and metal objects. This religion does not use a Bible or scriptures. Followers go to cemeteries to steal skulls and bones from graves to be used in their ritualistic ceremonies, and they form family-like groups that have a godfather. The rituals or ceremonies are conducted in a room containing many lit candles, and in most cases animals are sacrificed during these sessions. Rites and ceremonies used by Santeria include Trabajos (Works), Limpiezas (Cleansing), Rogaciones de Cabeza (Prayers of the Head), Hacer Santo (Making Saint), Cumpleanos (Birthdays), Feasts of Catholic Saints, Matanzas (Killings), Tanbores and Violines (Drums and Violins), and Ofrendas al Santo (Offerings to the Saint) (Dade County Sheriff's Department, 1991).

Many of the Marielitos practice Palo Mayombe, the committing of serious crimes during their mystical type of rituals. These ceremonies involve the use of altars, religious artifacts, human remains, burning candles, and the stabbing dolls. These criminals honor the god of hunting, Ochosi, whom they believe will guard them from apprehension after committing a crime and help them avoid being sent to prison. Members of the Marielitos gangs who continually practice these religious rituals gain a sense of invincibility, which has led to taking great risks during their criminal ventures. Their perception poses a dangerous threat to possible victims of their crimes as well as the police.

The rituals of the Palo Mayombe sect are centered around the Nganga and include the use of:

> the body parts of deceased human beings (skulls and bones) as religious artifacts; dirt collected from a cemetery; twenty-one (21) sticks that were gathered from a forest or wood lands (Palos de Monte); bird feathers and railroad spikes; an assortment of different types of animal bones; rakes, hoes, picks, and other types of small farming equipment; firearms, ammunition, and handcuffs; articles that have some type of unique meaning to the Palero members (known as sacred stones); pieces of paper containing peoples' names attached to small sticks (Amarres); cowrie shells; photographs; and various other items related to the ritual (DEA, 1990).

This group believes that some type of injury or sickness can be imposed on others, whether they be friends or enemies, by the gods. Malevolent witchcraft is a major part of the Palo Mayombe religious sect. An offshoot of the Palo Mayombe group is the Abacua, which is considered by many Marielitos to be an even more brutal group that attracted a number of ex-Cuban criminals. One major difference between this group and the Palo Mayombe is that the Abacua is far more selective in choosing new members. The Abacua also requires that all new members take an oath of silence and participate in a secret initiation ritual. During the ceremony the members of this gang are led to believe that they are instilled with special powers of invincibility.

A short time after the arrival of the Cuban refugees from the Mariel boatlift, the U.S. government realized that Castro had managed to "export" approximately 25,000 criminals. The U.S. Immigration and Naturalization Service (INS) has attempted to rectify this problem by confining all those who have been arrested for violent crimes until Castro agrees to take them back. Under federal law the INS is required to seize and incarcerate emigrant offenders after their release from state prison. Once imprisoned these criminals are held until they can be deported to their country of origin. The Castro government has thus far refused to allow the return of approximately 3,000 lawbreakers held in U.S. prisons (*Organized Crime Digest*, 1985; U.S. Senator, 1991).

## Cuban Communist Mafia

The Cuban Communist Mafia is the name given to Cuban leaders who have been, according to federal sources, actively involved in drug trafficking with the Colombian drug cartels since 1963. Information on the Cuban government's involvement with narcotics trafficking was originally collected by the U.S. Bureau of Narcotics and Dangerous Drugs. They trace the Cuban government's active interest in the drug business to a short time after Castro took power in 1961 (U.S. Senate Hearings, 1983, 1989; Arostegui, 1992). During the late 1960s and early 1970s, Cuban drug dealers controlled a vast majority of the cocaine trafficking in the United States. Police informers identified Cuban groups as the controllers of the cocaine market. Because supplies of cocaine were limited at that time, cocaine dealing turned out to be profitable business for the early Cuban gangs. In the early 1970s criminal organizations in Colombia realized the profitability factor of controlling cocaine distribution and, with this in mind, took over the cocaine market (Interviews of Confidential Informers, 1968–1972). In July 1971 information received by the U.S. government indicated that a narcotics operation working out of Havana was importing heroin to the United States in auto parts, various types of farm equipment, and medical provisions. Reports of the Cuban government's participation in drug trafficking activities with the Colombian cartels continued to surface during the 1970s, but no truly substantial evidence was provided by U.S. government enforcement sources. During late 1979, Jaime Guillot-Lara, identified as a major drug trafficker by the U.S. Drug Enforcement Agency (DEA) in 1976, formed profitable relationships with several Cuban officials (Fernando Ravelo Renedo and Gonzolo Bassols Suarez) in Bogota, Colombia. This affiliation put the Guillot-Lara drug-running planes and ships under the protective umbrella of the Cuban government while transporting narcotics in Cuban waters and airspace. According to DEA sources, Guillot-Lara paid the Cuban government $10 for every pound of marijuana transported through Cuba (U.S. Senate, 1989).

In November 1982, the U.S. District Court in Miami, Florida handed down indictments for conspiracy to smuggle drugs against 14 people including four Cuban government executives. Officials named in this indictment were Cuba's former Ambassador to Colombia (Fernando Ravelo Renedo), a vice admiral in the Cuban navy (Aldo Santamaria Cuadrado) and two high-ranking figures in both the Cuban Communist Party and the Cuban government (Rene Rodriguez Cruz and Gonzolo Bassols Suarez). These officials were named as active participants who assisted Jaime Guillot-Lara, a well-known Colombian drug trafficker, in expediting his drug activities. According to the U.S. indictment the Cuban officials participated in this venture in a number of different ways.

1. They agreed to let Cuba become a transshipment center for drugs being shipped from Colombia to the United States.

2. They allowed the use of specially designated Cuban airspace for the drug-carrying plane.

3. They granted permission to operate drug courier ships through Cuban waters in order to avoid detection by U.S. drug interdiction units.

4. They permitted off-loading from larger to smaller conveyors for shipment to the United States.

5. They purchased drugs at a cheaper price or received a specific percentage of the money retrieved from the drug sales.

6. They entered an agreement to transport weapons to the M-19 terrorist group in Colombia (President's Commission on Organized Crime, 1986; U.S. Senate, 1989).

Then in February 1983, David Lorenzo Perez, Jr. testified before a federal grand jury that he and Jaime Guillot-Lara plotted the scheme with Cuban officials to ship drugs from Colombia through Cuba to the United States. Lorenzo Perez, Jr. informed the government jury that he met with the vice admiral (Santamaria Cuadrado) and a high-ranking member of the Cuban Communist Party (Rodriguez Cruz) in Paredon Grande, Cuba, in October and November 1980 to forge a plan to smuggle $8.5 million of quaaludes into Florida. In the middle of this meeting, Rodriguez Cruz commanded Vice Admiral Santamaria Cuadrado to provide Cuban gunboats as protection for Guillot-Lara's drug operations in Cuban waters. During continuing testimony Lorenzo Perez, Jr. informed the grand jury that Rodriguez Cruz told him that the Cuban government would put up a portion of the money to buy 10 million quaaludes and 23,000 pounds of marijuana and ultimately received $800,000 from the sale of these drugs (U.S. Committee on Foreign Affairs, 1989).

A short time later, Mario Estevez Gonzalez, who had been a member of the Cuban Intelligence Service, informed federal and state law enforcement agencies that he had been selected, along with a number of other members of the Cuban Intelligence Service, to distribute cocaine, marijuana, and quaaludes throughout New York, New Jersey, and Florida. These agents had arrived in the United States during the Mariel boatlift in 1980. Estevez Gonzalez disclosed that during a 15-month period he had given Cuban diplomats residing in the United States somewhere between $2 and $3 million from the profits of these drug sales, which were used to promote terrorist activities in Latin America (Westrate, 1985; Committee of Foreign Affairs–House of Representatives, 1989). Hearings before the Senate Drug Enforcement Caucus in 1983 implied that Castro was involved with the drug traffickers and drug activities as were other Cuban government officials (U.S. Senate Commitee on Foreign Affairs, 1989).

Since early 1980, substantial information related to the active cooperation between Cuban officials and the Colombian drug cartels has surfaced. One report in 1987 indicated that Carlos Lehder Rivas, the renowned Colombian narcotics trafficker, convinced Cuban government officials to set up a cocaine processing plant in Cuba. According to this report, the Cuban government built this cocaine processing plant on a military base to provide greater security. The Cuban government also assured Lehder Rivas of safe passage for his drug boats traveling in Cuban waters on the trip from Colombia to the United States (*U.S. News and World Report,* 1987). A short time after a $15 million cocaine seizure in New York City, Sterling Johnson, the Special Narcotics Prosecutor for New York State, disclosed that the drugs seized had been transshipped through Cuba (*U.S. News and World Report,* 1987).

During Senate subcommittee hearings, Jose I. Blandon, a member of Gen. Manuel Noriega's staff in Panama, testified that Castro and Noriega worked in concert, using drug money to advance terrorist activities in Latin America. Blandon further stated that both Noriega and Castro fostered a strong relationship with the Colombian drug cartels. The association formed with the Colombian cartels proved extremely profitable to both Noriega and Castro. A portion of the money made by these dictators was eventually used to fund terrorist guerrilla movements in South America (Committee on Foreign Affairs–House of Representatives, 1989). In February 1988, the *Washington Times* reported that a Colombian drug cartel that had transported about a ton of cocaine through Cuba had been broken up by DEA agents. The story further revealed that Cuban-flown Russian-made MIG jet fighters were observed escorting Colombian drug planes, and Cuban military personnel participated in the off-loading and securing of the drugs. The *Times* also disclosed that during May 1987 members of the Cuban Air Force and Coast Guard, and a member of the Cuban General Intelligence Directorate (DGI) participated in a cocaine smuggling ring (Committee on Foreign Affairs–House of Representatives, 1989).

A great deal of evidence came to light in March 1989. Videotaped confessions by the gang leaders, Reinaldo and Ruben Ruiz, confirmed that Cuba was used as a safe refuge for the storage and transfer of drugs, as well as a refueling point for planes and boats. Ruben Ruiz characterized how on several occasions during 1987 he had piloted planes containing at least 1,000 pounds of cocaine from Colombia to Cuba and how he landed at a military air base in Varadero, Cuba. Cuban military, after off-loading the drugs, proceeded to transport the drugs to a coastal location where the drugs were transferred onto a boat named *The Florida* for shipment to the United States. The Ruizs also identified their contacts: Tony de la Guardia, Amado Padron, and Miguel Ruiz Pau (Committee on Foreign Affairs–House of Representatives, 1989).

The information gathered during research into the Cuban government's participation in drug trafficking indicates the following:

1.  An organized criminal group does exist within the Cuban government.

2.  The Cuban government's involvement in drug trafficking is real. Although Fidel Castro vehemently denies these charges, all the evidence gathered during this investigation indicates that both Fidel and his brother Raul are far more than participants in this drug conspiracy. Evidence gathered from hearings in the U.S. House of Representatives and the U.S. Senate indicate that both brothers have collaborated with other members of the Cuban government and the Colombian drug cartels to move drugs through Cuba to the United States. A number of ex-Cuban government officials as well as military officials have testified that nothing happens in Cuba or around Cuba without the okay of the Castro brothers. According to Susan Kaufman Purcell of the Americas Society, Latin American Affairs, it was impossible that Castro as "the leader of a highly centralized, personalistic autocracy, characterized by an intelligence and security apparatus that permeates all aspects of life on a small island of ten million people, remained in the dark about elaborate drug

trafficking maneuvers that involved the use of Cuban waters, air space and territory" (U.S. Senate Committee on Foreign Affairs, 1989). Another piece of evidence came from a former high-ranking State Department official, Elliott Abrams, who stated on the *MacNeil Lehrer Newshour* on July 6, 1989, "We know that when a yachtsman by accident edges into Cuban waters, he is immediately found and picked up by Cuban radar. We know that regularly boats from Colombia use Cuban waters, planes from Colombia fly over Cuba. This cannot happen without Cuban government knowledge." Abrams continued by stating, "The idea that this has been going on for ten years, and Fidel just learned about it just defies logic. Nobody in Cuba except Fidel Castro has the power to say 'Yes' for ten years. . . . No general, no admiral is going to risk doing that without Fidel's knowledge." The former U.S. Ambassador to Colombia, Thomas Boyett, testified during U.S. Senate hearings that "the Cuban government, as a matter of policy, for a long period of time—until exposed—was involved in drug smuggling. It was a [Cuban Intelligence] operation with the blessing of Fidel" (U.S. Senate, 1989: 104–105).

3. Robert Vesco, who is wanted in the United States for stealing more than $200 million, was granted asylum in Cuba by Fidel Castro in 1983. In 1984, Vesco set up a deal between the Colombian drug cartels and the Cuban government to transship Colombian drugs through Cuban territory for a fee. Law enforcement sources also believe that it was Vesco who initiated the Cuban government's involvement in shaking down drug boats passing though Cuban waters. Vesco, one must remember, was the person who created an almost faultless system of laundering money by moving currency in small bills from bank to bank and nation to nation. Vesco is presently under indictment in New York for embezzlment and in Florida for his involvement in the Cuban drug conspiracy (Sterling, 1994; U.S. Senate, 1991).

4. The easy money gathered from drug trafficking was used to purchase guns, ammunition, and explosives for terrorists' groups in both Central and South America. Drug money was easily available to Castro and by using these funds Castro avoided using money from the depleted Cuban economy. In the late 1970s Castro understood the relationship between drug money and the funding of revolutionary groups in Central and South American countries. The development of this relationship was fortified in the late 1970s and early 1980s when Jaime Guillot-Lara, a major Colombian drug trafficker, was given permission by the Cuban government to move his drugs through Cuba to the United States. Permission

also included protection for Guillot-Lara boats and planes, which was provided by the Cuban military. Guillot-Lara paid a specific fee for each pound of drugs transported through Cuba. This money, in turn, was used to pay Guillot-Lara to purchase and ship guns to the Colombian terrorist group M-19 (U.S. Senate, 1983). An article in *U.S. News and World Report* indicated that members of the Colombian cartels approached the Cuban Ambassador to Colombia in late 1975 in an effort to gain passage for their drugs through Cuba. The cartel members were informed that the fee would be $800,000 per boat load of drugs. Drug traffickers were told they could fly the Cuban flag and that their boats would be escorted through Cuban waters by Cuban Coast Guard gunboats. Monetary fees gained from the tolls paid by the drug cartels were then used to buy guns and explosives in the United States which were then transported back to Cuba for shipment to terrorists' groups in both Central and South America. According to the DEA, the Guillot-Lara case was only the "tip of the iceberg of Cuba's ultra-secret involvement in the drug trade" (May 4, 1987; 34–35). The DEA has documented more than 50 cases related to Cuban involvement in drug trafficking with the Colombian cartels between 1982 and 1987. A participant in one of these cases, Carlos Lehder Rivas, was forced by Cuban authorities to transfer his cocaine processing operations to Cuba. DEA intelligence indicates that the Cuban government has taken over the operation of this extremely lucrative cocaine processing plant (*U.S. News and World Report,* May 4, 1987).

5.  In 1989 an intriguing undercover drug operation was set in motion by the DEA. It was a trap to entice and then arrest Cuban Interior Minister Jose Abrahantes. Undercover DEA agents set up a meeting with Abrahantes on a yacht at a location outside of Cuban waters. At the last minute one of the Cuban informers, out of fear for his life, told the Cuban Ministries Intelligence Section that the people setting up the operation were U.S. drug agents. Abrahantes was the person who controlled drug operations for the Cuban government. He was also the person to whom Antonio de la Guardia Font turned over the drug profits ($3 million just prior to his arrest), and the person who controlled and stored cocaine in Cuba (Arostegui, 1992).

In response to pressure placed on him and his government, Castro instituted charges of corruption and larceny of government resources against 14 members of the Cuban military in June 1989. Four of the 14 defendants were close associates of both Fidel and Raul Castro. One, Gen. Arnaldo Ochoa Sanchez, had been selected by the Castro brothers to become the commander of the Western Army Forces, which is the most distinguished and highest-ranking position within the Cuban military forces known as the Fuerzas Armadas Revolucionarias (FAR) armies. The charges against Ochoa Sanchez and other members of the Cuban military included allegations of a joint conspiracy with Colombian drug dealers. According to the allegations, the collaboration between the Cuban military and the Colombian drug cartels included a combined narcotics smuggling operation in which airdrops, refueling stopovers for drug aircraft, and transferring of drugs from planes to boats was completed prior to shipment to the United States. All this activity took place under the guidance of the arrested members of the Cuban military and without the knowledge of the Castro brothers and the Cuban government (Lupsha, 1991; *Financial Times,* 1989; U.S. Senate Committee on Foreign Affairs, 1989).

This trial ended on July 7, 1989, with General Ochoa Sanchez, one of his aides, Captain Jorge Martinez Valdes, Colonel Antonio de la Guardia Font of the Ministry of the Interior, and de la Guardia Font's aid, Major Amado Padron Trujillo, being sentenced to death. All four of these convicts were executed on July 13, 1989, while the other 10 convicted military officers were sentenced to 10–30 years in prison. Since the completion of these trials it seems somewhat evident to members of the media and the Cuban community in exile that Ochoa Sanchez was aware of the drug trafficking but was not an active participant in any of the drug conspiracies. According to Granma neither Ochoa Sanchez nor his aid, Martinez Valdes, carried out any of the alleged drug schemes. It seems that Colonel Antonio de la Guardia Font and his aides had been designated to run the Cuban drug cartels' operations. If anything, de la Guardia Font and Ochoa Sanchez were in competition with each other and de la Guardia Font had successfully put Ochoa Sanchez in a position that eliminated him from any type of participation in the drug business (Lupsha, 1991). De la Guardia Font and other members of the Ministry of the Interior (MININT) were obviously active participants within a drug conspiracy. It also seems quite apparent from the evidence gathered during this research that the real coconspirators in the drug plot were the leaders of the Cuban Communist government and not Ochoa Sanchez and his aid. Arostegui informs us that a letter smuggled out of Cuba by Hector de la Guardia Font, the son of Patricio de la Guardia Font, implicates Castro's use of this so-called "war on drugs" to eliminate two of his major opponents in the military, Patricio de la Guardia Font and Arnaldo Ochoa Sanchez (1992). This article further indicates that the Cuba government is as deeply involved in drugs today as it was prior to the arrest and conviction of the 14 military leaders (Arostegui, 1992). In turn, we come to the same conclusion as Arostegui in that surely a Cuban Communist Mafia is involved in drug trafficking as well as money laundering. This gang, through the use of the Communist Manifesto, has created its own organized crime kingdom with tentacles that are always seeking new domains to control. Terrorist tactics that are supported through the use of drug money are used to take control of another country that is then used as another base for this gang's illegal activities.

As discussed, the Cuban groups vary in size, from actual organized crime families to what might be considered somewhat fanatical street gangs to government-organized political groups. As we move on to the Colombian groups we will see more groups fashioned after La Cosa Nostra.

## COLOMBIAN ORGANIZED CRIME

Just about every phase of cocaine trafficking, including cultivation, processing, and distribution, has expanded since the early 1980s. The world's cocaine supply is based out of South America with the coca being cultivated in Peru, Bolivia, Colombia, and Ecuador. The majority of the cocaine conversion laboratories are located in Colombia, Brazil, and Venezuela. This drug industry, as well as the long-established marijuana trafficking enterprises, have continued to flourish for the Colombian drug cartels over the past 15–20 years. Not to be outdone by the Asian drug rings, the Colombian cartels have recently created their own heroin business, going as far as to market their heroin at half the price of the heroin from both Southeast and Southwest Asia. A problem that persists with Colombian heroin is that, thus far, it does not have the same potency or substance that gives the addict the same high as the Asian heroin. Once again, the Colombian cartels only recently entered into the heroin industry, and their heroin will probably continue to improve until it reaches the same effectiveness as the Asian product. With their ever increasing participation in the drug trade, the Colombian drug cartels created an economy in Colombia that could no longer survive without the contributions of the drug traffickers.

The country of Colombia is located in the northwest part of South America and borders Peru, Panama, Ecuador and Venezuela. This country is also bordered by both the Pacific Ocean and the Caribbean Sea. Colombia is the fourth largest country in South America, with a land mass of approximately 440,000 square miles. As a nation, Colombia has a diverse population, which is the result of the blending of the native Indians, Spanish colonists, and African slaves. Approximately 31 million people presently live in Colombia.

As a country, Colombia survived 50 civil wars between 1850 and 1900, losing more than 100,000 people out of a population of 4 million during the last years of these revolutionary conflicts. These constant hostilities erupted into what is known as *La Violencia*. La Violencia started in 1946 and ended in the mid 1960s with an estimated 250,000 deaths. Ever since the early 1970s Colombia has been a nation overrun with violence and crime. The amount of violent crime in Colombia is exemplified by the number of homicides per year, averaging about 15,000 homicides annually since 1972. It means that approximately 68.2 murders are committed per 100,000 people in the population. In comparison, the United States' average is about 18 killings per 100,000 people. It seems commonplace to read about the murder of a Colombian political leader or judge. In fact, between 1979 and 1982 a total of 30 judges were viciously assassinated in Colombia. A great deal of regional strife has resulted along with terrorist attacks from either the 19th of April Movement, also known as M-19, or the Revolutionary Armed Forces of Colombia. A constantly elevated inflation rate, violence, and poor economic conditions have created a Colombian nation that depends on the drug cartels to support its ever-increasing monetary deficit (*Organized Crime Digest*, 1984).

Problems created by the inflationary trend and escalating crime problems have led to the immigration of a large number of Colombian citizens to the United States. This increased migration in the mid 1960s resulted in the takeover by the Colombians of the cocaine importation business. Almost all cocaine trafficking into the United States had been controlled by Cubans since the early 1960s. The immigration of a large number of Colombian citizens into the United States opened the door for the then small-time Colombia drug dealers to set up their own drug operations in the United States. At first these small operational bases were located in cities that had what the leaders of the drug groups considered a visible and viable Hispanic community. Colombian drug cartel bosses realized that couriers and dealers would be less conspicuous to law enforcement officials if they operated out of a Latin community. So as the immigration to the United States increased so did the amount of cocaine being smuggled into this country. One must remember that as a country Colombia:

1. is geographically well positioned in order to receive coca from other countries in South America.

2. has coastline on both the Pacific Ocean (900 miles) and the Caribbean Sea (1100 miles) for shipment to the United States.

3. benefits from a sparsely populated eastern area with vast central forests that effectively conceal clandestine processing labs and airstrips.

As the Colombian cartels continue to grow, so does their political power within that country. The Colombian organized crime groups have effectively transformed themselves from what could be considered trivial, unattached gangs into distinct organizations. Colombians who have immigrated to the United States and other countries throughout the world supply the cartels with access to those countries. In turn they then continue to assist workers within the Colombian drug systems. Two major Colombian drug trafficking groups have structured their organizations so that they maintain complete control over all steps involved in drug trafficking, from planting to street sale. Modeled after the traditional La Cosa Nostra organized crime groups, the Colombian factions are built of interconnected and required component groups. These groups require each specific sector to maintain its own responsibility for that area of productivity. Group participation in these gangs requires that members be involved as laborers, processors, transporters, financiers, and enforcers. Regular membership in most cases is supplemented through the use of outside criminal affiliates who perform certain tasks for a fee. Colombian gangs, in most cases, use other Colombians to carry out actions against group members who steal or cheat. When required the gang leaders will seek out the expertise of members of other ethnic organized crime groups.

In recent years we have seen the Medellin and Cali groups work together as one to overcome extradition proceedings against their leadership by the government of the United States. We have also observed a close relationship forming between the Cali cartel and members of La Cosa Nostra over the past several years. The Colombian and Italian factions have found that more may be gained financially by working together than by feuding. The Sicilian Mafia has formed a relationship with the Colombians that permits them to control a large portion of the fertile cocaine market in Europe. This arrangement has turned out to be a productive venture for both groups; the Colombians wholesale the cocaine to Sicilians and then let the Sicilians run their own drug operation. It frees the Colombians from setting up and running cocaine sales in Europe on a day-to-day basis. Colombian groups make their money up front and, basically, remove themselves from this operation.

The ability of the Colombian cocaine gangs to survive is indicated in a manual. These guidelines to protect drug traffickers were put together by Lizardo Marquez-Perez, who is presently serving a 45 year sentence for drug importation to the United States. The manual specifically lists standards to be followed by cartel members while participating in drug trafficking ventures:

1. Conduct all transactions in code.

2. In each person's possession should be security devices such as pocket alarms, beepers, electronic briefcases, mace, pepper spray, stun guns, security flares, tear gas, bullet proof vests, safety shields, and portable phones.

3. Distribute drugs prior to six o'clock in the morning and after six o'clock in the evening.

4. When conducting drug business out of a house, always identify yourself as either the butler or the handyman, and indicate that the people who own the house are away on vacation.

5. Use residential areas that have little street traffic, and find a house with a big lawn and a two-car garage that is out of any neighbor's sight.

6. Try to the best of your ability to imitate an American home owner. Wash your car, mow your lawn, and have barbecues. Stay away from extravagant social events and have some type of watchdog.

7. Avoid having furniture that you do not need.

8. Avoid using work vehicles for personal activities.

9. Never leave the house unguarded.

10. Always have available:
    a. airline tickets
    b. money
    c. safe house
    d. trusted lawyer
    e. nondescript vehicle (DEA, 1987).

During the early 1970s, a number of turf wars were fought over the control of the cocaine business in the United States. As previously stated the Cubans originally controlled most of the cocaine imported into the United States prior to the early 1970s. Once the Colombians took over control of the drug industry they successfully regulated drug trade through the use of high-profile violence and intimidation. Examples of this persisted through the late 1970s and early 1980s. In 1979 in East Elmhurst, New York, Susana Toro, a 5-year-old Hispanic girl, was found strangled and hung from a basement pillar in her residence with a Christmas wreath around her. Nine days later her 10-year-old brother, Oscar Toro, and the 17-year-old baby-sitter, Liliana Bustamante, were found strangled and stabbed, hanging frozen on mail bag hooks in a deserted post office in Long Island City, New York. Oscar Toro, Sr., the father of the murdered children, was a lieutenant in a Colombian drug group who had cheated the organization out of money. Then in January 1982, Orlando Galvez, his wife, and two children were found shot to death in his Mercedes-Benz alongside the Grand Central Parkway in Queens, New York. A search of the Galvez apartment turned up $980,000 in U.S. currency and $15 million worth of cocaine. Galvez had also been a dishonest employee of the Colombian drug cartels. Groups such as the Los Pistoleros led by Michael Sepulveda, were responsible for approximately 50–60 murders in both New York and Florida. Most of the members of this group were recruited hit men who came from Medellin, Colombia. Two members of this group, Hugo Echevirri and Carlos Arrango, would take their victims to an apartment in Queens, drain all the blood out of them in a bathtub, and put the bodies in discarded cardboard television or stereo boxes. These cardboard containers were then placed with other garbage on the street for pickup by sanitation workers. Such actions taken by the Colombian gangs certainly reveal their dedication to violence and intimidation for controlling the members of their organization.

## Medellin Cartels

Colombian cartels are basically nontraditional in character. They believe in conducting "in house" justice that is carried out through the use of vendettas, which are considered a legal principle of these organizations. Family members are active participants within their own drug group, and it would not be unusual to find a woman in a high-ranking position in any of the Colombian drug groups. Many leaders of the Colombian groups have become active participants in legitimate businesses including import/export, travel agencies, investment corporations, ranching, and the entertainment industry. Colombian groups over the past 25 years have managed to take over almost complete control of the marijuana (70%) and cocaine (90%) industries while they are still fairly active in the methaqualone trafficking (40%).

The Medellin cartel, formed in the early 1980s, was at one time considered the most powerful Colombian drug group. It was originally set up and run by Pablo Escobar-Gaviria, a former Colombian politician. Escobar-Gavaria started as an enforcer for a small drug smuggling group in Colombia. Within a short period of time, Escobar-Gavaria was able to save enough money to set up his own drug organization in Medellin. Escobar-Gavaria's drug ventures quickly made him into a billionaire who spent large amounts of money importing African wildlife into Colombia to stock his own personal zoo. Escobar-Gavaria was considered a "Robin Hood" type of character by some citizens of Colombia because he funded low-cost housing and soccer fields for the people. Yet, the other side of Escobar-Gavaria is illustrated in an article written by Jose De Cordoba a short time after Escobar-Gavaria's death. De Cordoba claims that Escobar-Gavaria was responsible for the bomb that exploded on an Avianca flight in 1989 that killed 107 people. He said that Escobar-Gavaria was the Colombian drug trafficker who instituted a great deal of the violent activities associated with the Colombian cartels. It was estimated that Escobar-Gavaria was responsible for 25,000 killings in Colombia in 1992 alone (De Cordoba, 1993). Although he was, at one time in 1991, confined to a Colombian correctional facility, Escobar-Gavaria still had enough free time to run his drug operations without any interference from government officials. Escobar-Gavaria escaped from prison in 1991 but was killed during a police raid on one of his hideouts in December 1993. Information has surfaced since his death that members of the Cali cartel, using a group known as *Pepes* (People Persecuted by Pablo Escobar), played a major part in locating and eliminating Escobar-Gavaria. As the Cali cartel took over the Colombian drug trafficking business, concerns over the extensive use of violence by the Medellin cartels also grew. Bombings, murders, and other violent acts brought too much attention to the Colombian cartels. Therefore, cartel leaders like Escobar-Gavaria were considered liabilities who could no longer be tolerated by the leaders of the new Cali drug cartels. These cartels are run on the basic management principles that advocate the use of bribery instead of violence (De Cordoba, 1993; Wilkinson, 1994).

As the drug ventures expanded so did the number of participants, and Escobar-Gavaria was soon joined in the drug business by Jorge Ochoa-Restrepo, his sons Fabio, Jorge, and Juan, and by Carlos Lehder-Rivas, each as a separate entity. Ochoa-Restrepo, also known as Don Fabio or El Gordo (the fat one) assumed national prominence as a drug cartel leader in 1977. He took over leadership by ordering the assassination of his boss. He is known not only as the father of international cocaine trafficking, but also as a "notable" millionaire businessman who has a number of legal investments in both agriculture and horse breeding. This murder plus many other acts of violence helped Ochoa-Restrepo become the "Godfather" of the Medellin cartels. Ochoa-Restrepo formed a profitable drug smuggling alliance with Escobar-Gavaria. As a result of this affiliation Ochoa-Restrepo was able to participate in an infinite number of drug smuggling endeavors that ultimately increased his wealth. Ochoa-Restrepo was also able to build a fleet of airplanes that included props as well as jets. In addition he had private and commercial sea-going vessels to ship his cocaine from Colombia to the United States. In 1991 Ochoa-Restrepo's sons took advantage of a Colombian government plea-bargain agreement for their prior participation in drug trafficking. During their stay in prison all of the food preparation for the brothers was taken care of by their mother, Margarita de Ochoa. The brothers were released from prison in 1995 and claim that all the money they made from their drug trafficking business was spent on lawyers and family security (Brooke, 1995).

Lehder-Rivas was originally arrested in Miami in 1973 for possession of 230 pounds of marijuana and indicted again in 1981 for shipping cocaine through Florida and the Bahamas. Lehder-Rivas, in the early 1980s, was smuggling an average of 500–1000 kilograms of cocaine each month into the United States. Lehder-Rivas has been given credit for setting up transshipment routes from Colombia through several Caribbean islands to the United States (*Organized Crime Digest*, 1984). Lehder-Rivas is currently serving a life prison sentence in a U.S. correctional facility.

Another group within the Medellin cartel deserves mention: it was formed by the now deceased Jose Gonzalo Rodriguez-Gacha also known as "the Mexican." Rodriguez-Gacha and his group emerged as a powerful force after the conviction of Carlos Lehder-Rivas in Florida in 1988. Rodriguez-Gacha's drug operation was run somewhat differently from other Medellin cartels. Rodriguez-Gacha personally maintained a tight control over both the transportation and dispersion networks of his drug operation. All the people who represent Rodriguez-Gacha's organization throughout the United States are true employees of his group. These workers put in regular business hours, they wear shirts, ties, and suits, and the organization requires that they maintain a low profile. Rodriguez-Gacha's employees are paid a weekly salary, unlike most other cartel employees who work on commission (U.S. Dept. of Justice: Office of Attorney General, 1989). Rodriguez-Gacha in 1989 offered to wipe out communism in Colombia if the Colombian government would give him amnesty for his past narcotics trafficking. In an effort to show that he would fulfill this promise, Rodriguez-Gacha went as far as to hire Israeli, American, and British mercenaries to train his own personal army to carry out the task of destroying communism in Colombia. Rodriguez-Gacha actually created a reign of terror with his paramilitary group. According to Colombian sources, his mercenary-trained military units were responsible for more than 200 killings, including Justice Minister Lara Bonilla, newspaper owner Guillermo Cano, radical leader Jaime Pardo Leal, and presidential candidate Senator Luis Carlos Galan. Rodriguez-Gacha's army was also responsible for the wanton killings of numerous other leftist leaders and political figures, judges, and police officials, who allegedly stood in his way in his effort to defeat communism in Colombia. In reality, the facts are that Rodriguez-Gacha was nothing more than a petty thief and hustler until he became associated with Pablo Escobar-Gavaria, who considered Rodriguez-Gacha, prior to his demise, as being totally out of control. During the search of his ranch, a short time after his death, the police found a large cache of Israeli-manufactured weapons and ammunition. An investigation revealed that these weapons had originally been sold to the Antiguan government. Eventually, the Antiguan government found that the shipment was made by two former Israeli Army officers who, through the use of a scam, managed to have the weapons shipped through Antigua to Colombia. One of the ex-

Israeli military officers is wanted in Colombia for both illegally transporting weapons into Colombia and teaching members of drug trafficking groups how to properly use subversive military procedures. Federal law enforcement officials have labeled Rodriguez-Gacha as a common crook who would steal or kill anyone (Eisner, 1989; *Narcotics Control Digest,* January 3, 1990). Rodriguez-Gacha's drug group operates on a smaller scale since his assassination in December 1989.

The Medellin cartels set up a family-oriented organization in which associates were carefully selected by family members. An example of the Medellin groups' ability to stay within their own friendly confines is illustrated by the drug alliance set up between Escobar-Gavaria and Ochoa-Vasquez. The Medellin cartel tightly controls their drug ventures from cultivation through distribution, including processing, transporting, and dispersal of the drugs. These drug groups were the first to:

1. purchase fields producing coca in Colombia, Bolivia, and Peru.

2. compensate the farmers through an agent.

3. employ chemists as associates in the group.

4. set up many small processing laboratories that were run by family associates instead of operating one or two major labs.

5. obtain coca paste, in most cases provided by growers.

6. arrange transportation that is devised and carried out by brokers who also supply aircraft, airstrips, pilots, and vessels.

7. distribute drugs through close associates of the group in the United States and Europe; lower-level distribution is usually done by members of other ethnic gangs.

8. make sufficient funds available to both bribe and intimidate politicians and other law enforcement officials.

9. maintain a strong home base operation that keeps tight reins on all overseas operations.

10. link the base of operations in Colombia with other locations throughout the world through the use of computers and fax machines; all supervisors are rotated from one location to another to avoid the temptations of cheating the cartels out of some of the large amounts of money they control daily.

11. remain open to forming business alliances with members of other criminal organizations in order to reach a specific goal.

12. accomplish money laundering through the use of diversified schemes such as:
    a. front businesses
    b. small deposits, less than $10,000
    c. computer transfers
    d. money orders
    e. money transferred through Panama, Switzerland, Colombia, and other foreign banks
    f. wire transfers of money (smurfing, which is breaking each transaction down to less than $10,000 so that it does not have to be reported to the U.S. Internal Revenue Service; storefront money transfer agencies usually get 8% for breaking down and wiring money)
    g. casinos.

Federal law enforcement agencies instituted a strict enforcement policy regarding the Currency and Foreign Transactions Reporting Act of 1970 and the Bank Secrecy Act in early 1980. The former act requires financial institutions, including banks, savings and loans, currency exchanges, currency brokers, and credit unions, to file Currency Transaction Reports with the U.S. Treasury Department on all cash transactions that exceed $10,000. Strict enforcement of the Bank Secrecy Act hindered the laundering of money by the Colombian cartels as well as other organized criminal groups. It did not take long for the members of these criminal organizations to come up with a "legitimate" way to launder their profits without government authorization. These criminals soon discovered that gambling casinos could be used to launder their unlawful profits. Casinos do not have to file any Currency Transaction Reports and, therefore, presented gang members with an effective remedy for their money laundering dilemma. The laundering of the money is done in several ways:

1. Bills in smaller amounts are exchanged for bills of a larger denomination, making it easier for drug groups to transport the money.

2. Casino personnel aware of the money laundering scheme wire clients' money to an offshore account. They can also make loans available to a patron knowing payback will be almost immediate and will include a monetary bonus for the casino employee.

3. Money deposited in one casino is then transferred to a specified account in another associated casino, usually outside the United States. After this transfer is completed credit can be issued to the person whose name is on the account. This person is, in most cases, a high-ranking member of the drug cartel.

4. A casino has the ability to proclaim that money in a person's account is the result of successful gambling. This method gives the money back to the depositor minus taxes, which is still to the advantage of the drug traffickers. Under what is designated as "high roller status," people can open accounts with the casinos. Under the guidelines set forth by the casinos, airline fare, room, and board are paid for by the casino but the gambler must put a specified amount of money in this "high roller" account. The gambler must also bet or spend a specific amount of money during this gambling venture. This person can win as well as lose money and large sums of money can be placed in the account and any money in the account can then be designated as winnings by the casino.

5. If a person gambles away small sums of money originally deposited in an account, usually $10,000, the casino will accept much larger sums of money deposited into a gambling account, usually $100,000 or more, which is then quickly withdrawn, in the form of a check or large bills (DEA, 1984).

## Cali Cartels

Cali drug cartels started their movement toward control of the Colombian drug industry during the late 1980s. Continuing violent and destructive acts by the Medellin cartels during the mid and late 1980s quickly deteriorated the working relationship agreed upon in the early 1980s by both the Medellin and Cali drug cartels. Suddenly in the late 1980s, the Medellin cartels found that their unchallenged power was eroding. The arrest and conviction of Carlos Lehder-Rivas in the United States was followed by the assassination of Jose Rodriguez-Gacha in 1989, the conviction and jailing of the Ochoa-Vasquez brothers, and the killing of Pablo Escobar-Gavaria by the Colombian police in December 1993. All these events hindered the Medellin cartels narcotic trafficking activities.

Leaders of the Cali groups have participated in some of the events that helped reduce the power of the Medellin cartels. These leaders quickly seized the opportunity to take over the Colombian drug business. Unlike the leaders of the Medellin cartels, the Cali groups have cautiously set up their drug operations in an attempt to avoid the mistakes made by leaders of the Medellin cartels. These groups have devised major corporation types of narcotic trafficking organizations that are, in some cases, run in the same clandestine manner as the U.S. Central Intelligence Agency (CIA). In order to avoid interception of either communications or drug shipments the Cali group has gone as far as attempting to purchase their own communications satellite. When they ship drugs they usually secret the drugs in another item such as Brazilian cedar boards. Using Brazilian boards was successful for the Cali group because it took U.S. Customs and DEA nine years to finally catch on to this diversionary method of smuggling drugs. The Cali group made sure these shipments contained a large number of these boards and then proceeded to drill out the centers of a very small portion of the boards to avoid detection. This method of smuggling was devised by members of the Santacruz-Londono Cali group in 1988, and it was only by a stroke of luck (the drilling of a board by a U.S. Customs official after observing some suspicious actions by a crew member), that U.S. Customs officials discovered that only a very small number (700 of 9,000) of the planks had been drilled out and filled with cocaine (Shannon, 1991).

The Cali drug organizations are structured to be patriarchal while maintaining an autarchic system that requires discipline to maintain total allegiance to the leadership. Although this organization has a great deal of discipline and control it still advocates the need for creativity within the drug trafficking business. An example of the inventiveness of this drug cartel surfaced when a drug sub washed ashore in Santo Domingo. These miniature submarines are anywhere from 17 to 30 feet long and are made of fiberglass and wood. They have no sharp edges which helps avoid radar detection. They hold two crew members and have a range of about 600 miles. It is estimated that these boats can carry up to several hundred kilos of marijuana, cocaine, or heroin. Intelligence information indicates that these miniature submarines are being built at the seaports of Santa Marta and Barranquilla and leased to the Cali cartel at some where between $100,000 and $200,000 per drug load (Copeland, 1994).

Jose Santacruz-Londono, also known as Don Chepe or El Gordo, is the leader of one of the Cali cartels. He along with Gilberto Rodriguez-Orejuela put the Cali drug operation together during the mid 1970s. This group set up their base of operations in the Cauca Valley city of Cali. Thus far, these groups have managed to work successfully hand in hand in taking over the importation of Colombian drugs worldwide. Santacruz-Londono and the other members of the Cali drug consortium groups have set up cell-type operations that are totally controlled by the group leaders residing in Cali. Cartel bosses in Cali go as far as to vigilantly check the expenditures and liabilities of each cell, oversee and make decisions on what tasks should be performed by hit men, and keep a watchful eye on the activities of their money couriers, and lab employees, and the transporting or smuggling of persons. Cali leaders feel that the control by the employer over the employee is made easier through the use of placing skilled and trusted workers from Colombia in charge of these cells. Cartel bosses also use the threat of violence against family members in Colombia to keep workers in line. The Cali leaders find it is important to keep each cell, the cell leaders, and the workers isolated from all other cell locations and employees. In fact, few high-ranking officials in each cartel are aware of the identity of the people who work in these cells.

Cells are set up in centralized locations throughout the United States. The DEA estimates that each Cali group has six to ten of these cells presently operating throughout the United States. These cells are made up of trusted employees from Colombia who have worked their way up the organizational ladder in either Colombia or the United States. All of the cells are supervised by a person who is known as a *Celeno*. Some of the cartels staff their cells with family members or close and trusted friends. Salaries for cell leaders and employees are deposited in banks in Cali and any monetary error made by a cell member is corrected by withdrawing the amount from the employee's bank account (Shannon, 1991).

Each one of these cells operates independently from all other cells. They are stocked like arsenals for the protection of the cell as well as its product, and they are set up to be impenetrable by outsiders, especially informers and law enforcement agents. The major task of each cell is to properly apportion either cocaine or heroin to distributors within its operational area, who will then ultimately retail the drugs out to street vendors. A Celeno or cell leader only sells drugs to people that he has been acquainted with over a period of time, usually other Colombians. Prospective drug purchasers must have been checked out and given an endorsement by cartel leaders in Cali prior to the sale of any drugs by any cell. Cali leaders may go as far as having a background and credit check done on prospective customers. Before receiving approval, these people understand that they must have some type of security to put up in case they are apprehended by law enforcement officials. Some of this collateral may include family members in Colombia. At the present time, the DEA estimates that the Cali cartels control 80 percent of the worldwide cocaine trafficking business (McGee, 1995; Shannon, 1991; *Newsweek,* 1989).

Gilberto Rodriguez-Orejuela and his brother Miguel Angel Rodriguez-Orejuela are the leaders of one of the Cali drug cartels. Gilberto is known as "El Ajedrecista" (the Chess Player) because of the way he methodologically maneuvers his drug operations to avoid detection by both U.S. and Colombian law enforcement agencies. Gilberto Rodriguez-Orejuela was arrested on June 9, 1995, by Colombian authorities but on two prior arrests he was released within a short period of time without any type of prosecution. A probable reason for Gilberto Rodriguez-Orejuela's arrest was a taped telephone conversation that involved the Cali cartels agreeing in 1994 to contribute $3,750,000 to the presidential election campaign of Ernesto Samper-Pizano.

Samper-Pizano, the newly elected Colombian president, denied any knowledge of a campaign contribution by the Cali cartels but suddenly encouraged a full enforcement assault on the Cali cartels (Rohter, 1995).

Gilberto and Miguel, like other members of the Cali cartels, have found that it is much easier, in most cases, to bribe someone than to kill him. Also, it is far more fashionable to work a member of the organization into an official position within the Colombian government. Yet, the likeliness of being killed by the Cali cartel is just as possible as being murdered by the Medellin cartel. A New York journalist, Manuel de Dios Unanue, did a continuing exposé on Cali cartel leader Jose Santacruz-Londono in the Spanish-language newspaper *El Diario-La Prensa* until he was assassinated while having a drink in a Queens bar in 1992. According to a DEA informer, John Harold Mena, Santacruz-Londono ordered the hit on Manuel de Dios Unanue (McGee, 1995). In many cases, when the Cali cartels have to use violence they attempt to keep it fairly low key, although intelligence information gathered from Colombian law enforcement officials indicates that Santacruz-Londono and his Cali group would sanction a terrorist-type action against the Colombian government. This type of terrorist action would probably be similar to the seditious type of campaign that Pablo Escobar-Gavaria carried out against the Colombian government (*New York Times,* 1995). Until now, the Cali cartels have stayed away, with one or two exceptions, from participating in mass killings and bombings to gain notoriety.

Another achievement of the Cali cartels is their inventiveness in seeking working agreements with other ethnic gangs, as evidenced by the Cali cartels' dealings with La Cosa Nostra in Italy.

1.  Connections to the Sicilian Mafia are well documented, including money laundering and a drug connection to Pasquale Locatelli, a Sicilian crime boss. He was arrested along with 60 other people for their involvement in laundering Colombian drug money through a bank set up by U.S. federal authorities to trap drug money launders. This operation, called "Operation Dinero," also led to the arrest of Roberto Severa, a member of the Banda Della Malgliana, a criminal group based in Rome. Through Operation Dinero, law enforcement agencies seized $40 million and expensive paintings by Picasso and Rubens (Janofsky, 1994).

2.  Another U.S. federal law enforcement drug money laundering operation set up in 1989 resulted in the arrest of members of the Sicilian Mafia, the Neapolitan Camorra, and the Calabian Ndrangheta. A person identified as Jose Duran (also known as Raul Grajales), who according to Italian law enforcement authorities is "the most important distributor in the world for the Colombian drug cartels," was also arrested in Italy. Appre-

hended with Duran was Betten Martens, a significant money launderer from the Netherlands, and Pedro Felipe Villaquiran, a Colombian national who was being introduced to organized crime connections in Europe by Duran (Ostrow and Montalbano, 1992: A1, A6).

3. FBI agents in Florida arrested several members of the "Calabian Ndrangheta" in Sarasota, who had been combined with a group of a Colombian traffickers to set up and run a heroin and drug trafficking conspiracy in the United States and Canada (*Narcotics Control Digest*, April 1993).

4. According to law enforcement sources, an alliance has been set up in New York City between members of both the Gambino crime group and Colombian organized crime cartels to deal both drugs and guns (Parascandola, 1995).

5. Russian drug enforcement chief, Aleksandr Sergeyev, documented information that indicates a direct working relationship between the Cali drug groups and the Russian and Israeli organized crime gangs in Europe. The Cali connection to the Israeli and Russian groups was evident during seizure of more than 2,400 pounds of cocaine packed in food containers marked "meat and potatoes" on a container truck in St. Peterburg, Russia. An Israeli, who had been a resident of St. Petersburg, was the only person arrested by Russian police (*Narcotics Control Digest*, May 1993; *Newsweek*, December 1993).

Seizures and arrests represent approximately 10 percent, if not less, of the total activities of organized crime groups in drug trafficking and/or money laundering. So the examples in the preceding list only give us a modest insight into the connections between organized crime groups. It seems likely that the total number of conspiracies involving these criminal groups is greater than most people can grasp.

An associate group of the Rodriguez-Orejuela family is the Orjuela-Caballero family. This group is led by Jaime Orjuela-Caballero who is a cousin of the Rodriguez-Orejuelas. Two other major Cali groups require mentioning. The first is the Pacho Herrera group whose leader is said to be the son of Afro-Colombian drug smuggler, Benjamin Herrera-Zuleta, also known as the "Black Pope." The other group, the Urdinola-Grajales family, known as the Northern Cauca Valley Cartel, operates out of the fairly wealthy sugar cane growing area north of Cali. The leader of this group, Ivan Urdinola-Grajales, was arrested by Colombian police in April 1993 and quickly pleaded guilty to drug charges for which he received a 5½-year prison sentence. Prior to his arrest and conviction Ivan Urdinola-Grajales was somewhat of an idol to local gang members. Ivan Urdinola-Grajales had built a reputation for killing people with a chain saw and then depositing their bodies in the Cauca river. These bodies, some of them with their hands tied behind their backs, would eventually turn up in villages and towns along the river. Colombian officials estimate that Ivan was responsible for well over 100 mutilation-type murders. Since his arrest and conviction on drug charges not one new body has turned up in the Cauca river (Wilkinson, 1994; De Cordoba, 1993).

Henry Loaiza-Ceballos, nicknamed the "Scorpion," and labeled "the Cali cartel's minister of war" by local Colombian newspapers, has become a notorious drug trafficker who surrendered to Colombian police authorities on June 20, 1995, in Bogota. According to Colombian police officials, Loaiza-Ceballos, celebrated by villagers in his home base of Venadillo, Colombia, because of the goodwill he spreads in that community, was involved in the killings of more than 100 of his workers who attempted to form a labor union on his ranch in Trujillo, Colombia, in 1990. Loaiza-Ceballos along with a group of Colombian army deserters allegedly tortured the victims with water hoses, blow torches, and chain saws. Most of the casualties were then cut up with chain saws and, like Urdinola-Grajales victims, dumped into the Cauca river (Brooke, 1995: A8).

Just as the Cali cartels have grown and increased their profits from drug trafficking so has the number of small-time drug dealers and their violent activities in Cali. Men known as *traquetos* (Spanish for machine gun fire) have popped up throughout Cali carrying walkie-talkies in their hands and semi-automatic pistols in their waistbands. A majority of the traquetos are in their early twenties and have made their money by smuggling drugs into the United States for members of the Cali cartel. Presently, the traquetos are licensed by the godfathers of the various Cali groups to operate, and will probably become more heavily involved in the drug trafficking business as the Cali bosses continue to franchise out their drug operations and move into legitimate business ventures. The problem with continuing to license the traquetos groups to operate under the umbrella of the Cali cartel is that in the future these groups will become direct clones of the Medellin cartels' Rodriguez-Gacha and Escobar-Gavaria—vicious and murderous (Wilkinson, 1994).

The ingenuity of the Cali cartels shows in their sudden move into the heroin market in early 1990 in an effort to increase their earnings. They had farmers in Colombia convert their crops from coca plants to poppy plants. Cali cartel leaders paid the farmers $3,000 for each pound of opium grown. Presently, the Colombian cartels have more acreage in Colombia, Peru, and Bolivia dedicated to poppy growing than every other country in the world except Myanmar, the worldwide leader in poppy production. In an effort to properly cultivate their heroin product, the Cali cartels imported Chinese chemists. Results seem to indicate that the procedures used by the Cali groups have yielded a poppy that produces more opium-containing bulbs than the opium grown anywhere else in the world. In addition, the highly fertile fields in Colombia make it possible to produce a new crop of poppy plants every five months (Ebron and Mustain, 1993).

The Cali cartels have compelled cocaine merchants to purchase heroin as well as cocaine from them. Since Colombian heroin first appeared on the drug scene, it has developed the reputation as the purest heroin produced in the world. The purity of the heroin makes it possible for it to be smoked or inhaled as well as injected into the body. Another factor that makes the Colombian heroin so inviting is that it is much cheaper on the street than heroin from either Southeast or Southwest Asia, which lacks the purity of the Colombian heroin. Colombian heroin traffickers are presently selling a kilo of heroin for $65,000 to $70,000 while the Southeast and Southwest Asian heroin usually costs about $130,000 per kilo.

## Other Colombian Cartels

Two other major drug groups operate in Colombia, although both have managed to keep a low profile and avoid media attention. The first cartel, the Bogota cartel, has over the past several decades maintained connections to both La Cosa Nostra and the Cuban groups, the Corporation and La Compania. Historically, the Bogota group formed a relationship with both La Cosa Nostra and the Cuban groups through Meyer Lansky during the late 1950s while running contraband items into Colombia. This group is probably the oldest organized crime group in Colombia. The Bogota group's first connection to drug trafficking involved the original cocaine dealers in the United States, who were Cubans. The Bogota cartel supplied them with cocaine during the 1960s and early 1970s. In most cases, the Bogota cartel is still supplying the Cuban and many La Cosa Nostra organized crime groups with cocaine. A major portion of its cocaine is processed through plants that adjoin coca plant farms in Colombia. As a group, the Bogota cartel has maintained its political contacts in Colombia over the years by staying out of the limelight and avoiding contact, whenever possible, with both Colombian and U.S. law enforcement agencies. Most of its profits from drug trafficking have been reinvested in properties outside of Bogota.

The last Colombian cartel is know as the North Atlantic Coast group. This group is small and lacks the cohesiveness that most of the other Colombian groups exhibit. As a group the members are spread out throughout the Colombian port cities of Cartagena, Barranquilla, Santa Marta, and Rio

Hacha. Similar to the Bogota cartel, the North Atlantic Coast cartel was originally involved in supplying contraband goods to Colombia. It was, as a group, one of the earliest participants in smuggling marijuana into the United States. Once the group observed the profits being gleaned by the other Colombian cartels, it also became involved in cocaine smuggling. Through the years the North Atlantic Coast cartel has set up solid drug bases in New York, Florida, Georgia, California, and Massachusetts. Since the late 1980s, this cartel has expanded its activities to include smuggling and money laundering assistance to both the Cali and Medellin cartels (Dept. of Justice, 1989).

Similar to other organized criminal groups, the Colombian cartels continue to survive and increase their profits from unlawful activities. The Medellin cartel has lost a number of its leaders over the past several years but will more than likely regroup in the near future in an effort to once again increase its participation in and profits from drug trafficking ventures. As far as organized criminal groups are concerned, the Cali cartels have to be considered one of the most well-managed and well-organized groups in the world. Like the Medellin cartels, however, they will ultimately get caught up in the violent activities that will destroy their alliances with other groups. One must also not forget the constant scrutiny of the Cali drug barons by tenacious U.S. law enforcement agencies. As indictments and money seizures continue so will the pressure on the Colombian government to arrest and extradite members of the Cali drug cartel to the United States for prosecution.

As we have seen in this section, the Colombian cartels' names may change, but they remain financially sound and politically strong in their homeland. For all the aforementioned reasons, Colombian cartels can be considered large corporations that profit from illegal activities.

Next we will view how Mexican crime groups, some of which have been modeled after the Colombian cartels, and groups that originated as prison gangs have developed as organized crime families.

## MEXICAN ORGANIZED CRIME

### Prison Gangs

The history of Mexican organized crime groups starts with the Mexican Mafia, "La Eme" (which is Spanish for the letter M). The Mexican Mafia's roots formed in East Los Angeles in the early 1950s. Prior to the Mexican Mafia, approximately 20 loosely knit gangs, most of which were created in the early 1940s, existed there. Some of these organizations were actually remnants of gangs, formed in the barrios of East Los Angeles during the mid 1920s. According to early gang observers some of these Mexican street organizations emerged from groups formed during the Mexican revolution. During the 1930s and 1940s gangs that came to be known as *Pachucos* sprouted up in Texas, New Mexico, Arizona, and Southern California. These gangs became modish because of their unique way of dressing. On most occasions the gangs' members wore "baggy, pegged pants worn high above the waist, patent leather shoes, knee length suit coats and broad brimmed hats." Many of these gangs, because of their style of dress, quickly attracted the attention of local police departments. In a majority of cases, these gangs were more of what today would be considered trendsetters, rather than criminal organizations. A murder in East Los Angeles during World War II resulted in off-duty police officers and military personnel roving through the streets of East Los Angeles preying on these gangs that were known as *zoot-suiters*. A segment of the present day Mexican gangs can be traced back in some ways to the earlier zoot-suiters gangs (Governor's Organized Crime Prevention Commission, 1991). Mexican street gangs continued to appear on the streets of East Los Angeles but the composition of these groups has changed somewhat since the mid 1940s. During the early 1950s the makeup of these groups was transformed to include hardened criminals who participated in numerous criminal operations in East Los Angeles. Many of these smaller gang members were ultimately linked into one large gang, the Mexican Mafia, through connections formed during the imprisonment of gang members in the Deuel Vocational Institute in Tracy, California, in the mid 1950s. Within a short period of time, members of these smaller gangs were assimilated into one big gang, creating a prison empire that victimized white, black, and northern Hispanic inmates. Not long after the incorporation of these smaller inferior gangs into one high-profile gang, this criminal organization started moving into more profitable unlawful activities.

At first the members of the Mexican Mafia set themselves up as a protection service to other members of the prison community. In an effort to follow up one successful endeavor after another the gangs quickly became active participants in gambling, drug dealing, and male prostitution rings within the California prison system. During the mid 1960s the Mexican Mafia took over complete control of the prison drug trade and a great portion of many of the other unlawful activities that take place within our penal institutions. A majority of the members of the prison population that the gang provided services for were either black or white. As the membership of the Mexican Mafia continued to increase so did their use of brutality against all nongang members, whether black, white, or Hispanic, within the California prison system. This type of treatment led to the formation of another Mexican prison gang, La Nuestra Familia, or Our Family, who objected to the actions of the Mexican Mafia against other prison groups.

La Nuestra Familia was originally comprised of U.S.-born Mexicans who lived outside of the major urban areas of California. This gang has been and still is involved in a fierce struggle with members of the Mexican Mafia that began with the inception of La Nuestra Familia in 1958. When La Nuestra Familia was originally formed as a prison gang, just about all members were from an area outside of Los Angeles, known as Central Valley. As time progressed so did the membership of this gang, which is now composed of urban as well as rural members. This organized crime group has managed to form a business relationship with several Chinese gangs including the Wah Ching and Chung Ching Yee. These alliances have helped the gang increase its involvement in the street sales of heroin (DEA, 1993).

As far as size is concerned the Mexican Mafia has to be considered a much more powerful gang than La Nuestra Familia. Its strength was built on its use of violence to protect gang members and other members of the prison community. In addition it prevented other groups from attempting to control unlawful prison and street operations. This reputation for violence has also helped the Mexican Mafia attract new members at twice the rate of La Nuestra Familia. Since the early 1970s both Mexicans and Mexican Americans entering the California prison system have been forced to become members of La Nuestra Familia, the Texas Syndicate, the Border Brothers, Fresno Bull Dogs, or the Mexican Mafia. The Mexican Mafia has, thus far, avoided being involved in any type of radical activities. They are working to make money and whenever possible continue to exploit the system whether it be inside or outside prison. Recent intelligence information indicates that the Mexican Mafia has formed a business relationship with La Cosa Nostra. These business operations include performing strong-arm activities, collecting debts, protecting gambling and prostitution establishments, and supplying heroin or cocaine to the Italian gangs. Members of the Mexican Mafia gang have always had a propensity to be more violent than their counterparts. This gang has found it easy to kill rival gang members, Mexican Mafia members who fail to follow gang policy, and any others who get in their way, including members or workers of another ethnic gang, whether hired to do so or just for the thrill of killing a rival gang member.

The members of the Mexican Mafia have a tendency to be arrested and charged at a far more frequent rate than members of other Mexican gangs. Of the several possible reasons for this high number of arrests, one is the inability of some gang members to cope with the world outside of prison. Another possible reason could be that when they are arrested and go back into the prison system they are going back to the only family relationships they know and to the only place where they feel safe. In turn, these feelings create a strong and structured "family" that produces a safe haven for the expansion of unlawful operations and attracts new members into the gang (DEA, 1989).

One early problem that Mexican gangs faced was the desertion of members after their release from prison. When the gangs were originally formed a person who was a member while serving time in prison could, upon release from prison, return to his home and have no further relationship with the gang. Gangs no longer tolerate disassocation; once a person becomes a gang member that person will remain a member until death. After release from a correctional institute a gang member will join with other members and participate in criminal activities. Members who desert the gang are usually found dead. All members have a responsibility to kill anyone who defects from the organization.

A large percentage of drug dealing in East Los Angeles is controlled by members of the Mexican Mafia. In most cases, the Mexican Mafia supplies the drugs to local Hispanic street gangs that then distribute the drugs to their members who sell the illegal substances at street level. East Los Angeles is the main location, outside of prison, controlled by Mexican gangs. The distribution of heroin, cocaine, and other drugs to these street gangs has resulted in the accumulation of large revenues for their leaders. Any intruders who think they can move into the gangs' territory to deal drugs are quickly eliminated by gang members. Another high-income producer for the gangs has been the armed robbery of businesses or banks within the gangs' area of control. The gangs have found that robbery is an easy way to increase their income and finance some other type of criminal activity.

The Mexican Mafia was controlled and run by Joe (Pegleg) Morgan for a greater part of the last 25 years. Morgan was a Slavic American who, while spending 40 years in prison, rose to the position of Mexican Mafia Godfather. Morgan's criminal career began in 1946 at the age of 16 when he was convicted of murdering his 32-year-old girlfriend's husband with a tire iron. He was released from prison after serving nine years but within a year Morgan was back in prison for bank robbery in West Covino, California. Morgan escaped from several correctional facilities in California, and one escape was facilitated by the tools that he had hidden in his prosthetic leg. In early 1993, Morgan threatened to use members of the Mexican Mafia as violent enforcers to stop the drive-by shootings by members of the Latino street gangs in Southern California. The number of drive-by shootings declined after Morgan's announcement, but a short time after his proclamation Morgan succumbed to cancer and died in early November 1993 (Katz, 1993).

Law enforcement officials in California consider the Mexican Mafia a well-established, highly meticulous, and most certainly a complex organized crime family. Each prison also has one specific leader who is answerable only to the principal leader. Many notable similarities can be observed between the Mexican Mafia's prison and street gangs' leadership and tactics and those of the different family groups within La Cosa Nostra. The basic structure includes two systemwide leaders, a godfather/president at the top with an underboss/vice president underneath him. Regional-level generals are in charge of each institution. Lieutenants and sergeants are at the unit level, with the soldiers or workers at the bottom along with associates or sympathizers. The prison and street leader will change, but are interchangcable, according to whether this leader is in or out of prison.

The Mexican Mafia has continued to grow over the past several decades and presently has about 700 hard-core members. In an effort to strengthen its control in the California prisons, the Mexican Mafia formed an alliance with the Aryan Brotherhood, a white supremacist gang. The Aryan Brotherhood will assist the Mexican Mafia in some of its criminal activities and on occasion take a contract to kill someone from the Mexican Mafia. This gang has no real written code to conform to but usually adheres to the following doctrine:

> A member is to share all and everything. I have one leader to boss all members and to swear their lives to the group with the understanding that death is the failure to comply with the codes of the group. Once an inmate is accepted into the group, he can no longer drop out (Office of Attorney General of California, 1991).

The Mexican Mafia, like other gangs, has become actively involved in acquiring government subsidized grants. Once the gang members become active participants in the project, they immediately take control of the grant. An example of the gang's activity within a project is illustrated by the following information gathered by the California Correctional authorities:

> In 1976, a project was established in East Los Angeles with $228,000 of government funds to help ex-convicts readjust to living in society. Vehicles bought by the project's funds for field counseling were used by Mexican Mafia members in at least seven murders. Funds were also used to purchase heroin in Mexico, which was then flown to California by couriers using the project's credit cards. Prison inmates released into the care of the project were provided with heroin by the Mexican Mafia and encouraged to establish dealerships in East Los Angeles. A percentage of the profits was then kicked back to the Mexican Mafia. When the wife of a Mexican Mafia member

threatened to tell the authorities about the misuse of the project's money, she was killed on the orders of her husband (LACSD, 1992).

Another prison gang, the Sindicato Nuevo Mexico (SNM) or the New Mexico Syndicate, is an expansion of the Mexican Mafia. The SNM gang is the largest gang operating in the New Mexico prison system. This gang follows the same philosophy as the Mexican Mafia and exerts influence throughout the New Mexico prison system by controlling drug operations, extortion, and prison violence. The objectives set forth by this group are explicit and they include the following:

1. Regulate all narcotics trafficking throughout the New Mexico prison system.

2. Direct all extortion and protection activities.

3. Achieve and maintain authority over the entire correctional facility, all inmates, and prison staff through the use of violence (Governor's Organized Crime Prevention Commission, 1991).

The SNM gang requires all new gang members to adhere to the following guidelines:

1. Sponsorship into the gang is mandatory and the sponsor should be of good character and willing to be accountable for the conduct of this newly sponsored member.

2. The new gang participant must be ready to devote his life to the gang.

3. A plurality of the membership's vote must be obtained to become a member.

4. Betrayal of the gang or disobeying an order by a member means death.

5. All new gang members have anywhere from six months to a year probationary period. During this time period the new member must perform different tasks to prove his worth to the gang.

6. It is mandatory that all members have a high regard for each other (Governor's Organized Crime Prevention Commission, 1991).

The SNM maintains a good relationship with the Mexican Mafia, and this alliance has helped the SNM strengthen its ability to recruit new members. The structural makeup of the gang includes a systemwide don and godfather. At the regional level, generals control prison and street activities, while unit-level supervisors are known as lieutenants. The soldiers, associates, and sympathizers are at the bottom level of the gang.

In 1984 the Texas version of the Mexican Mafia was formed in the Texas prison system. This gang is not only patterned after the California version of the Mexican Mafia, but also uses the name of Mexikanemi (Soldiers of Atzlan). Mexikanemi has been involved in continuous hostilities with the Texas Syndicate since the Syndicate declared war on the Mexikanemi in 1985. The administrative structure of the Mexikanemi is the same as its California forerunner, but it observes some differences in its guidelines:

1. Once a member always a member—"blood in, blood out."

2. All members must be ready to forfeit their lives or kill another if required.

3. Members shall struggle to conquer their faults in order to obtain and maintain control of the gang's membership.

4. No matter what happens a member must never disappoint or fail the gang.

5. A mentor to a new member is fully responsible for that member's actions, and it is the mentor's duty to dispose of any person he sponsors who turns out to be a defector or dropout.

6. The membership of Mexikanemi will strive to eliminate any person or group of people who take contemptuous actions against the gang or the gang's membership.

7. Maintaining honor and principles is essential to all gang members.

8. A member must never discuss the gang's activities to outside people or agencies.

9. All members have the right to participate in, agree, or disagree with the gang's philosophy or regulations.

10. Members of Mexikanemi have the right to guide and protect the gang.

11. Once a person has attained membership in the Mexikanemi, he can sport the gang's tattoo.

12. The Mexikanemi is an organized criminal group that will participate in criminal activities that will produce dividends for the gang (LACSD, 1992).

In the mid 1980s La Nuestra Familia experienced some serious disruptions within its ranks. Many of the problems were related to members deserting the gang. The gang leaders made several attempts to correct this problem by trying to influence the defectors to return to the gang and promising them that changes would be made to improve conditions within the gang. This attempt proved unproductive in that it enticed few members back into the gang. Two other issues affected the stability of La Nuestra Familia: the continuous growth of its number one adversary, the Mexican Mafia, which has been moving into territory once controlled by La Nuestra Familia, and the arrests and prosecutions of street leaders and members under the Racketeer Influenced Corrupt Organization (RICO) laws.

Mindful of all these difficulties, La Nuestra Familia leadership has tightened its control on the family environment within the organization. The gang leaders stress the importance of a disciplined and profit-making group. Within the prison environment, La Nuestra Familia formed a working relationship with the Black Guerrilla Family, which is a militant prison gang, and gained an ally in its war against the Mexican Mafia. One of the main aspects of this organizational change by La Nuestra Familia was to encourage a militaristic attitude within the rank and file of the gang. With this in mind, the leaders of La Nuestra Familia created a constitution known as the "Supreme Power Structure of La Nuestra Familia." The first, third, fourth, and fifth articles of this constitution describe the authority, competency, and obligations of all of the members of La Nuestra Familia. Rank structure in La Nuestra Familia is similar to that of the military with one leader who is designated as a general in command of all of the prison groups and another general who commands all of the gang's street activities. Each general has up to ten captains who control a large number of lieutenants who in turn supervise La Nuestra Familia soldiers or members.

Any member can become a gang leader after he performs or participates in a number of killings. Once a soldier (soldados) carries out a hit, usually the wounding of some specific person (leg or arm wound) with a gun, and not the killing of someone, this gang member is given the title of "warrior." The two ways to attain the rank of captain are to perform three killings or show executive abilities. It is not mandatory that a gang member be promoted under either one of these standards. A gang member can quickly achieve the rank of lieutenant by killing any person listed by La Nuestra Familia as one of its top ten enemies (LACSD, 1992).

The last two articles in La Nuestra Familia's constitution relate to the membership. The second article discusses the main objectives of the organization. The gang's purpose is to serve the membership, improve the conditions within the gang, and work toward solidifying an effective association. Guidelines related to the proper behavior of all gang members and the associated punishments for improper actions are described in article six, in addition to guidelines related to the denial of the gang's existence when questioned by law enforcement officials (LACSD, 1992).

La Nuestra Familia's constitution also outlines a three-part agenda that creates a financial equity "containing not less than $1,000 for each La Nuestra Familia 'regiment' and a main bank. The regimental bank, designed for each regiment's own use, will provide the payroll, pay attorney's and doctor's fees, pay bail money, and also buy into legitimate businesses. A main bank will exist as a financial resource for purchasing legitimate businesses. However, the businesses purchased through their main bank, unlike the regiment bank, are to be kept strictly legal" (DEA, 1990). It would be possible for the leaders of La Nuestra Familia to fulfill and maintain the first six articles of this constitution, but without building a large fund, implementing the three-part agenda would be difficult. The present strength of this gang is about 400 members. This gangs' area of operation includes Bakersfield, Fresno, San Francisco, Gilroy, San Diego, East Los Angeles, San Jose, Santa Barbara, Stockton, and Visalia. Like the Mexican Mafia, the major money-making activity for La Nuestra Familia is in narcotics trafficking both in the prisons and on the streets. Many gang members still participate in crimes such as burglary, robbery, and larceny.

## Street Gangs

In any discussion involving Mexican organized crime groups, some time must be spent reviewing Mexican street gangs, because many members of Mexican organized crime evolved from these street gangs. The East Los Angeles street gangs of today emerged from the original street gangs of the 1940s and 1950s, which were formed within the local Mexican communities to defend the local ethnic domains against attacks from outside ethnic groups. Participation in these Mexican groups has become a hand-me-down sort of practice. In fact, the Los Angeles County Sheriff's Department has found that grandfathers, fathers, and sons have held membership in the same street gangs. In fact, in some cases it is possible to have members who are third or fourth generation gang members. "Machismo" is another key factor that motivates membership in these street gangs (LACSD, 1992).

The enticements these gangs present to members include the following:

1. The member becomes part of a group/family and joins the gang in an attempt to gain self-identity.

2. Once attaining membership in the gang, this person becomes an acknowledged member of society, a "homeboy," who is set apart with a singular identity and more than likely a nickname that fits him/her.

3. The characteristic of the gang involves immersion in an existence that converts members into homeboys. The importance of being a homeboy is central to the new member's existence (LACSD, 1992).

A majority of the members use some type of drugs whether it is PCP, crack cocaine, speed, LSD, or heroin. Street gang members wear clothing that sets them apart from members of other gangs. Most Mexican street gangs prefer khaki pants that are baggy and pulled above the waist. At one time Pendleton shirts were a common part of their dress style but this trend has changed in recent years. Nicknames are a primary aspect of each gang membership. "Maton" (killer), "Gordo" (fat), "Toro" (bull), "Flaco" (skinny), and "Oso" (bear) are some examples of the names given to gang members by other gang members (LACSD, 1992).

The role of the leadership in most of these gangs is loosely structured and the leader's role is derived on the basis of the gang needs. A gang member who becomes a boss is usually only placed there on a temporary basis because of some unique talent that this gang member may possess. Seldom do any of the street gangs select a permanent leader. No substantial foundation supports a supervisory structure in most of these Mexican street gangs. In many cases, they are somehow under the guidance of older gangs like the Mexican Mafia. Some of the major differences between Mexican and other street gangs include the following:

1. Mexican street gangs are protective of what they consider their turf, which they will protect in any way necessary.

2. In most cases the gang will not leave its turf; mobility is not one of its assets.

3. Members are considerate to people and places within their own territory.

4. Loyalty to the gang is essential; the gang comes first and everything else is second (LACSD, 1992).

Graffiti, in most cases, is used to designate an area under a specific gang's controls. This wall writing leaves an explicit message to other gangs concerning what will happen if they attempt to infringe on this area. Most graffiti is used to heap praise on the gang and the membership. Mexican street gangs are prevalent along the West Coast and throughout the Southwest, California, and some cities in the Midwest, especially Chicago. Presently, 15 Mexican street gangs are active in Chicago. Most of these gangs are composed of Mexican, ethnic white, and black members while the gangs on the West Coast and in the Southwest are ethnically Mexican and Mexican-American (Chicago PD, 1993; LACSD, 1992).

## Mexican Drug Cartels

Organized crime groups in certain areas of Mexico are highly influential and heavily involved in drug trafficking, particularly in the city of Culiacan in the northwestern Mexican state of Sinaloa. Through the mid 1980s and into the 1990s, the DEA estimated that approximately two tons of cocaine was transported from Culiacan to the United States each month. In 1989, the Mexican army arrested Felix Gallardo, the leader of the Culiacan gang and a major cocaine smuggler, the chief of police in Culiacan, Robespierre Lizarraga Coronel, the director of the Sinaloa State Judicial Police, Arturo Moreno, the leaders of the Mexican state of Tamaulipus (on the border of Texas), the Federal Highway police unit, and the 300 members of the Culiacan police department (Rohter, 1989).

The drug gangs in the state of Sinaloa have been involved in the transshipment of narcotics from Colombia to the United States since the 1980s, as have the growers of Mexican brown heroin and marijuana since the late 1940s. The problem with the Gallardo drug gang is that the members have become completely out of control within the state of Sinaloa. Members of this gang were not only growing, importing, shipping, distributing, and selling drugs but were openly killing people who opposed them right on the streets of Culiacan. They also kidnapped and raped the young women of Sinaloa without any opposition from any police agency (Rohter, 1989).

The drug trafficking in and through the city of Culiacan in the Mexican state of Sinaloa has been steady since 1989. It fact, the city of Culiacan has been nicknamed "Little Medellin" because of the amount of drug activity in and out of the city. Until recently, Felix Gallardo was still controlling his high-profile drug organization from his prison cell in Mexico City's Southern prison. Gallardo's prison cell was equipped with a cellular telephone, fax machines, and body guards who performed clerical work. In 1993 in an attempt to control Gallardo's drug activities, the Mexican government transferred Gallardo to a high-security prison in the state of Mexico. Gallardo, who was a Sinaloa state police officer prior to his involvement in drug trafficking, still communicates with his gang by sending coded messages through his lawyers. DEA agents estimate that about 70 percent of all the cocaine that enters the United States is transported through Mexico (Golden, 1993).

Conditions in the state of Sinaloa have deteriorated over the past decade. The total number of people killed in Sinaloa since 1981 is over 7,000 (Golden, 1993). These murders, plus Gallardo's ability to operate openly while in prison, indicate that the drug gangs have adjusted well to the measures taken by the government to control the drug trafficking in the state of Sinaloa (Golden, 1993). The violence of the Mexican drug gangs came to a head in May 1993 when Juan Jesus Cardinal Posadas Ocampo was shot and killed along with five other people as he inadvertently walked through a drug shootout as he was leaving the airport in Guadalajara, Mexico. The person arrested for this crime was Joaquin Guzman Loera, also known as El Chapo or Shortie, who was the head of a Sinaloa-based drug cartel. Loera was apprehended in Guatemala along with five other gang leaders (Golden, 1993).

A short time after the murder of Cardinal Ocampo, the Mexican government pledged to dismantle the organized crime groups and the drug trade they control. This vow has apparently gone astray because the Mexican gangs continue to operate openly in Sinaloa. As of August 1994, the largest seizure made by the Mexican police was of marijuana on a 220-acre marijuana plantation in the Chihuahua desert, based on a tip to the Mexican police from the U.S. DEA (Golden, 1994). This seizure was followed up by the arrest in September of Antonio Abrego, the nephew of the boss of the Abrego organized crime family, and his associate Alejandro Diaz. A former Mexican government official has accused the Abrego cartel of being involved in the assassination of presidential candidate Donaldo Colosio (*New York Times,* 1994).

The latest action taken by members of the Mexican drug cartels involves the use of old Boeing 727s and French-produced Caravelle jets. An airport is usually built on short notice on a large farm area or in a Mexican desert by just flattening out and hardening the dirt surface with a steamroller. These planes can be loaded with six tons or more of cocaine in Colombia for a flight to Mexico. From there the Mexican gangs transport the drug by land or sea to the United States (Golden, 1995).

The organizational structure of the Mexican organized crime group is a combination of both La Cosa Nostra and the military. A leader is both a godfather and a boss. As a boss he runs the whole operation with the assistance of several underbosses and advisors, but as a godfather he has total control over the organization. Under his command are captains who control specific operations and are answerable to the godfather. Next in command are lieutenants who control the daily movements of the gang members, and underneath the lieutenants are soldiers or workers who perform the activities assigned to them by the lieutenants (DEA, 1993).

The Mexican drug cartels in Sinaloa have capitalized on their relationship with the Colombian drug lords. U.S. law enforcement officials estimate that 60–75 percent of the cocaine being imported into the United States is presently being transshipped through Mexico. This increase in cocaine distribution has made many members of the Mexican drug cartels millionaires. Along with this newfound wealth has come the power and the ability to corrupt both political and police authorities throughout Mexico, and increases in both crime rates and drug use. These organized crime gangs will continue to flourish in Mexico until their access to drug suppliers is cut off.

As the different types of Mexican organized crime groups continue to grow and flourish, it is questionable whether either the Mexican or U.S. governments will take strong steps to deter the gangs' criminal activities. The last criminal group we will look at is the Dominican gangs. These groups have built reputations as well-managed and violent organizations with total control over the product they sell and the activities of their employees. These qualities make the Dominicans the type of group that most drug organizations want to use for distribution and sale of their drugs at the street level.

## DOMINICAN ORGANIZED CRIME

The island of Hispaniola was originally discovered in 1492 by Christopher Columbus. Santo Domingo, the oldest European settlement in the Americas, was designated as the capital of La Hispaniola in 1496. The Dominican Republic has experienced a considerable amount of turmoil since the late 1700s. France controlled the colony from 1795 until 1801 when Haitian soldiers, under the command of Toussaint L'Ouverture, overthrew the French government. In a citizen revolt in 1808, local rebels seized Santo Domingo and immediately set up a republic. During the early 1800s Spain reacquired and lost power on several occasions, as did a number of local representative governments that disappeared as quickly as they surfaced. Haitians controlled the Dominican Republic again between 1822 and 1844. Spain, once again, seized control from 1861 to 1863. Then in 1916 U.S. Marines occupied this country until a democratic government was installed in 1924.

An unfortunate turn of events occurred in 1930 when Gen. Rafael Trujillo-Molina was elected president of the Dominican Republic. Within a short period of time, Trujillo quickly installed a military dictatorship that ruled through the use of murder, torture, and brutality. After 31 years of civilian torment by this military regime an assassin's bullet finally found and killed Trujillo in 1961. His successor Joaquin Balaguer was forced to step down in 1962, and Juan Bosch, who was elected in 1962, was overthrown in 1963. Then in 1965, Bosch and a group of his followers created their own rebellion in a coup. U.S. Marines were dispatched to the Dominican Republic within four days of these disruptions along with troops from several other South American countries, and they quickly quelled the activities of Bosch and his associates. Finally, in 1966 a presidential election was held in the Dominican Republic and Joaquin Balaguer defeated Bosch and took control of the new democratic government. A short time after the election the military teams left the Dominican Republic. In 1978, in an attempt to win a fourth term as president, Jaoquin Balaguer ordered the military to delay the processing of election ballots. President Jimmy Carter intervened and warned Balaguer to have all ballots counted as quickly as possible. A short time later, a member of the Dominican Revolution Party, Antonio Guzman, was named the winner of the presidential election. In 1986, Balaguer was once again elected as the president of the Dominican Republic on a platform that promised the creation of a diversified policy to improve and control the Dominican economy. Balaguer won his reelection campaign in 1990 and continues as president. The Dominican government is a democracy that consists of 30 delegates who are elected from the 29 provinces plus one national district. The president, who must run for election every four years, has executive power that was bestowed on him by a constitution created in 1966.

The Dominican Republic has suffered through years of distressing poverty and depression. It is located on the island of Hispaniola, which it shares with the country of Haiti. Haiti is probably the only country in the Caribbean that is poorer than the Dominican Republic. Its per capita income is $697, and it ranks as one of the four most poverty-stricken countries in the Northern Hemisphere.

This level of indigence within the Dominican Republic has created an increase in emigration to other nations within the Northern Hemisphere, including the United States. Many of these emigrants end up in New York City as a result of family sponsorship from residents of the large Dominican community there. Some Dominicans who do not have a legal way to gain entry into the United States obtain illegal identification and then enter from either Puerto Rico or Mexico. Information gathered by both the U.S. Customs Service and the INS indicates that illegal Dominican immigrants can set out from the Dominican Republic on a raft (yola) constructed of wood, and cross the Mona Passage on their voyage to the western shores of Puerto Rico. The cost of this trip would be $400–700. Another means of transportation would be to set sail in a legitimate vessel that sails north and then drops the illegal aliens off on the eastern shores of Puerto Rico for a mere $1,500 (DEA, 1993). The INS has observed a significant decrease in the number of visa applications from the Dominican residents since 1989 (more than 209,412 in 1989 to 60,000 in 1992). This decrease in visa applications, the INS believes, is an indicator of the increase in the number of Dominicans entering the United States as illegal aliens (INS, 1993).

The lifestyle in the Dominican Republic is very difficult for most inhabitants. The unemployment rate in the Dominican Republic is a constant 25–30 percent. In the early 1990s, the Dominican Republic also had the second highest total number of AIDS cases in the Caribbean. It has, however, maintained a literacy rate of 83 percent, which is good considering its economy and an ever-increasing population that is presently about 7.5 million people. The Dominican government has experienced difficulty decreasing its foreign debt because its economy lacks the agricultural base needed to supply its processing plants.

## Drug Activities

Dominican groups first began appearing in the mid 1960s on the west side of Manhattan between 105th and 109th Streets. Over the following 30 years the Dominican gangs expanded their activities throughout upper Manhattan. In fact, the criminal activities of these gangs are visible in four of the five boroughs of New York City. The Dominican gangs have taken over much of the drug trafficking from 110th Street to the northern tip of Manhattan, the west side of the Bronx, the Bushwick, and East New York sections of Brooklyn. They are also found in Elmhurst, Corona, and parts of the Jackson Heights sections of Queens.

With the incentive of $20,000 to $30,000 in daily profits from street drug operations, the Dominicans have continued to expand their street drug activities. The Dominican gangs employ addicts to deal the drugs at street level and use an armed supervisor to scrutinize the movements of the addict sellers. Observers are usually put in place to assure the boss of the drug operation that the seller is not leaving with either the drugs or the money. In most cases, addict-dealers are given small amounts of heroin/crack so that they must continually return to the stash or holder to replenish their supply. This type of operation almost guarantees that revenue from the drug sales will be turned over to the main operator within a short period of time. Most supervisors are put in charge of several addict-sellers within a small area. Gang bosses engage other Dominican gang members in mid-level positions and involve them in apportioning the heroin and/or cocaine. These positions of trust within the organization require the gang members to be accountable for the drugs they distribute and the amounts of money they collect from the street dealers.

The Dominican gangs have set up an area of Manhattan known as Washington Heights as the base of their criminal activities. An estimated 650,000 Dominicans live in the Washington Heights section of Manhattan. Dominicans have adapted to the New York City environment by creating a Dominican type of habitat within their Washington Heights surroundings. The focal point for each group's activities in these smaller neighborhoods is the local food store or bodega. These stores function as both a market and a cultural center for both legal and illegal aliens.

Members of most major Dominican organized crime gangs are originally from the villages of San Francisco de Macoris and Santiago de los Caballeros. Dominican gang members arrested for drug violations typically identify themselves as being from the village of San Francisco de Macoris, which is located 100 kilometers northeast of Santo Domingo and has received a great deal of notoriety over the past several years. The drug dealers that have flocked to this village are known as Dominican Yorks and are considered the nouveau riche. They gained their assets by workings as drug runners and dealers on the streets of New York City. Much of this village's economy is controlled by these rich opportunists who, after making their money on the streets of New York, come home to San Francisco de Macoris to create work for its citizens. The drug lords have built modern houses with turrets, balconies, skylights, statues, and geometric shapes that in some cases resemble spaceships. Gang members paint both the interior and the exterior of their homes in resplendent tropical colors like orange, raspberry, lime, peach, and mango. In many cases these colors are painted as stripes going up, down, or around the house. They use businesses, usually supermarkets or casinos, they have purchased in both San Francisco de Macoris and Santo Domingo to launder their drug money. The lack of respect that some of these drug cartel members have received in their hometowns in the Dominican Republic has forced them to move to other locations, primarily on the west coast of Florida and on Long Island in New York (O'Connor, 1992).

After they settled in the Dominican Republic, gang members would immediately start recruiting others to become part of their cartels. Recruiting new members was relatively easy because most of these young and poor local residents observed the fancy autos, the mansions, the expensive jewelry, and the free spending of families of the drug gang members. The gang newcomers were given a loan to pay for their passage and whatever type of identification required to enter the United States. A short time after arriving in New York, new gang members would be set up in the gang's drug enterprise.

As more and more illegal young Dominican aliens arrive in New York, the unemployment rate among these Dominican youths continues to rise to 300–500 percent higher than the U.S. national average. It is easy to see why these adolescents would find participation in the drug business a feasible money-making option. Sixty percent of the Dominican males living in New York are under 24 years old, and 41 percent of them are unemployed, explaining why they are likely to become actively involved in the drug trade. One unfortunate result of Dominican youths' involvement in the drug business has been their return to the Dominican Republic in caskets after being murdered in New York because of their participation in drug trafficking. In 1991, 122 drug-related homicides occurred in the Washington Heights section of New York City. A number of these murders were Dominican gang members killing other Dominicans over drug-related issues known as "business competitiveness" (NYDETF, 1992).

Washington Heights is the home base for Dominican drug dealing in the United States. According to local law enforcement, the Washington Heights area is separated into two sections with the purchasing and peddling taking place in the southern part of Washington Heights, while the storage or stash houses are located in the northern part. Almost all stash houses are equipped with various devices designed to hinder anyone seeking unauthorized admittance.

The law enforcement community has discovered that the Dominican drug gangs have set up complex systems to prevent easy detection and arrest. Specific code words and phrases created by the gangs are used to caution each other of some possible liability. The gangs will use gestures or special buzz words such as suviendo (coming up), agua (water) or bajando (coming down) to notify other gang members that the police are somewhere in the immediate area. Cellular phones also are used to transmit an alarm to gang members. The reasonable price of these phones enables each gang member who is watching a location to be easily notified of any nearby police activity.

Some of the gangs have reached into the future and are using surveillance equipment and special remote alarm mechanisms outside a location to warn them of police movement in the area. The same methods of protection are usually set up within a drug dealer's apartment door or in the hallway to observe movement there. Drug gangs will also use lookouts equipped with cellular phones or other alarm devices on rooftops, in doorways, on bicycles, and on street corners. These devices and lookouts are also used to avoid the "spot robbers" who pose as narcotics officers in order to rob the drug locations (NYPD, 1991).

The Dominican gangs use booby traps within their drug locations similar to those used by the Jamaican gangs. These booby traps are put in place to discourage police from raiding their locations, seizing the drugs, and arresting the employees. Booby traps are also a viable means to stop other drug gangs from entering the premises and stealing the money and drugs. Some devices used by the gangs include electrified wires on wet floors, electrified doors and windows, and hanging wires. Trip wires set up at entrances to darkened rooms and on the floors of these rooms are what the gangs call "pungi boards." "Pungi boards" are plywood boards that are full of 3- or 4-inch nails. These boards are set up on floors so that a person who trips on the wire will fall face forward into the nail-filled "pungi boards." Another deterrent used by the Dominican gangs is vicious pit bulls that have had their vocal cords extracted (NYPD, 1991).

Throughout the New York metropolitan area and most of the East Coast, the Dominicans have formed a beneficial alliance with the Colombian drug cartels. This relationship has progressed since the 1980s when the Colombian drugs traffickers designated the Dominican Republic as a refueling stop and a location from which to transship drugs. Since that time Dominican organized crime gangs have moved up the drug distribution ladder to the point of importing and allocating both cocaine and heroin for the Colombian drug cartels. Colombian drug cartels feel that the Dominican gangs can be trusted to handle the distribution of both cocaine and heroin because of the Dominican gangs' ability to regulate, supply, and dominate street-level drug operations of Dominican and other drug trafficking groups (NYDETF, 1992).

The Dominican gangs have stretched their operations throughout the New York State area, including the western portion of Buffalo. A large amount of the drugs they sell are imported from New York City and transported to Buffalo on the New York State Thruway. While in Syracuse, the Dominican gangs supply crack and cocaine to both black and white street drug dealers. Once again, the Dominicans bring the drugs to Syracuse from New York City. Recently, members of Colombian gangs have been attempting to remove the Dominicans from the drug business in Syracuse. In Rochester, the Dominican gangs have taken control of the cocaine market from Jamaican gangs. The Dominicans have set up their base for their drug dealing in the northeastern section of Rochester and have strengthened this foundation by importing and selling heroin in the Rochester area (NYDETF, 1992).

The Dominican gangs have formed relationships with several other organized crime gangs besides the Colombians. During incarceration in various prison facilities throughout New York State the Dominicans formed a working relationship with members of Chinese criminal gangs. A drug raid conducted by both federal and local law enforcement officers uncovered a large amount of heroin wrapped in Chinese newspapers in a Dominican drug house in Queens, New York. In 1989, an NYPD narcotics unit uncovered a Dominican heroin operation run by two ex-police officers from the Dominican Republic. This incident was followed up by an investigation conducted by members of the New York City Drug Enforcement Agency, which uncovered a Dominican-run heroin ring that supplied heroin to Rhode Island, New Jersey, Connecticut, Massachusetts, and New York. Evidence showed that this Dominican group was purchasing large amounts of Southeast Asian heroin from Chinese gang members (DEA, 1993). Dominican gangs have also formed a drug-related relationship with Nigerian organized crime groups who supply the Dominicans with heroin for street sales (NYDETF, 1992).

A 1993 article in the *New York Daily News* described the rise and fall of a Dominican drug gang leader in Washington Heights. The leader of this gang, Euclides Rosario Lantigua, a 30-year-old Dominican known on the street as "un rey" (a king), drove a flashy Toyota Pathfinder throughout Washington Heights and was assisted by his wife, Vanais, and his brother, Franklin, in running the gang. Lantigua would wear fancy jewelry, flaunt his money, and sport his silk shirts and linen pants. This gang, set up by Lantigua, had 50 different groups in Washington Heights alone. A great deal of the profits from drug trafficking by these gangs was sent back to the Dominican Republic for investment. Law enforcement official records show that the Lantigua organization set up an apartment building in Washington Heights that included:

1. a second floor where long wooden tables were used by employees to cut the drug, check its weight, bundle the drugs in plastic bags or containers, and record all necessary information in a book.

2. an eighth floor that was constantly patrolled by a special armed security force; Colombian, Nigerian, and Chinese drug importers were brought to this floor to arrange drug deals and finalize the transactions (Sennott, 1993).

The Lantigua drug operation was successful enough to eventually wholesale approximately 15 kilos each day at $20,000 per kilo. The Lantiguas made an estimated $3,000 per kilo. Some of the profits from these sales was invested into the purchase of the D'Cachet restaurant on Nagle Avenue and the Vanassiel Travel Agency on Amsterdam Avenue. A majority of the proceeds were sent back to the Dominican Republic through the use of either wire transfers from the Lantiguas' travel agency or through "smurfing," or money bundled in amounts less than $10,000 each and then forwarded to the Dominican Republic. Anyone shipping U.S. currency in amounts of $10,000 or more is required to file paperwork with the U.S. government prior to shipment (Sennott, 1993).

This drug operation was highly successful until the police overheard a telephone conversation on August 4, 1993, between Lantiqua and a Colombian courier that involved the purchase of 30 kilos of cocaine. Police moved in once the delivery was made and arrested two of Lantiqua's lieutenants and the Colombian courier. Lantiqua quickly paid the $50,000 bail on each of his lieutenants and shipped them both back to the Dominican Republic. Then on September 15, 1993, another telephone conversation between Lantiqua and a Colombian courier for the purchase of 10 kilos of cocaine gave the police the information they needed to arrest Lantiqua. Lantiqua and his wife, Vanais, were both arrested in their Wadsworth Avenue apartment where the police recovered $120,000 in U.S. currency. A search of the Lantiquas travel agency turned up drug records and $20,000 in U.S. currency. Lantiqua's drug headquarters, nicknamed the Heartbreak Hotel, was seized after the raid and is presently shut down and locked up (Sennett, 1993).

## Money Laundering

According to federal law enforcement agencies, approximately $800 million in U.S. currency is legally shipped to the Dominican Republic each year from the United States. A great deal of this money is sent home by legitimate, hard-working, native-born Dominicans. On the other hand, the true amount of money shipped to the Dominican Republic by the drug gangs can never be determined. Members of Dominican drug gangs use a variety of methods to ship money back to the Dominican Republic:

1.  Money is placed in a legal enterprise and currency can then be legitimately transferred anywhere in the world without attracting major attention. Once a business is set up by the drug lords the illegally obtained drug money is used to purchase commodities at a higher price in another country, which shifts money from one country to another under the guise of a legal business transaction.

2.  The gangs move the money out of the United States as U.S. currency or through the use of legitimate money orders. It is easy to secret the currency or the money orders in cargo being exported to the Dominican Republic.

3.  The Dominican drug cartels launder money through electronic transfer. Money is moved from the United States to the Dominican Republic by wire service, usually Western Union. This type of transfer was exposed when a New York County Grand Jury handed up indictments against three Dominicans who owned and operated the Dominican $ Express, Inc. The three were charged with unlawfully using 500,000 different transactions to transfer more than $70 million to the Dominican Republic (DEA, 1993). In many cases, the drug gangs purchase a large number of money orders in denominations less than $10,000 and usually in amounts that are much lower. In one case, Dominican drug dealers left U.S. currency with an electronic transfer company, which would then change the U.S. currency into money orders. The drug traffickers would

pick up the money orders several days later and then ship the money orders to relatives in the Dominican Republic.

Money laundering, through the use of money wiring, is far from complicated when the methods used by the Dominican drug gangs are reviewed:

a. U.S. currency is delivered to a messenger.

b. The messenger then delivers the cash, usually in tens, twenties, and fifties, to a corrupt money wiring agency.

c. The currency is broken down into amounts that are less than $10,000 each on separate money orders or invoices. Fraudulent identifications including residences and phone numbers are then placed on the money orders or invoices.

d. The money is deposited by the New York State licensed money transmitting agency into a bank account.

e. An authorization is given by the licensed money transmitter for the bank to shift the funds via wire to a foreign account.

f. This transfer is set up so that once the money reaches its foreign destination a representative, usually a lawyer, will show up at the transfer office with a document that enables him to take possession of the money. The person with the state authorized license to transfer the money receives about 7 percent of each transaction and the agent about 3 percent of the transferred amount (Guart, 1995).

4. The profits from drug enterprises that are not sent back to the Dominican Republic are usually invested in bodegas, laundromats, money transfer businesses, travel enterprises, beauty shops, and large food markets. Most of these businesses are operated somewhat legally only because they are used to launder drug money for the gang leaders.

5. The Dominican gangs, following the example of both the Colombian and Nigerian drug swallowers, filled the fingers of latex gloves with ten $100 bills. The gang leaders would then have one of their couriers swallow the fingers from the gloves and return to the Dominican Republic with the money. In one specific case, two of the gang's representative swallowers ingested 125 fingers containing a total of $125,000 in U.S. currency. In turn, many of these couriers would swallow heroin for their return trip to the United States (DEA, 1993).

6. The drug gangs have also been known to secret the money on the bodies of relatives or close friends and have them carry it back to the Dominican Republic.

## Other Criminal Activities

Robbery

Robberies committed in the Dominican community are called *tumbes*, which actually means "take downs." *Tumbes* is the expression used by members of Dominican gangs who participate in "push in" robberies. "Push in" robberies are one of the trademarks of Dominican gangs throughout the United States. Any area that has any type of Dominican population will soon find that "push in" robberies will also become part of this Dominican community. During 1993 more than 500 "push in" robberies were reported in the Washington Heights area of Manhattan and the Southeastern section of the Bronx. Both of these areas are densely populated Dominican communities (NYPD, 1993). Inquiries to the NYPD in relation to these types of "push in" robberies have come from other police agencies in Washington, D.C.; Lawrence, Massachusetts; Providence, Rhode Island; Reading, Pennsylvania; Bangor, Maine; and Westchester, Suffolk, and Nassau counties in the New York metropolitan area (NYPD, 1993).

This type of robbery usually targets a person who has large amounts of money or jewelry at either his or her home or business. Many of the first targets picked by the gangs were Dominican drug dealers who are known to hide money at their stashes or residences. Recently, the type of target has changed to include legitimate Dominican businessmen who own grocery stores (bodegas), restaurants, bars, jewelry stores, or supermarkets. The gangs have found that most legitimate business people are neither armed nor do they have body guards around them at all times. Once a target is chosen, observations of the target are conducted by gang members in an attempt to find out when the greatest amount of money will be present at the location where the robbery will take place.

A number of these robbers were originally part of the drug gangs' activities, but fearful of the harsh sentences that a second drug sale conviction presented to them, they moved over to the tumbes gangs. These Dominican tumbes groups usually have three to six members, and the victims are almost always Dominican. The gang members are aware that most Dominicans distrust the police and, with this in mind, realize that most of these crimes will not be reported to the authorities (Moses and Furse, 1991).

The gangs use two basic methods to gain entrance into a location without a notification to the police. The first method requires that gang members conceal themselves in close proximity to the victim's front door. They wait in seclusion until the target unlocks the door. The gang members, who are all armed, will then rush up behind the victim forcing all parties inside the location. Once inside the premises, gang members immediately disconnect all telephone wires and tie up the family members. Questions concerning the whereabouts of money and other valuables commence once all family members present at the location are bound with cord or wires. Some Dominicans like to keep large sums of money in their homes because they do not trust financial institutions, or because the money might have been earned unscrupulously or hidden to avoid taxes. Valuables are usually secreted in homemade vaults. A victim who fails to cooperate with the gang by telling them where the money is hidden will find that the gang will quickly terrorize other family members, especially female ones. These gangs have no compassion toward wives, daughters, or female relatives. They will assault, sexually abuse, rape, torture, or do whatever else is necessary until the location of the valuables is disclosed. In some cases, gang members have cut body parts off and have branded family members with hot irons or spoons (NYPD, 1991).

The second technique used by the gang involves a ruse to gain entry into the victim's residence. In many cases, the robbers identify themselves as police officers and actually display police shields and identification cards, or as Con Edison, building inspectors, postal carriers, UPS or telephone company employees to obtain entrance into the location. Once the gang members enter the victim's residence they use the same procedures as other tumbes robbers (Moses and Furse, 1991).

## Extortion

One specific Dominican gang found a better way to extort money. The C & C gang, in the Mott Haven section of the Bronx, set up an extortion racket that involved forcing the drug dealers on the streets of the South Bronx to pay rent in order to operate on these streets. Originally, the C & C gang was involved in street drug dealing using the name "D.O.A." on its heroin, but the leaders of this gang saw extortion as safer and almost as profitable as drug dealing. This gang was named for its two leaders, George Calderon and Angel (Cuson) Padilla, who together collected $100,000–500,000 weekly. Calderon and Padilla set up a complex blackmail system that made money using duress. It enabled them to totally control a seven block area in the South Bronx.

The first thing that Calderon did was set up a treaty within the community by forbidding the drug dealers to sell drugs during the times that children were going back and forth to school and in areas where the dealers could be seen from the school. A limit was also placed on the number of drug addicts who could assemble at one specific location at anytime. Anyone setting up business in the area controlled by the C & C without the permission of C & C would be kidnapped, assaulted, robbed, or murdered. Anyone dealing drugs in this area had to abide by the rules set forth by C & C and pay rent on his or her designated spot. In some cases, the gang would actually specify a site for the drug dealer to work. In most cases, the rent on each location is determined by the amount of money a dealer makes at a specific locale but in some cases a flat rate is paid each week (Faison, 1994).

Gang rule changed in 1992 when Calderon was shot and killed after leaving his parole officer in the Bronx. Two months later Calderon's sister, Lourdes Cintron, was shot and killed sitting inside a car in the Bronx. According to federal investigators both of these hits were ordered by Padilla (Purdy, 1994).

Homicide

A review of homicides in the Washington Heights section of New York City shows 122 murders in that area in 1991, 97 of which were Dominican. Of that total, 80 were killed with guns, and 54 of those shot were confirmed drug gang members. Most of these homicides were carried out by hit men brought in by the gangs from the Dominican Republic.

Information received from the Dominican National Directorate of Drug Control (DNCD) indicates that between January and August 1992, 144 bodies were returned to the Dominican Republic from the United States. The DNCD reports indicate all these citizens suffered violent deaths in the United States. The ages of these victims reveal that:

- 15 percent were 18–20 years old
- 70 percent were 21–35 years old
- 15 percent were 36 and older (DEA, 1993)

The location of the deceased person's residence or place of birth was judged by location of burial and reveals that:

- 57 percent were from Santo Domingo
- 29 percent were from San Francisco De Macoris
- 14 percent were from other locations in the Dominican Republic (DEA, 1993)

Investigators say one Dominican gang, the Wild Cowboys, are responsible for a number of the murders of other Dominicans over the past several years. Almost all these murders were connected to the control of drug trafficking in Washington Heights and the Bronx. In fact, the two gang leaders, Nelson and Lenin Sepulveda and their number one enforcer, Jose Llaca, are presently in prison awaiting trial on numerous charges. NYPD investigators pinpointed the leaders of the Wild Cowboys as having participated in more than 30 homicides in New York City (Faison, 1994). The Sepulveda brothers and seven of their appointed gang lieutenants were eventually indicted on 105 counts of murder, numerous counts of attempted murder, felonious assault, and drug trafficking. Both of the Sepulveda brothers claimed that they were destitute and could not afford to pay for an attorney. Court-appointed lawyers meant that tax-paying citizens of this city were responsible for the Sepulvedas' legal bills. Obviously crime does pay for the Sepulveda brothers who shipped millions of dollars in illegal drug money back to the Dominican Republic and then turned around and forced the New York City court system to pay for their attorneys.

In the Bronx, another Dominican drug gang led by Jose Reyes and known as "Reyes Crew" savagely controlled the University Heights community for more than five years. Reyes, paralyzed due to prior gunshot wounds, was nicknamed "El Feo" or the "Ugly One." This group was aware of police operations and was constantly moving its stash houses and distribution centers to avoid police surveillance. Reyes Crew still managed to profit over $500,000 a year from their drug businesses. Members communicated with each other through beepers and cellular phones, while all of the gang's records were kept on a computer by Reyes. The gang's drug operations were modeled somewhat like a big corporation with a different set of managers, steerers, and sellers for the heroin, crack, and cocaine divisions of their drug business. When Reyes was arrested in Miami he was in possession of records that showed all of his gang's drug transactions. Bronx Supreme Court indictments charged Reyes and his two lieutenants, Thomas "Cruel" Rodriquez and Francisco "Freddy Kruger" Medina, with murder, narcotics trafficking, and weapons possession (Parascandola, 1994; Perez-Pena, 1994).

The NYPD encountered another phenomenon in the Washington Heights community accompanied by a sudden surge in the number of Colombians being murdered in Washington Heights. Police believe the Dominicans tenaciously observed the movements of the Colombian drug dealers, and then, after the completion of a couple of drug deals, killed the Colombian couriers and kept the drugs and currency for their drug gangs (NYPD, 1993).

Auto Theft

The Dominican gangs have become increasingly involved in auto theft since the early 1990s. One gang designates Nissan Pathfinders and Toyota Forerunners as its choice of vehicles, mainly because these vehicles are somewhat easy to steal. In cases involving these vehicles one need only to get the car door open to procure the code number of the ignition key. Once the code number is obtained, the thieves need only acquire a portable key maker to reproduce the key and then quickly drive off in the auto.

The gangs use two other methods to steal vehicles. One method that is used is bumping a vehicle at a red light and then forcibly taking the car at gun point. Another technique involves stealing an auto from a parking garage by stealing the keys or paying the attendant for them.

A number of these vehicles are transported out of the United States. Shipping a stolen auto out of this country can be a difficult task. In most cases, the assistance of a person with some substantial knowledge of the shipping business is necessary, likely a freight forwarder. A freight forwarder receives fees to organize and then provide the necessary shipping papers. This person seldom has an opportunity to see the type of property being shipped, and therefore gang members can ship cargo without the freight forwarders having any knowledge of whether the property being shipped is stolen.

Shipping documents are typically poorly prepared and contain erroneous information. Car thieves give inaccurate vehicle identification numbers on the information supplied to the freight forwarders for listing on the shipping papers. A number of the stolen cars are taken to the Bronx Terminal Market where they are containerized. The cars are then shipped to Elizabeth, New Jersey, and finally transported to the Dominican Republic for resale. It was not long before local law enforcement officials realized what the car thieves were doing and shut down this type of operation.

Gangs realize a great deal of profit from stolen vehicles. A stolen car that would cost $25,000 new in the United States can be sold for $50,000 outside the United States. Therefore, stolen autos are pure profit for the gangs, especially with the escalating prices of the new and fancier vehicles.

A Dominican auto theft ring that was recently shut down by federal law enforcement authorities had stolen more than $8 million worth of luxury cars since early 1993. This gang, which worked out of an auto body shop in the Bronx, bribed officials in the Dominican Republic and stole hundreds of auto manufacturer certificates, or certificates of origin, that authenticate the age of the vehicles sold in the Dominican Republic. The stolen cars were a close match to the vehicle described on the certificate of origin. Vehicles were then taken to the body shop where workers removed the actual vehicle identification number plates and replaced them with plates that matched the vehicle identification numbers on the certificates. These stolen cars were then sold to unaware buyers by dealers in both the United States and the Dominican Republic. Types of autos stolen included Lexus, Infiniti, Jeep Grand Cherokee, Mercedes-Benz, and BMW. This investigation led to the arrests of 17 people including the gang leader, Fernando Pena, of the Bronx, two car dealership owners in New Jersey, a State Department of Motor Vehicles employee, the owner of two body shops in the Bronx, and the owners of four auto dealerships in the Dominican Republic (McKinley, 1995).

## Activities outside New York State

Dominican gangs have become the most active participants in cocaine trafficking throughout Montgomery and Prince George's County, and the city of Baltimore in Maryland. In New Jersey the Dominican gangs have teamed up with Colombian gangs in the cocaine trafficking business. Law enforcement officials in New Jersey conclude that the Dominican gangs are organized, and have pinpointed the Dominicans as the major suppliers of cocaine in the city of Trenton and the counties of Camden, Passaic, and Middlesex. Police agencies in both Camden and Middlesex counties have gathered evidence that the Dominican gangs are active participants in not only narcotics operations but also unlawful gambling businesses, illegal importation of Dominicans into the United States, and the counterfeiting of documents and U.S. currency (Magloclen, 1993).

Dominican gangs in Ohio have been active participants with Colombian groups in the dispersal of cocaine in the major urban centers of Ohio. The Dominican groups have worked out cooperative agreements with Hispanic as well as other street gangs in Philadelphia in order to conduct their drug trafficking business. These Dominican gangs have spread their tentacles throughout the state of Pennsylvania. They have operations in the Allentown/Bethlehem areas, Dauphin County, and the Lancaster/York/Reading areas of Pennsylvania. Almost all these operations are related to heroin and cocaine trafficking. Some of their other activities include counterfeiting of all types of federal, state and other documents, illegally bringing immigrants into the United States, money laundering, drive-by shootings, robbery, assault, and arson (Magloclen, 1993).

The Dominican gangs continue to operate as autonomous groups with loose-knit structures. Dominican gangs are basically all the same in that all members are citizens of the Dominican Republic and are from the same basic environment. These gangs, however, have been unable to combine their talents into a large organization with all members working together to improve the gang. Smaller Dominican gangs foster the characteristics of greed and rivalry, and these traits proscribe any banding together as one major organized ethnic gang. Sometime in the future these smaller Dominican gangs may unite to form one large, well-organized criminal enterprise, probably one similar to the Colombian cartels.

## CONCLUSIONS

Hispanic organized crime groups will continue to prosper due the vast drug market available to them whether they grow it, process it, smuggle it, distribute it, or sell it at street level. Most of the Hispanic gang groups come from countries run by governments whose integrity is questioned by the citizens as well as the media. So until drastic changes or laws are introduced and strictly enforced without corruption playing a major role, little will change in how successful these gangs can be.

# CHAPTER 12

# Russian and Israeli Gangs

Russian and Israeli organized crime groups are essentially similar but in reality quite different. Although based out of two different countries both groups have worked successfully in both the drug and money laundering businesses. The groups have also profited from scams they have perfected and worked on together. Yet each of these groups is controlled by a separate faction whose leadership is chosen by the membership. The first organization we shall view is the Russian groups.

## RUSSIAN ORGANIZED CRIME

### Early Activities

Historical records indicate that Russian organized gangs and their criminal operations have existed for several centuries. The earliest criminal groups that formed in Russia are patterned after procedures of the Russian Cossacks. Varery Chalidze, in his book *Criminal Russia: Essays on Crime in the Soviet Union*, compares what he considers to be the significant relationships between the members of the seventeenth century Cossacks and the original underworld gangs in Russia that later became known as Russian organized crime groups. Chalidze found the following:

1. Both groups conformed to policy set by the government, but each association had some kind of self-government that ruled from inside the organization.

2. Within the membership, members were treated the same, with little or no preferential treatment for anyone, although with leadership came some special recognition from the internal membership of the organization.

3. Leaders were selected and elected by the membership and sat on councils where every member had to express an opinion either for or against policy set by the council. This commentary on policy was done without any fear of retaliation.

4. No written procedures and policies relating to either the groups' legal or illegal activities existed, but each member understood the necessity of togetherness and punishment for members who committed some type of serious indecorous action (treason, cowardice, murder, etc.) against the association. Serious infractions against the organization usually resulted in the death of the offender.

5. As in other secretive associations a code of silence concerning the organization and its activities was maintained by all (Chalidze, 1977).

Early studies on crime in Russia indicate that almost all the previous criminal groups were considered to be Robin Hood-type of gangs who robbed the rich and seldom bothered the poor. As time passed members of these groups also became involved in extortion of businesses within their local villages. As times in Russia changed at the turn of the twentieth century, so did opinions of the leaders among the Bolshevik revolutionaries toward criminal groups. The gangs were used effectively by both the Bolsheviks and Social Revolutionaries as vehicles to procure collateral through extortion and robbery. Lenin went as far as to state that "we stole what had been stolen" (Chalidze, 1977: 22). Stalin created his own gang with Semyon Ter-petrosyan, an Armenian Bolshevik also known as "Kamo," as the leader, to carry out robberies to enrich the Bolshevik treasury and support the upcoming revolution (Chalidze, 1977). A short time after the revolution "Kamo" died under suspicious circumstances. Stalin denied any criminal association with "Kamo" as well as being involved in any criminal activities prior to, during, or after the revolution with "Kamo." Chalidze claims that Stalin had strong attachments to criminals and their organizations, which were built during the early days of the Bolsheviks' rise to power. During the early times, Stalin used these connections to carry out numerous robberies and other crimes that would bankroll the party and enhance his position within the revolutionary group (Chalidze, 1977).

As we continue to view Russian gangs we must also be aware of the way the Communist government in Moscow totally controlled all of the Soviet Socialist Republic over a period of 75 years. Many people in a "political" position in the Communist party were placed there to extort money from either businesses or citizens of the Soviet Republic, because they were politically connected to the Soviet regime. Only people trusted by government officials were placed in these posts. Corruption existed in every phase of governments operations. A Russian citizen in need of housing was given preference according to his or her ability to supply something to the person(s) in charge of assigning residences to citizens. In many cases those seeking housing had to participate in an auction-type situation of bidding on properties. In these cases a government official required a specific amount of money in order to obtain accommodations. This system also allowed the bribegivers, who in most cases managed public supplies, to barter their goods by way of either formal or informal markets. Back-door business deals were common as were the exchanging of items through an informal market place. The Communist party created a well-organized extortion-oriented system that evolved around bribery. Money obtained from corrupt activities moved up through the Soviet power structure and became a sort of tribute to the higher-ranking officials in the Communist party. The money was an "unofficial tax" paid in order to operate a business in the Soviet Socialist Republic (Leitzel et al., 1995).

Under the Bolshevik regime and the Communist party, the activities of organized crime groups in Russia gradually increased without any major intrusion into their operations by most members of the easily influenced Russian law enforcement establishment. Russian history does not acknowledge the fact that in many cases the clandestine and coercive activities of both the Soviet government and its secret KGB police were similar to those of La Cosa Nostra organized crime families. As time went on these tactics were found to be the most effective for the Soviet rulers in eliminating adversaries. It also assisted them in regulating the economy and assuring them of an ever-increasing corrupt income on top of their governmental salaries (Klebnikov, 1993). A considerable amount of organized criminal activity had always gone on within the Soviet Union but few of these groups' unlawful operations actually surfaced until the later part of 1970. Most parts of the old Soviet Republic had been aware of the actions of these organized gangs for decades (*U.S. News and World Report*, 1993a). Throughout Russia criminal operations are carried out on a daily basis by these gangs. In fact, during a recent meeting in Moscow members of the influential Roundtable organization demanded that something be done by the government to reduce the ever-increasing attacks on Russian businesspeople by the gang members. Since January 1, 1995, 90 assaults were perpetrated on rich business owners with 46 of these attacks being fatal to the victim (*New York Times*, 1995).

Most of the new gangs were built around a strong leader who in many cases had prior gang experience, had spent some period of his life within the confines of a prison, and had a strong autocratic disposition. Gang participants selecting a leader felt that these variables gave the newly appointed group boss sufficient criminal experience to run a profitable gang operation. Most of the early gangs had a power structure that included the boss, several lieutenants, workers, apprentices, and people who were considered the gangs' connections to legitimate society. They received and dealt in stolen property, acted as informers who set up places for people to rob, and participated in the escape of a thief or gang member after the completion of a crime. Although this latter group consisted of criminals, the gangs considered them legitimate citizens because they could never be considered true gang members.

The gangs in Russia that formed after the revolution had their own body of laws to guide their operations. Gang members:

1. lived segregated from the legitimate outside world.

2. rejected all responsibilities of a normal life.

3. vowed to never cooperate with state authorities in any way, and whenever possible found a way to rip off the state or one of its agencies.

4. were not permitted, although they were drafted, to be members of the Russian military during World War II.

5. avoided any connections that would interfere with the gang member's autonomy to properly perform.

6. maintained integrity when dealing with other gang members.

7. kept family members in a position where they understood that they were to avoid any type of contact with the outside world (Chalidze, 1977).

Russian gangs also use special terms to describe members and some of their activities. Some of these terms *pakhany* (bosses), *vory v zakone* (regulars or thieves professing the code), *vorovskoy mir* (thieves' world), *krestnii otets* (godfather), and *vory v ramke* (thieves in a frame), have different meanings to gang members than to outsiders. According to Russian police officials a person designated as a vory v zakone is a member of "thieves in law," which makes that person a leader in Russian organized crime throughout Russia (Raab, 1995).

Another characteristic of many members of Russian crime groups is their ability to withstand pain. This attribute seems to manifest itself when these gang members are confined to prison. In many cases the actions taken by the gang members are more of self-impairment than just infliction of pain upon oneself. While confined to a correctional facility a gang member will go as far as to swallow nails, barbed wire, mercury thermometers, chess pieces, dominoes, needles, ground glass, spoons, knives, and many other foreign objects. According to Chalidze, prisoners who are gang members will "sew up their lips or eyelids, nail their scrotums to a bed, cut open the skin on their arms or legs and peel it off their bodies." All of these activities are done in order for the gang member to be sent to the prison hospital. There the member will receive special treatment including better food and drugs, and he will be placed in a work-free environment for a period of time (Chalidze, 1977).

The actual activities and number of organized crime groups in Russia have increased dramatically since the 1960s. A great deal of the gang expansion was due to the lackadaisical attitude of a government that denied all allegations of the existence of organized crime in Russia. Many of these gangs were actually initiated in locations such as the Central Asian (Uzbekistan, Kazakhstan, etc.), Caucasus (Georgia, Azerbaijan, etc.), and Ukraine areas of what was then the Soviet Union. One of the most disreputable yet adaptable gangs within Russia has been the Chechen organized crime groups that originated in the Chechnya area of the Northern Caucasus. Although many of these Chechen gangs are not affiliated with each other, they manage to rely on each other and a corrupt government to avoid prosecution. The Chechen gangs have a force of an estimated 600 killers in Moscow where this group is feared and despised. They are considered a braggadocio bunch of hoodlums who are attempting to control the streets in Moscow, Prague, Warsaw, and Berlin. Over the past decade they have become involved in car theft throughout Europe and the United States. They have smuggled drugs all over Western Europe and created scams that have been used successfully to bilk money from both the public sector (government) and private enterprises in the United States (Sterling, 1994). Gang involvement in crimes such as robbery, extortion, fraud, murder, and prostitution continued to grow, but the increased participation in the lucrative Russian black-market enhanced the gang's treasury and helped expand the number of gangs and their total membership.

## Russian Gangs Since Glasnost

The formation of the Commonwealth of Independent States (CIS) that came with the fall of Communist rule in Russia has apparently caused a large increase in the number of organized crime groups. According to various law enforcement sources the number of gangs in the CIS is 3,500–5,700 with total membership somewhere in the area of 200,000 to 1,000,000, with 500 to

18,000 leaders. One must remember that within this Russian organized crime environment a majority of the gangs have an average of 2–5 members. Although some crime groups are large and organized, most are considered small cells that have some type of affiliation to the bigger groups. In most cases, an alliance with a larger gang requires some sort of monthly compensation for the protection afforded to the smaller group. Present-day Russian law enforcement has discovered that of the large number of groups in operation in the CIS, the vast majority of these gangs are under the control of 150–200 confederations. These confederations provide the necessary protection and guidance so that the smaller groups can avoid conflict within the various criminal environments or operations that most of these gangs are participating in at the same time (Klebnikov, 1993).

The Russian Ministry of Internal Affairs (RMIA) estimates that approximately 4,350 groups operate within Russia. Also, 275 intraregional gangs, 168 universal, approximately 150 "criminal communities" consisting of two or more gangs that work together, and about 150 ethnic gangs are part of Russian organized crime groups. Intelligence information gathered by the RMIA indicates that the four groups that have caused the most problems within the CIS were originally from the Chechen, Georgian, Azerbaijan, and Dagestan regions of Russia. A majority of the Russian gangs have profited fairly well because of their participation in banking fraud, auto theft, and contract murders.

Many Russian criminals who were deported during the 1980s under the guise of being Jewish emigrants, rushed back to Russia after the collapse of the Communist regime in 1991. These criminals, working hand in hand with a criminal element that never left Russia, have managed to infiltrate Russian bank operations through murder and kidnapping. Once these gangs took control of the banks they used them to launder money from unlawful gang operations and foreign drug cartels, and also to embezzle money from local business accounts. Gang members have used information obtained from bank records in order to decide what business to exploit and how much money to embezzle from this company. The gangs of former deportees have also successfully set up a systematic scheme that has forced 70 percent of all private sector enterprises to pay the gangs monthly fees for protection against anything happening that could hurt or destroy their businesses.

Researchers describe three basic types of group structures in organized crime groups in Russia. The first arrangement shows a pyramid-type of structure that has a combination of "elite" leaders at the top who control the activities and profits of the organization. These elite leaders live the "good life" and in many cases their street operatives are unaware of their identity. In actuality, the support and security part of this organization shields the identity of the leaders.

Members of the support and security part of the gang may include doctors, corrupt government officials, and individuals involved in the distribution of media information. All of the workers in both the support and security branches have an agenda to fulfill and it is their job to:

1. ensure that all orders given by the elite group are properly followed and the criminal activity planned is successfully completed by gang workers.

2. maintain peaceful coexistence within the gangs' lower ranks by ameliorating any disagreements or disputes.

3. perpetuate a peaceful coexistence between other criminal groups and other criminals.

4. distribute promotional information that helps expand the groups' illegal beliefs.

5. assure that members of the elite group receive the accolades they deserve and make sure that the local community is aware of the plaudits being heaped on each group leader; this type of notoriety is carried out in order to increase the productivity within a criminal society/group.

6. do whatever is necessary to hinder effective procedures that can or might be used by outside government agencies against the gang.

7. have a plan or people available to assist in confronting agencies that arrest and prosecute members of the gang.

8. provide all types of fraudulent documents to gang members whenever necessary either to bring a criminal act to a successful conclusion or to avoid arrest and/or prosecution (Serio, 1992).

The third and final group of members that works within a Russian organized crime group are the workers or street operatives. These workers, as members of the gang, are required to successfully complete all the criminal schemes formulated by the elite members of this criminal enterprise. In most cases, these members are usually career criminals who have an expertise in a specific type of crime (burglary, robbery, murder, fraud, kidnapping, etc.). It is possible for a member of the lower echelon to climb the ladder of success and join the elite group but it requires that person to be productive and capable of putting a lot of money or other assets into the group's accounts. Another alternative for an ambitious worker to gain status is to save a sufficient amount of money to start his own gang.

The second type of organizational structure is a tetrad-type of association. This four-tier criminal organization is controlled by a person identified as a boss. According to Russian police sources, approximately 500 crime bosses operate throughout the CIS (U.S. Dept. of Justice, 1993). An organizational boss/leader has directly underneath him (in this organizational structure) employees who are known as *spies*. Each boss usually controls two spies whose job it is to make sure that the next ranking person, a brigadier, maintains allegiance to the organization and that the brigadier does not become more influential with the workers than the boss. Workers within this structure are categorized into smaller units. These smaller units or cells may be labeled according to their specialties, as a narcotics unit, prostitution unit, governmental contacts unit, or an enforcer unit. Naturally, each specialized unit would control one specific area of organized crime activity for the gang. Russian organized crime bosses seem to feel that an organization that has specialty employees has the advantage in that each worker:

1. knows his job and how to perform it without being a "jack of all trades" and attempting to create new opportunities for this organized crime family in other areas.

2. can only supply particulars on one area of criminal activity even if arrested and turned into an informer.

3. can't blame his inability to perform a job properly on being overburdened with a number of tasks required of a generalist-type of worker.

4. finds it difficult to gain total knowledge of an operation so that he can form his own competing group using information gathered from this gang.

A third type of Russian organized crime group structure is the one used by the Chechen gangs, most of which are clannish groups. Most Chechens are Muslims. An estimated 1 million Chechens presently live in the northern area of the Caucasus. As a group they work throughout Russia, Germany, Saudi Arabia, and the United States. The Chechen gangs have five godfathers, four in Moscow and one in Groznyy. Each godfather controls four different underbosses who are usually placed in charge of all of the groups' operations in each country. The underbosses, in turn, control at least fifty gang leaders who control various gang members throughout the world. Gangs that these leaders manage are usually made up of criminals who perform specialized criminal tasks for each group. Most of the specialists are considered workers.

Intelligence gathered by U.S. law enforcement agencies indicates that the foundation of Russian organized crime groups is based on four different types of alliances:

1. A criminal enterprise modeled from the membership of the old communist party, which is a circle of dishonest ex-soviet officials who worked in various government positions under the old communist regime.

2. Regional ethnic groups that had been operating as organized gangs within the Soviet Union for decades even though the Communist government denied their existence. Some of the groups that fall into the ethnic organized criminal gang category are the Chechens, Georgians, Azerbaijanis, Ukrainians, Uzbeks, and Dagestans.

3. Regulars or thieves professing the code who came to power with their gangs after being elected a vory v zakone (thief professing the code) while serving a term in a Russian prison. These gang members are considered the leaders/bosses of most Russian organized crime groups and are elected by the membership to this position. They have the capacity to create their own organized crime gangs, and in doing so, have the ability to recruit membership to their gang from any other Russian group. The majority of these bosses avoid attention whenever possible to avoid identification by the government. After a person is selected to be a vory v zakove (a person is usually selected for this "honor" because of his prior history as a successful and notorious criminal and his leadership qualities) he is obliged to take an oath of office and, during an initiation ritual, is awarded the title of master thief and leader.

4. A criminal enterprise that is formed as an offshoot of one of the previously mentioned organizations. Many of these gangs have been formed since the downfall of the Communist regime. The leadership of these types of organizations is usually strong. Many of the members are career criminals who have spent a good portion of their careers in prison (FBI, 1993).

In an effort to legitimize their gang operations, the godfathers, bosses, or vory v zakone held a series of meetings in an attempt to eliminate the hostilities between some of the gangs and create one big happy family. The first truce was carried out during meetings between gang leaders in Dagomys on the Black Sea in 1988. Peaceful coexistence between the gangs lasted almost a year. Then during 1991 and 1992 more conferences were held with gang leaders. Peace was finally restored with the gangs being assigned different territories of authority by the leaders. Gang leaders felt that peace between all gangs was mandatory because opportunities were coming up for the gangs to purchase newly privatized businesses in Moscow. In doing so the gangs would create an even larger power base for themselves. In a combined venture, the gangs managed to purchase over 50 percent of the businesses that had been put up for auction after the government privatized these enterprises. Government officials in Moscow estimated that the sale of these businesses would bring approximately 1.6 billion rubles into their treasury. Gang leaders who were not interested in allowing the government to reap a large profit on these sales intimidated bidders on many properties. As a result, the government realized only 200 million rubles from these properties (Sterling, 1994).

A major advantage of organized crime groups in Russia is the inability of the newly reorganized government to set up or pass the legislative tools that are necessary to help police and prosecutors arrest and convict group members for their gang activities. As of yet, the new government has made no attempt to create laws comparable to anti-gang laws in the United States. An example is the Racketeer Influenced and Corrupt Organization (RICO) Act that allows government attorneys to prosecute bosses as well as workers. Russian leader Boris Yeltsin has called for legislation that would help the government prosecute members of the Russian organized crime groups. As of yet little has been accomplished because of the lack of support within the Russian parliament. An attempt has been made to strike out at the growing crime rate by strengthening prosecutors' offices in areas with high rates of criminal activity, but because of the staggering crime increase, augmentation of these office staffs has not helped the system.

Corruption within the Russian Criminal Justice system flourished even prior to the change in government. Indications of police corruption came to light in 1988 when the then old Soviet government eliminated 15 percent (100,000 members) of its police force because of corrupt activities within that agency. Yeltsin admonished the politicians and the police in Russia by commenting, "Corruption is devouring the state from top to bottom" during a speech (Sterling, 1994: 93). Three years later in 1991 more than 20,000 more police officials were terminated because they were participating in unlawful activities with members of organized crime. This action plus low or no pay and an ever-increasing number of serious assaults on police officers by members of organized crime has had an effect on law enforcement actions against member of these organized gangs. The number of attacks with guns on police officers increased from 186 in 1989 to 719 in 1991 in just one city, St. Petersburg, Russia. These figures are meaningful because the 386.5 percent increase within a two-year period cannot be matched even by the high number of police attacks that take place in other areas of the world, like Sicily or Colombia, that are also dominated by members of organized crime families (Sterling, 1994).

Since the change in government, the number of crimes committed within the old Soviet Union has increased significantly. The cause of this crime wave can certainly be blamed on either the sudden growth of organized crime groups or the lack of stability within the newly formed government. Researchers can find no definitive indicators as to which of these two factors has had the biggest effect on crime in Russia. Increased crime is indicated by the figures listed in Table 12-1.

According to a 1995 CNN special and several other reports, organized crime groups in Russia are:

1. a major factor in the ever-increasing crime rate in Moscow with a 40 percent increase in murder, 42 percent increase in rape and robbery, and 170 percent increase in fraud during the past year.

2. using crime as a tool to oppress the people just as the old regime used communism to instill fear into the citizens.

3. fighting over control of the wealth of natural resources within Russia.

4. in control of more than 40 percent of all Russian exportation of indispensable metals such as cobalt, copper, nickel, and uranium. Accomplished gang members stole an average of 50 train tank cars, each carrying 147 barrels of oil, every day during 1993 for sale on the black-market.

5. involved in the smuggling of both historical and religious icons and art treasures to the highest bidders throughout the world. During 1993 Russian Customs officials seized more than 400,000 antique art objects. According to Russian intelligence sources the gangs are connected to every security agency in Russia, therefore smuggling objects out of Russia is not a problem for the gangs.

6. extorting protection money from about 90 percent of the street vendors in Russia.

**TABLE 12-1**  Russian Organized Crime Statistics

| Type of Crimes | Crimes Reported to Police | | |
|---|---|---|---|
| | *1987* | *1989* | *1993* |
| Murders | 9,199 | 13,543 | 29,200 |
| Possession of firearm | 5,656 | 14,551 | 22,100 |
| Committed by organized gangs | 110,921 | 175,092 | 355,500 |
| Serious injury to victim | 20,100 | 36,872 | 66,900 |
| Total Crimes | 1,185,914 | 1,619,818 | 2,799,600 |

*Source*: Freedman, 1994.

7. in control of approximately 35,000 Russian businesses including 400 banks. Gang members have used these businesses in any way possible to increase their assets. One specific scam involves obtaining a 25 percent interest rate to pay employee wages or overdue accounts. This money is then put into a commercial banking establishment that is associated with the business. Then it lends the money out at a 250 percent interest rate with the excess interest money gained being placed in a gang members bank account outside of Russia.

8. involved in significant relationship with the Israeli organized crime groups and have strong ties to most U.S. gangs.

9. working hand and hand with Colombian drug cartels to distribute drugs throughout Europe and launder their drug money. They are also working with La Cosa Nostra organized crime groups from Italy in drug distribution, money laundering, and auto theft from both the United States and Europe.

10. controlling who does or does not get a visa at the U.S. Embassy in Moscow.

11. using violence and kidnapping to force citizens (older members of Moscow society) to either hand over the ownership papers or to sell their apartments and houses—now that tenants are being allowed to purchase apartments they rented from the old Soviet government for years—at a rate far below the average market price.

12. gaining control over the illegal movement of military equipment, specifically guns, which is apparent in the increase in crimes committed with guns in the past three years (from 4,000 to 22,500). Ammunition and explosive devices, plus if available, nuclear weapons and their energy supply, are then sold to the highest bidder on the world market. During 1994 German Customs officials seized 17.6 ounces of plutonium 239, which is the primary fissionable material used in atomic warheads, from three non-Russian citizens traveling from Moscow to Munich. This seizure, to date, is the largest of nuclear material (O'Connor, 1995; Gray, 1994; Klebnikov, 1993; Hersh, 1994; Handelman, 1994; Hockstader, 1995; Potekhina, 1994).

13. in control of the organ donor market from Russia. Gang members kidnap children, remove the children's organs, and offer the organs for sale in countries outside of Russia. Members of Russian organized crime groups have also been involved in the removal of organs from unclaimed bodies in the city morgues. The gangs then sell the highly profitable organs for use in either organ transplants or for medical experiments (Adams, 1993).

Several major gangs presently operate in Moscow. Dolgoprudny or Dolgoprudnaya, whose criminal activities were originally centralized in the northwest section of Moscow, is one of the oldest organized crime groups in Moscow. A major portion of this gang's income comes from its long-term protection rackets.

Lyubertsy was originally comprised of weightlifters from the southeastern section of Moscow who formed a gang in the mid 1980s. The members of this gang were initially considered to be a western type of cowboy who beat up on (what they considered) punks or hippies. Members of this gang eventually became involved in running prostitution rings, extortion operations, robbery rings and contract murder hits. Subsequently, a large number of the membership moved on to form their own gangs throughout Russia.

Solntsevo emerged from the southern part of Moscow where it became heavily involved in the illegal gambling and limousine businesses. This gang's vory v zakone was murdered during the fall of 1994 when a bomb exploded in his vehicle.

Ingushy gangs have been involved in the theft and illegal trafficking of leather and other animal skins to various parts of northern Italy.

Chechen gangs have been active throughout both the old Soviet Union and the new CIS, and are an ever-increasing worldwide operation. They participate in almost every type of criminal venture available to them and are presently considered the most powerful group in Moscow. They are feared and despised by the citizens of Moscow who think of them as nothing more than arrogant hoodlums who will not be quickly eliminated from the streets of Moscow. Chechen gangs have also expanded their horizons and have been taking over criminal activities on the streets of Berlin, Prague, Warsaw, and Stockholm. The criminal activities that these Chechen gangs participate in within these countries include auto theft, drug trafficking, fraud, and counterfeiting. This group has even expanded its unlawful behavior to the United States and is presently involved in swindles and drug trafficking. Chechen, Assyrian, and Azeris gangs control a majority of the drug trade in the present-day CIS (Hockstader, 1995; Sterling, 1994).

## Groups in the United States

During the early 1970s the United States government used a detente-type of policy in an effort to create a better relationship with the Communist government in the Soviet Union. Part of the agreement with the then-Soviet leadership involved the emigration of a large portion of the Jewish population in Russia to Israel or the United States. A short time after an agreement was reached a large number of these Soviet emigrants left Russia. Some settled in Israel while others ultimately ended up in the United States. In fact, by the mid 1980s more than 250,000 Russians who were members of the Jewish religion had immigrated to the United States.

The Russians, like their counterparts in Cuba did in 1980, sent along with the Soviet Jews who emigrated a large percentage (40%) who were not of the Jewish religion but were from the criminal ranks within Russian society. Many of these new immigrants had been arrested and convicted of serious crimes and had done time in Soviet prison. As it turns out, most of these Russian criminals ended up settling in major U.S. cities such as New York, Los Angeles, San Francisco, Chicago, and Miami. Once they settled into a large urban community it was not long before they established small criminally-oriented gangs involved in money-making ventures. At first it was robbery, extortion, burglary, larceny, and auto theft. Soon afterward they expanded their operations to include various con games, insurance fraud, medical scams, counterfeiting, credit card theft and use, forgery, and murder (Freedman, 1994; Adams, 1993; Sterling, 1994; Blumenthal, 1989; *Organized Crime Digest*, 1982).

A great deal of similarity can be noted between the newly established Russian gangs and other ethnic gangs that formed in the United States over the past 100 years. In fact, Russian gangs can be easily compared to other ethnic gangs in the United States because:

1. most members of the previous gangs were foreigners from another country.

2. they all made their bases of operations in modest areas of large urban centers.

3. these different groups were all from the same ethnic background and spoke the same language.

4. most were leaving countries suffering from both declining economic problems and the depletion of national resources.

5. most of the crimes were committed against other members of their own ethnic group.

6. the outlaws in each group banded together to form their own gang, without any affiliation with other outside ethnic groups; later on relationships were formed with other ethnic gangs that would benefit each gang.

7. in many cases, connections were made to organized groups in the homeland for support services and leadership whenever possible.

Brighton Beach in Brooklyn, New York, is the home base for most of the Russian organized crime operations in the United States, with more than 200,000 Russian immigrants within this community. According to intelligence gathered by members of local and federal law enforcement, three major groups operate out of Brighton Beach. A majority of the membership of the first group are Jewish and come from Odessa in Russia. The second group consists of immigrants from Tashkent in Uzbekistan and are allegedly Muslim. Most of the members in the third group are former citizens of the city of Ekaterinburg in Russia (Freedman, 1994). It has been alleged that a number of NYPD police officers from the 60th and 61st Precincts in Brooklyn work as chauffeurs and bodyguards for members of Russian organized crime. Roger Berger, an investigator for the New York State Department of Taxation and Finance, reports that these same NYPD officers work as bouncers at two local Russian nightclubs, Rasputin and Metropole, and that these officers are active participants in some of the phony accident scams staged by members of Russian organized crime (Freedman, 1994).

One of the first known members of organized crime to arrive in the United States was Evset Agron. Agron had been in jail in Russia for murder and had left Russia in 1971 to open up both gambling and prostitution operations in West Germany. He was one of 5,250 alleged Russian immigrants of the Jewish faith who came to the United States in 1975 who were really gangsters. A short time after his arrival in Brighton Beach Agron set up his own organized crime family. His first money-making venture was extortion. He hired the most violent members of the Russian community in Brooklyn to brutally intimidate Russians immigrants into paying protection money. Anyone who refused to pay tribute to Agron's gang was either beaten or tormented with an electric cattle prod until he or she paid the money demanded. This gang was bringing in more than $50,000 a week in extortion money by the end of 1980. Agron continued his successful extortion business from his offices in the El Caribe Country Club in Brooklyn until May 1985 when he was shot and killed in his Park Slope residence (Freedman, 1994; Adams, 1992).

Marat Balagula was quickly ordained Agron's successor. Balagula professionalized the gasoline bootlegging scam by setting up numerous dummy corporations and then moving the gasoline on paper from one spurious franchise to another until it reached a bogus company that was set up to pay the taxes. The only problem was that all this bogus corporation did was sell the gasoline and stamp "all taxes paid" on the bill. All of the money was then taken by gang members, and a company that had nothing more than a post office box and a corporate head who probably never existed disappeared from the face of the earth (Freedman, 1994). Balagula was convicted of credit card fraud in late 1986 and fled to Germany from where he was returned to the United States two years later to serve a prison term. Once Balagula no longer controlled the Russian gangs, one Boris "Papa" Nayfeld took over command. According to investigative sources Nayfeld was responsible for Agron's death in 1985 (Freedman, 1994). Nayfeld, as the leader of the Agron gang, has had an ongoing conflict with Monya Elson, an enforcer for the Zilber Brothers gang. Four unsuccessful attempts on Elson's life were allegedly engineered by Nayfeld. Included in these attempts were a hand wound to Elson, a perpetrator's jammed gun, a car bomb that exploded with the bomber still in the auto, and shotgun wounds received by Elson, his wife, and nephew in another botched attempt by an unknown assassin. Elson fled to Israel in order to escape the never-ending attempts on his life (Freedman, 1994). Elson was ultimately arrested for the murders of Vyacheslav Lyubarsky and Alexander Lyubarsky in January 1992, Alexander Slepinin in June 1992, and the attempted murder of Boris Nayfeld in 1991. Elson was seized in Italy in March 1995. Nayfeld was arrested in January 1994 for being the leader of a conspiracy that smuggled tons of heroin from Southeast Asia through Poland into the United States where the heroin was ultimately sold to members of La Cosa Nostra.

Identified as a vory v zakone in Russia, Vyacheslav Ivankov, known as "Yaponchik" or "Little Japanese" and "the father of Soviet extortion," had originally formed his own group, the Solontsevskaya gang, in Moscow in 1980. The members of this gang posed as Russian police officers in order to carry out robberies in Moscow. In 1982, Ivankov was arrested and convicted on robbery charges in Moscow and was sentenced to 14 years in a Siberian prison.

During the later part of 1991 Ivankov, in the ninth year of his prison sentence, managed, through the use of bribery, to get two prominent Russian politicians, one a member of the Russian parliament and the other a Russian supreme court judge, to shorten his prison sentence by five years. Within a short period of time after these two politicians intervened, Ivankov walked away from prison a free man and in early 1992 moved his operations to the United States (Raab, 1995; Hockstader, 1995).

Shortly after his arrival in the United States in 1992, federal law enforcement authorities described Ivankov as the most influential Russian organized crime leader in the United States. Intelligence information on Ivankov indicates that he was sent here by other Russian organized crime bosses to guide, control, and enhance the relationships between the Russian gangs throughout Europe and Russia and the expanding Russian gangs in the United States.

Ivankov set up his base of operations in Brighton Beach, Brooklyn, and because of his status within the structure of the Russian gangs has been clever enough to survive quite well on tribute paid to him by the gangs. He has also involved himself in several swindles including one for which the FBI arrested him. Ivankov and eight other Russian gangsters participated together in an extortion ring. Law enforcement sources state that Ivankov actively engaged in attempting to coerce $8.5 million from the owners of Summit International Corporation between November 1994 and May 1995. A demand was made for payments of $3.5 and $5 million as were threats of violence. Then in April 1995 one of the complainants, Vladimer Voloshin's father, was beaten to death on a Moscow subway station. A short time after this incident four armed males forced the complainants, at gun point, to accompany them to the Troika Restaurant in Fairview, New Jersey. Gang members then forced the complainants to sign a contract assuring the payments of $3.5 million to the gang members. A month later Ivankov and his eight associates were arrested and charged with extortion by federal authorities (Rabb, 1995; Ball, 1995).

One of the earliest and most successful fraudulent operations run by the Russian gangs to date has been a bootleg gasoline scam that has bilked federal, state, and city governments out of billions of dollars in excise taxes over the past 10 years. During the early 1980s a partnership was formed between the Russian gangs and members of four of the local La Cosa Nostra families (Gambino, Luchese, Columbo, and Genovese). Members of La Cosa Nostra families formed a coalition that allowed, in some cases, the Russians to maintain approximately 25 percent of the profit while La Cosa Nostra families were to receive about 75 percent of the profits, and in other cases members of La Cosa Nostra were to receive two cents for every gallon of bootleg gasoline sold by the Russians. One La Cosa Nostra connection to the Russian groups—Gambino family members—was used primarily as an enforcement agent for the Russian gangs. They collected 2.26 cents for each gallon of gasoline and fuel oil sold through the dummy corporations. A 1993 federal court indictment claimed that Gambino family members were paid a total of $6.7 million for their participation as enforcers for the Russian groups (Strom, 1993).

This unlawful scam was set up to avoid the collection of various excise taxes placed on gasoline by federal, state, and local government. The scheme used by these groups became known as a "daisy chain." It involved the setting up of numerous small corporations that were involved in a large number of sales and purchases of gasoline. One of these paper corporations was set up as a pony, or burn, company that was used to sell gasoline to a purchaser. This pony company indicated on paper that the taxes on this sale were included in the bill. This claim, of course, was not true because no taxes were paid on the gasoline at any time during any of these transactions. When the time came for a tax collector to collect the taxes allegedly paid, the pony company was no longer in existence.

As law enforcement agencies became wise to these illegal operations the gangs, Italian and Russian, changed their procedural methods. The groups started purchasing the facilities related to the operations of an oil company including transportation vehicles, gasoline stations, and petroleum terminals. Intelligence gathered by several law enforcement agencies indicates that a coalition of Italian and Russian mobsters were conspiring to obtain several tankers as well as an oil refinery. These groups have managed to buy a number of gas stations/truck stops throughout New Jersey and New York. An offshoot of this scam involves the gangs buying large amounts of number 2 oil, or home heating oil, which is tax-exempt and the equivalent of diesel fuel. Through the use of dummy corporations the home heating oil is moved from company to company until it is changed on paper from number 2 home heating oil to diesel oil. This newly designated diesel oil is either sold by gang members at their privately owned gas stations/truck stops or purchased by an unsuspecting retailer, and once again all of the tax money is pocketed by the gang members. Another scam contrived by the Russian gangs involved the purchasing of waste oil from both gasoline stations and oil container cleaning companies throughout the East Coast and Canada. Contaminated oil was combined with unadulterated oil and sold to unsuspecting customers. Law enforcement sources estimate that well over 8 million gallons of contaminated oil has been sold on the open market (Strum, 1993; Block, 1994).

Some of the other early scams run by the Russian gangs included what was called a "Potato Bag Scam" in which con men, who were members of a Russian gang from Odessa, posed as merchant seafarers and offered to sell antique Russian gold rubles at a bargain price. A genuine antique gold ruble is shown to a person, usually another Russian immigrant known to have money, for examination. Clients are permitted to totally scrutinize several antique gold Russian rubles prior to the completion of a deal. After an agreement is reached both parties decide on a delivery location where a bag of these antique gold rubles is to be handed over to this person. Once the exchange is made the gang members make off with the money while the victim opens the bag of rubles and finds that they have spent a lot of money on a bag of potatoes (Blumenthal, 1989). Another large swindle involved Jardinay, a watch and jewelry manufacturer in downtown Manhattan. Approximately 25 Russian immigrants managed to gain employment with the Jardinay Company and stole more than $54 million in diamonds and gold over a period of one year. Investigators theorized that most of the stolen jewelry was diverted to smaller jewelry stores owned by members of the ring that was stealing the jewelry. A similar type of swindle took place at the SoHo-based NGI Precious Metals company. Over the past ten years four members of a Russian organized crime syndicate have stolen more than $35 million worth of jewelry from NGI. Most of the stolen jewelry was smuggled to Europe were it was easily sold to jewelry dealers. Almost all of the money from this swindle was deposited in Swiss banks with a large portion of the money then used by this same group in a money laundering scheme (Smith, 1995; Blumenthal, 1989).

The Russian gangs have become active participants in both counterfeiting and forgery. Thus far members of Russian organized crime groups have been implicated in the production of more than $4.5 million worth of forged American Express checks and another $15.5 million in bogus checks from banks such as Citibank and Manufacturer's Hanover. These same Russian gangs have attained expertise in the forgery of art work. Shops were set up in Queens, New York, to scrupulously produce forged bejeweled Faberges eggs that are quite valuable and highly marketable throughout the world.

In Los Angeles, Russian gang members set up a scam that brought Russian immigrants, a good portion of them criminals, to the United States where they were then supplied with false identification and legitimate checking accounts. They were then sent out with a gang member to make numerous large purchases of goods at the foremost stores and auctions in Southern California. Russian con artists discovered several weaknesses within banks' checking account systems, including that an amount in a checking account may be verified over a phone but that it then takes a day or two for the bank to receive the check. The swindlers also realized that the check could be delayed several days longer if someone in the check clearing department at the bank put the check aside for a few more days. With all this information in mind, members of this Russian fraud gang proceeded to open checking accounts in several different banks in Los Angeles. People selected to work for the gang were permitted to operate for no longer than two weeks and the amount in the checking account was never exceeded at any shopping location. Merchandise purchased by the people working for the gang was ultimately sold off and the gang's members received 80% of the profits. Usually, just prior to the checks being presented for payment, the money in the accounts was removed by gang members. Profits from this swindle netted the gang more than $50,000 per month. The only problem with this scam was that the leaders of the gangs were viciously murdered by two of their employees. A search of the location of the murders turned up numerous items including camcorders, television sets, computer equipment, fax machines, highly valuable Persian rugs, antiques, and other works of art (Mitchell, 1992).

One of the most productive fraudulent schemes conducted by members of a Russian crime group involved a $1 billion Medicare/Medicaid billing scam. Approximately 350 front companies, phony companies incorporated to advance fraudulent activities, were instituted so that the members of this group could prevaricate their invoices. Customers were solicited by phone to participate in what they were told was a free medical examination to be conducted at one of the gang's mobile clinics. Once the consumer, either a senior citizen or a homeless person recruited off the street, appeared at one of the mobile clinics for the examination he or she was given several forms to sign that, as he or she was told, were for clearance to perform the tests. The papers signed were actually insurance claim forms that gave the clinics the right to submit bills to the customer's insurance company for the tests conducted on the policy holder. An average bill to an insurance company was $8,000. This group also set up scams throughout Russia. Fraudulent employment agencies were set up in Russia. People would respond to advertisements for employment opportunities in the United States and pay a fee to members of this group. A short time after the fee was paid both the employment company and the monetary fee would vanish (*Newsweek*, 1993).

Russian gang members, who come from an environment that feels it is only natural to steal from the government, have set up a variety of fraudulent activities against the U.S. government. Medicaid and Medicare fraud alone has brought millions of dollars into the Russian gangs' bank accounts. Many new immigrants from Russia who arrive in the United States and are somehow involved with the Russian gangs are immediately put on welfare, food stamps, and Medicaid. The gangs also have come up with another method of ripping off Medicaid by double and triple billing the government through the use of their own visiting nurse service. This nurse service, owned by gang members, bills the government using legitimate Medicaid numbers. These numbers have been obtained by people working for the gang or from drug addicts or homeless people that the gang paid off to gain this information.

Another Russian gang scam involved members of the gangs traveling throughout the United States. As the members reached specific destinations throughout the United States they would lease stores under false identities and immediately submit anywhere from 10 to 15 orders for gold and other jewelry to out-of-state jewelry vendors. In almost every case, the jewelry order was well over $5,000, and the vendor was informed that the bill for the jewelry would be paid upon delivery of the order. The only problem was that the cash on delivery was nothing more than a counterfeit cashiers check (Mitchell, 1992).

One other scam involving the use of credit cards was pulled off by the Russian gangs in Brooklyn. Gang members would get possession of the master keys to mailboxes in multiple dwelling buildings. They would check the mailboxes a short time after the mail delivery for credit cards in a tenant's mail box. Upon finding a credit card in an envelope the gang member would remove the envelope containing the credit card, unseal the envelope and run up as much as $10,000 on the account. The card would then be resealed in the envelope and the envelope containing the credit card would be re-deposited back into the original tenant's mailbox. Needless to say, within a couple of weeks the credit card holder would get a bill for several thousand dollars from the credit card company and then notify the credit card company that he or she had not run up these bills.

Members of the Russian Mafia have chosen Russian athletes as targets for extortion. Media and investigative reports indicate that the gangs are presently involved in targeting, for embezzlement, Russian hockey players who are active in the National Hockey League. Some of the players, Alexei Zhitnit of the Los Angeles Kings, Pavel Bure of the Vancouver Canucks, Viacheslav Fetisov of the New Jersey Devils, and Alexander Mogilny of the Buffalo Sabres, complained to authorities about being approached by members of Russian organized crime groups who attempted to extract extortion monies from them (Middleton, 1993; MacIntyre, 1993; Gray, 1994).

Some of the Russian gangs that have become highly visible within the United States include the Odessa Mafia group that originally set up operations in Brighton Beach in the mid 1970s. This gang then proceeded to set up other strong gang operations in both the Los Angeles and San Francisco areas of California while gang leadership remained based in Brooklyn, New York. The California Department of Justice has found this gang to be well controlled and organized. A gang known as the Evangelical Russian Mafia first appeared on the West Coast in early 1993. Law enforcement sources indicate that this gang has no roots in Russia and was formed by young Russian immigrants in Sacramento, California. The 60 current members of this gang have not, as of yet, expanded outside of California. A Russian/Armenian mafia group formed in New York City in the early 1980s and expanded their operations to both Hollywood and the San Fernando Valley in California during the 1980s. Gasoline bootlegging has been a profitable business for this group as has recent involvement in drug trafficking. Another group, the Molina/Organizatsiya, is a gang that combines ethnic Russians, Armenians, and Chechens, and any other person who has ethnic roots in the countries within the Commonwealth of Independent States. As a group, they have preserved their connections to other international organized crime gangs. Molina/Organizatsiya has remained active in credit card scams, drug trafficking, extortion, fuel tax and medical fraud, robbery, and murder (California Dept. of Justice, 1993; FBI, 1993).

Many members of Russian organized crime can be differentiated from other gang members by their distinct attributes. Some of these characteristics include:

1. Ethnicity, in that gang members are usually from the same city or country in the CIS.

2. Membership is small, 3–20 members.

3. Leaders and members are not confined to certain activities, but will participate in anything that will bring them some type of profit.

4. Members avoid any disclosure of assets that might draw attention to the gang.

5. Highly educated members who are fluent in several languages.

6. Violence that is somewhat controlled by the gang; most violent acts are used for expedient reasons, however, aggression, when necessary, will be used on anyone.

7. All gang business to be discussed outside of any area where a listening device can be installed or used.

8. All law enforcement agents can be bribed.

9. Neither the government nor elected officials can be trusted.

10. Members constantly use fraudulent activities as a tool to swindle private as well as public sector organizations (Mitchell, 1992; Freedman, 1993; Pennsylvania Crime Commission, 1990).

The participation of the Russian organized crime groups in drug trafficking in both the United States and Russia has been constantly increasing over the past five years. Some indications of the Russian gangs' expansion into drug dealing include the following:

1. Members of the Russian gangs have formed working relationships with the members of organized crime groups who are already heavily involved in drug trafficking (Colombians, Chinese, La Cosa Nostra, etc.).

2. The lack of any major drug enforcement agency within the newly formed CIS gives the Russian gangs an opportunity to set up new drug transportation routes into the CIS and Europe and then to participate in the distribution and sale of the drugs.

3. Areas within the CIS that have the proper soil and climate to grow and then process the drugs will allow the gangs to no longer be intermediaries for drug kingpins from outside the CIS. In some areas in Russia marijuana plants grow undomesticated in open fields in the country. Opium poppies are grown freely in the Central Asian Republics of Tajikistan and Uzbekistan, and a crop was recently planted in the Northern Caucasus. Approximately 40 percent of all the drugs coming into Russia in 1992 came from the former Soviet republic of Azerbaijan, and ethnic Azerbaijanis accounted for 82 percent of the people arrested for drug possession in Russia in 1992.

4. An ever-increasing demand in the CIS for drugs keeps the gangs "in business" with an estimated 3.5–4 million drug users. Networks are already in place that smuggle guns, precious gems, metals, art, and any other valuable materials taken from the CIS to Europe, Asia and the Americas. It would, therefore, be just as easy to smuggle drugs as any other items through these networks.

5. Russian gangs have been cautious in their dealings with almost all of the other organized crime syndicates throughout Europe, Asia, and North and South America. The Russian groups, in most cases, have gone out of their way to have continued peaceful negotiations with all the other crime groups. In the United States they have been more than willing to share any wealth with other groups in order to further camaraderie amongst all gangs. This willingness is obvious from their participation in the gasoline tax fraud scheme with La Cosa Nostra throughout the New York metropolitan area. In the CIS and Europe, the Russian gangs have been laundering money for both the Colombians and the Italian Mafia.

6. The ever-increasing maritime trade between members of the CIS and businesses in every major port city in the United States and Canada adds more routes to the expanding criminal networks of Russian organized crime groups. Indicators of the involvement of Russian sailors in the drug trade surfaced during 1992 when a Russian seaman was arrested in Melbourne, Australia, in possession of 12 pounds of heroin. Two other sailors were arrested in the Belgian port of Seebrugge with 24 pounds of cocaine in their possession. The U.S. Drug Enforcement Agency has received documented information that more than half the sailors in the Russian merchant marines that are on ships that run the Colombia-to-Russia route are smuggling cocaine back with them (Dahlberg, 1993).

Discussions involving Russian crime groups should always include Israeli organized crime groups. In many scams these groups have worked and profited together, but in reality they are two distinctly different crime families.

## ISRAELI ORGANIZED CRIME

During the late 1960s, a group of Israelis between the ages of 20 and 35 started migrating from Israel to California. This and later migration was probably due to a dynamic enforcement effort by the Israeli National police to rid Tel Aviv of some of these gangs. A major portion of the gang members had formed friendships while on active duty with the Israeli armed forces or while serving sentences in Israeli correctional facilities. Most members of this group were originally from a poverty-stricken suburb of Tel Aviv known as Bat-Yam, and most of the members are from the Sephardic Jewish sect that has family roots throughout the Middle East, North Africa, and Spain. In most of these cases, the families of the gang member or the member accompanying his family moved to Israel because of the religious persecution they were subjected to while residing in Arab countries.

As members of what is now known as the Israeli organized crime group, they did not come to the attention of the Los Angeles Police Department until 1975 when members of this syndicate were found to be actively participating in extortion, arson, bankruptcy scams, and insurance fraud operations. At first, most of this group's activities existed in either Los Angeles or Calexico but by 1978 this organization had expanded its activities throughout Southern California. Originally, gang members profited by extorting money from elderly Eastern European Jews who owned butcher and Judaica retail stores in what was then the predominantly Jewish community of Fairfax within Los Angeles. These gangs also increased their revenues by running bust-out schemes in which a business is set up and a credit line is opened by gang members. Once everything is in place the group members place large orders for jewelry, clothing, appliances, or whatever product they are supposedly selling.

Along with the extension of their criminal activities came an increase in membership and an expansion in the amount of violence used by members. For example, in 1979 Eli and Esther Ruven were brutally murdered in Los Angeles and their bodies cut up into pieces by three members of an Israeli organized crime group who were later arrested and convicted of this heinous crime. The Ruvens were dealing cocaine for the gang and failed to pay a $70,000 fee on a drug delivery to the gang members. Since this incident four other murders have been linked to this Los Angeles-based gang (*Organized Crime Digest*, 1982; Derfner, 1990).

The rapid growth of membership continued into the early 1980s as did the gang's participation in drug trafficking activities. During 1981 various federal, state, and local law enforcement agencies in Southern California arrested 33 gang members for narcotics-related offenses. Israeli gang expansion was apparent in 1986 when five gang members were arrested in Brooklyn, New York, for their involvement in a drug trafficking ring that supplied the New York metropolitan area with more than $1 million worth of heroin on a weekly basis. This gang is connected to the group in Los Angeles and in 1986 had more than 200 hard-core members. These Brooklyn gangs base most of their activities out of Brighton Beach but maintain headquarters in Bensonhurst. Most of the gangs average 5–25 members and are growing in number. One of the gangs, the Johnny Attias, formed in Brooklyn under the guidance of Johnny Attias, hence the group's name. This gang imported cocaine from Colombia and heroin from Southeast Asia. Attias, after a number of disputes over drug transactions, killed several of the members of this gang, and eventually other gang members, fed up with the actions of their leader, killed him (Ross and Gonzalez, 1994a).

The increasing participation of Israeli gangs in drug trafficking has led to a more active involvement in each aspect of the drug business by members of the Israeli crime organizations. In order to upgrade their drug operations in the United States, Israeli gangs set up bases in South America. Police officials and U.S. drug enforcement agents in Colombia have observed a conspicuous increase in the number of Israeli refugees in the Colombian cities of Barranquilla and Cali over the past ten years (Moses and Pelleck, 1986; Ross and Gonzalez, 1994a). Worldwide operations for drug trafficking and money laundering have been put in place by members of Israeli organized crime over the past decade. Intelligence gathered by members of the U.S. DEA on assignment in Europe and Asia indicate that members of Israeli organized crime groups have set up operations throughout Europe. Other bases for drug trafficking and money laundering, besides the United States, Colombia, Brazil, and Canada, have been operating in Germany, the Netherlands, Belgium, France, Poland, England, and Russia in Europe as well as Hong Kong and Thailand in Asia and Pakistan, Turkey, and Israel in the Middle East (DEA, 1993)

A U.S. narcotics enforcement agency has produced some fairly solid evidence that Rehavam Zeevi, a retired general from the Israeli military and appointed to the Israeli cabinet in 1991, has been a participant in trafficking deals with members of Israeli organized crime groups since the early 1980s. Information related to Zeevi was uncovered by Michael Levine, a retired undercover agent in the DEA, who stated that during an interview with an arrested member of the Israeli organized crime group, Sam Shapiro, he was told by Shapiro that the Israeli gangs had set up a working operation with La Cosa Nostra in both the United States and Italy. Shapiro also informed agents that Zeevi, who was appointed an advisor to Prime Minister Yitzhak Rabin on terrorism in 1974, traveled to Colombia in 1977 with antiterrorist advisors. Shapiro alleges that Zeevi had 1,000 pounds of hashish with him in order to exchange the hashish for cocaine, which was then shipped to Florida for distribution throughout the United States. This exchange, according to Shapiro, was the beginning of fruitful drug trafficking relationship between Colombian drug lords and members of Israeli organized crime groups. On his trip to South America Zeevi was accompanied by Betsalel Mizrahi, alleged to be the major financier behind the organized crime groups in Israel. According to a media report in the *Jerusalem Report,* information from Israeli police wiretaps published in February 1991 indicate that Zeevi is connected to a number of members of Israeli criminal groups including Tuvia Oshri, a major narcotics trafficker, who is presently serving a life sentence for two gang-related murders (Marshall, 1991).

Israeli gangs have been able to use varied routes to transfer heroin from either Southeast or Southwest Asia to the United States. One path takes heroin from Pakistan to Japan. Here a member of an Israeli gang creates a deceptive bill of lading to indicate that the product in which the heroin is hidden originally came from Japan. The product is then shipped to Europe, usually the Netherlands, where it is rerouted to France, Germany, Belgium, or North America for distribution. Another route sends the heroin from Turkey to the Netherlands and then on to the United States or Canada. A third path takes the heroin from Thailand to either France or the Netherlands and then on to the United States or Canada. An additional route will move the heroin from either Thailand or Pakistan into Italy where it is secreted in a shoe shipment and forwarded to the United States (DEA, 1993).

Cocaine purchased in Colombia by members of Israeli organized crime is transported through Mexico, with the cooperation of members of Mexican organized crime families, to California. Another variation involves the transportation of cocaine to Brazil from where it is secreted in shoes and conveyed to the United States or Canada. A third route takes the cocaine to Brazil where it is hidden in shoes and shipped to the Netherlands. Here it is distributed for sale in Europe or Israel or exchanged for heroin that is then transported back to the United States for distribution. In most cases, the Israeli gang members are not involved in the street sales of either heroin or cocaine. Almost all drugs brought into the United States by Israeli gang members are sold to other racial and ethnic groups who are involved in street sales (DEA, 1993).

The Brooklyn Israeli gangs have also been active participants in the gasoline tax scams since the early 1980s. In fact, the ability of the Israeli gangs to work these gasoline scams in concert with other members of the Israeli groups, as well as members of Russian and Italian organized crime groups, increased their credibility within organized crime groups in the United States. Israeli gangs quickly moved the profits from their gasoline scams into drug trafficking and money laundering schemes.

Israeli organized crime members in Los Angeles have found the use of credit card scams as a successful way to make money. One of the gangs' favorite schemes involved going through trash bins of retail stores in an effort to locate carbon paper and tissue from credit card sales. Once the carbon paper and/or tissue was discovered the gang members could then obtain names and card numbers from these items. A small factory was then set up with the necessary laminating equipment and plastic necessary to produce counterfeit cards using the names and credit card numbers of real people. Phony retail jewelry businesses with commercial bank accounts were devised, and credit card vouchers for bogus purchases were then submitted to the credit card companies. They in turn would reimburse the phony business where the credit card was used in this bogus scheme. A number of Hollywood celebrities' names turned up on these spurious purchases made with counterfeit credit cards.

Members of the Israeli gangs have found an excellent way to profit from drug trafficking. They launder money through the Diamond District businesses in New York. They also recruit leaders of Jewish religious institutions on both the East and West Coast to work money laundering scams with them. One Satmar rabbi, Abraham Low, charged a 30 percent fee on all the money he laundered through the Mogen Abraham Synagogue in Los Angeles. He openly bragged to an undercover FBI agent that he could launder approximately $5 million a week through a network of Charitable Satmar organizations throughout the United States and Europe. In another case, Joseph Krozer bragged that he was involved in a business that processed more than $300,000 in drug money on a daily basis. A DEA surveillance team followed Krozer to the offices of Ahron Sharir, a New York City gold manufacturer and an Israeli underworld figure, where Krozer picked up bags of cash and then delivered them to Congregation Chesed and Tsedeka, a schteebel (little place of worship) in Brooklyn. This group turned out to be one of the largest money laundering operations for the Colombian drug cartels in the United States. Federal prosecutors estimated that this group laundered over $3 billion for the Medellin drug cartels. One of the largest money laundering schemes involved Israeli organized crime member David Vanounou. He recruited Mendell Goldberger who set up a money laundering operation through the Mesivta Tifereth Jerusalem, one of the oldest Yeshivas in New York City, for Colombian drug traffickers. A total of $23 million was laundered through this Yeshiva. Ultimately, six different business firms and nine people, including Rabbi Yisrael Eidelman, the executive vice president of Mesivta, were convicted of various tax evasion infractions (Ross and Gonzalez, 1994c). These operations were set in place by Israeli gang members who shared the profits from the money laundering ventures equally with the participating religious institutions.

Federal officials were ultimately able to break up these Israeli organized crime money laundering rings and arrest the participants. One active member of a money laundering ring was Diamond District business owner and mob figure Ahron Sharir. Sharir set up one of the largest money laundering businesses in the world for members of Colombian drug cartels. Some of the methods included:

1. Direct deposit of monies into various banks as if the money had been a profit from his jewelry business.

2. Purchase of airplanes as an investment; these planes would eventually be used to ship drugs by the Colombian cartels.

3. Procurement of gold at inflated prices, which was sold to other associates in this conspiracy at a cheaper price.

4. Wire transfer of money throughout the world under the guise of business deals.

5. Exchange of cash for legitimate checks that were from the bank accounts of either other businesses or religious institutions (Ross and Gonzalez, 1994b).

The Israeli gangs have broadened their occupational environments and increased profits by participating in other unlawful activities.

1. Insurance fraud in which gang members operate businesses and report staged larcenies and burglaries to local law enforcement agencies in order to bilk an insurance company of money. The operator of the business purchases large quantities of the items the retail store is going to sell and then transfers the products to another location and reports the property stolen. Some store owners remove the property from the store and just burn the store to obtain insurance reimbursement.

2. Use of bogus identification to obtain large quantities of retail items, televisions, cameras, and video recorders. This equipment is picked up and taken to a storehouse owned by gang members. The supplier submits the bill to the credit card company or the check to the bank and finds out all the information, checks, or credit card slips are phony.

3. A business is set up by the gang members along with a business credit line. Payments are then made on small orders for about a three-month period. Once the company has established a good credit line the owners purchase large quantities of merchandise on the business' credit line. The newly purchased merchandise is moved to a different location and the company files bankruptcy.

4. Counterfeiting U.S. currency by both U.S.- and Israel-based members of Israeli organized crime. The gang members arrested had immigrated from Russia to Israel and had set up three counterfeiting money shops in Israel and one in Clifton, New Jersey.

## Russian-Israeli Relationship

At times it is difficult to estimate which gang made an appearance on the American scene first. Israeli gangs may have been working their scams in Los Angeles a short time prior to the arrival of the Russian gangs on U.S. shores. Some researchers actually contradict this theory by announcing that the Russian and Israeli gangs are the same, but the following factors seem to indicate that is not so.

1. Only recently members of the Russian Mafia started moving large amounts of money into the economy of Israel because of Israel's liberal money transfer policy. Four billion dollars had been transferred as of June 1995, which coincides with the mass immigration of Russians into Israel, approximately 35 percent of whom are not of the Jewish faith. Of the monies invested in Israel $2.5 billion has been placed in Israeli banks, while the other $1.5 billion was used to purchase land in the Tel Aviv area of Israel (Linzer, 1995; Agence France Presse, 1995).

2. Members of Russian organized crime have worked scams against the Israeli government. The Russians have prepared counterfeit Israeli immigration documents so that Russian immigrant gang members can enter Israel and receive the same benefits as a legitimate Jewish immigrant to Israel. Included in this package is a six-month grant, money to buy appliances, free medical insurance coverage, partial payment of rental fees, and "mashkanta" or a mortgage loan. Russian gang members set up these newly immigrated families so they can purchase apartments in Israel using the "mashkanta" fundings. The mortgage loan along with a bribe or threat of injury or death is supplied by a gang member, which most certainly helps with the quick acquisition of the apartment for the gang member. Once the apartment is officially owned by the gang member it is put

on the market at double the price and, in most cases, quickly sold for a large profit that is usually $50,000 to $100,000 (Polyak, 1994).

3. Russian gangs control 80 percent of the sex industry in Israel by using counterfeit documents to import prostitutes from the CIS (Walker, 1995).

4. Many of the original Brighton Beach gang members are ethnically Russian with a background in the Jewish religion.

5. Russian and Israeli gang members set up and ran the original gasoline tax scams during the early 1980s.

The information in the preceding list seems to indicate some type of a relationship between Russian and Israeli organized crime groups. Major connections have been made within the similar type of scams that both groups perpetrate against other Russians, Israelis, or the U.S. government. However, Israeli gangs have become deeply involved in money laundering and lightly involved in scams and drug trafficking; whereas Russian gangs have remained actively involved in crimes such as robbery, extortion, fraud, and drug trafficking. Several aspects point to a close relationship between these groups. One factor concerns how the Russian gangs had the ability to move all that money in and out of Israel. Another issue questions how the Russians could have such great knowledge of the social services system in Israeli that they were able to scam the government and take control of the sex industry without the assistance of the Israeli groups. A possibility does exist that the Israeli and Russian gangs could be the same, but at this juncture their differences make it truly doubtful. Yet these two groups will undoubtedly continue to work together right into the next century as long as they can both profit from the scams with which they are involved.

# 13

# Other Worldwide Organized Crime Groups

This chapter discusses the organizational characteristics and activities of what are to be considered smaller and somewhat unheralded—at least outside their own region or place of operations—ethnic organized crime groups throughout the world. Although many of these groups are interconnected with other criminal organizations, few of them are as well structured or run as effectively as La Cosa Nostra. Yet, all of these gangs are in the business of making as much money as possible for their leaders as well as the organization. The reader will see that some of these gangs, even though they are of the same ethnic background as other groups in the same area or country, have different agendas. One ethnic gang may be involved in murder, robbery, and drug trafficking, while another ethnic gang from the same country is involved in scams and terrorism. The use of fraud to support terrorism was demonstrated in a year-long inquiry conducted by investigative reporters of the television news show *West 57th*. This examination enlightened viewers about a loosely knit ethnic organized crime group, which will be discussed in the section on Palestinian gangs (*CBS News*, 1989).

## THIRD WORLD GROUPS

### Palestinian Groups

A Palestinian group that has received a good deal of attention throughout the United States over the past decade is the Deir Dibwan criminal organization. They are composed of a small group of citizens from the village of

Deir Dibwan on the West Bank in Israel. Members of this gang first came to the attention of law enforcement officials in the mid 1980s when the investigative television program *West 57th* did a segment on their criminal activities. This investigative program indicated that the members of the Deir Dibwan group work as an organized crime network involved in numerous unlawful business scams. Law enforcement sources believe a large portion of the money that is illegally obtained by this group is used to fund terrorist activities of the Palestinian Liberation Organization (PLO). Members of this criminal organization usually travel throughout the Arab world and the United States setting up their unlawful operations (*CBS News*, 1989).

During the 1980s stores were rented and legitimate businesses, either clothing or appliance shops, were opened throughout the West Coast of the United States. Some of the first "bust-out" operations by this Palestinian group appeared in eastern Washington state. These businesses were legitimately purchased by a gang member who then proceeded to stock the stores with products that were paid for within a short period of time after their purchase. Once group members were able to stabilize the business operations and show a profit they immediately ordered extensive amounts of merchandise that they were selling at these stores. The goods were purchased on the store's credit line, which was built up by paying for acquisitions on time. Upon delivery of the merchandise it was immediately transported to another was location to be either hidden or disposed of as quickly as possible. In most cases, the merchandise was sold off at anywhere from cost to 50 percent cheaper than cost. After a short time bills were received by the purchaser who claimed that the bills could not be paid because the items were no longer in his possession. The purchaser also claimed that due to other outstanding circumstances he no longer had any assets to assist him in paying this liability and he immediately filed for bankruptcy. The owner of the business then declared that either the money was lost gambling, the property was taken during the commission of a burglary, or the books and records were either misplaced or taken by a burglar. In cases in which the business owners presented either a gambling or burglary excuse, a purported bankrupt victim or a bankruptcy court investigator had little or no means to actually verify the claimed gambling losses. This inability to verify the claims was also true in the theft of money or property during the commission of a crime. For this reason, bankruptcy courts in some cases will not accept the bankruptcy claim (L. Williams, 1989).

Through these scams, the Deir Dibwan group found a way to ensure themselves profit for the PLO. Although the first three gang members to pull this scam off successfully were allowed to claim bankruptcy, which was accepted by the courts, the last five claims were not accepted. This result gives the creditors the opportunity to continue in their pursuit of the amount owed them until some or all of it is paid. The gang member or scammer either leaves the United States and returns to Deir Dibwan or adopts a new identity. Most members of the Deir Dibwan gangs are highly mobile and capable of traveling to any destination in the United States or Canada in order to set up a new business bust-out scam (L. Williams, 1989).

Another scheme instituted by a member of a Palestinian group involves the use of stolen telephone access codes. Telephone toll codes are accessed by Palestinian organized crime groups in several ways:

1. A search of businesses' dumpsters in an effort to locate telecommunication print-outs.

2. Shoulder surfing, which involves the theft of a phone code by watching a code subscriber input his or her credit card calling number at a pay phone.

3. Getting access to the codes by having office cleaning staff search desk tops, drawers, or trash containers for company or customer codes.

4. From pickpockets who obtain codes from stolen identifications.

5. From employees of telecommunication companies.

6. Through computer hackers who are paid by gang members to target a company's 800 number. Once the hacker has broken the security code through a computer modem and has programmed the computer to automatically dial numbers continuously until the computer locates and identifies the proper number grouping sequence, the hacker can then break into the private branch exchange (PBX). When the hacker has obtained this 800 number a second dial tone allows the hacker, gang member, or purchaser of the phone line time to make calls to anywhere in the world. The hacker will then give the access code(s) to a gang member who will sell the long distance lines to other illegal immigrants (Holmes, 1994; Mallory, 1994).

7. From cellular phones by using a scanner with special software that can be used along streets, parkways, expressways, and roadway overpasses in order to intercept the identification numbers from cellular phones in passing vehicles. Numbers obtained in this manner are then placed into a computer and transferred to another phone. It takes about five minutes to complete this procedure. The cloned phones use the identification numbers stolen from the authorized consumer whose account is ultimately billed for this illegal use (James, 1994).

The diverse illegal tactics just described led to losses of more than $1.8 billion for corporations throughout the world in 1993. Originally, the scheme was initiated by a scam artist named Frank Fahmi Amigo, a U.S. citizen of Palestinian ancestry. When this scam was uncovered by investigators from telephone company security and law enforcement they named it the "Amigo Scam" after Frank Fahmi Amigo. Fahmi Amigo was ultimately arrested, tried, convicted, and sentenced in August 1992 to 52 months in prison for setting up and perpetrating telephone swindles. In fact, in 1992 it was estimated that members of Palestinian and Jordanian organized crime groups in an average year swindled worldwide telephone service companies out of approximately $40 million (Lawlor, 1993; Holmes, 1994). Palestinian gangs continue to use workers to run these various telephone scams because they have become big money makers for these groups. It is what gang members call easy money that can be quickly reinvested in drug operations or other money-making schemes.

A second type of Palestinian gang is found on the West Bank in Israel. These gangs are similar to street gangs that operate in most major urban areas of the United States. Most of the gang members range in age from 12–30 years; older members are the gang leaders. Most members are armed and present a considerable threat to honest Palestinian and Israeli citizens on the West Bank.

Two major West Bank gangs are the Black Panther Brigades and the Red Eagles. Both of these gangs base their operations out of the West Bank town of Nablus. The Red Eagles was formed and is supported by the Popular Front for the Liberation of Palestine (PFLP). They are an extremist PLO faction that conducts most of its operations from a Syrian base and is totally opposed to any type of peaceful agreement or negotiations with Israel. The Black Panther's gang is affiliated with and supported by Yasser Arafat's Al-Fatah wing of the Palestinian Liberation Organization. Originally, these gangs were used to eliminate Palestinians who collaborated with the Israeli government. What happened was the PLO and the PFLP let the leadership of these groups get completely out of control. They killed anyone they thought was collaborating with the Israeli government and members of the Israeli police or military who got in their way. This indiscriminate killing resulted in an intervention campaign by the Israeli government that led to the killings of the leaders of both the Black Panther's and Red Eagles' gangs. In the first incident, Ayman Arruzeh, the boss of the Red Eagles gang, was shot and killed by Israeli soldiers after he had killed an alleged Israeli collaborator with an ax. Several weeks later members of the Israeli military, disguised as Arabs, killed Imad Annaser, the anointed leader of the Black Panther organized crime gang, during a shoot out in a Nablus barber shop (*Los Angeles Times*, 1989).

These killings slowed both gangs' criminal activities during the latter part of 1989. In early March 1990 gang activity picked up with a sharp increase in the number of robberies of jewelry exchanges in Nablus. Assets gained from these types of robberies supported unlawful gang activities against the Israeli government. Membership in the Black Panther's gang has increased to well over 300 since early 1990. This loosely organized criminal gang has also expanded its illegal activities to include extortion, kidnapping, and drug dealing. In fact, this gang went as far as to kidnap an Israeli soldier and kill him five days later during the Israeli/PLO peace talks in October 1994 (*Bergen Record,* 1994).

Although the Israeli military has attempted to crack down on these "street gangs," most of its actions have met with only a temporary decrease in gang activity. Usually within a short time after the strict enforcement policy is lifted, a sharp increase in the number of new members to older gangs and the creation of new gangs occur. As the number of gangs increases, so does the number of crimes being committed on the West Bank. The Israeli government seems hopeful that the recent peace agreement that affords the Palestinians the right to police their own territories will cause a decrease in the number of criminal activities and violence involving these street gangs.

## Syrian Groups

Although a great deal of information related to Syrian gangs is conjecture, a number of Syrian organized gangs are operating throughout the Middle East and most of them are involved in drug smuggling. DEA intelligence reports indicate that 25–35 percent of all the heroin imported into the United States is grown in the Syrian controlled Bekka Valley in Lebanon. In 1989 it was estimated that Lebanon's drug crop produced more than $600 million in profits for Syrian drug lords. Estimates in 1992 put the Syrian drug profit figure at more than $2 billion. Escalating drug trafficking occurred when members of Syrian drug gangs recruited Turkish and Iranian agricultural experts to help the Syrians convert the hashish drug crop to a heroin drug crop in 1986. These experts also convinced the Syrians to institute a crop rotation that would produce at least two drug harvests per year. This method would increase the total heroin crop in the Bekka Valley so that the drugs would be grown on 90 percent of the land instead of 10 percent of the land. According to published reports the recommendations by the Turkish and Iranian drug agriculturists were put into action when Rifaat Assad, brother of the president, and Mossar al-Kassar, a major Syrian drug trafficker, took control of drug production in the Bekka Valley in the mid 1980s. During this same time period the Syrian military was placed in charge of the security there (Builta, 1994; Widlanski, 1992; Rowan, 1992).

Syrian gang members then made connections with other members of ethnic Syrian gangs in South America, specifically Colombia. Coca base was shipped from locations in South America to locations in both Syria and Lebanon where the cocaine is refined, packaged, and shipped to both Europe and the United States. Syrian drug lords have an easy outlet for their heroin and cocaine in the United States through gang members already in place within the Syrian and Lebanese communities in and around Detroit, Michigan (Widlanski, 1992).

Some evidence indicates that the Syrian government has used the money derived from drug trafficking to support its participation in terrorist activities. An article by Michael Widlanski claims that the Syrian government, its leader, Hafez al-Assad, and the military are connected to the drug lords. Information gathered by Widlanski indicates that every member of the Syrian military receives some type of salary enhancement from the profits accumulated by the Syrian/Lebanese drug traffickers (1992).

An article in *Time* in 1992 goes as far as to make the connection between the terrorist bombing of Pan Am flight 103 over Lockerbie, Scotland, and a Syrian drug gang boss named Monzer al-Kassar. Kassar is connected to the Syrian government through his brother-in-law, Ali Issa Duba, Syrian Intelligence Chief, and President Assad, who is a blood relative of Kassar's wife. This article further states that that the U.S. Central Intelligence Agency (CIA) allowed Kassar to legally operate his drug trafficking business in exchange for his assistance in gaining the liberation of the U.S. hostages being held by terrorists in Lebanon. The DEA was also using Kassar's drug trafficking business in a sting operation targeted at persons participating in this drug conspiracy, usually other Lebanese or Syrian nationals, in the United States. According to a report from Mossad, an Israeli organization that gathers intelligence information related to terrorism and terrorist groups, Kassar was connected to Ahmed Jabril, leader of the Popular Front for the Liberation of Palestine–General Command (PFLP-GC). This group allegedly receives financial support from the Syrian drug enterprises. Jabril set up a meeting with Kassar in a Paris restaurant in 1988, and Kassar assured Jabril of his support for the terrorist attack on a U.S. airline. Kassar did notify the CIA of the intent of the PFLP-GC sometime in mid-December 1988, but it did not help because Pan Am 103 exploded in the air over Lockerbie, Scotland, on December 21, 1988, killing all the passengers and crew members (Rowan, 1992).

A member of the U.S. Military Defense Intelligence Agency (DIA), Charles McKee, along with the CIA's deputy station chief in Beirut, Matthew Gannon, were aboard Pan Am flight 103. They were en route to CIA headquarters in Virginia to condemn the CIA's association with Syrian drug trafficker Kassar. An investigation conducted by McKee and Gannon had discovered not only that Kassar was a major Syrian drug dealer but also that he was closely connected to Jabril and his PFLP-GC terrorist gang. The threat that Kassar presented to these two government agents was his terrorist connections to Jabril, for the two agents were in the process of setting up a plan to free the American hostages held in Lebanon. Kassar, in turn, fearing that without U.S. support his drug operations would be shut down once these agents reached Virginia, continued his support of the terrorist activities related to the bombing of Pan Am 103 (Rowan, 1992).

No matter how anyone views this information, it is disparaging enough to indicate a definite connection between the Syrian drug gangs, the Syrian government, and terrorist groups based outside of Syria. As previously stated in this book, numerous types of gangs participate in a variety of gang activities. The Syrian gangs, like some of the other gangs that will be described in this chapter, can be placed in the same category as the Cuban communist mafia that is controlled by the Castro government in Cuba. All these organized criminal groups participate in drug trafficking to both embellish their own assets as well as to support terrorist activities in an attempt to overthrow other governments, increase the power of their leaders, or just get even with another nation.

## Turkish Groups

When one discusses Turkish gangs the one group that comes to mind is the Kurdistan Workers Party, better known as the PKK. Originally instituted as a radical group for the overthrow of the Turkish government, this group has become known as a highly violent drug gang that thinks nothing of taking over small villages in eastern Turkey to extort money from local businesses. They also torture villagers who do not agree with their radical philosophy. Initiation of this gang began in 1974 in Ankara, Turkey, when a meager band of fanatics associated with a Turkish revolutionary youth group decided to start their own gang. The founder of this group, Ocalan, was eventually appointed the leader of the gang and, with the support of the other members, formed the Kurdistan Workers Party—Partiya Karkeren Kurdistan (PKK)—in 1978. This gang's motto since its inception has been that people who disagree with their fanatical logic are their enemies. In order to understand the systematic views of this group one must understand that their tactics include the wanton murders of all members of society who oppose their ideals. Some of their heinous crimes involved the killing of school teachers in front of a classroom of children as well as the murdering of women and children to maintain control over a village. The levels of violence involving the PKK gang members are more easily understood through reviewing the figures in Table 13-1.

Until the late 1980s, most of the funding for this gang was obtained through extortion, arms smuggling, smuggling of workers, or robbery. Gang leaders soon discovered the money that could be easily made in drug trafficking. Drug operations into eastern Turkey were quickly set up, and PKK members started importing drugs from both Southwest and Southeast Asia. Most of the drugs processed in Turkey come from Southwest Asia—Pakistan and Iran. In most cases, after the arrival of the morphine-based drugs in Turkey, gang members process the morphine into heroin in makeshift labs set up by the gang. Once this process is completed the heroin is shipped to either Europe or the United States.

Since 1990, arrests of members of the PKK have become more prevalent throughout Europe. In Germany, members of the PKK use juveniles to transport and sell drugs in most major urban centers. Hamburg police arrested children between the ages of 10 and 12 years for drug sales, and an eight-year-old for possession of a loaded firearm and drug sales. Police in Wandsbeck arrested 14- and 16-year-old youths for participating in drug trafficking. All these children had been transported to Germany from eastern Turkey by members of the PKK gang. Other members of the PKK have taken over drug trafficking activities in the German cities of Hamburg, Frankfort, Essen, and Bremen. German narcotics police reported in October 1994 that PKK members transferred 15 million Deutsch marks from Germany to their gang leaders in eastern Turkey. German police statistics further indicate that in 1991, 400 of 735 drug sale arrests involved PKK members. In 1992 of 735 drug sale arrests 450 were PKK members, and in 1993 the total PKK members arrested

**TABLE 13-1**   Killings Performed by the PKK

| Year | Terrorist | Civilian | Soldier | Police | Villager |
|------|-----------|----------|---------|--------|----------|
| 1984 | 11 | 20 | 24 | 0 | 0 |
| 1986 | 64 | 74 | 40 | 3 | 0 |
| 1989 | 165 | 136 | 111 | 8 | 34 |
| 1991 | 356 | 170 | 213 | 20 | 41 |
| 1993 | 1699 | 1218 | 487 | 28 | 156 |
| 1994 | 4114 | 1082 | 794 | 43 | 265 |
| 1995* | 2292 | 1085 | 450 | 47 | 87 |
| Total | 8701 | 3785 | 2119 | 149 | 583 |

*Figures for the first 6 months.
*Source:* Internet, 1995.

for drug sales was 300 of 457. Then in November 1993 a drug courier, Sengul Karacan, was apprehended in Caracas, Venezuela, carrying 3.5 kilograms of cocaine. During interrogation by Venezuelan police Karacan confessed that she was a courier for the PKK (Internet, 1995).

Turkish police investigators working with DEA agents seized the Panamanian registered ship, the *Lucky S,* in January 1993 and found 2.7 tons of morphine base hidden in the anchor chain storage area of this 200-foot boat. It was the fourth morphine base seizure by police in a two-month timeframe with a total of 7.5 tons of morphine base seized by drug authorities. Turkish police suggested that evidence from these seizures indicates a much closer connection than originally anticipated between the Turkish drug mafia and the PKK gangs in eastern Turkey within the drug smuggling market (Cowell, 1993).

The *Lucky S* seizure led to the arrest of Necat Des, the leader of the Des drug gang, and Derya Ayanoglu, part owner of this vessel, for drug smuggling. A leader of another major Turkish drug gang, Huseyn Baybasin, has been in hiding in eastern Turkey since the seizure of the *Lucky S.* Police have been able to establish direct connections between leaders of the Des and Baybasin drug gangs and the leaders of the PKK in the drug trafficking business (Cowell, 1993).

In an effort to destroy the PKK drug operations, the Turkish police and military initiated raids on PKK bases in eastern Turkey and northern Iraq. Knowing that PKK gangs had been conducting drug trading operations in Zaho, Iraq, the Turkish government decided to conduct some police/ military drug seizure maneuvers in that area. In fact during raids into PKK-controlled villages in eastern Iraq, the police and military authorities uncovered a cannabis cultivation center and farm located in the PKK's Pirvela Camp in the Bahara Valley of northern Iraq. A total of 4.5 tons of cannabis plants and hashish were seized by the Turkish police and military during this raid.

The expansion of the Turkish mafia's drug trafficking activities became even more prevalent in 1994 when an undercover member of the DEA purchased 23 kilograms of pure heroin from Seref Karanisoglu, a notorious Turkish drug trafficker. In an effort to eradicate both the Turkish mafia and the PKK drug rings the Turkish government has signed agreements to set up drug task forces to destroy PKK drug trafficking activities. These activities are the main monetary resource for this Turkish terrorist and drug gang. The Turkish government already has an agreement with the DEA and recently set up the same type of arrangement with the Israeli government (Reuters, 1994; Onishi, 1994).

## Lebanese Groups

In most cases, Arab gangs operate within their own countries except for the drug gangs. Lebanese drug gang members were arrested in Israel for smuggling more than a quarter of a ton of heroin with an estimated value of U.S. $21 million into Israel during the early 1990s. Police in Israel conducted a two-and-one-half-year investigation into these drug gangs. As a result of this inquiry, members of six different Lebanese gangs were arrested throughout Israel including members of two Bedouin gangs from southern Israel. This drug operation was originally set up by two Lebanese brothers who made sure that sufficient amounts of heroin were available at all times to supply most areas of Israel. Ramsi and Mufid Nahara had been previously arrested by the Israeli police for their participation in a hashish smuggling ring. The gang bosses, Itab Tuba and Shawki Latiff, owned a contracting company on the outskirts of the village of Rama in Galilee (Rudge, 1992).

## Iraqi Groups

During the later part of 1994 Lebanese police seized three members of an Iraqi gang who were involved in counterfeiting currency. When apprehended in the village of Ajaltoun on the outskirts of Beirut, Lebanon, the gang members had counterfeiting equipment and money in their possession. Law enforcement sources in Lebanon estimate that the gang members had produced well over 162 million Lebanese pounds, most in denominations of 50,000 and 100,000. A number of forged samples of other foreign paper money including Turkish liras, United Arab Emirates dirhams, and Kuwaiti dinars were also found. This gang of forgers did not stop with Arab currency; in their possession they discovered forged Swiss franks and German marks. Lebanese government officials roughly estimated that the forgers had placed about 45 million pounds of Lebanese currency in circulation prior to their apprehension (Reuters, 1994).

## United Arab Emirates Groups

The government of the United Arab Emirates recently faced its first problems with gangs when ten members of a local motorbike gang killed a night-security guard for no apparent reason. Apparently, the ten members of the gang, six of them born and raised in the United Arab Emirates, three Iranian nationals, and one Yemeni, were sniffing glue just prior to the savage attack on the security guard. Gang members between 15 and 18 years old first attacked the guard at a municipal car pound in the town of Sharjah. After being struck on the head with an iron bar the guard ran inside a building and bolted the door but the gang members proceeded to demolish everything in their way until they gained entrance into the room where the guard was hiding. Once the gang members entered the room, they proceeded to beat the security officer to death with sticks, bats, and iron bars. Prior to leaving the crime scene the gang members stole five motorbikes that had been taken from them during a previous confrontation with the police (Reuters, 1994). Prior to this episode the only gang activity in the United Arab Emirates involved drug gangs. These gangs in each case were made up of Pakistani nationals who found it easier and faster to smuggle drugs, heroin or hashish, through the United Arab Emirates en route to Europe.

## Iranian Groups

The Iranian government in 1989 passed strict drug laws that stipulated that any drug trafficker apprehended with 30 or more grams (1 ounce) of heroin or 5 kilograms (11 pounds) of opium would be sentenced to death. Once these laws were put in place, the government anticipated that the drug trafficking by Iranian gangs would cease, but it has not. More than 2,500 drug traffickers were hung between 1989 and 1994. Drug arrests have continued to increase steadily since the inception of the new laws, as has the quantity of heroin seized by Iranian police, with over half of the Iranian prison population serving time for drug infractions. Major General Reza Seifollahi, the chief of the Iranian law enforcement, stated that 14,612 narcotics traffickers and 43,464 drug addicts were arrested in Iran between April 1993 and February 1994. Seifollahi further stated that the police had seized more than 175,000 pounds of heroin (Agence France Presse, 1994).

The drug smuggling activities of these Iranian drug gangs continue even though the Iranian government has instituted a strict enforcement policy. This policy, however, has been less than effective. Some examples of the continuing activities of the drug traffickers in Iran indicate that as strict as enforcement is in Iran the drug gangs' trafficking businesses seem to be prosperous. On November 13, 1994, Iranian police arrested 89 members of an Iranian drug gang and seized more than 191 kilograms of heroin. In another instance on March 28, 1995, the Iranian police seized 2,058 kilograms of heroin and killed 20 members of an Iranian drug smuggling gang (Deutsche Presse-Agentur, 1994; Xinhus News Agency, 1995). Between March 1993 and February 1994 a total of 68 tons of drugs was seized by the police. Also between March 1994 and February 1995 the Iranian police seized more than 135 tons of drugs (Reuters, 1994). These statistics certainly seem to indicate that the tough drug laws are not a hindrance to most drug gangs.

Iranian drug gangs such as the Kamrani-Bameri are connected to drug growers in Afghanistan and Pakistan who can supply them with large quantities of both heroin and opium. They usually have 20–150 members who are well armed and distribute large amounts of heroin daily. The Kamrani-Bameri gang actually distributes more than 100 kilograms of opium a day. Drug gangs in Iran in many cases will kidnap local villagers, male and female, and force them to become slaves for the gang. The Kamrani-Bameri gang had 200 male and 300 female slaves when trapped by the Iranian military and police. Some of these slaves are ultimately sold back to their families while others are used to transport the drugs, carry weapons, clean the animals, or for forcible sex. Most of these gangs use camels as their transportation (Deutsche Presse-Agentur, 1994).

Most drug trafficking in Iran is confined to the Baluchins. A total of 1.5 million members of the Baluchin tribe live in Iran, and are Sunni Muslims, unlike most Iranis who are Shiite Muslims. Many members of the Baluchin tribe are involved as leaders and members of the Iran drug gangs. In fact, Baluchins who participate in the highly profitable drug trafficking business receive the blessing of the Baluchi clergy, who claim that Baluchins have a divine right to form drug gangs and participate in the drug trafficking business (Ghazi, 1991).

## Pakistani Groups

The involvement of Pakistani nationals in drug trafficking gangs has increased tenfold since the early 1970s. Customs officials in airports in New York, Houston, Newark, Miami, Chicago, Boston, Atlanta, San Francisco, Seattle, and Los Angeles as well as Canadian airports in Montreal, Vancouver, and Toronto have seized Pakistani gang members attempting to smuggle heroin into these cities. In most cases, the heroin is concealed in suitcases or briefcases that have either false sides or a false bottom, sewn into suits or jackets, or secreted in hollowed out items such as candle sticks or furniture legs. Heroin that gets past the customs officials is then given to a member of the Pakistani gang who is either a registered alien or naturalized U.S. or Canadian citizen.

Drug couriers leaving Pakistan for North American cities seldom carry the concealed drugs onto the plane with them. Most couriers pass through customs in Pakistan prior to being informed of the location of the heroin. Once the drug transporter reaches the departure area of the airport he is either handed a claim check for luggage that contains the heroin or given a carry-on item that holds the secreted drugs. Pakistani drug gangs usually place a member who is known as a controller on all planes that contain drug carriers to ensure the integrity of the courier. Once the plane arrives at the designated destination and the drug courier passes through customs one of two things will happen: first either the courier will pass the heroin onto the controller who then arranges to deliver the heroin to its final destination; or second, the courier will follow the instructions given to him that require him to register at a specifically chosen hotel and then call Pakistan for instructions on how to make the delivery to the purchaser (DEA, 1987).

An example of the drug gang smuggling operation took place in 1991 when U.S. drug agents seized 3 kilograms of pure heroin imported from Pakistan. They arrested Guiseppe DiFranco of New York City, the buyer and ultimate dispenser of the heroin on the streets of New York; Khalillullah Kakur, a native of Afghanistan and a resident of California, an associate gang member who received the heroin after its arrival in the United States; and Parvis Khan, a Pakistani sheep herder, who was the drug mule. Khan had arrived at JFK International Airport on Monday, November 4, 1991, and then proceeded to a Hauppauge hotel. He was joined at the hotel by Kakur on Tuesday, November 5, 1991. Kakur then proceeded to the Kew Motor Inn in Kew Gardens, Queens, where he held a meeting with DiFranco. Once the deal was consummated on Wednesday, November 6, 1991, federal drug agents moved in and arrested all three participants. Khan and Kakur were arrested in the Hauppauge hotel where the three kilos of heroin was recovered along with the $25,000 fee that Khan had received for smuggling the heroin into the United States. DiFranco was apprehended in his Brooklyn restaurant (Kessler, 1991).

In an effort to crack down on drug and kidnapping activities of organized crime groups in the southern province of Sindh, which is on the outskirts of Karachi, the Pakistani government, on June 19, 1992, staged raids on all locations that were known to be frequented by members of these criminal organizations. The police, with military assistance, conducted house-to-house searches in an effort to confiscate drugs and weapons that were hidden by local gang members. During this same time period, the Sindh province was experiencing an ongoing conflict between past and present members of the Mohajir Qaumi group over control of this gang's criminal activities. Police and military personnel in Sindh province suddenly found themselves in the midst of an all-out gang war. Within a short period of time this conflict spread into Karachi where the police dodged bullets being exchanged between opposing factions of the Mohajir Qaumi group. It took until Sunday, June 21, 1992, for the police and military to finally squelch fighting and subdue the rebellious gangs. Once peace was restored to this area the police announced that 10 people had been killed during the skirmishes and more than 700 gang members had been arrested by the police. Ruling government officials in Sindh were removed by Pakistani president Ghulam Ishaq Khan because of their inability to suppress gang activities in the province (Iqbal, 1992).

Problems with drug gangs in Sindh province are only one example of the Pakistanis' inability to control gang activities. A CIA report dated February 1993 indicates that Pakistani drug gangs have supplied funding to elect many of the past and present government leaders in Pakistan. Drug money is used to buy votes throughout the country, which in turn helps the drug gangs win seats in the Pakistani National Assembly. This money has even given drug gang leaders access to both the prime minister and president of Pakistan. One of the leading Pakistani drug gang leaders, Sohail Zia Butt, is the brother-in-law of Nawaz Sharif, the prime minister of Pakistan. One must remember the importance of a marital relationship in Pakistan. According to Pakistani custom, marriages are actually affiliations that in many cases are made in order to combine both prosperity and power. Since the Sharif and Butt alliance, both families have prospered to the extent that Sharif is now the prime minister, and Butt, a notorious heroin trafficker and influential multimillionaire, is protected from arrest and imprisonment by his family's political and monetary associations. Much of the prosperity has spilled over to other members of the Butt family. Aslam Butt has become the emissary to other drug trafficking groups. Haji Iqbal Butt, also a major part of the Butt narcotics trafficking gang, has become an effective and important advisor to Prime Minister Sharif (Royce, 1993).

The Butt family is not the only drug trafficking gang with connections in the Pakistani government. According to CIA documents Malik Mohammed Ayub Khan Afridi, also known as Haji Ayub Zakha Khel, the number one drug trafficker in Pakistan, has used his drug money to "buy" an elected seat in the National Assembly. Khel who is known as the "King of Khybur Heroin" has gained a great deal of influence throughout the Pakistani government. Through the use of corrupt methods Khel has gained direct access to the president of Pakistan, Ghulam Ishaq Khan, leaders of the ruling political party, as well as the high-ranking members of Pakistani military intelligence. Khel has compiled most of these benefits by spending large amounts of money to entertain as well as to support the reelection campaigns of high-ranking Pakistani politicians. Some previous government officials including former Prime Minister Benazir Bhutto, in an effort to take away Khel's power, had warrants issued for his arrest on drug trafficking charges, but Khel evaded arrest by remaining out of sight. Once the government of Bhutto was removed from office, Khel had members of the new government suppress these arrest warrants (Royce, 1993).

A 1993 CIA report indicated that one of the few Pakistani leaders who was not entangled in any of the Pakistani drug conspiracies was former dictator Zia ul-Haq who was killed when his plane exploded in 1988. Yet some of his associates, including the pilots of the presidential plane, were identified as coconspirators in a drug smuggling operation. CIA sources indicate that a large amount of drug money is used by the InterServices Intelligence Directorate (ISI) to support either Sikh radicals in India or Mashmiri revolutionaries in Kashmir. One drug gang controlled by Chaudhury Shaukat Ali Bhatti supplies large amounts of money to the Sikh revolutionaries to buy weapons. In return, the Sikh militants guarantee that the transportation of heroin across the Pakistani border into India is done without any interference from either other rebel groups or other drug gangs (Royce, 1993).

Similarities in religious laws related to opium cultivation, heroin production, and drug gangs within the Pakistani Muslim hierarchy is similar to that of Baluchin Muslims in Iran. The Koran, the Islamic bible, forbids the use of narcotics. It is noted that devout Muslim savants in the heroin production locations in Pakistan have declared that under Muslim law it is legally right to both grow poppies and produce heroin. What the religious leaders did was create a "fatwah" or legal doctrine that justifies the tillage of the soil to produce opium as long as the by-product, heroin, is not to be sold to or used by the Muslim drug addicts. This position is almost the same stance taken by the Islamic Shiite religious leaders in Iran and leads one to believe that the so-called fanatical Islamic religious leaders feel that violations of Islamic religious laws can only be committed against Muslims, and nothing is wrong with selling heroin to members of other ethnic and religious groups. This point is noteworthy only because most Muslim religious sects consider the Islamic religion to be the only pure and true religion on earth. In reality, what type of religion could justify drug gangs, violence, and drug trafficking?

Pakistani drug gangs have been operating since the late 1970s but the amounts of drugs being smuggled out of both Afghanistan and Pakistan have risen dramatically since the late 1980s. Opium production in Afghanistan for example has increased extensively since the Soviet military left in 1989. Pakistani heroin-producing labs process 70–80 metric tons of opium yearly. This heroin is then shipped to either a European or U.S. market.

Three major drug gangs operate out of Pakistan. The first gang is based out of the Lahore area of Pakistan and is known as the Haji Baig group. This gang has to be considered a loose coalition of major drug gangs that prospers in spite of the fact that the three major leaders were imprisoned in Pakistan on drug charges and that the U.S. government is involved in extradition proceedings against them. The first of the three leaders of this consortium is

Haji Mirza Iqbal Baig, who has amassed over $20 million in assets both legally and illegally over the past 30 years. Anwar Khan Khattak, the second member of this drug gang, is the mastermind behind the transshipment of the heroin from Lahore to Karachi and then by sea or air to either Europe or the United States. The third member of this coalition is Tariq Waheed Butt, who has provided the alliance with both a European and U.S. market for their drugs (Witkin and Griffin, 1994). In an effort to show that the Pakistan government is cooperating with the U.S. effort to prosecute foreign drug gang leaders, both Baig and Khattak were extradited to the United States in April 1995.

A drug gang leader who was at one time a member of Pakistan's National Assembly, Haji Ayub Afridi, has become possibly the mightiest drug lord in Pakistan. Afridi over the past decade has built his own drug barony 35 miles outside of Peshawar. Afridi's compound is surrounded by 20-foot walls that protect this fortress along with his own private drug army of more than 1,000 well-trained persons. This armed force plus a number of anti-aircraft guns protect Afridi from both ground and aerial attack. Within the confines of the Afridi estate are both a large ranch and a well-stocked zoo. To some extent Afridi seems to have modeled his drug operations after his Colombian counterparts (Witkin and Griffin, 1994).

A third drug gang, the Quetta Alliance, is similar to the first group. One major difference is that the Quetta gang has elected one of its members as the head of the gang. This gang's labs produce a morphine base product that is converted to heroin in Turkey. Sakhi Dost Jan Notezai, an elected member of the Pakistan Provincial Assembly, runs the day-to-day operations of the Quetta gang even though he is presently confined to a Pakistani prison awaiting trial on drug charges. The two other leaders of the Quetta gang are the Rigi family, who controls all of the transshipment of drugs in and out of Pakistan, and Mohammed Issa, an Afghan national who controls the markets for the gang's heroin in both North America and Europe. This group's base of operations is located in Pakistan, only several miles from the opium-rich Afghanistani province of Helmand (Witkin and Griffin, 1994).

Most of the heroin within these gangs' drug operations is transported across Europe from where it is transshipped to either Canada or the United States. Heroin produced by the Pakistani drug gangs is imported into the United States through New York, Newark, Los Angeles, and San Francisco. New York, Chicago, and Detroit contain the largest markets for Pakistani heroin because of their large populations of Pakistani nationals. In almost all cases, the heroin is sold to other ethnic groups who then sell it on the street.

Even though Islamic religious leaders in Pakistan have justified members of their religion dealing in heroin, they did not anticipate the increased use of heroin in their country. As of 1994, more than 1.5 million Pakistani citizens have become addicted to heroin, and they consume over 40 percent of all the heroin produced in Pakistan each year. In Karachi, for example, the heavily armed drug gangs have become so powerful that they control a major portion of the city.

Pakistan's problems with corruption from drug gangs has gotten so far out of hand that deposed Prime Minister Nawaz Sharif accused General Aslam Beg, military chief of staff, and General Assad Durrani, head of the ISI, of approaching him and proposing a plan to raise money for clandestine foreign campaigns by working with the local drug gangs (Anderson and Khan, 1994). According to the *Statesman,* money gleaned from narcotics trafficking has been used by the ISI to support dissident actions throughout India (1993). Other reports have indicated that drug gang leaders have managed to use money to reach the highest-ranking political officials in Pakistan in order to avoid arrest and prosecution for drug trafficking (Royce, 1993).

In early 1995 the Pakistan government, in an effort to take back control of the country from the drug gangs, staged raids throughout the Islamabad area of Pakistan. These raids resulted in the tearing down of 15 drug labs and the seizure of more than 6.3 tons of heroin. A prior raid by the military in January 1995 in Bara, Pakistan, resulted in the seizure of 480 kilograms of heroin and 165 tons of hashish. The only problem with these raids has been the way they have been viewed by both Pakistanis and western drug authorities. An opinion expressed by both groups seems to indicate that these raids were conducted against groups who were not involved in the major Pakistani drug market and most of the people seized were poor Khyber tribes. Some observers went as far as to say that in both cases the raids were orchestrated by the Pakistani government in order to gain U.S. support (Clerc, 1995). What these observers really want to know is why the government refused to go after members of the three major drug gangs who were still at large. Arresting members of the Khyber Pass tribes, who plant and gather the opium crop for sale to major drug traffickers for small amounts of money, is not the answer to Pakistan's drug gang problem. Neither is claiming that large quantities of heroin were recovered or drug labs destroyed without any visible evidence of these assertions. One must remember that a majority of the raids conducted by the Pakistan government were in inaccessible areas of the Khyber pass. Therefore all the information related to these raids and the amount of drugs confiscated was released by members of the Pakistani government's public information unit and not by any outside media or government agency.

Recently, criminal activities by Pakistani gangs have begun to appear outside of Pakistan. For instance, in Japan during 1994 the Japanese police arrested Mohammed Naeem, a Pakistani national and head of a Pakistani crime group that makes counterfeit 1,000 ruppe notes. It seems that Naeem set up a factory in Koshigaya in Saitama Prefecture and employed several Japanese workers who assisted him and his gang members in reproducing more than 4,000 counterfeit 1,000 ruppe notes. Many of these notes were smuggled out of Japan and then converted into either Japanese or U.S. currency in Bangkok. Tokyo police also arrested Jun Furusawa and four other Japanese suspects on extortion charges. Furusawa and his gang of four were hired by Naeem to pose as immigration officers and to seize four Pakistani nationals who were arriving at Tokyo airport. After the group's arrival they were approached by Furusawa and his associates who placed them in handcuffs for allegedly violating Japanese immigration laws. The four Pakistanis were then taken to Naeem who informed them that if they paid a specific amount of money to him he could assure them that they would not be charged with any violations of Japanese immigration laws. During interrogation by Japanese police Naeem informed them that he had made up counterfeit immigration officer identification cards for members of his gang as well as Furusawa and his four associates. He further stated that once the counterfeiting of money scheme had ceased he and his other gang members had a list of Pakistanis nationals living in Japan that they would extort money from sometime in the near future (Shimbun, 1994).

In the United States, besides the drug and extortion business, members of Pakistani organized crime groups have initiated scams to bilk the government, as well as other citizens, of U.S. currency. These gang members have instituted swindles that involve fraudulent automobile accidents with phony injury claims, with the claimants using medical clinics that only exist on paper. In most cases, a number of clinics are opened by gang members who then use both corrupt doctors to make up false reports and underhanded lawyers to file insurance claims. Gangs will employ members to act as "runners" who are issued fraudulent drivers' licenses, legitimate vehicle registrations, and insurance cards. A vehicle accident is then staged and three to four fictitious injured passengers are created by the "runner" when he reports this false incident to the police. This scam is successful in most major metropolitan areas because the "runner" has to go into the local police precinct to report this incident; in most cases, unless serious injury is involved, the police do not respond to vehicular accidents. Once the occurrence is reported to the police the gang member hands the information over to members running the clinic. They in turn forward medical bills to insurance companies for convalescent therapy that the gang's underhanded doctor states is necessary for all injured parties to successfully recover from the physical or mental impairments they suffered during or after the accident.

Gang members will set up a phony car service that is used by the injured driver and passengers for transportation to and from the clinic. The car service then bills the insurance company for these bogus services. The gangs also pay either illegal aliens or newly arriving immigrants to have X-rays taken so that there is a body available for the insurance company in case of any type of follow-up investigation. Most insurance companies will settle claims such as these as quickly as possible to avoid going to court and having to pay a larger settlement (Koleniak, 1995).

Pakistani organized crime groups are similar to all prior criminal gangs at this stage of their development. The U.S. market is new to the leaders and gang members but it has not, thus far, taken any great period of time for the gangs to adapt to the criminal opportunities within our environment. Almost all Pakistani gangs are loosely knit but the kinship within their ethnic and religious backgrounds may help create one tightly bonded organized crime group somewhere in the near future.

## Indian Groups

Organized crime groups first appeared in India in the early 1800s. Prior to the appearance of these organized crime groups, many of the wealthy people in India, known as zamindars, hired large groups of men known as paiks or lathials. They kept them under their control mainly for their own protection. These paiks or lathials were well trained and were used by the zamindars as enforcers to collect rents, forcefully take land back from renters, supply their bosses with women, and provide protection for the zamindars and their families. The first organized gang was known as Thuggees, and they were a secretive group of gangsters involved in robbery, extortion, and murder. Members of this gang traveled throughout India in smaller groups representing themselves as members of a religious sect in order to gain the trust of future victims. Through various types of deception, the gang members built up the victims' confidence in them. A short time after this goal was attained, the gang members would rob and kill the victim. These gangs got so far out of control by the mid 1830s that the British government in India passed special legislation that allowed the military and other law enforcement agencies to arrest the members on sight. Some gang members were put to death while others were banished from India and told that if they ever returned they would also be put to death (Ghosh, 1991).

Late in the 1850s the problem of loosely organized crime gangs again appeared in India. These gangs were bandits who roamed the highways and byways of India committing robbery, burglary, murder, kidnapping, and extortion. Gang members used trained dogs to protect their camps and hideouts from government attack. The gang leaders also extorted police coop-eration by using the female members of the gang to corrupt local members of the constabulary. During these times the gangs had approximately a quarter of a million members. They, like the Thuggees before them, forced the British government in India to enact what became known as Criminal Tribes Acts in 1871. This act was strictly enforced by the both the military and state police agencies. Stern enforcement of these acts led to a decrease in the crimes committed by these organized crime groups, but it was not long before other types of groups began appearing in India (Ghosh, 1991).

At the turn of the twentieth century information on a tightly run orga-nized crime group surfaced in Calcutta. Police intelligence information indi-cated that this group, known as the Bengal Goondas (thieves or gangsters), had formed a coalition with Indian revolutionaries as well as smugglers and drug traffickers. What this gang did was create its own criminal organization that supplied guns to the revolutionaries and drugs to local drug dealers. Once again, the British government stepped in and passed legislation that al-lowed the government to proclaim that if a person was a member of the Goonda gang, that person could be banished from the state of Bengal for an indeterminate amount of time. Again, punishment/banishment worked for a period of time but was not strong enough to totally remove the Goonda gangs from Bengal (Ghosh, 1991)

After the outbreak of World War II the Goonda gangs, which had been operating covertly in India since the Goonda Act of 1923, reappeared in Cal-cutta. These gangs immediately set up their own brothels and drug dens throughout what quickly became red light districts in Calcutta and every other major urban area in India. Goonda gangs established a protection racket for other ethnic brothels in India and became involved in supplying women to them. It led to the rape, kidnapping, and abduction of females of all ages and ethnic backgrounds in order to obtain enough women to stock the brothels of India. The abducted women were usually auctioned off to the brothel owner who bid the highest price. In many cases, the gangs' partici-pation in this type of crime provided all profit. In some cases the gang had a deal with the brothel owners that provided the gang with a small percentage of the abducted woman's earnings even after she was paid for by the brothel owner (Ghosh, 1991).

During this time, the gang activities not only increased because of the number of foreign military personnel, who were given leave from the war in Calcutta, but also because of the atrocities being committed by members of the Muslim community against members of the Hindu community. Muslims in Calcutta started by recruiting other gang members from throughout India to terrorize the Hindu community in Calcutta. These crimes included raiding

Hindu houses and robbing and killing the owner, abducting and raping all the females, and then burning the house to the ground. In retaliation for these crimes members of the Hindu community hired the Goondas to provide protection for them and their families (Ghosh, 1991).

Gang activities in India flourished. The gangs continued to establish themselves during the 1950s, 1960s, and 1970s. Until today the gangs have been as much a part of Indian society as the members of both the Muslim and Hindu religions. People who join the gangs are usually between 16 and 18 years old, unemployed, and most were previously involved in criminal activity prior to seeking gang membership. Once they become members of the Goonda gangs, they become totally faithful to the gang and its leaders. Some leaders are chosen from within but a majority of the leadership comes from what is considered the middle class of Indian society. Most leaders have reached this level in Indian society because of their criminal activities in a gang. A leader is called a *Dada* or *Mastan* and has extremely good abilities to organize and run a business/criminal association. Many gang bosses are between 40 and 50 years old and fairly literate. Bosses receive a specific percentage of the money made by their underlings for masterminding the criminal strategies used. They direct gang members on how to carry out these crime tactics without being apprehended by the police. They also make the proper connections to corrupt government officials in order to avoid the arrest and prosecution of members who participate in the gang's planned criminal activities. Once a gang member becomes somewhat prosperous he can break away and form his own gang. Organizing one's own group is done without any conflict from gang leaders, and usually with the leader's blessing, because the leader of a new group will remain loyal to his original gang and continue to support the old gang's criminal endeavors. Gang research done by Ghosh indicates that Indian gangs can be divided according to social stratum or religion (1991).

Like the wealthy people before them, members of India's political parties use the gang members to dissuade citizens to vote for certain politicians, discourage political opponents from seeking office, gather election funding for a candidate, and maintain the ability to manipulate the electorates. One Indian politician, Kapil Deo Singh, who is a minister in the Karpoori Thaker Cabinet, acknowledged on the floor of the Bihar Assembly that he had his own gang of Goondas and that without their assistance he would never have been elected to office. Goonda participation in political activities first appeared in 1969 when India's two major political parties were involved in a bitter dispute. During these times (1969–1980), gang leaders sought closer associations with politicians. At first, contributions were made by gang leaders to gain the confidence of the politicians, followed by gang members taking active roles in the election of their candidate. In many cases, this participation involved the use of intimidation to get people to vote for the office seeker supported by the gang.

In 1980, the association between gangs and politicians became more obvious when gang leaders decided it was cheaper and easier for them to seek election to office. After having acquired the necessary knowledge over the past eleven years by working for the politicians, the gangsters soon set up their own well-oiled political machine. Then, the gang leaders used whatever techniques were required to gain the votes necessary to be elected. What has happened since the gang leaders first started running for office in the early 1980s is that the gang leaders now control a great deal of the activities of both the politicians and the government. In many of the Indian states, the politicians are under the total control of the gangs and cannot vote on any controversial issue or do anything else without consulting gang leaders. The gangs have also established good relationships with lawyers, court officers, police officials, and members of the media. They have all the power they need to run their illegal activities without any interference from most government agencies or the media. Gang activities during an election have become more brutal as time passes. In 1989, during general elections in India, more than 150 people were killed by gang members during three days of voting because these people opposed the candidates supported by the gang leaders. Gang leaders have assured themselves continued political support by taking control of what is known as "booth capturing", a tactic we call stuffing the ballot box. Gang members, through the use of force, take over an election booth and then stamp all the ballots in that booth for their candidate. This election fraud is done without any government interference (Ghosh, 1991).

Organized crime gangs in India participate in numerous legal and illegal activities including the following:

1. *Unions* — During the mid 1960s the gangs were used to eliminate unions striking in Bombay. Since then gang members have penetrated the unions as both workers and union representatives. In this capacity gang members have used intimidation, kidnapping, assault, and murder to strong-arm management of the company. Gang members use the same tactics against union members who do not support them.

2. *Private companies* — Gang members are hired to eliminate competition, usually by murdering the owner of the other business. These private businesses also use gang members to help them bilk an insurance company. A businessperson will order an expensive piece of machinery and make sure it has insurance coverage. Once the businessperson

knows the location where the machinery will be dropped off for him to pick up, he will notify gang members who steal the machinery and deliver it to him. When the businessperson is informed that the property was stolen, usually from a shipping dock, he immediately informs the insurance company who will then reimburse the business for its loss. A percentage of the insurance claim is paid to the gang leader.

3. *Contract murders* — Members of the gang will murder anyone for a price.

4. *Real estate* — Landlords use gang members to remove anyone the landlord considers a problem tenant. In some cases, the gang leader offers to buy the apartment or house for half the price. A gang member then purchases the apartment, forcibly removes the tenant and the apartment is sold at its true price. Builders/contractors use gang members to assist them in removing tenants from slum area housing, which enables the builder/contractor, who has purchased the property, to knock down the old tenements and replace them with larger modernized buildings. A group of gang members will either continually beat up the tenant or defile the tenant's wife and daughters until he leaves the apartment.

5. *Hafta Collection* — This activity involves the extortion of businesses and stores including jewelry and diamond dealers, movie theaters, restaurants, hotels, limousine and taxi drivers, brothel owners, food stores, gambling dens, and money lenders. A set payment is compiled according to the profit made by the business. Refusal to pay this protection money will lead to assault, kidnapping, or murder.

6. *Movie Industry* — Owners of movie distribution centers use gang members to assure them that no one will counterfeit their movies. Gang members have also extorted money from Indian movie makers and movie stars, charging them a monthly fee for protection.

7. *Havala Business* — Essentially the same as loan-sharking, this operation is run by Indian gang members for stock market investors. An interest rate of 24 percent is charged on the money loaned out to these investors. Gang enforcers collect the debt in cases where investors refuse to pay the interest or repay the loan.

8. *Narcotics and Liquor* — Gangs control the distribution and sale of all drugs and alcohol throughout India. Indian organized crime gangs are also heavily involved in supplying drug gangs in Pakistan, Afghanistan, and Myanmar with a chemical known as acetic anhydride, which is used in the production of heroin.

9. *Smuggling* — All types of goods, from human beings, textiles, and drugs, or whatever else can make money for the gangs are smuggled by them (Ghosh, 1991; Hazarika, 1993).

The power of the gangs was evident during riots in Bombay in early 1993, which started out as a dispute between local Hindu and Muslim groups. Bombay police reported that organized crime gangs had spread the fighting and violence throughout Bombay. During these riots gang members robbed people on the streets, assaulted or murdered anyone who opposed their actions, and broke into stores to steal anything of value. In March 1993 Bombay was hit with 13 explosions that killed 317 and wounded 1,500 citizens. Bombs exploded in the Bombay stock exchange, three hotels, and several corporate offices including the central office of Air India. In the aftermath of these bombings the police investigation traced evidence located at and around these bomb scenes to a gang run by the Memon brothers. Another organized crime leader, Dawood Ibrahim, has been mentioned by the police as a coconspirator in this crime. Ibrahim became a power in organized crime in India in the late 1970s when he took over many smuggling and protection rackets in Bombay. In the mid 1980s Ibrahim moved his base of operations from Bombay to Dubai but was still able to control gang activities from there. A short time after the bombing the police responded to the Memon residence in Bombay to find that the family had packed up and left for Dubai (Gargan, 1993).

In August 1994 Yakub Abdul Razak Memon was apprehended by police at a New Delhi train station. The Indian government claims that the Memon brothers acted along with Ibrahim and other gang members to plant the bombs throughout Bombay and then watched as the bombs went off. Further information obtained from the Indian government indicates that both the Memon and Ibrahim gangs were contracted and paid by Pakistani militants to carry out these bombings. In fact, members of both gangs were trained and paid by Pakistani terrorist groups prior to the bombings (Burns, 1994; Bidi, 1994; Chakravarty, 1994).

The activities of most Indian organized crime groups have not yet impacted too heavily on the United States. Yet we must be aware that the Patel Indian organized crime group has been visible in this country since the mid 1960s. The Patel gang has been involved in loaning money to newly arrived Indians to open businesses in the United States. A government investigation in 1985 showed that the Patel groups owned 28 percent of motels and hotels in the United States. This gang owns about 90 percent of all the independently owned motels and hotels in this country. In most of their housing establishments, gang members also control and operate the prostitution business. Members of this organized crime group keep a low profile and avoid conflict with members of law enforcement. They are fairly well organized and in most cases operate as cell groups in most major cities throughout the United States. DEA sources indicate that the Patel groups also use their hotel/motel businesses as dropoff and pickup points for their hashish/heroin trafficking business (DEA, 1994).

Like many other ethnic groups before them, the Patel crime gangs are also involved in the forgery of documents that can be purchased by people looking for an easy entry into the United States. Members of this gang are also involved in the theft and/or forgery of food stamps, U.S. Treasury checks, travelers checks, and other checks. A recent scam by members of Indian organized crime involved the theft of thousands of copies of major magazines such as *Cosmopolitan, Time,* and *Good Housekeeping.* They then sold them to other members of the Patel gang who own and operate newsstands throughout New York City. A total of 13 members of this operation were arrested by investigators from the U.S. Department of Labor Racketeering Division for their participation in this theft (McCoy, 1994).

## Burmese Groups

Burmese organized crime groups first appeared in Burma (now known as Myanmar) about 30 years ago when Khun Sa organized the Mong Tai Army (MTA) or the Shan United Army to protect his newly established drug empire. Khun Sa's present base of operation is in the town of Homong in the southern Shan State of Burma. Sa over the past three decades has created his own personal military-type of gang, and he claims that he does not participate in the drug trafficking business but only extorts money from the growers and dealers to support his group. In reality, Sa has formed an alliance with local farmers who grow the opium for him, which he then refines in his refineries on the Burmese-Thailand border. Sa's gang is a military type of organized crime family, which includes him as the boss with three underbosses or lieutenants assisting him. One lieutenant runs the day-to-day operations of the gang, another lieutenant takes care of security and intelligence gathering, and the third lieutenant is the comptroller and runs the opium refineries (Witkin and Griffin, 1994).

With 20,000 members, the Sa gang is considered one of the most ruthless gangs in Burma. On occasion the gang has been known to kill or mutilate all the people in a village if they encountered opposition to their drug trafficking activities. These brutal activities plus the eccentricity of Sa brought a great deal of attention from the Burmese government, which sent a number of military detachments to confront and arrest Sa and to destroy his militaristic gang's drug operations (Lintner and Mai, 1994). During 1995 the Burmese government conducted an all-out attack on Sa and his army, which resulted in Sa surrendering to government troops in early 1996. An agreement reached by Sa and the Burmese government gives Sa amnesty from any government charges for his drug trafficking activities since the 1960s. (Shenon, 1995).

Following in the footsteps of the Sa gang came several other major drug trafficking groups, among them the United Wa State Army, a group formed by two former members of the Communist Party. The United Wa State Army has two wings, a political wing and a military wing. They have an elected leader, Chao Nyi-lai, and a military leader, Pao Ya-chiang. Total membership in this loosely knit group is estimated at 15,000–35,000 members. At one time the United Wa sold drugs to the Sa group, but over the past several years this gang has set up its own opium refining locations along the Burmese side of the Chinese border. A number of confrontations between the Shan United Army and the United Wa State Army during the past decade have erupted over both groups' desire to control Doi Lang, a drug-producing area near the town of Fang, Burma (Witkin and Griffin, 1994).

Probably the most dangerous up-and-coming drug gang leader is Lin Mingxian. Like the leaders of United Wa, he was originally a member of the Communist Party of Burma. Lin Mingxian established his home base in Mong La, Burma, from where he directs his heroin operations that run from deep within China across Laos and into Vietnam and Cambodia. No actual Burmese military presence can be found within miles of Lin's base in Mong La, which is considered part of the "lawless frontier" of Burma. The lack of any narcotics enforcement in this area provides Lin with total impunity to openly operate his drug business. Lin also owns and operates what can be considered the two largest opium processing plants in Burma with a third in Laos (Lintner and Mai, 1994).

Several other organized drug gangs presently operate in Burma, including the Yang and Pheung gangs in Kokang, the Lo Hsing-han gang in Lasho, and the Wei Brothers gang that works hand in hand with the United Wa State Army. Most of the notable gang leaders were at one time members of the Communist Party of Burma who saw a greater opportunity for moneymaking in drugs than in terrorism. The movement of these prior leaders into drug trafficking has more than doubled opium production over the past several years. These gangs, unlike the Shan United Army and the United Wa State Army, do not claim to be using drug money to support ethnic freedom for the people. They are strictly drug gangs that operate to make money, and they will kill anyone who interferes in their moneymaking business (Linter, 1994).

The activities of Burmese gangs have remained within Burma with virtually all of their heroin being brokered through locations such as Bangkok, Thailand, or Hong Kong. Most of these brokers run what seem to be legitimate businesses, while in reality they use these legitimate operations as fronts for brokering numerous drug transactions. One of the most notable drug brokers was Thai gangster Thongchai Sanguandikul, who is presently confined to federal prison in the United States. Sanguandikul shipped thousands of kilograms of Burmese heroin from Hong Kong, through his Mexican organized crime connections in Sinaloa, Mexico, to the United States. Much of the processed heroin is also sold to ethnic Chinese residents of the United States. Once the heroin arrives in the United States, it changes hands again and is retailed on the street by local drug dealers (Woolrich, 1993).

## EASTERN EUROPEAN GROUPS

Since the fall of the Soviet Union and its authority over Eastern European countries, the number of organized crime groups controlling the criminal activities in these countries has drastically increased. Prior to the fall of communism, most criminal actions were controlled by members of the Communist Party, the secret police, the military, or a combination of all three. After the demise of communism, these people remained in place in many cases, but they suddenly lost their communist or secret police classification and became the leaders or founders of some type of ethnic organized crime group in Eastern Europe. Besides gang involvement in extortion, forgery, fraud, prostitution, and people smuggling, they have shown a tremendous increase in their participation in drug trafficking. The countries in Eastern Europe have become major transshipment points for drug traffickers from both Southeast and Southwest Asia. Not a single country in Eastern Europe was prepared for the unlawful activities that have taken place since the fall of communism, especially the drug activity. Even today, most military and law enforcement agencies in these countries have little or no training, nor do they have the proper laws in place to deal with most of the crime. Therefore, what we are finding in just about every Eastern European country is that gang activity, drug use, and trafficking are out of control. They will remain that way until the government provides the military and the police with the necessary expertise and laws to eliminate these illegal activities.

## Albanian Groups

An estimated 300,000 Albanian nationals live in the United States today. Most of these immigrants have settled in major U.S. urban centers such as New York, Chicago, Detroit, and Los Angeles. Like most other groups, ethnic Albanians, most of them born in Yugoslavia, have also formed a loosely knit organized crime faction that is interconnected from city to city. Most Albanian gang members are illegal aliens who fly from Europe to Mexico. There they obtain forged documents, and then they illegally enter the United States. Once here, most will head toward a major U.S. city either to join up with other family members or to just disappear into an Albanian community. A number of the illegal Albanian immigrants smuggle drugs that are dropped off with a member of a Mexican drug cartel. The cartel then supplies the illegal aliens with the necessary forged documents and a contact person who will guide them across the border into the United States. Payments they receive for smuggling the drugs usually pay for the costs of their travel and fees to get to the United States.

Albanian gangs follow a code of honor similar to La Cosa Nostra's guidelines of honor and silence. The code, which is called either "Che Basa" or "Leke Dukagjini," sets forth for gang members and outsiders what honor and personal trust are and what will happen if someone violates this code of honor. In some cases, a violation of this code will result in some type of revenge. In most cases the revenge will involve the killing of the code violator, which is the primary reason why few, if any, Albanian gang members ever become police informants. Knowing this code and what will happen to them also impacts on legitimate members of the Albanian community who have nothing to do with gang activities. They refuse to cooperate with the police in apprehending these criminals because they are aware of the retaliation the gang uses against informers. One other Albanian practice that may have an effect on the social values of the male members of Albanian society is that right after birth a firearm is procured for the newborn infant. As the child grows up he becomes highly accomplished in both the handling and use of firearms. In most cases, it is as much a cultural thing as it is a bonding thing among the males in an Albanian family. About 90 percent of all Albanian males in the United States own some type of firearm. This custom, along with the code of honor/revenge, has led to a high number of serious assaults and murders among the males within most Albanian communities throughout Europe and the United States (Sherman and Goldfarb, 1996).

Along with the large influx of Albanian nationals into the United States came a sharp increase in the number of crimes involving Albanian males. New York police have found that Albanian gang members who form what they refer to as *crews* within the gang have become specialists in the crime of burglary. Gang members, acting as visiting tourists from Europe, go through various food markets, clothes outlets, jewelry stores, department stores, and banks throughout the New York metropolitan area videotaping the insides of the store. Within a short period of time after the videotaping, gang members return to break into these locations from the roof; they frequently climb down ropes into the store. They use a gang member who is an electronics expert to quickly disarm the alarm and video security system. They then attack the safe or other money holder with the equipment they used to gain entry to the safe. Gang members go as far as to purchase safes to practice techniques they use or plan to use to gain entry into a safe. Albanian gangs place well-trained lookouts equipped with walkie-talkies and police scanners outside the locations they are burglarizing in order to thwart any police efforts to apprehend them. In other cases, the gang has been known to set off an alarm in a business and wait outside to watch as the police respond to the scene. Once the police leave the scene the Albanian gang members enter the location and proceed to commit the burglary figuring that a second alarm will be viewed as nothing more than a nuisance by the police and that the police will not respond to the location again. Law enforcement agencies from throughout the East Coast and Midwest indicate that Albanian gangs have committed similar types of burglaries within many of their jurisdictions.

Police agencies have been able to substantiate their claims of Albanian participation in these crimes based on the use of the same types of equipment, personnel, and methods of operation used by the Albanian gang members in all their criminal ventures. In many cases, gang burglaries of super stores (large retail outlets and supermarkets) and cash-rich businesses usually give the gang a profit ranging from $500,000 to $10 million in U.S. currency on each burglary. The most recent activity by the gang has been breaking into automatic teller machines (ATMs) to gain instant cash. Members of the Albanian burglary gangs use what is known as a "slice pack," which consists of an oxygen-fueled device with burn rods that can be used to promptly reach a temperature of 10,000 degrees Fahrenheit allowing them to bore through a safe wall or an ATM in a short period of time. Always standing by during these safe jobs is another gang member known as a "hack and whack" artist with a 20-pound sledgehammer in case the gang needs physical force to gain entry into the safe. Recent law enforcement figures indicate that the Albanian gangs burglarized more than 200 large supermarkets, 50 ATM machines, and 35–40 jewelry manufacturers and stores in the New York metropolitan area in just two years' time (Purdy, 1994; Sherman and Goldfarb, 1996).

Albanian gangs use social clubs that they create as bases for their criminal activities. Gang members inform the Albanian community that these ethnic clubs will help them maintain their culture in a new and different environment, which is, in reality, far from the truth. Albanian gang members use these social clubs as locations where they plan all their criminal endeavors, recruit new members, and split the proceeds of their crimes. An outgrowth of these gang-run social clubs has been the formation of street gangs that spew hate against other racial and ethnic groups either inside or outside their neighborhoods. Unlike the Chinese street gangs who work for the Tongs, these Albanian street groups seem more inclined to work for their own benefit without a connection to the older Albanian gangs. This lack of connection exists because members of the street gangs are predominantly U.S. born and do not have the same maturity, discipline, understanding, or dedication as the foreign-born members of the established Albanian gangs. Most members of an Albanian gang come from the Eastern European environment where the law enforcement establishment could, under the old communist regime, do whatever it pleased to obtain a confession or stop criminal activity. The gang members who end up dealing with law enforcement in the United States have no fear of the police. They know that they can control most situations and that the police cannot threaten or use force to intimidate them (Gonzalez, 1992).

Members of Albanian organized crime have also become fairly active participants in the drug trafficking business. The group made a connection with the Colombian cocaine cartels in Florida. The Albanians obtain the cocaine in Florida and immediately move it to Detroit, New York, or Chicago. Upon the arrival of the cocaine, it is immediately cut by members of the Albanian gang who then retail it out to other ethnic groups to be sold on the street. Law enforcement sources in the Midwest consider the Albanian gangs the major suppliers of cocaine to the Chicago and Detroit areas (DEA, 1994). Some other activities of the Albanian gangs include alien smuggling, most of which is done through Mexico and Canada into the United States, forgery, and gun running.

## Polish Groups

Like other groups from Eastern Europe, most Polish organized crime groups appeared a short time after the fall of the Soviet Union. In Poland, almost all the members of these new criminal groups were active participants in the Communist Party, the military, and/or the Polish secret police. Organized criminal groups in Poland have become involved in bank frauds resulting in the loss of billions of dollars from the banking system.

In August 1994 shop owners in Warsaw closed their stores in protest over the actions of members of organized crime and the inability of the police to control gang activities. Gang members had set up an extortion ring requiring stores in Warsaw to pay $500 to $7,000 monthly to the group. In several cases gang members went to the homes of the shop owners and in one case actually threatened to chop off the hand of the child of one of their victims. Several days prior to the store owners' protest, gang members attacked several restaurant owners and vandalized half a dozen businesses. Apparently the protest worked because several days after these demonstrations the police arrested a gang member known as Pershing when he attempted to force a Warsaw businessman to pay him $40,000 (Turek, 1995).

The inability of the police to control the activities of organized crime gangs may be due to the corruption within Poland's police agency. This police corruption became visible in the summer of 1994 with the arrest of Mieczyslaw Grzybowski, the chief of the Polish police agency's economic crime section. He, along with several dozen Polish police officers, four state prosecutors, and a number of criminal court judges, was arrested and charged with taking bribes from members of organized crime. These arrests were followed by the arrests of several other high-ranking police officials for participating in the hijacking and selling of thousands of bottles of scotch (*New York Times*, 1994).

Corrupt police practices have forced the new prime minister of Poland, Jozef Oleksy, to select Jerzy Stanczyk to become the new leader of the Polish national police. Upon taking office Stanczyk immediately declared war on organized crime. He demanded that sufficient funding be apportioned by the government to support the police and prosecutors in their battle against Polish organized crime.

One major problem with the gangs has been their use of explosive devices. Since early 1994 the Polish gangs have planted 150 bombs throughout Poland in an effort to settle disputes with rival gangs. Thus far these bombing have caused the deaths of 10 people and the wounding of 36 other civilians. Police intelligence information indicates that the Pruszkow and the Wolomin organized crime groups are the two major factions involved in the bombings. Most of the explosions are the result of a battle over which gang should control drug trafficking, prostitution, auto theft, and extortion. As of yet, no arrests of any members of these gangs have taken place (Barker, 1995; Spolar, 1995).

Polish organized crime groups set out in the early 1990s to establish alliances with members of the international drug groups from Colombia, Nigeria, and both Southwest and Southeast Asia. Drug trafficking through Poland increased sharply once these affiliations were formed. Poland lacked any strict drug laws or enforcement methods police could use to cope with the transshipment of drugs through this country. Once the gangs planned their strategy to avoid detection and set the different routes to be used for drug transporting, the gangs started moving the drugs through Poland.

The extent of the participation of Polish organized crime groups in drug trafficking is shown by the increase in the number of drug seizures involving Polish nationals. During 1993, Polish customs agents seized 220 pounds of cocaine from a Polish ship in the port city of Szczecin. In January 1994, half a ton of cocaine was seized by customs agents from the Polish freighter, *Lublin II,* during a stopover in Antwerp. A member of a Polish organized crime group was arrested immediately after the seizure. In February 1994, British customs officials working hand in hand with Polish law enforcement officials, seized 1,200 kilos of cocaine in Liverpool aboard a ship bound for Poland. Then in May 1994, Polish authorities seized 88 pounds of heroin at the border of Germany and Poland being transported in two automobiles by members of Polish organized crime. Some recent seizures from members of Polish organized crime include 1.2 tons of Colombian cocaine aboard the Polish ship Jurata and 2.2 tons of hashish found in raisin containers on a train that arrived in Warsaw from Belarus. A seizure in Morocco netted 3,135 pounds of hashish secreted in containers of sardines and olives. Moroccan officials arrested Pawel Skowronski in connection with this drug seizure, and he was later identified by Polish authorities as a member of a Polish organized crime group. In one incident in February 1994, Polish customs officers apprehended two gang members at the Polish border attempting to smuggle into Poland 200 gallons of the ingredients used to produce amphetamines. In recent years Polish organized crime gangs have set up numerous labs to produce synthetic drugs. These illegal labs have made Poland the second largest producer of illegal synthetic drugs in the world behind Holland (Associated Press, 1994; *New York Times,* 1994; McKinsey, 1994; United Press International, 1994).

Ever-increasing participation in narcotics trafficking by Polish organized crime members has expanded the number of drug addicts in Poland. Since the collapse of communism the number of drug users in Polish society has increased from about 7 percent in the 1980s to approximately 25 percent in the 1990s. This trend certainly indicates that all of the heroin, cocaine, and amphetamines entering Poland from outside are not just passing through on the way to another country. It shows that Polish organized crime groups have sold a certain portion of the drugs they are smuggling for a profit on the streets of Poland (McKinsey, 1994).

Prior to their involvement in narcotics trafficking and still today the Polish gangs in both Europe and North America were and are operating successful car theft rings. Auto theft gangs in the United States base many of their operations out of Illinois. Gang auto theft activities first surfaced in Chicago in the late 1980s when the Chicago police department's auto crime unit discovered how they participated in these crimes. During an investigation that originated in August 1989, the Chicago police uncovered information related to the theft of vehicles by members of Polish organized crime groups. Members of the gang would steal luxury cars from showrooms and display lots in the Chicago metropolitan area. They would then transport the vehicles to a garage in Chicago where vehicle identification numbers on the autos would be altered and counterfeit license plates placed on the vehicle. The cars would then be transported to the Portsmouth, Virginia, marine terminal where the autos were containerized and shipped through Goteborg, Sweden, to their new owners in Poland. Gang members in Poland contact other members in the United States with vehicle orders received from clients in Poland. Usually the list consists of cars such as Mercedes-Benz, BMW, Lincoln, Volvo, Jeep Cherokee, Corvette, TransAm, and Harley Davidson motorcycles. Recently, Chicago police discovered that the Polish gangs ship cars in containers to Toronto; the vehicles are then shipped to Europe from Canada. While their gang counterparts in the United States are shipping autos back to Poland, the gangs in Poland are stealing cars throughout Europe and selling them in Poland and other parts of Europe (Skonie, 1991; Kiefer, 1992).

Organized crime activity throughout the rest of Eastern Europe is not yet on the same scale as in Poland and Albania, although some countries, including Hungary, are having problems with street gangs. In Hungary, the enormous increase in the number of crimes since 1991 is due to the involement of juveniles. Many of the gangs have the same ideology as their American counterparts, the skinhead gangs. The skinheads commit crimes primarily aimed at certain racial or ethnic groups. These gang robberies, assaults, or other encounters are against Arab, Turkish, or non-Hungarian people. These street gangs have also become heavily involved in street-level drug trafficking. Fun for gang members involves entering cemeteries at night, drinking or using drugs, and then vandalizing the graves and mausoleums. In many cases, the gang members wear black clothing, shaved heads, and have both their lips and cheeks pierced with metal objects (Viviano, 1994).

Hungary has experienced a drastic increase in the amount of activity involving organized crime groups, specifically, drug trafficking and money laundering. Like their Russian organized crime counterparts in the United States, the Hungarian gangs also participate in rings that sell heating oil, which is the same as diesel fuel but one-third cheaper at local petrol stations. To counteract the gangs' actions, the government put a harmless but observable red dye in the heating fuel. The placing of the red dye in the heating fuel did not deter the gang members who quickly found several oil refineries that removed the red dye from the fuel and the gang was back in business.

## Gypsy Groups

The mention of Hungary brings to mind another fairly well organized crime group/gang/family that is based out of this country and deserves some recognition, the Gypsies. Gypsy groups are an international organized crime group with tentacles spread throughout the world. They should be thought of as a nation of people as well as a large organized crime family. As both a nation and an organized crime family they have their own banks, bankers, courts, lawyers, and kings. Gypsy groups can be considered as much a traditional group as a nontraditional type of organized crime group. Their historical roots reach back to both Punjab Province in India over 1,200 years ago and Israel over 2,000 years ago. History indicates that the gypsies are descendants of two northern Indian tribes known as the Luri and Dom. Somewhere around 1000 A.D. these tribes left India and traveled through most of Southwest Asia, Northern Africa, and Western and Eastern Europe until they reached their final destination in what is now known as Hungary sometime during the fifteenth century. These Gypsy groups attempted to settle in many of the countries they traveled through but were not accepted by the citizens, who were apprehensive of the Gypsies because they were different.

The Gypsies were considered different because of their customs, language, and more than anything else, their purported mystical and esoteric powers. As the Gypsy groups traveled through many of the towns and villages of these countries, laws were passed by the rulers of these governments to either kill, imprison, or banish the gypsies from these areas. During the Hitler years in Europe, the Gypsies were singled out as one of the groups to be placed in concentration camps and killed. Hate and distrust for Gypsies remain even today and are evident in the apprehension and condemnation throughout the European community when it comes to dealing with Gypsies. Most of these feelings are a result of the skepticism surrounding their reputation as thieves who perform mystical feats.

According to legend, Gypsies became world wanderers and criminals because ethnic Gypsies refused to help Mary and Joseph while they were fleeing from Bethlehem with baby Jesus after King Herrod's proclamation to kill all newborn male children. Later, Gypsies were willing to forge the nails used to crucify Jesus while all other blacksmiths refused to make them.

When the Gypsy blacksmith who made the nails to crucify Jesus was informed by a Roman soldier that the fourth nail was to be used to pierce the heart of Jesus, he swallowed that nail. Myth has it that a short time after swallowing the nail Christ looked down on him from the cross and gave this Gypsy permission to wander the earth and live off whatever he could obtain illegally or steal.

Little actual Gypsy history has been recorded because most Gypsies are illiterate and live from day to day with no thought about their past history. For this reason, the veracity of the information as to why Gypsies are wanderers and thieves is at the very least questionable.

The lineage of a Gypsy family traces almost all members of a family as direct descendents of the eldest group leader who in most cases is known as the Vista Chief or Baro (Big Man) (see Figure 13-1). The families consist of a husband, wife, their sons and nonadult children. The father is responsible for the actions of his wife and children. Once a woman marries she is considered part of her husband's family and not her family of birth. Gypsies usually travel together in groups of anywhere from eight families to a larger assemblage consisting of 100 or more families. Besides their participation in criminal activities, these groups are also together because it enables them to survive economically and to locate and maintain living quarters during typically short stays in various locations. Groups that travel in this manner are known as Kumpanias (see Figure 13-2), and all members equally participate in the work as well as contribute and share the profits from their illegal activities. Members of the Kumpania elect a leader who is known as a King. This leader is chosen because of his leadership capabilities, moneymaking potential, maturity, and knowledge.

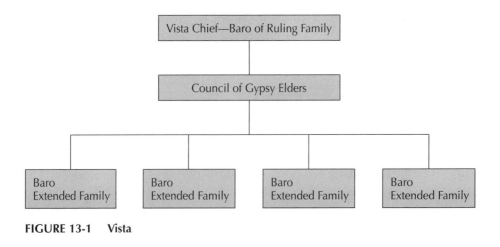

**FIGURE 13-1    Vista**

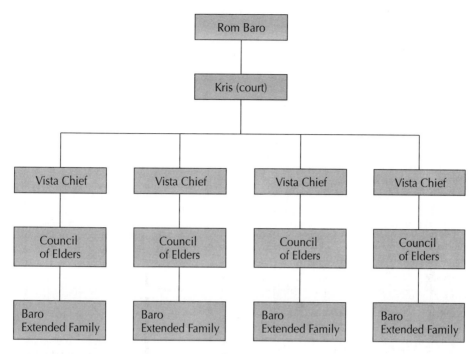

**FIGURE 13-2　Kumpania**

The Vista and the Kumpania figures each show a fairly strong correlation with the way the traditional organized crime groups are set up. A comparison of Figures 13-3 and 13-4 indicates the similarities in their setups.

Wandering from one location to another by an organized crime group is somewhat unusual because almost every suburban or urban center in which a Gypsy crime group operates or intends to operate usually already has a Kumpania in place. An outside Gypsy group entering one of these areas must seek the permission of the local Rom Baro, and before leaving this location the visiting Kumpania must pay some type of homage to the local Rom Baro. In many cases upon the visiting group's arrival a safe deposit box is rented and one key is held by the local Rom Baro while the other key is given to the visiting Rom Baro. When the travelers are ready to leave both Rom Baros go to the safe deposit box and the stolen property is removed and a certain percentage of the currency is given to the local Rom Baro.

One interesting part of the Gypsy lifestyle is the type of clothing they wear. Most of the older members of Gypsy families are fairly corpulent and they wear extra large clothing, usually suits, shirts, ties, and hats, that went

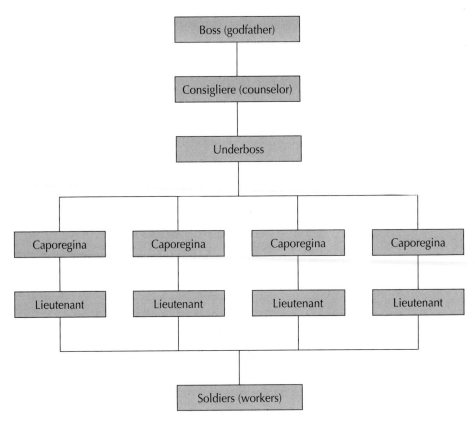

**FIGURE 13-3  Traditional Organized Crime Family**

out of style 20–30 years ago. Younger Gypsy males wear glittery clothing. During their youth Gypsy women wear traditional types of clothing. After their first menstrual cycle the female's mode of dressing changes. At this point Gypsy women wear customary clothing that consists of a long skirt and a sleeveless blouse with a low neckline that practically exposes their breasts. This low-cut blouse also gives the Gypsy women quick access to their undergarmets where they usually store small articles, such as the jewelry and money they steal. Skirt lengths on Gypsy women symbolize their age, with longer skirts indicating an older woman. An interesting anecdote states that the woman's body from the waist down is unchaste and, therefore, must at all times be hidden from view. The style of a Gypsy woman's hair also can indicate her age. Younger women wear their hair in a bun while older women wear braids. A successful Gypsy woman is easily identifiable because she wears a great deal of jewelry.

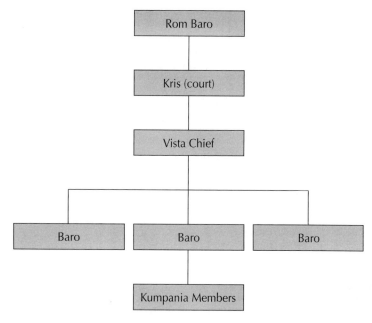

**FIGURE 13-4   Nontraditional Gypsy Organized Crime Family**

All Gypsies have three names with the first name given to the child right after birth. The mother whispers a secret name into the child's ear out of the earshot of any other person. According to Gypsy custom it is done to fool the evil spirits. A second name given to a Gypsy child is his or her given name. It is the name by which Gypsies can be identified by each other. Most Gypsies adopt a third name, usually a non-Gypsy surname, that can be changed each time they are apprehended for a crime. During their criminal careers most Gypsy offenders have 20–30 aliases that can be used at any given time.

Ethnically, Gypsies are divided into several groups: Polish, Romanian, Scottish, Hungarian, Irish, or American. Each ethnic Gypsy group has its special criminal method of operation. American Gypsies are noted for their ability to sell people remodeled used trailers as brand new models. Police estimate that this scam nets the Gypsies more than $2 million per year. Polish Gypsies are known for their deceptive methods of committing burglaries. Their most famous scam uses a deceitful method to gain entry, usually into the residence of a senior citizen. Two to three Gypsies, usually two women and perhaps a child, go to the door of a house occupied by an elderly couple. One of the women feigns sickness due to pregnancy and asks for a drink of water. In most cases entry to the home is easily gained. Once inside, the two women distract the person(s) who let them in, while the adolescent, who was hidden under one of the women's skirts, slips out and searches the house for valuables. Once the juvenile has completed the search and gathered some costly items from the house, he/she signals the two women who once again secret this child under their clothing and leave without the residents having any idea what took place. A similar scam in which three women state they are good friends of the next-door neighbor and need paper and pencil to leave a message has also been successful in gaining easy access for home burglaries. Each of these scams can net $1,000 to $50,000 in money and jewelry.

Yugoslavian Gypsies are experts at creating a distraction in order to steal property from stores. One of their diversions involves two to three different teams of 2–3 Gypsies who enter a store. The first team asks the salesperson to open a display case containing some valuable items. Once the salesperson opens the display case the second team enters the location. With their entrance, the second group distracts the clerk, usually by creating a disturbance. In an effort to quell the commotion the clerk leaves the first team alone at the open showcase. They quickly either raid the register or cash box, or take expensive jewelry from the showcase and replace it with zircons or costume jewelry. These thieves then quickly flee the scene and the theft is not discovered until the jewelry is examined, usually at a later date. This profitable scam often nets several hundred thousand dollars in jewelry or currency.

Other Gypsy crimes include house and auto scams in which two or three males pull up at a victim's house and offer to fix a roof, chimney, or siding for what seems to be a cheap price. In reality they only put a little tar on the roof or perhaps a small amount of glue or paint on the siding, collect the money, and leave. The auto scheme is similar in that the victim is told that a dent will be taken out of his or her car; however, the Gypsy just puts some plastic filler on the dent and leaves with the money. A short time later the plastic filler falls out exposing the original dent. Federal officials have also discovered that these wandering Gypsies collect welfare and food stamps in several states using some of their many aliases. It seems that during their travels they may stop off in a state and apply for welfare and food stamps.

## Bulgarian Groups

Bulgaria is facing the same problems with gangs as the rest of Eastern Europe. Bulgarian gangs have been involved in trafficking Turkish drugs into Western European countries. Since the ongoing armed conflict in Yugoslavia, members of Bulgarian organized crime have made thousands of dollars transporting gasoline across to the warring factions in Yugoslavia. Besides the activities related to black-marketing gasoline, the gangs have also become involved in extortion, drug trafficking, smuggling, prostitution, and counterfeiting. Thus far, estimates by Bulgarian law enforcement officials indicate that the gangs manage 70 percent of all gambling, 80 percent of all the alcohol and tobacco businesses, and 50 percent of cabarets and casinos. A large percentage of Bulgarian gang members are either wrestlers or weight lifters, which is why most Bulgarians call the gang members "bortsites" (wrestlers). Many of the gang leaders have attempted to pass their gangs off as security companies, without much success. One other problem the government faces in dealing with these organized crime groups is that members often have prior experience as members of the Bulgarian police. It has created a group of organized crime members who not only can act as Bulgarian police officers but also have available to them all the police equipment necessary to perpetrate crimes, wearing all the necessary police accoutrements (Perlez, 1995).

The power of the Bulgarian organized crime groups recently came to light after a shootout in a luxurious gambling club in Sofia owned by a former member of the secret police. The next day the Bulgarian police asked the leader of one of the gangs to stop in the local police station for coffee, but a short time after his arrival he was placed under arrest. A large group of gang members quickly gathered in the courtyard of the police station. In an attempt to calm this situation the police sent two supervisors out to attempt to settle this dispute. Unbeknownst to the police, another squad of officers was sent out from another location to apprehend the same gang leader. Ultimately, these two groups of officers confronted each other, which resulted in a shootout that caused the death of two officers. As an end result, the Bulgarian government had two police officers dead and the suspect in the shootout at the club was still a free man (Borger, 1994). This situation is indicative of what has happened in Bulgaria since the fall of communism. Like most of the rest of the Eastern European countries, Bulgaria is a democratic country that does not have the tools to deal with the problems presented by members of organized crime. They must, therefore, watch and wait until the proper adjustments are made to eliminate the criminal activities of Bulgarian organized crime groups.

## Czech Republic Groups

Since the fall of the so-called Iron Curtain (communist control) around Czechoslovakia, the activities involving what is known now as organized crime groups in the Czech Republic have increased. These newly formed organized gangs brought with them criminal activities such as narcotics trafficking, auto theft, prostitution, gambling, extortion, art theft, money laundering, fraud, blackmail, and people smuggling. Some of the favorite targets of these organized gangs are historical locations such as museums and castles from where the gang members can steal valuable works of art or ancient artifacts. These prizes, many of which are difficuilt to trace, are immediately sold on the black market for a quick and large profit.

## EMERGING HIGH-PROFILE GANGS IN THE UNITED STATES

### Almighty Latin King Nation

An organized crime group that has continued to expand since it was created in two Hispanic communities in Chicago about 50 years ago, the Latin Kings (Almighty Latin King Nation, or ALKN) was originally a loosely knit street gang. In many ways the early Latin Kings gangs are similar to the original Chinese street gangs in New York that were formed for the same basic reasons:

1. To protect their turf from being invaded and taken over by other ethnic groups

2. To prevent unwarranted attacks on Hispanic residents because of their ethnicity

3. To maintain the culture the Hispanic people brought with them into this community

Thus several small Hispanic communities in Chicago ended up with their own neighborhood security force that helped maintain the safety of all Hispanic residents. They also did their best to keep other ethnic groups outside of this area. The ultimate outcome was that these groups, over the years, expanded into locations outside of Illinois and turned into violent street gangs that would do almost any unlawful act for profit.

At one time many of the members of this gang were confined to correctional facilities throughout Illinois, New York, Connecticut, California, and New Mexico. Only within the past ten years has this gang set out on a major recruitment drive, resulting in a sharp increase in the number of gang members throughout the United States. This gang is primarily Hispanic, while the makeup of the gang is male as well as female. Members of the ALKN do most of their recruiting in Hispanic neighborhoods throughout most major metropolitan areas of the United States. Gang members appeal to the pride of young Hispanics, who should know and maintain their heritage. During their tenure as gang members they will be able to view their own as well as other gang members' personal, social, and economic growth. Juveniles between the ages of 10 to 12 are recruited into the gangs and are known as Pee Wee members while young teenagers between the ages of 12 and 14 are known as Juniors. Older adolescents between the ages of 16 and 20 are called Homeboys. Females who join the Almighty Latin Queen Nation (ALQN) become gang members and must follow the same codes as male members. Females are used by the male gang members as drug dealers, gun holders, and partners in sex.

New members are not informed of the consequences that they face as gang members if they step out of line. What they will find out is that if they make a serious mistake or fail to perform a task properly they will more than likely be either beaten on sight (BOS), tortured, or killed (terminated on sight—TOS) by other gang members. Two specific instances illustrate the danger faced by gang members who violate gang rules. In the first case gang member William Cartagena was decapitated, burned, and left in the bathtub of his Bronx apartment for violating gang policy by becoming a police informer. Another member, James Gonzalez, was shot to death in Manhattan for violating gang rules related to homosexual activities (Tabor, 1994; Executive Crown Authority, 1991; O'Shaughnessy, 1994).

As an organized criminal group the ALKN is well established with a hierarchical structure. They also have a chain of command to ensure that members strictly adhere to the group's charter. The hierarchy of this gang is described in the following sections.

## The Council Committee Structure

The Council Committee is the highest level of command within the ALKN's chain of command. Leaders of the ALKN are selected according to their rank to serve on the Council Committee. This council's major purpose is to provide the membership with an open line of communication throughout the organization.

*Crown Chairman.* Also known as Padrino (Father), the Crown Chairman has total control over the gang. He is the leader as well as the arranger of legitimate and illegitimate activities of gang members.

*Executive Crown.* As second in command, the Executive Crown runs the organization when the Crown Chairman is not available. He reviews and analyzes planned activities of gang members. He must also maintain order during council meetings.

*Prime Minister of Defense.* Whoever holds this role must stay on top of all security matters, provide security for all events involving the gang, and keep an updated list of all of the people who oppose or dislike the gang.

*Crown Treasurer.* The task of maintaining all the gang's financial records, collecting all back dues, and setting up a budget for all the gang's old and new projects falls to the Crown Treasurer.

*Crown Secretariat.* The major administrative official of the gang is the Crown Secretariat. This person must keep records relating to all gang meetings and assist the Executive Crown, Prime Minister, and Crown Treasurer. Any time records are inspected, the Crown Secretariat must be present to assure that everything goes smoothly.

*Regional First Crowns of all Chapters.* This position carries the responsibility of maintaining order in the gang and instituting social and business activities both inside and outside the gang's ranks. This leader must also solve any problems within each regional organization and distribute all policy changes to the members (Executive Crown Authority, 1991).

## Supreme Chapter Structure

A second level of leadership, known as the Supreme Chapter, is responsible for ensuring that all Council Committee mandates and recommendations are transmitted to and executed by all members of the organization. The hierarchy of the second tier of leaders includes some similarities and some differences from the Council Committee's structure.

*Supreme First Crown.* This leader is the highest-ranking crown. Whatever rules he proposes or mandates are considered the law to be followed by all members of the gang. He controls his region, and his main task is to make certain that everyone in the organization follows the guidelines set forth by both the Council Committee and him.

*Supreme Second Crown.* This person functions as second in command of the region and, like the First Crown, he makes sure that members adhere to gang policy. The Second Crown will run the organization anytime the First Crown is on leave.

*Supreme Warlord Nation.* The Supreme Warload is considered to be that gang's Defense Minister. This leader plans and implements a great deal of the strategy used by the gang during confrontations with other groups. Another assignment relegated to this leader is overseeing the behavior of members of the gang. The Supreme Warlords are responsible for the conduct of the members; it is their job to detect any wrongdoing within the organization. They are also responsible for punishing any subordinates who disobey organizational guidelines and/or standards.

*Supreme Crown of Arms.* As one who works directly for the Supreme Warlord, this leader's main function is to manage and review all security strategies related to the gang's field operations. This leader is also responsible for both the upkeep and upgrading of the gang's weapons, ammunition, and other defensive equipment.

*Supreme Captain Crown Advisor.*   This supervisory position requires the appointee to inform the crowns of the history, customs, regulations, and other conditions within the organization. As a leader within the gang, this supervisor's advice is also heavily relied upon by most higher-ranking members of this organization.

*Guardian Crowns.*   This group of members of the gang acts as a security force used to protect the crown and other superior officers within the organization.


## Regional Chapter Structure

The third and final level of this organization is the Regional Groups whose members work for the betterment of the whole gang (Executive Crown Authority, 1991).

*First Crown.*   As an appointed leader who controls a specified region, this leader is the highest-ranking crown in the organization. As leaders they must be accorded the same respect as other high-ranking bosses.

*Second Crown.*   This person substitutes for the First Crown whenever necessary and checks the membership to assure leaders that all members throughout the region are adhering to all gang procedures and policies.

*Minister of Defense.*   This person is in command of strategy, present and future, and maintains gang control over old or new territories, disgruntled members, business partnerships, or threats from other gangs. A minister must constantly be in contact with the Supreme Warlord who advises the Minister on tactics and/or strategy.

*Crown of Arms.*   This role is filled by the main advisor to the Minister of Defense. The person maintains security throughout the gang by controlling the procurement and allocation of weapons to gang members throughout this region, setting up security for all field operations, and keeping records on all chapter meetings.

*Captain Crown Advisor.*   As advisor to gang leaders on all activities—present and future—involving members of the gang, this person is sometimes considered the gang historian because of his knowledge of gang history, customs, and procedure.

*Crown Prince.*   This supervisor of all field operations requires all members to comply and participate fully when assigned to field operations (Executive Crown Authority, 1991).

Rank designation is denoted through the use of colored beads; black represents death and gold represents life. Members have five black beads followed by five gold beads while leaders of the gang have five black beads followed by two gold beads. Black beads are worn in respect of prior members who suffered and died for the cause of the ALKN. Gold represents the brightness of the sunlight that illuminates the crown. The gang's emblem is a five-point crown with each point representing one of the following five factors:

1. *Love* is carried in the hearts of the members for the crown as well as for all other members of the ALKN.

2. *Respect* for all other members of the nation and the crown. Respect for each other should coincide with the high esteem that the members hold for the Nation.

3. *Honor* for all other members as well as the leaders of the ALKN. Members must always respect and honor the organization.

4. *Sacrifice* means giving up everything mentally, physically, and emotionally for the benefit of the ALKN and its membership.

5. *Obedience* as a member of a close-knit family. It is very important that all obey and remain loyal to ALKN leaders as well as to the constitution set forth for all members by the ALKN (Executive Crown Authority, 1991).

Much of the income of the ALKN comes from member's participation in drug trafficking, which is done mostly at street level. Gang members, under the guidance of their leaders, also participate in extortion rings, weapons trafficking, and other violent activities. Once this gang moves an operation into a neighborhood it does not take it long to take over all the unlawful activities in that community. The ALKN moved into neighborhoods throughout New York, Illinois, and Connecticut.

Federal and local law enforcement agencies have arrested numerous gang members for illegal activities involving drugs and guns. One of the most ignominious incidents took place in Staten Island, New York, in 1995. During a drug raid at the Staten Island home of ALKN gang leader Jose Santos, police discovered a 15-month-old baby girl lying in a crib; not only was she wearing the traditionally colored gang beads but a semi-automatic pistol had been placed on each side of her head. Needless to say, four gang members were arrested for possession of drugs and weapons as well as for endangering the welfare of the child (Pierre-Pierre, 1995; New York City Housing Authority, 1994).

## Netas

Neta is a criminal organization similar to the ALKN. It was originally formed in the late 1970s in a correctional institute in Rio Pedras, Puerto Rico, by an inmate named Carlos Torres Irriarte, also known as "La Sombra" (the Shadow). This group was originally created by Irriarte to stop the violence and rights violations against Hispanic inmates at Rio Pedras prison by both the prison administration and other inmates. Irriarte taught other inmates that the only possible way to solve the problems facing them in the correctional institutions was by banding together in peace and accordance to stand up for their rights. According to Puerto Rican custom the word *Neta* is screamed out three times to properly commemorate the birth of a child, while the Neta gang will shout out the word *Neta* to venerate "La Sombra" and all other members of Neta who have sacrificed their lives for the gang (NYPD, 1994).

It did not take long for the Netas to form gangs in prisons throughout the East Coast. In Connecticut, as in most other federal and state correctional facilities, the Netas have formed tightly knit criminal organizations that are not only involved in criminal activities within the prison but also carefully protect all inmates who are members of the Neta organization. As with most other gangs, Neta members must specifically follow five major points set forth by gang leaders:

1. Members must always show respect toward Puerto Rico and its flag.

2. Members must know the Neta colors and understand what they mean:

    *White* — Peace and harmony
    *Red* — Blood shed by our members
    *Black* — Reverence for our departed members.

3. All new members must swear allegiance to the gang.

4. Any member who violates gang policy must be punished.

5. Members must demonstrate an ever-increasing devotion to the group along with a lasting desire to fight any attacks on the organization.

This gang also established 27 other specific rules that must be followed by all gang members (NYPD, 1994).

As a group, the Netas have become associated with the Los Macheteros, a revolutionary group that is seeking independence for Puerto Rico. Neta gang members also feel that they are part of an oppressed group of people who are being controlled by a government, the United States, that has no right to govern this island or its people. This gang holds their fallen leader and members in high esteem. On the thirteenth of each month a special service is held honoring those members.

Membership of this gang is predominantly Hispanic, but it has a sprinkling of black and white members as well. In fact, this gang does not recruit members according to race or ethnicity but instead tries to enlist new members who are humble and respect the rights of other people.

The gang leadership hierarchy in place includes a president, vice-president, recruiter, secretary, sergeant at arms, enforcers, and workers. Gang colors are the same as the Puerto Rican flag: red, white, and blue. Like their ALKN counterparts, the Neta membership is also considered a highly violent gang that funds their activities by drug trafficking, extortion, and intimidation. Gang members are limited in what they can do, which includes following a code of gang ethics in order to survive (NYPD, 1994).

## CONCLUSIONS

As this chapter indicates, gang activity worldwide has increased drastically over the past two decades. These types of organized crime groups and their unlawful activities will continue to flourish until all nations come together and institute national guidelines, laws and enforcement policies to make gang operations unprofitable and infeasible.

# CHAPTER 14
# Conclusions

This text attempts to provide a pragmatic look at all types of gangs. No discussion of working with gangs has been included because we believe that before one can work with a gang(s) one must understand the background, structure, and philosophy of the gang. Providing the basis for that understanding is what we have attempted to do here.

Even though each gang is unique, they all share one important element: they are a plague on our society, and are trying to take our children. However overused this statement has been during the Clinton administration and in the political process in general, with respect to gangs it is absolutely, positively true. Make no mistake, gangs seek out and recruit children in their efforts to continue and maintain themselves. Gangs also share another important element: crime, particularly violent crime. Crime is *the* defining characteristic. As Ryan (1998) noted, "Crime is what gangs do. Despite all the other activities they engage in [some legitimate] and despite their position statements of wanting to help and save the community, it is crime that they live for and crime that defines them."

The type of crime that most defines them is violent crime. Violence defines gangs and sets them apart from other criminal groups. Much of the time this violence is deadly violence, which sweeps innocent people along with it. It is violence in the name of the gang, violence that is mutually elaborating (Garfinkel, 1967). It defines the situation as a gang event, and the gang is seen as the generating force behind the violence.

Violence maintains gang solidarity; it keeps the gang together. However, even for the gang, the violence must be done in moderation. Too much external attention, which the violence will bring, can reduce cohesiveness, solidarity, and numbers. Gang members may go to jail or may die, neither of which is beneficial for the gang.

While it is violence that often brings the heat, violence often reduces the heat as well. One gangster in Chicago killed the "wrong person," thus bringing the full brunt of the Chicago Police Department into the area as they searched for the shooter. This police presence resulted in decreased drug sales, and therefore money, because gang members could not work their corner when the cops were there. Unfortunately the cops were not having any luck finding the shooter. Knowing that the cops would return to "normal" duties once the shooter was found, the gang found and delivered the shooter themselves, dead.

As a society we cannot stand for these kinds of behaviors. The time for handholding and rationalizing is over. We must adopt a zero-tolerance policy for gangs and gangsters. Only through this approach can the gang plague on our society be ended. The first step is to understand the gang. It is our hope that we have assisted in this first step.

# References

Abadinsky, Howard. *The Mafia in America: An Oral History*. New York: Praeger, 1981.

Adams, David. "The Organ Theft Scandal," *London Times*, November 18, 1993, p. 18.

Adams, Nathan. "Menace of the Russian Mafia," *Reader's Digest*, August 1992, pp. 33–40.

Agence France Presse. "Germans, Swiss Break Drug Ring, Seize Heroin," July 7, 1994.

Agence France Presse. "Billion Dollar Jewish-Moslem Money Laundering Ring Cracked," February 19, 1995.

Agres, Ted and Seper, Jerry. "Nigerian Nationals Are New Syndicate Plaguing the U.S.," *Washington Times*, January 27, 1986, pp. 1, 7.

Albini, Joseph L. *The American Mafia: Genesis of a Legend*. New York: Appleton-Century Crofts, 1991.

*Alcohol, Tobacco and Firearms Bulletin*. Jamaican ORCR, 1993.

Alexander, Shana. *The Pizza Connection: Lawyers, Money, Drugs, Mafia*. New York: Weidenfeld and Nicolson, 1988.

Anastasia, George. *Blood and Honor: Inside the Scarfo Mob—The Mafia's Most Violent Family*. New York: William Morrow & Company, Inc., 1991.

Anderson, John Ward and Khan, Kamran. "Heroin Plan by Pakistanis Alleged," *Washington Post*, September 12, 1994, p. A13.

Anslinger, Harry J. and Ousler, Will. *The Murderers: The Story of Narcotics Gangs*. New York: American Book–Stratford Press, 1961.

Arlacchi, Pino. *The Mafia Business: The Mafia Ethic and the Spirit of Capitalism*. Great Britain: Biddles, Ltd., Guildford and King's Lynn, 1986.

Arostegui, Martin. "Castro's Scapegoats," *National Review*, December 28, 1992, pp. 33–35.

Asbury, H. *The Gangs of New York*. New York: Capricorn, 1971.

Associated Press. "Robbery in Nablus Raises Fear New Gang Forming," March 12, 1990.

Associated Press. "Authorities Seize 1,422 Kilograms of Hashish," January 19, 1994.

*Australian Intelligence Journal*. "The Development of the Triads in Hong Kong," 1st ed., 1993.

Balagoon, K., et al. *Look for Me in the Whirlwind: The Collective Autobiography of the New York 21*. New York: Random House, 1971.

Ball, Karen. "Suspect Tells My Side of Story," *New York Daily News*, June 9, 1995, pp. 4, 34.

Ball, Karen. "He Swipes at Extort Rap," *New York Daily News*, June 11, 1995, p. 13.

*Baltimore Sun*. "Probe Uncovers Links of Drug Cartel, Mafia," December 17, 1994, p. 4.

Barboza, Joe and Messick, Hank. *Barboza*. New York: Dell Publishing, 1975.

Barker, Anthony. "New Polish Premier Declares War on Gangsters," Reuters, March 7, 1995.

Barr, Cameron W. "Japanese Extortionists Target Corporate Meetings," *Christian Science Monitor*, July 6, 1994, p. 2.

Barrett, Amy. "From Thefts of Art to Toilet Paper, Czechoslovakia Crime Wave Spreads," *Wall Street Journal*, November 6, 1992, p. 11.

Barzini, Luigi. *The Italians*. New York: Bantam, 1972.

Beacon, Bill. "Report Says Russians Forced to Pay Protection Money," *Times Colonist*, December 24, 1993, p. F2.

Beck, Simon. "Chinatown Godfather," *Sunday Morning Post*, August 21, 1994, p. 12.

Bell, Kenneth. "Insight," presentation, September 25, 1989.

Bell, Kenneth. "Black Gangs," presentation at Jacksonville State University, April 30, 1998.

*Bergen Record*. "Bumpy Road to Peace Takes Toll on Israelis," October 19, 1994, p. A22.

Berke, Richard L. "Bennett's Two Problems: Supply and Demand," *New York Times*, April 16, 1989, p. E2.

Bidi, Rahal. "Main Suspect in India Bombing Held at Station," *New Delhi Daily Telegraph*, August 6, 1994, p. 15.

Block, Alan A. *Space, Time and Organized Crime*. New Brunswick, NJ: Transaction Publishers, 1994.

Block, Alan A. and Scarpitti, Frank R. *Poisoning for Profit: The Mafia and Toxic Waste*. New York: William Morrow and Company, 1985.

Blum, Patrick. "Crime Claims Anger Czechs," *Financial Times*, August 25, 1993, p. 2.

Blumenthal, Ralph and Bohlen, Celestine. "Soviet Emigres in U.S. Fusing into a New Mob," *New York Times*, June 4, 1989, pp. 1, 38.

Bohlen, Celestine. "Russia Mobsters Grow More Violent and Pervasive," *New York Times*, August 16, 1993, pp. A1, A6.

Bonavolonta, Jules and Duffy, Brian. *The Good Guys*. New York: Simon & Schuster, 1996.

Bonanno, Joseph and Lalli, Sergio. *A Man of Honor: The Autobiography of Joseph Bonanno*. New York: Simon & Schuster, 1983.

Bonner, Raymond. "Poland Becomes a Major Conduit for Drug Traffic," *New York Times*, December 30, 1993, p. 3.

Borger, Julian. "The Spies Who Thumped Back in from the Cold," *Guardian*, February 19, 1994, p. 11.

Bosarge, Betty B. "White Heroin Pouring In: DEA, Police Trying to Cope, But Can't Stop the Flood," *Organized Crime Digest*, 1(6), June 1980, pp. 1–3.

Booth, Martin. *The Triads*. New York: St Martin's Press, 1991.

Brooke, James. "At Home (That's Prison) with Medellin's Ochoas," *New York Times*, February 28, 1995, p. A10.

Brooke, James. "Kidnappings Soar in Latin America," *New York Times*, April 7, 1995, p. A8.

Brooke, James. "Colombia Marvels at Drug Kingpin: A Chain-Saw Killer Too?" *New York Times*, June 21, 1995, p. A8.

Builta, Jeff. "Current Middle East Narcotics Activity," *Criminal Organizations*, 9(2), Summer 1994.

Burke, Dan. "Close-up of an Asian Gang Lord," *Gazette, Montreal*, March 30, 1991, pp. B1, B6.

Burns, John F. "India Pressing Bombing Case Against Pakistan," *New York Times*, August 11, 1994, p. A6.

Burns, John F. "Heroin Scourges Million Pakistanis," *New York Times*, April 1, 1995, p. 3.

California Department of Justice. "Russian Organized Crime," October, 1993.

Capeci, Jerry and Sennott, Charles M. "Snake Slithers to China," *New York Daily News*, June 20, 1993, p. 21.

*CBS News* (*West 57th*). "The Palestinian Connection: Dirty Business," June 27, 1989.

Chakravarty, Pratop. "Key Suspect in Bombay Blasts Arrested: Pakistani Involvement Alleged," Agence France Presse, August 5, 1994, p. 2.

Chalidze, Valery. *Criminal Russia: Essays on Crime in the Soviet Union*. New York: Random House, 1977.

Chalmers, D.M. *Hooded Americanism: The History of the Ku Klux Klan*. New York: Doubleday & Company, 1965.

Chan, Ying. "Crackdown Traps Asian Prostitutes," *New York Daily News*, May 17, 1993, p. 7.

Chan, Ying. "Queen of Smuggling is Fujian Hero," *New York Daily News*, June 17, 1993, p. 7.

Chan, Ying. "Chinatown Tong Tied to Scam," *New York Daily News*, June 25, 1994, p. 9.

Chan, Ying. "Grand Good-bye to a Godfather," *New York Daily News*, August 14, 1994, p. 10.

Chan, Ying and Dao, James. "Crime Rings Snaking into a New Biz," *New York Daily News*, September 23, 1990, pp. 32, 33.

Chan, Ying and Merzler-Lavan, Rosemary. "Global Mob Ran Scam," *New York Daily News*, August 30, 1994, p. 7.

Chan, Ying and Ross, Barbara. "Chinatown Big Dead," *New York Daily News*, August 7, 1994, p. 4.

Chicago Crime Commission. *Organized Crime in Chicago*. Chicago: 1990.

Chicago Police Department. "Street Gangs," 1993.

Chicago Police Department. "Auto Theft Gangs," November 1994.

Chin, James. "Crime and the Asian American Community: The Los Angeles Response to Koreatown," *Journal of California Law Enforcement*, 19(2), 1992, pp. 52–61.

Chin, Ko-lin. *Chinese Subculture and Criminality: Nontraditional Crime Groups in America*. Westport, CT: Greenwood Press, 1990.

Chin, Steven A. "Viet Youths Find a Niche in Crime," *San Francisco Examiner*, April 29, 1991, pp. A1, A6.

Chin, Steven A. "Scams Target Immigrant Investors," *San Francisco Examiner*, April 19, 1992, pp. A1, A8.

Christian, Shirley. "Central America: A New Drug Focus," *New York Times*, December 16, 1991, p. A10.

Clerc, Herve. "Government Announces Spectacular Drug Seizures," Agence France Presse, March 25, 1995.

Cleu Line Policy Analysis Division. November 1991.

Cleu Line Policy Analysis Division. "People Trade and Other Scams," November 1992.

Cleu Line Policy Analysis Division. August 1993.

Cleu Line Policy Analysis Division. "Crime Is Out of Control," Coordinated Law Enforcement Unit, May 1994, pp. 1–10.

Clines, Francis X. "Cops and Robbers, Gangs and Vice: Moscow Finds Out It Has Them All," *New York Times*, December 6, 1990, p. A20.

Coffey, Thomas A. *The Long Thirst: Prohibition in America*. New York: Norton, 1975.

Cohon, Mary Ellen. "New Mafia Bilks Credit System," *Northtown News*, December 30, 1985, pp. 1, 8.

Cole, Richard. "Asian Gangs Like a Giant Spider Web Spread Across the World,"*Seattle Times World*, July 17, 1994, p. A13.

Combined Agency Border Intelligence Network. "Nigerian Heroin Smuggling: An Overview, 1989," Cabinet, 1989.

Combined Agency Border Intelligence Network. "West African Narcotics Trafficking System," Cabinet, 1989.

Conly, C.H. *Street Gangs: Current Knowledge and Strategies*. Washington, DC: National Institute of Justice, 1993.

Connecticut State Police. "Prison and Street Gangs in Connecticut," December 1992.

Constantine, Thomas A. "Report to Subcommittee on Crime and Criminal Justice: Heroin Production and Trafficking Trends," U.S. House of Representatives, September 29, 1994.

Cooper, Michael. "U.S. Indicts a Fugitive over Drugs," *New York Times*, June 8, 1995, p. B3.

Copeland, Peter. "Drug Submarines Sneak Through Caribbean Waters," *San Francisco Examiner*, February 18, 1994, p. A17.

Cowell, Alan. "Heroin Pouring Through Porous European Borders," *New York Times*, February 9, 1993, p. 3.

Cressey, Donald R. *Theft of a Nation: The Structure and Operations of Organized Crime in America*. New York: Harper & Row, 1969.

Criminal Justice Institute: South Salem, New York. "Prison Gangs: Their Extent, Nature and Impact on Prisons," Washington, DC: U.S. Government Printing Office, 1985.

CTK National News Wire. "Seminar on Organized Crime Held," March 31, 1994.

Cullen, Robert. "Comrades in Crime," *Playboy*, October 1993, pp. 70–72, 130, 160–163.

Cummings, John and Volkman, Ernest. *Goombata: The Improbable Rise and Fall of John Gotti and His Gang*. Toronto: Little, Brown and Company (Canada) Limited, 1990.

Dade County Sheriff's Department. "Marielitos: A Religious Rite," August 1991.

Dahlberg, John-Thor. "Tracking the Russian Connection," *Los Angeles Times*, June 6, 1993, pp. A1, A12, A13.

Dao, James. "Asian Street Gangs Emerging as New Underworld," *New York Times*, April 1, 1992, pp. A1, B2.

David, John J. "Outlaw Motorcycle Gangs: A Transnational Problem," paper presented at the annual meetings of the conference on International Terrorism and Transnational Crime, Chicago, August, 1988.

Davis, R.H. "Cruising for Trouble: Gang-Related Drive-By Shootings," *FBI Law Enforcement Bulletin*, 64, 1995, pp. 16–22.

Decker, S.H. "Collective and Normative Features of Gang Violence," *Justice Quarterly*, 13, 1996, pp. 243–264.

Decker, S.H. and Kempf-Leonard, K. "Constructing Gangs: The Social Definition of Youth Activities," *Criminal Justice Policy Review*, 5, 1991, pp. 271–291.

DeCordoba, Jose. "End of Pablo Escobar May Slow Violence, But Not Cocaine Trade," *Wall Street Journal*, December 3, 1993, pp. A1, A4.

Dees, M. *Gathering Storm: America's Militia Threat*. New York: HarperCollins, 1996.

Dees, M. and Filler, S. *A Season for Justice: The Life and Times of Civil Rights Lawyer Morris Dees*. New York: MacMillan Publishing Company, 1991.

DeMaris, Ovid. *The Last Mafioso: The Treacherous World of Jimmy Fratianno*. New York: Avon Books, 1975.

Derfner, Larry. "Israeli Mafia 'Reaches All Over U.S.,'" *Jerusalem Post Reporter*, September 9, 1990, p. 3.

DeStefano, Anthony. "Asian Gangs Preying on Garment Factories," *New York Newsday*, June 2, 1991, p. 18.

Deukmajian, G. "Report on Youth Gang Violence in California," Department of Justice, State of California, 1981.

*Deutsche Presse-Agentur*. "Iranian Authorities Say They Smash Drug Gang in Southeast," November 20, 1994, p. 4.

Dicker, Fredric. "On the Cocaine Trail," *New York Post*, January 7, 1987, pp. 4–6.

Dobson, Chris. "Fears of Triad-Led War Hit New York," *Sunday Morning Post*, July 26, 1992, pp. 12–13.

Dobson, Chris. "Triads Bid for World Link-Up," *Sunday Morning Post*, September 6, 1992, p. 18.

Dobson, Chris. "China's Police Chief Met Top Triad Bosses," *South China Morning Post*, April 11, 1993, pp. 1–2.

Dobson, Chris. "Sun Yee On Incorporated," *Sunday Morning Post Magazine*, October 3, 1993, pp. 6–9.

Dobson, Chris. "The Shark's Fin War," *South African Sunday Morning Post*, July 10, 1994, p. 14.

Dobson, Chris and Chan, Quinton. "Beijing Chief's Triad Remarks Distorted," *Sunday Morning Post*, April 18, 1993, p. 9.

Dombrink, John and Song, John Huey-Long. "Hong Kong after 1997: Transnational Organized Crime in a Shrinking World," *Journal of Contemporary Criminal Justice*, 12(4), December 1996, pp. 329–339.

Drohan, Madelaine. "Russian Mafia Haunts Sweden," *Toronto Globe*, September 27, 1993, p. B7.

Drug Enforcement Administration. "Cocaine Trafficking Trends in Europe," Fall 1982, pp. 21–24.

Drug Enforcement Administration. "International Initiatives to Control Coca Production and Cocaine Trafficking," Fall 1982, pp. 6–9.

Drug Enforcement Administration. "Casinos and Drug Money: A Laundering Loophole," Summer 1984, pp. 22–24.

Drug Enforcement Administration. "Colombia," July 1985, pp. 1–17.

Drug Enforcement Administration. "Cocaine Trafficking by Colombian Organizations," April 22, 1987, pp. 1–14.

Drug Enforcement Administration. "Cuban Drug Activities," 1990.

Drug Enforcement Administration: U.S. Department of Justice. "Drug Trafficking by Nigerians," 4(8), 1984–1985, pp. 13–14.

Drug Enforcement Administration: U.S. Department of Justice. "Heroin Trafficking: The Nigerian Connection," February 1985.

Drug Enforcement Administration: U.S. Department of Justice. "Israeli Organized Crime," April 28, 1986.

Drug Enforcement Administration: U.S. Department of Justice. "Heroin Trafficking by Israeli Nationals," October 1986.

Drug Enforcement Administration: U.S. Department of Justice. "Mexican Organized Crime Groups," 1987.

Drug Enforcement Administration: U.S. Department of Justice. "Update on Pakistani Traffickers in the U.S," March 18, 1987.

Drug Enforcement Administration: U.S. Department of Justice. "Intelligence on Nigerian Heroin Traffickers," May 5, 1987.

Drug Enforcement Administration: U.S. Department of Justice. "Nigerian Heroin Smuggling Methods," May 12, 1987.

Drug Enforcement Administration: U.S. Department of Justice. "Statement to Robert M. Stutman Concerning Emerging Groups in Heroin Trafficking," July 10, 1987.

Drug Enforcement Administration: U.S. Department of Justice. "Dominican Narco-Traffickers," February 18, 1992.

Drug Enforcement Administration: U.S. Department of Justice. "Special Intelligence Report: Dominican Criminal Activity-A New York Perspective," February 1993.

Drug Enforcement Administration: U.S. Department of Justice. "Trends in Traffic," May 1993.

Drug Enforcement Report. "Asian Criminal Organizations Move into Heroin and Ice Trafficking," October 8, 1991, p. 8.

Duffy, Brian and Trimble, Jeff. "The Looting of Russia," *U.S. News and World Report*, March 7, 1994, pp. 36–47.

Duffy, John. "Nigerian Fraud," *IACCI News*, 91, March/April 1986, pp. 1, 2.

Duffy, John. "Fraudulent Applications," *IACCI News*, 92, May/June 1986, pp. 1–8.

Duga, Amanita. "The New Mob: Nigerian Mafia Feeding N.Y.'s Heroin Habit," *Staten Island Advance*, February 5, 1990, pp. A1, A6.

Duga, Amanita and Balsamini, Dean C. "The New Mob: $$ Scam—Island Banks Have Lost Millions to Nigerian Mafia Schemes," *Staten Island Advance*, February 4, 1990, p. A5.

Duga, Amanita and Balsamini, Dean C. "The New Mob: Nigerian Mafia Digs into Nation," *Staten Island Advance*, February 6, 1990, pp. A1, A17.

Dunn, Ashley. "After Crackdown, Smugglers of Chinese Find New Routes," *New York Times*, November 1, 1994, pp. A1, A24.

Ebron, Betty Liu and Mustain, Gene. "Cartels Cook Up Pipe Line to U.S.," *New York Daily News*, May 23, 1993, p. 20.

*Economist*. "Cuba and Drugs: Spot the Dots," April 18, 1992, pp. 23–24.

*Economist*. "Free to Cheat in Eastern Europe," March 11, 1995, p. 54.

Edgerton, R. Foreword. In J.D. Vigil, *Barrio Gangs: Street Life and Identity in Southern California*. Austin: University of Texas Press, 1988.

Efron, Sonni. "Vietnamese Girl Gangs Become Armed, Violent," *Los Angeles Times*, December 10, 1989, pp. A1, A53.

Ehrenfeld, Rachel. *Evil Money: Encounters Along the Money Trail*. New York: Harper Business, 1992.

Eisner, Peter. "Godfather and the Witch Key Cult Slaying Suspects," *New York Newsday*, April 14, 1989, pp. 5, 33.

Eisner, Peter. "Seeks Amnesty in Return for Fighting Communism," *Newsday*, September 10, 1989, pp. 7, 29.

Elliott, Dorinda. "Russia's Goodfellas: The Mafia on the Neva," *Newsweek*, October 12, 1992, pp. 50–52.

Erlanger, Steven. "Images of Lawlessness Twist Russian Reality," *New York Times*, June 7, 1995, p. A10.

*Executive Crown Authority*. "Charter of the Almighty Latin King Nation," January 1, 1991.

Fagan, J. Interview with Conly. In C.H. Conly, *Street Gangs: Current Knowledge and Strategies*. Washington, DC: National Institute of Justice.

Faison, Seth. "Head of Chinese Gang Re-entered the U.S. after Deportation," *New York Times*, June 10, 1993, pp. A1, B4.

Faison, Seth. "More Sought After Raid on Smugglers," *New York Times*, August 30, 1993, p. B1.

Faison, Seth. "Asian Gang Members Arrested in Kidnapping," *New York Times*, March 22, 1994, p. B3.

Faison, Seth. "Dominican Officers Arrest 2 Linked to Violent Drug Gang," *New York Times*, April 4, 1994, p. B7.

Faison, Seth. "U.S. Says 17 Ran Murder Gang That Ruled Heroin Sales in the Bronx," *New York Times*, May 27, 1994, pp. A1, B2.

Faison, Seth. "Charges Against Tong President Threaten a Chinatown Institution," *New York Times*, June 1, 1994, pp. A1, B5.

Faison, Seth. "Arrests in New York Are Said to Cripple a Huge Drug Gang," *New York Times*, September 9, 1994, pp. A1, B4.

Faison, Seth. "U.S. Indicts 2 Businessmen as Chinatown Gang Lords," *New York Times*, September 10, 1994, p. A23.

Farley, Maggie. "Turning a Profit on Human Cargo," *New York Newsday*, June 7, 1993, p. 19.

Federal Bureau of Investigation: U.S. Department of Justice. "Oriental Organized Crime," January 1985.

Federal Bureau of Investigation: U.S. Department of Justice. "Asian Organized Crime in the United States," 1987.

Federal Bureau of Investigation: U.S. Department of Justice. "An Analysis of the Threat of Japanese Organized Crime to the United States and Its Territories," July 1992.

Federal Bureau of Investigation: U.S. Department of Justice. "Organized Crime in the Americas," 1993.

Federal Bureau of Investigation: U.S. Department of Justice. "Vietnamese Criminal Activity in the United States: A National Perspective," March 1993.

Federal Bureau of Investigation: U.S. Department of Justice. "An Introduction to Organized Crime in the United States," July 1996.

Financial Crimes Enforcement Network. "Jamaican Organized Crime," August 1992.

*Financial Times*. "Castro's Executions Send Shocks Through Region," July 22, 1989, p. 12.

Fisher, Ian. "A Window on Immigrant Crime," *New York Times*, June 17, 1993, pp. B1, B8.

Fopiano, W. and Harvey, John. *The Godson*. New York: St. Martin's Press, 1993.

Foner, Philip S. *The Black Panthers Speak*. New York: Da Capo Press, 1995.

Franzese, Michael and Matera, Dary. *Quitting the Mob*. New York: Harper, 1992.

Freed, D. *Agony in New Haven: The Trial of Bobby Seale, Ericka Huggins, and the Black Panther Party*. New York: Simon & Schuster, 1971.

Freedman, Maurice. *Chinese Lineage and Society: Fukien and Kwangtung*. New York: Humanities Press, Inc., 1966.

Freedman, Robert. "The Organizatsiya," *New York Magazine*, November 7, 1994, pp. 50–58.

Fried, Joseph P. "2 Businessmen Indicted as Heads of a Crime Gang in Chinatown," *New York Times*, December 10, 1993, p. B7.

Friedland, Jonathan. "Traffic Problem: Rising Tide of Chinese Illegal Immigrants Worries Japan," *Far Eastern Economic Review*, August 4, 1994, p. 20.

Gannon, Kathy. "Pakistan's Thriving Drug Trade Earns Dealers 2.5 Billion Each Year," Associated Press, March 31, 1994.

Gargan, Edward A. "2 Suspects Held and 2 Flee in Fatal Bombay Blasts," *New York Times*, March 16, 1993, p. A3.

Gargan, Edward A. "India Bombings: Gangs Involved, But Who Else," *New York Times*, May 16, 1993, p. 1.

George, J. and Wilcox, L. *Nazis, Communists, Klansmen, and Others on the Fringe: Political Extremism in America*. Buffalo, NY: Prometheus Books, 1992.

Gerth, Jeff. "Israeli Arms, Ticketed to Antigua, Now in Colombian Drug Arsenal," *New York Times*, May 6, 1990, pp. 1, 23.

Ghazi, Katayou. "Drug Trafficking Is Thriving in Iran," *New York Times*, December 4, 1991, p. 13.

Ghosh, S. K. *The Indian Mafia*. New Delhi, India: Ashish Publishing House, 1991.

Giancana, Sam and Giancana, Chuck. *Double Cross: Inside Story of the Mobster Who Controlled America*. New York: Warner Books, 1992.

Gilbert, Andy. "Triads Flourish in an Industry Powerless to Act," *South China Morning Post*, November 30, 1993, p. 3.

Golden, Tim. "Violently, Drug Trafficking in Mexico Rebounds," *New York Times*, March 8, 1993, p. 3.

Golden, Tim. "Cardinal in Mexico Killed in Cross-Fire by Drug Traffickers," *New York Times*, May 25, 1993, pp. A1, A8.

Golden, Tim. "Mexicans Capture Drug Cartel Chief in Prelate's Death," *New York Times*, June 11, 1993, p. 1.

Golden, Tim. "Mexico's Drug Fight Lagging, with Graft Given as Cause," *New York Times*, August 7, 1994, p. 16.

Golden, Tim. "Tons of Cocaine Reaching Mexico in Old Jets," *New York Times*, January 10, 1995, p. 1.

Goldman, P. *The Life and Death of Malcolm X*. New York: Harper & Row, 1973.

Goldstein, A.P. *Delinquent Gangs: A Psychological Perspective*. Champaign, IL: Research Press, 1991.

Gonzalez, David. "Just Boys Being Boys, or Vicious Gangs?" *New York Times*, January 16, 1992, p. B1.

Goodspeed, Peter. "The Curse of the Triads," *Toronto Star*, February 2, 1992, pp. F1, F3.

Goodspeed, Peter. "Asian Gang Members Enroll in Scam School," *Toronto Star*, August 7, 1994, p. E6.

Gosch, Martin A. and Hammer, Richard. *The Last Testament of Lucky Luciano*. Boston: Little, Brown and Company, 1975.

Governor's Organized Crime Prevention Commission. "New Mexico Street Gangs," July 1990.

Governor's Organized Crime Prevention Commission. "New Mexico Street Gangs," May 1991.

Gray, Malcolm. "Capitalist Crimes," *Maclean's*, January 10, 1994, p. 17.

Gray, Malcolm. "Mob Rule," *Maclean's*, May 30, 1994, pp. 16–17.

Grennan, Sean A. "The Threatening Issue of Oriental Organized Crime," *IALEIA Journal*, 7(1), Fall 1992, pp. 1–17.

Gross, Jane. "6 Are Killed as 8 Hour Siege by Gang Ends in California," *New York Times*, April 6, 1991, p. 6.

Guart, Al. "Drug Bigs Wired to Launder Cash," *New York Post*, February 6, 1995, p. 8.

Gurr, T.A. *Violence in America: Protest and Rebellion*. Newbury Park, CA: Sage, 1989.

Hagedorn, John. "Gangs, Neighborhoods and Public Policy," *Social Problems*, 38, 1991, pp. 529–541.

Hamad, Haitham. "Palestinian Gangs Blamed for Murders," Associated Press, October 24, 1989.

Hamm, M.S. *American Skinheads: The Criminology and Control of Hate Crime*. Westport, CT: Praeger, 1993.

Handelman, Stephen. "The Russian Mafia," *Foreign Affairs*, 73(20), March/April 1994.

Hanley, Robert. "Teaneck Killings Linked to Chinese Gang's Power Struggle," *New York Times*, May 26, 1993, p. B5.

Harris County Sheriff's Department. "Nigerian Check and Credit Card Schemes," 1986.

Harrison, Eric. "Jamaicans New Faces in U.S. Crime," *New York Times*, January 17, 1989, pp. A1, A23.

Hazarika, Sanjoy. "Indian Heroin Smugglers Turn to New Cargo," *New York Times*, February 21, 1993, p. 11.

Hersh, Seymour, M. "The Wild East," *Atlantic Monthly*, 273(8), June 1994.

Hockstader, Lee. "Russia's Criminal Condition: Gangsters Spreading Web from Moscow to the West," *Washington Post*, February 26, 1995, pp. 1, 2.

Hockstader, Lee. "A Time of Thieves: Organized Crime in Post Soviet Russia," *Washington Post*, February 27, 1995, p. 2.

Hodgson, Liz. "Triads Linked to LA Car Thefts," *Sunday Morning Post*, August 22, 1993, p. 3.

Hogben, David. "Expert Puzzled by Home Purchase," *Vancouver Sun*, August 6, 1992, pp. B1, B5.

Hogben, David. "Japanese Gangsters Smuggled Heroin into B.C., Police Say," *Vancouver Sun*, August 28, 1992, p. B7.

Hogben, David. "Crime Chief Linked to Two City Companies," *Vancouver Sun*, March 20, 1993, p. A1.

Hogben, David. "Crime Boss Entered Canada Before Buying Home," *Vancouver Sun*, March 20, 1993, p. A5.

Holmes, Stanley. "Getting a Line on Phone Fraud," *Rocky Mountain News*, September 27, 1994, p. 30A.

Horowitz, R. *Honor and the American Dream: Culture and Identity in a Chicago Community*. New Brunswick, NJ: Rutgers University Press, 1983.

Horowitz, Ruth. "Sociological Perspectives on Gangs: Conflicting Definitions." In Ronald C. Huff, *Gangs in America*. Newbury Park, CA: Sage, 1990.

Howell, Ron. "U.S. Denies Posses Linked to Politics," *New York Newsday*, March 12, 1989, pp. 5, 21.

Huff, C. Ronald. "Denial, Overreaction and Misidentification: A Postscript on Public Policy." In Ronald C. Huff, *Gangs in America*. Newbury Park, CA: Sage, 1990.

Hughes, Mark. "Police Hold Mr. Big over Canada Drug Trafficking," *South China Morning Post*, September 16, 1993, p. 3.

Hughes, Mark and Li, Angela. "Suspected Drug King Extradited," *South China Morning Post*, November 30, 1993, p. 2.

Hundley, Tom. "Uprising Gets a New Front Line as Protests Die Down, Palestinian Gangs Gain Prominence," *Chicago Tribune*, May 5, 1992, p. 14.

Hunter-Hodge, Karen. "Rape and Rob Gang on Prowl," *New York Daily News*, February 26, 1992, p. QLI 2.

Illinois State Police. *Criminal Intelligence Bulletin*, no. 42, January 1989.

Iloegbunam, Chuks. "Run of Pot Luck," *Newswatch*, July 11, 1988, p. 25.

Imasa, Peter. "Business Fraud Surges," *Nigerian Economist*, October 14, 1991, pp. 9–10.

Inciardi, James A. *Careers in Crime*. Chicago: Rand McNally, 1975.

International Association of Asian Crime Investigators. "Eastern Region: Asian Crime Conference," December 11–13, 1991.

International Association of Asian Crime Investigators. "Korean Gang Problems: A Proactive Approach I," 6(1), January 1992, pp. 1, 3.

International Association of Asian Crime Investigators. "Korean Gang Problems: A Proactive Approach II," 6(2), March 1992, pp. 2, 6.

International Association of Credit Card Investigators. "Nigerian Fraud Groups," 1984, pp. 1–8.

Internet. "The Media vs. the Mafia: A Country-by-Country Perspective on the Problem," January 1996.

Internet. "The Formation of PKK," December 1995.

Internet. "Jails: The Source for PKK's Personnel," December 1995.

Internet. "PKK in Lebanon," December 1995.

Internet. "PKK and Terrorism," December 1995.

Internet. "PKK's Involvement in Drug Trafficking," December 1995.

Interpol. "Asian Organized Crime Activities in Europe and the United States," December 1993.

Interpol. "Worldwide Organized Crime," September 1998.

Iqbal, Anwar. "Pakistan Arrests Hundreds in the Southern Province," *United Press International*, June 20, 1992.

Irwin, Julie. "Just the Tip of the Iceberg: Bridal Shop Heist Part of Something Bigger," *Chicago Tribune*, August 31, 1994, p. 1.

Jackson, Pamela Irving. "Crime, Youth Gangs and Urban Transition: The Social Dislocations of Postindustrial Economic Development," *Justice Quarterly*, 8, 1991, pp. 379–397.

Jamaican Information Service, January 1998.

James, George. "33 Suspected Chinatown Gang Members Are Indicted," *New York Times*, November 22, 1994, pp. B1, B3.

Jamieson, Alison. *The Modern Mafia: Its Roles and Record*. London: Eastern Press Limited, 1989.

Janofsky, Michael. "Fake Bank Set Up by U.S. Agents Snares Drug Money Launderers," *New York Times*, December 17, 1994, pp. 1, 8.

*Japan Times Weekly International Edition*. "Yamaguchi-Gumi Opposes Anti-Gang Law," April 20–26, 1992, p. 5.

*Japan Times Weekly International Edition*. "Australian Embassy Blocks Sale of Property in Kobe to Yakuza," August 10–16, 1992, p. 18.

*Japan Times Weekly International Edition*. "Yakuza Muscle Their Way into China," September 19–25, 1994, p. 17.

Johnson, Elmer H. "Yakuza (Criminal Gangs): Characteristics and Management in Prison," *IALEIA Journal*, 7(1), January–February 1991, pp. 11–18.

Johnson, Richard. *Juvenile Delinquency and Its Origins*. Cambridge, England: Cambridge University Press, 1979.

Johnston, J.W. "Recruitment to a Youth Gang," *Pacific Sociological Review*, 24, 1983, pp. 355–375.

Jones, Clayton. "After Yakuza Threat Japanese Businesses Breathe a Sigh of Relief," *Christian Science Monitor*, July 1, 1993, p. 9.

Judson, George. "16 Charged as Members of Drug Ring," *New York Times*, June 30, 1994, p. B7.

Kaplan, David, E. and Dubro, Alec. *Yakuza: The Explosive Account of Japan's Criminal Underworld*. Reading, MA: Addison-Wesley, 1986.

Kata, Koji. *Japanese Yakuza*. Toyko: Daiwa Shobu, 1964.

Katz, Jesse. "Reputed Mexican Mafia Leader Dies in Prison," *Los Angeles Times*, November 10, 1993, pp. B1, B4.

Kehinde, Seye. "Nigeria: The Cocaine Epidemic," *African Concord*, May 13, 1991, pp. 31–37.

Kelly, Robert J., Chin, Ko-lin, and Fagan, Jeffrey. "The Structure, Activity, and Control of Chinese Gangs: Law Enforcement Perspectives," *Journal of Contemporary Criminal Justice*, 8(3), September 1992, pp. 256–278.

Kessel, Jerrold. "Israeli Raid on PLO Cell Condemned," *Guardian Foreign*, September 30, 1993, p. 12.

Kessel, Jochen. "Chinatown Crime Wave," *Ottawa Citizen*, March 16, 1991, p. B5.

Kessler, Robert E. "From Car Thief to Cocaine Kingpin," *New York Newsday*, February 15, 1987, pp. 6, 17.

Kessler, Robert E. "Agents Arrest 3, Seize Heroin in Hauppauge: Tip on Couriers from Pakistan," *New York Newsday*, November 8, 1991, p. 26.

Kiefer, Francine S. "Poland Is Now Key Link in Europe's Expanding Traffic in Stolen Cars," *Christian Science Monitor*, April 13, 1992, pp. 1, 4.

Kifner, John. "New Immigrant Wave from Asia Gives the Underworld New Faces," *New York Times*, January 6, 1991, pp. 1, 20.

Kirtzman, Andrew. "Chinatown on Gang War Alert," *New York Daily News*, July 9, 1990, p. 5.

Klebnikov, Paul. "Joe Stalin's Heirs," *Forbes*, September 27, 1993, pp. 124–134.

Klein, M.W. "Street Gang Violence." In N.A. Weiner and N.W. Wolfgang (eds), *Gang Delinquency and Delinquent Subcultures*. New York: Harper & Row, 1968.

Kleinfield, N.R. "Five Charged with Holding Thai Women Captive for Prostitution," *New York Times*, January 5, 1995, p. B1.

Kleinknecht, William, Sennott, Charles M., and Chang, Dean. "Empire of Terror," *New York Daily News*, June 20, 1993, pp. 6, 7, 20.

Koleniak, Mike. "The Mob's Crashing in with Scams," *New York Daily News*, February 28, 1995, p. 28.

Korean National Police. "Report of Organized Gang Activity in South Korea," July 1994.

Kraft, Scott. "A Gaping Gateway for Drugs," *Los Angeles Times*, Febuary 17, 1994, pp. A1, A8–A9.

Laub, Karen. "Palestinian Gangs," Associated Press Worldstream, October 18, 1994.

Lavgine, Yves. *Hell's Angels*. Toronto: Deneua and Wayne, 1996.

Lavgine, Yves. *Hell's Angels: Taking Care of Business*. Toronto: Deneua and Wayne, 1987.

*Law Enforcement News*. "Growing in Power and Viciousness, Vietnamese Gangs Flex Their Muscles," 17(336–337), May 15–31, 1991, pp. 1, 3.

Lawlor, Julia. "Quality Is Matter of Teamwork, Service—New York Telephone: Fraud Crackdown Rings Up Savings," *USA Today*, April 2, 1993, p. 4B.

Leitzel, Jim, Gaddy, Clifford, and Alexeev, Michael. "Mafiosi and Matrioshki: Organized Crime and Russian Reform," *Brookings Review*, 13(1), Winter 1995.

Leusner, Jim. "2 Accused of Using Florida for Mideast Call Forwarding," *Orlando Sentinel Tribune*, August 11, 1992, p. A1.

Levitsky, Melvyn. "Drug Trafficking in China," *U.S. Department of State Dispatch*, May 25, 1992, pp. 415, 416.

Levy, Clifford J. "Russian Emigres Are Among 25 Named in Tax Fraud in Newark," *New York Times*, August 8, 1995, pp. A1, B5.

Limb, Julia. "Colombians Here: Soccer Star Was Hit By Gamblers," *New York Post*, July 4, 1994, p. 4.

Lin, Wendy and Tyre, Peg. "A Gamble All the Way," *New York Newsday*, June 8, 1993, p. 7, 32.

Lintner, Bert. "The Volatile Yunnan Frontier," *Jane's Intelligence Review*, 6(2), February 1, 1994.

Lintner, Bert and Mai, Chiang. "Opium Wars," *Far Eastern Economic Review*, January 20, 1994.

Linzer, Dafna. "Police Chief: Israel Becoming Major Russian Mafia Center," Associated Press, June 28, 1995.

Lipset, S.M. and Raab, E. *The Politics of Unreason: Right-Wing Extremism in America, 1709–1970*. New York: Harper & Row, 1970.

Lorch, Donatella. "Hong Kong Boy: A College Student, and a Ghost Shadow," *New York Times*, January 6, 1991, p. A20.

Los Angeles County Sheriff's Department. "L.A. Style: A Street Gang Manual of the Los Angeles County Sheriff's Department," April 1992.

Los Angeles Police Department. "Asian Gangs in Southern California," October 1982.

*Los Angeles Times*. "Troops Kill 4 in West Bank's 'Black Panther' Gang," December 2, 1989.

*Los Angeles Times*. "The Shadows," August 8, 1992, pp. 28–30.

Lupsha, Peter A. "Cuba's Recent Involvement in Drug Trafficking: The Ochoa-LaGuardia Cases." In Susan Flood (ed.), *International Terrorism: Policy Implications*. Chicago: Office of International Criminal Justice, 1991.

Lyle, John P. "Southwest Asian Heroin: Pakistan, Afghanistan and Iran," *Drug Enforcement*, Summer 1981, pp. 2–6.

Maas, Peter. *Underboss: Sammy the Bull Gravano's Story of Life in the Mafia*. New York: HarperCollins, 1997.

MacFarquhar, Neil. "5 Held in Ring of Shoplifters at L.I. Mall," *New York Times*, March 11, 1995, pp. 25–26.

MacIntyre, Iain. "Bure Has Made No Payments to Russian Mobsters, Says Agent Salcer," *Vancouver Sun*, December 29, 1993, p. D7.

*Magloclen*. "Jamaican Criminal Activities," March 16, 1990.

*Magloclen*. "Special Report: Nigerian Organized Crime," January 1991.

*Magloclen*. "Asian Organized Crime Conference," December 5, 1991.

*Magloclen*. "2nd Quarterly Asian Organized Crime Regional Information Sharing Conference," February 26, 1992.

*Magloclen*. "Dominican Gangs," June 23, 1993, pp. 28–29.

*Magloclen*. "Jamaican Gangs," June 1993, pp. 30–32.

*Magloclen*. "Almighty Latin King Nation," January 14, 1994.

Mallory, Stephen J. "The Risks of Toll Fraud: Telephone Service Theft," *Risk Management*, 41(8), August 1994, p. 23.

Markham-Smith, Ian. "Police Smash Hong Kong Ransom Gang," *Sunday Morning Post*, March 22, 1992, p. 4.

Marshall, Jonathan. "New Israeli Cabinet Member Linked to Suspected Criminals," *San Francisco Chronicle*, April 30, 1991, p. 8.

Martin, M. L. "Asian Gang Activity," *Garden Grove Police Department*, 3rd ed., 1993.

Mascoll, Philip and Pron, Nick. "Drug Posse Leaders Rule with Terror," *Toronto Star*, July 17, 1991, p. 2.

McCoy, Kevin. "Really Hot Mags: Newsstand Raids Net 13 in Scam," *New York Newsday*, December 15, 1994, p. A33.

McFadden, Robert D. "Drug Trafficker Convicted of Blowing Up Jetliner," *New York Times*, December 21, 1994, p. B3.

McGee, Jim. "The Cocaine Connection: The Cali Cartel in America," *Washington Post*, March 26, 1995, pp. A1, A20.

McGee, Jim. "The Cocaine Connection: Murder as a Management Tool," *Washington Post*, March 27, 1995, pp. A1, A12.

McGee, Jim. "The Cocaine Connection: Lawyers Under Scrutiny," *Washington Post*, March 28, 1995, pp. A1, A8.

McGregor, Richard. "Police Links to Japan Garner Drug Arrests," *Australian*, August 11, 1992, p. 8.

McGuire, Phillip C. "Jamaican Posses: A Call for Cooperation Among Law Enforcement Agencies," *Police Chief*, October 1987.

McIllwain, Jeffrey Scott. "From Tong War to Organized Crime: Revising the Historical Perception of Violence in Chinatown," *Justice Quarterly*, 14(1), March 1997, pp. 25–51.

McKenna, James J. "Organized Crime in the Royal Colony of Hong Kong," *Journal of Contemporary Criminal Justice*, 12(4), December 1996, pp. 316–328.

McKenzie, Scott. "Australia Targets HK Triads in Drugs War," *South China Morning Post*, April 6, 1994, p. 5.

McKinley, James C. "U.S. Agents Seize 17 in Raids to Dismantle Jamaican Drug Ring," *New York Times*, December 8, 1990, p. 1.

McKinley, James C. "Bronx Ring Stole 100 Luxury Cars a Month, Officials Say," *New York Times*, February 1, 1995, p. B3.

McKinsey, Kitty. "Spate of Spectacular Raids Show Poland Is Now Drug Gateway to Europe," *Ottawa Citizen*, May 27, 1994, p. D14.

McKinsey, Kitty. "Changing Lifestyles: Poland Fights an Influx of Illegal Drugs from Abroad," *Los Angeles Times*, July 19, 1994, p. 6.

Meier, Barry. "Drug Trade's Army of Crack Gunmen," *New York Newsday*, March 12, 1989, pp. 5, 20.

Mercer, Pamela. "Colombian Who Made World Cup Error Is Slain," *New York Times*, July 3, 1994, pp. A1, A13.

Messing, Philip and Celona, Larry. "Ivankov the Terrible Reigns as City's New Czar of Crime," *New York Post*, March 20, 1995, p. 14.

Meyer, Josh. "Glasnost Gangsters in L.A.," *Los Angeles Times*, April 10, 1992, pp. A1, A30, A31.

Michelini, Alex. "8 Charged in Slaying of Drug Dealers," *New York Daily News*, March 25, 1993, p. 7.

Middleton, Greg. "Bure 'Mafia' Target," *Province*, December 23, 1993, pp. A82, A84.

Miner, Colin. "Bad Heart Earns Murder Suspect Flee Bargain," *New York Post*, August 3, 1994, p. 8.

Miller, W.B. "American Youth Gangs: Past and Present." In A. Blumberg, *Current Perspectives on Criminal Behavior*. New York: Knopf, 1974.

Miller, W.B. *Violence by Youth Gangs and Youth Groups as a Crime Problem in Major American Cities*. Washington, DC: National Institute for Juvenile Justice and Delinquency Prevention, 1975.

Miller, W.B. "Gangs, Groups and Serious Youth Crime." In D. Schicker and D.H. Kelly (eds.), *Critical Issues in Juvenile Delinquency*. Lexington, MA: Lexington, 1980.

Miller, W.B. *Crime by Youth Gangs and Groups in the United States*. Washington, DC: National Institute for Juvenile Justice and Delinquency Prevention, 1982.

Mitchell, Alison. "Russian Emigres Importing Thugs to Commit Contract Crimes in U.S.," *New York Times*, April 11, 1992, pp. 1, 28.

Mitchell, Chris and Marzulli, John. "Terror Ordeal," *New York Daily News*, June 9, 1993, p. 7.

Moneyclips, Ltd. "Crime on the Rise in UAE," *Arab Times*, May 15, 1993.

Moody, John. "A Day with the Chess Player," *Time*, July 1, 1991, pp. 32, 38.

Moore, J. Interview with Conly and Conly. In C.H. Conly, *Street Gangs: Current Knowledge and Strategies*. Washington, DC: National Institute of Justice, 1993.

Moore, J.B. *Skinheads Shaved for Battle: A Cultural History of American Skinheads*. Bowling Green, OH: Bowling Green State University Popular Press, 1993.

Moore, Jack. "Gangster's Murder No Surprise to Police," *Vancouver Courier*, December 1, 1993, p. 4.

Morgan, W.P. *Triad Societies in Hong Kong*. Washington, DC: The Government Printer, 1964.

Moses, Peter. "Asian Youth Gangs Are Setting Up Shop in the Sun Belt," *New York Post*, July 29, 1990, p. 15.

Moses, Peter. "Ghost Shadows Blamed for Cemetery Shootup," *New York Post*, July 30, 1990, p. 15.

Moses, Peter and Furse, Jane. "Dominicans Prey on Dominicans," *New York Post*, November 21, 1991, p. 18.

Moses, Peter and Pelleck, Carl J. "Kosher Nostra," *New York Post*, August 27, 1986, p. 7.

Mustain, Gene and Robbins, Tom. "The Return of a Killer," *New York Daily News*, May 23, 1993, pp. 4, 20.

Mydans, Seth. "For Vietnamese, a Wave of Gang Terror," *New York Times*, April 8, 1991, p. A11.

Mydans, Seth. "Racial Tensions in Los Angeles Jails Ignite Inmate Violence," *New York Times*, February 6, 1995, p. A13.

Myers, Steven Lee. "Life Sentence for Scourge of Chinatown," *New York Times*, October 24, 1992, p. 27.

*Narcotics Control Digest*. "Feds Indict 89 in Largest Case to Date Against Global Money Launderers," October 12, 1988, pp. 3, 5.

*Narcotics Control Digest*. "State Department Says Worldwide Drug Abuse Levels Continue to Increase," March 15, 1989, pp. 2, 9.

*Narcotics Control Digest*. "Nine Arrested in Reputed International Drug Ring," August 2, 1989, p. 2.

*Narcotics Control Digest*. "Evidence Links Medellin Cartel to Members of Sicilian Mafia," November 22, 1989, p. 4.

*Narcotics Control Digest*. "Andean Drug Summit to Be Held in Colombia, Despite Secret Service Worries," November 22, 1989, p. 5.

*Narcotics Control Digest*. "Italians Seize Pure Heroin, Crack Coke Smuggling Ring," February 28, 1990, pp. 8, 9.

*Narcotics Control Digest*. "Two-Year Probe Leads to East Coast Heroin Bust Involving Colombians, Italians," April 28, 1993, pp. 2, 3.

*Narcotics Control Digest*. "Cocaine Interception Uncovers Russian-Colombian Links," May 26, 1993, pp. 1, 4, 6.

National Police Agency of Japan. "Report on Sokaiya Activities," June 1993.

National Police Agency of Japan. "Report on Japanese Organized Crime," June 1994.

Nelli, Humbert S. *The Business of Crime: Italians and Syndicate Crime in the United States*. New York: Oxford University Press, 1976.

*New African*. "Shame of Nigerian Fraudsters," April 1992, pp. 30, 31.

New Jersey State Police: Intelligence Services Section. "Asian Criminal Groups," 1990.

New York City Housing Authority Police Department. "Gang Activity Briefing," July15, 1994.

New York City Police Department. "Dominican Gangs in New York City," November 1991.

New York City Police Department. "Asian Gang Activities," January 27, 1993.

New York City Police Department. "Nigerian/West African Narcotic Trafficking Organizations," April 8, 1994.

New York City Police Department. "Gang Intelligence," July 15, 1994.

New York City Police Department: Office of the Deputy Commissioner of Community Affairs. "Information on Jamaican Gang Activities," March 8, 1988.

New York Drug Enforcement Task Force. "Dominican Drug Activity in the Northeast," October 1992.

*New York Magazine.* "The People Collectors," January 16, 1995, pp. 15–16.

*New York Post.* "The Queens Connection," September 7, 1989, p. 13.

*New York Times.* "Drug Smugglers Use Cuban Base for U.S. Shipment, Jury Charges," February 27, 1988, p. 17.

*New York Times.* "Torrent of Violence," April 17, 1989, p. 14.

*New York Times.* "F.B.I. Says Los Angeles Gang Has Drug Cartel Ties," January 10, 1992, p. A12.

*New York Times.* "Warsaw Tourist Shops Close in Protest Against Crime," August 7, 1994, p. 11.

*New York Times.* "Police Forces Have Their Hands Full: Poland Purges Corrupt Cops," August 14, 1994, p. 32.

*New York Times.* "Asian Gang Leader Held in Plot to Kill 3," August 20, 1994, p. B7.

*New York Times.* "Mexico Arrests 2 in Drug Cartel," September 3, 1994, p. 4.

*New York Times.* "Russian Gang Chief Indicted in Slaying," March 9, 1995, p. B4.

*New York Times.* "Colombia Druglord Is Captured in Police Raid in His Hometown," June 10, 1995, pp. 1, 3.

*Newsweek.* "Cocaine's Dirty 300," November 13, 1989, pp. 36, 41.

*Newsweek.* "The Nigerian Connection," October 7, 1991, p. 43.

*Newsweek.* "Global Mafia," December 13, 1993, pp. 41, 48.

*Newsweek.* "Deals Too Good to Be True," September 26, 1994, p. 28.

Noble, Kenneth. "A Nigerian Racket Lures Foreigners," *New York Times*, April 5, 1992, p. 11.

Oakley, Robert B. "Combatting International Terrorism," *Drug Enforcement*, Summer 1985, pp. 25, 32.

O'Connell, Richard J. "California Reports on Rise of Israeli, Vietnamese, Japanese Organized Crime Activities," *Organized Crime Digest*, June 1982, pp. 1, 2–7.

O'Connor, Anne-Marie. "Empire of Norcotecture," *Gazette, Montreal*, April 6, 1992, pp. A1, A11.

O'Connor, Eileen. "The Wild, Wild East, the Battle for Russia," *Cable News Network*, March 12–13, 1995, transcript 467-1-5.

Office of Attorney General of California: Bureau of Organized Crime and Criminal Intelligence. *Criminal Information Bulletin*, January–March 1991.

Ogar, Maurice. "Nigerians Abroad: The Bad, the Good, and the Ugly," *Times International*, August 7, 1989, pp. 12, 16.

Omotunde, Dele. "War Against Junkies," *Newswatch*, August 20, 1990, pp. 10, 12, 15, 18.

Onishi, Norimitsu. "Heroin Trail: A Record Deal for an Agent," *New York Times*, April 20, 1994, p. B4.

*Organized Crime Digest.* "Israeli Nationals Suspected in New Credit Card Scheme," July 1981, p. 8.

*Organized Crime Digest.* "L.A. Police: Russian Mob at Work," February 26, 1982, p. 12.

*Organized Crime Digest.* "Ten Soviet Emigres Arrested in Counterfeiting Scheme," September 1984, p. 4.

*Organized Crime Digest.* "Organized Crime Commission Exploring Role/ Structures of International Cocaine Cartels," November 1984, pp. 1, 9, 12.

*Organized Crime Digest.* "The Mariel Boatlift," 1985.

*Organized Crime Digest.* "Germany Alarmed by Ruse of Chinese Crime Syndicate," February 9, 1994, p. 7.

O'Shaughnessy, Patrice. "Midtown Korean Extortion Ring Smashed," *New York Daily News*, May 9, 1993, p. 7.

O'Shaughnessy, Patrice. "The Kings' Empire Grows," *New York Daily News*, April 17, 1994, pp. 32, 33.

Ostrow, Ronald J. and Montalbano, William D. "Drug Agents Break Global Money Laundering System," *Los Angeles Times*, September 29, 1992, pp. A1, A6.

Parascandola, Rocco. "Bx Man Ran Killer Gang from Wheelchair: Cops," *New York Post*, December 21, 1994, p. 8.

Parascandola, Rocco. "Mobsters Unite to Wreak Havoc: Italian-Colombian Link in Brooklyn," *New York Post*, May 17, 1995, p. 18.

Parente, Michele. "Cops Grab 11 in Kidnapping Ring," *New York Newsday*, November 29, 1991, p. 23.

Parker, L. Craig, Jr. "Rising Crime Rates and the Role of Police in the Czech Republic," *Police Studies*, 16(2), Summer 1993, pp. 39, 42.

Paxton, John. "Federal Republic of Nigeria," *Stateman's Year Book 1984–1985*, 121st ed., pp. 922, 927.

Pear, Robert. "Cuban General and Three Others Executed," *New York Times*, July 14, 1989, p. 3.

Pearson, H. *The Shadow of the Panther: Huey Newton and the Price of Black Power in America.* New York: Addison-Wesley, 1994.

Penn, Stanley. "Con Artists: Nigerians in U.S. Earn a Reputation for Ingenious Scams," *Wall Street Journal*, June 5, 1985, pp. 1, 18.

Pennsylvania Crime Commission. "Organized Crime in Pennsylvania: A Decade of Change," 1990.

Perez-Pena, Richard. "35 Are Indicted as Members of a Hyper-Violent Drug Gang," *New York Times*, September 16, 1993, p. B3.

Perez-Pena, Richard. "From Afghanistan to the Bronx, Immigrant's Journey Ends in Gun Trafficking Charges," *New York Times*, November 29, 1993, p. B3.

Perez-Pena, Richard. "U.S. Indictment Charges 26 in Huge Drug Ring in Bronx," *New York Times*, December 21, 1994, p. B10.

Perlez, Jane. "Rogue Wrestlers Have an Armlock on Bulgaria," *New York Times*, January 12, 1995, p. A4.

Pierce, S.M. "Asian Crime in Victoria," *Victoria Police–Asian Division*, 1992.

Pierre-Pierre, Garry. "4 Reputed Gang Members Face Drug Charges," *New York Times*, September 2, 1995, p. 23.

Pierson, Randell. "Colombians in Big Heroin Push Here," *New York Post*, May 7, 1993, p. 3.

Pileggi, Nicholas. *Wise Guy: Life in a Mafia Family*. New York: Pocket Books, 1985.

Pinscomb, Ronald and Everett, Ernest M. "Hong Kong's Triads Move into Australia," *Criminal Organizations*, 6(2), Fall 1991.

Pistone, Joseph D. and Woodley, Richard. *Donnie Brasco: My Undercover Life in the Mafia*. New York: New American Library, 1987.

Pletka, Danielle. "Heroin Inc.: The Nigerian Connection," *Insight*, September 30, 1991, pp. 22, 24.

Polyak, Vladimir. "The Russian Mafia Pushes into Tel-Aviv," *Moscow News*, December 16, 1994, p. 12.

Porter, Bruce, "California Prison Gangs: The Price of Control," *Corrections Magazine*, 8(6), December 1982, pp. 6, 19.

Posner, Gerald L. *Warlords of Crime*. New York: Penguin Books, 1988.

Potekhina, Irina. "The Rise of Russia's Crime Commissars," *World Press Review*, June 1994, p. 13.

President's Commission on Organized Crime. *America's Habit: Drug Abuse, Drug Trafficking, and Organized Crime*. Washington, DC: U.S. Government Printing Office, 1986a.

President's Commission on Organized Crime. *The Impact: Organized Crime Today*. Washington, DC: U.S. Government Printing Office, 1986b.

Project North Star: Joint Coordination Groups. "1993 Drug Threat Assessment to the United States and Canada," 1993.

Puffer, J.A. *The Boy and His Gang*. Boston: Houghton Mifflin, 1912.

Purdy, Matthew. "New Way to Battle Gangs: Federal Racketeering Laws," *New York Times*, October 19, 1994, pp. A1, B5.

Purdy, Matthew. "Police Say Albanian Gangs Are Making Burglary an Art," *New York Times*, December 17, 1994, p. 1.

Queens District Attorney's Office. "Asian Youth Gangs: Queens," January 9, 1992.

Raab, Selwyn. "Influx of Russian Gangsters Troubles F.B.I. in Brooklyn," *New York Times*, August 23, 1994, pp. A1, B2.

Raab, Selwyn. "Reputed Russian Crime Chief Arrested," *New York Times*, June 9, 1995, p. B3.

Reckless, Walter. *Vice in Chicago*. New Jersey: Patterson-Smith, 1969.

Reuters World News Service. "Motorbike Gang Kills Watchman in UAE," March 29, 1994.

Reuters World News Service. "Turkey, Israel to Jointly Fight Terrorism," October 6, 1994.

Riverside County District Attorney: Gang Prosecution Program. "Asian Gangs," 1992.

Robbins, Tom. "The Bizman and the Thugs," *New York Daily News*, June 20, 1993, p. 21.

Roberts, Greg. "Yakuza Link with Casino Tender Feared," *Sydney Morning Herald*, September 18, 1992, p. 6.

Rohter, Larry, "Mexicans Arrest Top Drug Figure and 80 Policemen," *New York Times*, April 11, 1989, pp. A1, A8.

Rohter, Larry. "In Mexico, Drug Roots Run Deep," *New York Times*, April 16, 1989, p. 14.

Rohter, Larry, "As Mexico Moves on Drug Dealers, More Move In," *New York Times*, April 16, 1989, p. E2.

Rosario, Ruben. "FBI Has Dragons by Tail," *New York Daily News*, May 19, 1991, p. 13.

Rosenbaum, D.P. and Grant, J.A. *Gangs and Youth Problems in Evanston: Research Findings and Policy Options*. Evanston, IL: Center for Urban Affairs and Policy Research, Northwestern University, 1983.

Rosenberg, Howard. "Palestinian Network: A Full Report," *Los Angeles Times*, June 1, 1989, p. 6.

Rosenfeld, Seth. "U.S. Says It's Broken Key Asian Mafia Gang," *San Francisco Examiner*, October 13, 1993, p. 11.

Rosenthal, A.M. "In Eight Words, Bush Absolves Syria," *San Francisco Chronicle*, November 26, 1991, p. A16.

Rosenthal, A.M. "The Syrian Sanctuary," *Sacramento Bee*, March 13, 1993, p. B6.

Ross, Barbara and Gonzalez, Juan. "Multi-Ethnic Group Invades Drug Biz," *New York Daily News*, April 27, 1994, pp. 2, 20, 21.

Ross, Barbara and Gonzalez, Juan. "The Money Launderer Sang," *New York Daily News*, April 28, 1994, pp. 24, 44.

Ross, Barbara and Gonzalez, Juan. "Rabbis Laundered Money," *New York Daily News*, April 29, 1994, pp. 16, 33.

Rowan, C.T. *The Coming Race Wars in America*. New York: Little, Brown and Company, 1996.

Rowan, Roy. "PanAm 103: Why Did They Die?" *Time*, April 27, 1992.

Royal Canadian Mounted Police. "Organized Crime in Canada," December, 1992.

Royal Hong Kong Police. "Triads in Hong Kong: Past and Present," 1994.

Royce, Knut. "Country Run on Drugs," *New York Newsday*, February 23, 1993, p. 6.

Rudge, David. "Crackdown by Police Nabs Ring of 'Drug Baron,'" *Jerusalem Post*, March 16, 1992.

Ryan, P. Personal communication, March 1998.

Sachs, Susan. "West Bank's New Kind of Intifada: Palestinian Gangs on the Prowl," *New York Newsday*, May 12, 1992, p. 4.

Sanchez-Jankowski, M.S. *Islands in the Street: Gangs and American Urban Society*. Berkeley, CA.: University of California Press, 1991.

*San Francisco Examiner*. "Witness Ties Pebble Deal, Mob," August 11, 1993, pp. D1, D3.

Sanger, David E. "Top Japanese Party Leaders Accused of Links to Mobsters," *New York Times*, September 23, 1992, pp. A1, A5.

Sanger, David E. "$50 Million Discovered in Raids on Arrested Japanese Politician," *New York Times*, March 10, 1993, pp. A1, A11.

Sanders, W. *Gangbangs and Drive-bys: Grounded Culture and Juvenile Gang Violence*. New York: Aldine de Gruyter, 1994.

Sanders, Wiley. *Juvenile Offenders for a Thousand Years*. Chapel Hill, N.C.: University of North Carolina Press, 1970.

Sarnecki, J. *Delinquent Networks*. Stockholm: Research Division, National Swedish Council for Crime Prevention, 1986.

Savitz, L.D., Rosen, L., and Lalli, M. "Delinquency and Gang Membership as Related to Victimization," *Victimology*, 5, 1980, pp. 152–160.

Savona, Dave. "Waging War on Pirates," *International Business*, January 1995, pp. 42, 47.

Scammell, Michael. "Russia's Robber Barons," *Weekend Sun*, December 31, 1993, p. B5.

Schoenberger, Karl. "U.S. Probes How Japanese Bought Riviera Club," *Los Angeles Times*, May 2, 1993, pp. A1, A28, A30, A31.

Schoenberger, Karl. "Japanese Firm Agrees to Forfeiture," *Los Angeles Times*, October 3, 1993, p. D3.

Schut, Jan H. "Russian Roulette," *Corporation*, March 1995, p. 26.

Sciolino, Elaine. "State Dept. Report Labels Nigeria Major Trafficker of Drugs to U.S.," *New York Times*, April 5, 1994, pp. A1, A11.

Scott, K. *Monster*. New York: Penguin, 1994.

Seagrave, Sterling. *The Song Dynasty*. New York: Harper & Row, 1985.

Sebastian, Tim. "Carry on Drug Smugglers: Night and Day," *Mail on Sunday*, February 19, 1995, pp. 10, 12.

Sebeck, John. "Folks and People," presented at Jacksonville State University, April 30, 1998.

Sennott, Charles. "Colombia: Days of Death and Drugs," *New York Post*, September 5, 1989, pp. 4, 19.

Sennott, Charles. "Godfather of the Coke Clan," *New York Post*, September 6, 1989, pp. 3, 20.

Sennott, Charles M. "Anatomy of a Drug Gang," *New York Daily News*, February 14, 1993, p. 30.

Sennott, Charles M. "Chinatown Gang Linked to Voyage," *New York Daily News*, June 8, 1993, p. 4.

Sennott, Charles M. "Gang Has Global Reach," *New York Daily News*, June 9, 1993, p. 23.

Sennott, Charles, Robbins, Tom, Rosen, James, and Chan, Ying. "Wait in the Wings: Russian, Jamaican, Asian Syndicates Already Muscling In," *New York Daily News*, November 17, 1991, p. 33.

Serio, Joseph. "The Soviet Union: Disorganization and Organized Crime." In Ann Lodl and Zhang Longguan (eds.), *Enterprise Crime: Asian and Global Perspective*. Chicago: Office of International Criminal Justice, 1992.

Sexton, William. "Mob Links: How Organized Crime Took up Golf in Japan," *New York Newsday*, January 11, 1988, p. 66.

Shannon, Elaine. "New Kings of Coke," *Time*, July 1, 1991, pp. 29, 33.

Shenon, Philip. "Saudi Envoy Helps Expose Thai Crime Group: Thai Police," *New York Times*, September 19, 1994, p. A5.

Shenon, Philip. "Burmese Military Steps Up Drive Against Major Drug Trafficker," *New York Times*, April 10, 1995, p. A5.

Sherman, William and Goldfarb, Daniel. "Albanian Gangs Breaking into the Big Leagues," *New York Post*, January 11, 1996, p. 16.

Shigemasa, Kimikazu. "Land Boom Fallout Handicapped Ibaraki Club Members," *Japan Times Weekly International Edition*, September 21–27, 1994, p. 17.

Shimbun, Yomiuri. "Bogus Pakistani Money Found at Factory," *Daily Yomiuri*, November 27, 1994, p. 2.

Skonie, Sharon. "Hegewisch Cop Stings Polish Auto Theft Ring," *New York Times*, August 28, 1991, pp. A1, A7.

SLED. Personal correspondence with a variety of officers, 1997.

SLED. Gang training manual, 1997.

Smilon, Marvin. "Yellow Bird Caged for 20 Years in Bamboo Gang Trial," *New York Post*, January 4, 1987, p. 18.

Smith, Greg B. "Russians Face Gold-Smuggle Raps," *New York Daily News*, September 13, 1995, p. 10.

Smith, Greg B. and Chan, Ying. "Suspected Scam Firm Reopening," *New York Newsday*, August 31, 1994, p. 10.

Smith, Greg B. and Chan, Ying. "Chinatown Mob Bigs Arrested," *New York Daily News*, September 10, 1994, p. 5.

*South China Morning Post*. "Chinatown Tells Its Secrets," March 7, 1991, p. 15.

*South China Morning Post*. "The Nasty Business of Being Stung by the African Mafia," February 2, 1992, p. 10.

*South China Morning Post*. "Trio Face Yakuza Charges," June 2, 1992, p. 12.

*South China Morning Post*. "Turning up the Heat on the Yakuza," August 15, 1992, p. 13.

*South China Morning Post*. "Confessions of a Hitman," September 19, 1992, p. 4.

*South China Morning Post*. "Sun Yee On Branching Out," October 5, 1992, pp. 1, 2.

*South China Morning Post*. "Three Die as Gang Wars Flare Over Control of Tokyo," July 22, 1993, p. 12.

*South China Morning Post*. "Sun Yee On Membership Put at 56,000," January 29, 1994, p. 6.

*Southern Cross*. "Mafia Boss Hits Gold Coast," May 12, 1993, pp. 1, 2.

Southern Poverty Law Center. "Skinhead Violence: It's Come Back Again," *Face of Terrorism*, 85, 1997, pp. 14–16.

Soyinka, Kayode. "A Fork on the Road," *Newswatch*, July 11, 1988, pp. 21, 24, 26.

Speden, Graeme. "Kiwis Catch up with Asian Crime," *South China Morning Post*, February 25, 1994, p. 31.

Spergel, I.A. "Youth Gangs: An Essay Review," *Social Service Review*, 66, 1992, pp. 121–140.

Spergel, I.A. Interview. In C.H. Conly, *Street Gangs: Current Knowledge and Strategies*. Washington, DC: National Institute of Justice, 1993.

Spergel, I.A. Testimony before U.S. House Subcommittee on Juvenile Justice. *C-SPAN*, December 19, 1994.

Spergel, I.A., Curry, G.D., Ross, R.E., and Chance, R.L. *Survey of Youth Gang Problems in 45 Cities and Six Sites*. Chicago: University of Chicago, School of Social Service Administration, 1990.

Spolar, Christine. "Rogue Explosions Shake Warsaw as Gangs Vie for Power," *International Herald Tribune*, March 14, 1995.

Stallworth, Ron. "Music, Culture and Politics of Gangsta Rap," presented at the Second Annual Gang School, National Gang Crime Research Center, Chicago, July 10, 1998.

*Statesman*. "Pakistani Drug Money Aiding Militants in India, says CIA," February 25, 1993.

Sterling, Claire. *Octopus: The Long Reach of the Sicilian Mafia*. New York: Simon & Schuster, 1990.

Sterling, Claire. *Thieves' World: The Threat of the New Global Network of Organized Crime*. New York: Simon & Schuster, 1994.

Stovern, L.D. "Japanese Organized Crime," presented at the 15th Annual International Asian Organized Crime Conference, Las Vegas, March 30, 1993.

Strom, Charles. "13 Indicted in Oil Scheme Laid to Mob," *New York Times*, May 6, 1993, p. B6.

Sullivan, Ronald. "Five Indicted in a Robbery at a Church," *New York Times*, December 31, 1992, p. B3.

*Sunday Morning Post*. "Hong Kong Triads Take Root in U.S," November 24, 1991, p. 21.

*Sunday Morning Post*. "The Confessions of a Heroin Smuggler," August 3, 1992, p. 3.

*Sunday Morning Post*. "The Confessions of a Heroin Smuggler," August 9, 1992, pp. 2–5.

*Sunday Morning Post*. "Japan's Murky Revelations of Big Business and the Mob," December 13, 1992, p. 6.

*Sunday Morning Post*. "Wan Chai Sting Sheds Light on Dark World of HK Triads," November 28, 1993, p. 13.

*Sunday Morning Post*. "The North Korean Cash Connection," July 17, 1994, p. 15.

Tabor, Mary. "200 Members of Hispanic Gang Indicted in Multiple Killings," *New York Times*, June 22, 1994, p. B1.

Thrasher, F.M. *The Gang*. Chicago: University of Chicago Press, 1963.

Tierney, Ben. "Passport to Crime," *Ottawa Citizen*, November 8, 1992, p. B5.

Tierney, Ben. "Police Call the Big Circle Boys Chinese Gangs the Most Significant Development in Canadian Crime. All Came Here as Refugee Claimants," *Ottawa Citizen*, November 8, 1992, p. B5.

*Time*. "The Drug Thugs," March 7, 1988, pp. 28, 37.

*Time*. "Nigeria: Uncivil Disobedience," August 15, 1994, p. 27.

Torode, Greg. "Sun Yee On Move into Shenzhen," *South China Morning Post*, August 2, 1993, p. 3.

*Toronto Star*. "Gangsters Deliver Chilling Message with Slaying of Fuji Film Executive," March 3, 1994, p. F4.

Torres, D.M. "Chicano Gangs in the East Los Angeles Barrio," *California Youth Authority Quarterly*, 32, 1979, pp. 5–13.

Trachtman, Paul. *The Gunfighters*. New York: Time Life, 1974.

Train, Arthur. *Courts and Criminals*. New York: Scribner's Press, 1922.

Treaster, Joseph B. "Colombia's Drug Lords Add New Product: Heroin for U.S.," *New York Times*, January 14, 1992, pp. A1, B2.

Treaster, Joseph B. "Nigerian Connection Floods U.S. Airports with Asian Heroin," *New York Times*, February 15, 1992, pp. 1, 29.

Treaster, Joseph B. "U.S. Links Trail of Heroin to a 'Soviet Connection,'" *New York Times*, April 15, 1992, p. B3.

Treaster, Joseph B. and Myers, Steven Lee. "A Dozen Killings Tied to Colombia," *New York Times*, May 16, 1993, pp. 1, 38.

Treaster, Joseph B. "Behind Immigrants' Voyage, Long Reach of Chinese Gangs," *New York Times*, June 9, 1993, pp. A1, B2.

Treaster, Joseph B. "End to Gang Chief's Lavish Life on Run," *New York Times*, September 3, 1993, p. B4.

Treaster, Joseph B. "U.S. Says It Uncovered $100 Million Drug Money Laundry," *New York Times*, December 1, 1994, pp. B1, B8.

Treaster, Joseph B. "3 Arrested Smuggling Cocaine Found in Newark Cargo," *New York Times*, July 15, 1994, p. B3.

Turek, Bogdan. "Poland Blames Gangs for Bombings," *United Press International*, March 14, 1995, p. 2.

Turkus, Burton and Feder, Sid. *Murder, Inc.: The Story of the Syndicate*. New York: Farrar, Straus and Young, 1951.

Uhlig, Mark A. "Raul Castro Adds Spark to Cuban Trial," *New York Times*, June 22, 1989, p. A3.

*United Press International*. "Israeli Troops Kill Arab Ax Gang Leader," November 9, 1989.

*United Press International*. "Head of Palestinian Gang Killed by Israeli Soldiers," December 1, 1989.

*United Press International*. "Death Toll Crosses 200 in Sectarian Riots in India," January 10, 1993.

*United Press International*. "Poland Second Largest Producer of Synthetic Drugs," July 22, 1994.

U.S. Customs Service: U.S. Department of Treasury. "Heroin Smuggling from Nigeria Strategy," August 1989.

U.S. Customs Service: U.S. Department of Treasury. "Nigerian Drug and Money Laundering Activities," September 26, 1989.

U.S. Customs Service: U.S. Department of Treasury. "Asian Organized Crime: New York City Street Gangs," May 1993.

U.S. Customs Service: U.S. Department of Treasury. "Asian Organized Crime Organizations," June 1993.

U.S. Customs Service: U.S. Department of Treasury. "Asian Organized Crime: Korean Groups," January 1994.

U.S. Department of Justice: Bureau of Justice Assistance. "Developing and Managing Asian Informants," January 20–22, 1993.

U.S. Department of Justice: National Drug Intelligence Center. "Russian Organized Crime: A Baseline Perspective," November 1993.

U.S. Department of Justice: National Drug Intelligence Center. "Northwest Passage: Prospects for Russian Drug Trafficking to the U.S. Pacific Northwest," May 1995.

U.S. Department of Justice: Office of the Attorney General. "Drug Trafficking: A Report to the President of the United States," August 3, 1989, pp. 17–22.

U.S. Department of State: Bureau of Public Affairs. "Cuban Involvement in Narcotics Trafficking," April 30, 1983.

U.S. Department of State: Bureau of Public Affairs. "Nigeria," August 1992.

U.S. Department of Treasury: Bureau of Alcohol, Tobacco and Firearms (ATF). "ATF Overview of Asian Organized Crime 1993," 1993.

U.S. Department of Treasury: Bureau of Alcohol, Tobacco and Firearms (ATF). "Overview of Asian Crime in the United States," March 1995.

U.S. Department of Treasury: Federal Law Enforcement Training Center. "Organized Crime," October 1989.

U.S. News and World Report. "Narcotics: Terror's New Ally," May 4, 1987, pp. 31, 38.

U.S. News and World Report. "The Men Who Created Crack," August 19, 1991, pp. 44, 53.

U.S. News and World Report. "Coming to America," June 21, 1993a, pp. 26, 29, 31.

U.S. News and World Report. "Immigration Crackdown," June 21, 1993b, pp. 34, 38, 39.

U.S. Senate. U.S. International Drug Policy: Allegations of Increased Cuban Involvement in International Drug Trafficking. Washington, DC: U.S. Government Printing Office, 1991.

U.S. Senate Committee on Foreign Affairs. Cuban Involvement in International Narcotics Trafficking. Washington, DC: U.S. Government Printing Office, 1989.

U.S. Senate Committee on Governmental Affairs. *Asian Organized Crime: The New International Criminal*. Washington, DC: U.S. Government Printing Office, June 18 and August 4, 1992.

U.S. Senate Committee on Governmental Affairs. *The New International Criminal and Asian Organized Crime*. Washington, DC: U.S. Government Printing Office, December 1992.

U.S. Senate Minority Staff of the Permanent Subcommittee on Investigations. "Asian Organized Crime Groups," November 5, 1991.

*Vancouver Sun*. "Big Circle Operating in Canada," September 16, 1993, p. A1.

*Vancouver Sun*. "Crime Bosses from Russia Linking with Italy's Mafia," October 12, 1993, p. A13.

*Vancouver Sun*. "Zhitnik Admits He's Been Target of Extortionists," December 27, 1993, p. D1.

Vick, David. "International Alert Goes out for Nigerian Fraudsters," *African Business*, May 1992, pp. 10, 11.

Victoria Police–Asian Division. "Asian Crime in Victoria 1992," June 1, 1992.

*Victoria Times*. "Asia-Based Gangs Wave of Future in Organized Crime," July 18, 1994, p. B15.

Viviano, Frank. "Eastern Europe's Lost Generation," *San Francisco Chronicle*, September 19, 1994, p. A1.

Volsky, George. "Jamaican Drug Gangs Thriving in U.S. Cities," *New York Times*, July 19, 1987, p. 17.

Wade, B. Interview with Conly. In C.H. Conly, *Street Gangs: Current Knowledge and Strategies*. Washington, DC: National Institute of Justice, 1993.

Walker, Christopher. "Murders in Israel Blamed on Gangsters," *New York Times*, June 19, 1995.

*Weekend Australian*. "Asian Crime Gangs Lead Heroin Imports," November 20, 1993, p. 3.

Westrate, David L. "Drug Trafficking and Terrorism," *Drug Enforcement*, Summer 1985, pp. 19, 24.

Wethern, George and Colnett, Vincent. *A Wayward Angel*. New York: Marek Publishers, 1978.

Widlanski, Michael. "Assad Case," *New Republic*, February 3, 1992, pp. 8, 10.

Wilkinson, Tracy. "Colombia's New Era of Traffickers," *Los Angeles Times*, February 12, 1994, pp. A1, A13, A14.

Williams, Laurie, "Alarm Grows Over Similar Bankruptcies," *Tri-City Herald*, April 16, 1989, pp. A1, A2, A6, A8.

Williams, Phil, "Transnational Criminal Organizations and International Security," *Survival*, 36(1), Spring 1994, pp. 96, 113.

Williams, Phil, "The New Threat: Transnational Criminal Organizations and International Security," *Criminal Organizations*, 9(3–4), Summer 1995.

Wilson, James Q. *The Investigators*. New York: Basic Books, 1978.

Witkin, Gordon and Griffin, Jennifer. "The New Opium Wars," *U.S. News and World Report*, 117(14), October 10, 1994.

Wolf, Daniel. *The Rebels: A Brotherhood of Outlaw Bikers*. Toronto: University of Toronto Press, 1991.

Woodiwis, Michael. *Crime, Crusades and Corruption: Prohibition in the United States, 1900–1987*. New Jersey: Barnes and Noble, 1988.

Woolrich, Peter. "Chinese City Sells Its Citizens for 15G a Person," *New York Post*, June 9, 1993, p. 19.

Woolrich, Peter. "The Thai Connection," *Sunday Morning Post Magazine*, September 26, 1993.

X, Malcolm. *By Any Means Necessary: Speeches, Interviews, and a Letter by Malcolm X*. In G. Breitman (ed.). New York: Pathfinder, 1970.

X, Malcolm and Haley, Alex. *The Autobiography of Malcolm X*. New York: Grove Press, 1964.

*Xinhua General Overseas News Service*. "80 Tons of Drugs Destroyed in Syria," March 23, 1991.

*Xinhua General Overseas News Service*. "Suspected Drug Smuggler Arrested," March 7, 1992.

Yablonsky, L. *The Violent Gang*. New York: Macmillan, 1962.

Yglesias, Linda. "Vice Grip," *New York Daily News*, July 28, 1991, pp. 4, 5, 21.

Yglesias, Linda. "The Lust Roundup," *New York Daily News*, July 28, 1991, p. 21.

Yglesias, Linda. "Baby-Faced Boy, 13, Called Chinatown Thug," *New York Daily News*, November 28, 1994, pp. 4, 25.

Yunis, Khan. "PLO's Ability to Police Self Is Questioned: Arabs Fear Past Fighting Will Lead to Future Strife," *Dallas Morning News*, December 27, 1993, p. 1A.

Zellner, W.W. *Counter Cultures: A Sociological Analysis*. New York: St. Martin's Press, 1995.

# Appendix A

**THIRTY-SIX OATHS OF THE HUNG SOCIETIES**
*Source:* Booth, 1990.

1. After having entered Hung Mon, I ought to treat the parents, brothers, sisters, and wives of my brethren as my own home folks. I shall be killed by five thunderbolts if I do not keep this oath.
2. I shall help my brethren to bury their parents and brothers by offering or giving financial or physical assistance. I shall be killed by five thunderbolts if I pretend to have no knowledge of their trouble.
3. When Hung brethren come to my home, I shall provide them with board and lodging. I shall be killed by myriads of swords if I treat them as outsiders.
4. I shall accord recognition to all Hung brethren when they produce their signals, otherwise I shall be killed by myriads of swords.
5. I shall not disclose the secrets of the Hung family even to my natural parents or brothers or my spouse. I shall never disclose secrets for money. Otherwise, I shall be killed by myriads of swords.
6. I shall not betray my own brethren. If I happen to have arrested one of my brethren owing to a misunderstanding, I must release him at once. I shall be killed by five thunderbolts if I do not keep this oath.
7. I shall offer financial assistance to my brethren when they are in trouble, in order that they may pay their passage fee, etc. I shall be killed by five thunderbolts if I do not keep this oath.
8. I shall be killed by myriads of swords if I have done any harm to my brethren or incense master.
9. I shall be killed by five thunderbolts if I commit indecent assaults on my brethren's wives, sisters, or daughters.

10. I shall be killed by myriads of swords if I embezzle cash or property from my brethren.
11. I shall be killed by five thunderbolts if I do not take good care of my brethren's wives or children or other things when they are entrusted to my care.
12. I shall be killed by five thunderbolts if I have reported false particulars about myself for the purpose of joining Hung Mon tonight.
13. I shall be killed by myriads of swords if I change my mind about my Hung Mon membership after this night.
14. I shall be killed by five thunderbolts if I secretly assist an outsider or rob my own brethren.
15. I shall be killed by myriads of swords if I take advantage of my brethren's weaknesses and make unfair deals with them by force.
16. I shall be killed by five thunderbolts if, acting contrary to my own conscience, I convert my brethren's cash and property to my own use.
17. If I have wrongly taken my brethren's cash or property during a robbery, I must return them to my brethren. I shall be killed by five thunderbolts if I do not keep this oath.
18. If I am arrested for having committed an offense, I deserve punishment and should not pass the blame to my brethren. I shall be killed by five thunderbolts if I do not keep this oath.
19. If any of my brethren has been killed or arrested, or has gone some place else for a long time, I shall arrange to help his wife and children who appear to be helpless. I shall be killed by five thunderbolts if I pretend to have no knowledge of them.
20. When any of my brethren has been assaulted or scolded by others, I must come forward to help him if he is right, or advise him to stop if he is wrong. If he has been repeatedly insulted by others, I shall inform other brethren and arrange to help him financially or physically. I shall be killed by five thunderbolts if I pretend to have no knowledge of the matter.
21. If it comes to my knowledge that the government is seeking any of my brethren who have come from other provinces or overseas, I must immediately inform him so that he may make good his escape. I shall be killed by five thunderbolts if I do not keep this oath.
22. I must not conspire with outsiders to cheat my brethren by gambling. I shall be killed by myriads of swords if I do so.
23. I shall not sow discord among my brethren by making false reports about any of them. I shall be killed by myriads of swords if I do so.
24. I shall not appoint myself as incense master without authority. After having entered Hung Mon for three years, the loyal and faithful ones may be

promoted by the incense master or by the support of the brethren. I shall be killed by five thunderbolts if I do any unauthorized act of promoting myself.

25. If my natural brothers are involved in a dispute or lawsuit with my Hung brethren, I must not help any party against the other, but have to advise them against it. I shall be killed by five thunderbolts if I do not keep this oath.

26. After having joined Hung Mon, I must forget all previous grudges against any of my brethren. I shall be killed by five thunderbolts if I do not keep this oath.

27. I must not trespass upon the land occupied by my brethren. I shall be killed by five thunderbolts if I pretend to have no knowledge of my brethren's rights and consequently injure their rights.

28. I must not convert, or intend to share, any cash or property obtained by my brethren. I shall be killed if I have malicious ideas about it.

29. I must not disclose any address where my brethren store their wealth and have any malicious ideas about the address. I shall be killed by myriads of swords if I do not keep this oath.

30. I must not protect outsiders and oppress my Hung brethren. I shall be killed by myriads of swords if I do not keep this oath.

31. I shall not oppose others or act unreasonable or violently by taking advantage of the influence of our Hung brethren. I must be contented and honest. I shall be killed by five thunderbolts if I do not keep this oath.

32. I shall be killed by five thunderbolts if I commit indecent assault on the small boys and girls who are my brethren's family folk.

33. I must not inform the government, for the purpose of getting a reward, when my brethren have committed a big offense. I shall be killed by five thunderbolts if I do not keep this oath.

34. I must not take the wives and concubines of my brethren, and must not commit adultery with them. I shall be killed by myriads of swords if I do this purposely.

35. When speaking to outsiders, I must be careful never to use Hung phrases or disclose Hung secrets, which could cause trouble. I shall be killed by myriads of swords if I do not keep this oath.

36. After having entered Hung Mon, I shall be loyal and faithful, and shall endeavor to overthrow Ch'ing (Qing) and restore Ming by coordinating my efforts with those of my brethren, although my brethren and I may not be in the same profession. Our main aim is to avenge our Five Ancestors.

## THIRTY-SIX STRATEGIES OF THE HUNG SOCIETIES

*Sources:* Booth, 1990; Royal Hong Kong Police, 1994.

1. To cross the ocean without letting the sky know. To cheat all the people around.
2. To surround Wei country in order to rescue Chao county. If an ally is surrounded by enemy, attack the enemy's country to save the ally.
3. To kill a person with someone else's knife. To eliminate a victim without being personally involved.
4. To stay home and let the enemy come to attack you. To eliminate the tired enemy with your refreshed army.
5. To rob while there is a fire. To commit a crime amidst social unrest.
6. To pretend to hit the east and actually attack the west. To pretend to attack one place and strike the unguarded primary target.
7. To create something out of nothing. To confuse the enemy with false information.
8. To attack the enemy through the least suspected routes while launching an explicit yet fake attack plan.
9. To stay at a distance while two conflicting parties are attacking each other.
10. To pretend to be innocent when caught.
11. To put Chang's hat on Lee's head. To confuse the enemy by identifying Lee as Chang and vice versa.
12. To steal if the situation allows.
13. To beat the grass and scare the snake. To hit two enemies with one attack.
14. To utilize the identity of a deceased man.
15. To persuade the tiger to leave its mountain. To persuade the army or householder to leave the city or house so that one can attack the place off-guard.
16. To pretend to set loose a person right before arresting him.
17. To throw a stone to call forth the jade. Limited self-revelation or exposure to bring forth the hidden enemy.
18. To magnify one's own strength.
19. To solve a problem by treating the causes rather than the consequences.
20. To steal after creating chaos.
21. To transform oneself into a totally new person in a crisis situation.
22. To occupy a country while passing through it.
23. To make friends with groups from far away while conquering the surrounding groups.
24. To blame someone with whom you do not want to have open conflict, point the finger at someone else while you are making the verbal assault.

25. To steal the dragon and replace it with a phoenix. That means to steal a real thing and replace it with a fraudulent one, or to send an innocent marginal member to the authorities to bear the burden of the heinous crime of an important offender.
26. To kill a person and scare the rest.
27. To pretend to be an insane person when caught.
28. To destroy the bridge after crossing it, that is, to prevent the enemy from following.
29. To commit a crime in such a way that the incident seems to be caused by natural forces.
30. To overpower the host and take over his place.
31. To use women as bait.
32. To attack or rob a place while it is unguarded.
33. To obtain information about the enemy by counter-intelligence activities.
34. To lure the enemy's pity by intentionally hurting oneself.
35. To apply the domino principle.
36. To walk away from the scene if there is no better option.

## OATHS OF A CHINESE STREET GANG
*Source:* Royal Hong Kong Police, 1994.

I, Surname _____, First Name _____, Born 19_____, Month _____, Date _____, Time _____, State _____, County _____, now voluntarily and wholeheartedly join into the xxxxxxxxxx Association (Tong). After being admitted into the Tong (said of rulers), those who obey the mandate of heaven will live, while those who defy it will perish. As long as I live, I am a member of the xxxxxxxxxx Tong. We are all each other's brothers; even if I die, I am still a member. No remorse as long as I live. If I do, the heaven and earth will destroy me.

1. After I join, I am going to follow, to obey all of the rules and regulations of the Tong. If I do not, I will die under the condition of being shot.
2. Today I join the xxxxxxxxxx Tong. My date of birth must be true; if not, I will be destroyed by electric shock.
3. The secret of the association must be kept. If not, I will die under the condition of being stabbed a thousand times.
4. If the Tong runs into difficulty or is in danger, anyone who knows about it and does not provide assistance will be destroyed by electrical shock and/or burned by fire.
5. The Tong officer is the advisor of all events. If anyone tries to get rid of or kill him the punishment is death.

6. All brothers must unite as real brothers. If anyone is found to be a traitor, he will be punished by death.
7. If anyone overextends his authority and sends out an order to benefit himself or to gain more power, he will be punished publicly.
8. When our brothers run into trouble or danger, we must respond and provide assistance. Anyone who has money must give money; anyone who has strength must give strength. Give what you can; do your best. Anyone who ignores will be stabbed to death a thousand times.
9. We are all each other's brothers; we must never spy or sell out our brothers. If there is hatred and hostility between us, public judgment should rule. Never dwell on it. (Following the public judgment between the hateful brothers, put the feelings in the past.)
10. If one of our brothers is captured or goes on a long journey, leaving his wife and children behind and defenseless, we must try our best to help them. If anyone appears to do good but really means to deceive others, he will be punished. If anyone tries to take advantage of a member's wife, the punishment is death.
11. Never be disrespectful to your parents or abuse your brother, sister, or sister-in-law. Anyone who commits any of the above shall be punished.
12. If one is not authorized by the Tong's officer to know the Tong's secret, he shall not try to peep or spy on it. If he does so, he will be treated as a traitor and will be punished publicly.

Every member must follow the above rules and regulations. Now your name is displayed in heaven; you shall not try to ruin it on earth. Once you join the Tong, you should have confidence in it. You must be loyal to the Tong until you die. If anyone tries to betray the Tong, the punishment is death. If one acts positively externally and negatively internally, heaven is his justice; his death will be close. The sword and knife should cut him to pieces; lightning should destroy his identity (trace); therefore he will be in hell eternally with no hope for reincarnation. Since the sole judgment is heaven and God, one who is loyal to the Tong will be blessed by God. The heaven and earth are my parents; the sun and moon shine upon us. Following the brotherhood ceremony, we use the incense to pray to God to protect and look over us.

Display all of the names in heaven; if the incense breaks the heads fall.

I, Surname _____, First Name _____, Born 19_____, Month _____, Day _____, Time _____, State _____ County _____. Now we join our blood-brother ceremony before God-General Kwan. All of us hereby pledge to be loyal and to protect the xxxxxxxxxx Tong.

Tonight we pray to heaven as our father, earth as our mother, the sun as our brother, the moon as our sister, we all should enjoy everything together, resolve all of our anxieties together. Even though we are not born on the same day, we will die together on the same day.

# Appendix B

## BRIEF OF THE MOST ACTIVE ASIAN GANGS

*Sources:* California Department of Justice; Westminister Police Department; Garden Grove Police Department, 1993.

Asian gangs are nomadic. An Asian gang may be around one day, a week, or most of the time. The gang names may change, or the players may change gangs. The list of gang names are documented Asian gangs from across the United States and Canada. For the most part the gangs are from Southern California and Central California, however, you could come across one of the gangs at any given moment.

| Male Gang Names | Initials | Primary Race |
|---|---|---|
| 24 Hours | | Asian |
| Affil-East Side Boys | ESB | Filipino |
| Affil Oxnard Ban Boys | OBB | Filipino |
| Akrho Boyz Crazy | ABC | Filipino |
| All Brothers Together | ABT | Cambodian |
| Alpine Boys | ALPB | Vietnamese |
| American Burgers | AB | Korean |
| Asian Bad Boys | AB | Korean |
| Asian Bad Boyz | AB | Vietnamese |
| Asian Boys | AB | Cambodian |
| Asian-Born Americans | ABA | Vietnamese |
| Asian-Born Cambodians | ABC | Vietnamese |
| Asian Boy Connection | ABC | Asian |
| Asian Boys Club | ABC | Cambodian |
| Asian Boyz Insane | ABI | Vietnamese |
| Asian Boyz Hood | ABH | Vietnamese |

| Male Gang Names | Initials | Primary Race |
|---|---|---|
| Asian Boyz Club | ABC | Vietnamese |
| Asian Brotherhood Gang | ABG | Cambodian |
| Asian Crip Modesto | ACM | Asian |
| Asian Killers | AK'S | Cambodian |
| Asian National Gang | ANG | Asian |
| Asian Street Walkers | ASW | Cambodian |
| Asian Town Koreans | ATK | Korean |
| B-3 | | Asian |
| Bach 85 | | Filipino |
| Bad Boys Club | BBC | Asian |
| Bahala Na Gang | BNG | Filipino |
| Balboa Boys | BBS | Filipino |
| Barkadang Guam | | Filipino |
| Batang Los Angeles | | Filipino |
| Behind the Night Killers | KNK | Korean |
| Berendo Boys | | Filipino |
| Big Circle Boys | | Chinese |
| Big Time Asian Gang | BTAG | |
| Black Dragons | BNX | Korean |
| Black Eagles | | Asian |
| Black Ghosts | | Asian |
| Black Home Boys | | Asian |
| Black Jackets | | Asian |
| Black Orientals | | Asian |
| Black Shadow | BS | Asian |
| Blood of the Dragon | BOD | Asian |
| Born Before Crime | BBC | Cambodian |
| Born to Kill | BTK | Asian |
| Brothers of Dragon | BROD | Asian |
| Burgerking | BK | Korean |
| Cai Ban Santiago | CBS | Vietnamese |
| Cambodian Junior Gang | CJG | Cambodian |
| Cambodian Kid Gang | CKG | Cambodian |
| Cambodian Over Cook | COC | Cambodian |
| Cambodian Over Cooler | COC | Cambodian |
| Cambodians with Attitudes | CWA | Cambodian |
| Carson Boys | | Asian |
| Carson Pinoy Compadres | CPC | Filipino |
| Cerritos Korean Killers | CKK | Korean |

| Male Gang Names | Initials | Primary Race |
|---|---|---|
| Chang Jai | | |
| Chang Sha | | Chinese |
| Channat Phann Gang | | Cambodian |
| Cheap Boyz | CB | Vietnamese |
| China Town Kids | CTK | Chinese |
| China Town Rifa | CTR | Chinese |
| Clovis Thai Lai Boys | CTLB | Thai |
| Cold Blooded Cambodians | CBC | Cambodian |
| Contras | | Filipino |
| Cool Boys | | Asian |
| Cool Boyz Gang | | Asian |
| Cool Cats | | Korean |
| Cool Lover Boys | CLB | Asian |
| Cory Mafia | | Korean |
| Crazies | CYS | Filipino |
| Crazy Brothers Clan | CBC | Cambodian |
| Crazys | | Asian |
| Da Boyz | | Vietnamese |
| Dai and Tai | | Vietnamese |
| Dark Side | | Filipino |
| Diablo | | Filipino |
| Double Dragons | | Asian |
| Draculas Boys | | Asian |
| Dragon Boyz | DB | Asian |
| Dung Boyz | | Vietnamese |
| Easy Boys | EBS | Filipino |
| Electric St. Boys | | Asian |
| E. T.'s Boyz | | Asian |
| Ethnic Vietnamese | | Vietnamese |
| Exotic Foreign Cambodian Coteric | EFCC | Cambodian |
| Exotic Foreign Creation | | Cambodian |
| Fight to Kill | FTK | Asian |
| Flipside | FSB | Filipino |
| Fliptown Mob | FTM | Filipino |
| Flying Circle Boys | | Chinese |
| Four Seas | | Vietnamese |
| Fresno Fang Boy | FFB | Asian |
| Frogmen (organized) | | Vietnamese |
| Gamma Boys | GBS | Filipino |

| Male Gang Names | Initials | Primary Race |
|---|---|---|
| Garden Grove Boyz | GG Boyz | Vietnamese |
| Garden Grove Koreans | GGK | Korean |
| Garden Grove Local Koreans | GGK | Korean |
| Gardena PA | | Korean |
| Green-Brown | GB | Vietnamese |
| Hac Qui's Boys | | Vietnamese |
| Hak Kwai | | Vietnamese |
| Hak Kwai Chang | | Vietnamese |
| Hamburger | | Asian |
| Hard Core Bounty Hunter Locos | | Filipino |
| Hellside Gang | HSG | Filipino |
| Henry's Boys | | Asian |
| Hira Krisna Pinoy | HKP | Filipino |
| Home Boys | HB | Vietnamese |
| Hong Kong Triads | | Chinese |
| Hop Sing Boys | | Chinese |
| Hop Sing Tong | HST | Chinese |
| Hung Pho | | Vietnamese |
| I. D. Boys | | Asian |
| Jeffrox | JFX | Filipino |
| Jo Boys | | Asian |
| Joe Boys | | Chinese |
| Jr. Natoma Boyz | NB JR | Vietnamese |
| Jr. Santa Ana Boyz | JR SA | Vietnamese |
| K-Town | | Korean |
| Kalmege H. H. | | Korean |
| Karson Bad Boys | KBB | Filipino |
| Karson Matapang Pinay | KMP | Filipino |
| Khanh Bao That | KBT | Asian |
| Khmer Hamburger Boys | KHM | Cambodian |
| King Cobra Boyz | KCB | Laotian |
| King Kobras | KK | Asian |
| Kool Boys | | Asian |
| Korat Boys | KB | Laotian |
| Korean Crazies | CYC | Korean |
| Korean Killers | KK | Korean |
| Korean Mafia Association | | Korean |
| Korean Power | KP | Korean |
| Korean Town Crazies | KTC | Korean |

| Male Gang Names | Initials | Primary Race |
|---|---|---|
| Korean Town Mob | KTM | Korean |
| La Quinta Boyz | LQ Boyz | Vietnamese |
| Lao Boys | | Laotian |
| Lao Family | LF | Laotian |
| Lao Killer Boys | LKB | Laotian |
| Laos Home Boys | LHB | Laotian |
| Laos Viet Connection | LV | Laos/Viet |
| Laotian Oriental Punkers | LOP | Laotian |
| L. A. Oriental Boys | LAOB | Asian |
| LAPD Asian | | Asian |
| Little Nips | LN | Vietnamese |
| Local Korean Boys | LKB | Korean |
| Loco Boys | LB | Laotian |
| Lonely Boyz Only | LBO | Vietnamese |
| Long Beach Boyz | LBB | Vietnamese |
| Long Beach Local Boyz | | Filipino |
| Long Sang | | Asian |
| Los Angeles Viet Boyz | | Vietnamese |
| Lotus Gang | | Chinese |
| Mabuhay Pinoy | M13 | Filipino |
| Mag Ne Boys | | Korean |
| Merced Boy | MERB | Asian |
| Mercedes Boyz | MB | Vietnamese |
| Metal Warriors | | Cambodian |
| Mickey Mouse Club | | Korean |
| Midnight Shadows | MS | Cambodian |
| Mohawk Boyz | MB | Vietnamese |
| Mongolian Boy Society | MBS | Asian |
| Moonlight Strangers | MLS | Cambodian |
| Most Violent People | MVP | Asian |
| Mungs | | Asian |
| Natoma Boyz | NB | Vietnamese |
| Natoma Boyz Jr. | NB JR | Vietnamese |
| New Generation Wah-Ching | | Chinese |
| New Wave | | Vietnamese |
| Nicolle Street Boys | NSB | Filipino |
| Ninja Clan Assassins | NCA | Vietnamese |
| Nip 13 | | Vietnamese |
| Nip 14 | | Vietnamese |

| Male Gang Names | Initials | Primary Race |
|---|---|---|
| Nip 16 | | Vietnamese |
| Nip Boys | | Vietnamese |
| Nip Crip | | Vietnamese |
| Nip Family | NF | Vietnamese |
| Nip Wave | | Vietnamese |
| Nips with Attitudes | NWA | Laotian |
| Norwalk Boyz | | Vietnamese |
| OCJ Boys | OCB | Vietnamese |
| Orange Boyz | OB | Vietnamese |
| Oriental Bad Boys | OB | Vietnamese |
| Oriental Crips | OC | Asian |
| Oriental Killer Boys | OKB | Cambodian |
| Oriental Killers | OK | Cambodian |
| Oriental Lazy Boys | OLB | Asian |
| Oriental Raider Boys | ORB | Asian |
| Oriental Silence Boys | OSB | Asian |
| Oriental Toyz | OTs | Cambodian |
| Orientals in Black | OIB | Asian |
| OXO | | Filipino |
| Panangga | | Filipino |
| Peter's Boyz | | Vietnamese |
| Phanthom 13 | | Cambodian |
| Phillipino Island Boys | | Filipino |
| Pho Boyz | | Vietnamese |
| Ping On | | Asian |
| Pink Knights | | Asian |
| Pinoy N. Gang | PNG | Filipino |
| Pinoy Real | PR | Filipino |
| Placentia Boyz | | Vietnamese |
| Pomona Boyz | | Vietnamese |
| Rebel Boys | RBS | Filipino |
| Red Cobra | | Asian |
| Red Door | | Chinese |
| Red Dragons | | Filipino |
| Red Eagles Gang | | Chinese |
| Rolling Pinoys | RP | Filipino |
| Ruthless Heart Breakers | RHB | Asian |
| Ruthless Nips | | Laotian |
| Sacramento Bad Boys | SBB | Asian |

| Male Gang Names | Initials | Primary Race |
|---|---|---|
| Saigon Cowboys | | Vietnamese |
| Saigon Killers | | Vietnamese |
| Samahang Barilan Gang | SBG | Filipino |
| Samahang Royal Brotherhood | | Filipino |
| Santa Ana Boyz | SA, SAB | Vietnamese |
| Santa Ana Laos Boyz | | Laotian |
| Satanas | STS | Filipino |
| Satanas Ilocano Gangster | STSIG | Filipino |
| Sarzanas | SZR | Filipino |
| Scott Royal Brothers | SRB | Filipino |
| Sige Sige Commandos | | Filipino |
| Sige Sige Sigma | SSS | Filipino |
| Sige Sige Sputniks | | Filipino |
| Sika Bou | SKB | Asian |
| Simon's Boys | | Asian |
| South Bay Killers | SBK | Korean |
| South Side Asians | SSA | |
| South Side Boys | SSB | Filipino |
| South Side Koreans | | Korean |
| South Side Pinoy | SSP | Filipino |
| Stockton Loco Boys | SLB | |
| Street Killer Boys | SKB | |
| Supremo Pinoy Gangster | | Filipino |
| 4 Ts (prison gang) | TTTT | Asian |
| Tai Wah Ching | | Chinese |
| Teaser Mohawk Boys | TMB | |
| Teen Rapers | | Cambodian |
| Thai Killer Boys | TKB | Thai |
| The Boys | TBS | Filipino |
| Tiny Rascal Gang | TRG | Cambodian |
| Tiny Oriental Crips | TOC | |
| Totally Down Koreans | TDK | Korean |
| Tough Oriental Posse | TOP | |
| Tropa Ocho | | Filipino |
| Tropang Hudas | THS | Filipino |
| United Bamboo | | Chinese |
| United Killers | UK | Korean |
| V-Boys | V | Vietnamese |

| Male Gang Names | Initials | Primary Race |
|---|---|---|
| Valley Korean Killers | | Korean |
| Viet Boyz | | Vietnamese |
| Viet Ching | | Vietnamese |
| Viet Cong Boys | VC Boys | Vietnamese |
| Viet Skinheads | | Vietnamese |
| Vietnam Troublemakers | VTM | Vietnamese |
| Virgin Killers | VK | Vietnamese |
| Wah Ching | | Chinese |
| Western Boys | | Korean |
| Westside Islanders | WSI | Filipino |
| White Tiger | | Korean |
| Yakuza | | Japanese |
| Yellow Dragons | | |
| Yu Lees | | Cambodian |

| Female Gang Names | Initials | Primary Race |
|---|---|---|
| Alison Girls | | Vietnamese |
| Amazons | | Filipino |
| Asian Girlz Hood | AGH | Vietnamese |
| Bahala Na Chicks | BNC | Filipino |
| Banana Girls | | Vietnamese |
| Black Ladies | | Asian |
| Carson Pinoy Chicas | CPC | Filipino |
| Cho Cha Girls | | Vietnamese |
| Cindy's Girls | | Vietnamese |
| Dirty Punks | IBK | Vietnamese |
| Escandalosas | | Filipino |
| Girls from the Hood | GFTH | Vietnamese |
| Innocent Bitch Killers | IBK | Vietnamese |
| Innocent But Killers | IBK | Vietnamese |
| Jr. Wally Girls | | Vietnamese |
| Korean Girl Killers | KGK | Korean |
| Lady Rascal Gang | LRG | Cambodian |
| Lao Girlz | LGZ | Laotian |
| Oriental Raider Girls | ORG | Cambodian |
| Pomona Girls | | Vietnamese |
| Saddleback Girls | | Vietnamese |
| Silver Middle Girls | SMG | Vietnamese |

| Female Gang Names | Initials | Primary Race |
|---|---|---|
| South Side Scissors | SSS | Vietnamese |
| Supremo Pinoy Checks | | Filipino |
| Walley Girls | | Vietnamese |

A tattoo found on Vietnamese gangsters or criminals is the four Ts (TTTT):

- Tinh (love)
- Tien (money)
- Tu (prison)
- Toi (crime)
- Thu (revenge), if fifth T is with the four Ts

The four Ts have been found on the back of the neck (see Figure B-1), across the stomach, and on the back. This is usually found on a subject that has done time in CYA or a state prison.

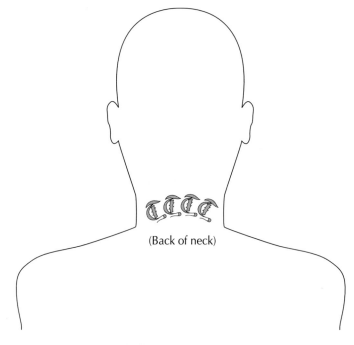

(Back of neck)

**FIGURE B-1** Four Ts Tattoo, Symbolizing Gang Membership

# Index

intragang hostilities
  Chinese street gangs, 205–207
  outlaw motorcycle gangs, 73–74
  Tongs, 199
investments. *see* legitimate businesses;
    money laundering
Invisible Empire, 104
Iranian groups, 376–377
Iraq, 374
Iraqi groups, 375
Irish criminals, 31–32
Israeli organized crime, 359–364
  Russian groups, 347, 364–365
  street gangs, 369–370
Italian organized crime, 19–53
  Black Hand, 28–30
  Chicago, 31–38
  five families from New York, 38
  narcotics, 47–48
Ito-Yokado Company, 240
Ivankov, Vyacheslav, 351–352
Ivory Coast, 177

**J**
Jackson, George, 95
Jamaica, 128, 130–131, 139–140
Jamaican organized gangs, 128–150
  activities outside of the U.S., 148–150
  Chinese groups, 217
  East Coast and Canada, listed, 149
  economic crimes, 140–145
    money laundering, 140–145,
      147–148
  immigration fraud, 145–147
  Nigerian drug trafficking, 174
Jamaican Posses, 129, 130, 131
  African Americans, 135
  Canada, 148–150
  currency violations, 140–145
  drug trafficking, 132–138
  legitimate businesses, 147–148
  weapons, 138–140
Jamal, Mumia Abu, 83
James Street Boys, 33

Japan, 177
  Pakistani gangs, 382–383
  Triads, 193
  World War II, 187, 191, 262
Japanese citizens, wartime U.S., 181
Japanese Defense Society, 241
Japanese organized crime, 219–223
  definitions, listed, 221
  gangs, 223–246
    Inagawa-Kai, 232–235
    Sumiyoshi-Kai, 231
    Toa Yuai Jigyo Kumiai, 235–239
    Yamaguchi-Gumi, 223–231
  Korean gang ties, 236, 243, 268
  Sokaiya (corporate extortion),
    239–241
  *see also* Yakuza
jewelry scams, 353–354, 355
Jewish emigration, from USSR, 348–349
Joe Fong Boys, 201
Johnny Attias gang, 360
joining a gang
  how people join, 18
  reasons for, 15–18
Junior Korean Power (JKP) gang, 269
juvenile gangs
  adult gangs versus, 13
  early historical, 3–5
  early immigrant, 52
  history, 5
  mafiosi, 25
  reasons for, 5–7

**K**
Kahl, Gordon, 82
Kamrani-Bameri gang, 377
Kassar, Monzer al, 371–372
King Cobra Boyz, 252
King, Martin Luther, Jr., 86
Kit Jars gang, 201
KK (Korean Killers), 265
Knights of the Ku Klux Klan, 103. *see
    also* Ku Klux Klan
Korean Flying Dragons gang, 270–271

Muhammad, Elijah (Elijah Poole, Elijah Karriem), 86, 87n
multiple marginality, 5–6
Murder, Inc., 42
music
  Jamaican, 130
  rap music, 94n, 126
  skinhead, 109
  white supremacist organizations, 106–107, 108
Muslim law, 380
Myanmar. *see* Burmese groups
Myong Dong gang, 262

**N**
Naeem, Mohammed, 383
narcotics. *see* drug trafficking
Nation of Islam, 81–82, 84–90
National Alliance, 116
National Association for the Advancement of White People (NAAWP), 103, 117
nationalism, 187, 188, 191, 196
Natoma Boyz, 252
Nayfeld, Boris (Papa), 351
near groups, 12, 14
neighborhoods, 17
nepotism, 81
Netas group, 411–412
New Obi Group, 273
Newton, Huey, 90, 91, 91n, 92–94
Nibiki–Kai group, 244
Nigeria, history, 152–153, 177–178
Nigerian organized crime, 150–180
  Dominican relationship, 326
  drug trafficking, 153, 155, 172–178, 178–180
  indicators of organized criminal group, listed, 156
  money laundering, 178–180
  recent scams, 165–172
Nippon Kominto group, 242
nonwhite supremacist organizations, 95–96

Noriega, General Manuel, 287
Nortes gang, 125
North Atlantic coast cartel, 307–308
Nuestra Familia. *see* La Nuestra Familia

**O**
Ob Pa gang, 264, 265
Ochoa-Restrepo, Jorge, 297
Odessa Mafia group, 356
oil painting market, 239
oil tanker scams, 170–172
Oklahoma City bombing, 82
"ol' ladies," 68–69
omerta (code of silence), 28
OMGs. *see* outlaw motorcycle gangs
Omnibus Crime Control and Safe Streets Act (1968), 51n
On Leong Tong, 196, 198–199, 205, 207, 208, 215, 217
On Leong Youth Club, 204–205
Ong, Benny, 199, 207
Operation CACUS, 75–77
Operation Self-Renewal, 195
The Order (Robert Matthews), 106n
Ordinance for the Suppression of Triads (Societies Ordinances), 186
organ donor market, 347
Organization of Afro-American Unity (OAAU), 87
organized crime
  Black Hand, 28–30
  brief history, 28–30
  Italian. *see* Italian organized crime
  organizational structure, 182
  structure, 22–28
  traditional family structure, 402
Oriental Boyz, 252
Oriental Raider Girls, 252
original gangster (OG), 2
outlaw motorcycle gangs (OMGs), 54–80, 73–74
  1% criminal element, 56, 56n
  Big Four, 56–57, 79
  criminal activities, 70–74